Revised
Standard Reference
for Secretaries
and Administrators

Revised Standard Reference for Secretaries and Administrators

Margaret H. Thompson

Extension Instructor in Writing,
Independent Study, University of California, Berkeley
Consultant, Office Practices and Communications
Formerly Faculty, Graduate School of Business Administration
University of California, Los Angeles

J. Harold Janis

Professor Emeritus of Business Communication
New York University

Macmillan Publishing Co., Inc.
New York

Collier Macmillan Publishers
London

Earlier edition entitled *New Standard Reference for Secretaries and Administrative Assistants*, copyright © 1972 by Macmillan Publishing Co., Inc.

Macmillan Publishing Co., Inc.
866 Third Avenue, New York, New York 10022

Collier Macmillan Canada, Ltd.

Library of Congress Cataloging in Publication Data

Janis, Jack Harold (date)
  Revised standard reference for secretaries and administrators.

  Edition for 1972, by J. Harold Janis and Margaret H. Thompson, published under title: New standard reference for secretaries and administrative assistants.
  Bibliography: p.
  Includes indexes.
  1. Secretaries—Handbooks, manuals, etc.
2. Commercial correspondence—Handbooks, manuals, etc.
I. Thompson, Margaret H., joint author. II. Title.
HF5726.J29   1980   6511'.3741   79-14818
ISBN 0-02-420660-1

Printing: 2 3 4 5 6 7 8   Year: 2 3 4 5 6

Preface

This Revised Edition is designed to help you work effectively in today's business environment. As an authoritative reference and guide for both secretaries and administrators, it will also answer many questions that arise daily in the work of supervisors, department heads, individuals in business for themselves, and others with secretarial, staff or management responsibilities. What these positions have in common—and what this book shares with them—is an overriding concern with effective communication: talking, writing, meeting with people, winning cooperation, finding and processing information, and managing the details of these operations smoothly and competently.

Though these broad aims are shared by all, the routes to accomplishment will vary in individual circumstances. Does the situation call for an impressively typed letter? Telephone tact? Speaking skill? Correct form in addressing a bishop? More efficient filing procedures? A good source of trade information overseas? The correct word? Parliamentary rules? Proofreading like a professional? Setting up a statistical table? The list could be carried to indefinite length. What this book has tried to do is organize much of the diverse information the business communicator may need, make it easy to find, and show how it can serve its intended purpose.

For the secretary, chapters having universal application are those on personal effectiveness, meetings, letter form, correct usage, punctuation, mechanical style, and typing pointers. Chapters, such as those on letter writing, information handling, report preparation, and publicity and editorial work are designed to help in advanced areas of competence.

For department heads and supervisors, the parts of greatest utility are probably those on group communication, supervision, conference arrangements, dictation techniques, improvement of correspondence procedures, data and word processing, report writing, and office services. For executives and proprietors of businesses, the value of the material is supplemented by chapters on financial and tax considerations, and international trade.

For those concerned with the training of personnel, the numerous sections on office practices, language usage, and communication skills may serve both as the text for in-service courses and as a guide to standards throughout the company.

For the professional person, for the writer of letters and reports, for the speaker, for the conference chairman or attendee, for the office editor, for the research assistant and for all others who need to know where to find business information, how to use and interpret technical business terms, how to phrase business ideas, and how to work with others—this book can be mined for a variety of useful data.

To help the reader in the search for information, there is first of all a table of contents that identifies the subject matter of each chapter and of each section within each chapter. In the text, the chapters and many of the sections also have their own table of contents. In some instances, an alphabetical arrangement is used within a section or chapter to permit easy reference. A shortened index on the inside covers and a complete index at the end of the book ensure that any topic treated can be found quickly.

The contents of this book rely heavily on the business and academic experience of both authors. Both have spent many years as writers, speakers, teachers, and consultants to business in areas related to communications, office and secretarial practices, and employee training and education. In all instances, material has been carefully selected to represent current usages and practices. A list of organizations to which the authors are especially indebted follows this preface. Much of the material has also been proved out in the courses and training programs the authors have conducted and in other books and manuals they have written.

Teachers will find ample coverage of the material needed in an advanced course in secretarial practice and office procedures. The additional business data may be viewed as a bonus useful for reference and special projects.

M. H. T.

J. H. J.

This book is helpful in preparing for the nationwide examination for secretaries sponsored by the National Secretaries Association through its Institute for Certifying Secretaries. Members and nonmembers alike may take a six-part examination for the title of Certified Professional Secretary. Information about the examination and the qualifications of candidates may be obtained from the Association, 2440 Pershing Road, Kansas City, Missouri 64108.

Acknowledgments

The authors appreciate the assistance given by the following organizations, including many individuals in them who willingly gave of their time to provide information and materials for this book.

A. B. Dick Company
Account-A-Call Corporation
Addressograph-Multigraph Corporation
Aerospace Corporation
American Airlines
American Express Company
American Telephone and Telegraph Company
Bank of America
Burroughs Corporation
Commercial Credit Corporation
Council of American Flag-Ship Operators
Dictaphone Corporation
Exxon Information Systems
Federal Reserve Bank of New York
Fortune Magazine
General Electric Company
Hobbs, Dorman & Company, Inc.
Honeywell Information Systems
International Business Machines Corp.
International Data Corporation
International Telephone and Telegraph Company
Lockheed California Company
Los Angeles Area Chamber of Commerce
The Macmillan Publishing Co., Inc.

Manufacturers Hanover Trust Company
NCR Corporation
New York Telephone Company
New York University, Libraries of the Schools of Business
Olivetti Corporation of America
Pacific Telephone Company
Pan American World Airways
Random House
Security Pacific National Bank
The Singer Company
Sperry Rand Corporation
3M Company
United States Government
    Department of Commerce
    Department of Health, Education and Welfare
    Department of the Treasury
    Federal Trade Commission
United States Postal Service
University of California, Los Angeles, Management Library
Vydec, Inc.
Wang Laboratories, Inc.
Western Union
The Wilson Jones Company
Xerox Corporation

Contents

Revised
Standard Reference
for Secretaries
and Administrators

1

Personal Effectiveness

A responsible job places a high premium on the ability of the individual to deal with others face to face and over the telephone. That is what this chapter is all about. Following a brief overview of the prospects offered by the modern office, it recommends effective procedures for making appointments, meeting visitors, maintaining poise, exerting personal influence, and improving administrative and human relations skills.

CONTENTS

1.1 OPPORTUNITIES IN THE CHANGING OFFICE ENVIRONMENT

The office environment is constantly changing, with new procedures and machines being developed every year. For those persons in administrative, supervisory, and secretarial positions, this fact of business life is important. Change shuts off opportunity for some and opens new avenues of advancement for others. This section is intended to help you measure your future course.

In summary, you can look for these developments:

1. Wider use of mechanical and electronic processes, placing additional value on human communication—in person, on the telephone, and by letter.

2. Advanced uses of business information, opening doors to talent in such areas as research, writing, and editing.

3. Closer interdependence of all parts of the organization, offering greater scope for the exercise of human relations and administrative talents.

1

4. Rapid changes in job descriptions and constant shifting of workers from job to job, placing additional responsibilities on key people to train others.

5. Growing ties between business and government and between domestic companies and international firms, creating needs for new kinds of data.

The Impact of Automation. The most revolutionary office development continues to be the introduction of labor-saving equipment, notably in the areas of data and word processing. The consequences are enormous. Work is redistributed. Jobs are eliminated or redefined. The executive's functions are updated and reshaped to take advantage of the efficiencies of computerized typing systems.

With the automation of functions formerly performed by people, the administrative secretary can now devote attention to human relations and to developing the necessary skills for a wide range of unprogrammed public relations and staff services, from greeting visitors and answering telephones to booking luncheons or arranging the details of meetings. Automation has not only reinforced the need for many of the secretary's traditional services, but it has also brought new responsibilities. Machines now absorb much of the time and drudgery previously spent in copying, calculating, and performing clerical chores. Favored by the trust and responsibility already enjoyed, the secretary finds opportunities to move up to creative or administrative work. The upgraded secretary often has a staff and the responsibilities of hiring, training, and supervising. This trend has been accelerated by a number of factors, such as the increase in administrative positions and the new professional status of the secretary.

The Information Explosion. Another important development in business is the dramatic rise in the production, accessibility, and use of information. The computer has multiplied the amount of information available and has aided in its processing. A great deal still needs to be done by hand, however, in the gathering, reporting, and interpreting of business data. Among the most interesting tasks performed by today's administrative secretary are those relating to report preparation, publicity, and editorial work. These tasks require a high level of verbal skills and expertise on sources of business information, research procedures, graphic techniques, and printing requirements.

The secretary protects the executive from the confusion and clutter of the avalanche of words produced by modern office machines; monitors incoming messages; screens and distributes incoming mail; and assures that essential information is given to the executive. As an administrator, the secretary may be required to answer letters and to initiate correspondence, often signing the messages personally.

Another consequence of the information explosion is the enormous growth in the number of meetings and conferences of all sorts and on all levels. The secretary's responsibilities for these events include setting up meetings and conferences, taking minutes, and following through to ensure that decisions made there are communicated to others and implemented. As an administrative assistant, the secretary also attends meetings and participates actively in them as chairperson, speaker, or member of a discussion group.

Interdependence and Cooperation. Especially evident to the executive is the increasing interdependence of all parts of the business organization. Before computerization and the systems approach to management, departments and offices worked more or less independently in their particular areas of responsibility. Today, there is strong influence of one function or event upon another, requiring a far greater coordination of effort and need for prompt communication among the various parts of the organization. Managers and executives need to know about techniques and events elsewhere in the organization. They must also have close contact with their associates through meetings, memorandums, and telephone conversations.

The changes in the executive's responsibilities are reflected in those of the secretary and the administrative assistant, who now have wider areas of responsibilities. Duties now require reaching out to all parts of the organization. In the process, one makes new contacts, increases one's usefulness to the company, broadens one's own knowledge and opportunities, and gains respect for one's personal qualities and the ability to communicate effectively.

Providing for Continuity of Service. In any list of changes taking place in business today, the growth of in-service training ranks high. Many factors account for this trend: the rapid movement of workers from company to company and job to job, business growth and change, and the requirement that workers be trained in the specific methods and operations of the company. Training may take place on the job, in company classrooms, or in independent schools and colleges. Such training is usually supplemented by written instructions in the form of memorandums, bulletins, manuals, and the like.

Key assistants share responsibility for training and counseling new employees and overseeing their work. For instance, the highly visible secretary should exemplify efficient standards of performance and be able to demonstrate to trainees how those standards can be met. To provide for contingencies of illness or business absences, all key personnel including the secretary are expected to train a backup person to take over when necessary. Such foresightedness actually works to one's advantage. Ensuring that a competent replacement is handling the office during an unavoidable absence means that office routines proceed in an orderly fashion and work does not pile up.

Business, Government—and the World.   Two more facets of modern business should be mentioned. The first concerns the increased involvement of business with governmental agencies—local, state, and national. The second relates to the growing international flavor of American business through dealings with foreign markets and foreign business organizations. Both developments contribute enormously to the complexity of business operations and put tremendous demands on the executive and the secretary for information not usually found in ordinary business sources. Such information ranges from methods of addressing letters to the military to knowing whether to call a native of the Netherlands a Dutchman or a Netherlander. Netherlander is the preferred term. Another side effect of government and world business concerns travel demands on the executive, with all that those demands mean to the administrative secretary in arranging for itinerary, tickets, hotel accommodations, and communications.

1.2   APPOINTMENTS AND VISITORS

The executive's appointments must be handled efficiently to avoid conflicts of time and to make sure visitors are received courteously and promptly. The secretary who arranges appointments and meets visitors sets an example of competence, poise, and friendliness.

Making Appointments.   Proficiency in making appointments for executives requires knowledge of their working day, work habits, business acquaintances and personal friends. The secretary must be able to classify and screen visitors according to the degree of accessibility the executive wishes to grant them. Such classification might follow a priority pattern like this:

1. Close business associates, friends, and members of the family, who may walk in unannounced if the executive is alone.

2. Employees and customers who may arrive to see the executive without an appointment.

3. Salesmen and others who may have prearranged special hours or days set aside for them.

4. Those in any category for whom an appointment must be made in advance.

5. Those whom the executive prefers not to see.

Records.   Systematic records are the best insurance that appointments will be honored (Figure 1-1).

1. Record every appointment on the executive's calendar and on your own. Include the name, the purpose of the call, the time, and—if not in the executive's own office—the place.

2. Also record on both calendars standing appointments and regularly scheduled meetings as far ahead as the dates are known.

3. Type a daily, weekly, or monthly appointment schedule for the executive to keep on the desk or in a briefcase or folder (Figure 1-2).

A MONTHLY CALENDAR for desk or wall shows at a glance the distribution of tasks for the period—makes it easy to balance the work load.

October					
	1	2	3	4	5
6	7	8	9	10	11	12
13	14	15	16	17	18	19
20	21	22	23	24	25	26
27	28	29	30	31		

A WEEKLY CALENDAR gives a clear view of activities within the Monday to Friday span—and on weekends, too.

March	Mon 1	Tues 2	Wed 3
	Thu 4	Fri 5	Sat 6
			Sun 7

A DAILY CALENDAR pinpoints specific tasks, appointments, meetings, etc. for specific times of the day. It also has space for notes.

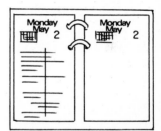

A POCKET CALENDAR allows the executive to check appointments when away from the office. It should include important names, addresses, and telephone numbers.

Figure 1-1 Types of calendars.

WEEKLY APPOINTMENT SCHEDULE

April 12 MONDAY   9:30 a.m.   Weekly staff meeting.
                                Board Room.

                    10:00 a.m. Mr. Denton Peters,
                                AVCO Mfg. Co.

                    12:30 p.m. Luncheon speaker,
                                City Bankers Associ-
                                ation, Union Club,
                                Park Avenue and 69th
                                Street.

                    3:00 p.m.   Telephone Mr. Paul
                                Smith, San Francisco
                                Office re Palo Alto
                                job.

                    8:00 p.m.   Opera.

April 13 TUESDAY   10:00 a.m. Pension Committee
                                meeting. Your office.

                    12:00 noon Lunch with Mr. David
                                Knauth, Lawyers Club,
                                115 Broadway.

                    2:30 p.m.   Telephone conference,
                                Regional Sales Man-
                                agers.

                    3:30 p.m.   Miss Doris Walley,
                                candidate for posi-
                                tion of Research
                                Assistant.

                    7:00 p.m.   New York Coliseum.
                                Inspection of com-
                                pany's Trade Show
                                Exhibit (Booth 29,
                                Main Floor, rear).

Figure 1-2 Part of a weekly appointment schedule.

4. Enter in the address file the names of all visitors with their business connections and phone numbers, so that you can contact them if necessary.

5. Keep a daybook in which to list all visitors, with the time, purpose, and outcome of their visit. This book is valuable in reconstructing events at a later date.

Coordination.   The success of any visit requires careful planning and much communication.

1. At the start of each day, review appointments and meetings, and gather necessary materials well in advance.

2. Check at least once a day with the executive to make sure no appointments were made without the other's knowledge.

3. When the executive's plans are changed, notify conferees immediately and arrange new appointments.

4. If the company receptionist screens visitors, prepare a list of appointments, so that visitors may be recognized by name and announced promptly.

5. In preparation for a luncheon meeting hosted by the executive, see that reservations are made well in advance and that the maitre d'hôtel is informed of the time of arrival; the number in the party; and any special seating, service, or menu requirements.

6. Be careful to make only appropriate appointments for the executive. If you have doubts, check first. If only the time is in doubt, make a tentative appointment subject to later confirmation.

7. When an appointment made in advance requires the executive to leave the office and meet elsewhere, telephone the day before the meeting— or at least before the executive leaves the office—to confirm the appointment.

Greeting the Visitor.   Whatever the executive's attitude may be toward individual callers, the secretary or administrative assistant is cordial to everyone, yet alert to ward off unwanted intrusions.

General Procedure.   The greeting accorded a visitor will range from normal courtesy to flattering attention, depending on the person's importance and relations with the executive. The following procedure is minimal.

1. Look up as soon as the visitor arrives at your desk and greet the caller by name, if known, or by asking pleasantly, "May I help you?"

2. An experienced caller usually gives his or her name; but if a caller does not, obtain it tactfully by asking, "Who shall I say is calling?"

3. If a visitor has an appointment, you will say, depending on the circumstances:

Mr. Brown is expecting you. Go right in.
I'll tell Mr. Brown you're here.
Mr. Brown is on the phone. Will you have a seat? I'll announce you as soon as
    he's free.

4. Take the visitor's coat and hat or offer the visitor the use of the wardrobe, if one is available.

5. If a wait is necessary, engage the visitor in light conversation for a few minutes. If the wait is to be extended, offer a newspaper or magazine.

Visitors Without Appointments. A visitor without an appointment must be handled with special care. The executive may be anxious to see the caller because the person's business or goodwill is important to the company. For that reason, ascertain who the individual is and the business matter to be discussed. When the visitor's identity and purpose have been weighed, you may decide to announce the caller at once. Such a situation occurs infrequently, however. More often, the visitor without an appointment would be asked (1) to wait until the executive is available, (2) to see another person, (3) to make a future appointment, (4) to let you handle the matter, or (5) to write a letter stating the nature of the business. The following comments may suggest what to say in a number of different situations.

> Mr. Brown is engaged now. Will you let me know what you wish to see him about? Perhaps I can help.
>
> Mr. Brown is working on a special project and can't be disturbed. But I'm sure that Mrs. Wiley will be able to assist you.
>
> If you'll let me know what you want, I'll see that Mr. Brown hears about it. You can call me later in the day for an answer.
>
> Mr. Brown has a personal list of charities. But if you would like him to consider your organization, the best thing to do is to write a letter enclosing some of your literature.
>
> Job interviews are customarily given in our Personnel Department. If you'd like to see someone there, I'll give Mrs. Blaine a ring and tell her you're coming.
>
> I'm sure Mr. Brown would be interested in your company's machine, but you'd stand a much better chance of getting him to consider it if you went through channels. The best man to see is Mr. McLean in the Purchasing Department.

When a visitor is offensively persistent after you have indicated that your superior is tied up all day, you might say in an even-tempered voice:

> I'm only carrying out Mr. Brown's instructions. He'll be angry with me and with you if I disobey them. I've already suggested the best way of reaching him. I'm sure you'll accomplish a lot more in that way than by any other.

Business Associates. Visits from persons in the company follow special rules. Many executives have open-door policies that permit close associates to walk in unannounced. Others who do not have this privilege may be told, "I'll see if Mr. Brown is free," or "Mr. Brown has a half hour free at 3 p.m. Come back then. I'll tell him you're coming," or "Mr. Brown has a caller right now. I'll phone you when to come back."

Announcing the Visitor. All visitors should be announced either through the telephone intercom system or by stepping into the executive's office. Use discretion when deciding which procedure is best and what is appropriate to say. When visitors arrive, the usual procedure is to notify the executive immediately through the intercom. You may say, "Your 10 o'clock appointment has arrived, Mr. Brown," or "Mr. Jones is here for his 10 o'clock appointment. May I bring him in?" If the executive already has a caller and cannot or does not wish to be disturbed, delay announcing the caller for a few minutes by asking the visitor to be seated. Within a reasonable time, use the intercom to announce the caller and the time of the appointment, or step into the executive's office with a note on which you have written the caller's name, purpose of visit, and time of the appointment. Leave immediately and wait for the executive to let you know when to send in the visitor.

Some executives prefer that visitors be escorted to their offices. The caller would be announced in the following way: "Mr. Brown, here is Mr. Jones to see you."

Routine business matters may be transacted by the secretary between appointments. An answer to a question, a signature on a letter, or delivery of messages and mail may be attended to before the visitor is brought in.

Refreshments. If a visit coincides with a morning or afternoon coffee break, bring two cups of coffee; but if the visitor refuses a cup, serve the executive anyway. If the visit is to be short or if it is undesirable to extend it, wait until the visitor leaves before serving coffee.

When you receive a visitor, offer coffee if the situation warrants; but if coffee is refused, postpone having any until the visitor leaves.

Interruptions. If it is necessary to interrupt the executive entertaining a visitor, use the telephone or take in a note instead of speaking in the presence of the visitor. The executive may not care to reveal the subject of the interruption to the visitor. If you do interrupt a discussion, excuse yourself first. In any case, make the interruption brief.

If a telephone call comes for a visitor who is already closeted with the executive, offer to take a message. If the caller, however, insists on talking to the visitor, interrupt the meeting by saying, "Mr. Brown, I have a telephone call for Mr. Jones." You may suggest that the call be taken in your office or in a more private place if the visitor prefers.

Ending the Visit. It is the secretary's responsibility to see that the executive is free for the next appointment. The procedure to follow may be established with the executive when the secretary first assumes the job. They may agree that the interruption should be in person with such a statement as, "Mr. Brown, your next visitor has arrived." When the executive expects a garrulous visitor, instructions may involve a ruse to end the visit. Thus you may be asked to telephone, take in a note, or go in and say, "It's time for your meeting, Mr. Brown."

The experienced host will usually anticipate the need to cut a visit short by saying to the visitor upon arrival, "I have a meeting at three, but I'm sure that will give us plenty of time to talk." During the visit the host may signal the end of the conversation by saying, "Let's continue this discussion some other time."

Hosting the Visitor.   Anyone talking with visitors has special responsibilities. Before the appointed time, consider what the objective of the meeting is and work out a strategy for achieving it most effectively. Brief yourself on the situation by consulting past records and have at hand papers and other materials that can be consulted during the meeting. Make a list of questions that should be asked and the answers to anticipated questions from the visitor. Arrange to have telephone calls held or redirected, if it is important to be undisturbed. If the visit is unexpected, make a quick appraisal of the situation to determine what objective the meeting will serve, send out for material from the files if necessary, and plan your remarks to bring the visit to a prompt and successful conclusion. The following points will apply in almost all situations.

1. Greet the visitor cordially. After the initial "hello," show the visitor to a chair and engage in light conversation for a few minutes. A matter of common interest makes a good starting point. It may be the weather, a reference to a mutual acquaintance, a compliment, or the reason for the interview.

2. Channel your remarks. Direct your own and the visitor's remarks into channels that will aid in completing the discussion as quickly as possible. Asking a question or briefly summarizing the visitor's main point may assist in bringing the interview to a conclusion.

3. Adapt to the visitor. Consider the visitor's feelings and don't let your impatience prevent you from suggesting what is best. For example, instead of telling a salesperson that the product offered is inferior to the one you are now using, perhaps you could say, "We are satisfied with the transcribing machine we are now using. Let us know when your company develops new products, however, and we will be interested in seeing them."

4. Avoid controversial issues. Try not to argue with a visitor who raises them. You might gloss over statements with which you disagree by such remarks as:

You're certainly entitled to your opinion.
I'm sure you have good reasons for thinking so.

5. Use caution in sharing your opinions. Avoid offering personal evaluations of people, especially members of your own organization. Do not discuss confidential information about your company unless you have previously cleared it with your superior. Talk about company matters that are commonly known through company brochures, advertising, annual reports, other published material, and news items.

6. Don't pass the buck. Handle as many matters within your jurisdiction

as you can. Refer the visitor to someone else in the company only when the matter being discussed can or should be handled by another department.

7. Close the interview conclusively and pleasantly. For example, you might end with statements such as these:

That's as much information as I can give you. I hope it will be useful.

Then I'll expect you to send me the specifications and price. Can you do that by Wednesday? Good. It was kind of you to give me so much of your time.

Now, if you'll put in a letter the information you just gave me, I'll be able to take up your request with Mr. Brown. You'll do that, won't you? It was so nice talking with you.

1.3 USING THE TELEPHONE

The telephone, an accessible and useful business machine, can save enormous amounts of time, reduce correspondence and travel, and make friends for the user and the company. No other machine makes possible such close human contact with customers, suppliers, employees, business associates, and others. Its use provides immediate response or feedback, and thus permits both parties to work out differences and reach agreement on the spot.

This section tells how to be personally effective when using the telephone. For a detailed description of available telephone services for business, see Section 12.3, "Telecommunication Systems."

Telephone Technique. Clear speech and a pleasing telephone personality are essential. Careful enunciation is important because the instrument often distorts sound, especially over long distances. Furthermore, the person at the other end of the line draws impressions only from what is heard. There is no opportunity to observe facial expressions that might assist in understanding the message. For best telephone results, start by observing these rules.

1. Speak directly into the mouthpiece in a normal voice, not too loud and not too soft.

2. Speak in an alert, animated way, not too fast to be understood clearly. A flat, monotonous tone adds to the distance between you and the listener.

3. Speak clearly. Because many letters sound alike over the telephone (for example, N and M, F and S), it is good practice to use key words when giving initials or spelling a name; for example, "R. E. Morris—R as in *Robert*, E as in *Edward*, Morris—M as in *Mary-O-R-R-I-S*." A list of key words can be found in Figure 1-3. A guide to the phrasing of telephone numbers is given in Figure 1-4.

4. Converse naturally. Speak to the other party as if you were in the same room. Use the tone and the vocabulary that are most expressive of your personality.

5. Be attentive, pleasant, sympathetic, patient, reassuring. The other party will appreciate it and be more receptive when a difficult situation arises.

6. Say "please" and "thank you" often. Say "sorry" for even slight inconveniences.

Telephone Listings.   Obtaining an unknown telephone number can be time-consuming. Therefore, keep a list of frequently called numbers and learn to find other numbers quickly in the telephone directory.

1. Maintain near the phone a card file of outside numbers frequently called. Keep it up to date and include such numbers as the following:

Accountant	Messenger service
Airlines	Personal services: barber, dentist, doc-
Attorney	tor, stockbroker, clubs, stores, and so
Bank(s)	on
Building manager	Post office
Business associates	Repair services for machines
Car rental agency	Restaurants
Express office	Stationers
Family and friends	Telegraph office
Garage	Theater ticket agency
Hotels, motels, and restaurants used for	Trade associations
company business	Travel agnecy
Insurance broker	

2. Keep the company's internal telephone directory handy and make necessary corrections and additions to keep it up to date. Note especially the extensions to call in emergencies and put the numbers on the cover.

3. Keep in a private place a list of home phone numbers of executives and office employees.

4. Have current telephone directories handy.

Locate the following numbers in the front of your local directory:

Directory assistance	Telephone company's business office
Emergencies: police, fire, ambulance	Time
Long distance	Weather forecast

A as in Alice	J as in James	R as in Robert
B " " Bertha	K " " Kate	S " " Samuel
C " " Charles	L " " Louis	T " " Thomas
D " " David	M " " Mary	U " " Utah
E " " Edward	N " " Nellie	V " " Victor
F " " Frank	O " " Oliver	W " " William
G " " George	P " " Paul	X " " X-ray
H " " Henry	Q " " Quaker	Y " " Young
I " " Ida		Z " " Zebra

Figure 1-3   Key words used in spelling names over the telephone.

SEVEN-DIGIT NUMBERS

674-1674 *Six seven four* (pause) one *six* (pause) seven four.

363-9500 *Three six three* (pause) nine *five* hundred.

555-6000 *Five five five* (pause) six thousand.

AREA CODE WITH NUMBER

212 393-4703 Area Code *two one two three nine three* (pause) four *seven* (pause) oh three.

919 232-4111 Area Code *nine one nine two three two* (pause) four *one* (pause) one one.

702 FA3-1256 Area Code *seven oh two F A three* (pause) one *two* (pause) five six.

Figure 1-4   Phrasing of telephone numbers.

Become familiar with the following directory listings:

Federal government: all offices, including post offices, listed under "United States Government."

State, county, and city offices: all listed under the names of the state, county, and city, respectively.

Consulates: listed under name of country, and in the classified directory (yellow pages) under "Government—Foreign Representatives."

Office buildings: listed under "Office Buildings" in the classified directory.

Public libraries: listed under the name of the city or the name of the library.

Radio and television stations: alphabetically listed; also found in classified directory under "Radio Stations and Broadcasting Companies."

Incoming Calls.   People are sensitive to the way their calls are received. They appreciate courtesy and seldom conceal their irritation when it is lacking.

1. Answer the telephone promptly, by the second ring, if possible, and acknowledge the call immediately. Be careful not to continue talking to someone else while the line is open.

2. Identify yourself. The conversation cannot begin until the caller knows that the right place or person has been reached. If you are working for a company that has no switchboard, give the firm's name, followed by your name, as "XYZ Corporation, Miss Johnson." In handling calls direct to your desk through Centrex, the direct-inward-dialing system, you should state your name only.

If the company has a switchboard, give your name when answering your own extension. When answering another's telephone, give that person's name, followed by your name, as "Mr. Brown's office, Miss Porter speaking." When answering an office or factory extension, identify the office or department and give your name.

Personnel Department, Mr. Drummond.

Assembly Station 14, Jenkins.

3. Take calls for others courteously. The person called may be in the building but unable to answer the telephone. Because the caller cannot see what is happening, give sufficient explanation, as, "I am sorry, Mr. Brown just stepped out of the office." Offer a choice between waiting or being called back, as, "Do you wish to wait, or may I ask him to call you?" Unless you have permission, it is better *not* to say:

He's in conference and can't be disturbed.	He's out.
He hasn't come in yet.	He's busy.
He hasn't come back from lunch yet.	He's ill.
I don't know where he is.	He's in court.
He took the afternoon off.	

These reports are more acceptable.

Mr. Brown is not at his desk right now.
He is talking with someone in his office just now.
I expect him back in a few minutes.
She is in a meeting. It will probably last until two o'clock.
She's out of town on business this week. I expect her back on Monday.
He stepped out for a few minutes.
She is talking on another line. Will you wait?

Always offer some kind of assistance.

May I help you?
May I take a message?
May I have her call you?
Mr. Erhard is handling Mr. Brown's calls while he is out of the city. Would you like to talk to him?

4. Screen calls tactfully. Most executives find it good public relations to be easily accessible by telephone. The use of Centrex, which bypasses the switchboard, promotes this trend. If, however, your superior wishes to have calls screened, you will have to use an extra measure of tact. By identifying yourself when answering, you may encourage the caller to do the same. If possible, provide some information before you ask the identity of the caller. If the person called is available say

Yes, Miss Hunter is in. May I tell her who is calling, please?

If the person called is not available, say

Mr. Brown is out of the office just now. May I help you or may I tell him who called?

5. Don't keep the caller waiting. If the called person is busy, ask the caller to leave a message or call back. Or, preferably, see if you can give whatever help is needed. If the caller is a person who should not be kept waiting, hand a note immediately to the called person with the caller's name and the extension number on which the call is being held. When the caller does wait, give frequent reports like these.

Mr. Brown's line is still busy. I'll connect you as soon as it is free.
Mr. Brown has not returned yet. Will you wait a little longer?
Hello, still waiting?
Here's Mr. Brown now. Thank you for waiting.

When you leave the line temporarily, you might say

Will you excuse me a moment while I answer another call?
Would you hold a moment, please, while I look up that information?

6. Transfer calls carefully. When an incoming call must be transferred, tell the caller why a transfer is necessary. Also, make sure the caller is willing to be transferred. If the person is not willing, offer to obtain the information and call back. If the caller agrees to the transfer, tell the caller the name of the person or department and the extension number to which the call is being transferred; then signal the PBX operator by depressing the plunger to the count of 1-2 pause, 1-2 pause. Give the operator enough information to complete the transfer to the proper person or department. Wait for the operator to acknowledge the request, then hang up gently.

If you wish to spare the caller the necessity of repeating to a second party information already given you, place the caller on hold and brief the other party on the situation; for example,

Mr. Brown, this is Miss Elliott. I have a call from Mr. Brennan, who would like some information on prices and quantities of our fall line. Will you speak to him please? He's on the phone now. Mr. Brennan, here's Mr. Brown.

7. Take messages accurately. If the caller leaves a message, take it down carefully and note the date, the time, the caller's name, the company, and the telephone number. Most companies provide a printed form for this information. In the interest of accuracy, repeat the information over the telephone and spell out names. When an incoming long distance, person-to-person call requires a call-back, be sure to get—in addition to the information already mentioned—the operator's number and the city and state in which the call originated.

8. Answer questions pleasantly—and cautiously. "I'll look it up" is better than "I don't know." If the caller asks for information that you are not sure may be given out, say

Let me find out and call you back.
I'll have to speak to Mr. Brown.
I'll do what I can to get that information for you.

Guard information about the company's business operations, sales, finances, personnel, and future plans. If there is some question about the legitimacy of the call, ask for the caller's name and telephone number, and offer to call back. Then secure permission to divulge the information sought. A great deal of business information is private even when it is the subject of common talk around the office.

9. Be courteous in other ways, too. The telephone offers many opportunities to make friends for the company. Callers like to feel they are receiving individual, rather than routine, consideration. Be especially tactful when handling complaints or refusing a request because of company policy. Be a good listener and remain calm even under provocation. When the situation

calls for it, give a full and sympathetic explanation, and offer assistance. Apologize for mistakes, as "I am sorry that happened." Avoid expressions such as "you have to" or "you must." A comment such as "If you'll come in Monday, we'll be happy to check that for you" is preferable to "You'll have to come in Monday if you want that checked."

10. Let the caller hang up first. If the call is prolonged beyond a reasonable time, you may drop a hint, such as, "Well, it was good to talk to you," or "Do enjoy that trip. I'll talk to you again when you get back." If the caller persists, you may then offer an excuse for getting off the line; for example:

Oh, I'm sorry, but I'm wanted on another phone.
I'd like to talk with you some more, but I'm due at a meeting now.
I'll have to say goodbye now. There's a letter I need to get off in the next mail.

11. Systematize the telephone routine. If you handle calls for others, set up a priority list for their telephone calls. The list will include:

Internal calls from superiors.	Calls from salesmen.
Internal calls from others.	Calls from civic and trade organizations.
Calls from customers.	Personal calls.
Calls from suppliers.	

Learn which calls executives wish to handle immediately, which ones they prefer to return, and which you can handle yourself. Even with such priorities set up in advance, however, there will be many occasions when you will have to use good judgment.

Many secretaries find it advantageous to keep a log, or list, of calls received with a note as to the action taken or yet to be taken. The log can be put before the executive several times a day. In this way, the executive always knows what business is being transacted and by whom. A decision can also be made as to who should handle the return calls. The log is useful for future reference, too, should a question about a telephone transaction arise.

Outgoing Calls.   Recognize the potential of the telephone calls you originate by using these techniques.

1. Plan the call beforehand. Decide to whom you want to speak and what you are going to say. Also, you should have alternatives ready if you do not get the party you want or the answer you anticipate. You may find it advisable to make notes for reference before you place the call.

2. Dial correctly. If you are not sure of the number, check the telephone directory or a personal list of numbers. Listen for the dial tone before dialing. And allow ample time for an answer. Give the person being called at least a minute to reach the telephone.

3. Identify yourself immediately. Give your name and the name of the company or the name of the person on whose behalf you are calling. At the same time, name the person to whom you want to speak.

Mrs. Smith calling Mr. Thomas.
I'm Miss Anderson of the Acme Corporation. May I speak to Mr. Peet?
Good morning, Mr. Burns. This is Dick Maxwell.
This is Mr. Jameson calling Mr. Bromley.
Mr. Harper? Mr. Brown would like to speak with you.

If you do not know what individual to talk to, ask for a particular department. Often, however, it is better to state your business and let the operator direct you to the proper party or department.

Adjustment Department, please.
I'd like to order a book, please.
This is Aiken and Company. We have a question about an invoice.

4. Be brief. The called party will appreciate it, and you'll free your phone for incoming calls. If a call is going to take more than a few minutes, it is advisable to state your business and then ask, "Is it convenient for you to talk to me now?" If the time is not convenient, arrange to call back at another time.

5. Arrange for a call-back. If you cannot reach the party you want, leave your name and number (or those of the person for whom you are calling), and ask to be called back. If a special time is best, name it. If, however, it will be inconvenient to receive the return call, ask when it will be best to call back and obtain a specific time, if possible.

6. Ask the person for whom you are placing a call to stay on the line. Dial the number and when connected, say to the called party, "Mr. Jones? Here is Mr. Brown." Or Mr. Brown may greet Mr. Jones without your intervention. In any case, Mr. Brown should be ready to speak. It is rude to keep the called party waiting when you initiated the call.

7. Speak in another's name. When you call on behalf of someone else, give the information or make the request in that person's name.

NOT: Will you please let me know . . .
BUT: Mr. Brown would like to know . . .
NOT: There'll be a luncheon on Thursday.
BUT: Mr. Brown asked me to tell you that there will be a luncheon on Thursday.

Out-of-Town Calls. Lower costs, telephone credit cards, and direct dialing have made out-of-town calls commonplace. To save time and money, however, you must place toll calls correctly. For example, it is important to know time zones in the United States and throughout the world. The map of the United States in Section 12.3 includes four time zones, telephone rate zones, and area codes for each state. International time is also shown in Section 12.3. Area codes for important cities in the United States and Canada are listed in the front of local telephone directories. Also included are typical charges for out-of-town and overseas calls, with rate schedules for day and evening calls and for unassisted and operator-assisted calls.

Unassisted Station-to-Station Calls. Because charges begin when the called telephone is answered, be careful to dial *1*, then the correct area code and the correct telephone number. Should you reach a wrong number, however, ask the person who answers for the name of the city. Then immediately dial the operator and give this information so that you will not be charged for the call. Always report any difficulties to the operator.

To locate a telephone number in a city outside your area, dial *1*, then the area code for that city and *555-1212*. For example, if you want to obtain the number of a company or a person in Detroit, dial *1*, then *313* (area code), and *555-1212*. There is no charge for this service.

Rates for unassisted calls (Direct Distance Dialing or DDD) are lower than for operator-assisted calls. If the called person is the only one who answers the phone or if anyone at the number can handle your call, use the less expensive unassisted station-to-station call.

Person-to-Person Calls. To place a long distance person-to-person call, dial *0*, then the area code and telephone number of the person you wish to reach. Before the connection is completed, the operator will interrupt to ask for the name of the person being called and your telephone number. The operator will wait for the phone to be answered and then will ask for the person being called. When the called person responds, the operator will relinquish the line to the caller. If the called person is not available, there is no charge.

Appointment and Sequence Calls. These two types of person-to-person calls, handled by the operator, enable one to specify a definite time to talk with a party in another city or with a list of variously located parties in a specified order. The operator will try to place an appointment call at the exact time designated. Sequence calls are put through in rapid succession by the operator from the prearranged list. The charge for each call is the same as for a person-to-person call.

Collect and Credit Card Calls. A collect or credit card long distance call may be dialed in the same manner as a person-to-person call. Dial *0*, then the area code and telephone number. On a collect call, the operator will ask the called person if he or she will accept the call. If the person refuses the call, the caller has the option to pay for the call or to cancel it. If it is cancelled, no charge is made. On a credit card call, the operator will ask for the card number. It is important that only authorized personnel have access to the credit card number.

Inward WATS. Station-to-station long distance calls may be made (without charge to the caller) to businesses that have wide area telephone service (WATS, described in Section 12.3). Dial *1*, area code *800*, then the number of the company that has this service. To determine whether the party you want offers this service, dial *1-800-555-1212*.

Conference Calls. Through the use of a conference call, an executive may be connected with a number of other telephones (up to ten) in different cities. All parties are able to hear each other and to exchange information. A speech to a large audience in another city may also be arranged by asking the telephone company to install loudspeaker equipment appropriate for the size of the audience. To place such conference calls, dial the operator, who will connect you with the conference operator.

Mobile, Aircraft, and Marine Service.   Local and long distance calls can be made to automobiles, trucks, aircraft, ships, and boats equipped for mobile telephone service. Ask the operator for the mobile, marine, or high seas operator.

Overseas Calls.   Overseas calls can be made to practically any telephone in the world. International Direct Distance Dialing (IDDD) is available from most prefixes in the United States to sixty-four foreign countries. See the introductory pages of your telephone directory for the list and dialing instructions. To telephone countries without IDDD service, dial *"0"* and give the name of the country being called. If you wish to secure an estimate of the charge before placing an overseas call, or after the call is completed, dial the *"0"* operator.

Calls to Alaska, Hawaii, Puerto Rico, Virgin Islands, Antigua, Bahamas, Barbados, Bermuda, British West Indies, Canada, Dominican Republic, Jamaica, and Mexico can be dialed in the same manner as Long Distance. Simply dial the appropriate area code plus the local number. The area codes are Alaska (907); Hawaii (808); Puerto Rico, Virgin Islands, Antigua, Bahamas, Barbados, Bermuda, British West Indies, Dominican Republic, Jamaica (809). For Canada and Mexico, check "Area codes for some cities" in your local telephone directory.

WARNING: Before making any maritime or overseas call, be sure to check the time zone of the area you are calling. Two o'clock in the afternoon at your office might be two o'clock in the morning at your destination. (See international time chart, Section 12.3.)

Long Distance Charges.   If you wish to know the charges for a long distance call, dial *0*, then the area code and telephone number. Make your request to the operator before the call is completed. After you have finished talking, the operator will call back and supply the exact charges. Keep an accurate record of long distance calls and include (1) the name of the person calling, (2) the name of the person called, (3) the date and the time, (4) the location and the telephone number, and (5) the charges.

A flat rate is charged for the first three minutes of a long distance call. After that, charges at another rate are made for each additional minute. Rates depend on the distance between calling points, the kind of call, and the time of day. Reduced rates are in effect every day between 5 P.M. and 8 A.M. and all day Saturday and Sunday.

1.4   TALKING TO GROUPS

A career in business offers many opportunities to attend conferences and participate in their proceedings. The nature of the participation varies with

BRAINSTORMING. A free-wheeling bull session in which all ideas, however wild, are listed and later examined more closely.

BRIEFING. A concise recital of all the facts needed to understand a situation; often a team of speakers, assisted by charts, slides, and other visual aids, is used.

BUZZ SESSION. One of a number of similar groups into which a larger, unwieldy group has been divided for a short discussion of a problem after a common briefing. Each buzz session consists of not more than six individuals who seat themselves in a circle, with one member acting as leader. When the allotted time has elapsed, the sub-groups come together again, reports from the leaders are heard, and general discussion leads to some conclusion.

PRESENTATION. A talk designed to influence a decision, often with the help of visual aids.

REPORT. A statement based on observation, investigation, or deliberation, often ending with a recommendation for action.

ROLE PLAYING. A technique employed in training, through which individuals act out roles assigned to them. The spontaneous nature of the performance (no rehearsal time is allowed) helps the participants understand the point of view of the persons they portray.

SENSITIVITY TRAINING. A technique in which several small groups (called T-groups) participate, spending as much as two weeks together in listening to lectures, seeing illustrative motion pictures, and engaging in experiments in group behavior. The purpose is to achieve a greater awareness of how the individual relates to others. It can be a corrosive experience.

Figure 1-5   Dictionary of terms for conference participants.

the kind of meeting and runs the gamut from attentive observance of proceedings to selling the group on a new idea (Figure 1-5). This section deals with improving individual effectiveness at meetings, whether held on company premises or elsewhere.

For information on conference arrangements, parliamentary procedure, and minutes of meetings, see "Meetings," Chapter 2.

Responsibilities of Attendees.   When you attend a conference, you have a duty to the sponsors and the chairperson to be an active participant. Here are some ground rules.

1. Arrive on time.

2. Come prepared. Know the purpose of the meeting, familiarize yourself with any available background material, and bring some tentative ideas and opinions.

3. Listen attentively. Be alert to what is going on. Look directly at those speaking and listen with interest. Because you can listen twice as fast as the speaker can talk, use the extra time to analyze the speaker's remarks by relating them to what you already know.

4. Take notes. Jot down information you want to retain and statements you may want to question, comment on, or rebut when given the opportunity. Do your writing, if possible, during pauses or interruptions in the speaker's presentation. Keep tuned to the speaker while you take notes.

5. Enter into the discussion. Without monopolizing the meeting, comment on the ideas of others, provide what information you can, and express your own thoughts and feelings. If you detect inconsistencies or errors, point them out tactfully. Do your part to keep the conference headed toward a satisfactory conclusion.

6. Be tolerant of others' views. Your fellow conferees have as much right to their views as you have to yours. If you listen without prejudice, you may actually change your mind. However, accept other people's views only after you have given the matter thoughtful analysis.

7. Object tactfully. If you do not agree with a speaker, avoid a head-on attack. Instead, ask questions that will clarify a point or expose the flaws. Address your arguments solely to the issues.

8. Keep a cool head. Avoid emotional debates with individuals. Talk to the whole group. The calmer and more reasonable you seem, the more persuasive you are likely to be.

9. Give up gracefully. If the discussion goes against you, accept your defeat in good humor. The group will respect you if you have held your view sincerely and maintained it even against great odds. Their regard may help you at other meetings and in other ways.

Chairing a Meeting. A meeting will be productive if the discussion is directed into purposeful channels.

1. Be prepared. Why has the meeting been called? What background information must you provide? What specific issues are to be discussed? What are the views of the various participants likely to be? The better prepared you are with the answers to these questions, the better you can anticipate the course of the meeting and direct it to your purpose.

2. Lead, but don't push. You want to lead the group step by step to the solution of the problem the meeting is designed to solve. In performing that task, call on particular individuals to give information or state their views. Also, ask questions, summarize arguments, and in general lead the meeting to a decisive conclusion. On the other hand, don't try to impose your views on the group. Let them talk freely and at length, provided they don't go off on tangents. If you see that the business of the meeting cannot be completed within the time allowed, settle for some lesser objective or arrange to continue the discussion at another time.

3. Assign tasks beforehand. To help the participants reach an informed conclusion, ask them to come prepared with ideas or information on the subject. Or direct your request to particular individuals who have special information to impart. Obviously, much more can be accomplished when participants are prepared to contribute than when they are not.

4. Avoid showing favoritism. Give everyone an equal chance to engage in the discussion, and be careful not to favor any one person with attention and comments. If some members of the group are not participating fully, or if the meeting is becoming a one-person show, draw out the shy ones by asking specific questions on matters in which they are expert or by asking their opinions regarding the ideas expressed by others.

5. Follow through. When the group has formed its conclusions or come to some agreement, sum up the results. Then take whatever action is necessary to implement the decisions. Thus you may appoint committees or assign individuals to specific tasks, or you may take on such duties as writing letters and talking to people. Memorandums should be sent to the individuals who are assigned duties, confirming their assignments and setting a date for completion. If other meetings are necessary, take the initiative in arranging them. Meetings of any kind almost invariably engender follow-up work. If there is no follow-up, the results of the meeting are lost along with the time of everybody who participated.

Giving a Talk. Everyone with responsibility will occasionally have to address a group, either introducing the speaker or giving the principal talk. The subject may be as simple as instructions on the care of typewriters, or as complex as the effect of new tariffs on imports. In such speaking situations, the assignment is usually known in advance, and there is time to prepare. Here are some suggestions.

1. Know the subject. If you are inclined to be nervous about the prospect of giving a talk, the best remedy is to know your subject thoroughly. Undoubtedly, you were chosen to give the talk because of your special knowledge. If your subject needs advance preparation or investigation, come to your talk well armed with data, then concentrate on what you want to say.

2. Look good. The audience will get a first impression of you from your dress and grooming. Make sure the impression is favorable. Look your best—but in a low-keyed way, so that the audience can concentrate on what you are saying.

3. Stand up straight and face the audience. Avoid fidgeting with clothes or objects on the rostrum. If there is a table in front of you, come around to its side to speak, unless it holds papers to which you must refer. Gesture naturally with hands or head but avoid moving around unnecessarily. Shift your gaze to various members and sections of the audience. Try not to look down at the floor, up at the ceiling, or out of a window.

4. Speak up. Enunciate clearly with sufficient volume so that everyone can hear without difficulty. Don't talk too fast or too slow, and pause now and then; speak slowly to stress an important word or phrase, and vary your pitch to give your speech color and interest. Flatness and lack of variety and vitality result in dull speeches.

5. Never memorize a speech. Instead, put an outline or salient points on small cards, which you can hold in your hand and refer to inconspicuously when necessary. Although technical and official papers are often read from manuscript, reading a speech tends to bore an audience and should be avoided. Without a manuscript the phrases may not be as polished, but they carry far greater interest.

6. Organize your thoughts. Have a definite purpose, and work in an orderly way through the important points to your conclusion. The advice often given speakers is to follow these three steps:

(a) Tell what you are going to talk about, and if there is more than one main point, enumerate the others.

(b) Discuss point by point in detail.

(c) Summarize by reiterating each point and its main argument.

7. Get and keep the interest of the audience. Speaking is always easier and much more pleasurable when the audience is entertained. Begin with some relevant story or anecdote, some dramatic facts, or a challenging statement. During the talk, support generalizations with specific facts, instances, and examples. Keep in mind, also, that the more narrative or personal experience you put into the talk, the more interesting it will be. Refer to actual people, places, and events. Engage the audience. Ask them questions and wait for a response. Also let them ask questions. Do all this without wandering from the purpose of your speech or using more time to make a point than it is worth.

8. Use visual aids intelligently. Visual aids can help to clarify points and add considerable interest to the presentation. But be sure they are big enough to be seen. Also keep them out of sight until you are ready to use them; otherwise they will be distracting. When showing them, see that there is an easel or some other fixture that will hold them properly. Stand off to the side and use a pointer so that the audience will see clearly what you are pointing out. When you are through using the aid, put it out of sight.

9. End conclusively. Sum up the main points, state what action is needed, or relate an anecdote that brings the talk to a relevant close. Thanking the audience for its attention is gracious, though not necessary.

Introducing a Speaker.   When you expect to introduce a speaker, find out what the subject is and the speaker's background or qualifications. Obtain this information from the speaker's office, either by mail or by phone, ahead of time. Information about the speaker may be supplemented from published biographies, such as *Who's Who in America*, newspaper files, or trade publications. Make notes for the introduction, including the correct pronunciation of the speaker's name and most recent official title.

The introduction may be brief; for example,

> As you know, we recently contracted with the Electrex Corporation of Cambridge, Massachusetts, to set up a computer program for our personnel records. I'm sure you would like to know the purpose of this program and how it will work. No one is better qualified to tell you about it than John Devers, vice president of Electrex, who has been working out the details for the past several weeks. Many of you already know him. Mr. Devers is a graduate of M.I.T. He has installed systems similar to ours in a number of large banks and insurance companies. Mr. Devers.

The introduction can be expanded with more details about the speaker's education, experience, community involvement, and, where appropriate, with references to origins, home, or family. Some cautions, however, are worth mentioning.

1. Do not present the speaker's credentials as if you were reading a catalog. Select only the points that you consider most relevant and important, and present them with warmth and appreciation.

2. Do not give a longer introduction than the speaker or the subject warrants. Avoid obvious flattery.

3. Do not oversell the audience. It is usually enough to say, "I'm sure you'll be interested in what Mr. Devers has to tell you." If you wish to praise the performance of the speaker, the time to do it is after the talk, not before.

1.5   OFFICE SUPERVISION

The supervisor is a key figure in managing the office and seeing that the work gets done. Many secretaries, administrative assistants, and professional staff are given supervisory functions because they have performed well in other duties assigned to them. They are likely to discover—sometimes to their chagrin—that the training that makes good workers is not necessarily the same as that needed to supervise. Then a period of adjustment including the acquiring of additional skills, must begin.

The most interesting change for the new supervisor is learning management rules, policies, and goals. In interpreting management's policies and attempting to achieve management's goals, the supervisor is required to display an extra measure of the qualities of orderliness, firmness, loyalty, patience, and fairness.

Supervisory duties vary considerably. Those described in this section are characteristic.

EMPLOYEE RELATIONS

Interviewing. The supervisor's communication duties include talking to individual members of the staff. On a formal basis, talks become interviews. Specific types of interviews are discussed under "Discipline," "Employment Interview," "Exit Interview," "Grievances," and "Merit Rating." Consider these guidelines in all interviews.

1. Planning the interview:

(a) Have a clear objective. Determine the objective in advance, and decide how to accomplish it with the least difficulty and a maximum of goodwill.

(b) Analyze the interviewee. What kind of person will you be talking to? What is the person's background? What attitudes and biases can you expect?

(c) Devise a strategy. List points to cover or questions to ask. Anticipate objections that will arise, and be prepared to cope with them. Decide in advance all the alternative courses of action.

(d) Arrange the time and place. Choose a place where there will be no outside interruptions or phone calls, so that the interview may be conducted in a relaxed atmosphere.

2. Conducting the interview:

(a) Begin with a pleasant greeting, an invitation to sit down, and an exchange of friendly conversation.

(b) If a conflict is expected, think of some constructive statements. These may be expressions of praise or appreciation or a review of areas of agreement. The conflict will be resolved more easily if both parties begin by recognizing they have much in common.

(c) When the interviewed person's help is desired, map out the problem, show how that person's interest will be best served, and invite participation in working toward a solution.

(d) Develop the interview by making points and asking questions. Questions are more relaxing than flat statements whenever some difference in views is suspected. Questions calling for "yes" and "no" answers are sometimes helpful in establishing facts, but better questions ask "how?" or "what?" or "why?" Avoid leading questions—for example, "Don't you agree that . . . ?"—that could call forth prejudiced answers or arouse resentment.

(e) Make brief notes during the interview of facts you want to remember.

Write a full report immediately after the interview, while details are fresh in your mind. Remember that it could be distracting and cause tension to make elaborate notes during the interview.

(f) Listen carefully to what is being said (see "Communication," page 29). Observe behavior and try to interpret the meaning and motives behind the words. Is information being concealed? Are personal feelings being repressed? Are comments sincere and truthful?

(g) End the interview as soon as its purpose has been accomplished, summing up the main points and indicating the next step, if any. Express appreciation for the interviewee's time and help.

3. Following up the interview:

(a) Review notes to make sure they are clear. If notes were not made or are incomplete, write a detailed record of the interview, being certain to include all information that will be useful for reference later on.

(b) Communicate the results of the interview to others, for example, to your superior, to the personnel department, the payroll department, the interviewee's supervisor, and others who need to know.

(c) Write a letter or memorandum to everyone affected when the interview has resulted in the delegation of a duty, the issuance of instructions, or an agreement on future action. In such cases, the letter records a decision and confirms the details. To prevent misunderstanding, be sure the interviewee agrees with its contents before it is issued.

(d) Follow up in person to see that the objectives of the interview have been met.

Employment Interviews. The purpose of an employment interview is to determine the qualifications of an applicant for a particular job. Keep in mind that both the interviewer and the applicant are forming opinions. What applicants are thinking has an important bearing on a company's ability to attract good workers. Some suggestions:

1. Know the requirements of the job.

2. Study beforehand the applicant's letter or application and review employment test results, when available. Use the information in the applicant's letter to begin the interview; use the company's application form as a checklist of qualifications.

3. See the applicant in private in a relaxed atmosphere.

4. Confine the discussion to matters related to the job. Seek further pertinent information not given in the application.

5. Let the applicant do most of the talking, but direct the conversation by an occasional question.

6. Describe the job and the conditions of work specifically, and observe the applicant's interest or lack of interest. Do not oversell the job.

7. Invite questions and answer them, adapting always to the interests and needs of the applicant.

8. Observe the applicant's manner, posture, and nervous movements. Check on personal habits by observing the condition of clothing, hair, hands, and so on. Expect the applicant to be under stress, and refrain from making unwarranted inferences from appearance or demeanor.

9. Avoid expressing or eliciting opinions about religion, politics, race, and other sensitive subjects.

10. Avoid hasty judgments about the applicant's personality. Try rather to evaluate such specific job-related facets of personality as intelligence, ability, ambition, industry, and imagination.

11. Tell the applicant what the next step will be. For example, the applicant is to return to the personnel department, or may start on Monday, or will hear from you shortly (you still have some applicants to interview), or you do not have anything suitable right now. Be tactful. Help preserve the applicant's self-esteem always.

12. End the interview pleasantly.

Training.   The supervisor sees to the proper induction and on-the-job training of employees who are newly hired, or transferred from another position in the company, or are filling a position temporarily for an absent employee.

Induction Training.   An employee must learn the specific duties of the job, as well as company policies and practices. It is usually best for a new employee to be given work that can be done without special training at first and then more complex duties as experience is acquired. This procedure builds confidence by allowing the employee to be productive immediately.

Information on company policies and practices can be imparted briefly in an orientation interview before the new employee begins work. At that time, distribute the employees' manual and any other literature designed to acquaint workers with their obligations and benefits. Encourage questions about the job and the conditions of employment.

On-the-Job Training.   Both new and seasoned employees must be given training on the job if they are to be able to handle tasks for which their experience is inadequate. A combination of the following training methods is often used.

1. Personal observation and coaching.

2. Counseling sessions designed to point up the employee's strong points and deficiencies.

3. Understudy to an experienced worker.

4. Self-instruction through study of company manuals, standard texts, and other training materials.

5. Formal instructions and practice, either individually or with a group (Figure 1-6).

The supervisor should be familiar with all available in-company training

INITIAL PREPARATIONS

1. Establish a timetable.

   Determine amount of skill worker needs by a certain date.

2. Break down the job.

   List steps in the task and select important key points for emphasis.

3. Have everything ready: equipment, materials, and supplies.

4. Arrange workplace as the worker will be expected to keep it.

STEPS IN INSTRUCTIONS

1. Prepare the worker.

   Put at ease.
   State the job and find out what is already known about it.
   Create interest in learning the job.
   Place worker in correct position at the desk or machine.

2. Present the operation.

   Tell, show, and illustrate one important step at a time.
   Stress each key point.
   Instruct clearly, completely, and patiently but give no more than
   can be mastered.

3. Try out performance.

   Have worker do the job.
   Correct errors.
   Have worker explain each key point as job is performed.
   Continue until worker knows exactly what to do.
   Allow the worker to take over the job.

4. Follow up.

   Designate a fellow worker to answer questions or give help.
   Check frequently. Encourage comments.
   Taper off extra coaching and end follow up.

Figure 1-6 How to instruct on the job (adapted from Training Within Industry Foundation).

programs so that recommendations can be made to subordinates. If additional training offered by outside institutions would be beneficial, the supervisor should explain company policies, if any, regarding reimbursement of tuition and time-off for daytime classroom attendance.

Because training is costly in time and money, it is important to assess its effectiveness. Check for the following results of effective training at the completion of a particular program or course and after a three- to six-month interval:

1. Improved quality of work.
2. Better morale.
3. Fewer errors.
4. Less absenteeism, lateness, and job turnover.

Such an evaluation will indicate whether the program was worthwhile, if instructions need to be expanded or changed, or if a refresher is necessary.

Training for Backup Duties.　　Training a backup person to fill in during the temporary absence of a regular employee requires a somewhat different approach. An effective method is to assign certain duties to an assistant, who then assumes responsibility for them. There remain, however, certain chores and special ways of doing things that such training will omit. Often, no suitable assistant is available for training, and one must rely on temporary help from another department or an outside employment agency.

Key employees, therefore, should be encouraged to compile a workbook or manual that details special facets of their jobs that are not covered by an office procedures manual. For a secretary, these might include the handling of the executive's mail, telephone calls, travel arrangements, and so on (Figure 1-7). Such information, arranged alphabetically, one subject to a page, and kept in loose-leaf form, can be updated regularly.

Communication.　　To avoid difficulties in supervisory communication, be sure to (a) let people know, (b) adapt to people and their circumstances, and (c) do not assume understanding when no understanding exists. Good communication principles include the following:

1. Develop two-way communication. This is the overriding principle. It is not enough to talk to people. It is also important for these same people to talk to you and for you to benefit from what you hear (Figure 1-8).

2. Ensure contact. Communication takes place only when a message is received. Make sure the other person hears you when you talk and fully understands what you are saying. Ask questions to find out. If there are special rules or instructions the worker is expected to follow, make sure these are known.

3. Use feedback. Carefully note responses to what you say, including instructions and orders. The response, called *feedback*, will let you know how well you are communicating. If necessary, repeat your instructions or try new approaches.

1. IDENTIFYING INFORMATION. Name of the department. Full name and title of immediate superior. Person authorized to make decisions in superior's absence. Names of other key persons in department and company.

2. MAIL. Time and place for pickup of outgoing mail. Handling of incoming mail: opening, routing, special treatment, and answering. Location of form letters, paragraphs, and communications manual.

3. TELEPHONE. Extension numbers and persons served by them. Special instructions for answering, screening, and announcing calls. Placing calls for superior and other key persons. Location of company telephone directory, key telephone numbers, and local telephone directories.

4. FILES. Location of centralized file department. Explanation of decentralized file system, if necessary. Location and explanation of materials kept in office files. Rules governing filing and withdrawal of confidential materials. Charge-out system followed for general materials. Location of keys and combinations for locks. Location and explanation of tickler file, if one is maintained.

5. DICTATION AND TYPING. Superior's dictation habits and preferences. Uses of various letterheads and other stationery. Number of copies to make and special distribution lists. Superior's preferences in letter format (include samples). Special instructions as to editing dictation, answering certain messages, and using form letters and paragraphs.

6. OFFICE. Names of principal contacts. List of office equipment and rules governing use. Number to call for repair service. Security measures for protecting person and property.

7. SUPPLIES. Location of supplies. Instructions for ordering. List of special items used in the office.

8. MEETINGS AND APPOINTMENTS. Instructions on arranging appointments for superior and other key persons in the office. Routine for reminding persons of their appointments and daily schedule. Location of calendar of meetings. Explanation of responsibility for sending out notices of meetings. Size and location of rooms available for meetings. Procedures for reserving them. Instructions for taking minutes and distributing copies of them.

9. TRAVEL AND MEALS. Instructions for setting up the travel itinerary; arranging for funds; selecting airlines, hotels, car rental, and restaurants. Arranging for payment by direct billing to company or use of credit card. Explanation of office petty cash fund and authorized disbursements from it.

10. PERSONAL. Time of lunch and coffee breaks. Where and when of approved smoking. Lunch schedules of superior and other key persons. Instructions for serving coffee to superior and visitors. List of organizations to which superior belongs and offices held in them. Duties, if any, performed in connection with these organizations.

Figure 1-7 Sample data to be included in workbook for guidance of back-up secretary. A similar pattern may be followed for other positions.

ONE–WAY COMMUNICATION

TWO–WAY COMMUNICATION

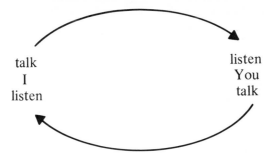

Figure 1-8   One-way versus two-way communication.

4. Invite feedback. Encourage your people to talk, give their opinions, and ask questions. Mistakes will be avoided and rapport improved.

5. Practice empathy. Good communication requires awareness of the behavior of others. Project yourself into the feelings and thoughts of your workers, so that you can interpret their responses and adapt to them.

6. Listen. When others talk, give them full attention (Figure 1-9).

7. Adapt your message. In framing your message, keep language on the listener's level and directed to the listener's interests and motives. If interests clash, seek a compromise.

8. Choose the time and place carefully. Attempt to approach a person who is receptive and to stay out of the way when you or your message is likely to irritate. A private room is better than an open office for some messages; other messages are best casually dropped in a lunchroom conversation or in a chance hallway meeting.

9. Follow up. Follow up on orders and instructions not only to ensure they are being carried out, but also to make sure they have been accurately understood in the first place.

Morale.   The morale of subordinates depends on many factors outside the supervisor's control, but morale can be reinforced in many ways.

1. Distribute work fairly. Show no favoritism of any kind.

2. Give clear and specific instructions for each job. Invite questions and answer them to the employee's satisfaction.

3. Take a personal interest in each subordinate's performance. Offer encouragement and express appreciation frequently.

WHEN LISTENING:

Pay Attention. Look at the speaker, hear what is said, and shut out distractions. Nod occasionally, smile, or use some other expression to show you are getting the message. A verbal response such as "yes" or "I understand" will perform the same function.

Learn. Learn about the speaker: kind of person, special needs and wants, how to gain his or her cooperation. Also, from the speaker's "feedback," determine how well your message is getting across. If responses suggest that you are not succeeding, try again.

Listen Without Bias. Listen with an open mind. Don't twist remarks to mean what they do not mean, and don't jump to conclusions. If you filter remarks through your prejudices, you'll never hear accurately what is being said.

Figure 1-9   Some rules for effective listening.

4. Follow through to see that work is done—and done properly.

5. Encourage observance of company rules. Set the example.

6. Plan ahead carefully so that rush work and overtime are kept to a minimum. Pitch in when an emergency arises.

7. Listen sympathetically to complaints and take care of those that are justified.

8. Keep subordinates informed of changes in company policies and rules.

9. Keep your superior informed of your supervisory activities.

Motivation. Every worker has emotional needs that must be satisfied through the job. If workers are not satisfied, performance will suffer and the worker will eventually seek satisfaction elsewhere. Through proper supervision, you can help implement the job satisfactions outlined here.

1. The need to feel that the work is important. Let the employee know how the job ties in with the work of others and benefits the entire organization. Help the worker maintain interest, improve performance, and develop pride in a completed task.

2. The desire for recognition. Show interest in the employee's work, appreciation for cooperation, and enthusiasm for a job well done. Recommend raises and promotions when deserved. Find opportunities to mention the worker's good performance to others.

3. The desire to know what is expected. Leave no doubt as to what an employee is to do, what standards are to be maintained and what your attitude is toward lateness, absenteeism, and other aspects of personal behavior on the job.

4. The desire for direction. Act with authority in your particular sphere.

Be firm but considerate. Know every job you supervise, and promote improvement in performance.

5. The desire for responsibility. Let the employee work out problems. Make sure instructions are understood, and leave the worker to handle a job from start to finish.

6. The desire for dignity and self-esteem. Never reprimand an employee in the presence of others. When an error is made, correct the way the work is done, not the individual. Instead of saying, "This is wrong," say, "Do you think there might be a better way?" Encourage the worker to find the solution. Keep criticism objective.

Merit Rating.   To be properly motivated, an employee needs to know how management rates performance and must be given incentives to improve. Merit rating helps fill this need. Usually twice a year, the supervisor reports to management on the performance of subordinates. The report will indicate areas of strength and weakness, will suggest means of improvement, and will serve as a basis for salary increase, promotion, or transfer.

Although several methods of evaluation are used, a rating chart is common to most. Selected traits are listed, along with a scale indicating the degree to which the employee exhibits each trait. Factors rated include job knowledge, quality of work, cooperation, initiative, adaptability, and dependability. The scale may consist of such simple terms as (1) outstanding, (2) above average, (3) average, (4) below average, and (5) unsatisfactory; or a short description of each point on the scale may be provided.

The ratings should be as objective as possible. If they are, a small number of employees will score low on a particular trait, an equal number will score high on the same trait, and a little more than half will score average. Rating nearly everyone "average" usually shows excessive timidity or poor judgment on the part of the evaluator.

Merit rating forms are supplied by the personnel department, which also oversees their use. It is up to the supervisor, however, to rate subordinates and to discuss the results with each worker in a private counseling session. Small offices and small companies can adapt the rating form in Figure 1-10 to their particular needs.

Grievances.   Whenever people work together, frictions and dissatisfactions will occasionally arise. If you have gained the confidence of the workers under your supervision, they will instinctively come to you with their complaints. Encourage frank discussions and lend a sympathetic ear. A complaint is always heard in private. The following techniques are suggested.

1. If, as is usually the case, the complainant comes in angry or upset, first calm the worker. Offer a chair and a glass of water to the worker. If tea or coffee is available, offer that. Another device is to excuse yourself while you make a phone call; the worker should remain seated in the room.

PERFORMANCE APPRAISAL

Name of Employee _____ Branch _____

Position _____ Department_____

Rated by_____ Date_____

Instructions: Carefully consider the definition of each quality and compare the employee with others doing the same or similar work in this company. Then place a check (✓) below the descriptive adjective that most nearly applies.

QUALITIES	REPORT				
	Out-standing	Above Average	Average	Below Average	Unsatis-factory
1. *Job Knowledge*. Understanding of work required and ability to perform it.					
2. *Ability to Learn*. Ability to learn new methods and follow instructions.					
3. *Industry*. Energy and application given regularly to each task.					
4. *Quality of Work*. Neatness, accuracy, thoroughness.					
5. *Initiative*. Ability to work without constant direction and contribute own ideas.					
6. *Cooperativeness*. Success in working together with others, including those with greater authority.					

Remarks:

Figure 1-10 Merit rating chart to be used by the supervisor in evaluating an employee's performance.

2. Encourage the complainant to talk freely while you listen. Ask questions to establish the facts clearly and to elicit views and opinions.

3. If the subject requires further investigation, assure the worker of your sympathy and promise to look into the matter promptly.

4. Try to correct the trouble without delay, but do not make promises that you may be unable to keep. If the final decision must go to a higher level, say that you will take it there and report back as soon as possible.

5. If the trouble cannot be corrected, explain the prevailing conditions or the appropriate policies and the uses they serve. Never refuse satisfaction because of personal prejudice.

6. If the satisfaction of a complainant requires concessions by other employees, talk to them also; then try to settle the matter on a cooperative basis. Never report to another employee any personal or negative remarks made by a complainant.

7. If there is no satisfactory alternative, you may offer to arrange a change in duties or a transfer to another department.

Discipline. Work is best accomplished when employees know their responsibilities and take pains to carry them out. Common disregard of rules leads to disorder and unhappiness. When infractions are detected, the supervisor must act promptly to correct the situation. An interview with the offender must be carefully planned to protect the rights of the employee while also effecting a positive change in behavior. Here are some suggestions:

1. Get all facts before the interview. Find out about the individual from personnel records and merit ratings. If others are involved, talk to them before the interview to obtain a complete background.

2. Conduct the interview in privacy.

3. Begin with some favorable report or observation about the employee.

4. Make clear the nature of the dissatisfaction, not by direct confrontation, but by questioning; for example, "Is it true that . . . ?" or "Can you explain . . . ?" After all, the facts you collected may be wrong, or you may have misinterpreted the situation.

5. Listen. Give the employee a fair chance to explain. Wait for a complete explanation before discussing the matter. Observe emotional reactions and respond sympathetically.

6. Be impersonal. Examine the action rather than the individual. Search for the causes.

7. Suspend judgment until all facts are in. You need not impose discipline at the first interview.

8. When discipline is required, it should be administered with a view toward educating, rather than punishing, the employee. Any penalty imposed must be one that you as supervisor have authority to exact, although you may want to discuss the matter first with your superior.

Penalties take many forms: a simple reprimand, a notation on the employee's personnel record, removal of some perquisite or privilege, apology to an injured party, docking wages or imposing overtime for excessive latenesses and absences, and even demotion, transfer, or dismissal.

Exit Interview. Interviewing departing employees is a way to obtain information that may be used constructively by the organization. The *exit interview* helps identify the causes of labor turnover and provide a way to check morale, working conditions, reactions to company policies, job satisfaction, and compatibility with fellow employees. Here are some special points to cover in the exit interview.

1. Find out whether a desirable employee may be kept if the cause for leaving can be remedied. If there has been a quarrel, a misunderstanding, or a failure to adapt, perhaps a transfer to another department can be effected. If the departing worker feels the opportunities for promotion are minimal, explain how one can advance to more responsible jobs within the company.

2. If the employee has a new job, try to find out why it is preferable to the present job: more pay, better working conditions, opportunities for advancement, more benefits, easier travel, closeness to friends. You may learn something to put to use in hiring new personnel.

3. If the employee has been discharged, emphasize that the action has been taken with regret. Mention positive qualities as you offer to suggest other sources of employment or vocational guidance. Tender a smile, a handshake, and good wishes upon departure.

OFFICE ROUTINE

Methods and Procedures. Efficiency is improved when the supervisor eliminates unnecessary work and finds simpler, better ways to do required work (Figure 1-11).

1. Encourage suggestions from workers. Ideas for improvement are always better when they come from the workers and are not imposed from above. Receive suggestions with an open mind and, wherever feasible, permit them

---

1. Eliminate unnecessary procedures.
2. Shift jobs to those in the best position to perform them.
3. Find the most efficient time and place to perform the job.
4. Change the sequence in which a job is performed or combine steps to improve efficiency.
5. Simplify forms and reduce paperwork.

Figure 1-11   Five keys to job simplification.

to be tried out. Reward those who offer work-saving suggestions with more interesting and more responsible work.

2. Avoid recopying information; it wastes office time and leads to errors.

(a) Write information received by phone on the same form that will be used in processing it—calendar, card, memorandum, sales slip, and so on.

(b) Use manifold forms to prevent rewriting. Copies of the form may be sent on for processing, filing, or informational purposes.

(c) Make machine copies instead of hand-typed ones.

3. Reduce unnecessary movement of persons and papers. For example, wait until there are several items before calling a messenger, bring machines and operators close together, or rearrange files and desks to minimize walking (Figure 1-12).

4. Observe an orderly pattern in assigning work to subordinates. Hand out work at a reasonably steady rate and, except in emergencies, permit one job to be finished before another is begun to let employees experience the satisfaction of completion. Keep a backlog of secondary tasks to provide work for slow periods.

5. Keep up to date on developments in office methods and machines. Browse through business periodicals regularly, read the literature provided by manufacturers of office equipment, and attend office equipment trade shows.

See also "Improving Correspondence Procedures," Section 4.4, and "Data and Word Processing," Section 5.1.

Maintenance of Office Machines.   The supervisor sees that office machines are in good working condition. Breakdowns in office machines cause work disruption and dissatisfaction on the part of both operators and executives. Preventive maintenance can reduce materially the number of breakdowns

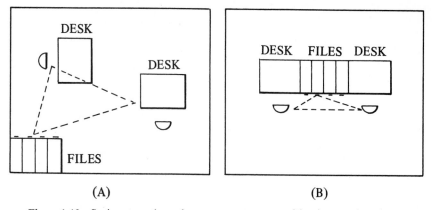

(A)   (B)

Figure 1-12   Saving steps through proper arrangement of furniture and equipment.

and keep machines running at maximum efficiency. The manufacturer's recommendations for cleaning, oiling, and periodic inspection should be followed.

Service contracts are available through the manufacturers or lessors of the machines or through independent contractors. Such contracts usually provide for regular inspection, cleaning, oiling, adjusting, and replacement of worn parts. They also provide for emergency repairs in case of breakdowns. Large firms often employ their own maintenance and repair crews.

The supervisor should welcome complaints about machine performance and should expedite repairs. Operators should be thoroughly trained in the use and care of the machines to prevent breakdowns through mistreatment.

Supplies.   Adequate supplies of paper, printed forms, envelopes, file folders, typewriter ribbons, note pads, pens and pencils, and other stationery items should be available at all times.

1. Establish maximum and minimum quantities for all items, based on use and ordering cycles. Take an inventory at regular intervals. (In a small office, a pad may be hung inside the door of the supply closet on which to note items in short supply.)

2. Reorder from the stationer or stockroom in ample time for delivery before the supply is depleted.

3. Inform the stockroom in advance when an especially large quantity of an item will be needed.

4. Look into any unusually heavy consumption of supplies.

5. Discourage the taking of office supplies for personal use.

6. If necessary, put one person in charge of the supply cabinet and require receipts for all items taken.

Housekeeping.   Work can be done efficiently when working conditions are comfortable, clean, and neat. Check for the following.

1. Windows, heat, or air conditioning should be adjusted for comfort within the guidelines set by the federal government for energy conservation.

2. Blinds and shades uniformly drawn; adequate light for each work area.

3. Access to work space clear; desks uncluttered.

4. Walls cleared of all but authorized pictures and charts. Hammering of nails into the wall by authorized persons only.

5. Clothing and personal belongings in lockers and wardrobes, inaccessible to intruders.

6. Plenty of wastebaskets, but out of sight.

7. Bookcases neat and frequently dusted.

8. Flowers and plants, if any, attended to regularly.

9. Typewriters covered and desks cleared of loose papers at the end of the day.

1.6 BUSINESS ETIQUETTE

Etiquette is no more than a decent regard for others. Good manners create harmonious working relationships, promote efficiency, and establish an atmosphere of friendliness and cooperation. Formal rules are less important than good instincts and genuine consideration for others.

Absenteeism. Most organizations allow an acceptable number of days off for personal reasons. They are intended to be used for emergencies caused by illness, death in the family, weather and road conditions, and business appointments. Extra days off, taken for frivolous reasons, place an unfair burden on others and make a negative impression on the employer.

Borrowing. Workers should have their own tools and supplies. If they must borrow, the items should be returned promptly with thanks. A note on one's calendar pad should serve as a reminder of the debt.

Borrowing money from co-workers should be done only in emergencies, and repayment should be made the next day. The lender should feel free to ask for the return of the money within a few days, if necessary.

Some companies and employee associations have funds from which money can be borrowed for emergencies and capital purchases. No stigma is attached to such borrowing when the loan is repaid in the required manner.

Borrowing and lending money are personal matters. They should never be discussed with co-workers.

Cafeteria. Diners should patiently wait their turn in line to be served; no urgency provides an excuse for breaking in ahead of others. Hovering over a diner to exert pressure for a seat is equally repugnant.

Tables are meant to be shared, and members of both sexes should feel free to join in polite conversation with co-workers, even though they may be strangers.

If there is waiting for tables, diners who are through should leave promptly; they may continue their conversation in the lounge or recreation area.

Complaints. Personal complaints should be kept under control. No one likes to work in an atmosphere of discontent. An employee with a legitimate complaint should see the supervisor. If conditions cannot be changed, the employee should try to adapt to them.

Large companies have regular grievance procedures to deal with complaints about work assignments, salary increases, promotions, benefits, and the like. Employees should learn the procedures and use them.

Confidential Information. Employees should not mention confidential company matters to family or friends and should not discuss such matters with other employees who have no right to the information. They should also avoid giving the impression that they have information that cannot be revealed. Employees who are able to keep confidences will gain respect from co-workers and management alike.

Confidential papers should always be put away in a desk or file drawer after use. If the nature of the papers requires, the drawer should be kept locked.

A person who asks for confidential information should be put off until the right to the information can be verified.

Telephone calls of a confidential nature should be handled discreetly. A visitor in the office may be courteously dismissed or seated in another room before the conversation proceeds; the call may be taken in another room; or the call may be returned later when the visitor is gone.

For treatment of confidential information in letters to the government and the military, see Section 3.2.

Cooperation.   If work cannot be handled cheerfully and on time, the reason should be discussed with the supervisor.

It is considerate to offer a helping hand to a fellow employee who is temporarily overloaded with work when the tasks assigned to you are finished. Co-workers should reciprocate when the occasion permits.

When requests for cooperation are received from outside one's own department, cooperation should be given cheerfully, at least to the extent that one's own work is not impaired.

Courtesy.   The rules of courtesy in the office are sometimes altered but never suspended. Greetings should be pleasant, and brief social conversation should be engaged in when chance brings co-workers together in halls, lounges, and elsewhere.

Kindnesses should be offered those in need and kindnesses received should be reciprocated. A pleasant demeanor, sympathy, patience, and normal consideration for the feelings of others also help to make the office a pleasant place for everyone.

Criticism.   It is rude and ego-damaging to criticize a subordinate or co-worker in the presence of others. (See also "Office Supervision," Section 1.5.)

An employee should not criticize company policies before strangers, for the critic as well as the company loses esteem. If a policy is believed to be wrong, it should be discussed with one's superior, but not before supportive evidence is obtained.

The suggestion systems operating in many organizations provide an orderly way for all employees to voice criticism and offer constructive ideas.

Death. The death of an employer, associate, or employee may be acknowledged by flowers and/or a personal note to the closest bereaved relative. (See "Condolence Letters," in Section 4.5.)

In addition to relatives, friends, and associates who attend the funeral, individuals or small groups may be sent as representatives of organizations to which the deceased belonged. A private funeral is, of course, confined to invited mourners only.

Dining Out. An expense account lunch is accepted by the guest with thanks, but without the need to reciprocate.

A reservation should be made in advance for a business lunch or dinner to ensure prompt seating. State the number in the party, the time of arrival, and any special instructions for seating or service.

If business is to be discussed, the host should introduce the subject. A guest who is pressed for time, however, may tactfully bring the conversation around to the business of the meeting.

In the matter of ordering, the guest takes cues from the host. The considerate host will say, "The antipasto here makes a tasty start for the meal," or, "The roast beef is a specialty here." The guest need not order what is suggested, but knows that an appetizer and main course as expensive as an antipasto and roast beef may be selected.

The host will usually offer the guest a drink. The considerate guest who does not want one will say, "No, thanks, but you go ahead and order one for yourself." The host may then order one or not.

A woman in management should have no compunction about inviting a man to be her guest for a business lunch. A credit card should be used to pay for the lunch. The male guest will thank his hostess, but should not offer to pay.

If one in the luncheon party has an engagement to keep, it should be mentioned beforehand to avoid the impression of rudeness if the meal must be concluded abruptly. Neither host nor guest, however, should schedule a meeting so early in the afternoon that a prior luncheon engagement must be rushed.

Dress (see "Grooming").

Elevator. Where a few individuals are involved, it is polite for men to let women enter and leave the elevator first. If there is a crowd, it is best for the persons nearest the door to enter and leave first.

A man need not remove his hat, especially in a crowded elevator.

Even if lighted cigarettes and cigars are not expressly forbidden, etiquette and safety require that smokers extinguish them before entering the elevator.

In a crowded self-service elevator, the person nearest the signal board may be asked to press the button for the floor desired.

Employer-Secretary Relations. The secretary is always polite, cheerful, and even enthusiastic in the presence of the employer. With exceptions for small talk, conversation should be brief and limited to business matters.

The employer is expected to treat the secretary with the consideration due the position and its responsibilities. Compliments should be offered freely, but criticism should be tempered. It is the employer's responsibility to schedule work so that it can be completed easily before the end of the day.

Gifts. A superior may give a small token of appreciation to a subordinate for a job well done or a special favor. A subordinate, however, rarely makes a gift to a superior. An exception is a gift to the superior from the whole staff, if it is the custom of the office.

Co-workers who exchange gifts should do so out of the office or at a time when others are not present.

Many companies and organizations have strict rules about accepting gifts from suppliers and others whose gifts may be construed as a bribe. When in doubt, one's superior should be consulted. A gift that is considered improper should be graciously returned.

Grooming. The best guide to dress and grooming for the office is to follow the current practice within the organization. Considerable individuality is often permitted in such professions as college teaching, science, and the arts. Professional offices, banks, and companies whose employees meet the public are somewhat more restrictive. In general, clothes should be clean, neat, and fashionable, but not eccentric. Business suits for men and tailored dresses and suits with skirts for women are almost always correct at work. Women going from the office directly to an evening engagement may wear a simple dress with a jacket that can be removed for the evening and dressed up with costume jewelry.

Hair should be clean, neatly combed, and conservatively styled for the office. Makeup should be understated. Perfumes and aftershave lotions should be subdued.

Husband and Wife Working in Same Company. When a husband and wife work in the same office or company, private feelings and personal problems are best kept outside the office. In addressing each other, the couple should follow the office custom, using either first or last names. Before the public, they should address each other as Mr. and Mrs., especially if other members of the group are addressing each other in this formal manner. In all situations, they should behave toward each other as naturally as other employees interact with each other in the day-to-day office routine.

Introductions. Business introductions differ from social introductions in that they are governed primarily by rank and importance rather than by sex or age. When one person is introduced to another, the person to whom greater deference is due is named first, for example, "Mr. Big, this is Mr. Little."

Introducing Individuals. The man is presented to the woman only when their ranks are equal or the woman has superior rank. Otherwise, the woman is introduced to the man.

Subordinates are introduced to their superiors.

No special order of precedence is followed in introducing men of equal rank or status, although it is courteous to mention the older man first. The difference in women's ages, however, is tactfully ignored. The following forms are correct.

Mrs. Jones, may I present Mr. Gordon.
Mr. Ford, may I introduce Mrs. Jones.
Mr. Parks, this is Mr. Gordon.

Introductions may give some helpful information about the persons being introduced. For example:

Mr. Falk, this is Mr. Gordon. He's the new assistant manager of our data processing center.
May Smith, I'd like you to meet Alan Elliott, who will give you the information you need.
Mr. Jackson, may I introduce Fred Thomas, who will be working on sales contracts. Jim Jackson is in charge of production, Fred.

As the last two examples suggest, when the first name of one party is given, the first name of the other is given, too, although judicious exceptions may be made when there are wide disparities in age or status.

Group Introductions. When a group is called together for a meeting, luncheon, or dinner, the host should be the first to arrive and should take charge of introductions. Each person is introduced upon arrival to the assembled group, or to one of the subgroups if it is a large meeting. The basic rules of introductions are observed.

A man introduced to women:

Miss Brown, Mrs. Fletcher, this is Mr. Weber.

Men introduced to a woman or to women:

Miss Brown, Mrs. Fletcher, this is Mr. Weber . . . and Mr. Green.

A man or men introduced to a group of men:

Mr. Weber, this is Mr. Curtis . . . Mr. Pepper . . . and Mr. Ogden.
Mr. Weber, Mr. Clark, this is Mr. Curtis . . . Mr. Pepper . . . Mr. Ogden.

A group of men and women introduced to men:

Mr. Weber, Mr. Clark, this is Mrs. Fletcher, Miss Floyd . . .Mr. Curtis . . . and Mr. Ogden.

Introductions to a Large Group. The introduction of an individual to a large group should be handled as easily and naturally as possible. Usually, the individual is introduced to a few people close by, and then to others as the situation permits. If there is a reason that a person must meet everyone present, the host introduces the guest a few people at a time, moving from one group to the next after a few words of conversation.

Self-Introduction.   A person introducing himself or herself should address the other person by name first, if known.

> Mr. Atkins? I'm Mr. Porter (or John Porter). Please come in.
> Mr. Atkins, I'm Miss Davis, Mr. Porter's secretary. Mr. Porter will return shortly. Please have a seat.

When the other person's name is not known, the introducer gives his or her own name, and may add his or her title or business connection.

> My name's Jones.
> I'm Miss Davis, Mr. Porter's secretary. May I help you?
> Hello, I'm Dave Reeves. I'm in the Securities Administration Division.

In a social situation, the introducer always uses his or her full name and omits the title *Mr., Miss, Ms. or Mrs.*

Acknowledging an Introduction.   When the introduction is completed, it is acknowledged verbally and perhaps by a handshake, depending on the circumstances and the wishes of the parties involved.

The proper response is, "How do you do?" or "How are you?" or "I'm glad to meet you." The phrases "Pleased to meet you" and "I'm glad to make your acquaintance" are considered stilted and should be avoided.

When one is introduced to a group of people, the acknowledgment may be varied, as, "How do you do, Mr. Gordon," "Mr. Smith," "Good to see you," "Hello," and so on.

Names.   In addressing co-workers, employees should take a cue from the practices observed in the department and the company. It is best not to use first names too quickly. If in doubt, consult other employees about individual preferences.

Usage is generally more formal in public and in the presence of strangers. Thus the person addressed by first name, *Judy* or *George*, in the office might better be addressed as *Mrs. Johnson* or *Mr. Morton* in more formal circumstances.

Parties.   When a party or social affair is held for employees, whether on company premises or not, some of the rules of protocol are relaxed to the extent that sociability becomes more important than the preservation of rank. This fact, however, should not lessen the deference customarily shown to others. Familiarities developed during the party should be forgotten when the participants return to work.

Personal Habits. Consideration for others dictates strict control over the application of makeup at one's desk and prohibits the cleaning of fingernails, the combing of hair, and the adjusting of clothing.

The feet-on-desk posture is acceptable only in a private office when there are no visitors.

The regular use of a deodorant by all employees is advisable.

Personal Phone Calls. Businesses discourage the use of the telephone for personal calls, but realize that some calls are legitimate and necessary.

Long, intimate conversations on company time and in the presence of others are never in good taste.

Relatives and friends should be discouraged from telephoning.

Personal toll calls at company expense are larcenous.

Urgent personal calls that cannot properly be made from the office should be made from a pay phone in the building lobby or in the employees' lounge.

Personal Visitors. Visits by friends or family are not encouraged. If a friend calls for lunch or at quitting time, the employee should be ready to leave promptly. If the friend is early, it is better to ask the friend to wait in the reception room than at your desk.

Those with private offices can, of course, feel somewhat freer to see family and friends during office hours than those who share space with others, but even executives prefer as little intrusion as possible during business hours.

Private Dining Room. Part of a company's private dining room is usually set aside for random seating of company executives. The seats are filled in order; a lone diner does not take a place removed from others. Where meal times are assigned, the diner should arrive promptly and leave within a reasonable time, so that someone else may have the place at the table.

Reservations are usually required when an executive has guests. The reservation should be made at least a day in advance, if possible, and the time of reservation should be observed by the host. If one of several guests is late, the others may start without waiting. In a crowded dining room, a specific period may be allowed for the meal, as between 12 and 1 o'clock. The host should tactfully close the luncheon meeting promptly. If necessary, the conversation can continue in the office.

The private dining room usually has a limited menu; however, a guest who is on a diet may feel free to ask for simple substitutes such as tomato juice, eggs, and toast. The waiter will probably have some other suggestions.

Ordering procedure varies. The waiter may take the order from each guest individually; the host may take the orders for all and write them on a card to be passed to the waiter; or each guest may be given a menu with instructions to check the items wanted.

No tips are left for the waiter. However, depending on the custom in the particular company, an executive who uses the dining room regularly will pay a sum monthly into a pool for the waiters or have it added to the sum charged for personal meals.

The guests' meals are always paid by the company and, except for the usual "thank you," no reciprocation is expected or necessary.

Punctuality.   Visitors should arrive promptly for all appointments. One who expects to be even a little late should call ahead before leaving the office. If an appointment cannot be met, the host should be notified as far in advance as possible and a new date arranged.

Employees should arrive promptly at work and return promptly from luncheon and coffee breaks. Punctuality shows consideration of fellow workers and helps to maintain everyone's morale.

Work promised, assigned, or contracted for should be completed on time, or the other party should be notified sufficiently in advance to permit the adjustment of plans accordingly.

Rising.   Common sense should govern the etiquette of rising to meet guests. The executive will rise as a special mark of courtesy for visitors of either sex and for women employees to whom special deference should be shown.

A secretary does not rise when the executive enters, and the executive does not rise when the secretary or associates enter.

A male subordinate will rise for his superior.

Tipping.   It is not necessary to tip porters, mail boys, and other service employees. However, an executive may offer a gift in cash or merchandise for special service rendered to him or her personally. A group of employees may take up a collection at Christmastime for service employees who have been helpful during the year.

It is not customary to tip outside messengers, repair men, and others who call at the office to render service.

2

Meetings

This chapter deals with the preparations for organized meetings and the formalities of minutes and parliamentary procedure.

CONTENTS

For further information on participation in meetings, see "Talking to Groups," Section 1.4.

For arrangements covering private meetings, see "Appointments and Visitors," Section 1.3.

Meetings provide a way of dealing with common problems by discussion and by the participation of all in the decisions of the group. This method has been found, in many instances, to be an improvement over the older process by which an individual unilaterally makes decisions and gives orders that they be carried out.

Common types of meetings are staff conferences and committee meetings. Another type is the task meeting, which brings together a number of individuals who do not ordinarily work as a unit, but who have been brought together to apply their particular skills to the solution of a problem. Corporate meetings include meetings of the directors and the annual meeting of stockholders. Other meetings are held for dealers and distributors, groups of consumers, civic leaders, and the press. Many companies and their personnel also lend their services to the running of meetings or conventions for the business or professional societies to which they belong.

Meetings may also be classified by the functions they perform or the nature of the business that takes place in them. These functions are easily identified.

1. Instructional. Attendees come to learn about new administrative procedures, changes in organizational personnel, and new developments in

their professional or technical specialty. All training sessions also come under this category.

2. Advisory. An administrator seeks the advice of peers or subordinates before making a decision.

3. Deliberative. A committee or other group meets to make decisions for which the whole group is responsible.

4. Persuasive. Those who call the meeting hope to sell their ideas, services, or products in a usually one-sided presentation.

5. Negotiative. Two sides with opposing views get together to reach a settlement. Labor negotiations fall into this category.

In addition, each group usually has a self-perpetuating function that may involve (1) electing officers, (2) adopting rules for its own conduct, (3) maintaining records, and (4) giving recognition to those who serve it well, for example, a gift, a citation, a vote of thanks, or a testimonial dinner.

2.1 CONFERENCE ARRANGEMENTS

The term *conference* is here used to denote the meeting of a relatively small group of individuals for consultation and discussion. Ordinarily, the routine associated with a conference will include these steps.

1. Arranging for the meeting place.
2. Sending out meeting notices.
3. Preparing the agenda.
4. Taking the minutes.
5. Following up on meeting business.

Division of Responsibilities. An executive is customarily responsible for holding conferences in his/her area of authority and makes whatever plans are necessary to ensure their success. As staff director, he/she runs the staff meetings. The chairman of a committee is responsible for calling meetings of that committee and presiding at them. A committee may have an elected secretary, although it is common in business for the chairman to ask the administrative secretary to assist in routine planning and to take minutes or less formal notes of the proceedings. How much the administrative secretary does depends on the authority assigned by the executive and on the freedom to use initiative. Certainly, the secretary can be of enormous help in practically every phase of conference planning and performance outside of the actual deliberations.

Informal Conferences. In anticipation of a small, informal meeting, the executive will ask the administrative secretary to assist in performing the following basic routines.

                                        October 10, 19--

To Members of the Personnel Committee:

There will be a special meeting of the Personnel
Committee on Thursday, October 24, at 3 p.m. in the
14th floor conference room. The purpose of the meeting is to discuss several proposals for disability
insurance.

Please notify the Secretary or Miss Farmer (Ext.
3201) if you are unable to attend.

                              James Gary
                              Secretary

Figure 2-1   Notice of a meeting.

1. Reserve the conference room. This is necessary if the executive's own office is not to be used. The room chosen should be large enough to accommodate the group comfortably. A check should be made of the seating, ventilation, lighting, and electrical outlets, if needed.

2. Invite the participants. This is done by telephone or mail. Those who cannot attend are usually asked to give notice to that effect. In some instances the participants are consulted beforehand so that a mutually convenient time may be set. The notification should tell the nature or purpose of the meeting and what contributions any individual participant is expected to make as, for example, to give a report or explain a procedure (Figure 2-1).

3. Prepare conference material. The secretary may be required to type the order of business, obtain or prepare data for the employer's presentation, and have reports duplicated for distribution at the meeting.

4. Check the room. The secretary should arrive shortly before the time set for the meeting and see that the room is in order. At the start of the meeting attendance should be taken and, if feasible, absentees reminded by telephone that the meeting is starting.

5. Take notes. The secretary may be required to keep notes of the course of the discussion and provide an oral summary from time to time during the meeting.

6. Follow through. When the meeting is over, a summary is usually typed and distributed to the participants (Figure 2-2). Either by the underlining of the applicable passages or by separate memorandums, the attention of individuals is drawn to tasks assigned to them at the meeting.

November 14, 19--

Memorandum to: B. C. Farnum   R. B. Sterling
                M. Greggson   H. S. Timmons
                C. T. Madow   G. Wanderly

A meeting of the Education Committee was held on
Monday, November 10, 19--, in Mr. Madow's office.
Present were Messrs. Madow, Sterling, Timmons, and
Wanderly.

Mr. Madow began by saying that fringe benefits were
becoming increasingly important in attracting and
holding ambitious young people and that unless we
liberalized our tuition refund plan, we would be
placing our future development in jeopardy.

Mr. Sterling said he hoped we wouldn't tamper with
the present policy of not refunding tuition for
courses in which D and F grades were received. He
said that part of the merit of the present plan was
that it offered a strong incentive for good work.
Mr. Wanderly said that such an incentive was built
into the grading system and that making an employee
pay tuition for a course in which he got a low grade
simply encouraged employees to take the easiest
courses.

Mr. Wanderly said that with the rising cost of text-
books, the company could most help its student employees by offering to pay up to $50 a term for
books.

Mr. Madow asked that Mr. Timmons and Mr. Wanderly
pool their information and design a new tuition refund package that would reflect the soundest modern
practices. This could then be presented at the next
meeting of the Education Committee, scheduled for
December 12.

                              Eleanor Drier
                              Secretary to Mr. Madow

Figure 2-2   Memorandum embodying notes of an informal meeting.

Formal Conferences. Many formally constituted groups meet to make decisions that are binding on the participants or their constituents, and they must therefore follow very orderly procedures to ensure the validity of their decisions. Even when the legal aspects of the meeting are minimal, there may be need for systematic planning, observance of rules, and careful record-keeping.

Preliminaries. The secretary is expected to assist with the following preparations.

1. Calendar. Formal conferences should be and usually are scheduled well in advance. Regular meetings of a committee or similar body may be announced for a full year ahead. Mark the dates on your calendar as soon as they are known; then, allowing the needed time for preparation, schedule the work on your calendar or in your tickler file.

2. Meeting file. Set up a folder for each scheduled meeting and put into it all the correspondence, notices, and other documents relating to it. A planning schedule should be included in the folder or stapled to the cover for easy reference (Figure 2-3).

3. List of conferees. Obtain a list of those who are to be invited to the meeting. If some people are to attend several meetings, keep their names and addresses on cards or put them on stencils for machine addressing. Sheets of gummed labels interleaved with carbon paper may be used for the same purpose. Keep the mailing list up to date by making changes in names and addresses as soon as they are known. Also make careful inquiry regarding special guests for each meeting and add their names to the list.

4. Room facilities. Reserve the room for the meeting as far ahead as possible. At the same time arrange for a tape recorder, a projector, or other equipment, if necessary. Remember to check the location of an electrical outlet and the possible need for an extension cord, and make a note to have an extra bulb for the projector handy in case of emergency. If an operator is needed, arrange for that, too. Just before the meeting, see that the equipment is in place and that the seats are arranged the way your superior wants them. Distribute pencils and pads. Have water pitchers and glasses strategically located, with such service available at least for the head table. Be sure there are enough ash trays. Check the air conditioning or ventilation.

5. Notices. Notice of the meeting should be sent out reasonably well in advance, the amount of time depending on the nature of the meeting, the business pressures on the participants, travel requirements, and other factors. When notices are sent out far in advance to ensure that busy recipients reserve the date, it is customary to follow up with a reminder close to the day of the meeting.

The meeting notice should include the name of the group or organization, and the date, time, and place of the meeting.

Unless only routine business is to be taken up, the notice should state the purpose of the meeting or the chief subject of discussion.

```
┌─────────────────────────────────────────────────────────────────┐
│                          MEETING                                  │
│                                                                   │
│  Group _____ Date _____ Time ____ to_____       │
│                                                                   │
│  Room _____ Reservation made (date) _____ No. of persons ____│
│                                                                   │
│  Seating Arrangements    ☐ Regular                                │
│                          ☐ Special  (If special room layout is required, send │
│                                      diagram to Building Dept. and file copy │
│                                      in folder.)                  │
│                                                                   │
│        Equipment Required                    Refreshments         │
│                          Ordered                        Ordered   │
│                                                                   │
│     ☐ Blackboard         _____    ☐ Coffee          _____     │
│     ☐ Pad and easel      _____                                  │
│     ☐ Lectern            _____    ☐ Tea             _____     │
│     ☐ Public address                                              │
│         system           _____    ☐ Soft drinks    _____     │
│     ☐ Neck microphone    _____                                  │
│     ☐ Slide projector    _____    ☐ Danish          _____     │
│     ☐ Overhead projector _____                                  │
│     ☐ Movie projector (__ mm.) ____ ☐ _____    _____     │
│     ☐ Screen             _____                                  │
│     ☐ Place cards        _____    ☐ _____    _____     │
│     ☐ _____      _____                                  │
│     ☐ _____      _____    ☐ _____    _____     │
└─────────────────────────────────────────────────────────────────┘
```

Figure 2-3 Form used in planning meetings.

The notice may include a tentative agenda and copies of any reports or other documents that need to be studied in advance.

Conferees may be asked to send information on any reports they wish to make or items of new business they would like to have taken up at the meeting (Figure 2-4). Those from whom reports are expected should be reminded by telephone if they do not respond promptly.

If it will serve a useful purpose, all recipients should be asked to reply by mail or telephone within a time limit. A postcard form may be included to ensure an answer. Another follow-up arrangement is to call each member of the group a few days in advance of the meeting to find out if he will attend, a procedure that is always necessary when members of the group fail to respond as requested.

6. Food and refreshments. If coffee or food is to be served at the meeting, special arrangements must be made with the catering service, preferably a

> July 24, 19--
>
> Memorandum to Mr. Collier:
>
> Mr. Huff is calling a staff meeting for Monday,
> August 9. If you as chairman of the Work Measure-
> ment Committee expect to have a report, please let
> me know so that the item may be included on the
> agenda.
>
> It would also be appreciated if you would let me
> have a copy of your report before the day of the
> meeting.
>
> > Evelyn Pawling
> > Secretary to Mr. Huff

Figure 2-4   Request for a report.

week or two, or several weeks, in advance. The exact number of persons to be served can be relayed by telephone a few days before the meeting. (See also "Food Service," p. 80.)

7. Agenda. Whether it is called the agenda, or the order of business, or the calendar, the plan of the meeting must be carefully outlined beforehand. Unless the bylaws of the group indicate otherwise, the usual order of business is as follows.

Call to order
Approval of the minutes of the last meeting
Announcements
Reports of standing committees
Reports of special committees
Old business (carried over from previous meetings)
New business
Adjournment

With the information already in your meeting file and in the minutes of the last meeting, you should know what business has been held over and, to some extent, what reports are to be made and what new business is to come up. With the help of your employer, you can then incorporate these and other specifics into the agenda for the meeting. (See example in Figure 2-5.) It is customary to have copies of the agenda for distribution to everyone at the meeting, especially if changes have been made in a previously distributed tentative agenda.

```
                COMMITTEE OF PROFESSIONAL WOMEN
                    FOR THE MUSIC CENTER

                Board Meeting--October 8, 19--


                            AGENDA


     I.   Call to Order

    II.   Introductions
              New Board Member
              Guests

   III.   Minutes of the June 22 Board
              Meeting                    Anita Reeves

    IV.   Treasurer's Report             Carol MacGregor

     V.   Old Business
              President's Advisory Board

              Bus-to-Bowl Event          Genevieve Carroll

              Membership Matters         Agnes Deringer

    VI.   New Business
              Fall Event - November 19   Genevieve Carroll

              The Orchestra
                 European Tour
                 Series W
                 Philharmonic Fund

              Annual General Meeting

              Publicity
                 Events
                 Officers
                 Newsletter

   VII.   Adjournment
```

Figure 2-5 A sample agenda.

The Meeting. You should be in the room before the first conferees arrive. Bring with you a list of the persons expected, copies of the agenda, copies of any reports to be distributed, and your meeting file.

1. Attendance. Methods of taking attendance vary, but you should be sure to have a record of those who attend and be able to tell the chairman if there is a quorum. The quorum is the number of the group required to be present for business to be transacted—usually a simple majority. Latecomers should be recorded as present and in cases where individual voting records may later be needed, notations should be made of those who leave the room.

2. Notes. A careful record must be kept of the proceedings of the meeting. Notes taken at the meeting will later be edited and written up as the minutes of the meeting (see "Minutes," Section 2.3).

If you are asked to take notes at the meeting, you will find some of the information you need already available in the agenda and in the reports and resolutions submitted in advance. However, you will have to pay strict attention to motions as they are offered and record them on the spot. Skeletal forms prepared in advance will ease the task of recording (Figure 2-6). Additional notes will include summaries of announcements and oral reports, arguments made for and against motions on the floor, and a brief record of the other matters discussed.

Many times you will be asked to repeat the phrasing of a motion or of amendments to it, and to tell the chairman what the state of any particular motion is. A knowledge of parliamentary procedure is useful for this purpose (see "Parliamentary Procedure," Section 2.2).

Motion no. _____

Proposed by:

Seconded by:

Voted for: Voted against:

Discussion:

Figure 2-6   Form to aid in taking of minutes.

The verbatim proceedings of a meeting taken by a stenographer or recorded on tape can be a valuable aid in the preparation of the minutes. However, it should be kept in mind that such records will not include many details, such as the date and time of the meeting, the time of adjournment, the attendance, the names of speakers, and individual voting records. You must be alert to fill in the gaps from your own notes.

Recorded proceedings of meetings are useful for purposes other than the writing of the minutes. They may be filed for the use of absent members and those who wish more details than the minutes provide. For convenience of reference, tapes should be transcribed, a task that may be turned over to the typing pool.

Post-Meeting Functions. After a meeting, there is always a considerable amount of follow-up work. Here is a quick checklist.

1. Prepare the minutes for the signature of the chairman or the organizational secretary.

2. Enter corrections of minutes of the previous meeting in the official minutes book (see "Minutes," Section 2.3).

3. Prepare vouchers to pay for any fees or expenses.

4. Send copies of resolutions of appreciation, condolence, and so on, to the affected parties, with a covering letter.

5. Notify affected individuals of election, appointment, or special assignment growing out of the meeting.

6. Remind the chairman or organizational secretary to write letters authorized by the meeting; or draft the letters and offer them for approval and signature.

2.2 PARLIAMENTARY PROCEDURE

In order to ensure the orderly conduct of business and the observance of democratic principles, formally constituted committees, clubs, and other organizations observe to some degree the rules of parliamentary procedure. The rules are so named because they have their origins in the practices of the British Parliament, and are set out in detail in *Robert's Rules of Order*.

Basic Principles

1. All members of the group have equal rights and obligations. Any member may offer motions and take part in the debate.

2. All officers of the group are elected by a majority vote, and majority rule prevails.

3. Meetings are conducted in an orderly fashion. The agenda shows what business will be taken up and in what order, and one item must be disposed of before another can be considered.

4. Personalities are avoided. The discussion is addressed to ideas rather than individuals. In keeping with the aim of objectivity, members are addressed not as "you," but as "the chairman," "Mr. Simmons," "the gentleman," "the previous speaker," and so on.

5. Full discussion is permitted as long as it relates to properly presented motions and resolutions.

6. Every member has the right to know the exact language and status of any motion being discussed, and it is up to the chairman to see that this right is preserved.

7. Impartiality requires that the chairman take no sides and that all members be given an equal opportunity to speak. The chairman never makes a motion while in the chair or debates a motion without having first called the next ranking officer to preside. In such an event, the chairman does not return to the chair until the vote has been announced.

Order of Business.   Unless otherwise stated in the bylaws of the organization, the usual order of business is as follows.

Call to Order.   The chairman says, "The meeting will come to order," and may add any opening remarks.

Approval of Minutes.   The chairman calls on the organizational secretary to read the minutes of the last meeting, then asks, "Are there any corrections?" If the minutes have been distributed before the meeting, the reading can be dispensed with. No motion is needed for approval of the minutes. The chairman says, "The minutes stand approved," or "The minutes stand approved as corrected."

Reports.   The chairman asks for reports from officers, standing committees, and special committees, in that order. After a report is presented by the officer or committee chairman, the meeting chairman asks if there are any questions or discussion. If not, the report is ordered filed. No motion is needed for the adoption of a committee report unless recommendations for action are made.

Unfinished Business.   The chairman announces that unfinished business is in order, and either he or others he designates present facts relating to matters held over from other meetings and included on the current agenda. At the conclusion, a member wishing to take up any other matter not concluded at an earlier meeting rises to be recognized, refers to the matter, and makes a motion.

New Business.   The chairman asks, "Is there any new business?" Motions relating to new business can now be made.

Announcements.   The chairman asks, "Are there any announcements?" and may add any necessary announcements.

Adjournment.   The chairman says, "If there is no further business, the meeting will stand adjourned." When the business of the meeting is not finished, however, the chairman must ask for a motion to adjourn, and the motion must be seconded, voted on, and passed.

Conduct of Business.   The business of a formal meeting is transacted by means of motions and resolutions (Figure 2-7). A *motion* is a proposal for a specific course of action. It may be stated, for example, as "I move that group life insurance benefits be extended to part-time consultants." A *resolution* is an expression of the views of a group. It usually consists of a preamble beginning "Whereas," followed by "Be It Resolved," and the resolution.

A *main motion* is one placed before the group when no other business is under consideration. Amendments to the main motion may be proposed, but they must be discussed and voted on before a vote is taken on the main motion. A very urgent or important motion takes precedence over other motions. All motions must have a single objective and must be presented in accordance with the rules of order.

Presenting a Motion.   To present a motion, a member stands and addresses the chair by his title, for instance, "Mr. President." The chairman recognizes the speaker by nodding to him or speaking his name. The presenter then says, "I move that," or "I move the adoption of the following resolution." In some instances, it is helpful to offer some explanation before the motion is made. In that case, the speaker may say, "I have a motion to make, but first I would like to say a few words by way of introduction."

After presentation of the motion, the chairman says, "You have heard the motion. Is it seconded?" Any member may, without rising, second the motion. If the motion is not seconded, the chairman says, "There being no second, the motion is not before the meeting." If the motion is seconded, the chairman states the question: "It has been moved and seconded that . . ." There can be no discussion or vote until the motion is so stated, at which time the motion becomes the *question* and is so referred to. The chairman now calls for discussion or vote, as the group wishes.

The Motion Considered.   Except for some motions relating to parliamentary procedure, all principal motions are subject to debate. The presenter should be given the opportunity to speak first if he claims the right promptly. Others should be given their turn, and no one should be permitted to speak twice when others desiring to speak have not yet been given the opportunity. Discussion must be confined to the question, and the chairman should be sure the assembly knows at all times what the issue is.

At the end of the discussion, a member may shout, "Question." Or the chairman may ask, "Are you ready for the question?" If some members still want to debate, a vote may be taken on a motion to close debate. This motion, which is not debatable, requires a two-thirds vote. When it passes, a vote is taken first on any amendments, and then on the main motion.

The chairman is required to repeat a motion before a vote is called for. In

Motion	Inter-rupt Speaker	Second Needed	Amend-able	Debate-able	Vote Required
Privileged Motions[1]					
Adjourn	No	Yes	Yes	Yes	Majority
Recess	No	Yes	Yes[2]	No	Majority
Question of privilege	Yes	No	No	No	No vote
Orders of the day	Yes	No	No	No	Majority
Subsidiary Motions[1]					
Lay on the table	No	Yes	No	No	Majority
Close debate	No	Yes	No	No	Two-thirds
Limit debate	No	Yes	Yes	No	Two-thirds
Postpone to a specified time	No	Yes	Yes	Yes[3]	Majority
Refer to committee	No	Yes	Yes	Yes	Majority
Amend	No	Yes	Yes	Yes[4]	Majority
Postpone indefinitely	No	Yes	No	Yes	Majority
Main Motions[5]					
General	No	Yes	Yes	Yes	Majority
Specific					
Reconsider	Yes	Yes	No	Yes[4]	Majority
Rescind	No	Yes	Yes	Yes	Majority
Take from the table	No	Yes	No	No	Majority
Change order of business	No	Yes	Yes	Yes	Two-thirds
Incidental Motions[5]					
Point of order	Yes	No	No	No	Chair
Appeal from decision of chair	Yes	Yes	No	Yes[4]	Tie or majority
Parliamentary inquiry	Yes	No	No	No	Chair
Request for information	Yes	No	No	No	Chair
Withdraw a motion	No	No	No	No	Chair[6]
Division of a question	No	No	Yes	No	Chair[6]
Division of the assembly	Yes	No	No	No	Chair[6]
Suspend rules	No	Yes	No	No	Two-thirds
Object to consideration	Yes	No	No	No	Two-thirds negative

[1] Arranged in order of precedence.
[2] Only length of recess is amendable.
[3] Only propriety of postponement is debatable.
[4] Only when specific motion to which it applies is debatable.
[5] No order of preference among themselves. Incidental motions rank above subsidiary motions and take precedence over the motions from which they rise.
[6] If an objection is raised, a majority vote is required.

Figure 2-7   Table of motions.

putting the motion to a vote, the chairman says, "All in favor, say 'Aye.'" The members cast their vote. Then the chairman says, "All opposed, say 'No.'" If the voice response is clear-cut, the chairman will say, "The aye's [or no's] have it. The motion is carried [or is defeated]." If the voice vote is questioned, the vote may be taken by a show of hands, by having members stand, by ballot, or by roll call. The last is used when a record of the vote is desired.

All main motions are decided by a majority vote. The chairman may cast a vote in a tie or whenever the vote is taken by ballot or roll call.

Other Actions. In addition to simple discussion and vote on the main motions, motions may be altered, delayed, or killed, and previous actions may be modified.

1. Amendments. A member of the group may change a motion by amending it or by dividing the question. An amendment may consist of an addition, a deletion, or the substitution of words, or any combination of these methods. The amender says, "I move to amend the motion to read *may* instead of *shall*." Like the main motion, the amendment must be seconded, opened to discussion, and voted by a majority. The initial or primary amendment may itself be amended by a secondary amendment, but no more than two amendments to the main motion are permitted. The secondary and primary amendments must be disposed of in that order before discussion of the main motion, as amended, can be resumed.

2. Division. Consideration of a complex question may be aided by a division into its parts, with discussion and a vote on each part separately. A motion to divide may be decided by the chairman without a vote.

3. Lay on the table. To postpone action on a motion, a member may move to "lay it on the table." The latter motion, which takes precedence over all others, is not debatable and is passed by a majority vote. A tabled motion must be offered again later at the same meeting or at the following meeting; otherwise it is considered dead. A motion to "take from the table" may be made when new or unfinished business is in order and no question is pending.

4. Postpone. A specified time for consideration may not be incorporated into a motion to lay on the table. If resumption of consideration is desired at a specific time, a motion to postpone until that time is in order. Such a motion may be amended and debated.

5. Commit. A motion requiring further investigation or discussion may be referred to a committee. A member says, "I move that the question be referred to a committee of three appointed by the chairman." If the number, composition, and method of selection of the committee are not stated in the motion, the decision must be made by the chair or on further motion by the assembled group. After consideration by the group, the committee chairman reports to the assembly and recommends the action to be taken.

6. Object to consideration. An objection may be raised to consideration of a motion, provided it is done before the first speaker is through talking. The chair responds by calling for a vote.

7. Postpone indefinitely. A vote to postpone a motion indefinitely has the same effect as a vote to defeat it.

8. Withdraw. A member may ask to withdraw the motion. The chairman responds by asking if there is any objection. If there is no objection, the motion is withdrawn. If there is objection, a vote must be taken.

9. Reconsider. Any action already taken may be reconsidered provided a member moves reconsideration on the same day as the main motion was adopted or defeated. The motion to reconsider is entered in the minutes for consideration at the next meeting.

10. Rescind. A member may move that an action already taken be rescinded.

Rights of Members. Some questions affecting the rights of members are so urgent that they may be raised even at the cost of interrupting a speaker.

1. Question of privilege. A member may get immediate attention to a request affecting comfort, heating, or the like, by rising to a "question of privilege." On action by the chairman, the regular business of the meeting is resumed.

2. Point of order. A member may call attention to a violation of procedure by saying, "I rise to a point of order." The chairman will ask for the point to be stated and then declare that it is either well taken or not.

3. Appeal. The decision of a chairman may be appealed. The chairman then puts the question to the assembly. "Shall the decision of the chair be sustained?" Debate is permitted, and a majority rules.

4. Inquiry. The chairman may be asked to rule whether a parliamentary procedure is in order or to explain the meaning of a motion.

5. Point of information. A member may interrupt a speaker to ask for clarification of a point, but not to offer information.

6. Division of assembly. When the tally of a vote is uncertain, a member may call out, "Division." The "aye's" and "no's" may then be asked to rise and be counted.

7. Orders of the day. When the scheduled order of business is not being followed, a motion for "the orders of the day" may be offered to ensure proper treatment of a measure. No vote is required.

Adjournment. A motion to adjourn is in order at any time except when a speaker has the floor or the assembly is occupied with important business. Forms of the motion include, "Mr. Chairman, I move that we adjourn," "I move that we adjourn at three o'clock," and "I move that we adjourn until Thursday, September 22, at four o'clock." The last type of motion is made to ensure another meeting when a regular meeting has not been scheduled. A break in any meeting can be obtained with a motion calling for a recess. Such a motion must state the length of the recess or the time the meeting will resume.

QUARTER CENTURY CLUB

Minutes of the Meeting of the Board of Directors

September 2, 19--

The regular quarterly meeting of the Board of
Directors of the Quarter Century Club was held in
the 14th floor conference room on Wednesday, September 2, 19-- at 4:00 p.m.

The meeting was called to order promptly by the
President, Eugene Kane. Present, in addition to Mr.
Kane, were Mary Blair, Marvin Denny, Eleanor Farber,
Roy Gilston, William Harrison, John Reynolds, and
Teddy Walhovic. Absent were Gloria Porter and Ste-
phen Simon. Miss Farber acted as secretary in the
absence of Mrs. Porter.

The minutes of the previous meeting, June 14,
19--, were read and approved without correction.

Mr. Kane announced that Jerome Daly, an active
member of the Board, had died after a short illness
on August 8. All stood for a moment of silence. Mr.
Kane asked Miss Farber to prepare a suitable letter
of condolence to be sent to Mrs. Daly on behalf of
the Board.

Treasurer's Report. Mr. Denny reported on the
statement of income and expenses as follows:

Income	$5,703.00
Expenses	8,672.78
Excess of Expenses Over Income	2,969.78
Credit Balance, June 30, 19--	4,963.52
Credit Balance, June 30, 19--	$1,993.74

The report was accepted as read.

Membership Committee. Mr. Harrison reported
that, as of September 1, four additional members
of the staff were eligible for membership in the
Quarter Century Club. They are Neil Goldberg, Henry
T. Grady, Lillian S. Harrison, and Benjamin Strom-
berg.

Upon motion of Mr. Harrison and duly seconded,
the four employees named were admitted to membership.
Mr. Kane asked that the Secretary so notify them.

Figure 2-8 Minutes of a formal meeting.

Annual Dinner Committee. Mr. Reynolds reported
that plans for the annual dinner were well under way.
The affair is set for January 25 at the Ambassador
Hotel. In response to a question, he said that complaints about slow service, heard frequently at the
last dinner, would be avoided; the hotel has promised to provide an extra staff of waiters.

Education Committee. Miss Walhovic said that
because of the increase in the cost of living,
tuition, and other expenses, the $500 scholarships
offered annually to sons and daughters of employees
now seemed inadequate. She therefore proposed the
following resolution:

> RESOLVED, That the value of the
> annual Quarter Century Scholarships be
> increased to $1,000 and that members be
> assessed $5 a year in order to cover the
> increased expense.

The motion was seconded and, after some discussion, carried.

President's Remarks. Mr. Kane noted that there
was general concern about the increasing cost of
living and the consequent erosion of the purchasing
power of anticipated pensions. He said the consequences would be felt particularly by those who, for
some reason, were not participating in the profit-
sharing plan or who had subscribed to the plan only
lately. He thought that if members were properly informed, they could still make adjustments in the
amount of their participation in the profit-sharing
plan in order to improve their retirement income.

After some discussion, Mr. Gilston introduced
a resolution asking the Treasurer to look into the
merits of Mr. Kane's proposal and report back to
Board at its next meeting, January 6, 19--.

There being no further business, the meeting
was declared adjourned at 4:50 p.m.

Eleanor Farber, Acting Secretary

September 5, 19--

Figure 2-8   (continued).

2.3 MINUTES

The minutes are the official records of the meetings of all kinds of groups (Figure 2-8). The more formal the group's organization and the greater the legal implications of its actions, the greater the necessity for formal and complete minutes. (See also "Conference Arrangements," Section 2.1.)

Mechanics. A distinction should be made between the minutes duplicated and sent to members of a group and the minutes kept as the official record.

1. The official minutes should always be the original typed copy, on plain white paper of good quality.

2. Minutes may be single- or double-spaced. However, double spacing makes it easier to write in corrections voted by the group at the following meeting. The use of marginal heads makes reference convenient. Numbered paragraphs may be used for the same purpose (Figure 2-9).

3. Number pages consecutively for each meeting or for the entire year. The latter practice is preferable when an index of the business of meetings is to be kept. Minutes of corporations follow separate rules (see pp. 67–74).

-3-

9.   In regard to the new production and backlog reports, Mr. Moses stated that the GRI ~~265~~ 255 Unit's cut-off dates are not consistent with the schedule. Mr. Davis said that each unit should use the actual cut-off dates for the runs reported on. He added that he will issue a schedule showing these dates.

10.   ~~Miss Knight asked if the Group Dept. would include the dollar amount for semi-private room and board benefit on the Group Issue Summary. Mr. Packer said he would look into it.~~ *Corrected statement on page 4 following*

11.   Miss Knight asked if the underwriters would forward any questions on the renewal rate memo through Mr. Packer. He *Mr. Greenfield* said he would try to get them to do this.

12.   The next meeting will be held on Monday, January 28, at 9:30 a.m. in the 16th floor conference room.

S. Berman

S. Berman
Secretary

Figure 2-9 Portion of official minutes showing use of numbered paragraphs and corrections ordered at the following meeting.

4. Type the name of the group in all capital letters, centered at the top of the first sheet. Below it, also centered, state the nature of the meeting and then the date of the meeting in upper- and lower-case letters (Figure 2-8).

5. In the body of the minutes, capitalize the titles of officers and such words as *Committee, Company, Corporation,* and *Board of Directors* whenever they relate to the assembly or the organization of which the assembly is a part.

6. Record each item of business or each separate action of the group in a separate paragraph. Indent motions and resolutions an extra five spaces at right and left.

7. The words *WHEREAS* and *RESOLVED* in resolutions should always (a) be typed all in caps, (b) begin a paragraph, and (c) be followed by a comma. The word *That* following *RESOLVED* should be capitalized (Figure 2-10).

Content.   Minutes vary in form from group to group, but the following content and order are fairly standard.

1. Name of the group.

2. Date, time, and place of meeting.

3. Regular or special meeting. If special, for what purpose.

4. Attendance: names of members present and absent; specially invited guests.

5. Name of the presiding officer and secretary.

6. Proceedings: a record of all announcements, reports, motions, and resolutions.

(a) Include only the *main motions* on which action has been taken (see "Parliamentary Procedure," Section 2.2), and the names of the proposers, if desired, but not of the seconders.

(b) Preserve the exact language of motions and resolutions, as passed.

(c) Reports may be summarized, or appended or filed elsewhere, with a proper reference in the minutes.

(d) A summary of the discussion is optional. It is especially helpful to absent members.

7. Date of the next meeting.

8. The time of adjournment.

9. The signature of the secretary and the date of signing. The close *Respectfully submitted* is not necessary.

Language.   The minutes should be expressed in an objective, businesslike way.

1. Exclude your personal opinions and interpretations.

2. Avoid qualifying adjectives like *enthusiastic, interesting,* and *well received.*

3. Avoid any suggestion of bias. In reporting a discussion, do not favor one side over the other.

1.

RESOLVED, That . . . .
. . . .
. . . .

2.

WHEREAS, the . . . .
. . . ., be it

RESOLVED, That . . . .
. . . .

3.

WHEREAS, it . . . .
. . . .; and

WHEREAS, the . . . .
. . . .; it is

RESOLVED, That . . . .
. . . .; and it is

FURTHER RESOLVED, That . . . .
. . . .

Figure 2-10   Forms of resolutions.

4. Adopt a formal but not necessarily legalistic tone, with emphasis on clarity and precision.

5. Use ordinary memorandum or report style for minutes of groups that are informally constituted or conducted (Figure 2-2).

Corrections.   When corrections of the minutes of a previous meeting are approved, the secretary enters the corrections in red ink on the original copy (Figure 2-9).

1. Draw a line through the words to be deleted and write the substituted words directly above.

2. If a whole paragraph or section must be recast, draw a line through each line of copy to be deleted and append the new paragraph or section. A note in red ink on the original should make reference to the addition to the minutes.

Indexing.   An index is helpful whenever the number of actions taken at meetings is so great as to present difficulties in finding the references desired. The index is kept on file cards, with one topic or subtopic to a card. References are then listed chronologically with the date of the meeting and the page number. The cards are brought up to date after each new set of minutes is approved (Figure 2-11).

Corporation Minutes.   The bylaws of a corporation prescribe the rules for meetings and tell for what purpose and at what times they will be held. The annual meeting of stockholders is traditional. Other meetings, held more frequently, are those of the board of directors and various committees of the board.

The corporate secretary, a high company officer, is required to see that the meetings are held and that the minutes are kept in good order. The administrative secretary, however, may assist in the actual preparations for the meetings, take notes at the meetings, and write up the minutes afterward. This job will be easier for the novice if the bylaws are carefully studied and the minutes of earlier meetings are reviewed beforehand. Tape recordings of the proceedings are near-necessary safeguards against omissions and errors.

```
Minutes of Personnel Committee

    Tuition Refund Plan

        April 12, 1969, p. 3
        May 7, 1969, p. 2
        October 15, 1969, p. 5
        September 8, 1970, p. 3
        October 19, 1971, p. 4
```

Figure 2-11   Indexed references to minutes.

METRO CORPORATION

Meeting of Shareholders

May 1, 19--

The annual meeting of the shareholders of the Metro Corporation was held at the office of the Corporation, 320 Park Avenue, New York City, on May 1, 19--, at 10:00 a.m.

CALL TO ORDER

The meeting was called to order by Mr. David Brown, President of the Corporation, who presided. Mr. Henry Green, Secretary of the Corporation, acted as Secretary of the meeting as provided in the bylaws.

NOTICE OF MEETING

The Secretary presented the order pursuant to which the meeting had been called, together with his affidavit showing that a notice of the meeting had been mailed to each shareholder of record, addressed to him as of the close of business April 10, 19-- at the address as it appeared on the books of the Corporation. Upon motion, the affidavit was approved and ordered to be appended to the minutes of the meeting.

LIST OF STOCKHOLDERS

The Secretary presented a certified list of shareholders, and upon a call of the list and inspection of the proxies, it was found that there were present in person or by proxy shareholders representing 48,325 shares.

APPROVAL OF MINUTES

The Secretary then read the minutes of the annual meeting of shareholders held on May 2, 19--,

Figure 2-12   Minutes of a meeting of stockholders.

whereupon a motion approving the minutes was made and seconded and unanimously approved.

PRESIDENT'S REPORT

The President then read his annual report. Following questions from the floor, the report was duly approved and ordered placed on file.

INSPECTORS OF ELECTION

Upon motion, Messrs. Thomas Wright and James Stacy were nominated and elected Inspectors of Election. Thereupon they subscribed their oaths, which were ordered to be appended to the minutes.

NOMINATIONS FOR DIRECTOR

The President then called for nominations for six directors to hold office for a term of two years and until their successors should be elected and qualify.

The following were nominated: (Names of nominees are listed.)

BALLOTING

The ballots were cast and then tabulated by the Inspectors of Election who reported the results as follows:

(List of names and number of votes for each.)

ELECTION

The President thereupon declared that Messrs. (names), having received the highest number of votes, were the duly elected directors of the Corporation for the ensuing two years.

ADJOURNMENT

There being no further business, the meeting was adjourned on motion properly presented, seconded, and approved.

David Brown, President   Henry Green, Secretary

Figure 2-12 (continued).

SIGMA INDUSTRIES, INC.

Report of Stockholders Meeting

June 12, 19--

The Special Meeting in lieu of the Annual Meeting of Stockholders of Sigma Industries, Inc., was called to order by Bernard Foy, Chairman of the Board and President, promptly at 2:30 p.m. on June 12, 19-- at the Statler Hilton Hotel, Buffalo, New York.

There were 84,884 shares of stock present at the meeting, in person or by proxy, representing more than 80 per cent of the total outstanding shares.

After the nomination of the nine Directors, Louis Brody, a stockholder, inquired as to the number of meetings held by the Board during the previous year and whether employee members received directors' fees. The Chairman advised Mr. Brody that ten meetings were held, lasting an average of two hours each, and employee Board members did not receive directors' fees.

The Company's proposals to amend the Certificate of Incorporation to increase authorized common stock from 200,000 to 500,000 shares and amend the Company's Qualified Stock Option Plan were acted upon favorably by the stockholders.

Mr. Brody's proposal for cumulative voting by stockholders in the election of directors was not carried.

Mr. Foy briefly reviewed the Company's activities during the year and plans for the future. Recalling that just four years ago the Company was in a weak financial position until present management took over, he described steps that had been taken to bring it into its present positive position. Mr. Foy

Figure 2-13 Minutes of a stockholders' meeting as reported to stockholders.

enumerated the companies which had been acquired since then and the roles they were playing in its growth.

In response to a stockholder's inquiry about the progress in the Datalab division, Mr. Foy explained that it was running well and "definitely on target." Mr. Foy concluded the question and answer period by stating that earnings increases in the near future would be attributed to acquisitions as well as to internal growth.

The inspectors of election reported the following results of stockholder votes:

(1)   Election of Directors:

80 per cent of the outstanding stock voted in favor (84,515).

(2)   Proposal Increasing Common Stock from 200,000 to 500,000 Shares:

For 81,373; Against 1,225—77 per cent of the outstanding stock voting in favor.

(3)   Proposal to Amend the 19-- Qualified Stock Option Plan to Increase the Number of Shares issuable thereunder to 6,500:

For 78,915; Against 2,405—75 per cent of the outstanding stock voting in favor.

The meeting was adjourned at 3:15 p.m.

Respectfully submitted

Jane E. Carson
Secretary

June 12, 19--
Buffalo, New York

Figure 2-13   (continued).

Minute Book. The minutes of stockholder meetings, directors' meetings, and committee meetings may be bound separately or not, but the minutes for each group should be kept together in chronological order.

1. Consecutive numbering of pages through the year helps prevent the loss of pages. In some instances, each sheet is also signed by the corporate secretary to ensure that no unauthorized substitutions are made.

2. The minutes are kept in a loose-leaf binder, often with a lock for security. The loose-leaf pages may be bound permanently at intervals of one or several years.

3. The minute book of a corporation may include a certified copy of its charter and bylaws. Other documents, referred to in the minutes, should be pasted in or bound in, or appropriate notes in the minute book should indicate where the documents are kept.

Minutes of Stockholders' Meetings. The minutes of the meetings of stockholders are generally characterized by the following details (Figure 2-12).

1. The place, date, and hour of the meeting; also the kind of meeting, for example, annual or special.

2. The names of the chairman and the secretary.

3. Reference to the proof of call and notice of the meeting. The proof of call is the legal authorization for the meeting, usually in the form of an order from the president of the company. The proof of notice of the meeting is an affidavit affirming that a notice was sent to every stockholder. Both documents are presented by the secretary of the meeting for inclusion in or as an appendage to the minutes.

4. The number of shares represented in person and the number represented by proxy. (If the number of stockholders is small, the names of those present may also be given.) A quorum is a majority of the number of shares outstanding and entitled to vote. Voting is by number of shares rather than by number of shareholders.

5. The names of inspectors of election, if any, and how they were chosen.

6. A record of all actions taken, including those on motions, resolutions, and reports duly moved and seconded. The discussion preceding a vote is not legally significant and need not be included except in the interests of good corporate relations with absent stockholders to whom the minutes are sent. (Minutes sent to stockholders may be written as a report, with any changes in language and order that may be needed to maintain interest. See Figure 2-13.)

The names of persons making and seconding motions should be omitted except on special request; sometimes a stockholder wishes his dissent to be recorded.

7. Record of adjournment.

8. Signatures of the secretary and the president.

METRO CORPORATION

Meeting of the Board of Directors

April 1, 19--

PRESENT

PRESIDING

NOTICE OF
MEETING

READING OF
MINUTES

FINANCIAL
STATEMENT

A regular meeting of the Board of Directors was held at the office of the Corporation, 320 Park Avenue, New York City, on Tuesday, April 1, 19--, at 2:30 p.m.

There were present the following directors:

(Names are listed.)

Messrs. Ralph Day and Emmett C. Dorp were absent.

Mr. David Brown, President of the Corporation, presided as Chairman of the meeting. Mr. Henry Green, Secretary of the Corporation, acted as Secretary of the meeting.

The Secretary presented the notice pursuant to which the meeting had been called, together with a certificate showing that a copy of the notice had been mailed to each director, as required by the bylaws; and, on motion, the notice and certificate were ordered filed.

The Secretary then read the minutes of the previous quarterly meeting held on December 31, 19--. The minutes were approved as read.

The President submitted to the Board a financial statement prepared by Joseph Blank & Co., certified public accountants, covering the operations of the Corporation for the quarter January 1, 19-- to March 31, 19-- and also showing the condition of the Corporation as of the close of business on March 31, 19--. Upon

Figure 2-14   Minutes of a meeting of corporation directors.

motion duly made and seconded, the
following resolution was approved:

DIVIDEND   RESOLVED, That a regular quar-
DECLARED   terly dividend of $1.00 per
                        share is hereby declared, pay-
                        able April 15, 19--, to all
                        shareholders of record at the
                        close of business on March 31,
                        19--.

REPORT OF   Mr. Donald E. Finley, Chairman
CHMN OF   of the Finance Committee, offered a
FINANCE COMM.   report on the prospects for bene-
                        ficial legislation affecting the
                        Corporation's financial plans. The
                        report was accepted and ordered
                        placed on file.

ADJOURNMENT   No other business having come
                        before the meeting, it was on motion
                        adjourned.

                        ─────────────────────────────

                        Henry Green, Secretary

Figure 2-14   (continued).

Minutes of Directors' Meetings.   The minutes of directors' meetings follow
the general pattern and style of those of stockholders' meetings, but these
specific comments may be added.

1. The minutes should show the names of the directors present and the
names of those absent.

2. All actions are taken on the basis of one-man–one-vote, not on the
basis of the number of shares held.

3. It is not proper for a director to vote on a matter involving his personal
interests (for example, a motion to compensate him for special services
rendered), and the minutes should show that he abstained.

4. It is not necessary to include the names of directors making or seconding
motions. However, a director making a dissenting or protesting motion may
want his name on the record, and his request should be honored.

See Figure 2-14 for an example of the minutes of a meeting of corporation
directors.

2.4   CONVENTIONS AND LARGE-SCALE MEETINGS

One of the most hectic and demanding experiences for an executive and the
secretary is to take charge of the details of a major meeting or convention.
Such an event may come about when the company decides to have a regional

or national meeting of its staff or its distributors. Or it may occur when the executive is selected to organize a meeting of some trade or professional society of which he is a member. In either case, there are usually months of planning, followed by active duty at the convention site.

The major administrative work and decisions are usually made by the convention chairman, but the secretary is always close by to see to the particulars. Normally, the planning for a convention will begin a year or more before the actual event, and the person in charge will have to perform these tasks:

Choose the convention site.
Engage hotel facilities.
Set up the program.
Invite speakers and guests.
Provide for off-hour activities.
Contract for displays and exhibits.
Arrange for hotel accommodations and transportation for VIP's.
Prepare and send out announcements.
Answer inquiries.
Take advance registrations.
Order printed programs, tickets, badges, and so on.
Contact the local Visitors' Bureau or Chamber of Commerce for maps and folders describing places of interest.
Ask local firms to contribute samples, souvenirs, useful product data, and so on.
Plan for personnel, supplies, and equipment for the office and for the registration desk at local headquarters.

A good convention chairman can often farm out many of these tasks to committees, but it still takes a great deal of energy to appoint the committees or their chairmen and to follow up to see that they perform their functions. Major help of another sort can be provided by the convention offices of hotels and airlines that serve the convention city as well as by the local chambers of commerce and visitors' bureaus. Early consultation will elicit planning guides, literature, and advice, as well as actual assistance in booking transportation and hotel rooms and running the meeting. For assistance in planning meal functions, a close working arrangement with the hotel's banquet office is indispensable. Early in the planning stage, the secretary should obtain the names of key people in every functional area, and then go directly to them when problems arise.

Some days in advance of the opening date, the convention chairman and the secretary and staff move to the convention site and set themselves up for the actual business of running the meeting. Figure 2-15 provides a facilities checklist that should be useful to anyone with responsibilities for the administration of a large conference.

Location.   Large meetings are held in locations that offer the greatest attractions for the participants. In many instances, the host organization has a plant or other facility in the area and is prepared to offer its hospitality and

Acoustics	Maitre d'
Air conditioning (noisy?)	Master switch location
Air Freight carrier	Meeting headquarters
Blackboard, easels, etc.	Piano availability (type)
Buses, taxis, limousines	Platforms
Capacity	Projection equipment
Carpenter	Reception and registration
Ceiling height	Rehearsal space
Chairs available	Rest room availability
Check cashing clearance	Room availability dates
Checkroom facilities	Room size and decor
Display area (room name)	Security
Door sizes (interior)	Sleeping rooms needed
Dressing rooms	Sound facilities
Electrician	Sound man
First-aid room	Special decoration
Floor plans	Special lighting equipment
Florist	Stage area
Food area (room name)	Storage space
Freight elevators	Tables available
Hotel representative	Traffic pattern
Lecterns	Traffic restrictions
Loading platforms	Transfer company (trucking)
Local model and talent agency	Union requirements (if any)

Figure 2-15   Checklist of convention facilities. (From American Airlines)

attend to many of the local arrangements. Be sure to check the meeting site for

Distance from airports and railroad stations.
Taxi, bus, and other local transportation facilities.
Parking facilities.
Restaurants, stores, and recreational facilities.

Hotel Liaison.   Arrangements must be made in advance for office space, hospitality suites, and meeting rooms, for which there is generally no extra charge.

Know the names of the people in the hotel convention office who have a direct interest in your meeting.
Request that confirmation of all reservations be sent directly to attendees.
Ask the desk for the room numbers of VIP's and others you may need to call frequently.
Get the numbers, names, and locations of the rooms to be used for all convention functions.

Supply a daily program for listing on the hotel bulletin board.
See that there are adequate checking facilities.

Meeting Rooms.   Preferably, meeting rooms should be just large enough for the purpose—neither too small nor too large. However, a little crowding is usually better than a sea of empty chairs. If a room is too large, the use of screens can effectively reduce the seating area. Other considerations:

Check air conditioning, lighting, and acoustics.
Avoid a location subject to noise interference from the outside, for example, the kitchen, construction work, main passageways, and so on.
If you need several rooms, see that they are close together, if possible, and easily accessible to each other.
Before engaging the rooms, try to inspect them while they are in use to see how well they meet the demands made on them.
See that the chairs are sturdy and comfortable.
Make sure posts don't interfere with the line of vision.
Check the availability of electrical outlets for audio-visual or other equipment.
Make provision in advance for the handling of an overflow. It may be possible to bring in extra chairs, open a partition to an adjoining room, or pipe the program into another location, using closed-circuit television or loud speakers alone.

Office Arrangements.   The hotel will usually provide a complimentary room or suite to serve as office headquarters for the meeting. The convention correspondence should be placed in transfer files and moved to this office several days before the meeting begins. In addition to telephone service, desks, chairs, and wardrobes for clothing, have the following supplies and equipment, or know where you can get them in a hurry.

Pencils, pens, erasers.
Letterheads with envelopes, plain paper, carbon paper, file folders, gummed labels, manila envelopes in several sizes, steno notebooks.
Staple machine with staples; paper clips, Scotch tape.
Stiff paper for signs, felt marking pens.
Typewriters; adding machine; Ditto or other duplicating machine.

Printing and Duplicating.   Programs, agendas, ballots, signs, and as many other forms as possible should be printed beforehand and shipped to the convention site in ample time for distribution.

On-the-spot printing needs, including bulletins and announcements, may be met in the convention office on a borrowed or rented duplicating machine. Be sure to arrange with the hotel in advance for such equipment and have the necessary supplies: paper, stencils, ink, and so on.

Registration.   Much of the secretarial detail centers on the registration desk. This must be set up as much as a day in advance of the meeting and staffed by at least a couple of shifts from early morning until the beginning of the last meeting each day.

Arrange with the hotel for phone service during registration hours.
Check the need for the following equipment:
Enough tables and chairs—for registrants and office help.

Typewriters (hotel can supply, usually without cost).

Notepaper, pens, pencils, ash trays, wastepaper baskets.

Cash box, with change, if fees are charged; receipts for fees received.

Badges or other identification, with provision for filling in names with large-type typewriter or felt-tip pen.

Registration cards, preprinted with space for name, title, business affiliation, fee paid, and so on.

Tickets of admission to various meetings and events.

Signs to instruct registrants and direct them to correct locations

Bulletin boards for emergency notices and last-minute instructions.

Set out programs and give-away materials for self-service, or prepackage sets of material.

In case of advance registration, have all materials for each individual in an envelope marked with his name, and arrange envelopes alphabetically for distribution at convention time.

Hospitality (Speakers and Guests).   Speakers and guests of honor always get special consideration. Check the following services.

Arrange for travel and hotel accommodations.

Provide necessary tickets for convention events.

Meet dignitaries at airport or send company car.

Assign some individual to look after the needs of each guest.

Arrange for reception and seating of dignitaries at the meeting.

Obtain in advance from each speaker a personal data sheet for use in publicity and in the introduction to the audience. If you will need a photo, ask for it at the same time.

Have flowers or fruit in VIP's room on arrival.

Hospitality (Conferees)

1. A local hospitality committee is best equipped to arrange for the ordinary amenities expected by convention visitors. Printed literature or a mimeographed bulletin prepared for distribution at the registration desk should give such information as the following.

Hotel directory.

Parking facilities.

Dining facilities in the area.

Entertainment available.

Points of interest.

2. Sometimes an interested organization or special group will provide a social hour or other special event for all attendees or for selected guests. Proper notice should be included with the registration materials or placed in the guest's mailbox or under the door.

3. Guest hospitality includes obtaining and distributing free literature and souvenirs not directly connected with the meeting. For example:

Complimentary notebook.

Pencil, ballpoint pen.

Key ring.

Small samples of locally grown or manufactured products.

Literature or products contributed by interested or participating companies.

Large envelopes or shopping bags for carrying such gifts.

Platform.   For a group of 20 or less, a round-table, oval, square, or U-shaped arrangement is usually most satisfactory. For larger groups, auditorium-style seating becomes necessary, with a raised platform for the speakers. A platform raised about a foot is usually better than a higher one, which gives the impression of a stage and removes the speakers too far from the audience.

Place the platform away from the entrances and exits so that latecomers and early leavers will not disturb the others.

Drape platform tables to the floor.

Provide a public address system, if necessary, with the choice of a neck or a standing microphone.

Check with the speakers in advance to determine the need for a blackboard, an easel, or other equipment.

For a panel session, provide a name card in front of each speaker and a table large enough for all speakers to be seated comfortably.

See that there is plenty of ice water and that there are enough glasses.

Audio-Visual Equipment

1. After the program has been arranged, the speakers should be asked to indicate (a) what kind of equipment they need, (b) whether they will bring their own equipment or want the convention management to supply it, and (c) whether they will need an operator. In large cities, union rules prohibit the operation of motion picture and other audio-visual equipment by any but union operators; the hotel can advise on this point.

2. Some additional suggestions:

Before bringing in equipment from the outside, check with the hotel to find out what is available there.

Ask the hotel to provide a lectern for the speakers and make sure the light on it works.

Check into the need for sound amplification and ask the hotel to provide any necessary equipment. Make the hotel responsible for the performance of any equipment it provides, but personally test it a half-hour before the meeting.

See that the room can be darkened for film presentations. Find out where the light switch is and have someone stationed there when needed.

Check the location of the wall outlets. Have the necessary extension cords and provide for emergencies with extra bulbs for the projection equipment. Make sure the power is adequate.

If talks are to be recorded, make proper arrangements for a microphone, a tape recorder, and an operator.

3. Now for a quick check of equipment needs.

Amplification system (necessary for large and noisy rooms).

Blackboard (provide chalk and eraser).

Easel for charts; large flip pads and felt marking pens.

Flannel board.

Lectern.

Microphones (stationary and lavaliere).

Motion-picture projector (for sound or silent films).

Opaque projector (projects original documents, but noisy and hot).

Overhead projector (requires transparencies).

Slide, sound-slide, or film-strip projector (have extension cord and extra bulb).

Tape recorder (with plenty of tape).

Videotape recorder (check lighting).

Program Assistance. Although the program content must be left to those in charge, staff assistance is needed to ensure the program's success.

Make sure session chairmen are provided with speakers' biographies well in advance.

Advise chairmen of the exact time for the beginning and end of each session, and impress on them the necessity of keeping speakers within the limits set.

See that the meeting rooms are set up as planned and that all equipment is in place and in good working order. After each session have the rooms cleared of the equipment no longer necessary.

Be sure that the signs at the entrances clearly identify the meeting rooms and the current programs.

Have ushers, if necessary, to collect tickets, distribute session programs, and assist in seating.

Check with the session chairmen to be sure their speakers are present and that their other needs are met. Use house telephone to round up tardy participants.

Advertise changes in program as promptly as possible through lobby posters, handbills, signs outside meeting rooms, and announcements at the beginning of meetings.

Food Service. A large meeting may require coffee breaks, luncheons, and dinner banquets. Except for coffee breaks, it is always best if separate rooms can be obtained for food service. If this is not possible, have tables set up in advance and screened off to avoid disturbance while the meeting is in session.

Coffee Breaks. Coffee is usually served between breaks in the morning and afternoon sessions (about 10:30 and 3:30). Doughnuts or Danish pastry may be served with it. If the Danish pastry is cut in advance, there is no need for plates or knives and fewer pastries are needed. In small meetings a coffee brewer may be kept standing for self-service at any time. Plastic cups prevent the nuisance of rattling china.

Bar Service. If a bar is to be available, it is best opened for socializing after the day's sessions or before dinner.

Drinks may be prepaid by the host or the guests.

A no-host bar collects from the guest for each drink served.

An open bar permits guests to serve themselves.

For convenience or quick service, selection of drinks may be limited and prepared in advance.

Meal Service. Arrange details with the hotel or caterer. Personally check table arrangements before every meal, and review special requirements with the maître d'hôtel. Give attention to these considerations:

Times of service.

Service or self-service.

Menu.

Special beverages.

Guaranteed price, including tips and taxes (based on guaranteed minimum number of persons).

General table positions and seating plan.

Desired set-up for dais, including lectern and microphone.

Table decorations, candles, flowers, and so on.

Place cards.

Elapsed time for service (the more waiters, the quicker the service).

Music, if desired, with instructions to leader on start and stop times.

Exhibits

1. Many meetings are enhanced by exhibits put up by the sponsors or participating organizations. Adequate space should be set aside for these exhibits, preferably outside the meeting rooms.

2. Make provision for receiving, storing, setting up, dismantling, and returning exhibits. Most exhibitors provide their own personnel to staff the exhibits.

3. Protect valuable exhibits against damage or loss. Provide guards, operators, or attendants, if required. Check with your attorney or insurance company to determine your liability and means of protection.

4. Check facilities and equipment needs:

> Tables with flannel tops.
> Vertical display boards.
> Room dividers.
> Shelves.
> Adequate lighting (including spotlights).
> Moldings or hooks for wall hangings.
> Outlets and sufficient power for electrically operated exhibits.

Publicity.   Wherever possible, the publicity chores should be put in the hands of the company's public relations department or a special publicity committee.

> Obtain biographies and glossy photos from principals at the time the program is arranged.
> Send advance press releases to editors of company publications, trade press, and daily newspapers, radio, and television. (See "The Press Release," Section 7.1.)
> Make arrangements with a professional photographer for convention pictures and prints. These may be used for current news stories and for release to principals and participating organizations.
> Obtain advance copies of principal talks.
> Release photos, news stories, and copies of talks to local newspapers, news magazines, trade press, and company publications.
> Set up a press room at the convention; have someone meet reporters, arrange interviews with principals, and provide food and beverages. Consider the need for telephones, typewriters, and writing supplies.
> Put organization's name on lectern, so that it will be included in news photos of platform speakers.

Post-Meeting Duties.   For those in charge, the end of the meeting signals another burst of activity.

> Check meeting rooms to make sure nothing has been left behind.
> Return borrowed and rented equipment.
> Dismantle and return exhibits.
> Pack records and ship them to home base. (Exception: put untranscribed steno notes in personal luggage.)
> Verify and pay bills.
> Write "thank you" notes.
> Write report of experience to guide those who take over convention duties the next time around.

3

Letter Make-up

An attractive letter reflects the total image of a company and its products. The typing should be neat and accurate, and such parts as the date, inside address, and complimentary close should conform to contemporary business practices. Special problems regarding the security of classified company and government documents and the format of correspondence to government agencies are discussed in detail in this chapter. Information and sample illustrations are given for framing the letter, setting up its principal parts, using the three patterns of punctuation, and preparing the letter for mailing, as well as styles used for office memorandums and envelopes.

CONTENTS

3.1 LETTER FORM AND STYLE

The rules for the mechanical form of business letters have their roots in custom and etiquette, as well as in the more practical considerations of convenience, effectiveness, and the necessities of recordkeeping. Departures from approved forms are sometimes made for good cause in individual instances but, on the whole, conformance to the guidelines in this section should relieve any uncertainty about correctness.

Placement of the Message.   Center the letter on the page. In modern business practices, equal left, right, and bottom margins are used. Whether the message is to be typed on standard $8\frac{1}{2}'' \times 11''$, executive $7\frac{1}{4}'' \times 10\frac{1}{2}''$, or any other size stationery, the margins should be carefully worked out. Before starting to type, judge the approximate number of words or the length of the message. You can make your estimate from your shorthand notes, from the length of dictated tape, from the used portion of the dictation disc, or from the rough copy. If necessary, reset the right and left margin stops for each letter. Margins can be changed in seconds on either manual or electric machines once you are familiar with the stops for short, average, and long letters. Manufacturers of media typewriters suggest that a standard writing line of six inches, for instance, be adopted for the majority of work to save time and avoid duplication of costly machine setup activities. Some adjustment for document body length may be necessary. Secretaries who use media equipment should consult the manufacturer's instruction manual for specific directions.

The letter placement guide (Figure 3-1) shows the correct placement of short, average, and long messages. The right and left margin stops for both pica (10 pitch) and elite (12 pitch) type are given. Before setting them, be sure that the left edge of the paper is at *0* on the paper guide scale. The term *10 pitch* means that there are 10 spaces to an inch across the typing line; 12-pitch machines have 12 horizontal spaces to an inch. The date is typed from 2 to 4 lines beneath the letterhead.

Vertical spacing is also important because the bottom margin should be approximately the same as the left and right margins. In planning for the bottom margin, remember that there are 6 vertical lines to an inch on all typewriters. For instance, to have a one-and-a-half-inch bottom margin, leave 9 blank lines. Place a light pencil line near the bottom before inserting the paper to remind you to leave space for the margin. On the second and succeeding pages of a long letter, leave 6 blank lines, or one inch, at the top and start typing on line 7.

Letter Formats.   Most companies that have word processing centers choose one letter style or format for all outgoing correspondence. Smaller companies allow each typist to choose the style. Recent studies have found that approximately 95 percent of business letters use a variation of the block style. The following forms are generally accepted.

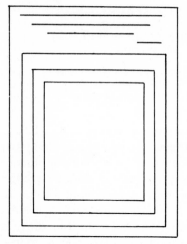

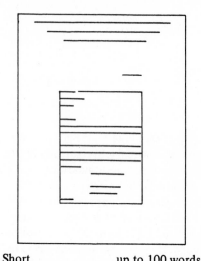

In General. Side and bottom margins at least 1" to 2". The shorter the letter the wider the margins and the more space between the date and inside address.

Short.   up to 100 words
Length of line: 50 spaces
Margin stops: Pica   17-67
              Elite   25-75
Side margins: 2"

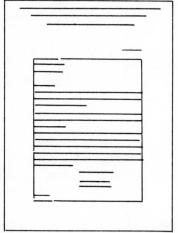

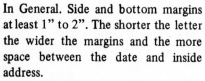

Average.   100-300 words
Length of line: 60 spaces
Margin stops: Pica   12-72
              Elite   20-80
Side margins: 1½"

Long.   over 300 words
Length of line: 65 (pica)
                             78 (elite)
Margin stops: Pica   10-75
              Elite   12-90
Side margins: 1"

Figure 3-1 Letter placement guide.

WOODS BROTHERS
662 North Euclid Avenue
Anaheim, California 92806

February 1, 19--

Mr. James A. Jones
12205 Sunnybrook Street
Anaheim, California   92813

Dear Mr. Jones:

In answer to frequent requests we have had from
businessmen for a conservative suit that would incorporate the important new styling trends, Woods
Brothers is introducing the Executive Model.

This new model sharkskin suit is made of fine quality imported worsted (feel the swatches). It has
softly padded shoulders, three buttons, flap pockets,
and the popular plain front trousers. The suit is
available in a wide range of colors and sizes including medium gray, dark gray, navy, olive, and dark
brown.

Come in soon and see our new Executive Model. You
would expect to pay much more than our low price of
$170 for a suit of this quality.

Sincerely yours,

Stephen C. Shulheimer
President

SCS:mt

Enclosure

Figure 3-2   Block style. Mixed punctuation.

1. Block. All lines except the date and the complimentary close begin at the
left margin. The date and the complimentary close are indented. This is
probably the most popular letter style (Figure 3-2).

2. Semiblock. Along with the block style, the semiblock has won wide
acceptance. This style has indented paragraphs in addition to the indented

date and complimentary close. A 5-space paragraph indention is usual, although the paragraph may be indented as many as 10 spaces (Figure 3-3).

3. Full block. All lines in the letter begin flush with the left margin. The advantage of this style is its simplicity for the typist. However, there is some objection to the imbalance on the left side (Figure 3-3).

4. Indented. In this style, all principal lines are indented: the date, second and succeeding lines of the address (five spaces more than the preceding line). first line of each paragraph, complimentary close, each line of the signature (three spaces more than the preceding line). The indented style is used infrequently in modern correspondence (Figure 3-3).

5. Hanging-indented. The block style is sometimes modified for advertising letters in order to attract the reader's attention. The date and the complimentary close are indented as usual. The paragraphs begin with the first line blocked at the margin, and the second and succeeding lines indented five spaces. This style is not used for ordinary correspondence (Figure 3-3).

6. Simplified. This variation of the full block style uses a subject line in place of the salutation. The complimentary close and the dictator's initials are omitted. The typist's initials, *cc* (carbon copy), and *Enclosure* may be omitted or used as preferred (Figure 3-4).

Punctuation Patterns. Three accepted punctuation patterns (*open, mixed, and close*) may be used with the letter styles already described. Most business letters are typed with mixed punctuation.

Open. No punctuation mark is added at the ends of lines in the date, address, salutation, complimentary close, and signature. If a line, however, ends with an abbreviation, a period follows the abbreviation as usual. Any punctuation marks within the lines themselves are retained. Many companies are adopting the open punctuation style, as it saves time and does not detract from the clarity of the letter. Open punctuation is always used with the simplified letter style and is often used with the full block style (Figures 3-3 and 3-4).

Mixed. The popular mixed punctuation pattern uses two marks of punctuation. A colon follows the salutation and a comma follows the complimentary close (Figure 3-2).

Close. With this pattern, punctuation marks are used with all principal parts of the letter. A period follows the date line. Commas are placed at the end of each line of the address except the last, which ends with a period. A colon follows the salutation. Commas are placed after the complimentary close, after the firm name (if used), and after the typed signature if a title is to follow. Periods are used after the typed signature if no title follows or after the title of the person signing the letter. No punctuation mark is used after the identification initials or the enclosure notation. Close punctuation is often used with the indented style. Fewer and fewer letters written in the United States use these extra punctuation marks (Figure 3-3).

Full block style.   Open punctuation    Semiblock style. Mixed punctuation

Indented style.   Close punctuation    Hanging-indented style. Mixed punc-
                                         tuation

Figure 3-3   Four letter formats.

FIRST NATIONAL BANK
201 South Main Street
Butte, Montana 59701

March 15, 19--

Mr. John H. Willow
896 Fletcher Avenue
Butte, Montana 59701

APPLICATION FOR EXTENDED CREDIT

Your application for extended credit has been referred to this
department for processing. As you know this new plan guarantees
a checking account additional funds during times of heavy spending or in case of an emergency.

Extra funds from $1,000 to $5,000 are made available to our customers upon approval of the evaluation committee. In order to
determine the amount of extended credit we may offer you, the
following information is needed:

1. A copy of last year's income tax form
2. Verification of present employment and your employment from
    1968 to date
3. The names and addresses of five credit or character refer-
    ences
4. A list of places of residence during the past ten years plus
    an indication whether rented or owned

To take advantage of a protected checking account as soon as possible, please send us the requested information within the week.

Herbert A. Downie

HERBERT A. DOWNIE - Manager, Accounts Department

mt

cc: J. A. Smith, Frances Humes

Figure 3-4 Simplified style. Open punctuation.

Principal Parts of a Letter.   The principal parts of a letter are the date line,
the inside address, the salutation, the body or message, the complimentary
close, the signature line(s), the reference initials, and the carbon copy or
enclosure notation.

Date Line.   The date line is typed two to four spaces below the letterhead. If
the date is not blocked at the left margin as in the full block and simplified

styles, many companies prefer to block it at the right margin (Figure 3-2). To do this, move the typewriter carriage to the right margin and depress the backspace key once for every letter, number, punctuation mark, and space in the date. Set a tabular stop for the date when you type the first of several short, average, or long letters.

Abbreviations are never used in the date line. No punctuation is needed at the end of the line unless close punctuation is used with the other principal parts. The military-style date line (e.g., 10 November 1981) is used by the United States military and in the United Kingdom.

Some companies prefer the date line to be a part of the design of the letterhead; others begin the date at the center point and use this same placement for the complimentary close to speed typing. Attractive placement is the criterion to use in deciding where to place the date in the block, semiblock, and indented business-letter styles (Figure 3-5).

Inside Address. Begin the inside address at the left margin, approximately four to eight lines below the date line. Additional blank lines may be left after the date when needed to place the message more attractively on the page. If possible, always use the street address or post office box number with the city and state. If no street address is available, type the city on the second line and the state on the third. Avoid using more than five typed lines for an address. No line in the address should extend beyond the middle of the page. Long company names may be typed on two lines; indent the second line two spaces. All inside addresses are single-spaced, even though a short message in the same letter is double-spaced.

Mr. Robert R. Smith
The Smith, Needham, Walters
    and Clark Corporation
6289 Spruce Street
Philadelphia, Pennsylvania 19142

Married couple; professional names:

Dr. Constance Thompson	Dr. Sam Henry Jones
Dr. Robert Norris	Dr. Lillian M. Jones
25 Sunnyvale Road	527 River Road
Trenton, New Jersey 08609	Rochester, New York 14611

(Salutations: Dear Dr. Thompson and Dr. Norris, Dear Drs. Jones)

AEROSPACE CORPORATION

Post Office Box 95085, Los Angeles, California 90045, Telephone 648-5000

2641-122
January 15, 1982

Figure 3-5 Positioning the date and reference number in harmony with the letterhead design.

Individual and company names are both used in the inside address of the majority of letters written today. To ensure prompt and proper handling, address the letter to an individual in the company. Type the person's name on the first line and the company's on the second. Be sure to use the correct first name and/or initials of the addressee. The company name should be typed exactly as printed on its letterhead or on one of its official publications.

Department names are often used in the inside address when the writer does not know the name of the person who handles the matter discussed in the letter. In such instances, type the company name on the first line and the department name on the second.

Union Carbide Corporation	S. M. Roth & Company
Public Relations Department	Accounting Department

Special titles, such as *Dr.*, *Professor*, *Reverend*, or *Senator*, may precede the addressee's name. If not, *Mr.*, *Mrs.*, *Miss, or Ms.* should always accompany an individual's name. *Ms.* is recommended especially if you do not know the marital status of the woman addressed.

Business titles are not used in the address block today unless needed for identification. If one is included, however, use the placement that gives the best balance. The title may be placed as follows.

1. On the second line of the address block:

Mr. F. O. Morehead
Vice President and Manager
Burnham Associates, Inc.
1212 Olive Street
Des Moines, Iowa 50324

2. On the first line after the addressee's name:

Mr. B. B. Birch, Director
Technical Research Corporation
804 Orange Grove Avenue
Pasadena, California 91107

3. On the second line preceding the company name:

Mrs. Leslie K. Corrothers
President, Fashion Fair, Inc.
101 Fifth Avenue
New York, New York 10006

Do not abbreviate business titles or positions, and do not hyphenate a civil or military title denoting a single office.

NOT:		BUT:	
	Sec'y		Secretary
	Bus. Mgr.		Business Manager
	Vice-president		Vice President
	Brigadier-General		Brigadier General

CORRECT: Secretary-Treasurer (two positions)
          or
          Secretary and Treasurer

When addressing a person who holds several offices in a company, use the same title from the signature line in the letter you are answering or the title of the highest office held if you originate the correspondence. If you can ascertain a preference (possibly from previous correspondence), use the title the addressee prefers. See Section 3.4 for additional information on titles.

Street addresses should not contain abbreviations. Use figures for house numbers (except *one*) and numbered street names beginning with thirteen. Spell out number *one* if it is a house number and *one* through *twelve* if they are street names. When a numbered street name follows the house number, put a spaced hyphen between them.

1824 North Vine Street	208 West 42 Street
One West Eighth Street	2945 - 29 Street
2310 H Street NW	5 Boulevard Place

Cities and states should be spelled out, unless the official spelling is abbreviated as in *St. Louis*. The only exception, *D.C.*, is always abbreviated. The ZIP Code, a five-digit coding system that identifies each post office and each delivery unit at large post offices, follows the name of the state. The first three digits identify the sectional center or major city, and the last two identify the post office or other delivery unit. The ZIP Code need not be included in the address box on the letter but *must* be typed as part of the address on the envelope. The preferred place is two spaces after the state name.

Salutation.   The salutation is typed flush with the left margin, two spaces below the inside address or the attention line if there is one. Capitalize only the first word, title, and surname or special title.

Dear Mr. Grant
My dear Senator Anderson
My dear Madam Mayor

Although most business letters use a colon after the salutation, a growing number of companies are adopting open punctuation, which omits the colon. A comma may follow the salutation in personal and social letters, and must be used if they are handwritten.

The form of salutation may vary with the tone of the letter and the degree of acquaintanceship between the writer and the addressee. The current emphasis on the personal, friendly approach in business writing calls for the use of the addressee's name instead of the formal *Sir, Dear Sir, Dear Madam,* and the like.

1. If the letter is addressed to an individual, use the title only with the surname.

Right	*Wrong*
Dear Dean Jacoby	Dear Dean
My dear Dean Jacoby	My dear Dean Jacoby, Ph.D.
Dear Mrs. Hughes	Dear Treasurer
Dear Dr. Wanous	Dear Doctor

Personal acquaintances of the writer may be addressed by their first names.

Dear Bob
My dear Frank
Dear Mildred

2. A letter addressed to two persons with the same or different names will have one of the following salutations.

Dear Messrs. Tyler (two men with same name)
Dear Mesdames Smith (two married women with same name)
My dear Misses Smith (two unmarried women with same name)
Dear Mr. Jones and Mr. Wilson
Dear Mrs. Rice and Mr. Jones
My dear Mrs. Heath and Miss Heath
Dear Ms. Smith and Ms. Herbert (marital status unknown)
My dear Mrs. Carlson and Mrs. Stahl
Dear Ms. Jasper and Mr. Atkins (married couple with wife retaining maiden name)

3. Use *Gentlemen* as the salutation in a letter addressed to a company, even though it contains an attention line naming an individual.

4. When writing to a women's organization, either of these two salutations is acceptable: *Ladies* or *Mesdames.*

5. In a letter addressed to a group of men and women, use *Gentlemen* or *Ladies and Gentlemen.* In a letter addressed to a man and a woman, use *Dear Miss Hunt and Mr. Morgan.* The salutation for a married couple reads *Dear Mr. and Mrs. Cetner.*

6. Use the salutation appropriate for a man when in doubt as to the sex of the addressee.

7. The salutation *To Whom It May Concern* is written in capitals and lower case. Where this salutation is used, the complimentary close is omitted.

8. The correct salutations to use for people in official or honorary positions are given in Section 3.4.

9. A subject or catchline may replace the salutation. The simplified letter style (Figure 3-4) uses a subject line typed flush with the left margin. Three blank lines are left before and after the subject. Examples of catchlines used in advertising or form letters are these.

$7 is little to pay   But First, Ask Yourself
for one new concept . . .   If This Is an Invitation
    a solution to a problem . . .   You Should Accept . . .
        even a useful fact!
May we help you
help your students?

Body of the Letter.   Business letters are single-spaced unless they are unusually short. Double-space between paragraphs. In double-spaced letters, paragraphs should be indented or set off by triple spacing. Begin each line flush with the left margin in full block, block, and simplified letter styles. First lines of paragraphs may be indented five to ten spaces in semiblock and indented styles. Five-space indention is preferred.

Tabulated material. Tabular inserts, such as lists, quoted matter, addresses, and short tables, are usually indented five to ten spaces from the left and right margins in order to set them off from the message. Double-space before and after the insert. If the insert contains several items, these may be single-spaced if each item can be typed on one line. Items that take several lines should have a double space before and after them for clarity. In enumerated material, the number may be followed by a period or enclosed in parentheses. Space twice after the period or the right parenthesis before typing the information.

Dear Mr. _____ :

--- .

-- .

--- :

    1. --

       ------------------- . .

    2. --- .

    3. --

       ----------------- .

-- . .

                                      Yours very truly,

Enumerated items that are complete sentences should end with a period. Those that are not sentences, but words or phrases that complete a sentence, may be followed by commas, except for the last, which is followed by a period. Other enumerated items that are merely lists used as an illustration or definition need no punctuation after the last word (Figure 3-4).

Indented quoted matter may begin and end with quotation marks, but common practice omits these marks if it is obvious from the previous paragraph that the material is a quotation.

The letter we received from the Los Angeles Civic Light Opera Association gave the following reason that the guarantors are being contacted:

Because some very promising prospects will need aid to cover the cost of tuition, and some out-of-town students may be worthy of help in dormitory living on the campus, it occurred to us that some of our guarantors might enjoy undertaking the sponsorship of a full or partial scholarship.

If you desire to help these talented young people, please fill in and mail the enclosed form to us as soon as possible.

In order to make special information stand out, such as an address for the reply or a source to contact, indent the information in block style.

Please contact our local retail outlet in your city:
    Jones & Jones
    515 Perkins Street
    Memphis, Tennessee 38103
Your reply to this letter should be addressed to:
    Mr. John H. McIlroy
    Engineering Sales
    General Electric Company
    Penn Square
    Philadelphia, Pennsylvania 19102

A table should be centered on the page in a manner similar to the format of tabulated material in reports. (See Section 11.3 for suggestions on arranging tables.)

Dear Mr. _____:

--..

-----------------------------   ------------------------------
-----------------------------.:

Europe	April 22	41 days	$5,160
West Indies	Weekly	11 days	$985
Alaska	July 9, 23	20 days	$1,995
Mexico	Weekly	13 days	$1,155
South America	July 10	38 days	$4,165

--------------------.

When using the simplified letter style, begin each line of the tabulated material at the left margin. If an item takes more than one line, type to the right margin and then start the second line under the first word of the preceding line. If the letter is long, you need not double-space between items (Figure 3-4).

Hyphenation at end of line. It is sometimes necessary to divide a word at the end of a line in order to keep the right margin as even as possible. Check the rules for hyphenating words in Section 10.5 to be sure that you divide each word correctly. In order to speed up your production and make reading easier, avoid dividing words at the end of lines. Do not divide words at the ends of more than two consecutive lines. Do not divide the last word on a page or the last word in a paragraph.

Complimentary Close. A courteous business phrase, called the complimentary close, is used to end the writer's conversation with the reader. Reflecting the tone of the letter, it may be the conventional *Very truly yours,* or a more personal phrase, such as *With all good wishes.* Always write the close dictated by the writer. If the close is not dictated, use one that fits the message or the person addressed (see Section 3.4).

Capitalize the first word of the close and use lower case for all other words. Use a comma after it if a colon is used with the salutation. In most business letters the close is typed two spaces below the last line in the message. Sometimes three or four spaces are left in order to frame the letter more attractively on the page. Here is a list of the positions usually occupied by the close:

1. In the full block style, the close is typed flush with the left margin.

2. In block, semiblock, indented, and personal styles, the close may be typed (a) five spaces to the left of page center to allow ample space for long signature lines, (b) at center or five spaces to the right of center, (c) at a predetermined spot that assures the ending of the longest line in the signature block at the right margin, or (d) in direct line with the date or some portion of the letterhead.

The following complimentary closings are used most frequently in business.

1. For formal and diplomatic correspondence.

Respectfully
Respectfully yours

2. For less formal situations.

Yours truly
Very truly yours
Yours very truly

3. For friendly situations.

Sincerely
Sincerely yours
Very sincerely
Very sincerely yours
Most sincerely
Cordially
Cordially yours
Most cordially
Yours cordially

4. For special situations.

Best wishes
Best regards
Kindest regards
Kindest personal regards
With all good wishes
With kindest wishes
With the season's greetings
With best wishes to you and Mrs. _____

Firm Name.   Ordinarily, a letter on the firm's printed letterhead should *not* have the firm name typed below the complimentary close. Its omission saves time and space. If the letter is considered a formal document or a contract, or if it contains professional advice, the firm name may be typed in all capitals or written by hand after the complimentary close. If a business letter is typed on blank paper, the firm name in all capitals is typed two spaces below the complimentary close.

Signature Line.   The name of the person signing the letter is typed four spaces below the complimentary close (or below the firm name). In capitals and lower case, type the signature exactly as the writer signs his or her name and, if necessary, include any degrees or titles that indicate how the person wishes to be addressed in the reply.

TYPED SIGNATURE:	IN REPLY:
George P. Tucker, M.D.	Dear Dr. Tucker
L. W. Erickson, Associate Dean	Dear Dean Erickson

If the signer's name and title are part of the letterhead, they need not be typed again. The *only* titles that may precede the typed signature are *Miss*, *Ms.*, or *Mrs.*, even though they are not included in the handwritten signature.

Women's signatures may be written as follows.

1. An unmarried woman or a married woman using her maiden name may precede her typed signature with *Miss* or *Ms.* If no title is included, she may be addressed by either title.

2. A woman using her married name should precede her typed signature with *Mrs.* She may use either her first name and/or initial(s), or her husband's name and/or initials. In social correspondence she should always use her husband's name.

	Business	Social
Preferred:	Mrs. Ruth J. Barrons	Mrs. Donald A. Barrons

3. A widow may use either her first name and/or initials or her deceased husband's name with *Mrs.*

4. A divorcee may sign her maiden name if regained, may sign her first name with or without the initial of her maiden name and her former husband's surname, may use her maiden name and former husband's surname.

Ruth R. Jones
Ms. or Miss Ruth R. Jones
Mrs. Ruth J. Jenkins
Mrs. Jones Jenkins
Mrs. or Ms. Ruth Jones Jenkins

5. When signing a letter for someone else, you may sign the name followed by your initials immediately below. When signing a letter in your own name for someone else, include the other person's title and surname only below your typed signature.

Right	Wrong
Robert T. Levin	Robert T. Levin
Assistant to Mr. Berkowitz	Assistant to Mr. O. L. Berkowitz
Eleanor M. Doan	Eleanor M. Doan
Secretary to Mr. Wagner	Secretary to T. J. Wagner

Title of Addressor. It is customary to place the title and/or department of the person signing a business letter on the line below the typed signature. The title indicates that the person is acting in an official capacity for the company.

U. C. Bruin, Supervisor	Paul L. Thomas
General Offices Services	Secretary-Treasurer

On personal letters written on company letterhead, the title is usually omitted. Also, if the signer's title is included in the letter, it may be omitted in the signature block. There appears to be a trend toward the omission of the typed title, especially in large companies. It should be apparent, however, in the message, letterhead, or reference numbers where the signer may be reached in reply.

Identification Initials.   Initials of the dictator and the transcriber are placed two spaces below the last line in the signature block at the left margin. They indicate the persons responsible for the information in the letter. The dictator's initials are written first, followed by two initials of the transcriber. The easiest setup is all caps with a colon, which requires only one shift of the typewriter. Documents typed on media typewriters will include special coding following the typist's initials to indicate the location of the document on media.

    EMD:JK   EMD:JK1127B

Some companies prefer that the dictator's initials be in caps and the transcriber's in lower case.

    EMD:jk   DB/mo

A letter dictated by one person and signed by another may use the following style of identification—the signer's initials, followed by the dictator's, and then the transcriber's.

    DDC:TRW:bb

Or, if the signer prefers, the identification may use only the initials of the dictator and the transcriber.

There appears to be a trend to omit the dictator's initials if the name is typed in the signature block. When the typist's initials appear alone, it usually means that the typist composed the letter or telegram or that it is a form letter. The latest accepted business practice is to show identification initials on carbon copies only. If the dictator signs the letter, only the typist's initials are shown on the carbon. The dictator's initials are shown if someone else signs the letter.

Miscellaneous Parts of a Letter (Figure 3-6).   *Personal or Confidential.*   The *personal* notation is used in cases where the message should be seen by the addressee and no one else. The *confidential* notation applies to the information in the message; the confidential letter may be seen by others who have been approved to handle such matters. Type the personal or confidential notation in all caps approximately four lines above the inside address at the left margin.

Attention Line.   Use the attention line only when the letter is addressed to the company and contains information concerning the company's business that you want acted upon should the person named be absent. In modern practice, the majority of letters are addressed to individuals within the company.

If it is necessary to use the attention line, type *Attention* followed by the name two spaces below the address at the left margin for all letter styles. Do not underline *Attention* or write it in all caps, or follow it with a punctuation mark. Use *Gentlemen* as the salutation with an attention line because the letter is addressed to a firm. Use the person's given name or initials, if known (Figure 3-6). Type the attention line on the envelope as either the first or second line of the address block (Figure 3-10).

Subject Line. A subject line briefly summarizes the message. Most business letters contain a subject line to alert the reader to the message that follows and to assist in routing and filing the letter in both the sender's and receiver's offices. The federal government asks that all incoming and outgoing letters contain subject lines.

Type the subject line in capitals and lower case two spaces below the salutation at the left margin or centered on the typing line. Auxiliary words are not used with the subject line except for *In re* or *Re* which are used in legal correspondence. A few companies prefer to use *Subject* or *Reference* followed by a colon. Other companies feel that the position of the line clearly indicates its nature.

PREFERRED: Marketing Plans for the XB100
ACCEPTABLE: Subject: Marketing Plans for the XB100

Letters prepared in the simplified format use a subject line in place of the salutation. In these letters the subject is preceded and followed by three blank lines (Figure 3-4).

A letter should cover only one subject. If two or more subjects are included, sideheadings may be substituted for the subject line. Be sure to make sufficient carbon copies for each subject file.

Reference Line.   Often a file, correspondence, order, invoice, or policy number is placed on the letter for control and ease of handling. The preferred position of a reference line is from one to four spaces below the date line. A few companies prefer to type the reference line immediately above the date line (Figure 3-5). If the date line ends at the right margin, type the reference line to end at the right margin also.

PREFERRED: October 10, 1982
                    L-123-2
OR: October 10, 1982
            Policy No. C18972
ALSO USED: 71G0641-122A
            October 10, 1982

Many large companies, in order to process correspondence and reports more efficiently, assign control numbers, such as the ones illustrated above, to all incoming and outgoing letters, memorandums, and reports. The mailroom or file department usually assigns the number based on the following information: addressee, author, subject, date, and classification. On outgoing correspondence, the typist uses the date the number is assigned and not the date the letter or memorandum is prepared. For example, if the number is obtained on Monday, May 1, but for some reason the correspondence is not typed until Wednesday, May 3, the date of May 1 is still used. The control

AMCO AIRCRAFT CORPORATION

10789 Space Park

Seattle, Washington 98119

September 22, 19--

CONFIDENTIAL

General Corporation
1121 Lincoln Boulevard
Chicago, Illinois

Attention Mr. John J. Jones

Gentlemen:

Conditions of Sub-Contract for XYZ Project

In awarding your company the sub-contract to manufacture Part No. 145WK, we are sending you specific

_____

_____

If you have any questions regarding these operating
procedures, please write us and we will do our best
to clarify them.

Yours very truly,

AMCO AIRCRAFT CORPORATION

Frank A. Patton Hwk

Frank A. Patton, Administrator
Sub-Contracts Department

FAP:mt

Enclosure

cc: James T. Pierce
      Elwin O. Slaughter

Figure 3-6 Placement of miscellaneous parts of a contractual letter requiring typed company name in signature block and showing initials of person who signed the letter for the dictator.

number usually expires after five calendar days. The typist notifies the proper person to cancel the number and obtains a new one.

Enclosure Reminder. Letters accompanied by an enclosure or an attachment should have the word *Enclosure* (or the abbreviation *Enc.*) typed flush with the left margin one or two spaces beneath the identification line. For more than one, indicate the number of items enclosed, for example, *Enclosures 4.* If the enclosures are of special importance, list and describe each one individually. The word *enclosures* may be followed by a colon.

> Enclosures: 1. Annual Report (1978), 2 copies
> 2. Vendor List
> 3. Profit and Loss Statement 1/1/78–6/30/79

It is recommended that a notation such as the following appear in the upper right corner on each page of each enclosure:

> Enclosure (1) to (*Company name*) letter No. L-2645, dated
> May 17, 19—, page 1 of 5 (if enclosure has several pages).

Such a notation will ensure that the addressee can locate the letter to which a particular enclosure was attached. If the enclosure is a bound item and too bulky to insert in the typewriter, place a handwritten notation in the upper right corner of the first page only. See Section 3.2 for special information on how to list enclosures to the military.

Mailing Notation. If the letter is to be sent by any method other than regular mail, type the mailing notations—for example, *Air Mail, Special Delivery,* or *Certified Mail*—flush with the left margin two spaces below the enclosure reminder. Some companies prefer this notation to appear on all copies of the letter, and others type it on the carbon copies only. See Figure 3-10 for placement of the mailing notation on envelopes.

Carbon Copy Notation. The distribution of carbon copies should be typed at the left margin below all other notations. If space permits, double-space after the last notation. The preferred carbon copy notation is *cc:*, except in the simplified letter style, which omits the *c*'s before the distribution list.

All recipients of a carbon copy should be listed alphabetically. Include addresses if there is a possibility the addressee might need this information. If the person receiving a copy of the letter is also receiving an enclosure, indicate which enclosure and how many copies.

> cc: Mrs. Carlton Howes (2 copies Training Questionnaire)
> Houghton School
> 123 South River Street
> Portland, Oregon 97214
> B. A. Morningfield
> T. B. Shaw

To save space, the address of a recipient of a carbon copy may be typed across the page instead of in block form.

Blind Carbon Copy Notation. If the addressor wishes to distribute carbon copies without indicating the distribution to the addressee, the blind carbon copy notation *bcc:* together with the alphabetical list of names is placed on internal copies only. It may be placed in the upper left corner of internal carbon copies or in the usual position at the bottom of the page.

Postscript. A postscript may be added to a letter two spaces below the last notation. Indent five spaces and type the message single-spaced. Be sure to use the same margins as in the body of the letter. If the paragraphs of the letter are blocked, block the postscript. If the paragraphs are indented, indent the first line of the postscript. The abbreviations *P.S.* and *P.P.S.* (second postscript) may precede the message, but the present trend is to omit these abbreviations because placement indicates the addition of another thought.

Second and Subsequent Pages of a Letter. When a letter has two or more pages, type the second and subsequent pages on a plain sheet of bond paper of the same size and quality as the letterhead. At least three typewritten lines of the message must be carried over to the second page. Never place the complimentary close and signature lines by themselves on the second page. The heading for additional pages of a letter may be written in either of the two styles shown in Figure 3-7.

Type the heading for the second and subsequent pages approximately one inch, or six lines, from the top of the page. Space down four to six lines after the heading and continue the message. Be consistent and use the same heading and spacing for each additional page. To be sure that the pages of a letter do not become separated, you may staple them together in the upper left corner.

Personal or Diplomatic Letters. Personal and diplomatic letters use the same format to distinguish them from ordinary business correspondence. The address block is moved to the bottom of the page; and identification initials, if used,

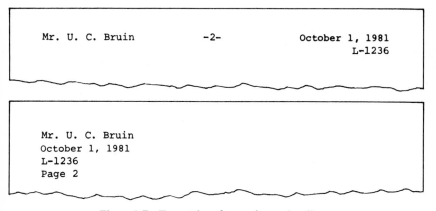

Figure 3-7 Two styles of second-page headings.

are double-spaced below the address. The date, salutation, and complimentary close are typed in their regular positions. Usually, the typed signature
line and the identification initials are omitted. They may be typed on the
carbon copy, however. If the writer's signature is difficult to read or if the signer
is not well known to the reader, type the name beneath the signature as usual
(Figure 3-8).

THE NATIONAL HISTORICAL SOCIETY
78 Constitution Avenue
Washington, DC 20016

December 15, 1981

My dear Ambassador Manos

You and your wife are cordially invited to a
reception on January 27, from six to eight in the
evening, in honor of The President and The Vice
President of the United States.

We look forward to greeting you at this fes-
tive occasion.

Respectfully

James A. Miller
Chairman of the Board

R.S.V.P.

His Excellency Alberto P. Manos
Ambassador of Honduras
332 Ambassador Row
Washington, DC   20005

Figure 3-8   Personal and diplomatic style.

These letters are usually typed on executive stationery. If this stationery does not include a street address in the letterhead or if the message is typed on plain bond paper, the address of the writer may be typed immediately above the date (Figure 3-9).

Addressing Envelopes.   The addressee's address is typed in the approximate vertical and horizontal centers of the envelope. Most address blocks are placed a little to the left (five spaces) of horizontal center in order to allow for exceptionally long lines. Single-space the address block in block form (Figure 3-10).

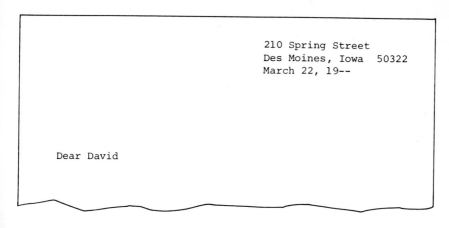

```
                              210 Spring Street
                              Des Moines, Iowa   50322
                              March 22, 19--




      Dear David
```

OR

```
                              Cordially


                              James A. Dillon
                              210 Spring Street
                              Des Moines, Iowa   50322



      Mr. David A. Peters
      3150 Sunset Plaza
      Washington, DC   20022
```

Figure 3-9   Position of return address on unprinted executive stationery.

```
Thomas R. Jones
North American Van Lines
700 East Imperial Highway
El Segundo, CA   90241
   HOLD FOR ARRIVAL
                                                  SPECIAL DELIVERY
                                                  REGISTERED



                              PERSONAL
                                   Mr. T. W. Platt
                                   Harrison Manufacturing, Inc.
                                   2500 North Hanson Road
                                   Dallas, TX   75204
```

```
Thomas R. Jones
North American Van Lines
700 East Imperial Highway
El Segundo, CA   90241




                              Harrison Manufacturing, Inc.
                              Attention Mr. T. W. Platt
                              2500 North Hanson Road
                              Dallas, TX   75204
```

Figure 3-10   Envelope address styles.

The ZIP Code, required by post office regulations, should appear two spaces after the state name in both the address of destination and the return address. A comma should not be inserted between the state name and the ZIP Code (Figure 3-10). The *National ZIP Code Directory* lists ZIP Codes for all post office addresses. It may be secured from the Superintendent of Documents, Washington, D.C. Special rules for ZIP Code addressing, including authorized state abbreviations, will be found on pp. 105–106.

The information on the envelope may include the class of mail or special service you wish the correspondence to receive. This type of information should be typed in all capitals below the stamp so that post office personnel will see it immediately. First class mail to all 50 states, Canada, and Mexico is shipped by air.

| Class of mail:
FIRST | Special services:
SPECIAL DELIVERY
REGISTERED
CERTIFIED
COLLECT-ON-DELIVERY
AIR MAIL
(foreign mail only) | SPECIAL HANDLING
EXPRESS MAIL
(guaranteed next day
delivery) |

See Chapter 15 for an explanation of classes of mail, special services, rates, and other postal information.

The *personal* notation should be written in all capitals to the left and one line above the address block (Figure 3-10). The *attention* line is written as the first or second line of the address block. Any other special handling instructions to be followed when the letter reaches its destination should be typed in the upper left. For instance, *holding* or *forwarding* instructions may need to be given. Another notation to be included is the sender's name and possibly department name immediately above or below the printed return address of the company. If the letter is undeliverable, it can be returned quickly to the person who sent. it.

Window envelopes permit the inside address on the letter to be used for the mailing address. Additional information to be included on the envelope, however, must be typed before the letter and/or its enclosures are inserted.

ZIP Code Addressing. Advancements in the electronic processing of mail have prompted the Postal Service to issue updated rules governing envelope addresses.

1. The following state abbreviations are recommended on envelope addresses showing destination. The name of the state should *not* be spelled out. However, the full name of the state and conventional abbreviations may be used in the return address, as well as in the inside address and other parts of the letter.

Alabama	AL	Kentucky	KY	Ohio	OH
Alaska	AK	Louisiana	LA	Oklahoma	OK
Arizona	AZ	Maine	ME	Oregon	OR
Arkansas	AR	Maryland	MD	Pennsylvania	PA
California	CA	Massachusetts	MA	Puerto Rico	PR
Colorado	CO	Michigan	MI	Rhode Island	RI
Connecticut	CT	Minnesota	MN	South Carolina	SC
Delaware	DE	Mississippi	MS	South Dakota	SD
District of Columbia	DC	Missouri	MO	Tennessee	TN
Florida	FL	Montana	MT	Texas	TX
Georgia	GA	Nebraska	NE	Utah	UT
Guam	GU	Nevada	NV	Vermont	VT
Hawaii	HI	New Hampshire	NH	Virginia	VA
Idaho	ID	New Jersey	NJ	Virgin Islands	VI
Illinois	IL	New Mexico	NM	Washington	WA
Indiana	IN	New York	NY	West Virginia	WV
Iowa	IA	North Carolina	NC	Wisconsin	WI
Kansas	KS	North Dakota	ND	Wyoming	WY

2. The last line of the envelope address should consist of the name of the city, the recommended two-letter state abbreviation, and the ZIP Code number (Figure 3-10). The city and state names should not be put on separate lines.

3. A room, suite, or apartment number should be typed immediately after the street address on the same line.

    Example: 2344 Courtland Place, Apt. 2B

4. The address should cover an area no larger than $1\frac{1}{2}$ by $3\frac{3}{4}$ inches and leave at least a half inch of space from the right and bottom margins. Where a window envelope is used, nothing but the address should appear in the window space, and there should be at least a quarter of an inch between the address and the right, left, and bottom edges of the window space.

Steps to Take Before Folding and Inserting

1. Proofread the letter carefully to be sure it is correct and has been signed.

2. Check to see that all enclosures mentioned in the letter are noted in the enclosure notation. Verify that the proper enclosures have been collected and, if necessary, duplicated. If the enclosures are to be a permanent part of the letter, staple them to it in the upper left corner. Do not use pins. If the enclosures are to be returned, or are to be circulated by the addressee, or are bulky, clip them to the letter with a paper clip. Be sure to fold the clip inside the letter and insert the papers into the envelope so that the clip is underneath the return address on the envelope. If the clip is underneath the stamp, it will interfere with the stamp-canceling machine.

3. Check to see that the address on the letter corresponds to the address on the envelope. Now, you may insert the material into the envelope and seal it.

Folding Letters. To fold a one-page $8\frac{1}{2}'' \times 11''$ letter to fit the small or short business envelope (No. $6\frac{3}{4}$, $6\frac{1}{2}'' \times 3\frac{5}{8}''$), follow these steps.

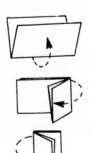

1. Place the letter flat on the desk, face up.

2. Bring the bottom edge to within one-fourth inch of the top edge and crease.

3. Fold the right edge a little less than a third of the width toward the left edge and crease.

4. Fold the left edge within one-half inch of the now creased right edge.

5. Place this last fold in the envelope first.

A one-page letter with enclosures or a letter of two or more pages should be placed in a No. 10 envelope, $9\frac{1}{2}'' \times 4\frac{1}{8}''$. To fold an $8\frac{1}{2}'' \times 11''$ letter to fit the large or long business envelope, follow these steps.

1. Place the letter on the desk, face up.
2. Fold a little less than a third of the sheet from the bottom toward the top and crease.
3. Fold the top third down to one-fourth inch from the first crease.
4. Insert the last fold into the envelope first.

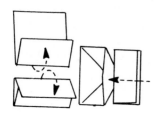

A letter to be mailed in a window envelope should initially be folded the same way for either a small or a large envelope.

1. Place the letter face up on the desk.
2. Fold up the bottom third of the letter and crease.

3. Turn the letter over and fold the top third down even with the first crease. The inside address is now visible, upside down on the right.

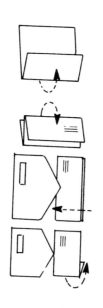

4. Insert this last crease into a large window envelope so that the address is visible.

For a small window envelope, make one additional fold of approximately two inches opposite the address to make the folded letter a little smaller than the envelope.

Ascertaining Correct Postage. Each piece of mail that contains three or more pages should be weighed to determine the correct postage to use. Office postal scales should be checked for accuracy before you weigh the piece you are sending. An adjustment screw at either the top or the side will allow you to balance them. The post office counts every ounce or fraction of an ounce for regular postage. Every half ounce or fraction of a half ounce is counted in figuring foreign air mail postage. Do not estimate weights. Mail may be delayed because of insufficient postage, or the addressee may resent receiving postage-due mail. See Chapter 15 for postal rates.

Chain-Feeding Envelopes. Approximately 150 envelopes an hour may be addressed if they are fed continuously into the machine. Place a stack of envelopes with flaps up and toward you on the left of the typewriter. Next, position the first envelope to be addressed in the machine about two inches (12 lines) from the top edge. Insert the second envelope on top of the disappearing portion of the first envelope and next to the platen or roller. Space down to type the address at the middle and slightly to the left of center. Be sure to set a margin stop instead of a tabular stop at this point in order to save carriage return time. As the address is typed on the first envelope, the second will move into position. The left hand should be used to feed a new envelope into the machine as the addressed envelope is removed from the machine with the right hand. Stack the finished envelopes face down at the right of the typewriter.

Use a chain of two if you must add information in the upper portion of the envelope; otherwise use a chain of three. Practice the steps slowly at first as you build speed and economy of movement. You should not have to turn the envelope over or twist the hand around to place it properly in the machine; the left and right hands work together.

Internal Communications. Information transmitted within a company is set up as a memorandum on either blank paper or a printed form, preferably in a color other than white. The form may include the company name or symbol together with a caption such as *MEMORANDUM* or *INTEROFFICE CORRESPONDENCE* and essential headings such as *To, From, Date, Memo No., Subject,* and *Copies to.* These headings may be arranged at the discretion of the designer of forms within the company. Three examples of typical memorandum forms are shown in Figure 3-11.

If a printed memorandum form is not available, type *MEMORANDUM, INTERDEPARTMENTAL COMMUNICATION,* or *INTEROFFICE CORRESPONDENCE* in capital letters on the seventh line from the top of the page. The heading may be centered or typed at the left margin. Triplespace and type the address information. Spacing between the headings *To* and *From* may be expanded to permit the typing of a number of names. It is good practice to use a person's first name and initial or both initials to ensure that the memorandum reaches the right person. Margins may be set where desired and single- or double-spacing used depending on the length of the memo. A half sheet is used for short messages. In a large company, it is good practice to note the addressee's and the writer's locations, such as department, room, and building numbers (Figure 3-11).

The carbon copy distribution list may be typed at the top of the page. Arrange the names alphabetically in one or two columns in both the *copies to* list and the addressee list. If there is not enough room on the printed form for either the addressee list or the *copies to* list, these lists may be placed at the bottom of the page (Figure 3-12).

Interdepartmental communications may or may not show reference initials, and most of them are not signed. If the originator feels that the

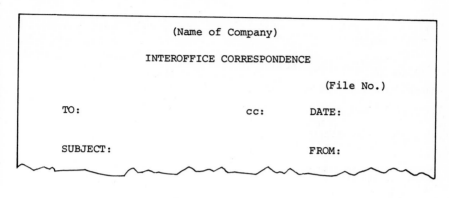

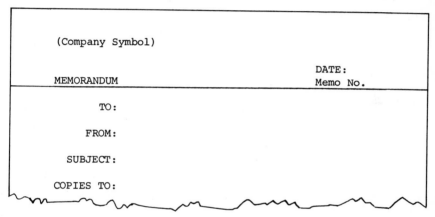

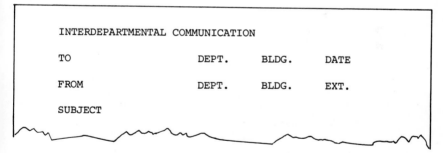

Figure 3-11   Examples of internal correspondence forms.

message would carry more weight or its instructions would be followed more carefully if a personal signature were included, he may place his initials or complete signature by his name on the *from* line or at the end of the message. Second and subsequent pages are typed on a plain sheet the same size, weight, color, and texture as the first page. The format for these pages is the same as that of the second page of a letter (Figure 3-7).

MEMORANDUM

71-54

TO: Distribution List   DATE: April 10, 19--

FROM: John R. Drew, 82-01

SUBJECT: Memorandum Format

COPIES TO: Distribution List

xxxxxxxxxxxxxxxxxxxxxxxxxxxxxxxxxxxxxxxxxxxxxxxxxxxxxxxxxxxxxxxxxxxxxxxxxxxx
xxxxxxxxxxxxxxxxxxxxxxxxxxxxxxxxxxxxxxxxxxxxxxxxxxxxxxxxxxxxxxxxxxxxxxxxxxxx
xxxxxxxxxxxxxxxxxxxxxxxxxxxxx.

xxxxxxxxxxxxxxxxxxxxxxxxxxxxxxxxxxxxxxxxxxxxxxxxxxxxxxxxxxxxxxxxxxxxxxxxxxxx
xxxxxxxxxxxxxxxxxxxxxxxxxxxx:

    1.   xxxxxxxxxxxxxxxxxxxxxxxxxxxxxxxxxxxxxxxxxxxxxxxxxxxxxxxxxxxxxx
         xxxxxxxxxxxxxxxxxxxxxxxxxxxxxx

    2.   xxxxxxxxxxxxxxxxxxxxxxxxxxxxxxxxxxxxxxxxxxxxxxxxxxxxxxxxxxxxxx
         xxxxxxxxxxxxxxxxxxxxxxxxxx

xxxxxxxxxxxxxxxxxxxxxxxxxxxxxxxxxxxxxxxxxxxxxxxxxxxxxxxxxxxxxxxxxxxxxxxxxxxx
xxxxxxxxxxxxxxxxxxxxxxxxxxxxxxxxxxxxxxxxxxxxxxxxxxxxxxxxxxxxxxxxxxx.

JRD:mt

Enc. (3)

To: J. B. Adams, 25-02   Copies to: P. W. Anderson, 11-2
         S. Booth, 25-02   J. K. Johnson, 25-02
     J. D. Davis, 102-5   Susan Parsons, 82-01
     Janet Dunn, 82-01   Security
     B. W. Perkins, 82-01   D. A. Weaver, 11-4
     D. J. West, Customer Sales

Figure 3-12 Sample memorandum form showing distribution and "Copies to" lists.

Classified memorandums require proper classification stampings and usually an accompanying receipt form. A declassification stamp or downgrade notation should be used when appropriate. See the discussion on marking classified information in Section 3.2.

File copies must be prepared for memorandums also. Carbon pack memorandum forms can be secured from your stationer in a variety of sizes and numbers of carbon copies. The use of these printed packs saves time in assembling copies and typing introductory headings.

3.2 LETTERS TO GOVERNMENT AND THE MILITARY: FORMAT AND SECURITY PRECAUTIONS

Of concern to the government and the military, as well as private business, is the security of letters and other documents. The main problem is safeguarding confidential information from those who might misuse it. A related problem, especially acute in large bureaucracies, is ensuring that all documents, whether confidential or not, are marked in a way that ensures their delivery into the right hands and, subsequently, their prompt and efficient attention.

All correspondence to any agency or department of the United States government should conform to the requirements of the agency addressed. Communications incorrectly prepared or addressed may be misplaced and delayed or may be rejected and returned. Because the return of a letter for correction would result in loss of time and perhaps interfere with a company's production schedule, care must be taken to prepare each letter as requested by the agency.

Nonmilitary Government Correspondence.   Most letters to departments of the government follow the business-letter format used in the business world. Also, the same informal conversational tone is used in correspondence to government officials as you would use with business associates. A letter should be as clear and concise as possible, yet maintain a friendly, courteous approach. It is important to use a comprehensive subject and a reference number when initiating the correspondence. The government agency or department will then be able to route your message correctly and refer to it specifically in reply. It is also important to address elected and appointed officials correctly as illustrated in Section 3.4.

Military Government Correspondence.   Letters to various agencies of the Department of Defense, however, are set up in special formats, designed by the agency involved. The military letter styles are similar in the order of introductory parts. The differences in format will be pointed out in the discussion that follows. Of more importance than format, however, is compliance with military security regulations established by the Department of Defense.

Importance of Security.   Much of the correspondence between a firm and the government concerns unclassified information that in no way jeopardizes national security. However, the security of classified information that passes between the United States government and business firms must be ensured by both the government and the firm involved. Every employee of a firm who handles or has knowledge of classified information is responsible for protecting and accounting for it. This responsibility extends to the safeguarding of classified information against unlawful or unauthorized dissemination, duplication, or observation. Classified information is released to persons on the basis of security clearance and need to know.

Company Control Numbers. In order to ensure the maximum security of documents, companies that have been granted government contracts set up a system of control numbers. These numbers are assigned to:

1. All classified documents that have been so designated by the government agency.

2. All communications concerning the negotiation or administration of contracts covering projects for the Department of Defense.

3. All communications from the company's engineering department relating to military procurement and projects.

A control number may be any arrangement of digits and letters that a company wishes to use. Generally, the year, department initials, and a numerical count number make up the control number. For example, *79ENG124* is the number given to the one-hundred-twenty-fourth incoming or outgoing document from/to the engineering department in 1979.

Responsibility for classified documents is vested in a classified-documents office. This office keeps records of the receipt, dispatch, and internal accountability of all classified documents. It is also responsible for the destruction of these documents and the maintenance of related records for a specified period of time. In order to keep adequate records, the following information should be gathered before a control number is assigned.

1. Date (date that will appear on document).

2. Type (e.g., letter, report, interdepartmental communication, photograph, and so on).

3. Destination.

4. Company cross-reference (e.g., previous company correspondence and enclosures, if any, to which this document refers).

5. Subject.

6. *Signed by/Dictated by.*

7. Classification (e.g., confidential, secret, top secret, and so on).

8. Control station number.

9. Name of person asking for the control number.

10. Number of copies to be made (e.g., original and five copies, ditto master and twenty-five copies, and so on).

11. Where document is to be duplicated.

Classification. Classified information is official information that requires protection in the interest of national defense. Materials bearing the following designations are safeguarded according to prescribed rules and regulations set up by the Department of Defense.

1. Top secret. Information or material that, if disclosed without authorization, could cause exceptionally grave damage to the nation.

2. Secret. Information or material that, if disclosed without authorization, could cause serious damage to the nation.

3. Confidential. Information or material that, if disclosed without authorization, could be prejudicial to the defense interest of the nation.

4. Restricted data. In addition to classification markings, this designation is applicable to any information or material subject to the provisions of the Atomic Energy Act of 1954. It may be used with top secret, secret, or confidential classifications.

Marking Correspondence. The security classification is always stamped in letters not less than one-fourth inch in height at the top and bottom of each page (Figure 3-13). In addition, each document is grouped in one of four categories as required by the automatic downgrading system and is stamped accordingly. Department of Defense security regulations determine the assignment of specific information to one of the four categories (Figure 3-14).

The espionage clause must appear on all classified correspondence to companies, organizations, and agencies other than the military (Figure 3-16). On classified letters, interdepartmental communications, and similar correspondence not having covers and title pages, the espionage clause is placed on the first page in the lower right corner. It need not appear on any other pages. On classified reports, proposals, and other bound documents, the espionage clause should be typed or stamped on the outside front cover (if one is used),

TOP SECRET   CONFIDENTIAL

SECRET   CONFIDENTIAL
MODIFIED HANDLING AUTHORIZED

| TOP SECRET |
RESTRICTED DATA
ATOMIC ENERGY ACT — 1954
SPECIFIC AUTHORIZATION FOR ACCESS REQUIRED

| SECRET | | CONFIDENTIAL |
RESTRICTED DATA   RESTRICTED DATA
ATOMIC ENERGY ACT — 1954   ATOMIC ENERGY ACT — 1954
SPECIFIC AUTHORIZATION FOR ACCESS REQUIRED   SPECIFIC AUTHORIZATION FOR ACCESS REQUIRED

Figure 3-13   Security classification stamps.

the first page, and the title page. If a stamp is not available, the following may be typed on the appropriate pages in the lower right corner.

THIS DOCUMENT CONTAINS INFORMATION AFFECTING THE NATIONAL DEFENSE OF THE UNITED STATES WITHIN THE MEANING OF THE ESPIONAGE LAWS, TITLE 18 U.S.C., SECTIONS 793 AND 794. ITS TRANSMISSION OR THE REVELATION OF ITS CONTENTS IN ANY MANNER TO AN UNAUTHORIZED PERSON IS PROHIBITED BY LAW.

All classified material must bear a classification marking at least as high as the highest class of its contents. All classified documents must be accompanied by a transmittal or covering letter stamped with the appropriate classification. Unclassified correspondence that is attached to or enclosed with other data that are classified must be marked with the highest classification of the attached or enclosed material. It should be marked to indicate that it becomes declassified when removed from the attachments or enclosures. The following declassification stamp should be placed in the lower left corner of the letter.

IF ENCLOSURES ARE WITHDRAWN OR NOT ATTACHED, THE CLASSIFICATION OF THIS CORRESPONDENCE WILL BE CANCELED IN ACCORDANCE WITH THE INDUSTRIAL SECURITY MANUAL FOR SAFEGUARDING CLASSIFIED INFORMATION.

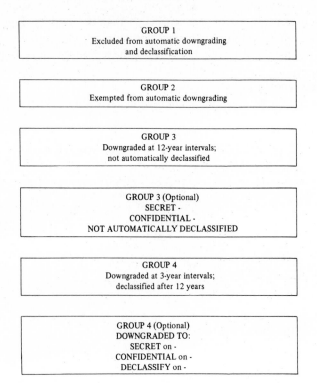

Figure 3-14   Automatic timephased downgrading and declassification stamps.

A classified letter or memorandum transmitting enclosures that bear a higher classification than the letter or memorandum itself is marked with the following stamp placed in the lower left corner of the letter.

DOWNGRADE TO _____ WHEN DETACHED FROM ENCLOSURES.

Figure 3-15 indicates the markings that should be placed on military letters according to their classification and the classification of their enclosures.

Format of Military Correspondence.   Letters to the U.S. Army, Navy, and Air Force use the same general format. The *subject* and *to* lines are required on all formal military letters. Letters to the Air Force should list the subject first whereas letters to the Army and Navy start first with the *to* address and the *via* routing information (if needed). The full block or block letter styles are used. The date is written in the military style—25 October 19—. Control numbers are assigned to assure proper handling of these important messages. A model form is shown in Figure 3-16.

Subject Lines.   In a letter to the U.S. Air Force, the subject lines follow the date and control number, at least three to six lines below depending on the length of the letter. The appropriate contract number, when applicable, is typed on the first line after *Subject:* (or abbreviation *Subj.:*). The project or program name, when applicable, is typed on the second line. The subject of the message is placed directly below and should be limited to two typewritten lines, if possible. Military letters are designated by the originating agency as either classified or unclassified. On a *classified* letter, the subject itself must bear a security designation. The parenthetical abbreviations *(U), (C-MHA), (C), (S),* and *(TS)* should be used, respectively, for unclassified, confidential-modified handling authorized, confidential, secret, and top secret.

    18 September 1980
    71G0987
    Subject: Contract AF 13(108)-1125
               Air Defense Command Program
               Computer Programs for SQUID (U)

In letters to the Army and Navy, the subject lines come after the address and the routing instructions.

Address Lines.   The inside address begins two spaces below the subject in letters to the Air Force or four to six spaces after the date in letters to the Army and Navy. The word *to* followed by a colon is typed at the left margin, and the lines in the address are blocked at the same point as the subject information and other preliminary parts of the letter. If the correspondence must be directed to a specific person within the office addressed, the attention line is typed after the name of the office.

    To: BSD (BSRR)
          Attention John H. Jones
          Air Force Unit Post Office
          Los Angeles, California 90045

Classification of Letter	Classification of Enclosures	Markings on Letter			
Unclassified	Unclassified	None			
Unclassified	Confidential	Confidential		Declassification	
Unclassified	Secret	Secret		Declassification	
Unclassified	Confidential and Secret	Secret		Declassification	
Confidential	None or Unclassified	Confidential	Espionage		Timephase
Confidential	Confidential	Confidential	Espionage		Timephase
Confidential	Secret	Secret	Espionage	Downgrade to Confidential	Timephase
Confidential	Confidential and Secret	Secret	Espionage	Downgrade to Confidential	Timephase
Secret	None or Unclassified	Secret	Espionage		Timephase
Secret	Confidential	Secret	Espionage		Timephase
Secret	Secret	Secret	Espionage		Timephase
Secret	Confidential and Secret	Secret	Espionage		Timephase

Figure 3-15 Guide to classification and marking of letters to the military.

SECRET

T H O M P S O N   M A N U F A C T U R I N G ,   I N C.
12456 Arizona Highway, Phoenix, Arizona 85007

Date
Control number   OR In reply refer to:
                                      (Control number)

Subject: xxxxxxxxxxxxxxxxxxxxxxxxxxx

To: xxxxxxxxxxxxxxxxxxxxxxxxxxx
           xxxxxxxxxxxxxxxxx

Through: xxxxxxxxxxxxxxxxxxxxxxxxxxx
           xxxxxxxxxxxxxxxxxxxxxxxxxxx
           xxxxxxxxxxxxxxxxxxxxx

Reference: (a)   xxxxxxxxxxxxxxxxxxxxxxxxxxxxxxxxxx
             (b)   xxxxxxxxxxxxxxxxxxxxxxxxxxxxx

1.   xxxxxxxxxxxxxxxxxxxxxxxxxxxxxxxxxxxxxxxxxxxxxxxxxx
xxxxxxxxxxxxxxxxxxxxxxxxxxxxxxxxxxxxxxxxxxxxxxx

     a.   xxxxxxxxxxxxxxxxxxxxxxxxxxxxxxxxxxxxxx

     b.   xxxxxxxxxxxxxxxxxxxxxxxxxxxxxxxxxxxxxxxx
          xxxxxxxxxxxxxxxxxxxxxxxxxxxxxxxxx

2.   xxxxxxxxxxxxxxxxxxxxxxxxxxxxxxxxxxxxxxxxxxxxxxxxx
xxxxxxxxxxxxxxxxxxxxxxxxxxxxxxxxx

THOMPSON MANUFACTURING, INC.

Signer's name, Title
Department

(Initials, optional)

Enclosures: (1)xxxxxxxxxxxxxxxxxxxxxxxxxx
              (2)xxxxxxxxxxxxxxxxxxxxxxxxxx

cc: xxxxxxxxxxxxxxxxxxxxxxxxxxxxxxxxxxxxxxxx

SECRET

Figure 3-16   Form of classified correspondence to the Air Force.

If the correspondence must be sent through another office or agency before transmittal to the addressee (for information, approval, or other reasons), the office name, initials, or symbol (in parentheses) is typed two spaces below the inside address. Use the word *through* in letters to the Air Force: use *via* in letters to the Army and Navy. A colon follows the word. If the correspondence must be handled by a specific person or section in that office, the attention line is the second line of the block.

```
Through:  Chief, U.S. Air Force Liaison Office
          Attention John H. Jones
          c/o System Development Corporation
          Santa Monica, California 90312
                         OR
Through:  SSD (SSKMA) Mr. A. M. Rossbo
```

Reference Line.   The reference line (when required) is two lines below the inside address (or coordination office, if applicable)—or two lines below the subject block in letters to the Army and Navy. The designation *Reference* or the abbreviation *Ref.* is followed by a colon. Referenced items should be listed chronologically.

```
Reference:  (a)  AFLC letter MCFD/AJ dated 4 May 1979
            (b)  AFLC letter MCFD/AL dated 22 October 1978
            (c)  NavAirSysCom ltr (add complete file code, serial, and date)
```

Salutation.   Salutations are *not* used in letters to the military.
Body of the Letter.   Start the body of the letter two spaces below the inside address, the coordination office, or the last line of the reference, as applicable. Each paragraph is usually numbered consecutively. The numbers are flush with the left margin. In a one-page letter, you have the option of omitting paragraph numbers; however, it is a good idea to identify subparagraphs. To facilitate the referencing of letters over one page in length, number the main paragraphs (*1., 2., 3.,* and so on) and identify subparagraphs (*a., b., c.,* and so on).

```
1.  xxxxxxxxxxxxxxxxxxxxxxxxxxxxxxxxxxxxxxxxxxxxxxxxxxxxxxxxxxxxxxxxxxxx
xxxxxxxxxxxxxxxxxxxxxxxxxxxxxxxxxxxxxxxxxxxxxxxxxxxxxxxxxxxxxxxxxxxxxxxxxx
xxxxxxxxxxxxxxxxxxxxxxxxxxxxxxxxxxxxxxxxxxxx:

     a.  xxxxxxxxxxxxxxxxxxxxxxxxxxxxxxxxxxxxxxxxxxxxxxxxxxxxxxxxxxxxxxxx
         xxxxxxxxxxxxxxxxxxxxxxxxxxxxx

     b.  xxxxxxxxxxxxxxxxxxxxxxxxxxxxxxxxxxxxxxxxxxxxxxxxxxxxxxxxxxxxxxxx
         xxxxxxxxxxxxxxxxxxxxxxxxxxxxxxxxxxxxxxxxxxxx

         (1)  xxxxxxxxxxxxxxxxxxxxxxxxxxxxxxxxxxxxxxxxxxxxxxxxxxxxxxxxxxx
              xxxxxxxxxxxxxxxxxxxxxxxxxxxxxxx
         (2)  xxxxxxxxxxxxxxxxxxxxxxxxxxxxxxxxxxxxxxxxxxxxxxxxxxxxxx

2.  xxxxxxxxxxxxxxxxxxxxxxxxxxxxxxxxxxxxxxxxxxxxxxxxxxxxxxxxxxxxxxxxxxxxxx
xxxxxxxxxxxxxxxxxxxxxxxxxxxxxxxxxxxxxxxxxxxxxxxxxxxxxxxxxxxxxxxxxxxxxxxxxx
```

Closing Lines.   The complimentary close is omitted on letters to the U.S. Army, Navy, and Air Force. The company name, however, is typed in all capitals two spaces below the last line in the body of the letter. The addressor's name is typed four spaces below the company name. The title may be typed on the same line as the name or one space below with the department title, if used. Use the placement that gives the best balance. The addressor on letters to the military is a person officially authorized by the company to sign on its behalf.

xxxxxxxxxxxxxxxxxxxxxxxxxxxxxxxxxxxxxxxxxxxxxxxxxxxxxxxxxxxxxxxxxxxxxx
xxxxxxxxxxxxxxxxxxxxxxxxxxxxxxxxxxxxxxx.

LOCKHEED-CALIFORNIA COMPANY

C. C. Jones, Manager
Contracts and Proposals
DDD:CCJ:aa

Identification Initials.   Initials may appear on the original copy of a letter to the U.S. Army, Navy, or Air Force; or they may appear solely on the internal copies of the letter. The signer's, dictator's, and typist's initials should be shown. Some companies omit the dictator's initials on the carbon copy if he also signs the letter. In these cases the typist's initials are the only ones that appear on the copies of the correspondence.

Enclosures.   In military correspondence, all enclosures should be listed and identified carefully. Arabic numerals, followed by a period or enclosed in parentheses, are used to list two or more enclosures (or groups of enclosures). Use *Enclosure* or the abbreviations *Encl.* or *Enc.* in letters to the Navy and Air Force; use *Inclosure* or *Inc.* in letters to the Army. Each enclosure should be identified on each page either in the upper right corner or centered one inch from the bottom of the page. The notation should be "Enclosure (1) to (your company name) letter (control or file number, if any), dated _____, page 1 of 5."

Enc: (1) 3 copies of Report XXxx dated 27 December 19—
       (2) 2 copies of Contract 12345 (Copies 12 and 14)
       (3) (SC) 1/c ea. photographs listed in paragraph ___

Enclosures sent under separate cover should be listed and identified by (*SC*) immediately preceding the description. Be sure that the information given in the body of the letter agrees with the manner in which the enclosures are described in the enclosure block. The enclosure block may be double-spaced below the identification initials, or it may appear immediately after the reference information at the beginning of the letter.

Carbon Copies.   Following the abbreviation *cc:* or *Copy to:* list alphabetically all persons or agencies receiving carbon copies, with addresses if necessary. The *copy to* line is placed at the left margin two spaces below the last line in the signature block or the last line in the enclosure block. On military letters, the list on the original contains only the names of persons or agencies outside the company receiving copies. Internal copies of the correspondence contain both external and internal distribution lists. Those addresses (both external and internal) receiving one or more of the listed enclosures should show the following information—*cc: Col. J. K. Patrick, Edwards AFB (w/enc. (1)—2 copies).*

Approval Line.   An approval line may be added as the last item on the page when it is necessary for the correspondence to be returned to the originator with an approval signature and date. Two copies of the letter should be sent to the addressee if one is to be returned with the approval signature.

APPROVED:

_____

Date   (Type in addressee's title)

Second-Page Heading.   Headings for the second and succeeding pages of letters to the military should include all pertinent information. The control number, subject, abbreviated inside address, date, and page number should be included. The security classification, if any, must be stamped at the top and the bottom of each page. Several ways to head second pages are shown in Figure 3-17.

Copies of Military Correspondence.   Because most government agencies require several copies of each piece of correspondence, it is usually economical to type the communication on an original company letterhead and make a vellum or ditto master as the carbon copy of the original for reproduction purposes. No tissue copies are needed unless specifically requested. Ditto masters with appropriate security classifications imprinted on them can be secured. If a blank ditto master is used, all copies made from it must be stamped with the appropriate classification. The originator of a communication should carefully determine the number of copies required. Care should be taken to reproduce no more copies than are absolutely necessary. An original and four copies are usually asked for by the Army, Navy, Air Force, and Space Agency. The external distribution list for government agencies and other companies appears on both the original letterhead and the master ditto. The identifying initials and the company internal distribution list, however, appear on the master ditto only.

Transmission of Classified Correspondence.   Most companies handling classified government material require a receipt for the transmittal of secret material within or outside the company. They also require a receipt for the transmittal outside the company of confidential material. A receipt for the transmittal of confidential material within the company is not necessary. Top secret material is never sent by mail but is handled according to special instructions issued by the Department of Defense.

The transmittal and receipt form should contain the information shown in Figure 3-18.

```
(Subject line(s))                              15 January 19--
(Abbreviated address)                               70ENG-445
                                                       Page 2
```

```
To:       AFLC Plans Office, Dir. Plans & Programs      Page 2
          Hq., AFLC, Wright-Patterson AFB, Ohio      6 June 19--
          Attn.:  Colonel J. Jensen, MCFD              70GO-1111

From:     North American Aviation, Inc., General Offices
Subject:  Customer Letter Format (Air Force) (U)
```

```
                        S E C R E T


NASA, ASPO, MSC, Houston, Texas
Attention Mr. C. D. Sword
6 June 19--
70GO-1112
Page 2
```

```
To:       Chief, BuWeps, Washington, D. C.             Page 2
          Attention:  WEPS                           6 June 19--
From:     North American Aviation, Inc.                70GO-1113
          General Offices
Subject:  Customer Letter Format (Navy) (U)
```

Figure 3-17 Styles of second-page headings for military correspondence.

Addressor's name and complete address
Addressee's name and complete address
Project or contract number
Unclassified subject or brief description of material being transmitted
Identification or control number
Copy number
Security classification
Date of material
Originator's name and department or room number
Mailing or delivery instructions
Acknowledgment section for signature and date
Postal registry number, if applicable

Mailing Classified Material. Government security regulations require that classified material be enclosed in two opaque envelopes before it is mailed through the facilities of the U.S. Postal Service or before delivery by a commercial carrier. Both envelopes should bear the names and addresses of the

TRANSMITTAL AND RECEIPT FOR CLASSIFIED MATERIAL S 1001		CLASSIFICATION SECRET	Log. No. Out ____ In
Date	Page of Pages	Postal Registry No.	
From		To	
Originator Room No.		☐ Airmail ☐ First Class	

Material listed below is being transmitted as enclosures _____

Classification	Copy No.	Identification Number and/or Title	

If enclosures are withdrawn or not attached the classification of this correspondence will be cancelled in accordance with industrial security manual.	RECEIPT OF THE ABOVE IS HEREBY ACKNOWLEDGED
Classification SECRET	Signature Date

Figure 3-18 Transmittal and receipt form for classified material.

addressor and the addressee. The inner envelope must be marked with the security classification of the documents and the restricted data stamp, when applicable. The classified document should be protected from direct contact with the inner envelope by a cover sheet or by being folded inward. Check to see that the classification stamp is not visible through the outer envelope. The inner envelope must contain a classified-material receipt and must be sealed and inserted into the outer envelope, which is also sealed.

Security regulations require that confidential material be sent by certified mail and that secret material be sent by registered mail. The outer envelope must be stamped "Certified Mail No. ____" or "Register No. ____" before it is placed in the outgoing mail basket or taken to the post office.

For *material that cannot be folded,* use two manila envelopes, one slightly larger than the other (sizes $8\frac{3}{8}'' \times 11\frac{1}{2}''$, $9'' \times 12''$, $10'' \times 12''$, or $12'' \times 16''$) and type two identical mailing labels. Then follow the steps outlined above.

For *material too bulky for manila envelopes,* prepare two mailing labels. Double-wrap the documents, enclose the receipt, affix the labels, stamp the proper classification on the inner wrapping, register or certify the package, and mail it.

Handling of Classified Material. The transmission, destruction, accountability, storage, and marking of classified material follow certain specific procedures. Figure 3-19 is a chart of recommended procedures for handling top secret, secret, and confidential material. Anyone who has clearance to work with classified information must be familiar with these procedures.

Security regulations require also that all secret and confidential waste generated during the preparation, typing, or reproduction of classified information be destroyed. Usually the classified-documents control office is responsible for the destruction. Classified waste includes preliminary drafts; carbon sheets; carbon typewriter ribbons; plates; stencils; Azograph, ditto, vellum, and other masters; composition recording tapes; stenographic notes; work sheets; and similar items containing classified information.

Safeguarding classified material during use, storing and filing it carefully, and seeing that only authorized personnel have access to it are security controls that must be exercised by everyone cleared to handle these documents. Tips on how to avoid security infractions are listed below.

1. Never leave classified material exposed or unattended.
2. Use a cover sheet with each classified document.
3. Use file markers on all classified files and containers.
4. Do not take classified material home to work on.
5. Be certain of three facts before discussing classified information with anyone: the person's identity, his or her level of clearance, and whether or not the person "needs to know" the information.

	Top Secret	Secret *or* Confidential	All Classifications
TRANSMISSION	Distribution and transmittal handled by a corporate officer or his representative. Special instructions issued by the Department of Defense.	*Inside Company:* 1. Use red-bordered interoffice envelope; send via interoffice mail or deliver personally. 2. Double wrap if hand-carried between buildings. 3. Include receipt (secret only). *Outside Company:* 1. Double wrap. Address inner wrapping and stamp both sides with classification. 2. Include transmittal and receipt form. 3. Send only by U.S. registered mail. 4. Do not send classified material marked *Personal.* 5. All materials must be sent through a control station. 6. Special instructions are issued for courier authorization.	1. Classified information may not be transmitted via telephone or telegram. 2. Follow instructions covering transmission of bulky classified material.
DESTRUCTION	All Top Secret materials is destroyed by the responsible corporate officer.	1. Prepare a record of items being destroyed. 2. Destroy by burning or pulping in the presence of a witness. 3. Accountability records should be retained for ten years.	Deposit in classified waste closets or containers all nonaccountable classified materials (notes, working papers, carbon paper and ribbons, etc.).

ACCOUNTABILITY	The responsible corporate officer receives, records, and is responsible for all accountable Top Secret material. He or his representative must authorize access to Top Secret material.	1. A corporate office should keep master records for company authored documents.
		2. The files or the library should keep master records for documents written and published outside the company.
		3. The mailroom and the files should keep master records for documents sent out of company and those sent to company via U. S. mail.
		4. An inventory should be made and an accounting submitted periodically.
		5. All classified mail should be logged in by the mailroom.
		6. Maintenance of incoming and outgoing mail logs is recommended.
			1. An employee is responsible for all documents for which he signed a receipt.
			2. Before releasing classified information make sure:
			  a. of recipient's identity.
			  b. of his need to know.
			  c. of his clearance level.
			  d. that he signs a receipt for the material.

STORAGE	Top Secret material should be returned to responsible corporate official or his representative at a specified time, such as 4:30 p.m., for overnight storage. No Top Secret items should be left in other offices or files overnight even though these may be securely locked.	1. Return material to filing cabinet for overnight storage or when person responsible leaves office during working hours. Use an approved combination-locked, steel file safe which has been recommended by the Defense Department. 2. Physical custody or surveillance by authorized personnel is required when not stored.	1. When material is in use, protect it from being seen by an unauthorized person. 2. Return to locked file cabinet as soon as practical after use.

Figure 3-19 Recommended procedures for handling classified material.

Top Secret	Secret *or* Confidential	All Classifications
1. Copy numbered in series. 2. Each page numbered in series. 3. Total number of copies in existence marked on each document. 4. Classification stamped on top and bottom of each page.	1. Bound documents: Classification stamped on top and bottom of front and back covers, title page, and first and last pages of the volume. 2. Unbound documents: Classification stamped on top and bottom of each page. 3. Charts, maps, drawings, and photographs: Classification shown on both top and bottom. 4. Films: Classification shown at beginning and end of each roll, and on film containers. 5. Letters of Transmittal: a. Show same classification as material it accompanies. b. Include notice of downgrading, if applicable: *If enclosures are withdrawn....* 6. Documents sent outside company: Stamp notice of espionage laws on cover: *Notice: This document contains information...* 7. Documents containing restricted data: Stamp *Restricted Data Atomic Energy Act 1954* in addition to Classification markings. 8. Records of recipients and copy numbers of author-delivered information should be filed in mailroom or some other control office. 9. Recommend stamping of classification, not typing.	Refer all technical questions to the corporate officer or his representative who is responsible for classified documents.

MARKING

Figure 3-19 (continued).

6. Commit your safe combination to memory.

7. Erase all classified information from blackboards.

8. Never store classified material in a desk or table drawer.

9. Know that your area is secure with all files locked, whenever it is unattended during the day or night.

10. Do not discuss classified material over the telephone, at home, or in public.

11. Store, handle, and destroy typewriter ribbons; steno pads; media tapes, cards, belts, and discs; rough drafts; and other classified waste with the same precautions as you would the finished documents.

12. Perform classified work only in classified facilities.

13. Don't pry into classified projects that are not your direct concern.

14. Don't leave classified documents or unopened mail in your mail trays overnight.

15. Use the facilities of a classified-documents control office for recording incoming and outgoing documents, and for mailing classified material; or keep complete records yourself if such an office has not been established.

3.3 SECURITY OF COMPANY DOCUMENTS

Certain information circulated within the company is of a private nature. The disclosure of this type of information to unauthorized persons would be contrary to the best interests of your company. Company private information includes, but is not limited to, certain financial records, payroll records, employee investigation records, personnel records, minutes of executive- and policy-committee meetings, patents, plans for new projects, some engineering drawings, geology surveys, proprietary information, and any other facts or figures judged to be private in nature.

The discussion in the previous section illustrates how the military and the government protect classified information vital to the United States. It should be read carefully because many of their procedures could be adopted by a company seeking to protect its own interests. The usual corporate designations used to limit and control access to specific information follow.

Proprietary Information. Information or material that, if disclosed without authorization, could be prejudicial to the interests of the corporation is proprietary. This designation is used to protect patentable information and information concerning the competitive technological processes of private organizations.

Sensitive. Information or material that, if disclosed without authorization, could be detrimental to the interests of the corporation or an individual is sensitive. Both the reproduction and the distribution of copies are controlled by the author.

Limited. This designation allows control of the distribution of a document by the author. It does not control the handling or the safeguarding of the document copy itself.

Many companies prefer to use either *Private Data* or *Private Information* on all material in the nature of private company business. The terms *confidential, secret, top secret,* and *restricted* are reserved for classified government material. A company's security designation is never stamped on a document having a military or government security classification. Private information of a company should be handled in much the same way as government classified material.

3.4 FORMS OF ADDRESS

The titles *Mr., Mrs., Ms.,* or *Miss* are correct when you are not sure of the recipient's official, appointive, honorary, or earned title. If you are familiar with a person's special title or position in the government, the military, or the educational and religious fields, it is courteous to use the appropriate form of address. Correct statements of titles and their forms of address may be quickly checked in the alphabetical listing at the end of this chapter.

General Practices. The inside address and the address on the envelope should be identical as to content and form, except that the ZIP Code may be omitted from the inside address. Ordinarily, a person's business title is omitted unless he or she holds an official or honorary position. With the emphasis on the informal, friendly tone in business letters, the salutation should be one that uses the recipient's name. *Dear Sir* and *Dear Madam* are rarely used today, and *Sir* and *Madam* are used only for a very formal situation. *Sir* establishes a cold atmosphere, whereas *Dear Mr. Jones, Dear General Jones,* or *My dear Ambassador Jones* establishes a warm relationship between the correspondents.

Every effort should be made to learn the exact title and correct address of the person with whom one is corresponding. Correct titles of United States officials may be verified in the *Congressional Directory,* the *United States Government Organization Manual,* the *Biographic Register of the Department of State,* and the military service registers. Titles of foreign dignitaries may be found in the monthly *Diplomatic List* published by the Department of State, in the quarterly *Foreign Consular Offices in the United States* also published by the Department of State, and in the *Congressional Directory.*

Copies of these publications are in most public libraries and in the government publications sections of university libraries.

When addressing private individuals in a foreign country, it is common practice to use the appropriate American forms when the letter is worded in English. If the letter is written in a foreign language, appropriate foreign titles should be used. The *Department of State Correspondence Handbook, Part III* is a helpful guide for United Nations diplomats, who are also listed in the United Nations official directory. The correct forms of address for members of royalty and nobility in the United Kingdom may be found in the *Department of State Correspondence Handbook, Part III.*

Titles of Courtesy.   *Mr.* is reserved for a man (Mr. Everett Jones). The plural is *Messrs.* (Messrs. Everett Jones and Henry Gray).

Miss is correct in addressing an unmarried woman (Miss Theresa Jones). The plural is *Misses* (Misses Theresa Jones and Clare Drew).

Mrs. is correct in addressing a married woman using her own maiden first name and maiden middle name or initial and her husband's last name, or her husband's full name (Mrs. Lucille V. Jones or Mrs. Cary S. Jones). The plural is *Mesdames* or *Mmes.* (Mesdames Lucille V. Jones and Louella Briggs).

Ms. is well established in addressing a single woman, a married woman using her full maiden name, or any woman whose marital status is unknown or not pertinent (Ms. Theresa Jones, Ms. Lucille V. Jones). The plural form is the same as the singular (Ms. Dora E. Jones and Ellen Truslow).

Special Titles
Excellency.   This title is not used very often in America. *His Excellency* is the complimentary diplomatic title to use in addressing foreign presidents, foreign ambassadors, foreign cabinet officers, and foreign high and former high officials. *His Excellency* is used in the address; *Excellency* in the salutation; and *Your Excellency* in the body of the communication. In ecclesiastical correspondence, *Excellency* is used in addressing all Roman Catholic archbishops and bishops.
Honorable.   This title is used in addressing the following American officials: former Presidents, Presidents-elect, and all high ex-officials; governors; cabinet officers; senators; congressmen; American ambassadors; American ministers; secretaries or assistants to the President; under secretaries and assistant secretaries of the executive departments; judges; and mayors. *Honorable* must be followed by initials or a first name and may be abbreviated (*Hon.*) when *the* is omitted.
Esquire.   This title is used sometimes in the United States for professional men and women, such as architects and attorneys. The person's full name without a title, such as *Mr.* or *Ms.*, is followed by a comma and *Esquire* or *Esq.* It may be used for foreign-service officers below the grade of career

minister, for a clerk of the Supreme Court of the United States, and for officers in other courts.

In the United Kingdom, *Esquire* is often used after the names of persons prominent in the social, diplomatic, and business worlds.

Military. In official and formal correspondence, all military officers should be addressed on the envelope and letter by their complete titles. These titles may be abbreviated when followed by the given name, or initials, and the surname. In the salutation, brigadier generals, major generals, lieutenant generals, and generals are all addressed as *General;* lieutenant colonels and colonels, as *Colonel;* the fleet admiral, full admirals, vice admirals, and rear admirals of the U.S. Navy and Coast Guard, as *Admiral.* In conversation, officers of the U.S. Medical and Dental Corps may be addressed as *Doctor,* and officers of the Chaplain Corps as *Chaplain.*

When addressing correspondence to an enlisted person in any of the five services, use the abbreviated title plus the full name on the first line; and on the second indicate branch of the service followed by the designation of the military division.

M. Sgt. John J. Jones
Company B, Headquarters Wing U.S.A.F.
Kelly Air Force Base
San Antonio, Texas 78200

The comparative ranks and abbreviations of the five services are shown in Figure 3-20.

Additional Pointers on Forms of Address

1. Retired officials and holders of honorary positions are extended the courtesy of *The Honorable* in the address but are called *Mr., Ms., Mrs.* in the salutation. Even a former President of the United States reverts to *Mr.* unless he has a military title and is addressed by it.

2. Judges and persons holding officer rank in the military retain these titles for life.

3. When a person has been officially appointed to act for another, use the word *acting* preceding the title in the envelope and letter address but do not use *acting* in the salutation or in spoken address.

4. Address a person by his/her highest title.

5. The spouse of an official does not share the partner's title when the two are addressed jointly. The titled name is given first: *The Honorable Jane A. Jones and Mr. John C. Jones* or *The Honorable and Mrs. John C. Jones* and the salutation *Mayor and Mr. Jones* or *Mayor and Mrs. Jones.*

6. Women are addressed just as men are in similar positions. The formal salutation is *Madam.*

7. The use of a formal or less formal salutation and complimentary close depends on (1) the nature of the message (official, routine, personal, civic, or social) and (2) the relationship between the writer and the addressee.

	ARMY (U.S.A.)		NAVY (U.S.N.)		MARINE CORPS (U.S.M.C.)		AIR FORCE (U.S.A.F.)		COAST GUARD (U.S.C.G.)	
(1)	General of the Army (wartime)		Fleet Admiral (wartime)		No Equivalent		General of the Air Force (wartime)		No equivalent	
(2)	General	Gen.	Admiral	Adm.	General	Gen.	General	Gen.	Admiral	Adm.
(3)	Lieutenant General	Lt. Gen.	Vice Admiral	Vice Adm.	Lieutenant General	Lt. Gen.	Lieutenant General	Lt. Gen.	Vice Admiral	Vice Adm.
(4)	Major General	Maj. Gen.	Rear Admiral	Rear Adm.	Major General	Maj. Gen.	Major General	Maj. Gen.	Rear Admiral	Rear Adm.
(5)	Brigadier General	Brig. Gen.	Commodore (wartime)		Brigadier General	Brig. Gen.	Brigadier General	Brig. Gen.		
(6)	Colonel	Col.	Captain	Capt.	Colonel	Col.	Colonel	Col.	Captain	Capt.
(7)	Lieutenant Colonel	Lt. Col.	Commander	Comdr.	Lieutenant Colonel	Lt. Col.	Lieutenant Colonel	Lt. Col.	Commander	Comdr.
(8)	Major	Maj.	Lieutenant Commander	Lt. Comdr.	Major	Maj.	Major	Maj.	Lieutenant Commander	Lt. Comdr.
(9)	Captain	Capt.	Lieutenant	Lt.	Captain	Capt.	Captain	Capt.	Lieutenant	Lt.
(10)	1st Lieutenant	1st Lt.	Lieutenant (jg.)	Lt. (jg.)	1st Lieutenant	1st Lt.	1st Lieutenant	1st Lt.	Lieutenant (jg.)	Lt. (jg.)
(11)	2nd Lieutenant	2nd Lt.	Ensign	Ens.	2nd Lieutenant	2nd Lt.	2d Lieutenant	2d Lt.	Ensign	Ens.
(12)	Chief Warrant Officer	CWO	Chief Warrant Officer	CWO	Chief Warrant Officer	CWO	Chief Warrant Officer	CWO	Chief Warrant Officer	CWO
(13)	Warrant Officer	WO	Warrant Officer	WO	Warrant Officer	WO	Warrant Officer	WO	Warrant Officer	WO
(14)	Staff Sergeant Major or Specialist E9	S. Sgt. Maj. / Spec. 9	Master Chief Petty Officer	MCPO	Master Gunnery Sergeant	MGySgt.	Chief Master Sergeant	CMSgt.	Master Chief Petty Officer	MCPO
(15)	First Sergeant or Master Sergeant	M. Sgt.	Senior Chief Petty Officer	SCPO	Sergeant Major	Sgt. Maj.	Senior Master Sergeant	SMSgt.	Senior Chief Petty Officer	SCPO
(16)	Sergeant First Class or Specialist E7	Sfc. / Spec. 7	Chief Petty Officer	CPO	Master Sergeant	M. Sgt.	Master Sergeant	M. Sgt.	Chief Petty Officer	CPO
(17)	Staff Sergeant or Specialist E6	S. Sgt. / Spec. 6	Petty Officer First Class	PO1c	1st Sergeant	1st Sgt.	Technical Sergeant	T. Sgt.	Petty Officer First Class	PO1c
(18)	Sergeant or Specialist E5	Sgt. / Spec. 5	Petty Officer Second Class	PO2c	Gunnery Sergeant	Gy Sgt.	Staff Sergeant	S. Sgt.	Petty Officer Second Class	PO2c
(19)	Corporal or Specialist E4	Cpl. / Spec. 4	Petty Officer Third Class	PO3c	Staff Sergeant	S. Sgt.	Airman First Class	A1c.	Petty Officer Third Class	PO3c
(20)	Private First Class	Pfc.	Seaman	S1c.	Sergeant or Corporal	Sgt. / Cpl.	Airman Second Class	A2c.	Seaman First Class	S1c.
(21)	Private 2	Pvt.	Seaman Apprentice	SA	Lance Corporal	Lance Cpl.	Airman Third Class	A3c	Seaman Apprentice	SA
(22)	Private 1	Pvt.	Seaman Recruit	SR	Private First Class	Pfc.	Airman	A.	Seaman Recruit	SR

Figure 3-20 Ranks and abbreviations of the five services.

131

Alphabetical List of Important Titles and Their Forms of Address

Inside Address	*Salutation and* *Complimentary Close*

Alderman
　Alderman John C. Blank　　　　　　　　　Dear Alderman Blank
　　　　　　　　　　　　　　　　　　　　Dear Mr. Blank

　The Honorable John C. Blank
　Alderman, City of Philadelphia　　　　　Yours very truly
　　　　　　　　　　　　　　　　　　　　Sincerely yours

Ambassador
　*The Honorable John C. Blank　　　　　　Sir
　American Ambassador　　　　　　　　　　Dear Mr. Ambassador
　London, England　　　　　　　　　　　　My dear Mr. Ambassador
　　　　　　　　　　　　　　　　　　　　My dear Madam Ambassador

　Central and South America:
　　　　　　　　　　　　　　　　　　　　Very truly yours
　The Honorable John C. Blank　　　　　　Sincerely yours
　The Ambassador of the United States
　Bogotá, Columbia

Archbishop
　The Most Reverend John C. Blank　　　　Your Excellency
　　　　　　　　　　　　　　　　　　　　Most Reverend Sir
　　　　　　　　　　　　　　　　　　　　Dear Archbishop Blank

　　　　　　　　　　　　　　　　　　　　Respectfully yours
　　　　　　　　　　　　　　　　　　　　Respectfully
　　　　　　　　　　　　　　　　　　　　Sincerely yours

Armed Forces Officers
　General John C. Blank, U.S.A.　　　　　Sir
　Admiral John C. Blank, U.S.N.　　　　　Dear General Blank
　General John C. Blank, U.S.M.C.　　　　My dear Admiral Blank
　Colonel John C. Blank, U.S.A.F.
　Captain John C. Blank, U.S.C.G.

　Chaplain:
　Lieutenant John C. Blank (Ch.C.), U.S.N.　My dear Chaplain

　Chaplain John C. Blank　　　　　　　　My dear Chaplain Blank
　Captain, U.S.A.

　Retired Officers:
　Colonel John C. Blank, U.S.A., Retired　Dear Colonel Blank

Associate Justice of the U.S. Supreme Court
　Mr. Justice Blank　　　　　　　　　　　Sir
　The Supreme Court　　　　　　　　　　My dear Mr. Justice
　Washington, D.C. 20543　　　　　　　　Dear Mr. Justice Blank

　　　　　　　　　　　　　　　　　　　　Very truly yours
　　　　　　　　　　　　　　　　　　　　Sincerely yours

　　* If the ambassador holds a military rank, omit *The Honorable* and use the military rank.

Inside Address	*Salutation and Complimentary Close*

Bishop (Catholic)
The Most Reverend Bishop Blank

Your Excellency
Dear Bishop Blank

Respectfully yours
Sincerely

Bishop (Protestant)
The Reverend Bishop Blank
The Right Reverend Bishop Blank

Most Reverend Sir
My dear Bishop Blank

Respectfully yours
Sincerely yours

Cabinet Member
The Honorable John C. Blank
Secretary of State
Washington, D.C. 20520

Sir
Dear Mr. Secretary
Dear Madam Secretary
Dear Mr. Blank

Yours very truly
Sincerely yours

Cardinal (Catholic)
His Eminence, John Cardinal Blank
Archbishop of New York
New York, New York 10022

Your Eminence
My dear Cardinal Blank
My Lord Cardinal (*to Cardinals of foreign countries*)

Respectfully yours

Chaplain (See "Armed Forces Officers")

Chief Justice of the United States
The Chief Justice
The Supreme Court
Washington, D.C. 20543

Sir
My dear Mr. Chief Justice

Yours very truly
Sincerely yours

The Honorable John C. Blank
Chief Justice of the United States

City Attorney
Hon. (or Mr.) John C. Blank
City Attorney
Denver, Colorado 80202

Dear Mr. Blank

Very truly yours
Sincerely yours

Commissioner, Director, or
    Chief of Government Bureau
The Honorable John C. Blank
Director, Bureau of the Budget
Executive Office Building
Washington, D.C. 20503

Dear Mr. Blank

Very truly yours
Sincerely yours

Mr. John C. Blank
Commissioner of Labor Statistics
Department of Labor
Fourteenth Street and Constitution
    Avenue NW
Washington, D.C. 20210

Inside Address	*Salutation and Complimentary Close*
Commissioner (City) The Honorable John C. Blank Commissioner of the City of Buffalo New York 14202	My dear Mr. Blank Dear Mr. Blank Very truly yours Sincerely yours
Congressmen, Territorial **Delegate, Resident Commissioner** The Honorable John C. Blank House of Representatives Washington, D.C. 20515	Dear Representative Blank My dear Mr. Blank My dear Mrs. Blank
The Honorable John C. Blank Representative in Congress 5312 Wilshire Boulevard Los Angeles, California 90036	Yours very truly Sincerely yours
Consul Mr. John C. Blank *American Consul Moscow, Russia	Sir Dear Mr. Blank Respectfully yours Sincerely
County Officials Hon. (or Mr.) John C. Blank Supervisor, Ventura County	Dear Mr. Blank Very truly yours Sincerely
Dean of a School Dean John C. Blank School of The Arts New York University Washington Square New York, New York 10003	Dear Dean Blank Dear Dr. Blank
Dr. John C. Blank Assistant Dean, School of Law Stanford University Palo Alto, California 94305	Dear Dr. Blank Dear Dean Blank Sincerely yours
District Attorney The Honorable John C. Blank District Attorney, Sunflower County County Courthouse Indianola, Mississippi 38751	Dear Mr. Blank Very truly yours Sincerely yours

* In Central and South American countries: *Consul of the United States of America.*

Inside Address	*Salutation and Complimentary Close*

Foreign Officials

His Excellency The Ambassador of Germany Washington, D.C. 20035	Excellency My dear Mr. Ambassador
His Excellency Mr. John C. Blank Minister of Luxembourg Washington, D.C. 20046	Sir My dear Mr. Minister My dear Mr. Blank Respectfully yours Sincerely yours
His Excellency Count John C. Blank Ambassador of Italy Washington, D.C. 20046	

The Right Honorable John C. Blank,
  C.M.G.
Prime Minister of the Dominion
  of Canada
Ottawa, Canada	

Governor

The Honorable John C. Blank Governor of North Dakota Bismarck, North Dakota 58501	Sir Dear Governor Blank Very truly yours Sincerely yours

Judge

The Honorable John C. Blank Judge of the Circuit Court The Honorable Judy C. Blank Judge of the District Court	Dear Judge Blank Respectfully yours Sincerely

Lieutenant Governor

The Honorable John C. Blank Lieutenant Governor of Ohio Columbus, Ohio 43200	Sir Dear Mr. Blank My dear Governor Blank Respectfully yours Very truly yours

Mayor

The Honorable John C. Blank Mayor of Los Angeles Los Angeles, California 90054	My dear Mayor Blank Dear Mr. Mayor Respectfully yours Very truly yours

	Salutation and
Inside Address	*Complimentary Close*

Minister
The Reverend John C. Blank

My dear Mr. Blank
Dear Mr. Blank

With Scholastic Degree:
The Reverend John C. Blank, D.D.,
Litt.D.

My dear Dr. Blank
Dear Mr. Blank
My dear Dean Blank

The Very Reverend John C. Blank, D.D.
Dean of St. Luke's Cathedral
New York, New York 10008

Respectfully yours
Sincerely yours

President of a School
Dr. John C. Blank
President, University of California
Berkeley, California 94700

Dear Dr. Blank
Dear President Blank

Very truly yours
Sincerely

President of a Catholic College
The Very Reverend John C. Blank,
S.J., D.D.
President, Loyola University

Dear Father Blank

Very truly yours
Sincerely yours

President of the United States
The President
The White House
Washington, D.C. 20500

Mr. President
My dear Mr. President

The Honorable John C. Blank
The White House
Washington, D.C. 20500

Respectfully yours
Faithfully yours (official)
Very respectfully (private
  individual)

Priest
The Reverend John C. Blank
St. John's Church

Dear Reverend Father
Dear Father Blank

The Reverend John C. Blank, Ph.D.
Notre Dame University

Dear Dr. Blank

Sincerely yours

Professor
Professor John C. Blank

Dear Mr. Blank
Dear Professor Blank

Dr. John C. Blank
Associate Professor, Department
  of Chemistry

Dear Dr. Blank

Very truly yours
Sincerely

Rabbi
Rabbi John C. Blank, Ph.D.
Dr. John C. Blank
Rabbi John C. Blank

My dear Rabbi Blank
My dear Dr. Blank
My dear Rabbi Blank

Sincerely yours

Inside Address	*Salutation and Complimentary Close*
Secretary or Assistant to the President of the United States The Honorable John C. Blank Secretary to the President The White House Washington, D.C. 20500	My dear Mr. Blank
Major General John C. Blank The Assistant to the President The White House	My dear General Blank Very truly yours Sincerely yours
Senator The Honorable John C. Blank United States Senate Washington, D.C. 20510	My dear Senator Blank Very truly yours Sincerely yours
Retired Senator: The Honorable John C. Blank (home address)	My dear Mr. Blank
Speaker of the House The Honorable John C. Blank Speaker of the House of Representatives Washington, D.C. 20515	My dear Mr. Speaker Respectfully yours, Sincerely yours
State Legislator The Honorable John C. Blank State Senate Oklahoma City, Oklahoma 73100	Dear Senator Blank Dear Mr. Blank Very truly yours Sincerely yours
The Honorable John C. Blank House of Representatives Oklahoma City, Oklahoma 73100	
State Officials The Honorable John C. Blank Secretary of State of Iowa Des Moines, Iowa 50300	Sir My dear Mr. Secretary Dear Mr. Blank
The Honorable John C. Blank Superintendent of Banks San Francisco, California 94100	Very truly yours Sincerely yours
Under Secretary and Assistant Secretary of a Federal Department The Honorable John C. Blank Under Secretary of the Treasury Department of the Treasury Washington, D.C. 20510	My dear Mr. Blank
The Honorable John C. Blank Assistant Secretary of Labor	Very truly yours Sincerely yours

Inside Address	*Salutation and Complimentary Close*
United Nations	
His Excellency John C. Blank	My dear Mr. Secretary General
Secretary General of the United Nations	
United Nations, New York 10021	Respectfully
	Sincerely yours
The Honorable John C. Blank	My dear Mr. Blank
Under Secretary of the United Nations	
United Nations, New York 10021	Very truly yours
	Sincerely yours
His Excellency John C. Blank	My dear Mr. Ambassador
Representative of Great Britain	
to the United Nations	Respectfully
United Nations, New York 10021	Sincerely yours
The Honorable John C. Blank	My dear Ambassador Blank
United States Permanent Representative	
to the United Nations	Respectfully
United Nations, New York 10021	Sincerely yours
Vice President of the United States	
The Vice President	My dear Mr. Vice President
United States Senate	
Washington, D.C. 20510	Respectfully
	Very truly yours
The Honorable John C. Blank	Sincerely yours
Vice President of the United States	
Washington, D.C. 20501	

4

Letter Writing

Over the years amazing improvements have been made in typewriters and dictating machines that result in more efficient letter production. Telephone and machine dictation, coupled with word processing centers, provides maximum convenience for large and busy offices. The magnetic media typewriter makes it possible to correct transcripts to any extent without retyping the entire message and to store messages for later recall. The business letter itself, however, remains unchanged. It still poses a challenge to the dictator to say the right things and to find the right words. Correspondence secretaries can be of great help, and administrative secretaries can take over much of the composing and dictating load. This chapter has a wealth of ideas for all who dictate letters, take dictation, or have an interest in the improvement of correspondence and correspondence procedures.

CONTENTS

4.1 EFFECTIVE LETTERS

The test of an effective letter is the impression it makes on the reader. The letter is effective when (1) it moves the reader to take positive action, and (2) it leaves the reader with good feelings toward the writer and the organization represented. Such results depend largely on the content of the letter and the controlling business policies. They also depend on the writer's ability to express ideas in ways that are acceptable to the reader. Here is a review of the writing techniques that influence the effectiveness of a letter.

For additional help with the style of business writing, see "Writing the Report," Section 6.2.

An effective letter is
1. Timely.
2. Reader-oriented.
3. Clear.
4. Well organized.
5. Courteous.
6. Tactful.
7. Natural (not stereotyped).
8. Positive (not negative).
9. Concise.
10. Persuasive.

Figure 4-1 Ten qualities of effective letters.

In General (Figure 4-1)

1. Before you write, learn as much as you can about the reader and the situation you are dealing with. Be sure you have examined previous correspondence and other pertinent records.

2. Recognize the importance of timeliness. Deal with situations as they arise and answer incoming letters promptly. If you don't have all the information you need for a prompt reply, send an interim letter to reassure the reader that the matter has not been forgotten (Figure 4-2).

3. Set a goal for each letter; for example, to build goodwill, to help the reader, to collect the debt, to sell the goods. Then carefully choose the content and language that will accomplish the goal.

```
Dear Mr. Farnum:

     We're pleased that you want a copy of Mr.
Leffler's speech before the Buffalo Chamber of
Commerce last week.

     Copies of the talk in an attractive format
should be off the press in about ten days, and you
may expect a copy shortly thereafter.

                         Sincerely,
```

Figure 4-2 An interim letter.

4. Use the "you" approach, that is, express ideas from the reader's point of view rather than yours. For example, don't say, "The new forms save *us* money," if you can say, "The new forms will save *you* time."

5. Use the language that sounds most natural, almost as if you were talking. There should be no special vocabulary for business letters.

6. Be concise, but use all the words you need to express yourself clearly and effectively. Avoid any suggestion of haste.

7. Put a full measure of tact and courtesy in every letter. Say "please" and "thank you" often. Be considerate of the reader's interests and feelings always.

Planning the Letter

1. Plan a long or formal letter in three parts: the beginning, the body, and the ending.

(a) The beginning introduces the subject and sets the mood.

(b) The body provides the necessary information. It may consist of one or several paragraphs.

(c) The ending is designed to produce a particular action or emotional response.

2. The body paragraphs are usually longer than the opening and closing paragraphs, but avoid paragraphs that run beyond 10 or 12 lines.

3. Arrange ideas in a logical and consistent way, for example, chronologically or in the order of interest or importance.

4. When details are numerous, list and number related ideas (such as reasons, steps, advantages) in order to simplify the organization of the letter and save time and space.

5. If a very short letter sounds abrupt, try adding a few pleasant words at the beginning or end (Figure 4-3).

6. Unrelated messages for a single addressee are best put in separate letters. In that way, each message gets individual attention at the reader's end. The reader is also spared needless recopying of parts of a letter for the attention of others in the organization.

The Beginning (Figure 4-4)

1. Try to introduce the subject in a pleasant and natural way. Avoid such lame beginnings as "In reply to your letter" and "We are in receipt of your letter." It is better to say:

Thank you for your letter
We appreciate your notifying us that
We are glad to send you

The phrases in Figure 4-4 suggest natural (unhackneyed) ways of beginning and ending many types of routine letters. They should not be used when individual circumstances require different treatment.

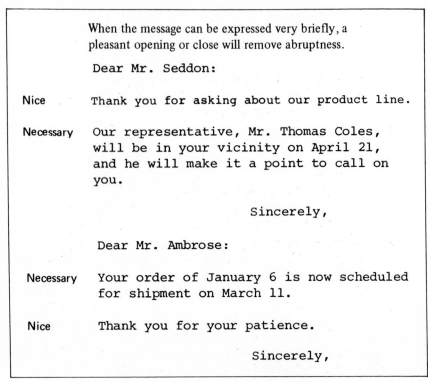

Figure 4-3   Brevity without abruptness.

2. Instead of using the opening to acknowledge the incoming letter, try using it to *answer* the letter. The reference to the incoming letter can be either subordinated or implied.

> The pamphlet you refer to in your recent letter has been out of print for several months.
> The delay in shipping the binders to you has been caused by

3. Don't put a negative comment or decision in the opening. If you have to say "no" or refer to a negative situation, do it later on in the message.

> NOT: We regret to inform you that your suggestion is not acceptable.
> BUT: The suggestion made in your letter of (date) deserves careful consideration.
> OR: We have carefully considered your suggestion.

4. When you are initiating the correspondence, use the opening to tell why you are writing.

> In looking over our records, we find that it is some months since you last called on us for service.
> Can you help us locate a nozzle for a Dietrich Blower, Model 3206?
> We recently received a request for credit from the Superior Frame and Door Company, Racine, Wisconsin, who gave us your name as a reference.

BEGINNINGS

I am (sorry, glad) to learn from your letter of (date) that
We appreciate your telling us that
Your letter of (date) asks
As you requested, we are (tell what you are doing)
You will be glad to know that
Thank you for your prompt reply to our letter of
I have your letter of (date) in which
In the absence of Mr. Jones, who is away on business, I am pleased
   to answer your letter of
Mr. Jones has asked me to reply to your letter of (date) regarding
I am enclosing–Enclosed is–You will find enclosed
We appreciate your request for
We have given careful consideration to your request for

ENDINGS

(For Action)

May we hear from you soon.
Will you please give this matter your (prompt, urgent) attention.
We shall appreciate your writing and telling us your wishes.
Please send us your answer by (date).
We shall appreciate your prompt answer.
I am looking forward to hearing from you soon.
Will you please let us know what action you want us to take.
Your promptness in replying will be much appreciated.

(For Goodwill)

We appreciate your interest.
It is a pleasure to be of help.
Thank you for giving us the opportunity to be of service.
We look forward to the opportunity of serving you again.
If we can be of any (further) help, be sure to let us know.
Please tell us if there is anything more we can do.
It was nice to hear from you. Please call on us again.
You may be sure that we appreciate your efforts on our behalf.

Figure 4-4   Useful letter beginnings and endings.

The Ending (Figure 4-4)

1. A formal ending is often not necessary. Just stop after you've given the last piece of information.

2. In any case, avoid such hackneyed phrases as, "Hoping this is satisfactory, I remain." If that's all you want to express, it would sound more natural if you said, "I hope this is satisfactory."

3. The ending is usually the best place to tell the reader what action to take. You can be as mild or as forceful as the situation requires.

> If you will give me a call, we can arrange a mutually satisfactory date.
> Please return the card at your convenience.
> Don't delay another minute. You must send your check now to avoid serious trouble.

4. Whether or not the close seeks action, it can often be used to express your goodwill or otherwise leave a pleasant feeling.

> We appreciate your writing to us.
> Thank you for giving us the opportunity to serve you.
> If I can be of any further help, please let me know.
> We'll most certainly keep your product in mind.

5. If you have been at fault, try to smooth things over with a careful explanation in the body of the letter. Do not refer to the matter again in the close. End a letter on a positive, optimistic note.

Language

1. Use the pronouns *I, we,* and *you* to help make your letters personal and interesting. However, don't overdo the *I* and *we. You* is better if the phrasing can be made to accommodate it.

Impersonal	*Personal*
Please communicate with the *undersigned*	Please write to *me*
As requested	As *you* requested
It is believed	*We* believe
This pamphlet deals with estate problems	*You* will find this pamphlet helpful in dealing with estate problems

2. Avoid business-letter clichés. They rob your letter of individuality (Figures 4-5 and 4-6).

Stereotyped	*Natural*
We wish to acknowledge receipt of your letter of recent date.	We have received your recent letter.
Please be advised that this charge was made by the collecting agency.	This charge was made by the collecting agency.
Replying to yours of the fourth, we are herewith sending you the form you requested.	We are pleased to send you the form you requested in your letter of August 4.

Stereotyped	*Natural*
We have your order and thank you for same.	Thank you for your order.
Under date of February 10, we returned to your goodselves a check in the amount of $50.	On February 10 we returned to you a check for $50.
Thanking you for your courtesy in this matter, we are,	Thank you for your courtesy.

3. Use pleasant words as often as possible. For example:

thank you	promptly
please	benefit
appreciate	considerate
glad	generous
pleasure	happy
service	delighted

4. Keep to a minimum, or avoid altogether, unpleasant or tactless words.

Tactless	*Softer*
you claim	your letter states
your delinquency	your oversight
you failed to	you did not
your complaint	your letter
we must refuse	we are sorry we cannot
you must have misunderstood	apparently there was an oversight

NOT: We are sorry for the inconvenience caused by our mistake and hope there will be no recurrence of this unfortunate incident.

BUT: We are sorry for the inconvenience caused you.

Dear Mrs. Pastor:

Here is the Summary of the Annual Stockholders'
Meeting of the Excelsior Pictures Corporation. It is
the report that should have been enclosed in the envelope you received from us. Please excuse the over-
sight.

We have changed your address as you requested.

                                   Very truly yours,

Figure 4-5   Natural—simple—friendly. The way a good letter should sound.

AVOID THESE EXPRESSIONS

Do you use any of the following expressions in your letters? They usually indicate a lack of freshness and should be replaced with expressions that are more original or more natural. Some exceptions may be made in legal and other very formal documents.

in reply to, replying to, with reference to
contents carefully noted
hand you herewith
enclosed herewith
attached hereto
pursuant to
deem it advisable
at your earliest convenience
thereto, therefor, therein, thereunder
per, as per
in lieu of
hereinbelow set forth
re, in re
reference is made to
relative to
wish to say, wish to state, wish to advise
advise you further, please be advised,
in receipt of, receipt is acknowledged
acknowledge receipt of
the undersigned
thanking you, we are
thanking you in advance
we remain, yours truly
your favor (for "letter")
esteemed favor
same (as in "please return same")
kindly (for "please"), kindly advise
in due course
hereby
above-captioned, above-mentioned
aforesaid, aforementioned
subject (as in "the subject policy")
duly
yours of the 23rd
this day (for "today")
trusting, hoping (in the letter close)
your goodselves
and oblige

Figure 4-6 Stereotyped expressions.

5. Rephrase negative ideas to make them positive.

Negative	*Positive*
I cannot send you the information because you failed to give your account number.	I'll be glad to send you the information as soon as you give us your account number.
We hope there will be no further delay in shipping your order.	We're trying very hard to get your order to you promptly.
You'll have no reason to regret your decision.	This is a wise decision.
It is against our policy to sell direct to the consumer.	It is our policy to sell only through retailers.

6. Adapt the language to the reader.

TECHNICAL: Will you please acknowledge payment by receipting and returning to us the voucher accompanying the check.

NON-TECHNICAL: Will you please sign the blue slip accompanying the check and return it to us in the enclosed envelope.

Writing for Someone Else's Signature. When you draft a letter for someone else's signature, write the letter in that individual's style, not yours.

1. Go to the files for samples of similar letters written by the prospective signer.

2. If there are no guide letters, think of the language the other person would use when dictating a letter. If you have any doubts, lean toward a simple, unaffected style.

3. Never use the occasion to change the prospective signer's or the company's way of dealing with the situation. If you think the traditional way is wrong, discuss it with the person before you write the letter.

Editing Dictation. A secretary not only *may* edit the dictation but is *expected* also to make corrections in facts, figures, and English usage. That goes for errors in dates, amounts, and other facts; obvious errors in grammar and word use; and any faults in word order or sentence structure that distort the intended meaning.

On the other hand, the language should not be changed to the point that it sounds artificial or uncharacteristic of the signer. The sound of a real person talking should be reflected in the tone of the message.

Letters Signed by the Secretary. In letters personally written or dictated and signed by the secretary, the language and tone of the message should be friendly but formal and should follow the patterns used by other persons who write for the company.

1. Be as polite, considerate, and courteous in your letters as you would be in person. Use your own natural, friendly style of expression.

2. Be correct in every detail, including your use of language. Any errors you make will reflect on your superior and on the company.

3. Be brief. State your business, offer a pleasant word if the situation permits, and sign off. In that way you'll give the impression of a busy, efficient person.

4. Phrase letters written on behalf of another person so that the message appears to be sent at that person's request.

> NOT: I am sorry that Mr. Dempsey will be out of town next week and will not be able to keep his appointment with you.
>
> BUT: Mr. Dempsey regrets that he will be out of town next week and will not be able to keep his appointment with you.
>
> NOT: I should be pleased if you would have lunch with Mr. Dempsey next Friday at noon at our Park Avenue headquarters.
>
> BUT: Mr. Dempsey, who is out of town for a few days, has asked me to extend to you an invitation to be his guest at lunch next Friday at noon at our Park Avenue headquarters.

4.2 DICTATION TECHNIQUES

Dictation is the modern way to "write" letters. Dictation gives the advantage of speed; it also helps letters sound natural because talking is a more natural process than writing.

Dictating Person to Person. Although the use of machine dictation is rapidly increasing, some executives still prefer to dictate in person to their secretaries. Under the right conditions, personal dictation can provide maximum flexibility and individual attention to the dictator's needs. For those who dictate to a secretary, these suggestions are offered.

1. Organize your dictation beforehand, so that you do not waste the secretary's time. Keep handy any records of correspondence needed for reference. Make brief outlines of long or involved letters. *Know* what you are going to say before you start dictating.

2. See that your secretary has a comfortable place to work, preferably a straight chair and a desk top or pull-out shelf on which to rest the shorthand notebook.

3. When you start dictating, concentrate on the first idea, and express it as simply and clearly as you can. Then go on to the second idea, the third idea, and so on. The *think-then-speak* formula will ensure a logical progression throughout the letter, and it will help you avoid the stereotyped openings and closings that are largely the result of not thinking about the content.

4. Speak distinctly, facing the secretary. Maintain an even rate. Watch your speed when dictating from printed material; you may talk too fast for the secretary's ability to take notes.

5. Give the secretary explicit instructions at the beginning with respect to name, title, and address of the receiver, as well as enclosures, number of copies, and special mail handling. If convenient, let the secretary find names

and addresses from past correspondence. Spell out other names and technical or unusual words.

6. If you have any special instructions regarding paragraphing, punctuation, underlining, and the like, indicate these as you dictate. Otherwise, the secretary will paragraph and punctuate according to conventional rules.

7. If you are dealing with a difficult situation or have trouble with a message for any reason, ask the secretary to type a double-spaced draft. You will then have a chance to make corrections and changes on your own time before returning the draft for final typing.

8. If you are interrupted by a telephone call or a visit that may take some time, give the secretary permission to leave until you are ready to dictate again.

9. Avoid overlong dictating sessions. Two dictating sessions, morning and afternoon, permit rush letters to get out the same day and provide morning transcription the next day for the secretary.

10. When typed letters are delivered to you, read them over carefully for content, form, spelling, and punctuation. If you find an error, mark the correction on a file copy or another sheet of paper, not on the original. The secretary may be able to correct the error without retyping the entire letter. Try not to place blame for an error. Compliment your secretary whenever an especially creditable job has been done.

Machine Dictation.   Machine dictation imposes special responsibilities on the dictator, especially when there is no personal contact with the transcriber. Thus, instructions to the correspondence secretary must be explicit and follow a particular pattern. You can imagine the waste of time, for example, if you fail to give—before you begin dictating—reference numbers, mailing instructions, or similar information that appears on the first page of a letter. Changes in the text that are made well past the place where copy is to be reworded can cause an entire letter to be retyped.

To avoid these mistakes and others, you should follow the instructions of the manufacturer in the use of the dictation machine. Although machines and systems differ, the suggestions that follow may be considered generally applicable to all. Be sure to refer to the preceding section on dictating to a secretary for additional pointers.

1. Know your machine and follow the instructions for its use. Remember that extraneous noises or failure to speak directly into the mouthpiece may interfere with clear reception.

2. Modulate your voice, so that it is neither too loud nor too soft, and articulate clearly. Talk directly into the mouthpiece, keeping it about three inches away from your lips. The speed of the dictation is not important, one way or the other, because the transcriber can adjust the playback to a comfortable speed.

3. If you want a particular letter or report to have priority, note the fact

on the indicator slip that accompanies some types of machines. In other instances, explain the priority to the transcriber at the beginning of the message. Correspondence secretaries search the tape for rush messages before beginning to transcribe.

4. Start by giving such basic information as (a) your name, department, location, telephone extension; (b) type of message, for example, letter, memo, schedule: (c) number of copies needed; (d) name and address of addressee, including attention line, if any; (e) salutation, for example, *Dear Mr. Dunn, Dear George, Gentlemen;* and (f) subject line, if desired.

5. Preface any corrections or special instructions with the word *correction* or *operator* (or *Miss Jones* or *Mary*), so that the words in the instructions won't be confused with those in the letter. For example:

Our tapes are packed six boxes *operator, make that eight boxes* to the carton.

A good sales correspondent was in 1963 worth about $75 per week and whereas today his salary is closer—*correction, please—begin this paragraph again—* Back in 1963 the average salary of a good sales correspondent was $75 a week. Today it is closer to $250 a week.

*—correction, please—insert the following after the first paragraph in the letter to Jones and Company—*It was thoughtful of you to arrange for theater tickets for Mrs. Brown while we were at the sales banquet.

6. If you wish, indicate paragraphing and uncommon punctuation, such as semicolons, colons, dashes, parentheses, and quotation marks. Be sure to indicate the *close parentheses.* Voice inflection as in normal conversation may indicate commas and periods, but experience will tell you whether it is best to indicate these, too.

7. Dictate long or uneven figures by digits. For example, .0035 per cent would be *point double-oh three five per cent.*

8. Spell out difficult and confusing words.

(a) Spell out unfamiliar names and addresses unless they appear in the correspondence forwarded to the transcriber.

(b) Spell out technical and unfamiliar words. Indicate initial capital letters with instructions in the style of *Operator, cap J Jacksonville,* or *Operator, initial caps Mary Jones.*

(c) When sounds may be confusing, use a phonetic key, for example, *V, as in Victor.* (For key words see page 12.)

9. When you get to the end of the letter, indicate:

(a) the complimentary close, for example, *Very truly yours;* (b) the signer's name and title; (c) enclosures, if any; (d) distribution list; and (e) instructions for marking copies.

A Dictation Model.   The following model will give you an idea of how the recording of a dictated letter might sound to the transcriber. What it cannot convey is the voice inflection, which can be as valuable as the instructions themselves in guiding the operator.

Operator, this is David Green of the Stock Transfer Department. My telephone extension is 3347. I have a letter requiring an original and two copies. Please address the letter to the United States Fidelity and Guaranty G-U-A-R-A-N-T-Y Company, 100 Maiden Lane, New York, New York, Zip Code one double-oh three eight. Attention Mr. Arno A-R-N-O Tauck T-A-U-C-K, Gentlemen, Subject National Foods Corporation.

We have your letter of September 6 regarding the issuance of a replacement certificate for—operator, cap C Certificate cap N oh period two nine eight five B—operator, B as in Bertha—for twenty shares of common stock registered in the name of Laurence L-A-U-R-E-N-C-E Nostrand N-O-S-T-R-A-N-D. Paragraph. Both the affidavits and the bond forms should be executed in three counterparts period—operator, counterparts is one word. They should include—operator, change they should include to the bond forms should include as obligees O-B-L-I-G-E-E-S —operator, initial caps National Foods Corporation comma Metropolitan Trust Company comma and the City Trust and Savings Bank of Geneva G-E-N-E-V-A New York. Paragraph. We will be glad to issue a replacement certificate as soon as these requirements are met. Very truly yours, David Green, Stock Transfer Department. Operator, please mark one copy for Mr. D. R. Granger at our 60 Broad Street Office, third floor.

Here is a copy of the same letter, as transcribed:

September 9, 19—

United States Fidelity and Guaranty Company
100 Maiden Lane
New York, New York 10038

Attention Mr. Arno Tauck

Gentlemen:

National Foods Corporation

We have your letter of September 6 regarding the issuance of a replacement for Certificate No. 2985B for 20 shares of common stock registered in the name of Laurence Nostrand.

Both the affidavits and the bond forms should be executed in three counterparts. The bond forms should include as obligees National Foods Corporation, Metropolitan Trust Company, and the City Trust and Savings Bank of Geneva, New York.

We will be glad to issue the replacement certificates as soon as these requirements are met.

Very truly yours,

David Green
Stock Transfer Department

DG:rh
Copy to Mr. D. R. Granger

4.3 TAKING AND TRANSCRIBING DICTATION

As the person responsible for the transcription of dictation of company correspondence and other documents, the secretary handles some of the most important tasks in the office. The following suggestions will help you perform your job effectively.

Taking Dictation.

Establish Harmonious Working Relationships. Whether you take dictation from one or several persons, you should build a friendly, courteous relationship between yourself and the dictator. A smile and a pleasant word will establish a good climate for the dictation session. You should be poised and confident, but unobtrusive. Control mannerisms and nervous habits that might distract the person who is concentrating on what must be said next. When the dictator pauses to think, keep alert and refrain from staring or daydreaming. Your eyes should be on your notebook, perhaps rereading the copy, and your pen should be ready to write. Do not supply a word when you sense that the executive is searching for one, but be ready in case you are asked for help. Learn when to interrupt during dictation. Some dictators prefer to be interrupted immediately when a question occurs, others prefer to complete the thought before being interrupted, and still others prefer to wait until all dictation is completed. When the session is over, gather your materials quickly and indicate that you will get right to work on a rush job or the most important letter. Or indicate the approximate time you will have the work transcribed.

Be Available. Many times a dictator must send a telegram immediately or dictate before leaving the building for an unexpected meeting elsewhere. Consequently, you should be at your desk the major part of the working day. When you must leave the immediate area, arrange for someone to cover your desk and contact you if you're needed. Or, if no one is available, leave a note in your typewriter indicating where you have gone and when you will return. If you will be gone for a considerable length of time, it is a good idea to tell the people from whom you take dictation the approximate amount of time that you'll be away from your desk. Then they will be able to give you dictation before you leave, if they plan to leave before you return. By being thoughtful in these ways, you can avoid much friction.

Be Prepared. Preparation means that the supplies needed for taking dictation are immediately available. A separate spiral notebook should be kept for each dictator by name on the outside cover. Use a rubber band to secure the used pages to the stiff cover. When only a few unfilled pages are left, take a fresh notebook with you. Date each notebook on the cover with the beginning and ending dates of dictation. Several sharpened shorthand pencils or shorthand ball-point pens should be ready to be picked up as you leave your desk. Take at least two with you together with a sharpened colored pencil to mark insertions in the dictated copy, a point that will be discussed later.

Help the dictator prepare for dictating sessions by supplying the files and other information needed to answer the correspondence. Many times the file is sent along with a letter or other type of message when it first arrives. If this is not the procedure in your office, read the incoming correspondence as you prepare it for your superior and try to determine whether additional material will be needed when the answer is being composed. Collect what you can without overstepping your authority.

Be Attentive. When taking dictation, listen carefully. Ideally, a secretary should face the dictator in order to hear clearly what is being said. Often, however, the executive will walk around or shift the chair, making this impossible. By being alert, you can hear every word. If a few words are missed or need clarifying, read back a few lines at the next pause so that your notes may be corrected if necessary. Listen for copy changes and directions. Be sure to write these immediately with the red pencil and leave nothing to memory.

Take Notes Efficiently. Your notebook should rest on the corner of the desk or on the extended arm rest. If this is not possible, learn how to support it firmly on your lap while maintaining a businesslike posture. Enter the date and time on the first page of a day's dictation, preferably at the bottom so that you can see it when flipping through pages. Before each message leave two or three lines in which to write special instructions, such as number of copies, special mailing, or order of transcribing. Number each message.

Take Messages Exactly As Dictated. Use shorthand symbols for most of the words. When you hear a new word, don't panic; it might be wise to write the first few letters or the complete word in longhand. Abbreviations might also come to mind faster than shorthand outlines. It is permissible to write both longhand and shorthand in your notes. Accurate transcription is your goal. Names and initials should be written in longhand and numbers in figures. Be especially careful to write numbers as heard in order to avoid transpositions. If you are having difficulty recalling shorthand symbols, practice writing shorthand from materials in the files during slack periods of the day. Work out in advance the shorthand symbols for technical words used in your company. And take a refresher course at night, if your skill is not adequate for the dictator and the job.

Most persons dictate at an uneven rate of speed, sometimes as fast as 150 words a minute but more often at an average of 70 words a minute. By concentrating on the message, you will be able to catch up during pauses. When portions of previously dictated material are changed, you are usually given time to find the place and cross out the unwanted words. Use the colored pencil to indicate where to place the insert. Number each insert and place the corresponding number at the place where the revision is to be made. At other times, the dictator will give you instructions to look up additional information and insert it at a particular place. Write as exact a description as possible of the needed material, and leave a few blank lines on which to write it when found. Pages containing rush work should be folded diagonally so that the edge protrudes from the notebook. Usually the dictator will hand you a piece of correspondence or a file that concerns the message just dictated. Place each piece face down on top of the last one to keep the stack in the same order as the dictation. Use a second notebook for dictation of technical materials, reports, and other work that extends over several days.

When interruptions such as telephone calls or visitors occur, you should usually remain with the dictator and spend your time reading your notes; correcting shorthand outlines; and inserting punctuation, paragraphs, capitalization, and other transcription aids. Your presence gives the dictator a reason for cutting the interruption short. If, however, you sense that the matter is private or will take considerable time, you may quietly leave and begin transcribing at your desk. Do not wait to be called back, but when the executive is again free, reenter the office and be seated ready to take dictation. Read back the last paragraph or a few sentences to refresh the dictator's memory after each interruption.

Transcribing Notes and Tapes.
Get Ready to Transcribe

1. Set aside a portion of the day when interruptions are at a minimum. If this is not possible and interruptions do occur, mark your notes at the last typed word with a colored pencil so that you may find your place easily when you return to them. When you are using transcribing machines, there is no problem because the tape, disk, or belt remains at the point where the machine stops.

2. Clear your desk of other tasks you might be working on and stack them in a neat pile in order of priority. Thus, you will be able to complete these tasks later with little need to review the work already finished.

Follow a Transcription Routine

1. Assemble the correspondence to be answered in order of priority as indicated by the dictator or as determined by information you possess. For instance, if you know you will not be able to complete all the transcription before quitting time, you should first work on messages that should go out that day. Always transcribe rush jobs first and take them to the dictator for approval and/or signature when they are ready.

2. Check the typewriter keys to see that they are clean, and be sure the ribbon is fresh and makes a strong, black copy.

3. Place your shorthand notebook in an upright position so that you may easily flip the pages when necessary. If a metal copyholder is not available, make your own support by attaching a button at each end of a six-inch length of string. Stand your steno book between the two buttons to keep it from slipping. If you are doing machine transcription, insert the tape casette or disk and place the index strip on the machine. Put on the earphones.

4. Read your notes (or listen to the tape) to locate any special instructions and to decide on the number of copies to make. Be sure to check this number against established company procedures regarding distribution of copies and records retention.

5. Arrange supplies so that a minimum of effort is necessary in collating the sheets of paper or in locating erasers, correction fluid, pencils, and other supplies. Assemble the paper pack and insert it into the machine.

Type the Message

1. Gauge the length of the message from the number of columns used in your shorthand notebook or by the marks on the transcription machine strip in order to set the margin stops. Be especially careful to pick out long letters or medium-to-long letters. These may take two pages or more. In deciding what margins to set, leave adequate left and right margins. A well-framed message is attractive to the reader. Recall that the closing parts of a letter usually take 10 to 12 lines, and that the bottom margin has at least six lines in it. Therefore, the last line of a message should end about three to three and a half inches from the bottom of the page. If the message is too long to allow sufficient space for the closing parts and the bottom margin, set the margin stops for wider margins, leave a one-and-a-half- to two-inch bottom margin, and carry at least three lines of the message to the second page. (See Chapter 3 for the correct placement of letter parts.)

2. Use the right date. Letters to be signed and mailed at the end of the day should bear that date. Letters that are to be signed the next day or when the dictator returns in several days, however, should bear the date of mailing.

3. Type the correct inside address. A check of the correspondence being answered or the file will reveal the recipient's name, its spelling, and the initials; the person's title; and the company name and address or box number.

4. Transcribe your shorthand notes by reading them rapidly in thought units, or by listening to the tape in thought units. Apply the rules of English composition as you read or listen. Check grammar, spelling, and punctuation in this reference book. Be sure that all names, figures, dates, and addresses on finished copies are the same as those in your notes and on letters or memorandums that you are answering. When listening to dictation on tape, be certain that you hear names and figures accurately. A secretary is responsible for the correctness of all transcribed messages. Most dictators expect the secretary to reword awkward and ungrammatical passages. However, to avoid overstepping your authority, ask the dictator about your exact responsibilities when you first take dictation.

5. Type in rough form the transcription of technical or complicated messages and reports. It is also a good idea to make a rough draft the first time you transcribe work for a new dictator. Making a rough draft is good practice when you have questions about the copy and must wait for an opportune time to talk to the dictator. You can type the final copy from the corrected rough draft quickly.

Secretaries who use media typewriters need not make rough drafts but can apply the procedures and codes for recording material that may subsequently be edited and corrected on hard copy as well as on media.

6. Proofread copy in the machine, and correct any errors.

Complete the Transcription Task

1. Type the correct size and kind of envelope. See "Letter Form and Style," Section 3.1.

2. Arrange in correct order the original copy, all enclosures, the envelope, and copies of a distribution list that need to be signed in a folder for the dictator's signature. The flap of the envelope may be placed over the original and/or enclosures and a paper clip affixed to the top left corner to hold the papers together. The folder keeps the pages neat and clean and offers a certain amount of privacy. Submit transcribed material to the dictator several times a day instead of in a large batch at the end of the day. When transcribing for several dictators, attempt to give the same service to each one. Transcribe rush jobs for all dictators before transcribing the regular correspondence for any one of them.

3. Draw a diagonal line through notes (or on the transcription machine strip) that have been transcribed.

4. After letters have been signed, fold them as explained in Section 3.1 and insert in envelopes. Place the sealed envelopes in the out or mail basket or deliver them to the mail room. You are responsible for seeing that important or rush messages leave the company in the next mail pickup. Therefore take the time to speed messages on their way by doing some of the messenger work yourself or by calling for company messenger service.

5. See that carbon copies and/or file folders are forwarded to the file department, if you have a centralized filing system. Or place the file copies and/or folders in your department files as soon as possible.

6. At the end of the day, check your shorthand notebook or the transcription tapes to make sure that you haven't overlooked something. This rechecking is particularly important if you have been transcribing material in a different order than that in which it was dictated.

Store Filled Notebooks and Tapes. File filled notebooks (and tapes) for possible future reference. Place the dictator's and your own name plus the beginning and ending dates of use on the cover. Set up a realistic retention schedule for these notebooks and destroy the older ones when you file a new one. Often they need not be kept more than three or four months. Many transcription tapes, belts, and disks are reusable; therefore, they should not be stored very long but should be placed back in circulation as soon as they are not needed for reference.

Accept End-of-Day Dictation and Transcription. Be gracious when asked to handle end-of-the-day dictation and transcription. Often the securing of a contract or the sale of a product depends on the correspondence reaching the client within a certain time period. Decisions regarding the matter may take all day to reach, and yet the executive still must close the deal that day. Your willingness to stay after closing will be rewarded by time off later, a commendation that will be noted at promotion time, or some other expression of appreciation.

4.4   IMPROVING CORRESPONDENCE PROCEDURES

Estimates put the cost of a single letter between $4 and $6. But the cost cannot be measured in dollars only. Inefficient correspondence procedures take up a disproportionate part of a company's energies, cause delay, and create dissatisfaction among the parties to the correspondence. In this section you will find a roundup of tested ideas that will save time and money, and at the same time promote good relations with the reader.

Acknowledgments.   Distinguish between situations that require letter acknowledgments and those that do not.

1. Omit the letter acknowledgment when the acknowledgment is already taken care of satisfactorily by such documents as statements, credit slips, and receipts.

2. Omit the letter acknowledgment when the action you take itself provides the answer to a letter, order, request, and so on. Just be sure to act promptly; otherwise an interim acknowledgment might be needed.

3. When routine acknowledgments are necessary, consider a form letter or write the acknowledgment on the incoming letter and mail a machine copy to the sender.

4. Don't acknowledge an acknowledgment unless a discrepancy is discovered.

5. Continue to use personal letters or the telephone for acknowledgments in the instance of favors, complaints, and similar situations in which goodwill depends on your giving the matter your individual attention.

Copies.   The distribution of needless copies clogs the mails, increases filing expenses, and wastes the time of recipients who have no need for them. Ingenious office machines make it so easy to produce copies that strict control must be exercised.

See also "Reprographics," Section 12.2.

1. Make as many copies as required, but not more.

2. Send copies of letters or other documents only to persons who need them and will use them to advantage.

3. Destroy extra copies when they are no longer needed to prevent them from getting into the files.

4. Use a color code for carbon copies distributed internally. The color of

the tissue will indicate which copy is to go into the permanent files and which copies can be thrown away after they have served their purpose. The color code is also helpful in the sorting and distributing of copies.

Follow-Ups

1. When you anticipate the need to follow up a letter, make an extra carbon to use for this purpose. If an extra carbon is not available, a machine copy of the file carbon will do. Then write or type at the top, "Did you receive this letter? A reply would be appreciated," or words on that order. An alternative is to attach to the copy a business card or note sheet with the same message. (Be sure the copy or attachment bears your return address.)

2. To cut down on the need for follow-up correspondence, make it easy for the reader to respond. For suggestions, see "Reply Copy" and "Return Envelopes."

3. Use the telephone for local or toll-free calls when you don't receive an answer promptly. Before making a toll call, weigh the cost against the advantage to be gained.

Form Letters.   Probably the biggest savings in correspondence can be obtained through the use of form letters, guide letters, and form paragraphs.

The idea behind the use of these forms is that a great deal of routine correspondence is repetitive. Because the same situations arise time and again, the same or similar phrasing can be used at each occurrence. The advantages of form letters may be summed up as follows.

1. They can compensate for a staff inadequate in numbers or training.

2. They can often be expressed in better English and with less risk of offending than letters personally dictated by staff members.

3. They can provide a standard way of dealing with matters involving company policy.

4. They save time and money.

Two objections to the use of correspondence forms usually arise.

1. Form letters lack originality and spontaneity.

2. Form letters look impersonal.

There are answers to both objections. So-called original letters quickly lose their originality when they have to be dictated over and over again. Form letters can be made to sound less hackneyed because they have to be written only once, and more time can be given to their composition. Also, through the use of alternative phrasing and optional forms, they can be individually adapted to a particular reader.

The second objection—that form letters look impersonal—can be attacked in two ways. Form letters do not have to look impersonal. They can be personally typewritten from the standard phrasing provided, or they can be reproduced by media typewriters. But even if form letters are printed—and there are times when efficiency requires it—there is still something to be said for a printed letter that promptly, completely, and satisfactorily handles a situation, as against a typewritten letter that may be late in coming or indifferently written.

If a disadvantage is to be found in form letters, it is that they offer a correspondent the temptation to use them when they, in fact, do not accurately fit the situation. In those circumstances, the form letter must be altered or a new letter must be dictated.

Printed Form Letters.   The printed form letter (or card) is valuable in the handling of an especially large volume of correspondence of the same kind. For example, it may be used to answer complaints or inquiries, to acknowledge orders, to give notice of shipment or delivery, to notify customers of a change of address or telephone number, and the like.

Three kinds of printed form letters are common.

1. Printed without blanks for fill-in. In these, the same situation is handled without variation.

2. Printed with blanks for fill-in. These permit the insertion of names, dates, and other individual details.

3. Check-off form. These have a list of statements. When one or more of the statements are checked off, they constitute a notice to the reader, an inquiry, or the answer to an inquiry. Blank lines at the end permit the writing in of additional information.

Guide Letters.   Guide letters are precomposed to handle a variety of anticipated situations; they are personally or electronically typewritten as the need arises. Changes in phrasing can be made at any time to adapt the letters to particular individuals and cases. Alternative forms can also be provided to prevent the necessity of sending the same letter in rapid succession to the same reader. When many guide letters are used, putting them in a loose-leaf binder with an index makes reference easy. Some companies suggest that their correspondents dictate guide letters to the typist or secretary instead of specifying them by name or number. In that way they are forced to read the letter and at the same time can make any changes necessary to fit it to the particular situation.

Form Paragraphs.   The greatest flexibility in mechanized correspondence is offered by form paragraphs. These paragraphs are written in advance to handle particular situations, they are carefully indexed, and then they are called forth by the correspondent in any combination that suits the letter requirements. Blank spaces in form paragraphs afford the opportunity for individual details. Typing is done by hand or on a media typewriter that has alternative paragraphs stored for retrieval when proper instructions are given to the machine. The machine can be set to stop at any point for the insertion of handtyped material. Even so, the uniform appearance of the letter is not disturbed because the same type and ribbon are used.

A sample page of a form paragraph manual is shown in Figure 4-7. An

Cr 100-200   INCORRECT REMITTANCES
    Cr 180-190   Error in Check

Openers

Cr 181   Your check for $ - - - - sent us in   Cr 181
            payment of our invoice of   (date)
            just arrived.

Cr 182   Thank you for your check for $ - - - -   Cr 182
            sent us in payment of our invoice of
             (date)   .

Check Not Signed

Cr 185   We notice, however, that through an   Cr 185
            oversight your signature was omitted
            from the check.

Numerical and Written
Amounts Disagree

Cr 186   We notice, however, that the written   Cr 186
            amount does not agree with the
            amount in figures—the correct amount.

Closer

Cr 188   Your check is being returned with   Cr 188
            this letter, and we ask that you send
            us a corrected check promptly.

Cr 190-200   Follow-Ups to Secure Stamps or Check

Opener

Cr 190   On (date)   we wrote you about an   Cr 190
            error in your remittance of   (date)
            for $ - - - - .

Awaiting Stamps

Cr 193   On   (date)   we asked that you send   Cr 193
            us the balance of - - cents in stamps
            owed on your account.

Awaiting Corrected Check

Cr 194   We returned your check in our letter   Cr 194
            of (date)   and asked you to mail us
            a corrected check for $ - - - - .

Figure 4-7 A page from a form paragraph manual. The same forms can be adapted for use with media typewriters.

index to all the paragraphs is available to the correspondent. Instructions to the typist will look like this.

Calvin Dryer
    Cr 190   April 16, April 13, $8.93
    Cr 193   50 cents
    Cr 197

Handwriting.   Even in this electronic age, the human hand is sometimes more efficient than the machine. Handwriting is fairly standard for "Speed Letters" and routing slips. It is also permissible in business for short informal notes to people you know.

A typewritten letter containing errors should never knowingly be submitted for signature. When an error is discovered in a typewritten letter, however, the signer may wish to correct it by hand rather than wait for retyping. A postscript may also be added by hand. The personal touch shown by the handwriting often overrides any impression of carelessness. But, of course, individual circumstances should always control the decision.

Printed Enclosures.   Do not write long letters containing material that is already available in printed form. Where possible, answer an inquiry with a folder or booklet sent with a short covering letter. If the printed form is one of a kind, perhaps it can be photocopied. Another point: if you find yourself or your co-workers repeating the same data in letter after letter, why not suggest that the data be put into a printed leaflet for enclosure, or that a processed form letter be used.

Reply Copy.   When agreement is required, it is common practice to enclose a copy with the original letter and request that the reader sign and return it to signify approval.

Return Address and Telephone Number.   Many company letterheads do not have adequate addresses, and some do not include telephone numbers. Delays in receiving mail and phone calls are the inevitable result, not to speak of the inconvenience to the other party. If the information on your company's letterhead is deficient, type in the building name or number, the room number, the street address, the ZIP Code, or your particular extension, as the need indicates. The information can be fitted neatly into the letterhead design or blocked above the date.

Return Envelopes.   When a reply is essential, the use of a prepaid envelope will materially increase the chance of response and cut down on the need for follow-up letters. This technique, however, is more successful in dealings with private individuals than with those in business.

Routing Slips.   Routing slips are printed memorandum forms usually about $3\frac{1}{2}'' \times 5\frac{1}{2}''$ in size (Figure 4-8). Some have a checklist of instructions as well as space for a personal message. Routing slips are especially useful within

Date _____

From: **ROGER B. KELLETT,** *Assistant Secretary*
350 Park Avenue - 14th Floor - 350-5109

To:

Date _____

To _____

Of _____

From _____

Please

☐ Attend to
☐ Note and return
☐ Note and forward to files
☐ See (phone) me re attached
☐ Prepare reply for my signature

☐ For your information
☐ For your files
☐ As per conversation
☐ As requested
☐ For your comments and suggestions
☐ Does attached meet with your approval?
☐ For signature, if you approve

Other remarks:

Figure 4-8   Routing slips.

the organization as a cover for letters, reports, clippings, and other attachments. But they serve just as well to carry attachments or independent messages—handwritten or typed—to friends outside the organization.

Sheet Size. By a kind of Parkinson's Law, messages are expanded to fill the size of the sheet. Letters are shorter when limitations of space are kept in mind. Use half-size letter sheets whenever possible for your own correspondence, and encourage others to use them, too. Also keep handy a small note pad and post cards for informal use, when copies are not needed. Like routing slips, they save time and free stenographic help for other chores.

"Speed Letters." Available from stationers are carbon-interleaved forms for internal correspondence or for correspondence with close members of your business family (vendors, for example). These forms, sometimes called "Speed Letters,"[1] have space for a reply and provide a copy for each party. Either handwriting or typing can be used. (Figure 4-9).

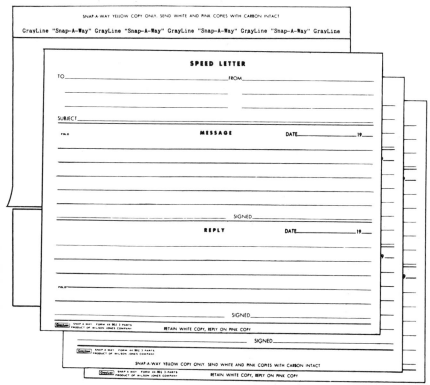

Figure 4-9 "Speed letter"—message-and-reply form. (Reproduced by permission of Wilson Jones Company).

---

[1] "Speed Letter" is the registered name of forms printed by the Wilson Jones Company.

Telephone.   Where telephone service is efficient, it's faster, and often cheaper and better, to call than to write. Here are some handy guidelines.

Use the telephone:

1. When speed is of controlling importance.

2. When the situation has a number of uncertainties that can best be resolved by instant two-way communication.

3. When the nature of the information to be imparted makes it undesirable to put it in writing (unfavorable credit information, for example).

4. When voice communication will help the business relationship.

Write a letter or memo:

1. When a telephone call requires confirmation.

2. When you must have a permanent record of the message.

3. When a phone call may embarrass the other party or come at an inconvenient time.

4. When the message can be expressed more tidily on paper.

5. When the difference in cost, or the difficulty of reaching the other party, favors writing.

Training Aids.   Manuals, bulletins, and other training aids are accepted ways by which a company sets standards for its written communications and encourages good performance. The standards relate particularly to format, English usage, and phrasing.

Manuals.   Unless a company has special requirements or special rules it wishes its employees to follow, this handbook can serve as its official style manual for both secretaries and correspondents.

Bulletins.   Many companies use bulletins to maintain the interest of their correspondents in effective writing. Consisting of a page or more and issued on a fairly regular basis, a bulletin usually concentrates on a single point or theme and offers examples from current letters (Figure 4-10). One of the most productive themes is the systematization of correspondence through the development of forms and guides. As discussed earlier under "Form Letters," these offer the best route to saving time and money and improving the quality of correspondence as well.

4.5   A TREASURY OF MODEL LETTERS

Here is a collection of many different types of letters, accompanied by special instructions for the person who is called on to write letters similar to them.

Although the letters cannot cover every contingency, they have been selected for their general utility and can easily be adapted to a large number of similar situations. The content of the letters will usually indicate whether they are to be signed by the assistant, the secretary, or the executive. In some instances —with a slight change or none at all—the letters would be equally appropriate from any one of those sources.

The Need to Know

The recent mail strike has made everyone more aware of the value of letters. Not to know—to be deprived of the comfort of words—is one of the cruelest predicaments to confront a citizen in a time that has been called "the age of communication."

If a lesson can be learned from our experience, it is that letters have a value beyond what they actually say. They give the reader a sense of community, of being in touch. To ask a question and not get an answer is to feel a loss of security. To suffer pain or experience pleasure without someone to share either increases the one and diminishes the other.

What you as a correspondent can do to help is fairly simple:

1. Answer incoming letters promptly, courteously, and helpfully.

2. Anticipate the customer's banking needs and problems, and show that you are ready to assist in meeting them.

3. Write the letters you don't <u>have</u> to write— the letter of condolence, the letter of congratulation, the letter of appreciation.

A recent issue of <u>Time</u> magazine says, "Nothing seems to work any more." We'd like to claim an exception. Letters work. Just use them and see.

Figure 4-10 A letter improvement bulletin for employees. (Manufacturers Hanover Trust Company)

Acknowledgments. *Of Documents Received.* When valuable papers are received, an acknowledgment should be sent whether or not it is requested.

   1. Acknowledge receipt.

   2. Name the document.

   3. If the situation requires, state the disposition of the document.

   4. Unless the matter is strictly routine, express appreciation or offer some other personal comment.

Dear Mr. Stewart:

   Thank you for sending us the will of Mr. Henry F. Connelley for safekeeping. It will be kept in our vaults, from which you may obtain it at any time

                                       Sincerely yours,

Dear Mr. Hill:

   We have received our copy of the contract putting into effect our participation in the 19— National Marketing Survey.

   Many thanks for your efforts in our behalf.

                                       Sincerely yours,

Dear Mr. Ryder:

   Thank you very much for sending us a copy of your audited report as of December 31, 19—.

   We have been most interested in reviewing these figures and wish to extend our congratulations on the way you have maintained your fine condition. I observed particularly the substantial increase in sales and profits and know how gratifying this must be to you.

                                       Kindest regards,

Of Letters Addressed to Key Employees. Whenever key employees are away and letters are received that require their personal attention, they should be acknowledged immediately.

   1. Identify the letter by date or subject.

   2. Tell how long the addressee will be away.

   3. State that a reply can be expected by a certain date.

   4. If you wish, give the reason for the absence ("away on business," "on a brief vacation," and so on); but do not refer to illnesses.

   5. Answer the letter yourself if you have the necessary information.

Dear Mr. Dorfman:

   Your letter of November 8 about the Carpenter project will be brought to Mr. Farnum's attention as soon as he returns from a short business trip.

                                       Very truly yours,

Dear Mr. Tyndall:

   I am answering your letter of May 12 in the absence of Mr. Ryan, who will be out of the office for a few days.

   Mr. Ryan customarily receives sales representatives on Thursday mornings from 9 to 12. If you would like to call on him any Thursday after May 20, I am sure he would be glad to talk with you. To arrange a definite appointment, please call me a day or two in advance.

                                       Sincerely yours,

Dear Mr. Gulton:

Because Mr. Fisher is away on business, he is unable to answer personally your letter of August 18 regarding the error in the printing run he specified in our Purchase Order No. 3257.

I have, however, taken up the matter with Mr. Sampson in our advertising department, who assures me that the figure should be 200,000, just as you surmised. A corrected purchase order will be sent to you in a few days.

Sincerely,

Of Personal Letters.   Many letters that have to be answered are those of a personal nature, for example, letters of condolence, sympathy, and congratulations. These require a special touch and are never as easy to write as they sometimes seem. They should always be signed personally by the person to whom the original message was sent.

1. Be brief and use a natural style of expression.
2. Be personal.
3. Be gracious.

Reply to Congratulatory Note

Dear Mr. Brown:

Thank you for your letter conveying the good wishes of your company and your own in particular. These anniversaries come rather frequently when one has had as many as I have. However, they will never come close enough together to make the good wishes of friends less appreciated than they were in my younger days.

Sincerely,

Dear Fred:

Thank you very much for your congratulatory note. I don't know how good the work has been, but I know that there has been plenty of it.

If and when you happen to be in Washington, please stop in, for Elwood and I would both be happy to see you.

Cordially yours,

Reply to Letter of Compliment

Dear Mr. Sadler:

Thank you for your kind comments on my talk. I would like you to know that your generous and encouraging words are very much appreciated.

Sincerely yours,

Replies to Letters of Condolence

Dear Mr. Stevens:

Your expression of sympathy on the death of our president, Mr. George C. Grady, is very much appreciated.

Sincerely,

Gentlemen:

We are deeply touched by the fine tribute your organization paid to Ellen Fox at the time of her death.

Miss Fox always had a keen interest in your association and spoke enthusiastically of the inspiration she received from her fellow members.

Your kind words have been a source of consolation to all who knew her, and we thank you for them.

Sincerely,

Appointments. Letters and the telephone provide able assistance in making appointments. A good appointment letter will

1. Indicate the reason for the appointment (or for the inability to make it or keep it).

2. Seek to set the exact time and place and to obtain confirmation.

Dear Mr. Gray:

Mr. Sims would like to see you in his office on Monday morning, October 17, at 10 o'clock to discuss the reorganization plan you have suggested. He would like you to stay for lunch after the meeting.

Will you please let me know if the time is convenient. My telephone number is (212) 435-6666.

Very truly yours,

Dear Mr. Tomes:

Mr. George Howard, our treasurer, is going to be in your city on Tuesday, March 22, and would like the opportunity to chat with you for about a half hour in the morning. He believes that you may be of some help to him in working out a problem in connection with our company's employee pension plan. Mr. Howard will be staying at the Hilton Plaza Hotel and will be pleased to see you there or at your office. He is taking a one o'clock plane back to Chicago.

Will you please telephone me at the above number to let me know whether a meeting would be agreeable to you and when and where you would like it to take place.

Very truly yours,

Dear Mr. Ames:

I will be glad to see you about your job application in my office at 3 p.m. Monday, January 14. If this time is agreeable, please telephone my secretary, Miss Jane McGorry, collect. She will see that you receive your round-trip plane fare.

I am looking forward to our meeting.

Sincerely yours,

Appreciation (also see "Acknowledgments").
For Gift

Dear Mal:

You are indeed a thoughtful person and I am a fortunate and grateful one. The package that was delivered to me yesterday came as a most pleasant surprise. I am very happy with the generous supply of Creston's excellent products and the container that housed them.

With my thanks, I send you the season's greetings and every good wish for a happy, healthful, and prosperous New Year.

Sincerely,

For Personal Favor

Dear Mr. Graham:

I appreciate your sending me the newspaper clipping containing the announcement of my promotion. It's very flattering that anyone so far away would take notice.
Best wishes.

Sincerely,

Dear Mr. Morrison:

I enjoyed the use of your office and the proximity to the many nice people in Room 1050. Carol Black was especially helpful in enabling me to produce a great deal of work I could not have done under other conditions.
Thanks very much for your kindness—and welcome back.

Sincerely,

Dear Mr. Crutchfield:

I have been intending for some time to write and express to you my appreciation for the consideration you have shown to Bob Ellison, whom you hired on my recommendation. He has often told me how much he enjoys working under you, how much he learns by being associated with you, and how many interesting opportunities are being afforded him.
I do hope that Bob is reciprocating in the best way—by doing his job well.

Kindest regards,

Complaints. Some complaint letters relate to office maintenance and services; others, to products bought and used in the office.

1. State clearly the nature of the complaint and any relevant facts.

2. Appeal to the reader's motives.

3. Ask for specific action to be taken.

4. Display cool determination, but avoid abuse. (An offended reader is not the most cooperative.)

Memorandum to the Office Maintenance Department:

I have called several times about the condition of the sofa in Mr. Platt's office. If the sofa cannot be satisfactorily cleaned or slip-covered, then it should be recovered with new fabric or replaced. As things stand, this piece of furniture is an embarrassment to Mr. Platt and does not speak well for the company or your department.
Will you please send someone to examine the sofa and let me know promptly what action you propose, so that I can tell Mr. Platt.

Gentlemen:

For several weeks now we have been using your Super-X carbon paper in our Mogul Electric Typewriters. It leaves a broad streak on second and third copies that we are unable to erase or eliminate. We still have a considerable supply of this carbon and are reluctant either to continue using it or to discard it and take the loss. Perhaps if your service representative could see your carbons in use, he would have some remedy to suggest. We certainly would not consider ordering any more carbon paper from you until the problem is solved.
Will you please have your man call on me personally as soon as possible.

Very truly yours,

Condolence Letters.   It is customary and thoughtful to send a letter of condolence to the family or close business associate of a deceased employee, customer, or other friend.

1. Keep it brief.

2. Include other members of your family or organization in the expression of sympathy.

3. Be sympathetic but not maudlin.

4. Recall the achievements or character of the deceased, or a particular episode in your relations with him.

5. In writing to the family, offer your assistance if appropriate.

Dear Jim:

I do not need to tell you of our profound sorrow at the news of Al Bowen's death. He was a banker of great quality and left a heritage and tradition at First National that will long be remembered. I count it a privilege to have known him as a friend.

I want to express to you and your associates and to his family my very deep sympathy.

Sincerely,

Dear Mrs. Fellow:

It was with sincere regret and surprise that I read in this morning's paper of Jim's passing. I had spoken with him only last Friday, at which time we had tentatively arranged for a get-together yesterday. His friendship will be sorely missed.

My staff joins me in extending our deepest sympathy. If we can be helpful in any way, please be sure to call on us.

Sincerely,

Dear Mrs. Mayer:

It is with deep sorrow that we have received the sad news of your loss. We, in some measure, share your loss, for your father was a charter member of our club.

The officers and members of the Quarter Century Club extend to you their deepest sympathy in your bereavement.

Sincerely yours,

Dear Mr. Troy:

I am extremely sorry to learn of the recent passing of your president, Mr. George S. Farmer, and on behalf of the officers and directors of the Steele Manufacturing Company, I wish to extend to you and your associates our deepest sympathy.

Sincerely yours,

Confirmations.   When a personal conversation or telephone call results in some understanding, it is usually wise to confirm the agreement by mail. If the other party obtained a different impression from the conversation, he then has the opportunity to correct it before any serious damage is done.

1. Tell how and when the agreement was reached.

2. Tell specifically what the agreement covered.

3. Add any details necessary to carrying out the agreement.

4. Express your goodwill or, more specifically, your desire to carry out your part of the arrangement.

Dear Mr. Greer:

This will confirm the arrangements we agreed on today pertaining to the Community Chest Drive. If you will send us the printed circulars, we will enclose them in our weekly payroll envelopes to be distributed on January 3. We will need 3,500 of the circulars, and they will have to be in our hands by December 30.

We're very glad that we can offer this kind of cooperation, and we hope our employees will respond generously.

Sincerely yours,

Dear Mr. Saxe:

As Mr. Sattler mentioned to you today when you visited him, our messenger will pick up the framed portrait of John Applegate on Friday morning in Room 1011, 660 Fifth Avenue. I will appreciate your leaving the necessary instructions with your public relations department for the release of the painting.

The portrait will be well cared for while in our possession and will be returned to you as soon as the photoengraver is through with it, probably in a week or ten days. Thank you for lending it to us.

Sincerely,

(The letter that follows, signed by the secretary, is somewhat informal because of the informal nature of the "agreement.")

Dear Mr. Traube:

Just a reminder that you are going to be Mr. Field's guest at the Finance Club's monthly luncheon at the Waldorf on Tuesday, March 20, at 12:30 p.m.

Very truly yours,

Congratulatory Letters.   Business anniversaries, elections and appointments to office, and personal achievement of any sort provide the opportunity for writing congratulatory letters. These are most effective when they are warm, personal, and concise, with a minimum of the customary clichés.

Business Anniversary

Dear Jack:

I am pleased to learn that on Tuesday you will have completed 25 years with the company. May I extend my best wishes to you on this anniversary and congratulate you on your eligibility for membership in our Quarter Century Club.

This is an occasion of great significance to both you and the company. I am sure you can look back with a great deal of satisfaction to your record of accomplishment and to the lasting friends you have made among your associates.

My best wishes for your happiness now and through the years to come.

Sincerely yours,

Dear Mr. Caine:

We're very proud to note that tomorrow, December 9, will mark the tenth anniversary of the opening of your account with us.

I do not want to let this occasion pass without again thanking you for the business that you sent our way and telling you how highly we value a relationship that extends over so many years. In looking forward to the next ten years of our association, I hope you will continue to prosper while calling on us to be increasingly helpful to you.

To you and Mr. Cornell I send my very kind regards and best wishes.

Sincerely,

New Job

Dear Mr. Marston:

My warm congratulations and best wishes to you as you assume the vice presidency of Clinton Manufacturing Company. You bring to this high post a splendid background of achievement and I am happy to join your many friends in every best wish for the years ahead.

I hope you will be coming our way soon. It will be a privilege to welcome you at 10 Wall Street.

Sincerely,

Dear Jim:

I am sorry that an out-of-town engagement prevented my joining in the toast to you at the Metropolitan Club last night.

I should have liked to tell you how much your association has meant to us and how much we are going to miss you. Please know that you carry with you to your new assignment my best wishes for your success and the hope that it will give you every bit of personal satisfaction you ever wanted from your work.

Cordially,

Promotion

Dear Rod:

I am pleased to read in this morning's news of your election as Treasurer of the Bliss Lighting Corporation. This is most assuredly a well-merited promotion and one that must give you a great deal of personal satisfaction.

Congratulations and my very best wishes for the future.

Cordially,

Dear Mr. Sampson:

The good news of your recent promotion has just reached us here. My associates and I want to join your many friends in extending our heartiest congratulations and sincerest wishes for your continued success.

Cordially yours,

Special Honors

Dear Stanley:

I learn from the *Alumni News* that you have won the Alumni Meritorious Service Award.

As one who has been privileged to work with you for a long time, I want to add my congratulations to the many you will receive. I hope your period of usefulness to the university has only begun and that you and your family will enjoy the benefits of your good health and good works for many years to come.

As ever,

Dear Mr. Plimpett:

Just a note to express my congratulations and best wishes on your election as President of the Commerce Club. You have a fine opportunity for public service, and I know you will make the most of it.

Sincerely yours,

Speech, Article, and So On

Dear George:

I enjoyed your talk the other night, as did the rest of the audience. Your remarks on the businessman's responsibility to his employees couldn't have been more apt or more interestingly put.

In the weeks and months ahead, I hope you will be given other opportunities to express your views. Everybody would benefit. Again, my most sincere congratulations.

Cordially,

Dear Mr. Winston:

I have just had the pleasure of reviewing the report that you have made to the stockholders of the Chambers Corporation for the fiscal year recently ended, and I compliment you on this informative and attractive document. The results clearly reflect the vigor and foresight of Chambers' management.

My congratulations to you and your associates and best wishes for the years ahead.

Cordially yours,

Follow-Up Letters. When a reply to a letter is expected but not received, the matter should be followed up by phone or mail. The person who signed the original letter should also sign the follow-up letter. Sometimes, however, it is less embarrassing to both principals if the secretary takes over the follow-up.

1. State the purpose of the letter.
2. Describe the letter to which an answer is wanted.
3. If the situation requires, ask the reader to investigate the matter.
4. Request a reply.

Signed by Secretary

Gentlemen:

On July 12 Mr. Henry Flint sent you his subscription to the *Standard Business Review* and enclosed his check for $20 in payment. Although more than two months have now passed, he has yet to receive his first issue.

Will you please look into this matter and see what you can do to put the subscription in force. A prompt answer will be appreciated.

Sincerely yours,

Signed by Originator of First Letter

Dear Mr. Felton:

Some time ago, responding to your request, I filled out a long questionnaire on the subject of hiring sales personnel. Your letter indicated that a copy of your study, when completed, would be sent to all respondents.

The subject of your investigation is one of great interest to me. If the results are available and have somehow been sidetracked, will you please send me a copy. If your report is not yet completed, perhaps you can tell me when I may expect it.

Sincerely yours,

Dear Mrs. Dawson:

May we have a reply to our letter of September 4 asking for approval of our purchase of stocks for your account. A copy of the letter is enclosed. Please sign it in the space marked and return it in the envelope we have provided.

We look forward to hearing from you by return mail.

Very truly yours,

Introductions. A letter of introduction is written to a business acquaintance on behalf of an employee, customer, or other person who desires some help from the addressee.

1. State the business connection of the person introduced.

2. Give the reason for the introduction.

3. Ask the reader to provide such assistance as may be required.

The following letters are intended to be presented personally by the individual who is being introduced.

Dear Mr. Mornet:

May I introduce Mr. William Haley, chairman of the Haley Manufacturing Company, Akron, Ohio.

As I write this letter, Mr. Haley is preparing to leave on a trip to Europe. While he is in your city, he may have occasion to call on you for some information or advice.

Any courtesy you may be in a position to extend to Mr. Haley will be very much appreciated.

Sincerely,

Dear Mr. Rose:

This letter will serve to introduce its bearer, Mr. Philip Denton, a Detroit businessman with whom we have had the pleasure of doing business for the past seventeen years.

Mr. Denton is President of Denton Plastics, Inc., a leader in the design and production of molded plastic containers for prepackaged liquid consumer products. He is now visiting the Southwest for a purpose that he will explain to you in person. I am sure you will receive him cordially and give him, to the best of your ability, the help he is seeking.

Sincerely,

A copy of the letter of introduction with a covering letter is customarily sent ahead to the person addressed.

Dear Mr. Rose:

Early next month you will receive a visit from Mr. Philip Denton, a very good customer of ours, who would like to establish business connections in your part of the country. Enclosed is a copy of a letter with which we have provided him.

As the letter indicates, we have a high regard for Mr. Denton, and we believe that his plans will be of considerable business interest to you. We will be grateful for any help you give him.

Sincerely,

Invitations.   Invitations may be classified as formal or informal. The formal invitation is either printed or typewritten on an engraved letterhead in a series of centered short lines. The informal invitation is set up as a letter, but usually on small engraved stationery, with the inside address at the bottom. (See Figure 3-8). The following invitations are arranged in order of descending formality.

Formal

Mr. James S. Patterson
cordially invites you to attend
a reception in honor of
Chancellor Carl V. Kronenberg
on Monday, the tenth of February,
from 5:00 to 6:30 p.m.
at the University Club
50 West 54th Street
R.S.V.P.

Informal

Dear Hobart:

The pleasure of your company is requested at the Annual Reports Awards Banquet to be held at the Statler Hilton Hotel on Monday, October 25, at 7:00 p.m. I hope you can be with us and shall look forward with pleasure to your acceptance.

Cordially yours,

Dear Fred:

I am arranging a small luncheon on April 23 to mark the retirement of our Executive Vice President, Mr. Samuel Treadwell. We'll be meeting in our Executive Dining Room on the 44th floor at 12:30 p.m.

Will you please let me know if you are free to join us.

Sincerely,

Invitations Answered.   All written invitations of a personal nature require an answer. If time permits, the answer is best given by letter. As a precaution against error, it is usually a good idea to repeat the time and place.

Answer to Formal Invitation.   The answer to a formal invitation takes the same form as the invitation. For example:

Mr. and Mrs. Charles S. Stratton
are pleased to accept
(or) regret that they are unable to accept
your kind invitation to
the reception in honor of
Chancellor Carl V. Kronenberg
on Monday, the tenth of February,
at the University Club

Answer to Informal Invitation (Accepted)

Dear Gary:

I am pleased to accept your invitation to attend the Annual Reports Awards Banquet to be held at the Statler Hilton Hotel on Monday, October 25, at 7:00 p.m. It was nice of you to think of me.

Sincerely,

Dear Arthur:

I'll be very happy to join you at the luncheon for Mr. Treadwell on April 23, at 12:30 p.m. in your Executive Dining Room.

Thank you for the invitation.

Cordially,

Answer to Informal Invitation (*Declined*)

1. Give a tactful reason for being unable to accept.
2. Express appreciation for the invitation.

Dear Gary:

Because I will be away on business on the evening of October 25, I am sorry that I will not be able to accept your kind invitation to attend the Annual Reports Awards Banquet.

Thank you anyway. It was nice of you to think of me.

Sincerely,

Dear Arthur:

Another engagement, made some time ago, will prevent me from attending the luncheon for Mr. Treadwell on April 23.

I'm especially sorry because I have the highest regard for your executive vice president and would like to join in honoring him.

Thanks for inviting me. I'll convey my good wishes to Mr. Treadwell separately.

Sincerely,

Invitations Confirmed.   When a luncheon or dinner involves several different parties, and especially when such arrangements have been made by telephone, a confirming letter is helpful in preventing misunderstandings.

Dear Mr. Bliss:

I am very glad that Mr. Carroll Dennis will be able to join us for dinner next Monday, November 1, and that you and Mrs. Bliss as well as Mr. R. M. Clouder will also be with us on this occasion.

As I have confirmed separately with Mr. Dennis, we will meet at the Maisonette Russe at the St. Regis Hotel, Fifth Avenue at Fifty-fifth Street, where I have made dinner reservations for 8 p.m.

Mr. and Mrs. Hartman and my wife and I are looking forward to seeing you all then.

With kindest personal regards,

Recommendations.   A letter of recommendation is an endorsement usually given to an employee or friend who is seeking other employment or preferment. The letter may be addressed to a particular individual or "To Whom It May Concern." If addressed to an individual, it should be mailed directly to the office; otherwise, it is given to the subject, who may show it or send copies at his or her discretion.

1. State the reason for the letter.
2. Indicate the relation of the subject to the writer.
3. Describe the qualifications of the subject.
4. Offer your endorsement.

Dear Mr. Crawford:

Mr. Nelson F. Connelley informs us that he has applied to your company for the position of trainee in your management development program.

We know Mr. Connelley as a former employee who worked in our plans department from the time of his graduation from Bard College in June of last year until he left us about a month ago. Although his duties were mainly clerical, we learned to respect his accuracy, his thoroughness, and his capacity for hard work. We particularly liked his pleasant personality and his ability to get along well with others. We were sorry to see him go, but we understood his desire for a position in a business that could offer more rapid advancement.

We have no hesitation in recommending Mr. Connelley for any responsibility you may see fit to assign him in the position you have open.

Very truly yours,

To Whom It May Concern:

To our great regret, the bearer of this letter, Mr. Alfred Cummings, has tendered his resignation as he is terminating his Wall Street career to enter industry, where he believes there is a broader field for knowledge and advancement open to him.

Mr. Cummings entered our employ in April 19— and became a registered representative in October 19—. During the entire period of his association with us, we knew him as a gentleman of the highest integrity and of most pleasing personality. He is intelligent, intuitive in grasping ideas, and most enthusiastic in everything he undertakes. For these reasons we believe he will be a success in any enterprise in which he is engaged.

Dear Mr. Sabin:

As an alumnus of Excelsior University, may I add a personal word to the application of Mr. Ernest S. Carr for admission to the Graduate School.

I have been a friend of Mr. Carr's family for more than twenty years, and I can recommend Ernest for your consideration, confident that his character and scholarship measure up to the University's high standards. Ernest's father, Dr. Ralph M. Carr, is himself an outstanding alumnus of our College of Medicine.

Any consideration you give to Mr. Carr's application will be most appreciated.

Sincerely yours,

References. A letter of reference is different from a letter of recommendation in that it reports rather than recommends. It is useful in answering routine inquiries about former employees who have applied for work elsewhere.

Dear Mr. Clark:

Mrs. Jane Dammler, about whom you inquire in your letter of September 21, was employed by us from June 26, 19— until May 18, 19—, when she resigned to remain at home.

Mrs. Dammler served as a typist-clerk and performed her duties in a satisfactory manner.

We found no reason to question her honesty or integrity.

Very truly yours,

A more complimentary letter of reference follows.

Dear Mrs. Graves:

Your letter of April 10 asks about our experience with Mr. Oscar Welford, who has applied for a position in your advertising department.

Mr. Welford was employed as a production assistant in our advertising department from November 19— to January 19—, when he left to go into military service.

We liked Mr. Welford personally and considered his work to be of superior quality. He was offered the opportunity to return to work with us when his military service was completed.

Our experience with Mr. Welford suggests that he will be an asset to your company.

Very truly yours,

Refusals.   Turning down a request represents one of the most difficult of all writing jobs. It is best to follow these rules.

1. Keep the refusal out of the opening.
2. Be sympathetic.
3. Give a reason.
4. Say "no" tactfully.
5. Close on an affirmative note.

Charity Solicitation Turned Down

Gentlemen:

Your invitation to take advertising space in the souvenir program of the annual dinner of the League for the Underprivileged has been given our careful consideration.

Much as we are in sympathy with the aims of your organization, we regret that our advertising budget does not include funds for such a purpose. As a corporation we regularly contribute to a list of charities approved by our Board of Directors. On their own, our executives and other employees also contribute to a large number of worthy causes, and we don't doubt that the League shares in their benevolence.

With all good wishes, we are

Sincerely yours,

Job Refused

Dear Mr. Williams:

It was good to talk with you the other day about the possibility of a job in our operations department.

We have now seen a number of candidates for the job and we are impressed with the qualifications they offer. The choice was especially difficult, but we had to make it. We are sorry that you missed out by a small margin.

We believe, however, that you have much to offer an organization and wish you much success in achieving your career goals.

Sincerely,

Employee's Suggestion Turned Down

Dear Mr. Conway:

The Suggestion Committee acknowledges your proposed plan for a consolidation of our "Weekly Management Bulletin" and the biweekly "RDC Review," which also reaches management personnel.

After careful weighing of both the advantages and the disadvantages, we came to the conclusion that the need to retain the double forum for management views outweighed all considerations of economy and efficiency. We have therefore decided to retain the publications in their present form.

Although your suggestion did not win you an award, we compliment you on the thought you gave it and hope you will continue to give us your ideas for improvements in any area of the company's operations.

Sincerely yours,

Customer's Suggestion Turned Down

Dear Mrs. Belmar:

Thank you for your suggestion for improving the package of Gordon's Wheat Nibbles.

We have tried a number of ways, including the method you suggest, for making the package easier to open, but we have found no way that would keep the product as fresh in use as the present package.

We are pleased to know that we have such a loyal and interested customer and hope you will continue to enjoy the freshness that every package of Gordon's Wheat Nibbles affords.

Sincerely yours,

Requests. A request for information, copies of printed materials, samples, and the like, represents an imposition on the reader and therefore requires special courtesy and tact.

1. Tell what provided the impetus for the request.

2. State specifically what you want. Keep the request within reasonable limits. Obviously, you can ask more from a reader who is in some way dependent on you than you can from one who has no ties with you at all.

3. If you think it will help, tell how you will use the material you are requesting.

4. If what you want has a monetary value, offer to pay for it or to reciprocate in some other way.

5. Express your appreciation.

Gentlemen:

Yesterday's *Times* reported a speech by Mr. William Rathbone before the Foreign Trade Association. If a copy of the full talk is available, I would appreciate your sending it to me, so that it may be circulated among some of our export people here.

Thank you for your trouble.

Sincerely,

Gentlemen:

I have learned through trade sources that your company has initiated a programmed course in customer relations. We have been thinking of doing the same and would welcome any ideas from a company we regard as well as we do yours.

Could we impose on you to send us a copy of your manual and any instructions that go with it? Also, is there anything you can add in the way of advice to a company contemplating a similar program?

If you prefer, we could arrange to send one of our training personnel to see you and discuss the matter with you. In any case, we hope you will give us the opportunity to reciprocate in some way soon.

Sincerely yours,

Sympathy. A letter of sympathy may be sent to a friend or colleague who has suffered through illness or accident.

1. Express regret.
2. Indicate that the person is missed and is thought about often.
3. Offer encouragement.
4. If the situation permits, try a little quiet humor or facetiousness.

Dear Doug:

I received encouraging news about you in the last few days and hope to hear soon of your complete recovery.

Many of your friends have been asking about you. Only the other day Miss Feller and Mrs. Corrigan were reminiscing about the "old days" when your work frequently brought you to their department. Your many kindnesses are still very affectionately remembered.

We all send our regards and good wishes.

Sincerely,

Dear Morris:

I was sorry to hear about your accident and hope this letter finds you much improved.

At first I thought the whole incident was part of a well-conceived plot to obtain an extra vacation, but on sober consideration, I decided that you wouldn't voluntarily patronize any place that didn't offer golf and fishing.

Do hurry and get back soon. We miss you.

Cordially,

Letters Ordering Tickets. Tickets to theatrical presentations and sporting events may be obtained directly from the box office or from a ticket broker with whom your employer may already have a charge account. The broker charges a premium for his service but is often able to get better seats and on shorter notice than the box-office customer.

Letter to Box Office

1. Order well in advance.
2. State the preferred location, date, and whether it is for matinee or evening.
3. Give alternative dates, if possible.
4. Enclose payment and a return envelope stamped and addressed.
5. Address the letter to the theater or stadium box office.

Gentlemen:

Please send to Mr. Walter Field two orchestra seats for the musical for Friday evening, November 12. Mr. Field prefers a center location. Alternative dates are November 10 and 11 in that order. Mr. Field's check for $45.00 and a stamped return envelope are enclosed.

Very truly yours,

Letter to Ticket Broker

1. Give the name of the attraction.

2. State the preferred location and date—alternative dates for a very popular show.

3. State an alternative attraction if tickets for the first are not available.

4. Ask for a bill or direct that the amount be charged to the individual or to the company account.

Gentlemen:

Mr. Walter Field would like two orchestra seats for *The Misanthrope* for Saturday evening, February 16. Please mail the tickets directly to him and charge his account.

If tickets are not available, please try *Pygmalion* or *Roman Holiday* in that order.

Very truly yours,

Transmittal Letters.   Do not send documents or other material without a covering letter. If the letter cannot feasibly be enclosed with the material, send it separately.

Letter with Documents

1. Tell what is enclosed.

2. Tell why it is being sent.

3. Ask for acknowledgment, if desired.

Dear Mr. Grimes:

Mr. Fields thought you would be interested in the enclosed copy of the talk he gave to the Aurora Merchants Association about a week ago. He thinks you will be especially interested in the underlined portions, which touch on political activity by business organizations—a topic on which you and he have had some discussion.

Sincerely yours,

Dear Mr. Somers:

I am enclosing a suggested draft for the press of a statement relating to our joint participation in the purchase of the stock of the Mercer Company, Inc. I think this will be more satisfactory than separate statements, which may lead to some misunderstanding about our mutual interests.

Please return the statement as soon as you can with your corrections, amendments, or comments. We'll aim for a November 25 release date.

Sincerely,

Letter Sent Separately.   Send the letter separately when (1) it might be overlooked in a bulky or odd-shaped package, (2) when you want it to be received before the material to which it refers, or (3) when postage costs would be considerable if the letter, requiring first-class postage, accompanied material that could otherwise qualify for third-class or parcel post rates.

NOTE: Postal rules permit fastening a first-class letter to the outside of a package sent by third- or fourth-class mail (Figure 15-5).

Dear Mr. Hammond:

I am sending you separately a copy of our new "Employees Handbook." In past discussions you have mentioned the need for such a manual in your own business, and I thought you might like to see what we have done.

Sincerely,

Travel Arrangements. Hotel accommodations and transportation may be obtained through the employer's travel agent or directly from hotels and transportation companies. There is no charge for the services of the travel agent, who is often able to command scarce accommodations for clients. When arrangements are made directly with hotels and airlines, the telephone is often more satisfactory than writing because confirmation can be obtained immediately. Further, if desired accommodations are not to be had, there is no waiting to learn the available alternatives. Large hotels and hotel chains, like the airlines, have instant reservation services in many cities. Consult your local telephone directory. If you find it more convenient to write for hotel accommodations, follow these instructions.

1. State whom the reservation is for, including the number of persons.
2. Tell what type of accommodation is desired.
3. Give arrival date (also time, if later than 6 p.m.) and date of departure.
4. Ask for confirmation—by wire if time is too short for a mail response.

See also "Travel Arrangements," Section 12.4.

Gentlemen:

Please reserve for Mr. John Regan a suite consisting of living room, bedroom, and bath for two nights beginning Thursday, July 17. Mr. Regan, who is traveling alone, expects to arrive about 9 p.m.

A confirmation of this reservation is requested.

Very truly yours,

Gentlemen:

Please reserve for Mr. and Mrs. John Regan and their two young children two twin-bedded rooms for arrival on Monday, April 14. Connecting rooms with separate baths are desired. Mr. Regan and his family expect to stay until 5 p.m. Thursday, April 17. May I have your prompt confirmation.

Very truly yours,

5

Handling Business Information

Collecting business information and processing it have always been characteristic office operations. If the work is different today, it is because it has two distinctly different modes. One is the traditional way, with individuals painstakingly gathering and presenting information for nonroutine business reporting needs. The second is the application of computer science to routine and repetitive paper work. This chapter begins with an overview of machine processing methods and follows with instruction in the still-needed human techniques of finding information, documenting it, and displaying it in tables and graphs.

For assistance in writing reports, see "Report Preparation," Chapter 6.

CONTENTS

5.1 INFORMATION PROCESSING

Spurred by new developments, the paper revolution has reached the stage where it impinges on every aspect of office work. From electronic data processing, it was but a short step to the union of the typewriter and the computer. Now the concept of *word processing* has placed the secretary and the dictator at the center of the action.

Data Processing. The computer is at the heart of the new information technology. Doing its work by electrical impulses rather than by the movement of mechanical parts, the computer is especially useful in performing repetitive clerical functions, making information instantly available, and bringing out significant relationships among data for decision-making purposes (Figure 5-1).

A common application of data processing is seen in the preparation of payroll records and checks. The computer, given a list of employees, hours worked, rates of pay, and deductions, can prepare an earnings statement and a check for each employee. At the same time it can store and accumulate the information and, when needed, produce records for Social Security, unemployment insurance, and income tax purposes. It also has built into it the capacity to recognize errors and inconsistencies.

A more inclusive application is that used by a large industrial sales department. Orders from customers are fed directly from the sales office to the computer, which prepares customers' invoices and at the same time transmits shipping instructions to the appropriate warehouse. The computer also keeps track of stock at the warehouse, so that requisitions for replenishment can be sent to the factory. The same computer can determine the factory's needs for the materials of production and, on cue, issue the proper orders to suppliers. Meanwhile, at any stage, executives have available current information about sales and inventory and can use the machine to help with decisions about future strategy.

Minicomputers—many of them portable—make data processing available even to small business and professional offices. A computerized management system for a dental office, for example, can maintain records of treatments, charges, and payments by patients; prepare third-party (insurance) claim

Accounts payable	Job costing
Accounts receivable	Market analyses
Addressing	Payroll processing
Balance sheet	Personnel recordkeeping
Bid estimating	Production scheduling
Billing	Productivity reports
Breakeven analyses	Programmed instruction
Calculating and summarizing	Purchase order processing
Collections	Quarterly payroll reports
Credit management	Record retrieval
Data storage	Sales forecasting
Income statement	Sales order processing
Inventory control	Sales reports
Inventory management reports	Tax reports

Figure 5-1   Some tasks for the computer.

forms; keep track of overdue payments from patients and third parties; scan patients' records and produce printed reminders of their next examination; and provide the doctor with twice-a-month summaries of accounts receivable. All the computer tasks can be handled by the office secretary or nurse.

Understanding the Computer.   A computer system entails a number of interrelated components—the *hardware*—which are useless until they receive some direction. Much of this direction comes from a ready-made program repertoire that enables the computer to perform a particular set of functions in a fixed sequence. The programs are the *software*.

The computer components consist of input devices, a central processing unit (CPU), and output devices (Figure 5-2). Supplemental equipment temporarily stores data outside the CPU for use when needed.

Input.   Data are fed to the computer from a console typewriter linked to the CPU by wire or, with the help of a reading or scanning device, from a *common language medium* such as punched cards, disks, magnetic tape, or optical characters.

Central Processing Unit.   The CPU consists of a console or control unit; an arithmetic unit, which manipulates the data in response to signals from the control unit; and an internal memory, from which stored data and instructions can be recalled at will. At the console terminal, the operator can type instructions for the computer to follow, and the same machine can automatically type out instructions to guide the operator.

Output.   The console typewriter used for input may also receive the output. Because it is too slow for most computer needs, however, its use is often limited to typing out special messages concerning the status of the computer job. Heavy printing is done by a machine that assembles and prints whole lines in rapid succession. Other devices may convert the output to such computer-compatible media as magnetic tapes and disks. Data may also be relayed to the user by a voice-response unit, like a telephone, or displayed visually by a cathode-ray tube (CRT) on a TV-like screen.

Computer Programming.   The routine by which a computer performs a given task is called the program. Some programs are especially designed to meet unique needs. On the other hand, standard programs are available for accounts receivable, purchasing, payroll preparation, and other tasks common to many businesses. These can be obtained either from the manufacturer of the original equipment or from companies specializing in software. The needed programs are stored in the computer. In most instances, all the operator has to do to activate a particular program is to type the instructions and enter the data on the console keyboard. The answers—and any questions the computer must ask to arrive at the answers—are automatically typed out at the same console.

In the instance of consoles with a visual display unit, the data appear on the

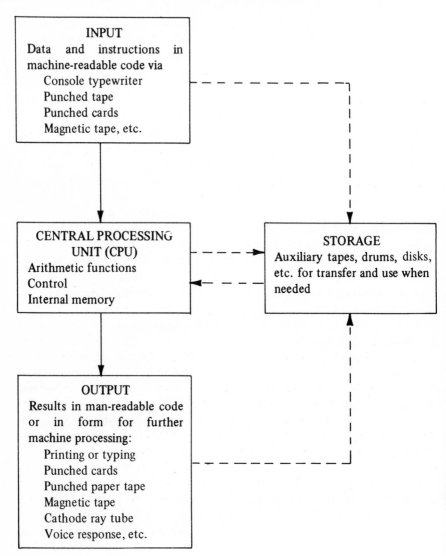

Figure 5-2 Organization of a computer system.

screen. Such a procedure is commonly observed when a store clerk enters a transaction in a computerized cash register. Using the register keyboard, the clerk follows the directions flashed on the screen. The machine checks the customer's credit and records the transaction in a way that gives management all the information it needs for billing, accounting, and stock control.

Operating Systems. *Time sharing* permits the use of a single computer from a number of scattered terminals. For example, branch bank lending officers, using the company's central computer, may have their own deskside terminals to permit them to check immediately on the credit record of a loan applicant. Through *real-time processing*, the computer performs its work as it receives its instructions. An airline computer used for passenger reservations works on this principle. A clerk at any reservation console can find out immediately what seats on any flight are available and stand by while the central computer books reservations and withdraws the seats from the available pool. Through *batch processing*, information is accumulated over a period of time before being entered into the computer. Thus, withdrawals and additions to inventory may be accumulated during the day for processing the same night. This method permits the use of a computer during otherwise slow or idle hours.

In some instances it is more economical for an organization to farm out work to a computer service company than to process it themselves. A terminal at the client's location is linked by regular telephone or telegraph lines to the service company's computer. Smaller companies may accumulate data on punched cards or other media and send them to the processor by mail or messenger. For the names of computer service companies, consult the yellow pages under the heading "Data Processing Service."

For a glossary of terms used in data processing, turn to Section 16.3 of this handbook.

Word Processing.   Computer-assisted typewriters are used in the production of letters, reports, proposals, briefs, and similar documents. Word processing incorporates in a single system the tasks of dictation, transcription, keyboarding, revising, proofreading, copying, duplicating, filing, and distribution.

The specially designed typewriters are *word processors*. Many different models with varying capabilities are available from numerous manufacturers. The same manufacturers offer full courses of instruction in the use of their machines. Using one word processor—a *memory typewriter*—the correspondence secretary transcribes dictated material, usually from magnetic tapes or disks, at rough draft speed. Minor errors are easily corrected; when the carriage is backspaced, the error is automatically lifted off the page and the correction is typed over it to produce a clean draft copy. Meanwhile, everything typed is simultaneously captured in the typewriter's computerized memory. The memory sets margins and tabs, centers, underscores, and indents automatically. It also automatically aligns columns of figures at decimal points, simplifying the typing of complex charts and other statistical material.

After an original draft is typed, the copy can be held indefinitely in the typewriter's electronic storage file until the author changes are complete. To make a correction, an addition, or a deletion, the information is recalled to memory with the push of a button. The correspondence secretary then electronically advances to the point of change and makes the required revisions. Finally, the machine automatically plays back a letter-perfect typescript incorporating all the changes.

Depending on the capacity of the memory, 100 or more pages of typed material can be stored in the typewriter. Thus, standard letters, documents, and forms can be stored and played out as necessary; the secretary need only add such variables as names and addresses. With the memory it is possible to maintain lists and update them electronically and to assemble entire documents from similarly stored standard sentences and paragraphs.

A machine of the same family, but with greater capability, is the *magnetic card typewriter*. In addition to its memory, which permits revision and reformatting without retyping, it records typestrokes on magnetic cards to provide a convenient card-to-page reference. The cards can be stored outside the typewriter for use at any time and on any compatible machine. They are especially convenient for automatically recapturing material for repetitive typing tasks.

The capacity of many word-processors is remarkably expanded when they use flexible (called "floppy") magnetic disks, each of which holds some 130 pages of typed material that is totally accessible in seconds. Other features permit transmission of typed data over telephone lines and provide for automatic feeding, printing, and stacking of both letters and envelopes. With a CRT display unit, the editing of copy is dramatically simplified. Without paper, keystrokes are transferred to a screen for instant verification and revision in preparation for a final hard-copy (paper) printout (Figure 5-3).

Operational features of a word processing center are described in Section 11.1, "Word Processing and Media Typewriters."

The Office in Transition. To put the information processing revolution in perspective, one need only compare the typical office of today with one that uses the most advanced automatic equipment. In most offices, documents begin as longhand drafts or dictation to a secretary. The work is typed, revised, and typed again. For the most part, carbon copies have given way to machine copying, but documents are still filed in cabinets, cross-indexed, and manually retrieved. Written interdepartmental messages are collected and delivered by hand.

The large complex office using the latest automatic equipment is primarily an information processing center consisting of three major areas (Figure 5-4).

Transmission of Information. Dictation is recorded by machine dictation systems and sent to word processors who transcribe it on media typewriters. These typewriters make possible error-free copy, the printout of any desired number, and the storage of copy for later retrieval. The dictator may use portable or free-standing dictation machines, but more often transmits directly by telephone to a central receiving unit.

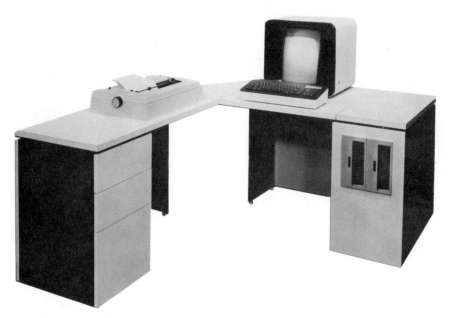

Figure 5-3 A typical word processing system with simultaneous input/output, display screen, and storage. (Courtesy of Addressograph—Multigraph.)

Stored Data Retrieval. Any stored data, including printed documents reduced to microfilm, may be instantly displayed on a viewing screen or automatically printed in any desired type size. See "Micrographics," pp. 413–415.

Reprographics. Automatic machines are used for copying, phototypesetting, and printing. Communicating word processors send copy by wire to distant points, and telephone systems transmit whole page facsimiles of text or pictures. (See also "Reprographics," Section 12-2.)

At least 100 companies are engaged in manufacturing word processing equipment. The list that follows names only a few leaders, but it provides a good start for anyone seeking current information about machines, tools, and materials in this fast-growing field. In addition to the address given, there may be a branch office near you. Consult your local telephone directory.

A. B. Dick Company (word processing). 5700 West Touhy Avenue, Chicago, Il 60648.

Addressograph Multigraph Corporation (text processing systems). 11 Mt. Pleasant Avenue, East Hanover, NJ 07936

American Telephone and Telegraph Company (information transmission systems). 195 Broadway, New York, NY 10007.

Dictaphone Corporation (voice processing). 105 Oak Street, Norwood, NJ 07648.

Digital Equipment Corporation (word processing). 129 Parker Street, Maynard, MA 01754.

Honeywell Information Systems (word processing). 200 Smith Street, Waltham, MA 02154.

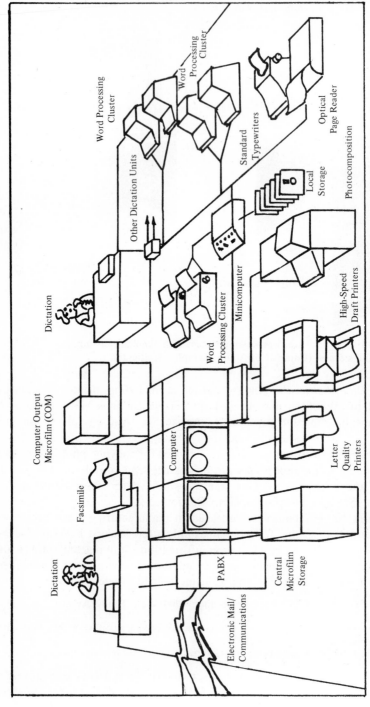

Figure 5-4 Artist's representation of a technologically advanced word processing center. Printed messages can be received and sent via the private automatic telephone exchange (PABX), shown at the left. Reprinted by permission from "Information Processing and the Office of Tomorrow," a special FORTUNE magazine advertising section prepared by International Data Corporation, Waltham, Mass.

IBM Corporation, Office Products Division (word processing). Parsons Pond Drive, Franklin Lakes, NJ 07417

Lanier Business Products (voice processing). 1700 Chantilly Drive NE, Atlanta, GA 30324.

NCR Corporation (word processing). 1700 South Patterson Blvd., Dayton, OH 45479.

Olivetti Corporation of America (word processing). 500 Park Avenue, New York, NY 10022.

Qyx Systems, division of Exxon Information Systems. 1270 Avenue of the Americas, New York, NY 10020.

3M Company (word processing, copiers, microform systems and supplies). 3M Center, St. Paul, MN 55101.

Vydec, Inc., division of Exxon Enterprises, Inc. (word processing). 9 Vreeland Road, Florham Park, NJ 07932.

Wang Laboratories, Inc. (office systems and word processing). One Industrial Avenue, Lowell, MA 01851.

Xerox Corporation (word processing, communicating typing systems, and tele-copiers). Stamford, CT 06904.

5.2 INFORMATION SOURCES

Knowing where to go for information and how to extract it is a valuable business asset. The occasions for the personal collection of data are many

—when researching a problem on your own.

—when obtaining data for someone else.

—when checking the facts in the draft of an employer's report.

—when writing a report for your employer.

—when preparing a background paper for use by your employer in making a presentation or speech.

Personal Inquiry. A useful way to get certain kinds of information is to go directly to people. You may use the telephone, see people in person, or write for information. You may go to co-workers in your own organization or to persons in other organizations who may have the answers you seek. You may also observe certain processes, procedures, conditions, and human activities in order to report on them. Another method is to make up a questionnaire in order to get the experiences and views of others in a form that permits the tabulation of results.

Here are some points to keep in mind as you make personal inquiries.

1. Don't pry or in other ways arouse suspicion of your motives. State frankly and clearly what your purpose is and what use will be made of the information you obtain.

2. Be courteous, attentive, and brief.

3. Take notes of points you may forget.

4. Ask questions when necessary to clarify the facts, but refrain from arguing. Weigh the information you receive against what you believe to be true.

5. Don't ask questions about salary, religion, or other personal matters.

6. If you want confidential information, be sure your authority or your right to it is well established. Use the name of your employers if you are acting on their behalf.

7. If you are going outside your organization for information, offer to reciprocate.

See also "Interviewing," Section 1.5.

Company Files. The necessary information may already exist in the company's files. Care should be taken, however, to distinguish between the public and private records of the organization.

Unrestricted Company Records. The information you need may be found in readily available published documents such as these:

    The annual and quarterly reports to stockholders
    Reports of annual meetings of stockholders
    SEC registration applications
    Proxy statements
    Company newspapers and magazines
    Catalogs
    Advertisements
    Handbooks and manuals
    Press releases
    Public speeches of company officers

An important advantage of material from these sources is that it is both official and public and does not have to be cleared with anyone before it can be used. Watch for the exception, however, in published bulletins intended for private circulation among top executives.

Restricted Company Records. Other information originating in the company may be obtained from the files. Such materials include:

Letters	Bookkeeping records
Memorandums	Personnel records
Reports	Purchase orders
Estimates	Sales slips
Proposals	Appointment books
Instructions	Diaries
Procedures	Contracts
Minutes	Leases

Most of these documents are private and should be obtained through regular channels. Documents removed from the files should be promptly returned. Any copies made should be kept securely and destroyed when they are no longer needed. Confidential information in the documents should never be communicated to unauthorized persons.

Library Sources. The number and variety of books, pamphlets, and periodicals is so vast that any researcher must be prepared to set aside some time just to discover what is available. A useful all-round collection of reference books would surely include a dictionary, an atlas of the world, a trade directory, and an up-to-date almanac. Your company's library, if there is one, should have these and other reference books and periodicals, especially those relating to trade and economic matters (Figure 5-5). The reference division of your public library will have an even more comprehensive collection of publications and information as to where and how any published data may be obtained.

Many trade associations and other business, philanthropic, and professional organizations maintain libraries that contain valuable printed materials in their own areas of interest. For lists of such libraries, consult publications

---

BOOKS

World Almanac and Book of Facts
U.S. Bureau of the Census, *Statistical Abstract of the United States*
U.S. Government Organization Manual
Rand McNally Commercial Atlas and Marketing Guide
Christine Ammer and Dean S. Ammer, *Dictionary of Business and Economics* (Macmillan)
Lorna Daniells, *Business Information Sources* (Berkeley: University of California Press)

PERIODICALS AND NEWSPAPERS

Business Week
Newsweek, Time, or *U.S. News and World Report* (weekly)
Fortune (biweekly)
Monthly Economic Letter, Citibank, New York (free)
Forbes (monthly)
Harvard Business Review (bimonthly)
Wall Street Journal (every business day)
New York Times (daily)

MISCELLANEOUS

Your company's annual report, catalogs, and other published data
Business and technical periodicals in your company's area of interest
Publications of your trade or professional association(s)
Handbooks covering special fields of interest, as accounting, marketing, management, foreign trade
A trade or professional directory in your organization's product or service area
A dictionary of business or technical terms in your company's specialty
Government publications touching on your organization's interests

---

Figure 5-5   A basic business research library.

of the Special Libraries Association, New York, as well as the *Directory of Special Libraries and Information Centers*, edited by Margaret L. Young (Detroit: Gale Publishing Co.) and *Subject Collections*, edited by Lee Ash (New York: R. R. Bowker). Colleges and universities are also known to extend library privileges to alumni and community organizations. Consult the librarian.

At least two cautions are necessary in connection with all published sources of information.

1. Note carefully the publisher and the author. Some sources are more reliable than others. Government publications and the publications of university presses and research bureaus are usually highly authoritative. Commercial publishers and other enterprises should be judged individually.

2. Note the date of publication. Old information may have historic value, but it may be useless as an indicator of present conditions. Many printed works are issued periodically or in revised and updated editions. Try to obtain the latest editions. This caution should be applied to the works named in this section as well as to any others you might consult.

Library Tools.   To tap the library's riches, you must know how to use the tools the library provides

1. The general catalog. All printed works in a library are listed in its catalog. Books are listed by author, title, and subject. If you want to see if the library has a particular book, you will look for it in the catalog by author or title. A book issued by a "corporate author"—that is, a government body, a corporation, an institution, or a society—will be listed under the name of the organization. For example:

U.S. Department of Commerce
American Management Association
Museum of Modern Art

If you have no particular book in mind, but want to know what the library has to offer in a particular subject area, you will look up the subject. The card file will also tell you what periodicals the library stocks and, in some instances, what issues are available. Some publications—including the *New York Times*—will be available on microfilm, for which the library will provide viewing facilities.

2. *Books in Print*. *Books in Print*, an annual publication, is a handy reference to all books currently published in the United States. In separate two-volume sets, it lists books by title and by author. Two additional volumes, *Subject Guide to Books in Print*, complete the set. For a list of soft-cover editions, see *Paperbound Books in Print*.

3. *Cumulative Book Index* (*CBI*). Consult the CBI index for books in English published throughout the world. Published monthly and cumulated twice a year, it lists books alphabetically by author, title, and subject. For current works published in the United States, you will find *Books in Print* more convenient to consult. For titles published before 1928, see the *U.S. Catalog of Books*.

4. *Vertical File Service Catalog*. Because much material is published in monographs, pamphlets, or leaflets, rather than in books or periodicals, it is good to know that you can go to the *Vertical File Service Catalog* for information on the availability of such materials. Many of the pamphlets listed in the *Catalog* will probably be found in the library. Because of the difficulty of handling them, they are filed in boxes, which are stored vertically on the shelves.

5. Indexes to periodicals. If you want to know what materials are available in newspapers and magazines, look up the subject in any of a number of indexes that are available. The *New York Times Index* and the *Wall Street Journal Index* are guides to the articles printed in those publications. They will tell you in what issue an article appears and on what page. A similar index to articles in general periodicals will be found in the *Reader's Guide to Periodical Literature*. Articles in business publications are indexed in the *Business Periodicals Index*. Other specialized indexes include the *Accountant's Index*, the *Index of Economic Journals*, the *Management Index*, and the *Public Affairs Information Service*.

6. General guides. Every library has a number of volumes that are, in fact, directories to books and other publications in particular subject areas. Some of the most useful are the following:

Business Books in Print (New York: R. R. Bowker; annual).
Daniells, Lorna, *Business Information Sources* (Berkeley: University of California Press).
Johnson, H. Webster, *How to Use the Business Library, with Sources of Business Information* (Cincinnati: South-Western Publishing Co.).
Management Information Guides (Detroit: Gale Research Co.). The many volumes include information sources relating to accounting, building construction, business trends and forecasting, commercial law, computers and data processing, food and beverage industries, government regulation of business, real estate, transportation, and other specific areas of business interest.
Statistics Sources (Detroit: Gale Research Co.).

Another useful guide of a more general sort is Constance M. Winchell's *Guide to Reference Books* (Chicago: American Library Association). It is regularly brought up to date.

Reporting Services. Several organizations specialize in providing continually updated digests and analyses of the impact on business of legislation, court decisions, and the rulings of regulatory bodies. Their various publications also include guidelines for dealing with problems in such areas as taxation, accounting, personnel, and communications. The most prominent publishers in this field are Prentice-Hall (P-H), the Commerce Clearing House (CCH), and the Bureau of National Affairs (BNA). The following list of publications represents only a fraction of the output of these organizations.

P-H

Federal Tax Service
State and Local Tax Service
Executive's Tax Report
Insurance Service
Labor Relations
Personnel Policies and Practices
Union Contracts and Collective Bargaining
Real Estate Service
Securities Regulation Service
Wills, Estates, and Trust Service
Prentice-Hall Management Letter
Lawyer's Weekly Report

CCH

Atomic Energy Law Reports
Aviation Law Reports
Federal Banking Law Reports
Stock Transfer Guide
New York Stock Exchange Guide
American Stock Exchange Guide
Food, Drug, Cosmetic Law Reports
Government Contracts Report
Federal Carriers' Report
Utilities Law Reports
Insurance Law Reports
Workmen's Compensation Law Reports
Legislative Reporting Service
Federal Tax Guide Reports
All-State Sales Tax Reports
Payroll Tax Guide
State Tax Guide
Unemployment Insurance Reports

BNA

Antitrust and Trade Regulation Report
Environment Reporter
Government Security and Loyalty
Tax Management
Construction Labor Report
Labor Arbitration
Labor Relations Reporter
Retail Labor Report
Union Labor Report
Executive Library Service
United States Patents Quarterly
Standard EDP Reports
International Trade Reporter
Collective Bargaining Negotiations and Contracts

A more general service catering to business information needs is The Information Bank, a subsidiary of the *New York Times.* By tapping its vast store of computerized information, a business client can obtain abstracts of current data on any subject of interest appearing in the *New York Times* and more than seventy other cooperating publications. The information is available through existing telephone lines linking the Information Bank's central computer and the client's own terminal, from which the printouts are obtained. Data on a particular subject can also be obtained from the Bank by mail.

Government Publications.   Information on almost any subject, including valuable statistics, is published by the federal government, but it is not always easy to obtain. Most current publications can be ordered through the Superintendent of Documents, Washington, D.C. 20402, or from one of several Public Documents Distribution Centers. Publications of the U.S. Department of Commerce can also be obtained from any of its field offices located in more than twenty leading cities throughout the United States, including Anchorage, Alaska, and Honolulu, Hawaii (see Figure 14–1). Libraries in these offices are open to the public. In some large cities, the Government Printing Office operates retail stores in which the most popular current publications are sold over the counter. For the address, consult the white pages of your telephone directory under the heading United States Government, Government Printing Office Bookstore.

Your public library will have many government publications and reference works as well as general surveys of government publications and guides to their use. The following books are recommended:

Andriot, John L., *Guide to U.S. Government Statistics* (Arlington, Va.: Documents Index).
Government Publications and Their Use (Washington, D.C.: The Brookings Institution).

Valuable government bibliographies are *United States Department of Commerce Publications* (supplemented annually), and the *Catalog of United States Census Publications*. A comprehensive list of all government publications will be found in the *Monthly Catalog of U.S. Government Publications*. The semi-monthly list of *Selected United States Government Publications* is free; write to the Superintendent of Documents, Washington, DC 20402.

The Small Business Administration of the U.S. Department of Commerce publishes a large number of management and technical aids, many of them free, for small businesses. To receive lists of available publications, write to the SBA office nearest you or the Small Business Administration, Washington, DC 20230. SBA's *Survey of Federal Publications*, also for owners of small businesses, can be obtained from the Superintendent of Documents, Washington, DC 20402.

The *Statistical Abstract of the United States* gives information on population, vital statistics, education, employment, military affairs, Social Security, income and prices, manufacturers, commerce, and other topics. The *Cities Supplement to the Statistical Abstract* gives special data for cities with a population of more than 25,000.

Other popular sources of business data are the *Survey of Current Business* (monthly) and the *Foreign Commerce Weekly,* both published by the U.S.

Department of Commerce, and the *Monthly Labor Review*, published by the Department of Labor. The President's Council of Economic Advisers publishes the monthly *Economic Indicators*, which gives current statistics and forecasts trends and indications of government action.

The *Congressional Record* gives in full the daily proceedings in both houses of Congress. The *Federal Register*, published daily by the National Archives, contains the official pronouncements of the many government agencies and regulatory bodies. The *United States Government Organization Manual*, the official handbook of the federal government, describes agencies in the legislative, executive, and judicial branches. The *Congressional Directory* is the official guide to the Senate and the House of Representatives; congressional committees; government agencies, departments, and commissions; the diplomatic corps; and foreign diplomatic representatives in the United States. Names, positions, and official duties are given.

Directories.   Information about individuals and organizations can be obtained from directories. *Who's Who in America* gives biographical information about distinguished living men and women. Regional biographical sources include *Who's Who in the East, Who's Who in the West,* and *Who's Who in the South.* The *Directory of the American Medical Association* is the best known of the many directories of members of professional organizations. The professional and academic communities are also represented in the *Directory of American Scholars* and *American Men of Science.*

The *National Directory of Addresses and Telephone Numbers* (New York: Bantam Books) lists about 50,000 important businesses, government agencies, foreign consulates and embassies, trade associations, financial institutions, foundations, unions, communication media, and cultural organizations throughout the United States.

The most complete and up-to-date listing of associations is contained in the *Encyclopedia of Associations* (Detroit: Gale Research Co.).

Some useful directories of individuals in business are *World's Who's Who in Commerce and Industry, Who's Who in Finance and Industry, Poor's Register of Corporations, Directors and Executives of the United States and Canada, Rand McNally's Bankers Directory,* and the *Directory of Directors in the City of New York.* Other directories of leaders in particular fields include *Who's Who in Advertising, Who's Who in Banking, Who's Who in Labor, Who's Who in Insurance, Who's Who in Personnel Administration and Industrial Relations, Who's Who in the Public Utilities Industry,* and *Who's Who in Transportation and Communication.*

Leading directories in publishing and advertising are *Ayer's Directory of Newspapers and Periodicals,* the *Standard Directory of Advertisers,* the *Standard Directory of Advertising Agencies,* and the *Standard Rate and Data Service,* whose numerous directories cover all advertising media.

General business and industrial directories include the following:

Thomas Register of American Manufacturers. A useful guide to products, trade names, and manufacturers.

MacRae's Blue Book. Information similar to that in the *Thomas Register.*

Kelly's Directory of Merchants, Manufacturers and Shippers. Covers companies in Britain, the British Commonwealth overseas, and other countries.

The Fortune Directory of the 500 Largest Industrial Corporations. Also includes companies in merchandising, banking, transportation, life insurance, and public utilities.

Million Dollar Directory. A Dun & Bradstreet publication that lists all firms with net worth of more than $1,000,000.

Middle Market Directory. Another Dun & Bradstreet publication that lists American business enterprises having total assets of $500,000 to $1,000,000.

Economic and Financial Services. The *Value Line Investment Survey,* published by Arnold Bernhard & Co., provides a weekly update on some 1,700 stocks rated for price performance, investment safety, projected yield, and appreciation potential. More comprehensive financial services are provided by Moody's and Standard and Poor. Moody's Investment Service provides for each organization listed detailed information on financial condition and corporate history, organization, and activities. Kept current with weekly and semiweekly supplements and cumulated annually, its separate components are the *Bank and Finance Manual, Industrial Manual, Municipal and Government Manual, Over-the-Counter Manual,* and *Public Utilities and Transportation Manual.* Other Moody publications include *Moody's Bond Record, Moody's Dividend Record,* and *Moody's Handbook of Common Stocks.* Standard & Poor's *Corporation Records* consists of a number of loose-leaf volumes, alphabetically arranged by company and continually revised. It provides detailed data on financial structure, securities, and corporate background. Standard & Poor also publishes the *Bond Outlook, Daily Dividend Record, Industry Surveys, Convertible Bond Reports,* and other financially oriented services. Many of the volumes mentioned here are available for reference in stockbrokers' offices.

Other subscription services supplying current information on business, economics, and finance, include the following.

The Conference Board (New York)
Babson's Business Service (Babson Park, Mass.)
Bureau of National Affairs, Inc. (Washington, D.C.)
Dun & Bradstreet, Inc. (New York)
The Kiplinger Washington Letter (Washington, D.C.)
Research Institute of America (New York)

Dictionaries, Encyclopedias, Atlases, and so on. In addition to the standard dictionaries of the English language, the researcher has access to special dictionaries of various kinds. Examples are *Dictionary for Accountants, Thomson's Dictionary of Banking, Encyclopedic Dictionary of Business and Finance, Computer Dictionary and Handbook, Dictionary of Modern Economics, Black's Law Dictionary, Marketing Dictionary, Modern Real Estate*

Dictionary, Dictionary of Statistical Terms, and *Dictionary of Systems and Management.*

Comprehensive sources of information on many subjects are the *New Encyclopaedia Britannica, New International Encyclopedia,* and *Encyclopedia Americana.* The one-volume *Columbia Encyclopedia* is handy, but its brevity limits its usefulness. *The World Almanac and Book of Facts* and the *Information Please Almanac* are annual compendiums of miscellaneous data. *The Economic Almanac,* published by The Conference Board, is strong on statistics.

Among the atlases, the *Rand McNally Commercial Atlas and Marketing Guide* ranks high for business use. Others are the *Rand McNally Cosmopolitan World Atlas, Odyssey World Atlas, National Geographic Atlas of the World.* and *The Times* [of London] *Atlas of the World.* Good geographical dictionaries are the *Columbia Lipincott Gazetteer of the World, Larousse Encyclopedia of the World,* and *Webster's New Geographical Dictionary.*

Handbooks of information relating to particular business functions are published in profusion. Examples are the *Accountants' Handbook, Encyclopedia of Banking and Finance, Encyclopedia of Management, Data Processing Handbook, Financial Executive's Handbook, Handbook of Modern Personnel Administration, Marketing Handbook, Dartnell Public Relations Handbook, Production Handbook, Purchasing Handbook,* and *Dartnell Sales Manager's Handbook.*

Useful in the preparation of speeches and articles are *Bartlett's Familiar Quotations,* Burton E. Stevenson's *Home Book of Quotations,* and the *Oxford Book of Quotations.*

International Reference Works.   Many kinds of information available about the United States are also available about foreign countries, industries, and individuals. Some representative publications follow.

Statesman's Year-Book. Information about nations, governments, and diplomatic representatives.
Worldmark Encyclopedia of the Nations.
United Nations Statistical Yearbook.
Yearbook of Labour Statistics (Geneva).
Europa Yearbook.
Who's Who (British).
Whitaker's Almanack. The British parallel to the American *World Almanac and Book of Facts.*
Whitaker's Cumulative Book Index. The British parallel to the American *Cumulative Book Index.*
Kelly's Directory of Merchants and Manufacturers. (British).
The Canada Yearbook.
McGraw-Hill Directory and Almanac of Canada.
Year Book Australia.
New Zealand Official Yearbook.
The South American Handbook.
Japan Register of Merchants, Manufacturers and Shippers.

For reference to U.S. Department of Commerce publications on foreign countries and foreign trade, see "International Trade," Chapter 14.

5.3 FOOTNOTES AND BIBLIOGRAPHIES

In a formal report, sources of information are often listed for reference under a heading such as "Sources Consulted" or "Bibliography." Particular statements or quotations are cited in numbered footnotes.

Footnotes and a bibliography are indispensable in research reports based at least partly on the printed word. They show from what sources the author has received help, they establish the authority for the author's statements, and they guide readers to sources they may wish to consult for themselves. Footnotes and bibliographies should never be used for pretension, however, and should be kept to a minimum or avoided completely. In many instances, the reference to a source can be woven into the text, so that a footnote is not needed. Also, when only a few works are to be acknowledged in a report, they can be mentioned in the letter of transmittal or the introduction to the report instead of in a formal bibliography.

Where footnotes and bibliography are used, they should conform to accepted rules of style to ensure that they are complete, clear, and consistent.

Footnotes.   Footnotes are of two kinds. An *explanatory footnote* gives a cross-reference to another part of the same report or contains some incidental remarks of the author. Examples:

[1] For a fuller discussion of this point, see page 23.

[2] The situation is analogous to that frequently encountered in officer candidate schools during World War II.

A *reference footnote* gives the specific source of a quotation or other borrowed material.

[1] John A. Meyers, "A Letter from the Publisher," *Time*, July 17, 1978, p. 2.

[2] Wassily Leontief and Herbert Stein, *The Economic System in an Age of Discontinuity* (New York: New York University Press, 1976), pp. 64–65.

General Style.   Footnotes are separated from the text by two blank lines. A line of one and a half inches (15 pica spaces or 18 elite spaces) is typed after the first blank line, beginning at the margin (Figure 5-6).

1. Identify footnotes by arabic numbers raised a half space above the line. Similarly identify the corresponding reference points in the text. If possible, the number in the text should be placed at the end of a sentence or paragraph, but in any case it should immediately follow the point to which the footnote refers.

for commercials and advertisements on tire safety. The public, through this advertising, is to be informed that no tires are safe under all conditions of use and that in order to have adequate tire safety, the consumer must take necessary measures for proper maintenance.[2]

Government actions have been accompanied by those of private parties. Women's groups have taken advertisers to task for their depiction of women.

[1] Louis Banks, "Taking on the Hostile Media," *Harvard Business Review* (March–April 1978), pp. 124–25.
[2] *Trade Cases,* 1976–1 (Chicago: Commerce Clearing House, 1976), p. 68.

Figure 5-6   Placement of footnotes.

2. Number footnotes successively throughout the report or throughout a chapter or section.

3. Indent the first line of each footnote five spaces. Use single spacing, with preferably a double space between entries.

4. Use standard abbreviations to save space (Figure 5-7).

5. See that footnotes end even with the bottom margin—at least one inch from the edge of the paper.

6. A footnote should appear on the same page as the text reference. When space is limited, however, the last footnote on a page may be continued beneath the text on the following page.

7. If there are many footnotes, they may be separated from the text pages and listed as "Notes" or "Endnotes" at the end of the report as shown in Figure 5-8. Some publications require that articles be documented in this manner. When you use endnotes, you may omit a separate bibliography.

Content.   A footnote consists of the following information arranged to form a single sentence.

1. Identifying number.

2. Name of author or authors as given in the work. If no author is given, begin with the title of the work; or, in the instance of a corporate author—a company, association, or other sponsoring organization—name the organization as the author.

3. Title of the work. Underline the titles of books, magazines, and other self-contained works. Put in quotation marks the titles of chapters, articles, and other parts of longer works. The edition of a book, other than the first, and the volume number follow the title.

4. Facts of publication. For a book, show in parentheses the place of publication, the name of the publisher, and the date of publication (last copyright date). For a magazine article, give only the date of the issue, but

ca. (*circa*)	about. Used when the exact date is unknown, as in "ca. 1918."
cf. (*confer*)	compare.
ch., chs.	chapter(s).
ed.	edition, editor, edited by.
e.g. (*exempli gratia*)	for example.
et al. (*et alii*)	and others, as in "Carl I. Hovland et al." to signify other authors.
f., ff.	and the following page(s), as in "pp. 28ff."
fn., fns.	footnote(s). Also abbreviated n.
ibid. (*ibidem*)	in the same work. Refers to the immediately preceding footnote.
i.e. (*id est*)	that is.
infra	below.
l., ll.	line(s). "Lines," however, is better spelled out because of possible confusion with the number 11.
loc. cit (*loco citato*)	in the place cited. Used with the author's name to refer to the same passage cited in an earlier footnote.
MS., MSS.	manuscript(s), as in "Biddle MSS."
n.d.	no date of publication given.
op. cit. (*opere citato*)	in the work cited. Follows the author's name and precedes the page number. Usually superfluous.
p., pp.	page(s).
passim	here and there. Denotes scattered references, as in "pp. 35–52 passim."
rpt.	reprint, report.
ser.	series.
supra	above.
trans.	translated by, translator, translation.
vol., vols.	volume(s).

Figure 5-7 Abbreviations and Latin terms commonly used in documenting reports. The English terms are almost invariably preferred in business usage.

NOTES

1. James O'Toole, *Work, Learning, and the American Future* (San Francisco: Jossey-Bass, 1977), p. 85.
2. Louise Kapp Howe, *Pink Collar Workers: Inside the World of Women's Work* (New York: G. P. Putnam, 1977), p. 104.
3. Ibid., p. 212.
4. William D. Guth, "Toward a Social System of Corporate Strategy," *Journal of Business* (July 1976), pp. 374-78.
5. The Boston Consulting Group, Inc., *Perspectives on Experience* (Boston: The Boston Consulting Group, 1970).
6. For some of the adjustments made during the 1975 recession, see "Shifts in Supermarket Buying Patterns," *The Nielsen Researcher* 2 (1975), pp. 2-12.
7. O'Toole, p. 208.

Figure 5-8 References collected at end of report take the place of footnotes.

if the periodical is a scholarly journal, give the volume number followed by the date in parentheses.

5. Page reference.

The correct form of footnotes for various types of material is shown in Fig. 5-9.

NOTE: Material underlined in typewritten work is ordinarily set in italics by the printer. In the text examples that follow, the italicized material would be underlined if typewritten.

Subsequent References. When additional references are made to works already footnoted, highly abbreviated forms are used. Although Latin terms are sometimes preferred for this purpose in scholarly works, business reports tend to use plain English. Examples:

[1] Brookshire, Michael L. and Michael D. Rogers, *Collective Bargaining in Public Employment: The TVA Experience* (Lexington, Mass.: D. C. Heath, 1977), pp. 212-214. [First reference.]

[2] Ibid., p. 35. [Same work as previously cited, but another page.]

OR [2] Brookshire and Rogers, p. 35. [Preferred form.]

[3] John Kenneth Galbraith, *The Age of Uncertainty* (Boston: Houghton Mifflin, 1977), p. 112. [First reference.]

[4] Brookshire and Rogers, *Collective Bargaining*, p. 54. [This form, with shortened title, is useful when footnotes cite more than one work for an author.]

[5] Galbraith, loc. cit. [Same passage as cited earlier.]

OR [5] Galbraith, p. 112. [Preferred.]

[6] Brookshire and Rogers, op. cit., p. 98. [This is a variant of footnote 2; the Latin abbreviation is considered unnecessary in business reports but is used in books.]

Book (One Author)	[1]W. Allen Wallis, *Our Overgoverned Society* (New York: Free Press, 1976), pp. 85–86.
Book (Two Authors)	[2]Margaret Hennig and Anne Jardin, *The Managerial Woman* (New York: Doubleday, 1977), p. 55.
Book (Three or More Authors)	[3]Richard V. Farace and others, *Communicating and Organizing* (Reading, Mass.: Addison-Wesley, 1977), p. 27.
Book with Subtitle; Later Edition	[4]Joe Kelly, *Organizational Behavior: An Existential Systems Approach*, rev. ed. (Homewood, Ill.: Irwin, 1974), pp. 124–26.
Edited Work	[5]Henry J. Aaron, ed., *Inflation and the Income Tax* (Washington, D.C.: The Brookings Institution, 1976), pp. 285–86.
Chapter or Article in Collected Work	[6]Estelle James, "Effects of Women's Liberation," in *Sex, Discrimination, and the Division of Labor,* Cynthia B. Lloyd, ed. (New York: Columbia University Press, 1975), pp. 389–90.
Volume in Series	[7]James P. Northrup, *Old Age, Handicapped, and Antidiscrimination Legislation,* Labor Relations and Public Policy Series, No. 14 (Philadelphia: University of Pennsylvania, 1977), pp. 187–89.
Article in Encyclopedia	[8]"Malta," *Encyclopedia Americana,* vol. 18 (1978).
Pamphlet (No Date)	[9]Speakers Guide (Washington, D.C.: Department of the Navy, n.d.), p. 35.
Article in Learned Journal	[10]Robert T. Green and Isabella C. M. Cunningham, "Feminine Role Perception and Family Purchasing Decisions," *Journal of Marketing Research,* vol. 12 (August 1975), pp. 325–26.
Signed Magazine Article	[11]Marylin Dammerman, "The Story of the Phantom Smelter," *Forbes,* April 3, 1978, pp. 36–37.
Unsigned Magazine or Newspaper Article	[12]"Single-Minded Dollar Strategy," *Business Week,* April 3, 1978, p. 36.
Unpublished Work	[13]Minutes of the Summer Meeting of the Environmental Preservation Society, May 12–13, 1979 (in the files of the Association).

Figure 5-9   Correct form of footnotes.

Footnoting Public Documents.   Because of differences in the nature of documents, references to government publications, legislative proceedings, and legal decisions vary considerably. Whatever the document, however, it is well to keep in mind that the purpose of a footnote is served if it gives the reader, who so wishes, enough information to locate the material in question.

Agency Publications.   In citing books and pamphlets issued by public agencies, begin with the name of the agency; if the work carries an author's name, place the name after the title of the work in the manner shown in footnote 3 here. In other respects, the style follows closely that of the footnotes already treated.

[1] U.S. Department of Commerce, Bureau of Domestic and International Business Administration, *A Basic Guide to Exporting* (Washington, D.C.: Government Printing Office, 1976), p. 45.

[2] U.S. Department of Commerce, Bureau of the Census, *Population Estimates and Projections: 1975–2050*, Current Population Reports Series P–25, No. 601, October 1975 (Washington, D.C.: Government Printing Office, 1975), p. 77.

[3] U.S. Department of Labor, Employment and Training Administration, *Women at Work*, R and D Monograph 46, by Patricia C. Cato (Washington, D.C.: Government Printing Office, 1977), pp. 49–50.

[4] International Labour Office, *Protection of Workers Against Noise and Vibration in the Working Environment* (Geneva: International Labour Office, 1977), p. 62.

Legislative Bills, Hearings, and Reports.   Congressional bills are referred to by the name of the chamber (House or Senate), the session number (sometimes also the date), and the number of the bill. Testimony and reports are identified by the name of the document, the volume or part, and the page number.

[1] 96th Cong., 2d Sess., H. R. 6143 [House bill]

[2] 96th Cong., 1st Sess., S. 2228 [Senate bill]

[3] 95th Cong., 2d Sess. (1978), J. Res. 335 [Joint Resolution]

[4] U.S. Congress, *Social Security Amendments of 1977: Conference Report to Accompany H.R. 9346*, 95th Cong., House Document No. 95–837, December 15, 1977 (Washington, D.C.: Government Printing Office, 1978), p. 8.

[5] U.S. Congress, *State and Local Government Credit Problems, Hearings Before the Joint Economic Committee*, 94th Cong., 1st Sess., June 20, 1975 (Washington, D.C.: Government Printing Office, 1975), p. 245.

[6] Council of Economic Advisers, *Economic Report of the President*, transmitted to Congress, Jan. 22, 1978, p. 12.

[7] New York State, *Report of the New York Joint Legislative Committee to Revise the Banking Law* (Albany: 1976), p. 22.

Laws and Regulations.   Citations of federal and state constitutions, statutes, and regulations will include the name of the document and the number, date, chapter, article, and section—whatever the identification of the document requires. The name of the document is not underlined or italicized either in text references or in footnotes.

[1] 28 U.S. Code, sec. 2202 (1970). [References to the U.S. Code, often abbreviated U.S.C., are preceded by the title number.]

[2] U.S. Constitution, art, 6, par. 2.

³ Internal Revenue Code (1954), sec. 901(b).
⁴ U.S. Social Security Act (as amended 1977), sec. 202(a).
⁵ Louisiana Civil Code (1870), Book 3, Title 2, Chap. 1, Art. 1468.

Cases at Law. Citations of legal cases, including the decisions of regulatory bodies, identify the cases by name, legal body, volume, initial page number, and date. Names of cases are underlined or italicized in the text of a report, but *not* in the footnotes. As the examples show, legal citations are greatly abbreviated and highly technical. *A Uniform System of Citation*, published by the Harvard Law Review Association, Cambridge, MA 02138, contains numerous examples of the correct forms to use.

¹ Parker v. Brown, 317 U.S. 341 (1943). [The reference is to volume 317 of the official records of the United States Supreme Court, page 341.]
² Bates v. State Bar, 97 S. Ct. 2691 (1977). [The document cited is the *Supreme Court Reporter* (S. Ct.), an unofficial record; the official United States Supreme Court record had not yet been published.]
³ Ingraham v. Wright, 498 F. 2d 248 (5th Cir., 1974). [A decision of a United States District Court is invariably cited, as this one is, from the unofficial *Federal Reporter Series* (F), currently in the Second Series.]
⁴ Cade v. State, 237 Ark. 927, 377 S.W. 2d 816 (1964). [This citation refers to the official records of the Arkansas Supreme Court and also to the unofficial *South Western Reporter*, 2d Series.]
⁵ Kemp-Barclay Co. v. Commissioner, 26 T.C. 582 (1956). [Citation of a U.S. Tax Court case from the official source.]

Bibliographies. A bibliography lists works alphabetically by author and title (Figure 5-10). A long list is divided according to the type of materials as, for example, books, periodicals, government documents, and miscellaneous sources. For the style of bibliographical entries, follow these rules.

1. Give the author's last name first. If there is more than one author, the names of other authors are usually written with the given names first.

2. Start each entry at the margin, but indent succeeding lines several spaces. Single-space individual entries, but double-space between entries.

3. When an author is represented by more than one work, use an underscore line of ten spaces to denote the author's name in the second and succeeding entries.

4. When no individual is credited for a work, list as author the name of the sponsoring organization or, if none is given, the title of the work in the correct alphabetical sequence.

5. Give the facts of publication as in footnotes, but set them off with periods instead of parentheses. You may use parentheses, however, to enclose an isolated date.

6. Give the inclusive pages of an article or chapter in a work that contains other material, but omit page references otherwise.

BIBLIOGRAPHY

"Advertising Portraying or Directed to Women." *Advertising Age*, April 21, 1975, pp. 72, 75, 78.

Bell, Griffin. Address Before the American Bar Association, Antitrust Section, April 14, 1977.

The Conference Board. *Top Executive Compensation.* Conference Report No. 640. New York: The Conference Board, 1974.

Drucker, Peter F. *Management: Tasks, Practices, Responsibilities.* New York: Harper & Row, 1974.

_____. *People and Performance: The Best of Peter Drucker on Management.* New York: Harper & Row, 1977.

Mobil Corporation. *Annual Report, 1979.* New York: Mobil Corporation, 1980.

Rutner, Jack L. "The Federal Reserve's Impact on Several Reserve Aggregates." *Monthly Review.* Federal Reserve Bank of Kansas City, May 1977, pp. 14–22.

Silk, Leonard and David Vogel. *Ethics and Profits: The Crisis of Confidence in American Business.* New York: Simon and Schuster, 1976.

U.S. Congress, Joint Economic Committee. *Foundations for a National Policy to Preserve Private Enterprise in the 1980's.* Prepared for the Subcommittee on Economic Growth and Stabilization, 95th Cong., 1st Sess. Washington, D.C.: Government Printing Office, 1977.

U.S. Department of Labor. Bureau of Labor Statistics. *The U.S. Economy: A Summary of BLS Projections.* Washington, D.C.: Government Printing Office, 1980.

Vernon, Raymond, ed. *The Oil Crisis.* New York: W. W. Norton, 1976.

Figure 5-10   Correct form of a bibliography.

5.4 TABULAR PRESENTATION

A collection of figures can best be communicated by means of a table. A table saves many words of description and permits easy reading and comparison.

See also "Typing Statistical Material," Section 11.3.

For information on positioning tables in a report, see "The Report in Finished Form," Section 6.3.

General Design. Tables are often classified as spot tables or reference tables. Spot tables, invariably limited in scope, are integrated into the text (Figure 5-11). Reference tables, regardless of their scope, are positioned independently, either close to the text to which they refer or in appendixes; each bears a title and, if there is more than one table, a number (Figure 5-12).

For additional instructions regarding the position and labels of tables and charts, see "Exhibits," in Section 6.3.

The design of a table requires much thought and care. The main objective is to show relationships among the data in the rows and columns.

1. Data may be arranged geographically, numerically, alphabetically, chronologically, or by class, rank, or size.

2. When arranged by size, magnitudes usually diminish from left to right or top to bottom.

3. A table is better read across than down and is better long than wide.

4. In general, quantities should occupy the columns, whereas the things being studied (the *variables*) are named in the stubs on the left side of the table.

5. A column containing percentages, averages, ratios, and the like should be placed to the right of a column containing the base figures.

6. Coordinate columns—that is, columns containing the same kinds of information—should be the same width.

7. Horizontal rules are used to separate the column heads from the body of the table, but other horizontal rules and vertical rules between columns are used only to improve display or prevent the confusion of figures. In any case, the sides are usually left open.

A survey of 127 typical plants and offices in the East showed that companies paid their employees' tuition as follows:

	Plants	Offices
In advance	16.8%	26.9%
After completion of courses	71.2%	57.7%
In installments	12.0%	15.4%

Most companies (about two-thirds of the firms having percentage formulas) specified a flat percentage for all reimbursements. Fifty per cent is the most frequently mentioned figure; seventy-five per cent is the next.

Figure 5-11 Sample of text showing spot table.

Table 2

PERCENT OF FUEL USED IN EACH CONSUMING SECTOR

Fuel/Energy Source	Industrial	Commercial-Residential	Transportation	Electric Utility
Coal	24	2	*	43
Gas	53	46	*	22
Oil	10	34	100	16
Hydropower	—	—	—	16
Nuclear	—	—	—	3
Electricity	13	18	*	—
	100	100	100	100

*Negligible amounts.

Figure 5-12 Reference table.

Parts of the Table. The parts of a reference table are shown in Figure 5-13. The following is a description of the parts, with additional commentary on tabular techniques.

Title. The title and number of a reference table are centered in one or several lines. Roman numerals may be used for the table number. Unit values, if applicable, are placed in parentheses below the title.

Columns. Each column has a descriptive heading or caption centered in one or several lines to fit the width of the column. A caption may also span several columns, each with its own subcaption. Unit values applicable to any of the columns should be included tersely in parentheses, as, for example, (*000's*), when three ciphers are to be added to the figures given.

Column totals should be placed at the top or bottom to suit the convenience of the reader. Subtotals within a column should be underlined.

Column spaces should not be left blank. If there are no figures to be supplied, the fact should be indicated by a long dash (—) or by the abbreviation n.a. ("not available").

Stubs. Headings in the left-hand column are called *stubs*. The stub caption is the descriptive word or phrase at the top of the column. When stubs are subdivided, the main entry is the line caption; the subentries, indented two spaces, are the group captions. A space is left above the group caption. If a space cannot be left below the group caption, it may be underlined to separate it from the line captions. In a closely packed table, a space should be left between every five rows to make reading easier. Leaders, or spaced periods,

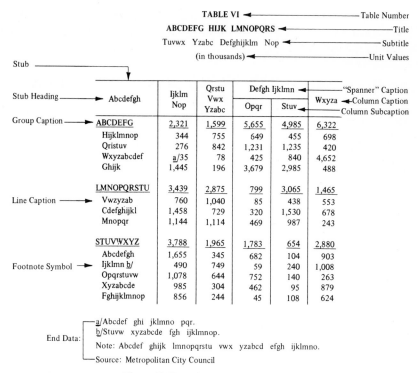

Figure 5-13   The parts of a table.

may also be used to carry the eye from the stub to the column data. The periods should be aligned vertically.

End Data.   A single footnote reference in a table may be marked by an asterisk (*). If there are several footnote references, alphabetical symbols are more practical (numbers would be confusing). The alphabetical symbols are usually placed to the left of column figures to avoid disturbing the column alignment. All three of the following styles are correct, but a single style should be adopted for use throughout a table or set of tables.

a/1,956   (A)1,956   1,956a
b/ 560   (B) 560   560b

The symbols are repeated at the bottom of the table before the respective footnotes.

5.5   GRAPHIC PRESENTATION

Graphs and other types of charts are often used in reports as well as for independent use and presentation at meetings. Although some companies have specialists prepare these materials, the preparation of the drafts—if not the finished charts—may be assigned to a secretary or administrative assistant.

Graphs and charts cannot present the detailed information found in tables. Graphic exhibits do have an advantage, however, in their dramatic appeal to the eye.

Chart-Making Materials.   The following materials are useful for making simple charts.

Graph paper	Black India ink
Ruler	Lettering guide
Protractor	Drawing board
Compass	T-square
Ruling pen	Triangle
Speedball pens	

Printed graph paper is available in a variety of rulings, principally 5, 6, 8, 10, and 12 to the inch. The 6 ruling corresponds to the vertical spacing on the typewriter; the 10 and 12 correspond to the horizontal spaces of pica and elite type.

Other chart-making aids include colored cellophane tapes for use in making lines and bars, acetate film for use in shading, and alphabet packs with transferable letters and symbols. Some of the trade names under which these materials are available are Chart-Pak, Pretype, Formatt, and Letraset.

General Techniques

1. Draw the graph in pencil on graph paper; then copy the draft on plain white paper. Keep grid lines to a minimum. Intermediate values can be shown, where necessary, by ticks along the horizontal or vertical axis.

2. The use of color for lines and bars helps to emphasize distinctions, but is impractical if the graphs are going to be reproduced in black and white.

3. Typewrite the title and other data on the graph or hand-draw them in block letters. For position and labels of graphs, see "Exhibits," in Section 6.3.

4. Explain distinctions in color, shading, or line quality by a legend on a convenient part of the chart.

5. Generally, time is indicated by the horizontal scale of a line or column graph, and quantity by the vertical scale. Clearly mark the points on both scales and place the index or unit of measure (examples: "1960 = 100"; "Thousands of Dollars") above the vertical scale or below the horizontal scale, as the chart requires.

6. Choose the scale range to represent conditions accurately. Figure 5-14 shows how the choice of range may accentuate a rise or drop.

7. Be consistent in your scale. Don't, for example, show five-year intervals at the beginning of the scale and one-year intervals at the end. All the measures should be uniform.

8. Don't crowd the chart. Select carefully the few details to be shown and the few relationships to be established. Cut the number of words and figures to a minimum and make sure they are clearly visible.

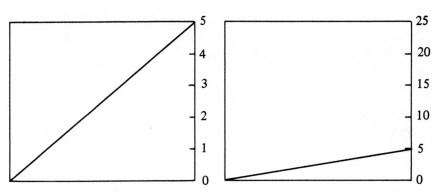

Figure 5-14 Visual effect of differences in scale.

The most common types of charts are the pie chart, bar chart, column chart, and line chart.

Pie Charts (Figure 5-15). A pie chart is a full circle that divides a whole quantity into its parts. Thus it might show the distribution of a dollar of income, the proportion of men to women in the employ of an organization,

DISTRIBUTION OF ADVERTISING DOLLAR

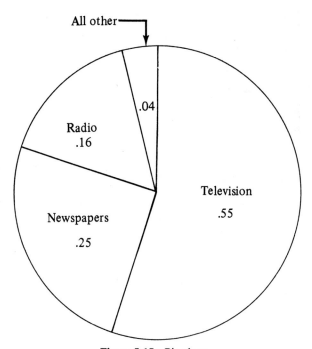

Figure 5-15 Pie chart.

or the relative sales of a company's several product lines. To make a pie chart:

1. Convert all figures into percentages.

2. Beginning at "12 o'clock," mark off the required segments, going from the largest to the smallest, unless emphasis requires some other arrangement.

3. In allocating space, consider the circumference of the circle as 100 percent and determine the size of each segment by using a protractor or by making a close estimate. Reasonable accuracy is possible if the circle is quartered,

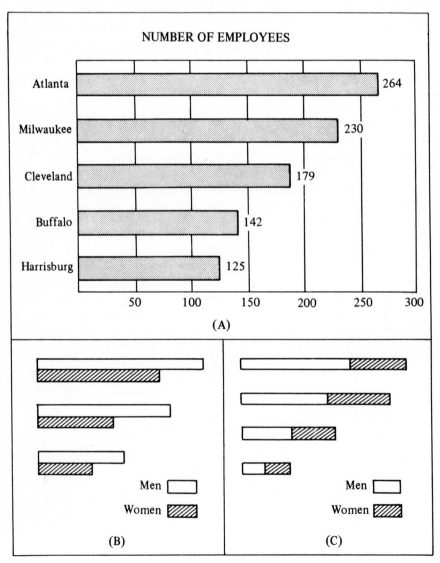

Figure 5-16   Bar charts.

then each quarter halved, and each half quarter halved again. Each of the 16 segments is then equal to 6.25 percent. If you use a protractor, keep in mind that the circumference of the circle is 360°; so 10 percent would be 36°, 20 percent 72°, and so on.

4. Place segment captions and percentages inside or outside the circle, depending on the space available. Segments may be shaded for contrast.

5. Type all captions horizontally. Draw arrows, if necessary, to the segments to which they apply.

Bar and Column Charts.   The bar chart shows the magnitude, or quantities, of different things. A sequence of dates or amounts is marked off on the horizontal axis, and the things being compared are represented by the bars extending from the vertical axis. The bars may be subdivided to show their components, or they may be clustered in groups of two or three (Figure 5-16).

Although the bar chart may be set upright to form a column chart, the column chart is technically reserved for two-scale representations, that is, those that permit measuring both horizontally and vertically (Figure 5-17). As in bar charts, the columns may be subdivided or grouped.

FIVE-YEAR SALES RECORD

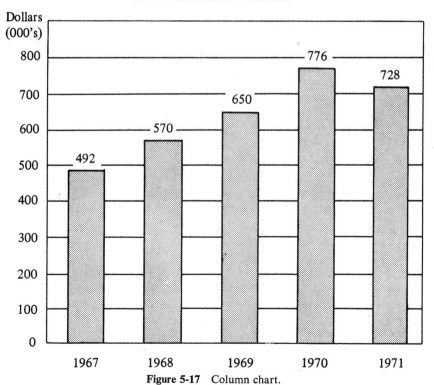

Figure 5-17   Column chart.

The following suggestions apply to both bar and column charts.

1. Space the bars from one-half to a full bar width apart. Use narrower spaces or none at all between grouped bars.

2. Arrange the bars in ascending or descending order, or any other order consistent with the purpose of the chart or the emphasis you desire. A time sequence, however, must be plotted in chronological order, beginning with the earliest period.

3. Use a consistent shading scheme for the parts of divided bars and the members of grouped bars. For simple bars and columns, draw outlines or solids.

4. If you prefer, you may type the charts instead of drawing them, using ordinary symbols to make the bars or columns (Figure 5-18).

Line Charts (Curves).   When points along a horizontal scale are too close for a column chart to be feasible, the points may be connected to form a curve (Figure 5-19). Two or three curves may also be overlaid on the same grid to show other variations in quantity over the same period. Some applicable suggestions:

1. Plan the chart so that it is about half again as wide as it is high to prevent visual distortion.

2. Begin quantity scales at zero; otherwise a rise or fall will seem steeper than it is. If curves are too high on the chart, the chart may be broken near the bottom to show the omission of part of the scale.

3. When several curves are superimposed, use a different color for each, or use a solid line for one and broken or dotted lines for the others.

```
                     EMPLOYMENT OF TEMPORARY HELP

                       October-November, 19--

        OCT. ))))
        NOV. ####

                                          Man-Hours

                     0     50    100    150    200    250
                     |     |      |      |      |      |

34th Street    120   )))))))))))))))))))
   Store       179   ###########################

59th Street     96   )))))))))))))))
   Store       168   ########################

86th Street     39   )))))))
   Store       109   ################
```

Figure 5-18 A typewritten bar chart. The upper bars are made of superimposed parentheses.

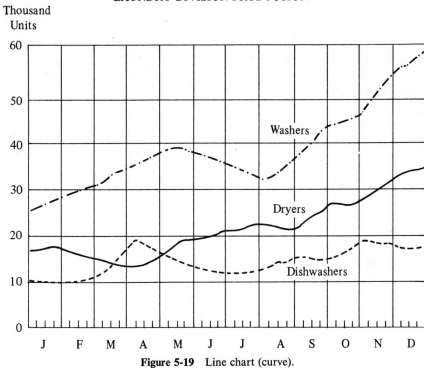

Figure 5-19   Line chart (curve).

6

Report Preparation

Reports play an important part in the communication and decision-making processes of all large organizations. As office functions are taken over by the computer and other machines, the executive spends more time studying data and writing reports on the findings. Others, including administrative secretaries and the professional staff, are also called on to write, assemble, or edit reports on their own behalf or on behalf of their superiors. This chapter is designed to help with those tasks. The first three sections cover the requirements of the long-form report. The last deals with the short, internal report, commonly referred to as the memorandum.

CONTENTS

Information regarding other aspects of reports will be found in Chapter 5 as follows: "Information Sources," Section 5.2; "Footnotes and Bibliographies," Section 5.3; "Tabular Presentation," Section 5.4; and "Graphic Presentation," Section 5.5.

6.1 PLANNING THE REPORT

A report can be only as good as the planning behind it. The planning requires a specific objective, a search for the relevant data, and logical organization of the content. For all but the shortest reports, some form of working outline is indispensable. Fleshed out with suitable language, supporting exhibits, and attractive typographical display, the outline is transformed into an effective report. (Figure 6-1.)

Report Objectives. The chief criterion for judging reports is "Does it do its job?" (Figure 6-2). For that reason the report objective should be clearly

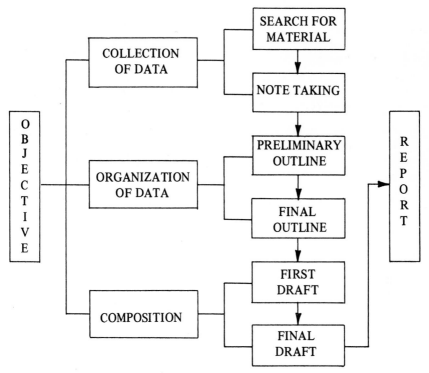

Figure 6-1 The report-writing process.

defined in the first place. Several of the following objectives may be combined in a single report.

1. To preserve information for legal or reference purposes.
2. To provide information for high-level decisions.
3. To evaluate performance.
4. To record individual, group, or machine performance for later evaluation.
5. To analyze current procedures.
6. To make recommendations.
7. To predict future results.

Developing Report Data. The heart of any report is the information it contains. A reader may disagree with the writer's conclusions or recommendations, but the data should be complete, specific, and incontestable. Generally, two kinds of data are used: primary and secondary.

Primary Data. This type of information is most desirable because it comes from an examination of original documents and the writer's own research and personal experience. Primary data include the following.

Company records and files
Original letters, estimates, and proposals
Public records
Legal documents
Personal interviews
Questionnaires
Personal observation
Experimentation
On-the-job experience

Secondary Data. In many cases, the writer does not have access to original sources, or the research work has already been done by the government or other reliable sources outside his control. The following may be classified as secondary sources.

Government documents and statistics
Books
Newspapers and periodicals
Records and reports of private agencies
Business services (e.g., Standard & Poor's)
Published reports of surveys, interviews, and questionnaires

See also "Information Sources," Section 5.2.

---

1. **UTILITY**
   (a) The report serves the purpose for which it was prepared.
   (b) It provides information in a convenient form.
   (c) It is helpful to the reader.

2. **RELIABILITY**
   (a) The information is specific, accurate, and dependable.
   (b) The report includes all data that would affect the conclusion.
   (c) Unimportant data are not given undue weight.

3. **PERSUASIVENESS**
   (a) The conclusions and recommendations are adequately supported by the data presented.
   (b) The reasoning is logical.
   (c) Adequate consideration is given to contrary evidence and conclusions.

4. **READABILITY**
   (a) The report is organized for easy comprehension.
   (b) The language is as clear and simple as the subject permits.
   (c) The technical vocabulary, if any, is suited to the reader.
   (d) Ideas are expressed concisely.
   (e) Tables and charts are used where applicable.

Figure 6-2 Criteria of good reports.

Organization of Data. Generally, the thinking that goes into a report is inductive; that is, it proceeds from an examination of the facts to the formation of conclusions based on those facts. The same method may be followed in the actual writing. However, for reasons of emphasis or convenience to the reader, the conclusions and recommendations are often placed ahead of the

METHOD	*EXAMPLES*
Time	Chronology of events. Conditions before—conditions after. Present system—proposed system.
Space	First floor—second floor. Eastern sales—western sales. North America—South America.
Classes	Kinds of accounts. Classes of products.
Parts	Parts of a machine. Steps in a process.

Support	General statement or conclusion followed by
	   specific details (deductive order).
	Specific details followed by general statement or
	   conclusion (inductive order).

Balance	Cause—effect. Need—fulfillment. Problem—solution. Question—answer. Point-by-point comparison of two or more things.
Importance	Most important to least important. Least important to most important (climax).
Interest	Most interesting points to least interesting.
Familiarity	Most familiar material to least familiar. Simple to complex.
Acceptance	Most acceptable ideas to least acceptable.

Figure 6-3   Methods of organizing data.

supporting data, and sometimes the supporting data are either omitted or put in an appendix to form a subordinate part of the report.

The most important steps in organizing a report are dividing or classifying the data and arranging the parts in logical order. The following patterns, though general, should prove useful in a great variety of situations.

Useful Report Patterns

I. Introduction	I. Introduction
II. Data	II. Data
	III. Conclusions and/or Recommendations

I. Introduction	I. Abstract or Summary
II. Conclusions and/or Recommendations	II. Background (Introduction)
III. Supporting Data	III. Discussion of Data
	IV. Conclusions and/or Recommendations

I. Statement of problem	I. Background
II. Proposed solution(s)	II. Faults of Present System
III. Anticipated results	III. Alternatives
IV. Recommendations	A. Advantages
	B. Disadvantages
	IV. Conclusions
	V. Recommendations

Within the various parts of the report, data may be arranged in a number of different ways for order and consistency (Figure 6-3).

Suggestions for Content.   Once the general outline is conceived, the particulars of the report can be distributed through the various parts. The following lists suggest not only the allocation of details, but also some of the kinds of information the report may contain.

1. Introduction
   (a) Authorization for the report.
   (b) Purpose of the report.
   (c) Scope and limits.
   (d) Statement of the problem.
   (e) Organization of the report.
   (f) History or background.
   (g) Methods of investigation.
   (h) Sources of information.
   (i) Definition of terms.
   (j) Acknowledgments.
   (k) Abstract or synopsis.
   (l) Summary of findings (conclusions).
   (m) Summary of recommendations.
2. Discussion (main body of data).
   (a) Analysis of present conditions; strengths and weaknesses.
   (b) Details of structure, functions, methods.
   (c) Proposals.
   (d) Evidence, reasoning, and other forms of proof.
   (e) Use of models: mathematical or graphic.
   (f) Narrative or chronology.
   (g) Procedures: past, present, proposed.

(h) Causes and effects.
(i) Comparison of data.
(j) Alternatives.
(k) Advantages and disadvantages.
(l) Summary tables and charts.
3. Conclusion.
   (a) Summary of purpose and main points.
   (b) Detailed conclusions.
   (c) Detailed recommendations.
   (d) Anticipated results.
4. Appendix(es).
   (a) Original documents (or copies).
   (b) Reference tables and charts.
   (c) Pictures and diagrams.

Outline Techniques.   Except for the most simple report, it makes good sense to prepare an outline before writing the report proper. The outline serves a number of purposes: (1) it provides a step-by-step plan for the presentation of

---

THE NEED FOR WORK MEASUREMENT
IN THE OFFICE

I. Evolution of work measurement

II. Purposes of work measurement

   A. Provide basis for evaluating and appraising performance
   B. Permit more efficient scheduling of work
   C. Allow for more effective cost control

     1. Screening of projects
     2. Budgeting

III. Work measurement techniques

   A. Subjective method
   B. Observation time study
   C. Historical records
   D. Stop watch studies
   E. Work sampling
   F. Standard time data
   G. Predetermined time data

IV. Conclusions

   A. Work measurement aids productivity
   B. Techniques must be carefully weighed
   C. Timing, personnel resources, and cost play important roles

V. Recommendation

Figure 6-4   A topic outline.

data; (2) it can be submitted for approval before time is spent (and perhaps wasted) on the finished report; and (3) it is useful in coordinating data when parts of the report are assigned to different persons to prepare.

An outline may consist of a few informal jottings on a scrap of paper or of a list of topics carefully phrased, arranged, and numbered. The exact form will depend on the length and complexity of the report and the use that will be made of the outline. The suggestions that follow should prove helpful in the framing of a formal outline but, in general, it should be kept in mind that a good outline is one in which the organization of ideas is logical, simple, and readily apparent.

1. Decide whether you want the outline to be in complete sentences (sentence outline) or phrases (topic outline); then be consistent in sticking to one or the other (Figures 6-4 and 6-5). The topic outline is usually preferred because of its simplicity and convenience, but the sentence outline gives more information and may therefore be preferred if it is to be submitted to others for examination.

2. Use roman numerals for identifying first-degree headings, capital letters for second-degree heads, arabic numbers for third-degree heads, and small letters with or without parentheses for fourth-degree heads. A further subdivision of material is usually not desirable. If only two levels of heads are used, you may prefer a combination of arabic numbers and small letters, or capital letters and arabic numbers, in the order named.

THE POST OFFICE BOX COLLECTION PLAN

I. The present method of handling cash receipts is far from efficient.
    A. Handling incoming checks takes three to five days.
    B. Steps taken to shorten time have not succeeded.
    C. The Post Office collection box plan offers a possible solution.

II. The proposed method consists of these steps.
    A. Mail is picked up by the company's trucks at local post offices.
    B. A cash report is prepared for the cashier by the mail department.
    C. The cashier examines each check for
        1. Post-dating.
        2. Name of payee.
        3. Signature
        4. Agreement of written and figure amounts.
    D. Verified checks are deposited, with each check listed on the deposit slip.

Figure 6-5 Part of a sentence outline.

NOTE: In outlining technical and scientific papers, it is customary to use a decimal numbering system or pure number code (Figure 6-6).

3. Avoid the use of a single subhead. If a second subhead cannot be created, the single subhead can be absorbed into the immediately preceding head. An exception can be made when a single subhead is used to denote the use of an example.

NOT: A. Number of employees   BUT: A. Number of employees: 60
        1. 60   B. Volume of mail
     B. Volume of mail   1. 100–150 pieces daily
        1. 100–150 pieces daily   2. 1,500 pieces at end of month
ACCEPTABLE: A. Public-service advertising
              1. Example: Georgia-Pacific

4. Show the logical relationship of ideas by the ranking you give them in the outline. Instead of giving unequal ideas the same rank, try to combine related ideas under suitable headings. The outline on p. 226 is confusing because it does not equate the present system with the proposed system

TITLE

1. _____
   1.1 _____
   1.2 _____
   1.3 _____

2. _____
   2.1 _____
      2.1.1 _____
      2.1.2 _____
   2.2 _____

3. _____
   3.1 _____
      3.1.1 _____
      3.1.2 _____
   3.2 _____
      3.2.1 _____
      3.2.2 _____
      3.2.3 _____

Figure 6-6 Outline using pure number code.

signified in the title. It also lists the parts of the subject as if all were of equal rank. The outline to the right corrects these faults.

<table>
<tr><td>Poor</td><td>Improved</td></tr>
</table>

Poor	*Improved*
Proposed Mechanization of Bakery Order Procedure	Mechanization of Bakery Order Procedure
I. Present method described	I. Present method
II. Need for change	A. Description
III. Store processing	B. Need for change
IV. Office procedure	II. Proposed method
V. Bakery platform handling	A. Daily processing
VI. Weekly processing	1. At store
VII. Cost comparisons	2. At bakery
VIII. Other considerations	a. Office
	b. Shipping platform
	B. Weekly processing
	III. Cost comparisons
	IV. Other considerations

5. Apportion space in the outline about as you would in the report. Don't exaggerate minor ideas by giving them a long string of subtopics. Save the details for the report proper.

6.2 WRITING THE REPORT

When all the information has been gathered and assessed, and at least a rough outline has been made, the next step in the preparation of the report is writing the first draft. In the instance of a short, simple report, the first draft will probably be the final draft also. In a long report, however, there will probably be further editing and rewriting.

Report Language (General)

Title or subject.   The title should be short and specific. If a short title does not identify the subject sufficiently, a subtitle should be added. Examples:

Space Requirements of the Legal Department
Investigation of the Delay in Shipments of R-200
Proposed Different Procedure in the Sorting and Counting Division: Interim Report No. 1
Excelsior Electronic Calculator, Model 320S: Evaluation for Use in Domestic Research Division

References to author.   In a short report that takes the form of a letter or memorandum, reference to the author is made with the pronoun *I* (*we* if others are included). In a more formal report the author who wishes to avoid the first person may use such terms as *the writer*, *the analyst*, and *the investigator*. With a little editing, however, it is possible to avoid references to the author altogether, as the following illustrations show:

Informal: I found . . .
Formal: An inspection showed . . .
Informal: I recommend . . .
Formal: It is recommended . . .
Informal: We propose three flexible alternatives.
Formal: Three flexible alternatives are proposed.

NOTE 1: A person of high position or unquestioned authority in the field of investigation should not hesitate to use the first-person ("I") style, even in a formal report.

NOTE 2: A formal report written in the name of an official group will refer to the signers as *we, the Committee, the Commission, the Board,* and so on.

We have stated on many occasions that we would not impair safety, or reduce standards of service, or cut service merely to keep down operating costs.

The Committee is unanimously of the opinion that all concessions should be let as the result of competitive bidding.

Objectivity.   The value of a report is in the facts it presents, rather than in the writer's personal opinions or unsupported conclusions. If opinions are offered, they should be backed by convincing evidence and stated in temperate language.

NOT: The conditions we found were disgraceful.
BUT: We found that 60 per cent of the orders received during May were unattended to for periods ranging from nine days to three weeks.

NOT: Mr. Smith proved himself to be thoroughly incompetent in the new job.
BUT: Mr. Smith was charged with four errors last month. One of them involved a difference of $2,800. In another instance. . . . All in all, Mr. Smith's performance is well below that which we expect from an employee in his position.

Adaptation to the Reader.   Technical language is necessary and desirable in a report written for someone familiar with the writer's special subject, but it should be modified for the less knowledgeable reader. Reports originating in technical departments often have to be rephrased when they go to management. There is usually some loss of meaning in the transition.

TECHNICAL: Most refractory coatings to date exhibit a lack of reliability when subjected to the impingement of entrained particulate matter in the propellant stream under extended firing conditions.
NONTECHNICAL: The exhaust gas eventually chews the coating off existing ceramics.

Connecting Ideas.   The interconnection of ideas should be shown by sentence and paragraph structure and the repetition of key words. More specifically:

1. Let the heads and subheads give the reader clues to the relation between the parts of the report. For example, do not give two heads equal position and weight when one is actually subordinate to the other.

2. List and enumerate coordinate ideas, such as points, conditions, advantages, and so on. This technique saves words and shows clearly that all the listed units are part of the same category of information. As an example, note the list of points, of which this paragraph is a part.

3. Use topic, or summary, sentences to alert the reader to what follows. The repetition of key words will emphasize the connection. Example:

TOPIC SENTENCE: The application of electronics to banking falls into two distinct areas: (1) *deposit accounting*, and (2) *all other bank recordkeeping functions*, including general accounting, loans, trusts, and mortgage activities.

FIRST POINT REPEATED
AND DEVELOPED: The problems involved in *deposit accounting* . . .

SECOND POINT REPEATED
AND DEVELOPED:* The problems incident to *all other bank recordkeeping functions* . . .

* Repetition of the word *problems* also helps to link the points and show their relation to each other.

4. Now and then use a connecting sentence or paragraph to sum up what you have said and to pave the way for what you are going to say. Example:

(reference to preceding point)
↓
In addition to *a decrease in telegraphic traffic volume*, the new system would also require *a substantial reduction in clerical time*.
↑
(reference to following point)

5. Use connecting words and phrases to signal the relation between ideas.

Relationship	Connectives
ADDITION	*and, also, too,* *besides, furthermore, moreover,* *first, second, third,* *one, another,* *finally, in conclusion*
EXAMPLE	*for example, for instance,* *to illustrate*
CAUSE AND EFFECT	*because, since, thus,* *for this reason,* *therefore, consequently, accordingly*
COMPARISON	*similarly, in the same way,* *likewise, in a like manner*
CONTRAST	*but, however, in contrast,* *on the other hand,* *in spite of*

Paragraphs

1. For reading ease, try to avoid paragraphs of more than 120 words (about 12 lines). Exceptions may be made in highly technical discussions, where the separation of qualifying details may adversely affect the sense.

2. Vary paragraph length, when possible, to make the page look interesting. An occasional paragraph of only a few lines provides a welcome break in a series of long paragraphs. However, except in an enumeration or for emphasis, avoid a series of very short paragraphs; they suggest a lack of development.

3. Ideally, each paragraph should develop a single idea or several closely related ones. A good method of development is to start with a general statement, or topic sentence, and then expand the statement in an orderly fashion. For an example, see "Connecting Ideas," point 3, in this chapter.

Sentences

1. Keep sentences reasonably short. An average of twenty to twenty-two words per sentence would be considered fair for most subjects.

NOT: The four-part continuous "Advice of Charge" forms were placed in the Flexowriter while the punched tape containing the consolidated shortages of the previous day's differences was placed in the auxiliary tape reader, which mechanically sensed codes punched in the tape and automatically typed "Advice of Charge" forms without an operator. (One sentence of 51 words)

BUT: The four-part continuous "Advice of Charge" forms were placed in the Flexowriter. Then the punched tape, containing the consolidated shortages of the previous day's differences, was loaded in the auxiliary tape reader. The reader mechanically sensed codes punched in the tape and automatically typed "Advice of Charge" forms without operator attention. (Three sentences of 13, 20, and 19 words, respectively)

2. Rework sentences to simplify the structure.

NOT: The information collected from all branch offices as to actions taken to cope with short-run disruptions will be summarized and distributed in the form of a "Guidelines for Action."

BUT: The actions taken by all branch offices to cope with short-run disruptions will be summarized in the report, "Guidelines for Action."

NOT: Our report to the manufacturer will incorporate a request that they inform us of any product improvements they have made relevant to several serious shortcomings in their central dictation system.

BUT: We will ask the manufacturer what they have done to correct the serious shortcomings in their central dictation system.

3. Use similar grammatical patterns (parallel structure) to express parallel ideas in the simplest, most readable form.

NOT: The lack of training of the personnel, often too few to carry out their functions efficiently, coupled with an indifference toward enforcement policies, indicates the need for a reorganization of the office.

BUT: The office should be reorganized. The employees are *insufficient in number, improperly trained,* and *indifferent toward enforcement policies.* [Series of adjective phrases]

4. Express ideas concisely.

Wordy	*Concise*
The policy of the company . . .	The company's policy . . .
We are of the belief that . . .	We believe that . . .
The procedure is in the process of being reviewed.	The procedure is being reviewed.
The work that is of greatest interest to them . . .	The work of greatest interest to them . . .
During the course of their research in connection with the feasibility of . . .	During their research on the feasibility of . . .

Words

1. Use the simplest words consistent with precise expression and easy reading.

Compare		*Compare*	
aggregate	total	inadvertency	slip-up
approximately	about	modification	change
assistance	help	substantiation	proof
causative factor	cause	remuneration	pay
commence	begin	subsequently	later
converse	talk	termination	end
demonstrate	show	utilization	use

2. Use strong verbs. In each of the following examples, note how the meaning of the noun is transferred to the verb, with resulting force and conciseness.

Compare	
made a decision	decided
came to a conclusion	concluded
placed an order for	ordered
sending the enclosed	enclosing
be of service	serve
showed an increase	increased
for the conservation of	to conserve

3. Keep to a minimum expressions containing "it is," a common sign of official jargon.

NOT: It is the intention of the Budget and Expense Committee to . . .
BUT: The Budget and Expense Committee intends to . . .
NOT: It is realized that numeric codes can be supplied in all messages originating in the clearing banks.
BUT: Numeric codes can be supplied . . .

4. Avoid stilted language. If you wouldn't use an expression in speaking, don't use it in writing.

Stilted	*Natural*
per their request	at their request, *or*
	as they requested
as per company policy	in accordance with bank policy
the cost of said repairs	the cost of the repairs
in view of the above	in view of these facts
the subject study	this study

Also avoid *thereof, thereto, therefor, therefrom, therein, further to the above, under date of, same* (as in "have received *same*"), *deem, pursuant to, aforesaid.*

6.3 THE REPORT IN FINISHED FORM

Close attention to the final typing and assembly of the report returns extra dividends in the strong impression it makes. The instructions that follow apply chiefly to the long formal report. Moderate variations are always permissible, provided the results are clear and consistent.

General Considerations.   *Binding.*   A heavy paper cover protects the report and adds to its attractiveness. If your company does not have a standard report cover, use one that is commercially available. It should be heavy enough to support the weight of the report, but simple in construction and conservative in texture and color. It should call attention to the report, not to itself.

Margins.   The typed pages should have a margin of at least one inch at the top, right side, and bottom, and one-and-one-half inches at the left side to allow for the binding. Leave two inches at the top of the first page and of every other page that marks the beginning of an independently titled major section.

Headings.   The main title of a report or chapter is usually typed in all capitals and the subtitle is typed in capitals and lower case.

MARKETING INFORMATION SYSTEMS

A New Era in Marketing Research

Chapter headings and subheadings should follow a consistent pattern to show the reader the organization of the subject and the relative importance of each topic. Several systems are in use. Probably the most common system uses five degrees of headings as shown here.

FIRST-DEGREE HEADING

Second-Degree Heading

Third-Degree Heading

    Xxxxxxx xxxxxx xxx xxxxxxxxxx xxxxxxx xxx xxxxxxx xxx xxxx xxxx xx. Xxxx xxxx xxx xxxxxxxxxxxxx xx xxxxxxxxx.

    Fourth-Degree Heading.   Xxx xxxxxxx xxxxxxxxxx xxx xxxxxxxx xxx xxxx xxx xxx xxxxxxxxxx xx xxxxxx xxx.

        The Fifth-Degree Heading is set up, with additional indention, as the first few words of a subdivision of the fourth-degree topic.

Another system omits the second-degree heading and goes directly to the third-degree heading. Still another starts with the second-degree heading. Considerable latitude is permitted provided consistency is observed throughout.

Generally, two blank lines (triple spacing) are left before and after the first- and second-degree headings. Two blank lines are usually left before a third-degree heading within the copy. Because all other copy is double-spaced, the extra line alerts the reader to the start of another major topic.

Underscoring of headings is optional but should be used whenever necessary for emphasis or attention, but again consistency of use is required. When a long heading is broken into two or more lines, the underscoring is placed only under the last line to preserve the neat appearance. However, the underscoring extends to the limits of the longest line.

This Is a Second-Degree Heading
Underscored for Emphasis

This Is a Third-Degree Heading
Underscored for Emphasis

Xxxx xxxxxxxxxxx xxx xxxxxxxxxxx xxxx xxxxxxxxx xxxx xxxxxx xxxxxxxx xx xxxxx xx xxxxxxxx xxxxxx xxxx xxxxxxxxxxxx.

Spacing. Double-spacing produces the most readable pages. However, good reading qualities may also be achieved with single-spacing if lines are kept short and double-spacing is used to set off paragraphs and heads. Even when double-spacing is used in the report proper, single-spacing is conventional in these parts: the letter of transmittal, the abstract, the footnotes, the bibliography, and the appendixes.

Page Numbers. A report containing a number of preliminary features (like a title page, an introduction, and a table of contents) is best numbered in the following way.

1. Beginning with the title page, allot a number to each page, and type the number on each page except the title page.

2. Center the small roman numeral *ii* a half inch from the bottom edge of the page following the title page, and number consecutively in the same manner all the pages up to the first page of the report text.

3. Number with arabic numerals all pages of the text of the report continuing through the exhibits, the bibliography, and the index, if such parts are included. Center the number of the first page of every independently titled major division (for example, section, chapter, bibliography, index) a half inch from the bottom edge. Type all other page numbers a half inch from the top at the right margin.

Quotations. Set off from the text, by indention and single-spacing, a quotation of more than three or four lines unless it is closely interwoven with the narrative. An example is shown in Figure 9-1.

Footnotes. The customary place of footnotes is at the bottom of the page. (See "Footnotes and Bibliographies," Section 5.3.) In the draft of a report, however, a footnote may be placed immediately following the line in which the footnote reference appears. A solid rule above and below the footnote will mark it off from the text.

Exhibits. Follow these rules for positioning and labeling exhibits.

1. The position of reference tables and charts should serve the convenience of the reader.[1] The best place is usually as close as possible to the reference in the text. On the other hand, either custom or convenience may require that

---

[1] Spot tables and charts are always placed with the text. See Figure 5-11.

PROPOSED USE OF

REGIONAL BANK DEPOSITORIES

Dorothea R. Jordan

Administrative Assistant
Finance Department

Ace Chemical Company
Stamford, Connecticut

October 9, 19--

Figure 6-7 Title page.

HARBOR TRANSPORTATION CO.
785 Front Street
New York, New York 10005

July 8, 19--

Mr. George A. Fenton, President
Harbor Transportation Company
New York, New York

Dear Mr. Fenton:

At your request, contained in your memorandum of May 15, 19--,
I have made a survey of the office operations of our Routing
Department. My findings and recommendations are embodied in
the accompanying report.

During my study I directed my attention to these specific aims:

1. Improvement of service to customers.

2. Cost reductions wherever possible.

3. Adequate supervision and controls.

4. Improved personnel relations.

The adoption of my recommendations should do much to reduce
complaints and improve the overall efficiency of our operations.

I should like to thank Mr. Morton Fairbanks and Miss Arlene
Brody for their assistance in research and writing.

Should any questions arise concerning the content of this
report or the implementation of my recommendations, I will
be glad to discuss these matters with you.

Sincerely yours,

Egbert H. Grayson

Egbert H. Grayson
Vice President-Operations

Figure 6-8 A letter of transmittal.

they be placed at the end of the report. In some instances, special-purpose exhibits are put with the text, whereas general-purpose exhibits are put in an appendix. The difference is largely one of relevancy; the more pertinent the exhibit, the more reason for placing it close to the corresponding text.

2. "Close to the text" means immediately following the text or, if it cannot be fitted on the same page as the text, then at the top of the next page. Exhibits occupying a page without text should be positioned right after the reference page. If you want the exhibit page to face the text page, cut off the top left corner of the exhibit page at a right angle, so that the number of the reference page shows through. In this arrangement, the exhibit page is referred to by the same number as the reference page.

3. Other considerations aside, it is more efficient to put exhibits on separate pages from the text. The reasons are (a) it is often hard to estimate the exact amount of space that will be needed for an exhibit, and (b) an error in drawing an exhibit would otherwise require the retyping of the page.

4. If it is necessary to place a table or drawing sidewise to fit the page, the top should be at the bound edge.

5. If necessary, an extra-wide sheet may be used to accommodate an exhibit, provided the sheet is folded forward eight-and-a-half inches from the

```
                        TABLE OF CONTENTS

    Letter of Transmittal                                    ii

      I.  THE PROBLEM DEFINED                                 1

     II.  PRESENT METHODS OF HANDLING WRITTEN COMMUNICATIONS  3

    III.  DEFICIENCIES IN THE PRESENT SYSTEM                  6

     IV.  OPERATION OF THE MAGNETIC TAPE TYPEWRITER           8

      V.  INSTALLATION COST                                  10

     VI.  ANTICIPATED RESULTS                                11

    VII.  CONCLUSIONS AND RECOMMENDATIONS                    12

          EXHIBITS

              A.   ILLUSTRATION OF MAGNETIC TAPE TYPEWRITER  14

              B.   SAMPLES OF WORK PRODUCED                  15
```

Figure 6-9   Table of contents.

TABLE OF CONTENTS

Preface

I. Control Division Tabulating Department 1

Equipment Requirements 2
Clerical Requirements 2
Space Requirements and Miscellaneous Costs . . 3
Personnel Displacement Resulting from Adoption of Tabulating Procedures 4
Advantages of Tabulating Procedures 5

II. General Bookkeeping 6

Standardization of Proof Procedures 6
Preparation of Daily Statements 7
Treasury Tax and Loan and Federal Tax Accounts 9
Time Deposits 10
Account Classification 11

III. Accounts Payable 12

Application of Tabulating Procedures 12
Signing Expense Checks 14
Miscellaneous Recommendations 15

Figure 6-10 Table of contents in another style.

left edge. The sheet can be folded back again, accordian-style, to keep it free from the binding.

6. When only a few miscellaneous exhibits are included in a report, label them Exhibit 1, Exhibit 2, and so on; or Figure 1, Figure 2, and so on. Otherwise, use a different series for each class of exhibit; for example, Table 1, Table 2, and so on; Chart 1, Chart 2, and so on; Map 1, Map 2, and so on. Roman numerals may be used for a single series, preferably tables, but arabic numbers should be used for all others. The number and title of a table are always placed above it, but the numbers and titles of other exhibits may be placed above or below, as long as consistency is observed.

Assembling the Report. The following report features, with notes on their content and use, are discussed here in the order in which they are generally to be found.

Cover
Title page
Letter of transmittal
Preface
Table of contents
List of exhibits

Summary
Report body
Appendix
Bibliography
Index

PROPOSED USE OF REGIONAL BANK DEPOSITORIES

I. The Problem and Its Significance

Several months ago the Ace Chemical Company found that under the present method of handling cash receipts it was taking from three to five days to list checks, reconcile the cash report, prepare the checks for deposit, and deposit the checks to its account at the bank.

Immediate steps were taken to correct the situation, and the delay was cut somewhat. It is a fundamental fact that money from receivables cannot begin earning until it becomes a deposit in the bank. For that reason, float time and clerical time must be held to an absolute minimum.

The system now in use is the result of several refinements put into effect during the past few months, but it is essentially the same as it has been for the past 25 years. Lengthy delays have been eliminated, but money is still kept out of the banks one or two days longer than necessary. Since it will be difficult to achieve further speed in handling the present methods, an alternate method of handling should be examined.

The system recommended is a banking service known as the lock box or post office collection box plan. Though not a new concept, lock box operations have only in recent years come into their own and are today accepted as an excellent means of speeding up the collection of checks, providing additional working cash, and reducing clerical work in the preparation of deposits.

1

Figure 6-11 The introduction to a report.

Cover and Title Page (*Figure 6-7*). The cover gives at least the title of the report. It may also include the date, the name and title of the author, the name of the author's organization, and the client or company for whom the report was prepared. Some of the latter details, however, are usually reserved for the title page. The title is typed in capital letters a little above the center. The other details, in caps and lower-case letters, are arranged in one or two spots below it.

2

At the start, some firms designated a single bank, often in or near the city in which the home office was located. The single-bank method has two great disadvantages. First, little or no time was saved in the process, so that the speed-up in cash flow was negligible. About all that was gained was the convenience of having the bank receive and process the customer's remittances. Second, a single bank handling all the receivables found itself so burdened with volume that the company was required to carry heavy compensating balances, offsetting any tangible gains in availability of funds.

Experience has demonstrated that best results can be obtained from the lock box plan only when it is employed on a <u>regional</u> basis. Should Ace adopt a regional plan for handling deposits?

That is the problem toward which this report is directed. The purpose is to examine the present method of handling cash and explore the alternate method of using regional depositories. Specific recommendations will be offered.

Information for this report was obtained from several banks in each region, which were able to describe the plans they offered. Through questionnaires and personal visits, companies already using the plan gave the benefit of their experience with the system.

Figure 6-12   The introduction concluded.

10

department, and the local bank. The entire procedure
can be followed through an examination of the work
done by each group in turn.

Mail Department

All mail is picked up at intervals during the
day by Company trucks at the local post office. The
mail is brought to the mail room and sorted. Any envelope which is marked to the attention of an individual is sent to him unopened. All mail addressed
to the Company is opened and the contents are
scanned.

Any check contained in an envelope addressed to
the Company is removed and placed in an alphabetical
sorting bin and set up in strict alphabetical order.
Any check reaching an individual is sent back to the
mail room to be recorded on the cash report.

After the checks have been set up, they are
then listed by typewriter on a cash report showing
the date of check, company name, detail, if any, and
amount of check (Figure 2). An adding machine tape
is run on both the checks and the listing to verify
the total. Copies of the cash report are given to
the accounting department, accounts receivable, the
cashier, and credit departments. The cashier is
given all the checks with his copy of the report.

Cashier

On receipt of the cash report and accompanying
checks, the cashier must look at each check for the
following:

1. Is the check postdated?
2. Who is the payee?
3. Is the check signed?
4. Do the written and figure amounts agree?

The amount of each check is then compared against

Figure 6-13 A report page showing use of single spacing with side heads.

```
     Subject:   Computer Rental Charges
                Your memorandum of July 8
                      * * *



In a conversation last week you asked me to look in-
to the need for an additional typist to assist Mr.
Greer with his year-end report.
                      * * *



At the request of the Control Division, I have con-
ducted a study on the General Ledger area. The ob-
jectives of the study were twofold:

      1.  To find ways of speeding the filing of cur-
          rent material.
      2.  To devise an improved system for putting
          dated file material into storage.
                      * * *



Yesterday I received a visit from Mr. William Hopper,
the local representative of the 3M Company. He made
some suggestions for handling our copying needs, and
they were so interesting I would like to pass them
on to you.
```

Figure 6-14 Examples of memorandum beginnings.

Letter of Transmittal. The letter of transmittal, if bound into the report, should be placed right after the title page. It is usually typewritten on the company's letterhead with full mechanical treatment, including date, inside address, and signature. The contents of the letter of transmittal may include:

1. Notice of submission of report
2. Authorization for report
3. Purpose and scope of report
4. Sources of information
5. Acknowledgment of help received from others
6. Offer of further assistance

Figure 6-8 shows a sample letter of transmittal.

240

Preface.   A preface may be used as an alternative to the letter of transmittal. It may also be used when the letter of transmittal is merely a notice of submission.

Table of Contents (Figures 6-9 and 6-10).   A table of contents is helpful in a report consisting of numerous sections and subsections. The table should list all the features of the report, including the main heads and, optionally, the second-degree heads.

List of Exhibits (Figure 6-9).   Reference tables, charts, and other illustrations should be listed immediately after the table of contents, either on the same page or on the next page.

Summary.   Paralleling the abstract in scientific and technical reports, a summary of a business report is helpful when the report is long or complex. A common substitute for a summary of the whole report is the "Summary of Findings" or "Summary of Conclusions and Recommendations" at the beginning of the report body.

Report Body (Figures 6-11, 6-12, and 6-13).   Here is the main part of the report, complete with introduction, discussion, and conclusions and recommendations.

Appendix.   The appendix (or appendixes) should include any documents, details, summary tables, illustrations, or other materials not included with the text. Each item should be clearly identified and a reference to it should be made somewhere in the report discussion.

Bibliography.   The bibliography is more useful in academic papers than in business reports, but if a number of books and articles have been consulted, they should be listed at the end of the report. (See "Footnotes and Bibliographies," Section 5.3.)

Index.   The index is an alphabetical list, with page references, of all the topics covered in the report. It is usually reserved for published reports of some length and complexity. Subtopics in the index are listed alphabetically under the main headings, and cross-references are frequent.

6.4   MEMORANDUMS

A memorandum is a short report intended usually for readers within the organization. It satisfies a number of important needs.

1. It permits continuing communication between subordinates and their superiors.

2. It provides a medium for communication between departments and between individuals on similar levels of authority.

3. It records data for permanent reference, and guides and controls staff activities.

4. It records temporarily information to be included in a broader study and report.

Subjects Treated.   Memorandums are versatile. Some of the uses to which they can be put include:

Report of a meeting or conference
Report of a visit
Credit report
Instructions
Policy statement
Official procedure
Change in policy or procedure
Notice or announcement
Inquiry and follow-up
Analysis of a job or procedure
Analysis of human or machine performance
Analysis of organizational structure
Results of a test or questionnaire
Suggestion
Proposal
Recommendation

Mechanical Form.   The format of memorandums is treated in "Letter Form and Style," Section 3.1. These additional points are relevant.

1. The readability of a memorandum may be improved by (a) wide margins, (b) paragraphs of varied length, (c) occasional lists and enumerations, and (d) in a long memorandum, centered or side heads to mark the major divisions of the content.

2. Tables and other exhibits that are part of a memorandum may be positioned, labeled, and numbered in the same way as if they were part of a long-form report. (See "The Report in Finished Form," Section 6.3.'

3. The memorandum has no cover; its pages are stapled in the upper left corner.

Organization of Data.   A memorandum is organized in the same way as a longer report (see "Planning the Report," Section 6.1). It has an introduction, a body, and, more often than not, a conclusion.

Introduction.   The subject line in the heading may provide all the introduction that is necessary. If not, the opening lines should include such data as (1) the purpose of the memorandum, (2) the authorization for the memorandum, and (3) the background history or data. Figure 6-14 shows several ways of handling the introduction. If no introduction is necessary, the memorandum begins with the discussion or body of the report.

Body.   The body paragraphs give the writer's findings. Even a short memorandum requires an orderly arrangement of the data in order to prevent wordiness and confusion. For tight organization, try these simplified techniques (see also "Planning the Report," Section 6.1).

1. Arrange discussion in chronological order, for example:

(a) History   (Past)
(b) Current status   (Present)
(c) Recommendation
(d) Anticipated results   (Future)

Please let me know if there is any further information you need.
                          ✳✳✳

I'd appreciate your following this practice in the
future.
                          ✳✳✳

My investigation showed a definite lapse in our service to the Farmhill district agencies. I suggest
this matter be discussed at our next monthly meeting.
                          ✳✳✳

From the evidence it would appear that a few simple
changes in procedure would help us meet our publication schedule without difficulty:

    1.   Advance the initial planning of the catalog
         to August 1 of each year.
    2.   Use a second printer for the color insert
         and send the printed inserts to the primary
         printer for binding into the catalog.
    3.   Employ a mailing house for addressing, wrap-
         ping, and mailing.

I'll be glad to discuss these proposals with you any
time.

Figure 6-15   Examples of memorandum endings.

STILTED (BAD)
Pursuant to your memorandum re above, notice has been taken of the faulty carbon ribbons and said supplies will be returned forthwith to the stationer. Upon due receipt of a satisfactory explanation and replacement of same, the undersigned will contact you and advise.

INFORMAL (BETTER)
I am returning to the stationer the faulty carbon ribbons you mentioned in your memorandum of October 8, and I am asking for an explanation and satisfactory replacement. I'll let you know the results.

FORMAL (ACCEPTABLE)
According to the Manual of Procedures governing the operation of the cafeteria, bids on meat and poultry are to be obtained on a quarterly basis.

During the recent three-months' absence of the unit head, his duties were taken over by the chief of the Services Division. The chief, on his own authority, asked for bids on a weekly basis. When the cook prepared the weekly menu to determine the quantities needed, she submitted the list to the chief. He then telephoned three vendors and received quotations on the items. This method resulted in a saving of $1,775 over food costs for the same three-month period (January-March) last year.

In view of the indicated savings, it is recommended that the Service Division continue the practice of obtaining bids on meat and poultry on a weekly, rather than quarterly, basis.

Figure 6-16   Memorandums written in different styles.

2. Work for a simple balance of elements. For example:

(a) Problem—Solution
(b) Cause—Effect
(c) Fault—Remedy
(d) Need—Fulfillment
(e) Question—Answer
(f) Plan A—Plan B
(g) Old Way—New Way

3. Treat parallel points in parallel fashion, as in this list.

A good system for organizing the company's publication needs should have a threefold objective:
   A. Service to the company
   B. Economy of production
   C. Coordination among designer, user, and producer

Conclusion.   Whether or not there is a formal conclusion, the memorandum should have some significance that is expressed or implied.

1. The information may speak for itself and require no conclusion.

2. The conclusion (or recommendation) may have been stated at the beginning of the report so that restatement at the end is unnecessary.

3. Most likely, however, the memorandum will end with some conclusive statement as (a) a bid for cooperation, (b) an assurance of action, (c) a summary of the main points, or (d) a recommendation. Some examples appear in Figure 6-15.

Language.   Ordinarily, the memorandum uses informal or conversational language with normal contractions (*I'll, can't, won't*) and the personal pronouns *I* and *you*. In no circumstances, though, is it considered good form to use the stilted and outworn expressions that have already been so discredited in letter writing. The best style is always a natural one, though it may be pitched on a lower or higher level of dignity depending on the circumstances (Figure 6-16).

See also "Writing the Report," Section 6.2.

7

Publicity and Editorial Work

Office duties often entail a variety of editorial tasks. These may include editing manuscript, preparing copy for the printer, reading proof, and—on occasion—writing press releases and other material for publication. Work of this kind requires a good command of English and some special reserves of creativity, resourcefulness, and mental discipline. This chapter is designed to give office editors the basic information they need to carry on their work with confidence and proficiency.

CONTENTS

7.1 THE PRESS RELEASE

A press release is information sent to the press in the hope that it will be published as news. The "press" may be the company's own newspaper or magazine, local daily or weekly newspapers, trade or professional publications, or the official organs of social and fraternal organizations. Many publications look to press releases for much of their news and publish them as received or with some editing to conform to their space and style requirements. For the source, the press release means valuable free publicity and often the difference between success and failure when a meeting or other event is announced.

Press releases for use outside the organization should always be cleared by the organization's public relations department or by the official in charge. This procedure permits control over the number, content, and timing of stories and ensures conformance with company policies. The control of stories sent to the editors of company publications usually rests with the individual departments in which the news originates. In any case, the chances of acceptance are increased when the story is prepared in a form suitable for publication.

Subjects of Press Releases. In a dynamic organization, there is so much activity that an alert reporter has more trouble in choosing his stories than in finding them. Besides the news of sales, earnings, appointments, and organizational changes that show up in the company's official records, additional news is made all the time in the peripheral activities of employees and of all who sell and use the company's products. The following topics will only suggest the range.

Election of officers
New appointments
Promotions
Transfer of personnel
Organizational changes
Property and plant improvements
Mergers and acquisitions
New plants, stores, and offices
Ground-breaking and cornerstone-laying ceremonies
New lines, products, and services
Reports on sales, earnings, and dividends
Government contracts
New stock issues
Unusual product displays and sales stories
Unusual uses of the company's products and services
Prominent visitors
Honors, awards, and prizes
Contests
Company philanthropies
Charity and community work by employees
Professional and educational attainments of employees
Speeches and reports

Mechanical Form (Figure 7-1). The form of the press release should serve the convenience of news editors.

1. Use white paper, size $8\frac{1}{2}$ by 11 inches, with a heading consisting of the name, address, and telephone number of the news source. Preferably include the name and telephone number of the individual to be called if more information is wanted. There is no advantage in using the regular company letterhead.

2. Type the release directly on the sheet or mimeograph it, but do not send carbons.

3. Double- or triple-space copy, with margins of at least an inch. The editor can be expected to do a lot of revising and cutting.

4. Type the release date under the heading in such form as "For Immediate Release," "For Release Wednesday, April 24," or "For Release at Will." A story sent to out-of-town newspapers usually carries a dateline at the beginning of the first paragraph, for example, "Athens, Ohio, March 16." The

AMERICAN FAMILY INSTITUTE
5200 Sunset Boulevard
Los Angeles, California 90027

                              FOR IMMEDIATE RELEASE
For further information:
                              September 7, 19--
  Mrs. Leslie M. Peters
  (213) 461-2345

                    NEW HOMEMAKING COURSE

     "Less Work, More Fun in Homemaking" is the

title of a five-week series to be presented each

Tuesday afternoon from 1:30 to 3:00, beginning Sep-

tember 18, at the American Family Institute, 5200

Sunset Boulevard, Los Angeles. Designed for the

young wife and mother who is beset by dishes, dia-

pers, and dirt, the course will have as its motto,

"Run your house; don't let your house run you."

     The informal lectures and discussions will

deal with such problems as fatigue, the common

enemy of homemakers, and how to prevent it; making

a work schedule that is flexible yet efficient; and

teaching children to enjoy helping around the house.

     Reservations for the course may be made by

writing or telephoning the Institute, 461-2345.

                    # # # # #
          Figure 7-1   Form of the press release.

place named is that of the story source, and the date is the anticipated date of release, not the date of mailing.

5. Number at the top all pages after the first. At the bottom of all pages except the last write the word *more* to indicate that there is additional copy. Mark the end of the story by a series of *x*'s or number signs (# # #) several spaces below the last line. Clip or staple pages together in the upper left-hand corner.

Writing the Release.   A press release is written in the same style as a story in a good newspaper. It presents the facts in an interesting way, but without expressing the writer's opinions or judgments. The news values are achieved by giving the reader the answers to the questions *Who? What? Where? When?* and *Why?* or *How?* For example:

WHO is the central participant in the event?
WHO is making the announcement?
WHO is the authority for the statement?

WHAT is the title or other identification of the persons named?
WHAT happened (or will happen)?
WHAT are the details?
WHAT is the significance of the event?

WHERE did (or will) the event take place?
WHERE does the central participant live or work?
WHERE does the announcement originate?

WHEN did (or will) the event take place?
WHEN was the announcement of the event made?

WHY is the event taking place—what are the reasons or causes?

HOW will the event or proposal be accomplished?

The Lead.   The nub of the story is stated in the headline, if one is supplied, and in the *lead,* or first sentence or two.

Richmond, Va.—Allen G. McCabe, Jr., office manager and assistant treasurer, Crawford Manufacturing Co., has been elected president of the Richmond Chapter of the Administrative Management Society. He succeeds J. W. Montgomery, assistant controller, Southern States Cooperative, Inc.

The stories an editor is most likely to print are those specifically adapted to the publication and its readers. Although the following story originated in Boston, the lead capitalizes on the home address of the subject in order to appeal to East Orange residents.

John S. Talbert of 200 Grove Street, East Orange, an associate of the David Marks, Jr., agency in New York City of the New England Life Insurance Company, has qualified for the company's Hall of Fame.

The honor is awarded to the company's field representatives who, in the course of giving outstanding service to their clients, have placed with New England Life at least one million dollars' worth of life insurance protection on their policyholders during the preceding calendar year.

Portraits of those honored are displayed in a special hall at the company's home office in Boston.

In sending this story to the subject's college alumni newspaper, the writer added the following sentence to the first paragraph.

Mr. Talbert is a graduate of New York University, Class of '76.

The following brief story ran in the monthly house organ of the subject's company. The interest for Mr. Berger's co-workers is self-evident.

PROTESTANT COUNCIL HONORS BERGER

Philip H. Berger, executive vice president, was honored at a testimonial luncheon held in the Regency Hotel by the Factors and Finance Division of the Protestant Council of New York.

Additional Details. When paragraphs are added, it is good practice to put the most important details first and to make each paragraph self-contained. This permits an editor to cut off a story at the end of any paragraph without serious loss.

Details suitable for the expansion of a story include the following.

1. Biographical details.

Mr. Astor is with the Metropolitan Division and supervises the development and promotion of retail banking and special corporate services.

He is a 1976 graduate of the Stonier Graduate School of Banking at Rutgers University and has been with the bank since 1972.

2. Historical details.

Put together six years ago as an advertising promotion for the April auto loan campaign, the "sponge on wheels" has led to a number of awards. These include the Town Crier Award for the best ad by a commercial bank and trust company and the SCB Award for the best magazine ad by a commercial bank.

3. Description.

The new facility has a total of 7,500 square feet as opposed to the old quarter's 5,700 square feet. The building is constructed of poured concrete, with exposed concrete as part of the interior design.

4. Quotation.

Lawrence Ross, sales training coordinator, emphasizes that the primary objective of the program is fact finding, but he notes that collateral advantages add to the success of the program.

"Naturally," he says, "during the week that a management trainee is assigned to the program, he absorbs an invaluable amount of on-the-job training in the highly developed skill of customer contact. He can thus broaden his knowledge of business and businessmen in the greater Los Angeles area."

Special Suggestions. Press releases that do not meet the requirements of the publications they are intended for are a waste of time and may even antagonize the editors. Follow these rules to avoid some common mistakes.

1. Study the publication carefully to discover what kinds of material are suitable for it.

2. Check every statement and every name and date for correctness. The editor must be able to rely on your accuracy.

3. Send out the story in time for publication on the release date. If possible, let newspapers have it several days in advance, but in no case later than several hours before press time. Magazines need more time—sometimes several weeks—to plan their editorial content.

4. When such words as *today, tomorrow,* or *next Wednesday* appear in the story, prevent confusion by putting the actual date in parentheses immediately after them. For example: "The annual meeting of the D. M. Kirby Corporation will be held tomorrow (March 15) at its national headquarters, 60 Wall Street, New York."

5. Adapt your language to the reader. Use the simplest language for most stories, but be sure to write to technical and professional people on their own level.

6. Avoid puffery. Let the facts speak for themselves.

7. See that all photographs carry suitable captions. Typewrite each caption on a separate sheet of paper; then tape or paste the top to the back of the photograph so that the caption can be read at the bottom when the photograph is held face up. Never write on the back of the photograph.

7.2 EDITING

An editor is a person who reviews and revises or corrects reports, speeches, articles, and other manuscripts prepared by others. One reason an editor is needed is that, the office writer, although an expert in a particular subject area, often lacks proficiency in written expression. Another reason is that even with a mastery of written expression, the writer is usually too pressed for time to be able to give the writing the careful review it requires. A third reason is that with many people in an organization turning out manuscripts of different sorts, only an editor can ensure that uniform standards and a consistent style will be maintained.

The Editor's Functions. A good editor is a genuine friend of the author, essentially, performing two functions.

1. Examines the manuscript for content and organization, and either suggests changes to the author or makes the changes contingent on the author's approval.

2. Copy-edits the manuscript to ensure consistency in style and correctness in names, facts, punctuation, grammar, and the like.

Some editors perform one function or the other; some perform both. In either case, an important asset for the editor is tact. Assuming that you have been chosen for the role of editor, you should not try to impose your ideas on the author. A better approach is to make suggestions of such a kind and in such a manner that the author will recognize the improvement and will be grateful for the assistance offered. Of course many, if not most, of the errors you find will be so obvious that clearance with the author is not necessary; you are expected to find them and the author will be disappointed if you do not.

Editing for Content and Structure.   You should not attempt to make suggestions about the content of a manuscript unless you have some familiarity with the subject area and the audience. If you feel insecure in these matters, you may consult with the author to resolve any doubts you may have or, with the author's permission, seek the opinion and advice of some other person with the necessary qualifications. Taking the latter course is no reflection on the editor, who is not expected to be an expert in every field.

JUDGING A MANUSCRIPT

The Beginning
> Does it spark the reader's interest?
> Does it adequately suggest the content of the paper?
> Does it lead quickly to the main point?

The Body
> Is the organization logical and consistent?
> Is the relation between the parts readily apparent?
> Is the text clear and convincing?
> Is enough use made of detail, example, comparison, and the like?
> Can anything be left out, with resultant improvement?
> Is interest maintained throughout?

The End
> By summary or otherwise, does the end pull together the whole piece?
> Is the end conclusive?
> Is the conclusion warranted by the evidence presented in the body?

General
> Is the title reasonably short, and does it accurately describe the tone and content of the text?
> Is reasonable use made of tables, charts, and other illustrations to support and clarify the text?
> Where appropriate, has the author made adequate use of headings and enumerations to add to the attractiveness of the text and make reading easy?

Figure 7-2   An editor's guide.

Questions you should be able to answer (or find the answers to) with respect to the content of any manuscript are these.

Does the author have a worthy subject?
Is the author competent to write on the subject?
Is the paper factually correct?
Is the subject matter up-to-date?
Is the treatment of the subject on a level suited to the reader?

Even without a great deal of expertise in a technical field, you should be able to judge the structure of a paper and make suggestions for improvement. An editor's guide to the organization of a manuscript—which may be equally useful to the writer—will be found in Figure 7-2. (See also "Report Preparation," Chapter 6.)

Copy Editing.   In most instances your editing chores will probably be confined to copy editing. In this task, you will correct errors and inconsistencies, but you will not attempt to evaluate the content or organization of the material.

Reference Tools.   You should have a good dictionary (preferably unabridged), a handbook of English, and a thesaurus. Some specific titles are suggested in Figure 7-3. If you are working in a specialized area (like accounting or insurance), you should also have a handbook on the subject, if one is available, and a dictionary or glossary of the technical terms used. (See the book lists in "Information Sources," Section 5.2, and the "Dictionary of Business Terms," Chapter 16.) Other reference materials you should have are instructions on style published by your own company for the guidance

---

AN EDITOR'S REFERENCE SHELF

Bartlett, John. *Familiar Quotations.* Boston: Little, Brown & Co.
The Doubleday Roget's Thesaurus in Dictionary Form.   New York: Doubleday & Co.
Fowler, H. W. *A Dictionary of Modern English Usage.*   Revised by Sir Ernest Gowers. New York: Oxford University Press.
GPO Style Manual. Washington, D.C.: U.S. Government Printing Office.
Manual of Style. Chicago: University of Chicago Press.
Perrin, Porter G., and others.   *Writer's Guide and Index to English.* Chicago: Scott, Foresman & Co.
Random House Dictionary of the English Language (Unabridged).   New York: Random House.
Webster's New Dictionary of Synonyms.   Springfield, Mass.: G. & C. Merriam Co.

Figure 7-3   Standard reference works for the copy editor.

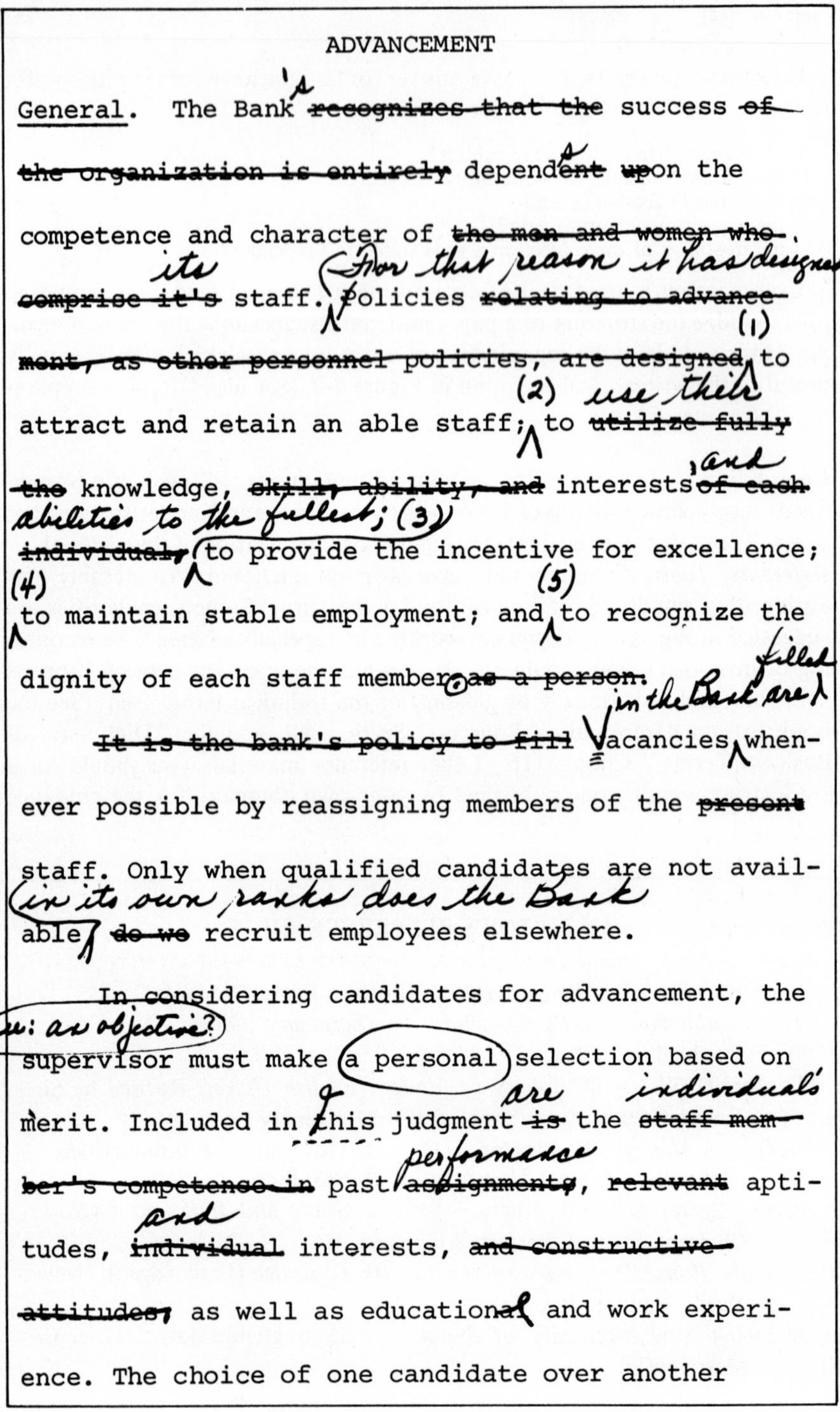

General. The Bank*'s* ~~recognizes that the~~ success ~~of the organization is entirely~~ dependent ~~up~~on the competence and character of ~~the men and women who~~ *its* ~~comprise it's~~ staff. *(For that reason it has designed)* Policies ~~relating to advancement, as other personnel~~ policies, are designed *(1)* to attract and retain an able staff; *(2)* to ~~utilize fully the~~ *use their* knowledge, ~~skill, ability, and~~ interests ~~of each~~ *, and abilities to the fullest; (3)* ~~individual,~~ to provide the incentive for excellence; *(4)* to maintain stable employment; and *(5)* to recognize the dignity of each staff member ~~as a person.~~

~~It is the bank's policy to fill~~ *filled* Vacancies *in the Bank are* whenever possible by reassigning members of the ~~present~~ staff. Only when qualified candidates are not available *in its own ranks does the Bank* ~~do we~~ recruit employees elsewhere.

In considering candidates for advancement, the

are: an objective?

supervisor must make (a personal) selection based on merit. Included in this judgment ~~is~~ *are* the ~~staff member's competence in~~ *individual's performance* past ~~assignments,~~ ~~relevant~~ aptitudes, ~~individual~~ *and* interests, ~~and constructive attitudes,~~ as well as educational and work experience. The choice of one candidate over another

Figure 7-4 Example of an edited manuscript.

of its writers, secretaries, or typists. Unless there are good reasons for doing otherwise, you should adhere to the rules prescribed in those instructions.

Making Corrections. Working with a lead pencil, rather than a pen, gives you the opportunity to change your mind without messing up the manuscript. You should indicate small corrections by drawing a line through a word or punctuation mark and inserting the replacement between the lines, using a caret (∧) to show where the insertion belongs. If more room is needed, you may use the top or bottom margins. Queries for the author should be put in the side margins next to the copy to which they apply, and they should be circled to prevent confusion with actual corrections. If changes are heavy, retype pages or parts of pages to make the amended version.

Editing Procedure. The following steps are recommended.

1. Correct typographical errors.

2. Correct dates, proper names, and obvious errors in fact. If you think the author has to be persuaded, note the source of your information in the margin.

3. Correct errors in spelling, punctuation, grammar, and word usage. If a usage is optional, be guided first by the need for clarity, then by consistency with your standards. If there is some question, give the author the benefit of the doubt.

4. Take out or rearrange words to achieve conciseness and relieve awkwardness of expression, but be sure you preserve the sense and general tone of the manuscript. If in doubt, query the author on the proposed change.

5. Keep an alphabetical list of stylistic peculiarities. For example, *May 23rd* (as opposed to *May 23*), *advisor* (as opposed to *adviser*), *COD* (as opposed to *C.O.D.*). When you come across a question relating to these forms later in the manuscript, you will be able to follow the style you chose earlier. Otherwise, disturbing inconsistencies will result.

6. Question, in the margin, apparent inconsistencies in reasoning, seeming omissions, and dubious assertions. Unilaterally changing the author's statements can lead you into serious error.

An example of an edited manuscript is shown in Figure 7-4.

7.3 PREPARING COPY FOR THE PRINTER

Manuscripts of reports, speeches, and other documents need special attention if they are to be sent to a commercial printer for typesetting. Similar attention must be given to any manuscript prepared for publication in a book or magazine. The principal objective is to ensure accuracy, but another aim is to obtain a printed appearance that accords with the wishes of the author and the editor.

It is assumed that the printer has some model to follow or that he or a designer has planned the printed product with regard to form, paper, page

by setting forth the responsibilities and authori-

ties delegated to particular positions, the rela-

tionships that exist among positions, and the ac-

countabilities of the incumbent managers.[1]

---

[1]For a fuller discussion see "What's in a Posi-

tion Guide?" <u>Management Record</u>, September 1980.

If there is confusion about accountability, a

manager may fulfill only part of his responsibilities

under the impression that other parts of the job are

in another bailiwick. He may . . .

Figure 7-5 Placement of footnote in printer's copy.

size, and typographical treatment. The editor's attention may then be confined to the manuscript itself. For best results, the following suggestions should be followed.

1. See that the copy is typed on one side of plain white 8½ by 11 inch paper, heavy and strong enough to withstand rough treatment.

2. Leave at least a one-inch margin all around, and preferably an inch and a half at the left.

This is set in Roman.

This is set in italic.

THIS IS SET IN ALL CAPS.

This Is Set in Caps and Lower Case.

THIS IS SET IN CAPS AND SMALL CAPS.

This is set in boldface.

Figure 7-6 Type styles.

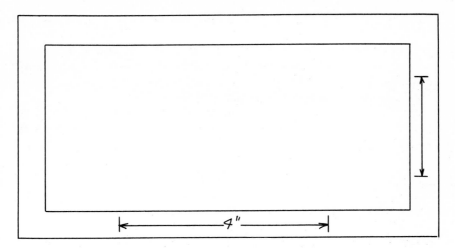

(A) Cropping

Extraneous background on photographs and drawings may be eliminated by cropping. Draw arrows in margin to show what portions are to be retained. Mark size desired along one dimension and the other dimension will be reduced in proportion.

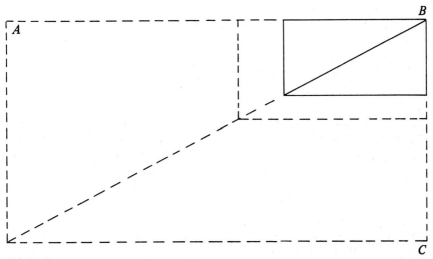

(B) Scaling

Pictures always reduce or enlarge along their diagonal. To scale a picture to fit a given space, draw a rectangle the size of the space to be filled; then draw a diagonal line from the upper right corner to the lower left corner and extending for some distance beyond. Any rectangle formed by angle *ABC* along the diagonal will have the same proportions. If it is desired to retain the proportion of the original drawing or photograph, the size of the reduction or enlargement may be ascertained in the same way.

Figure 7-7 Instructions for cropping and scaling pictures.

3. If several persons type the manuscript, see that the same style and size of type are used throughout; otherwise it is difficult to estimate the number of words—a matter of some importance to the typesetter.

4. Use double-spacing throughout.

(a) If the copy includes a long quotation that is to be set off from the text by indentation or a smaller type face, draw a pencil line down the left-hand margin for the entire length of the quotation. This will call the printer's attention to it.

(b) Start a footnote directly following the line in which the reference to it appears; double-space the footnote and separate it from the text by a rule above and below the note (Figure 7-5). Footnotes in manuscripts for books and other printed matter are numbered with superscripts and typed at the bottom of the text page. It is helpful to the editor and the printer if these are double-spaced. See also Section 5.3, "Footnotes and Bibliographies."

5. Use upper and lower case (capitals and small letters) throughout the manuscript, including titles and heads. That leaves the editor or designer free to style the copy in any way desired. If your mind is made up, however, you may use the standard printers' marks to specify boldface, italics, all caps, caps and small caps (Figure 7-6).

6. Underline on the typewriter all words in the text that should be set in italics (see "Underlining," Section 10.4).

7. If the copy includes printed matter from other sources, paste the copy neatly on the regular manuscript paper with rubber cement. (Typing the copy takes time, requires proofreading, and involves the danger of error.) If both sides of a printed page are to be used, obtain two copies of the original or make a photographic copy of the second side.

8. Number all pages consecutively in the upper right-hand corner. If pages must later be inserted, mark them with the number of the preceding page and the letters *A, B, C,* and so on. Thus, if you insert two pages after page 12, you will mark them *12A* and *12B*. Also, at the bottom of page 12 write "Pages 12A and 12B follow"; at the bottom of page 12B write, "Page 13 follows." Handwriting in dark pencil or ink will make these notations stand out.

9. If photographs or drawings are to be reduced in size, mark the desired size in the margin. If a photograph is to be *cropped,* that is, if part of the sides or top or bottom is to be cut off, draw arrows in the margin to show the part you want omitted (Figure 7-7).

10. Do not write on the back of a photograph. Type the caption on a separate slip of paper and paste it to the back of the photograph so that it hangs from the bottom edge.

7.4 PROOFREADING

Except when typewritten copy is photographed directly for reproduction, the printer will set the copy and submit proofs for correction before the work is put on the press.

Two kinds of proofs are offered: galley proofs, which are long sheets containing about three pages of material, and page proofs, which include the corrections made in the galleys and represent the final submission before printing. Unless you ask for more, the printer will submit two sets of both galleys and page proofs. One set will contain queries. These are marginal notations that may question a word or spelling or alert the proofreader to the possibility that some copy has been omitted. The queried set should be returned, corrected, to the printer. The other set, with all the corrections carefully copied, should be kept for reference. The original manuscript always accompanies the galley proofs. It should be used for checking the proof and returned to the printer with the corrected galleys, but no marks should ever be added to it.

Proofreader's Marks

1. Use a sharp black pencil, but one that will not smudge. Ink or crayon is also acceptable if the color is different from that used in the printer's queries. Pencil corrections can of course be changed more easily.

2. Answer every query by (a) striking out the query if it does not apply and writing "O.K. as set"; (b) striking out only the question mark if the printer's correction is valid; or (c) striking out the query and writing in the copy correction.

3. Draw a line through the incorrect material, insert a caret, and use other standard proofreading marks to call attention to an error; then write the correction in the nearer margin. Do not squeeze corrections between the lines, as you do in correcting manuscript (Figures 7-8 and 7-9).

4. If only a letter requires correction, write only the letter, not the whole word in the margin; but if you think the correction may be misunderstood, write the whole word as well, and circle it.

5. When a line contains more than one error, place corrections in the margin in the same order as they occur in the line, and separate them by a slant (/).

Galley Proofs

1. Read galley proofs for content, and then again for typographical errors. The first reading will ensure against inadvertent omissions, misplacement of material, and perpetuation of substantive errors in the original copy. The second reading will uncover errors in spelling, punctuation, numbers, spacing, type style, and so on.

2. Make only necessary changes. Because the pages have not yet been made up when the galleys are submitted, there is some leeway permitted in changing copy and making additions to the original. The author and the proofreader should be aware, however, that these changes may be costly, and that it is always preferable to make changes before the copy goes to the printer. Changes in format also require expensive resetting of copy. A way to

Mark	Explanation	Sample of Marked Proof	Corrected Proof
Punctuation Marks			
˅	Apostrophe	The author˅s work.	The author's work.
[/]	Brackets	He∧the author]wrote.	He [the author] wrote.
: /	Colon	The author wrote∧	The author wrote:
∧	Comma	The author wrote∧	The author wrote,
¦—¦	Dash	The author∧John Smith.	The author—John Smith.
· · · /	Ellipsis	The author∧wrote.	The author . . . wrote.
! /	Exclamation point	He has style∧	He has style!
= /	Hyphen	The author∧editor relationship.	The author-editor relationship.
˄	Inferior letter or figure (subscript)	CO∧	CO_2
(/)	Parentheses	The author∧John Smith∧ wrote.	The author (John Smith) wrote.
⊙	Period	The author wrote∧	The author wrote.
? /	Question mark	Is he the author∧	Is he the author?
ˇˇ ˅˅	Quotation marks	He wrote˅Fantasy in F.˅	He wrote "Fantasy in F."
; /	Semicolon	He wrote∧he spoke.	He wrote; he spoke.
˅	Superior letter or figure (superscript)	The author∧wrote.	The author[1] wrote.
Type Style			
ital	Set in italic	The author wrote.	The *author* wrote.
rom	Change from italic to roman	The *author* wrote.	The author wrote.
l.c.	Set in lower case	The Author wrote.	The author wrote.
caps	Set in capitals	the author wrote.	The author wrote.
c. & l.c.	Set in capitals and lower case	THE AUTHOR SPEAKS	The Author Speaks.
s.c.	Set in small caps	The author wrote.	THE AUTHOR wrote.
c. & s.c.	Set in caps and small caps	The author speaks.	THE AUTHOR SPEAKS.
b.f.	Set in boldface	The author wrote.	The **author** wrote.
l.f.	Set in lightface (not boldface)	The **author** wrote.	The author wrote.

Meaning	Mark	Example
Delete; take out	ℓ	The author wrote. — The author wrote.
Close up; no space	( )	The aut hor wrote. — The author wrote.
Delete and close up	⊖	The author wrote. — The author wrote.
Insert	∧	The auth wrote. — The author wrote.
Turn inverted letter	⊙	The author wrote. — The author wrote.
Let it stand; change made was wrong	stet	The author wrote. — The author wrote.
Spell out	sp	23¢ — 23 cents
Transpose	tr	The wrote author — The author wrote.
Start new paragraph	¶	in this manner. The author — in this manner. The author wrote.
No paragraph; run in	No ¶	manner. The author wrote. — manner. The author wrote.
Push down unwanted type slug	⌄	The author wrote. — The author wrote.
Make a space	#	The authorwrote. — The author wrote.
Equalize space	eq#	The author wrote. — The author wrote.
Broken letter	⊗	The author wrote. — The author wrote.
Wrong font (type style)	w.f.	The author wrote. — The author wrote.
Indent one em	□	The author wrote. — The author wrote.
Center copy on line	Center	The Author Speaks — The Author Speaks
Raise the word or letter	⌐ ¬	The author wrote. — The author wrote.
Lower the word or letter	⌐ ¬	The author wrote. — The author wrote.
Bring matter to the right	⌐	The author wrote. — The author wrote.
Bring matter to the left	⌐	in this manner. The author wrote. — in this manner. The author wrote.
Align type	=	The author wrote. — The author wrote.
Straighten line	=	The author wrote. — The author wrote.

Figure 7-8 Proofreader's marks.

PRODUCTION ═══════════════════ *flush right*
c. + l.c.

no ¶/s.c. ⌐ From the day the manuscript is turned over to the production division to the day the finished book is published, usually nine to twelve months will elapse. In the first few weeks of
this time, a final check is made on the length of the manuscript and the cost of production, including composition, printing and binding of the text and the engraving of the illustrations. At the same time, sample pages, which show the typography and format chosen for the book by the designer, are prepared.

b.f. Sample Pages

Indent 1 em ☐ The material for sample pages is carefully chosen to show
y all typographical examples to appear in a book: sections of the body of the text, sections of extract material, footnotes, bibliography, mathematical, chemical and phonetic symbols, running heads, tables, etc.
run in On approval of the the sample pages by the department, they are forwarded to the author for his examination and checking. It is essential that the author make his suggestions for changes at this time. It is too late to make changes after the compositor has started setting the book.

b.f. Copyediting

Before composition is ordered, a copyeditor indicates in the *l.c.* manuscript the typography for each section of the text and corrects errors in grammar, spelling and punctuation, and the
OK as set? major inconsistencies that invariably occur. As a result of his *tr.* work, the manuscript may be more accurate technically and
rom. more consistent, but the quality of writing will not be significantly improved. It is the author's responsibility to present his work clearly and effectively. If in the opinion of the copyeditor
stet and the department, the manuscript needs further work, it may be returned to the author, but only after the editor has discussed the problem with the author.

The copyedited manuscript is returned to the author for final checking, along with a list of the stylistic standards which were followed by the copyeditor. The copyeditor / may query *∂#* the author on points of style or fact that the author may need to reconsider; these queries may be indicated in the margins of the manuscript, flagged, or listed on a separate sheet. All such queries must be answered before the manuscript is returned.

As will be noted later under Corrections, an author's altera- *b.f./∨* tions in proof can be expensive to him.

Figure 7-9 A typeset page after proofreading.

avoid such changes is to consult with the printer beforehand on the typographical design, even to the extent of having sample pages set.

3. Plan changes for minimum resetting of type. When copy changes or additions are to be made in the galleys, it is better if they occur toward the end of a paragraph. If a change is made near the beginning of a paragraph, the whole paragraph may have to be reset. When a phrase must be changed, it is desirable that the substitute copy occupy the same amount of space. In that way, resetting can be restricted to a line or two. The best way to measure space in a line of set copy is to count the number of type characters, including the spaces between words.

4. When lengthy additions are to be made, type each addition on a separate slip of paper, marking the slips with the galley number and the letters *A, B, C,* and so on. Then, using paste or Scotch Tape (not clips or staples), attach each slip to the appropriate place in the margin of the galley, and mark the proof to show where the copy is to be added.

Page Proofs

1. Check to see that the corrections in the galleys have been made as marked.

2. Proofread carefully any parts that have been added (for example, titles, running heads, and page numbers).

3. Read the end and the beginning of each page to make sure that the sequence is correct and that no lines have been omitted. (If the galleys have been read carefully in the first place, it is not necessary to reread the whole proof, although that may be done as a precaution.)

4. Make small copy changes, if necessary, for typographic reasons. For example, a very short top line ending a paragraph (called a *widow*) should if possible be filled out a bit with additional words, and copy that overruns the bottom margin by a line or two should be shortened. (Discretion must be used here; obviously a speech or article that is being reprinted verbatim cannot be altered without the consent of the author.)

8

Correct English Usage

Business, always sensitive to its image, places a high value on the use of good English in its communications. Careful writing builds trust and confidence. On the other hand, misspelling, incorrect word choice, or errors in grammar may not only distort the meaning but also convey a poor impression of the company, its products, and its employees.

For those who want to use English correctly, a good dictionary is indispensable (Figure 8-1). To use it to best advantage, study the introductory notes, acquaint yourself with the pronunciation key, and note the meanings of the many symbols that explain the forms, definitions, and usages of the words (Figure 8-2).

Collected in this chapter are some quick guides to the questions of usage that are most likely to arise in the business office.

Unabridged Dictionaries

Funk & Wagnalls New Standard Dictionary of the English Language
Random House Dictionary of the English Language
Webster's Third New International Dictionary of the English Language

Abridged Dictionaries

American Heritage Dictionary of the English Language
Funk & Wagnalls Standard College Dictionary
Random House College Dictionary
Webster's New Collegiate Dictionary
Webster's New World Dictionary (College Edition)

Figure 8-1 Dictionaries suitable for office use.

CONTENTS

For "Punctuation," see Chapter 9. For guides to "Mechanical Style" (abbreviations, capitals, numbers, underlining, and word division), see Chapter 10.

8.1 SPELLING GUIDE

The need to make a good impression gives business people a special incentive to spell correctly. Fortunately, some of the most troublesome words do conform to a few reasonably simple rules, and the others can at least be isolated and identified. An occasional review helps to fix the correct forms in mind.

Useful Rules. *Words Ending in Silent E.* A silent *e* at the end of a word is usually dropped before a suffix beginning with a vowel but is retained before a suffix beginning with a consonant.

advise, advisable	advise, advisement
continue, continuous	bare, barely
imagine, imaginary	care, careless
make, making	judge, judgment (exception)
sale, salable	hope, hopeful

Words ending in *ce* or *ge* retain the silent *e* before a suffix beginning with *a* or *o*.

advantageous	enforceable
changeable	manageable
courageous	noticeable

The silent *e* is also retained when mispronunciation or confusion with other words might result.

eyeing (*not* eying)   lineage (ancestry)
mileage (*not* milage)   linage (number of lines)
       dyeing (changing the color)
       dying (expiring)

Final Consonant. Before adding a suffix to a word ending in a single final consonant following a single vowel, double the consonant if (1) the accent is on the last syllable, and (2) the suffix begins with a vowel.

allot, allotted, allotting
begin, beginning
control, controlled, controlling
occur, occurred, occurring
refer, referred, referring

| percept | provender |

Catchword — percept

Vocabulary entry — per·cept (pûr'sept), n. 1. the mental result or product of perceiving, as distinguished from the act of perceiving. 2. that which is perceived; the object of perception. [< L perceptum) something perceived, n. use of neut. of perceptus. pp. of percipere to PERCEIVE]

Etymology

Syllabication dots

Pronunciation

per·cep·ti·ble (par sep'ta bal) adj. capable of being perceived, recognizable, appreciable. [< LL perceptibil(is)] —per·cep'ti·bil'i·ty, per·cep'ti·ble·ness, n. —per·cep'ti·bly, adv. —Syn. discernible, apparent.

Loan phrase — per di·em (par dē'am, dī'am), 1. by the day. 2. a daily allowance, usually for living expenses while traveling in connection with one's work. [< L]

Variant plural pronounced — per·i·car·di·um (per'a kär'dē am), n., pl. -di·a (-dē a). Anat. the membranous sac enclosing the heart. [< NL < Gk perikárdion, n. use of neut. of perikárdios heart-surrounding. See PERI-, CARDI-, -OUS] —per'i·car'-di·al, adj.

Diagram and caption — per·i·carp (per'a kärp'), n. 1. Bot. the walls of a ripened ovary or fruit, sometimes consisting of three layers, the epicarp, mesocarp, and endocarp. 2. a membranous envelope around the cystocarp of red algae. 3. a seed vessel. [< NL pericarp(ium) < Gk perikárpion pod] —per'i·car'pi·al, per'i·car'pic, adj. —per'i·car·poi'dal, adj.

ABC, Pericarp of fruit of peach; A, Epicarp; B, Mesocarp; C, Endocarp

Definition

Variant principal parts — per·il (per'al), n., -iled, -il·ing or (esp. Brit.) -illed, -il·ling. —n. 1. exposure to injury, loss, or destruction; risk; jeopardy; danger. —v.t. 2. to expose to danger; imperil; risk. [ME < OF < L pericul(um) trial, test, danger] —Syn. 1. See danger.

Grammatical information — per·i·o·don·tics (per'ē a don'tiks), n. (construed as sing.) the branch of dentistry dealing with the study and treatment of diseases of the bone, connective tissue, and gum surrounding and supporting a tooth. Also, per·i·o·don·tia (per'ē don'sha, shē a). [< NL; see PERI-, -ODONT, -TOM, -ICS] —per'i·o·don'tic, adj.

Variant spelling

Homograph number (separates words spelled identically but of different derivation) — perk¹ (pûrk), v.i. 1. to act, or carry oneself, in a jaunty manner. 2. to become lively or vigorous, as after depression or sickness (usually fol. by up): She began to perk up during dinner. 3. to put oneself forward briskly or presumptuously. —v.t. 4. to raise smartly or briskly (often fol. by up or out): to perk one's head up. 5. to dress smartly; make trim or natty (usually fol. by up or out): to perk up a suit with a new scarf. 6. perk; jaunty. [ME perke(n); ? akin to PEER²] —perk'i·ly, adv. —perk'ish, adj.

Syntactic information

Example sentence — perk² (pûrk), v.t., v.i. Informal. to percolate: Is the coffee perking yet? [by shortening]

Alternate pronunciation

Capitalization style — pil·grim (pil'grim, -gram), n. 1. a person who journeys, esp. a long distance, to some sacred place as an act of devotion. 2. a traveler or wanderer. 3. (cap.) one of the Pilgrim Fathers. [early ME pilegrim, peligrim, c. OFris pilegrim, MLG pelegrim, OHG piligrīm, Icel pīlagrīmr, all < ML pelegrīnus, dissimilated var. of L peregrīnus alien < peregrē abroad = per- PER- + -egr- (comb. form of ager field; see ACRE) + -e adv. suffix]

Synonym list — —Syn. 2. wayfarer, sojourner.

Geographical entry (location, population and date, foreign name) — Pil·sen (pil'zan), n. a city in Bohemia, in W Czechoslovakia. 141,736 (1963). Czech, Plzeň.

Verb inflected forms (past tense and past participle; present participle) — pin (pin), n., v. pinned, pin·ning. —n. 1. a short, slender piece of metal with a point at one end and a head at the other, for fastening things together. 2. a small, slender, often pointed piece of wood, metal, etc. used to fasten, support, or attach things. 3. any of various forms of fasteners, ornaments, or badges consisting essentially or partly of a pointed or penetrating wire or shaft (often used in combination): a fraternity pin; a tiepin. 4. a short metal rod, as a linchpin, driven through the holes of adjacent parts, as a hub and an axle, to keep them together. 5. a short cylindrical rod or tube, as a wristpin or crankpin, joining two parts so as to permit them to move in one plane relative to each other. 7. the part of a cylindrical key stem that enters a lock. 8. a hairpin. 9. (usually pl.) See tenpin. 10. a peg, nail or stud marking the center of a target.

Cross reference to multiple-word entry — 11. Bowling. one of the rounded wooden clubs set up as the target in tenpins, duckpins, etc. 12. Golf. the flagstaff that identifies a hole. 13. Usually, pins. Informal. the legs. 14.

Usage label — Music. peg (def. 2). 15. Wrestling. a fall. 16. Naut. See

Cross reference to one-word entry — belaying pin. 17. a very small amount; a trifle. —v.t. 18. to fasten or attach with or as with a pin or pins. 19. to hold fast in a spot or position. 20. to give one's fraternity pin to (a girl) as a pledge of one's fondness or attachment. 21. Wrestling. to obtain a fall over one's opponent. 22. pin down, a. to bind or hold to a course of action, a promise, etc.

Idiomatic phrase — b. to define with clarity and precision: to pin down a vague intuition. 23. pin something on someone, Slang. to blame someone for something. [OE pinn; c. D pin, G Pinne, Icel pinni; ? akin to MIr benn (for *bend), now beann peak, steeple, gable, etc.]

Adjective inflected forms (comparative, superlative) — pin·y (pī'nē), adj. pin·i·er, pin·i·est. 1. abounding in, covered with, or consisting of pine trees. 2. pertaining to or

Example phrase — suggestive of pine trees: a piny fragrance. Also, piney.

Mythological entry — Pi·rith·o·us (pi rith'ō as), n. Class. Myth. a prince of the Lapithae and friend of Theseus, in whose company he attempted to abduct Persephone from Hades.

Abbreviation — pk, pl. pks. (in dry measure) peck.

Parts of speech ——

Consecutive definition numbers ——

Italicized entry ——

Language label ——

Historical entry ——

Etymological cross reference to foreign word ——

Archaic label ——

Antonym list ——

Synonym study ——

Cross reference to hidden entry ——

Symbol ——

Example in synonym study ——

Hyphenated entry ——

Subject label ——

Usage study ——

Comparison ——

Example in usage study ——

Combining form ——

Stressed multiple-word entry ——

Run-on entry ——

Biographical entry (dates, nationality, profession) ——

Illustration and caption (taxonomic name and size) ——

Foreign pronunciation ——

Lower-case style ——

Regional label ——

Spot map ——

Chemical formula ——

Hidden entry ——

Etymological cross reference to dictionary entry ——

Variant form ——

Cross reference to synonym study ——

Pronunciation key ——

---

per'manent press', (of a fabric) wrinkle-resistant and requiring little or no ironing after washing.

per men·sem (per men'sem; *Eng.* par men'sem), *Latin.* by the month.

Per·sia (pûr'zha, -sha), *n.* **1.** Also called **Per'sian Em'·pire**, an ancient empire located in W and S Asia: at its height it extended from Egypt and the Aegean to India; conquered by Alexander the Great 334–331 b.c. **2.** former official name (until 1935) of **Iran**. [< L, var. of *Persis* < Gk < OPers *Pârsa*]

per·spi·ca·cious (pûr'spi kā'shəs), *adj.* **1.** having keen mental perception; discerning. **2.** [*Archaic*] having keen sight. [PERSPICACI(TY) + -OUS] —**per·spi·ca'cious·ly**, *adv.* —**per·spi·ca'cious·ness**, *n.* —Syn. 1. perceptive, acute, penetrating. —Ant. 1. dull, stupid.

Pe·ru·vian rhat'any, See under **rhatany** (def. 1)

Ph., *Chem.* phenyl.

phase-out (fāz'out'), *n.* the act or an instance of phasing out: *A phase-out of obsolete production methods is essential.*

phase' rule', [*Physical Chem.*] a law that the number of degrees of freedom in a system in equilibrium is equal to two plus the number of components less the number of phases. Thus, a system of ice, melted ice, and water vapor, being one component and three phases, has no degrees of freedom. Cf. **variance** (def. 4)

-phasia, a learned borrowing from Greek, used in the formation of compound words to refer to speech disorders: *aphasia.* Also, **-phasy**. [< Gk, comb. form akin to *phánai* to speak]

Ph.D., See **Doctor of Philosophy**. [< L *Philosophiae Doctor*]

pheas·ant (fez'ənt), *n.* **1.** any of numerous large, usually long-tailed, gallinaceous birds of the family *Phasianidae,* of the Old World. **2.** [*Southern U.S.*] the ruffed grouse. **3.** any of various other birds that resemble or suggest a pheasant. [ME *fesaunt* < AF, OF *faisan* < L *phāsiānus* < Gk *phāsiānós* (*órnis*) (bird) of the Phasis River]

Ring-necked pheasant, *Phasianus colchicus* (Length to 3 ft.)

phe·no·bar·bi·tal (fē'no bär'bi tal', -tôl', -nə-), *n. Pharm.* a white powder, C₁₂H₁₂N₂O₃ available also as the sodium salt [**Phenobar'bital so'dium**] for greater solubility: used as a sedative, a hypnotic, and as an antispasmodic in epilepsy. Also called **phenylethylmalonylurea**.

---

plan (plan), *n., v.,* **planned, plan·ning.** —*n.* **1.** a method of action or procedure. **2.** a design or scheme of arrangement: *an elaborate plan for seating guests.* **3.** a project or definite purpose: *plans for the future.* **4.** a drawing made to scale to represent the top view or a horizontal section of a structure or a machine: *a plan of a floor of the dock area.* **6.** (in perspective drawing) one of several planes in front of a represented object, and perpendicular to the line between the object and the eye. —*v.t.* **7.** to arrange or project a plan or scheme for (any work, enterprise, or proceeding): *to plan a new recreation center; to plan one's vacation.* **8.** to draw or make a plan for, as a building. —*v.i.* **9.** to make a plan: *to plan for one's retirement.* [< F: *plane, plan,* groundwork, scheme < L *plān(us)* level *plānum* level ground. See PLANE¹, PLAIN¹]
—Syn. 1. plot, formula, system. PLAN, PROJECT, DESIGN, SCHEME imply a formulated method of doing something. PLAN refers to any method of thinking out acts and purposes beforehand: *What are your plans for today?* A PROJECT is a proposed or tentative plan, often elaborate or extensive: *an irrigation project.* DESIGN suggests art, dexterity, or craft (sometimes evil and selfish) in the elaboration or execution of a plan, and often tends to emphasize the purpose in view: *a disturbance brought about by design.* A SCHEME is apt to be either a speculative, possibly impractical, plan, or a selfish or dishonest one: *a scheme to swindle someone.* 4. draft, diagram, chart. 7. design, devise.
—Usage. Many teachers object to the phrase PLAN ON (followed by a gerund) considering it poor style for PLAN TO (followed by an infinitive): *I had planned to go to the movies tonight* (not *I had planned on going to the movies tonight*).

pop' art', a style in the fine arts characterized chiefly by forms and images derived from comic strips and advertising posters. —**pop'art'ist.**

Pow·ys (pō'is), *n.* John Cowper, 1872–1963, and his brother, Theodore Francis, 1875–1953, English authors.

Pro·ven·çale (prō'vən säl', prô văn-; *Fr.* prô văn sȧl'), *adj. Cookery.* (*sometimes l.c.*) prepared with garlic and tomato. [< F; fem. of PROVENÇAL]

Pro·vence (pəð väns'; *Eng.* prə väns'), *n.* a region in SE France, bordering on the Mediterranean: formerly a province; famous for medieval poetry and courtly traditions.

prov·en·der (prov'ən dər), *n.* **1.** dry food for livestock or other domestic animals. **2.** food; provisions. [ME *prov- endre* < OF, var. of *provende* prebend, provender < ML *pr(ae)benda,* b. *praebenda* PREBEND and *providere* to look out for, PROVIDE] —Syn. 1. See **feed**.

act, āble, dâre, ärt; ebb, ēqual; if, ice; hot, ōver, ôrder; oil; book; ōōze; out; up, ūrge; ə = a as in alone; chief; sing; shoe; thin; thad; zh as in measure; ə as in button. See the full key inside the front cover.

Figure 8-2 A page from a desk dictionary, with explanatory notes. (From the *Student Guide* of the Random House Dictionary, College Edition, Copyright 1969, 1968, by Random House, Inc. Reprinted by permission.)

267

But no doubling of the consonant occurs when the accent is *not* on the last syllable.

benefited
canceling
profited

If the accent shifts to an earlier syllable when the suffix is added, do not double the final consonant.

prefer, preferred, preference

Some exceptions:

write, writing, BUT written (change in pronunciation)
train, trained, training, trainee (final consonant preceded by two vowels)
tax, taxes (NOT taxxes; word ending in *x* excepted from rule)

Final Y.   When a final *y* is preceded by a consonant, change the *y* to *i* before adding any suffix except one beginning with *i*. When the final *y* is preceded by a vowel, keep the *y*.

carry, carries, carrying   *y preceded by vowel:*
happy, happier, happiness   dismay, dismayed, dismaying
likely, likelihood   employ, employer, employing
marry, marriage, marrying   stay, stayed, staying
plenty, plentiful   survey, surveyed, surveying
worry, worrisome

Some exceptions:

day, daily   lay, laid   say, said
dry, dryly,   pay, paid   wry wryly

The Rule of Addition.   When you add a prefix or suffix, or combine two words, and the last letter of the first part of the word is the same as the first letter of the second part, be sure that you retain both letters.

dissatisfied   barrenness
illiterate   meanness
immaterial   soulless
irresponsible   universally
misspelling   woolly
transship
underrated   bathhouse
unnamed   bookkeeper
withholding   roommate

Exceptions:

eighteen (NOT eightteen)
cross-section (NOT crosssection; never put three identical consonants together)

Ei and Ie.   When *ei* and *ie* are pronounced *ee,* place the *i* before the *e,* except after *c* use *ei.*

achieve   ceiling
believe   perceive
field   receipt
series

Some exceptions:

neither, species, leisure, seize, eight, weight (*ei* pronounced *ay*)

-Able, -Ible.   There is no fast rule for choosing between these word endings, but it may help to know that *-able* is much more common than *-ible*. Furthermore, the *-able* ending usually follows a full word or a full word minus the final *e*.

acceptable	dispensable	credible
believable	likeable	deductible
changeable	questionable	intelligible
considerable	valuable	irresponsible

-Ance, -Ence.   A *verb* ending in *er, or,* or *ur* and accented on the last syllable forms its noun by the addition of *-ence*. There is no other reliable guide to distinguishing between *-ance* and *-ence*, except your dictionary.

abhorrence	deference	allowance
concurrence	preference	guidance
conference	recurrence	performance

-Cede, -Ceed, -Sede.   The only word ending in *-sede* is *supersede*. The only words ending in *-ceed* are *exceed, proceed,* and *succeed.* That leaves just eight words ending in *-cede:*

accede	intercede
antecede	precede
cede	recede
concede	secede

-Ic.   When a suffix beginning with *e, i,* or *y* is added to a word ending in *ic,* a *k* is usually inserted to prevent mispronunciation.

mimic, mimicked, mimicking (*but* mimicry)
panic, panicked, panicky
picnic, picnicked, picnicking
politic, politicking
traffic, trafficked, trafficking

Plurals.   Many questions of spelling arise because of uncertainty about ending plural nouns. For example, is it *tomatos* or *tomatoes, editor-in-chiefs* or *editors-in-chief?*

Most nouns form their plurals by the addition of *s* or *es* to the singular (*books, taxis; sashes, taxes*). However, there are many exceptions and divided usages, as explained below.

Final Y.   When a final *y* follows a consonant, change the *y* to *i* and add *es.*

blueberries	ferries	plies
countries	Januaries	twenties

When a final *y* follows a vowel, just add *s.*

attorneys	displays	moneys (*also* monies)
buys (purchases)	keys	parleys

Final O.   When a final *o* follows another vowel, add *s* to form the plural.

cameos   duos   folios   patios   radios

When the final *o* follows a consonant, practice is divided between adding *s* and *es*.

dittos	mottoes (*or* mottos)
dynamos	noes (*plural of* no)
mementos	potatoes
pianos	tomatoes

Final F.   To form the plural of many words ending in *f* or *fe* (but not *ff*), change the *f* to *v* and add *es*.

calves   halves   knives   leaves   selves   wives
BUT: briefs   chefs   proofs   roofs   tiffs   whiffs

Compound Words.   When a term consists of two or more words, with or without hyphens, only the significant word takes the plural form. If both words are equally significant, both take the plural; and if no word is particularly significant, the plural form is placed on the last word.

Significant word first:

adjutants general	mothers-in-law
attorneys-at-law	notaries public
attorneys general	rights-of-way
commanders in chief	sergeants at arms

Significant word in middle:

assistant attorneys general   deputy chiefs of staff

Significant word last:

assistant directors	provost marshal generals
assistant secretaries	trade unions
brigadier generals	under secretaries

Both words equally significant:

coats of arms	secretaries-treasurers
menservants	women buyers

No word especially significant:

forget-me-nots	pick-me-ups
hand-me-downs	will-o'-the-wisps

NOTE 1:   When a noun is hyphenated with a preposition or adverb, the noun takes the plural.

droppers-in	hangers-on	passers-by
goings-on	listeners-in	runners-up

NOTE 2:   When neither word of a compound is a noun, the last word takes the plural.

also-rans	fill-ins	higher-ups
come-ons	go-betweens	tie-ins

NOTE 3: Single words ending in *ful* are pluralized at the end.

armfuls bucketfuls cupfuls pailfuls spoonfuls

BUT: Separating the parts and pluralizing the initial word changes the meaning.

2 cupfuls (an amount equal to the content of two cups)
2 cups full of (two cups filled with)

Common Singular and Plural.   Some nouns, many with a final *s* sound, have the same form in the singular and the plural.

gladiolus	Chinese	deer
series	Japanese	salmon
species	Portuguese	sheep

NOTE 1: Words ending in silent *s* have the same form in the singular and plural, though the *s* may be sounded in the plural.

chassis	faux pas	Bracques
corps	patios	Dumas

NOTE 2: Some nouns ending in *s* are used only in the plural.

goods means proceeds scissors thanks

NOTE 3: Other words ending in *s* are regularly construed as singular.

aeronautics economics news

NOTE 4: Still other words ending in *s* are either singular or plural, depending on the sense.

Acoustics [the study] is a modern science.
The acoustics [the sound qualities] of Philharmonic Hall have been improved.

Other words in the same class include:

athletics	physics	statistics
ethics	politics	tactics

Proper Names.   Proper names, including those ending in *y* form their plurals by the addition of *s* and *es*.

Mr. Daly	the Dalys	Prof. Haney	the Haneys
Dr. March	the Marches	Mr. and Mrs. Kelly	the Kellys
Frank Vance	the Vances	Mrs. Prentis	the Prentises

ALSO: the Drs. March (two or more doctors by that name)
  Professors Haney and Carvell (two professors)
  the Messrs. Daly (two or more men by that name)
  the Mesdames (or Mmes.) Prentis (two or more women by that name, married or single)
  the Misses Hopkins and Joyce (two single women)
  Ms. Hopkins and Ms. Joyce (two single women or marital status unknown)

NOTE: When a name ends in Jr., II, III, and so on, add the plural ending to either the last name or the suffix. The first practice is considered somewhat more formal than the second.

Martin J. Beckley II
the Martin J. Beckleys II (*or* the Martin J. Beckley II's)
Henry Fairfield, Jr.
the Henry Fairfields, Jr. (*or* the Henry Fairfield, Jrs.)
John H. Marks, Jr.
the John H. Marks, Jrs. (*less awkward than* the John H. Markses, Jr.)

Words Used as Words. In referring to words as words, form their plural by adding *s* (*es* if the word ends in *s*). If there is a chance that the word may be misread, add an apostrophe and *s,* or use quotation marks. Add the *s* alone to words that already have an apostrophe.

ands	the or's and nor's	the don'ts (*not* the dont's *or*
ifs, ands, and buts	the who's and which's	the don't's)
whereases	the "why nots"	the mustn'ts

Letters, Figures, Signs, Abbreviations. Form the plural of letters by adding an apostrophe and *s*. However, there is a trend toward the omission of the apostrophe where no misreading would result. (See also "Abbreviations—Plurals," Section 10.1.)

p's	2's (*or* 2s)	*X*'s (*or* *X*s)
q's	Ph.D.'s (*or* Ph.D.s)	CPA's *or* CPAs
s's (*not* *s*s)	BTU's (*not* BTUs)	Mfrs. (*not* Mfr's)

Foreign Words. The plurals of some words of foreign origin often cause difficulty. As the list below indicates, some of these words have both an Anglicized and a foreign plural.

Singular	*Plural*
addendum	addenda
adieu	adieus
agendum	agenda
alumna	alumnae
alumnus	alumni
analysis	analyses
antenna	antennas (*also, in zoology,* antennae)
appendix	appendixes (*also* appendices)
automaton	automatons (*also* automata)
axis	axes
bacterium	bacteria
basis	bases
beau	beaus (*also* beaux)
cactus	cactuses (*also* cacti)
crisis	crises
criterion	criteria
curriculum	curriculums (*also* curricula)
datum	data
dilettante	dilettantes (*also* dilettanti)
erratum	errata
executrix	executrices
focus	foci

Singular	*Plural*
formula	formulas (*also* formulae)
fungus	fungi
genius	geniuses (*also in sense of guardian spirit,* genii, *often capitalized*)
genus	genera (*also* genuses)
hypothesis	hypotheses
index	indexes (*also, in science,* indices)
insigne	insignia
larva	larvae
lira	lire
locus	loci
madam, madame	mesdames
matrix	matrices (*also* matrixes)
maximum	maximums (*also* maxima)
medium	mediums (*also, esp. in advertising,* media)
memorandum	memorandums (*also* memoranda)
minimum	minimums (*also* minima)
minutia	minutiae
monsieur	messieurs
nucleus	nuclei (*also* nucleuses)
oasis	oases
opus	opera
parenthesis	parentheses
phenomenon	phenomena
plateau	plateaus
podium	podiums
radius	radii (*also* radiuses)
radix	radices (*also* radixes)
referendum	referendums (*also* referenda)
residuum	residua (*also* residuums)
stadium	stadiums (*also* stadia)
stimulus	stimuli
stratum	strata
syllabus	syllabuses (*also* syllabi)
symposium	symposiums (*also* symposia)
synopsis	synopses
tableau	tableaus
terminus	termini (*also* terminuses)
testatrix	testatrices
thesaurus	thesauri (*also* thesauruses)
thesis	theses
ultimatum	ultimatums (*also* ultimata)
vertebra	vertebras (*also, in zoology,* vertebrae)
virtuoso	virtuosos (*also* virtuosi)

8.2 WORDS OFTEN CONFUSED

Many words in English sound alike, and even look alike, but mean different things. The chance of confusion is likely to increase when the secretary is transcribing from dictation. The following list contains the words most likely to cause "double trouble."

Key to Abbreviations

adj	adjective	part	participle
adv	adverb	prep	preposition
conj	conjunction	pron	pronoun
n	noun	v	verb

Key to Pronunciation

a	mat	ē	eat	ō	loaf	th	then
ā	day	er	mother	ô	bought	u	up
â	air	i	sir	oo	tool	û	urge
ä	arms	ī	bite	ou	loud	uh	data, alone
e	set	o	on	th	thin		

accept	(v) Receive. "I *accept* the honor."
except	(v) Leave out. "Only Jones was *excepted*."
	(prep) With the exclusion of, but. "All came *except* him."
access	(n) Means of approach. "*Access* to the files."
excess	(n) Immoderate quantity. "*Excess* baggage."
ad	(n) Advertisement (shortened form).
add	(v) To make a sum. "Let's *add* the figures."
adapt	(v) Modify. "One must *adapt* to conditions."
adopt	(v) Take. "They *adopted* a new name."
admittance	(n) Permission to enter. "They gained *admittance*."
admission	(n) 1. Right of entry, as by paying. "*Admission* is free."
	2. A point conceded. "A damaging *admission*."
advice	(n) 1. Counsel. "We gave our *advice* freely."
ad vīs′	(n) 2. Notice or communication. "Our *advice* is enclosed."
	"*Advice* from abroad."
advise	(v) To counsel, to inform. "Please *advise* us."
ad vīz′	
affect	(v) To influence. "The weather *affected* sales."
effect	(v) To bring about. "They will *effect* a change in strategy."
	(n) Result. "The *effect* of the change was noticeable."
all ready	All prepared. "We are *all ready* to leave."
already	(adv) Previously. "He had *already* offered his apologies."
all together	In a group. "They arrived *all together*."
altogether	(adv) Entirely. "The fuss was *altogether* unnecessary."
allusion	(n) A reference. "An *allusion* to Shakespeare."
illusion	(n) A deceiving appearance. "Easy profits are an *illusion*."
all ways	In every way. "He is in *all ways* a gentleman."
always	(adv) At all times. "He is *always* a gentleman."
ante-	Before, as in *antedate* (to put an earlier date on).
an′tē	
anti-	Against, as in *antisocial*.
an′tē, an′tī	
any way	In any one way. "*Any way* you look at it."
anyway	(adv) At least, nevertheless, in any manner. "*Anyway*, he tried."
a piece	(n) A thing or part. "*A piece* of pie is 50 cents."
apiece	(adv) For each. "We had one slice *apiece*."
appraise	(v) To put a value on. "He was asked to *appraise* the ring."
apprise	(v) To inform. "They were *apprised* of their rights."
arraign	(v) To bring before a court of law. "The prisoner was *arraigned*."
uh rān′	
arrange	(v) To put in order. "His lawyer *arranged* the transaction."
uh rānj′	
assay	(v) To make a test. "They *assayed* the situation."
	(n) An analysis. "An *assay* of the metal showed. . . ."
essay	(v) To try. "Only Smith would *essay* the difficult feat."
	(n) An attempt, a composition. "The *essay* was brief."
assistance	(n) Aid. "We need *assistance*."
assistants	(n) Helpers. "We had many *assistants*."

baring bâr′ing	(part) Exposing. "The witness is *baring* the details."
barring bär′ring	(part) Excluding. "*Barring* an upset, we expect to win."
bearing bâr′ing	(part) Carrying. "Kevin is *bearing* a difficult responsibility."
beside	(prep) Next to. "He sat *beside* us."
besides	(adv) In addition, furthermore. (See Section 8.5)
biannual	(adj) Occurring twice a year.
biennial	(adj) Occurring every two years. (See Section 8.5.)
born	(part) Brought into being. "He was *born* into a good family."
borne	(part) Carried. "The burden was *borne* by the treasurer."
breath breth	(n) Air inhaled and exhaled. "A *breath* of air."
breathe brēth	(v) To inhale and exhale. "*Breathe* deeply."
breadth	(n) Width, extent. "I admired the *breadth* of his interests."
Britain	(n) Great Britain (England, Northern Ireland, Wales, and Scotland).
Briton	(n) An inhabitant of Great Britain.
calendar	(n) A table showing the days, weeks, months, and so on.
calender	(n) A smoothing machine used in paper manufacture. (v) To press in a calender.
canvas	(n) A coarse cloth.
canvass	(n) A solicitation or inquiry. "A *canvass* showed. . . ." (v) To solicit. "He *canvassed* the district for votes."
capital	(adj) Of primary importance. "A *capital* idea." (n) 1. Principal city. "The *capital* of New York is Albany." 2. Wealth invested in a business. "Started with $100,000 *capital*."
capitol	(n) Statehouse. "The legislature meets in the *capitol*."
Capitol	(n) The building in which Congress meets, in Washington, D.C.
censor sen′ser	(v) To review for purposes of changing or expurgating. (n) A person who censors or censures.
censure sen′sher	(v) To blame or condemn. "I will not *censure* him."
click klik	(n) A slight, sharp sound.
clique klēk, klik	(n) A small exclusive group. "He belonged to a *clique*."
climactic klī mak′tik	(adj) Constituting the climax. "A *climactic* event."
climatic klī ma′tik	(adj) Relating to the climate. "*Climatic* conditions."
clothes klōz	(n) Apparel.
cloths klôths	(n) Pieces of cloth.
coarse	(adj) Common, vulgar, rough, or harsh. "A *coarse* remark."
course	(n) Path, progress. "Followed an even *course*."
complement	(n) That which completes. "The scarf is a *complement* to her dress."
compliment	(n) An expression of courtesy or praise. "He paid her a *compliment*."

compose	(v) Constitute.
comprise	(v) Consist of. (See Section 8.5.)
comptroller kun trō′ler	(n) A person in charge of expenditures and receipts (finance).
controller kun trō′ler	(n) Another (but preferred) form of *comptroller*.
confidant kon fi dänt′	(n) A person in whom one confides.
confident kon′fi dent	(adj) Full of confidence, assured.
contemptible	(adj) Deserving of contempt, despicable. "A *contemptible* slander."
contemptuous	(adj) Showing contempt, disdainful. "*Contemptuous* of authority."
correspondence	(n) An exchange of letters. "A secretary handles her employer's *correspondence*."
correspondents	(n) Writers of letters.
costumer ko stoo′mer	(n) 1. A clothes rack. 2. One who makes costumes.
customer kus′tuh mer	(n) A patron.
council	(n) A body of advisers. "The *council* meets on Thursdays."
counsel	(n) 1. Advice. "We sought his *counsel*." 2. A person or persons giving advice, a lawyer. "Our *counsel* is Mr. Brown."
consul	(n) A government representative in a foreign country.
credible	(adj) Believable. "He told a *credible* story."
creditable	(adj) Deserving of credit. "His action was entirely *creditable*."
credulous	(adj) Easily convinced. "Only a *credulous* person would believe that story."
credit	(v) To put confidence in, to give credit. "They *credit* him for the savings." "We'll *credit* your account for $20."
accredit	(v) To authorize, to give credentials to. "An *accredited* agent."
critic kri′tik	(n) One who forms judgments. "The *critic* was severe."
critique kri tēk′	(n) A judgment or evaluation. "His *critique* was very perceptive."
cue	(n) A signal. "The bell was a *cue* to begin the performance." (v) To signal, give an indication to. "We *cued* him on his answers."
queue	(n) A line. "The patrons formed a *queue* at the box office." (v) To form a line. "The patrons *queued* up at the box office."
decease di sēs′	(n) Death.
disease di zēz′	(n) Illness.
decent dē′sent	(adj) Proper, respectable. "He came from a *decent* family."
descent di sent′	(n) 1. Downward motion. "The *descent* was steep." 2. Ancestry. "Of English *descent*."
dissent di sent′	(n) Disagreement. "He expressed his *dissent*." (v) To disagree. "He *dissented*."
decree	(n) An official order. (v) To issue such an order.
degree	(n) A step, stage, or rank.
depository	(n) A place for the safekeeping of money, jewels, and other valuables.

depositary	(n) 1. A person or organization entrusted with something for safekeeping. 2. A synonym for *depository*.
deprecate	(v) To express disapproval of. "He *deprecated* the action."
depreciate	(v) 1. To lessen in value. "The stock *depreciates*." 2. To disparage. "He *depreciated* his own achievements."
desert dez′ert, de zert′	(n) A dry, sandy area. (v) To abandon. "We will not *desert* our friends."
dessert di zurt′	(n) A course at the end of a meal.
deserts di zurts′	(n) Deserved reward or punishment. "He got his *deserts*."
device	(n) 1. A mechanical instrument. 2. A plan. "It was just a *device* for stimulating sales."
devise	(v) To contrive or plan. "They will *devise* a substitute for the broken part."
die (died, dying)	(v) To stop living.
dye (dyed, **dyeing)**	(v) To color. "The fur was *dyed* muskrat." (n) A coloring agent. "The *dye* ran."
disapprove	(v) To express an unfavorable opinion of. "I *disapprove* of such conduct."
disprove	(v) To prove something false. "The theory has been *disproved*."
disassociate	(v) To separate. "You should *disassociate* yourself from him."
dissociate	(v) Same as *disassociate*, but preferred.
disburse	(v) Pay out. "Window 9 *disburses* petty cash."
disperse	(v) Scatter. "The crowd *dispersed*."
discomfit	(v) To embarrass. "We did not intend to *discomfit* him."
discomfort	(v) To cause discomfort. "A tight shoe would *discomfort* anyone." (n) Lack of comfort. "Tight shoes cause *discomfort*."
discreet	(adj) Tactful. "A *discreet* inquiry."
discrete	(adj) Separate and distinct. "*Discrete* symbols.
done	(part) Finished, accomplished. "The job was *done*."
dun	(v) To ask for payment. "We *dun* delinquent accounts on the first of every month."
dual	(adj) Double. "He played a *dual* role in the merger."
duel	(n) A fight, contest. "They fought a *duel*."
egoist	(n) A person who is self-centered (not necessarily a term of reproach).
egotist	(n) A conceited person (usually signifies disapproval).
elder, eldest	(adj) Refer to the seniority of members of a family. "The *eldest* son."
older, oldest	(adj) More general terms relating to seniority in age, rank, and so on. "We could use an *older* man for the job."
emigrate	(v) To leave one's country and settle in another. "*Emigrate* from Ireland."
immigrate	(v) To come into a country. "*Immigrate* to Canada."
migrate	(v) A more general term meaning to move from one place to another; used of animals as well as people. "They *migrate* every spring."
eminent	(adj) Outstanding, distinguished. "An *eminent* surgeon."
immanent	(adj) Remaining within, inherent. "He had an *immanent* faith in the power of good works."
imminent	(adj) Threatening. "He was in *imminent* danger of bankruptcy."

enormity	(n) Great wickedness. "The public was appalled by the *enormity* of the crime."
enormousness	(n) Great size. "Visitors are astonished by the *enormousness* of the Pan Am Building."
envelop en vel′up	(v) To cover completely. "In this test the flames *envelop* the car."
envelope en′vuh lōp	(n) A container for letters.
equable ek′wuh bul, ĕ′kwuh bul	(adj) Uniform, serene. "An *equable* temperament." "An *equable* climate."
equitable ek′wi tuh bul	(adj) Equal, fair. "An *equitable* division of the profits."
exceptional	(adj) Unusual. "It is an *exceptional* example."
exceptionable	(adj) Open to objection. "An *exceptionable* remark."
exercise ek′ser sīz	(n) Physical activity. (v) To engage in such activity.
exorcise ek′sôr sīz	(v) To drive away, usually some evil spirit. "The masks are intended to *exorcize* the devil."
exhausting	(adj) Tiring. "An *exhausting* job."
exhaustive	(adj) Thorough. "An *exhaustive* search."
farther	(adv) Used in expressions of distance. "*Farther* down the road."
further	(adv) 1. Used in expressions of degree. "You can carry that reasoning even *further*." 2. Used as a synonym for *farther*. (See Section 8.5.)
fete fāt, fet	(n) A festival. "A *fete* marked the end of Lent."
feat fēt	(n) A remarkable accomplishment. "Lindbergh's *feat* was marked by wild acclaim."
feet fēt	(n) Plural of *foot*.
flaunt flônt	(v) To display ostentatiously. "He *flaunted* his wealth."
flout	(v) To show contempt for. "He *flouted* the law."
flounder	(v) To struggle awkwardly. "He *floundered* around on the slippery floor."
founder	(v) To sink, said of a ship; to collapse or fail. "The business *foundered*."
forbear fôr bâr′ fôr′bâr	(v) To refrain from. "We will *forbear* criticism." (n) An ancestor, same as below.
forebear fôr′bâr	(n) An ancestor. "His *forebears* came from Sweden."
forcefully	(adv) Vigorously. "He spoke *forcefully*."
forcibly	(adv) By means of force. "The thief entered the premises *forcibly*."
forgo	(v) To do without. "Let's *forgo* the long introductions."
forego	(v) 1. To go before, usually found in such expressions as "a *foregone* conclusion" and "the *foregoing* statement." 2. Used as a synonym for *forgo*.
formally	(adv) In a formal manner. "The mayor *formally* takes office on January 1."
formerly	(adv) In the past. "Mr. Cain was *formerly* a salesman."
forth	(adv) Forward.
fourth	(adj) Next after third.

gourmet goor'-mā	(n) A person who likes fine foods. "He fancies himself a *gourmet*."
gourmand goor'-mand	(n) Also a person who likes fine foods, but often used in the sense of *glutton*.
guarantee gar un tē'	(n) A pledge of assurance that something meets specifications. "The maker's *guarantee* accompanies every purchase." (v) To give such a pledge. "The company *guaranteed* the article."
guaranty gar'un tē	(n) 1. A pledge to pay another's debt in case of default. "Mr. Dawson's *guaranty* of the loan will be accepted." 2. An agreement that gives assurance of performance, same as *guarantee*. (v) To guarantee. NOTE: *Guaranty* is used as a synonym for *guarantee* in all senses.
hardy **hearty**	(adj) Bold, durable, robust. "A *hardy* traveler." (adj) Vigorous ("a *hearty* laugh"); satisfying ("a *hearty* meal"); sincere ("a *hearty* welcome").
healthy **healthful**	(adj) Having good health. "A *healthy* man." (adj) Helping to promote health. "A *healthful* diet."
holy **wholly**	(adj) Consecrated, sacred. (adv) Entirely, as in "*wholly* fitting."
hypocritical hip uh krit'i kul	(adj) Not sincere. "He engages in *hypocritical* doubletalk."
hypercritical hī per krit'i kul	(adj) Too critical. "The *hypercritical* review seemed undeserved."
immanent **imminent**	See eminent.
inapt	(adj) Not suitable, lacking skill, awkward. "If he proves *inapt*, we will transfer him to another job."
inept	(adj) Same meaning, but usually in the sense of foolish, absurd, or clumsy. "The performance was so *inept*, we were embarrassed."
incidence	(n) Degree of occurrence. "The *incidence* of lung cancer is increasing."
incidents	(n) Occurrences. "The number of traffic *incidents* involving taxis is increasing."
incredible **incredulous**	(adj) Unbelievable. "An *incredible* number of errors." (adj) Unbelieving, skeptical. "You must be wary of the *incredulous* reader."
indention **indentation**	(n) A notch or recess. The words are used synonymously.
ingenious in jēn'yus	(adj) Clever, resourceful. "They devised an *ingenious* plan."
ingenuous in jen'yoo us	(adj) Frank, artless, naïve. "His *ingenuous* remarks were not amusing."
interstate	(adj) Between states. "The federal government controls *interstate* commerce."
intrastate	(adj) Within a state. "He thought the governor should concentrate on *intrastate* affairs."
isle **aisle**	(n) A small island. (n) A passageway.
its	(pron) Possessive of *it*. "We've seen the rise of railroad passenger traffic, and we've seen *its* decline."

it's	Contraction of "it is" or "it has." "*It's* no longer true." "*It's* been so long since we've seen you."
jibe jīb	(v) Colloquial for "being in agreement." "Our views *jibe*."
gibe jīb	(n) A jeer or taunt. "We ignored his *gibes*." (v) To jeer or taunt. "He *gibed* at us constantly." Sometimes spelled *jibe*.
karat or **carat**	(n) A unit of weight for diamonds and other precious stones.
caret	(n) An inverted *v* (∧) to show where something is to be added.
later lāt′er	(adj, adv) Occurring after, relating to time. "We'll call you *later*."
latter lat′er	(n, adj) The last mentioned. (See *former, latter*, Section 8.5.)
lead lēd led	(n) 1. A metal. "*Lead* is heavier than aluminum." 2. Front place. "We plan to take the *lead*." (v) To show the way. "This staircase will *lead* you to the shelter."
led	(v) Past tense of *lead* (v). "We *led* the way to the shelter."
leased	(v) Given by lease. "*Leased* to the Jones Company."
least	(adj) The smallest in size, degree, or amount. "The *least* trouble." (n) The smallest amount. "The *least* you can give is $10."
lessen	(v) To make less. "The insulation will *lessen* the noise."
lesson	(n) Something to be learned.
liable li′uh bul	(adj) Exposure to some disadvantage. (See *apt, likely, liable*, Section 8.5.)
libel	(n) A written or printed defamation. "A suit for *libel*."
liqueur li kûr′	(n) A sweet, syrupy, alcoholic drink. "We'll have a *liqueur* after dinner."
liquor lik′er	(n) Any distilled alcoholic drink. "Prices for *liquor* have gone up."
loath lōth	(adj) Reluctant. "I am *loath* to do it."
loathe lōth	(v) To detest. "I *loathe* the new fashions."
local lō′kul	(adj) Confined to a certain place. "The condition is *local*."
locale lō kal′	(n) A place. "The *locale* of the story is Monte Carlo."
lose looz	(v) To be unable to find. "Try not to *lose* the key."
loose loos	(adj) Not tight. "The knot was *loose*."
luxuriant	(adj) Fertile, lush. "A *luxuriant* garden."
luxurious	(adj) Rich. "*Luxurious* surroundings."
material muh tēr′ē ul	(n) Substance. "Have you ordered enough *material* to redo the entire roof?"
materiel muh tēr ē el′	(n) Equipment, supplies, especially those used by the armed forces. "War requires men and *materiel*."
militate	(v) To work (against). "His quick temper will *militate* against his success."
mitigate	(v) To make less severe. "The loan will help to *mitigate* the effects of the flood."
moral mor′ul	(adj) Good, right. "The employer viewed the raise as a *moral* necessity."

morale muh ral′	(n) Mental condition, spirit. "The *morale* of the work force was high."
motif mō tēf′	(n) Theme. "The *motif* of the party was the gold rush of 1849."
motive mō′tiv	(n) Inner drive, incentive. "Money has always provided a strong *motive* for work."
ordinance	(n) A statute law. "The *ordinance* called for a $50 fine."
ordnance	(n) Artillery and ammunition.
past	(adj) Gone by. "The *past* president introduced his successor."
passed	(v) Moved forward, went through. "Mr. Dee *passed* here a moment ago."
personal	(adj) Private, individual. "It is a *personal* decision."
personnel	(n) Employees. "All *personnel* were affected by the decision."
perspective	(n) Objects "in *perspective*" are drawn to show their relation in space; also used in the sense of "mental view or prospect." "Seen in *perspective,* the decision was a wise one."
prospective	(adj) Expected, likely. "A *prospective* customer."
plaintiff	(n) A complainant, one who brings a suit.
plaintive	(adj) Mournful. "A *plaintive* voice."
post card	(n) A private mailing card.
postal card	(n) A mailing card issued by the Post Office, with imprinted stamp.
practical	(adj) Not governed by theory. "A *practical* solution." "A *practical* man."
practicable	(adj) Capable of being done, feasible. "The plan is *practicable.*"
practice	(v) To perform; (n) a performance or exercise.
practise	(v) Another form for *practice;* not to be used as a noun.
precedence pres′i dens, pri sēd′ens	(n) Preceding in time; priority. "The law takes *precedence* over company regulations."
precedents pres′i dents	(n) Acts that establish rules or serve as justification. "The *precedents* for his action are many."
prescribe	(v) To give rules or directions. "Doctors *prescribe* rest in bed for flu patients."
proscribe	(v) To forbid. "The laws *proscribe* campaign contributions by government employees."
presentiment	(n) A premonition. "He had a *presentiment* of impending catastrophe."
presentment	(n) A presentation, especially the report of a grand jury, in the phrase, "handed up a *presentment.*"
principal	(adj) First in rank. "Mr. Gray is the *principal* partner." (n) 1. The head person. "He is the *principal* in the transaction." 2. An amount invested or bearing interest. "Your *principal* earns 5 percent a year."
principle	(n) A rule or doctrine. "I am against the transaction on *principle.*"
prophecy prof′i sē	(n) A prediction. "Your *prophecy* came true."
prophesy prof′i sī	(v) To make a prediction. "What do you *prophesy* for 1990?"
proportional	(adj) In proportion to, relative; used with reference to a number of related things. "*Proportional* representation." "*Proportional* shares."

proportionate

(adj) 1. In proportion to; used with reference to the relation between two things. "The effort was *proportionate* to the salary."
2. Same as *proportional.*

queue

See **cue.**

quiet

(adj) Still, not noisy.

quite

(adv) Entirely, truly, very. "*Quite* warm."

receipt
  ri sēt´

(n) 1. The receiving of something. "We are in *receipt* of your letter."
2. The acknowledgment of something received. "We will send you a *receipt* for your payment."

recipe
  res´uh pē

(n) A formula, instructions for preparing food or drink. "Follow the *recipe* carefully."

residence
residents

(n) A dwelling place.
(n) People who live in a place.

respectfully
respectively

(adv) Showing respect. "*Respectfully* yours."
(adv) Relating to two or more in the order named. "Mr. and Mrs. Reese opened their individual accounts in the amounts of $1,000 and $500 *respectively.*"

rout
  rout
route
  root, rout

(n) A disorderly flight. "Our competitors were put to *rout.*"
(v) To put to flight. "Our competitors were *routed.*"
(n) 1. A course traveled over. "Take the shortest *route.*"
2. A newspaper delivery business. "He bought the *route* from his brother."
(v) To send over a certain course. "We'll *route* the car through the turnpike."

sensual
sensuous

(adj) Relating to the senses or appetites. "*Sensual* images."
(adj) Affecting the senses aesthetically. "*Sensuous* rhythm."

sight
site

(n) Something seen; (v) to see.
(n) Location. "The *site* of the new building has not yet been chosen."

cite

(v) To refer to or quote. "We can *cite* the dictionary as our authority."

sometime

(adv) At some time or other in the future. "I'll see you *sometime.*"
(adj) Former. "Dr. King is a *sometime* professor of English."

some time

1. A period of time. "*Some time* ago."
2. Same as *sometime.* (adv)

sometimes

(adv) Occasionally. "He is *sometimes* tardy."

special

(adj) 1. Particular, specific. "He wanted no *special* favor."
2. Outstanding. "This is a *special* treat."

especial

(adj) Not ordinary or common. Sometimes used as a synonym for *special.*

stable

(adj) Firm, steady. "The economy is now *stable.*"
(n) A place where animals are kept.

staple

(n) 1. A regularly stocked or used item. "Meat is a *staple.*"
2. A wire fastener.

stationary
stationery

(adj) Standing still; not movable.
(n) Writing materials.

straight
strait

(adj) Not crooked; upright, undeviating.
(n) 1. Dilemma or predicament, usually *straits.* "Difficult *straits.*" [Related usages include "strait-laced" (prudish), and "straitened circumstances" (financial difficulties).]
2. A narrow waterway connecting two larger bodies of water; also *straits* (construed as singular).

suit
  soot
	(n) 1. A set of clothes or cards.
	    2. A court action. "He promised to bring *suit* against our client."

suite
  swēt (*or,*
  for 1, soot)
	(n) 1. A set of matched furniture.
	    2. A group of rooms.
	    3. An instrumental form.

than **then**	(prep) Used in a comparison. "Taller *than* average." (adv) At that time; next in order.
therefor thâr fôr'	(adv) For it, for that. "Payment *therefor*."
therefore thâr'fôr	(adv) For that reason.

through
 	
thru
threw
	(adj) Finished. "They're *through* with the painting."
	(prep) By way of, by means of, from one end to the other.
	    Informal for *through* in prepositional sense.
	  (v) Past tense of *throw*.

to
too
 	
two
	(prep) Used largely to indicate direction. "Walk *to* work."
	  (adv) 1. Also.
	    2. Overly, as in "worked *too* hard."
	 (adj) A couple.

tortuous **torturous**	(adj) Twisting. "A *tortuous* road led through the mountain." (adj) Causing torture. "It was a *torturous* experience."
typography **topography**	(n) The use of type. (n) The surface features of a region. "The *topography* of the area includes a five-thousand-foot mountain."

use
  yoos
usage
  yoo'sij
	(n) A way of using. "His *use* of the word *flustrated* raised some eyebrows."
	(n) Customary use or practice. "The word *flustrated* is not in good *usage*."

waive **wave**	(v) To give up or forgo. "To *waive* immunity." (v) To move to and fro. "To *wave* the flag." (n) A moving ridge or swell, as in a lake or ocean.
weather **whether**	(n) Atmospheric conditions. (conj) If it be the case that. "He asked *whether*. . . ."
who's **whose**	Contraction of "who is" or "who has." " *Who's* going with you?" " *Who's* got the keys?" (pron) Possessive of who. " *Whose* keys are they?"
your **you're**	(pron) Possessive of you. " *Your* order will be filled promptly." Contraction of "you are." " *You're* paid up until June 1."

8.3   GLOSSARY OF COMMON GRAMMATICAL TERMS

Terms in boldface are defined in this glossary. Starred items (*) are discussed more fully in "Grammar Review," Section 8.4.

active verb   A verb whose subject performs the action indicated by the verb. Example: We *mailed* the check yesterday. (*Mailed* is an active verb because its subject, *we,* did the mailing.) See also **passive verb.**

*adjective   A word that describes or limits the meaning of a noun. An adjective usually precedes the noun it modifies (but see **predicate adjective.**) Example: *a large black* box (the italicized words are adjectives modifying *box*).

*adverb   A word that modifies or limits the meaning of a verb, adjective, or another adverb. It usually signifies time, place, degree, or manner. Example: The *heavily* overloaded truck arrived *very late*. (*Heavily* modifies the adjective *overloaded; very,* the adverb *late;* and *late,* the verb *arrived.*)

article   The articles are *a, an,* and *the.* They are adjectives.

case   An attribute of nouns and pronouns that shows their relation to the rest of the sentence. Thus the subject of a verb is in the *nominative case,* the object of a verb or preposition is in the *objective case,* and a noun or pronoun showing ownership is in the *possessive case.* Nouns have the same form for the nominative and objective cases, but pronouns often have different forms. For example, *I* and *he* are nominative, but *me* and *him* are objective.

clause   Any part of a sentence containing a subject and predicate. If the clause can stand alone as a sentence, it is a *main* (or *independent*) *clause;* if it cannot stand alone as a sentence, it is a *subordinate* (or *dependent*) *clause.* Main clauses are often introduced by coordinate conjunctions or conjunctive adverbs; subordinate clauses are introduced by subordinate conjunctions. See **conjunction.**

> We would appreciate it if you raised the discount.
> ←——— Main clause ———→ ←——— Subordinate clause ———→
>
> We asked for the first edition; we got the second.
> We asked for the first edition, but we got the second.
> We asked for the first edition; however, we got the second.
> ←——————— Main clause ———————→ ←——————— Main clause ———————→
>
> Although we asked for the first edition, we got the second.
> ←———————Subordinate clause ———————→ ←—— Main clause ——→

collective noun   A noun that stands for all the members of a group, for example, *company, management, team, herd, flock.* Use of a collective noun often raises the question of whether it is to be treated as singular or plural. For the answer, see "Subject-Verb Agreement" and "Pronouns," in Section 8.4.

common noun   The generic or class name for persons, places, or things. See also **noun, pronoun,** and **proper noun.**

> The *spirit* of the *workers* is high.
> The *books* were a *shambles.*
> No *stencil* is needed.

complement   Any word or group of words that completes the meaning of a verb. It may be **object, predicate adjective,** or **predicate noun.** The italicized portions of the following sentences are complements.

> He signed *the letter.* (Object)
> The machine is *inoperable.* (Predicate adjective)
> It was *a beautiful performance.* (Predicate noun)

compound sentence   A sentence having two or more main clauses. For examples, see **clause.**

compound subject Two or more subjects having the same verb. The verb is usually plural. For exceptions, see "Pronouns" and "Subject-Verb Agreement," in Section 8.4.

> Both the *employer* and the *employee* benefit from this plan.
> A *hammer* and a *screw driver* are all the tools you need.

compound predicate Two or more verbs having the same subject.

> He *stopped* the truck and *asked* for directions.

conjunction A word that connects words, phrases, or clauses. Coordinate conjunctions connect units of equal rank; subordinate conjunctions introduce subordinate clauses; conjunctive adverbs introduce main clauses. See **clause.**

> Coordinate conjunctions: *and, but, for, or, nor*
> Subordinate conjunctions: *since, because, after, that, if,* and so on.
> Conjunctive adverbs: *however, therefore, accordingly, furthermore, so,* and so on.

exclamation A grammatically independent word or phrase expressing feeling, often followed by an exclamation mark, sometimes by a period or comma.

> *Ouch!*
> *My goodness!*
> *Yes,* I am in accord.
> *No.* I did not agree.

*gerund A form of the verb ending in *-ing,* for example, *writing, comparing, asking.* A gerund is always used as a noun, that is, it performs the function of a subject or object.

> *Hiring* is the function of the personnel department. (Subject of verb *is*)
> Let's see what comes of *talking* with him. (Object of preposition *of*)

indirect object A noun or pronoun that answers the question to whom? or to what?, for whom? or for what? after the verb. It is not preceded by a preposition. See **object.**

> We will allow *them* the discount. (*Them* is the indirect object, *discount* the direct object.)

*infinitive A form of the verb usually preceded by *to* (the sign of the infinitive). It may perform the function of a noun, an adjective, or an adverb.

> He asked *to see* the new models. (Noun)
> She hadn't a thing *to wear.* (Adjective)
> Having fought *to win,* he was dejected in defeat. (Adverb)

nominative case See **case.**

noun The name of a person, place, thing, or abstract quality. A noun can be the subject or complement of a verb, or the object of a preposition.

> *Mr. Smith* rented a *home* in *Medwick.*

Nouns are singular or plural (*man, men; book, books*) and, as modifiers, may show possession (*men's* shoes, *ladies'* handbags, the *manager's* order). They are often preceded by *a, an,* or *the* (a *hat,* an *opening,* the *choice*).

object A *direct object* names the receiver of the action of a verb or verbal (participle, infinitive, or gerund).

> We sent the *invoice.*
> Selling *radios* is our business.

An *indirect object* tells to whom or to what or for whom or for what the action of the verb or verbal is performed, but is not preceded by a preposition.

> We sent them an invoice. (If the sentence were, "We sent an invoice to them," *them* would be the object of the preposition *to.*)
> Selling *dealers* radios is our business.

objective case See **case.**

*participle A verb form, usually ending in *-ing, -ed, -en,* or *-t,* which performs the function of an adjective.

> I noticed him *collating* the sheets. (Modifies *him*)
> *Bought* two years ago, the typewriter is still in excellent condition. (Modifies *typewriter*)

passive verb A verb whose subject is the receiver of the action of the verb. Active verbs are usually preferred. See also **active verb.**

> He *was given* a plaque by the Bowling Club. (Compare with, "The Bowling Club *gave* him a plaque.")
> The bill *was sent* by us. (Compare with, "We *sent* the bill.")

person An attribute of nouns and pronouns indicating the direction of discourse. The first-person pronoun is the speaker (*I, we*); the second-person pronoun is the person spoken to (*you*); the third-person pronoun is the person or thing spoken of (*he, it, they*). All nouns (*factory, book, chair*—anything) are regarded as in the third person. Verbs change their form to accommodate the person of the subject: I *am,* you *are,* he *is;* I *type,* you *type,* he *types.*

phrase Any group of related words without a subject and predicate. See also **clause.**

> Noun phrases: a suitable premium, the Multilith operator
> Verb phrases: have been tried, won't be able, has gone
> Prepositional phrases: in the room, from my desk, under the table
> Infinitive phrases: to fit the individual, to try my hand
> Participial phrases: walking across the aisle, working two nights

*possessive case A grammatical relationship usually, but not always, shown by the apostrophe (*Altman's, Max's; ours, theirs; a day's work*).

predicate That part of a sentence or clause that makes a statement about the subject. It consists of at least a verb, and usually of a verb and complement.

The letter *expresses our point of view fairly accurately.*
Although he *is still under 35,* he *seems certain to win a place on the Board.*

predicate adjective   An adjective following certain verbs, including *be, seem, appear, look, taste.* Its chief characteristic is that it describes the subject rather than a following noun.

The cartridge is *empty.* (Versus, "The *empty* cartridge.")
He seems *intelligent.*
The pie tastes *good.*

predicate noun   A noun (or pronoun) following a verb and representing the same thing as the subject. The predicate noun is in the nominative case. See **complement.**

He became *president* at 35.
It is *they.* (Not *them*)

*preposition   A preposition links a noun or pronoun with another word in the sentence. The noun or pronoun following a preposition is called the object of the preposition. Prepositions include *in, at, by, for, into, with, from, after, before, behind, toward, against, beyond, around, through, beside.*

at the desk   *behind* the counter   *with* great speed

*pronoun   A substitute for a noun. Some examples:

I, you, he, she, it, you, they; me, him, them (See **Case.**)
who, which, what
this, that, these, those
someone, somebody, anyone, anybody
myself, yourself, himself, oneself, themselves

Pronouns also have a possessive form:

mine, yours, his, hers, its, theirs, whose
anyone's, anybody's

proper adjective   An adjective form of a proper noun, usually capitalized.

American know-how
Victorian morality
Keynesian theories

proper noun   The distinctive name of a person, place, or thing; always capitalized.

David Kingsley
a tube of *Colgate* tooth paste
an office in *Rockefeller Center*

*sentence   A word or group of words that, in its context, can stand as a complete thought. It is followed by a period, a question mark, or an exclamation point. Customarily, a sentence has a subject and a verb; however, some sentences have neither a subject nor a verb, or have one or both understood.

I will write tomorrow.
Will I write? Of course. (Two sentences. "I will write" is understood to follow "Of course")
My goodness! How sales have risen! (Two sentences)

*subject That part of a sentence, usually at the beginning, about which a statement is made. The complete subject may consist of a single noun or pronoun, a noun phrase, or a noun clause. See also **phrase** and **clause.**

> *Workers* are getting scarce. (Noun)
> *Too many men* fail to realize their full potential. (Noun phrase)
> *Eating on the job* is prohibited. (Noun phrase)
> *To work for oneself* is my idea of independence. (Noun phrase)
> *That he was capable* was immediately apparent. (Noun clause)

subjunctive A form of the verb used for special purposes, for example, in resolutions, requests, conditions, and wishes. See "Verbs," in Section 8.4.

> I wish he *were* here. (Not *was*)

subordinate elements Any phrase or clause that cannot stand alone as a sentence, as illustrated by the italicized word groups below.

> *If you order now,* you will receive an extra 10 percent off.
> I'll let you know *after I study the details.*
> He did it *knowing that he would be criticized.*
> *To offer a commission only* does not seem fair.

tense The time (present, past, or future) shown by the verb, as I *write,* I *wrote,* I *will write.* See "Verbs," in Section 8.4.

*verb A word or words, expressing action or state of being, through which an assertion is made about a noun or pronoun. With the complement, it forms the predicate.

> The secretary *takes* dictation.
> Free samples *will be distributed.*
> The auditors *are* Brown, Henderson & Co.

verbal A form of the verb: **infinitive, participle,** or **gerund.**

> They propose *to sell* the entire stock. (Infinitive)
> *Having worked* for the company for 40 years, he retired. (Participle)
> He had some regrets after *signing* the letter. (Gerund)

8.4 GRAMMAR REVIEW

In grammar, as in word use, there is no absolute standard of correctness—only a general and sometimes highly disputed consensus of how people use the language. For that reason it would be a mistake to follow slavishly any given set of "rules." Still, the following review provides sensible norms for using language with clarity and precision—and some degree of formality—especially in writing.

For a "Glossary of Common Grammatical Terms," see Section 8.3.
For a "Dictionary of English Usage," see Section 8.5.

CONTENTS

Sentence Structure

Sentence Fragment.   When an essential part of a sentence is missing, or when one part is incorrectly separated from another by a period, an incomplete sentence, or fragment, is created. Fragments are avoided by careful writers except in special cases.

FRAGMENT: Your letter of February 12 regarding our fall merchandising plans. (What about the letter?)
FRAGMENT (IN ITALICS):   I have your letter of February 12. *Regarding our fall merchandise plans.*
COMPLETE: I have your letter of February 12 regarding our fall merchandising plans.

NOTE: Fragments are sometimes used to save words or for stylistic effect, especially in advertising copy. Examples:

Over the calf hose. Cotton lisle. Four popular colors. $2.00.
Thunder and lightning. Zero to 60 in 9 seconds. What kind of family sedan is this?

See **sentence,** in Section 8.3.

Run-On Sentence.   Two independent clauses not joined by the words *and, but, for, or,* or *nor* should be separated by a period or a semicolon, not a comma.

RUN-ON: Mr. Jones will be in on Thursday, I suggest you call beforehand if you want to see him.
IMPROVED: Mr. Jones will be in on Thursday. I suggest you call beforehand if you want to see him.

And as a Connective.   Do not join ideas with *and* unless they are closely related. Either split the sentence, or find a more exact connective.

BAD: The company was founded in 1926 *and* manufactures steel furniture.
IMPROVED: The company was founded in 1926. It manufactures steel furniture.
BETTER STILL: The company, which was founded in 1926, manufactures steel furniture.

Ambiguous Connective.   If you use the connectives *as, since,* or *while,* be sure that they can be interpreted in only one way.

DOUBLE MEANING: *As* I was going to lunch, I took the letter with me to mail. (*As* could stand for *when* or *inasmuch as.*)
SINGLE MEANING: On my way to lunch, I took the letter with me to mail.

DOUBLE MEANING: *Since* we are without a sales manager, we have experienced a sharp drop in orders. (Does *since* mean *because* or *from the time that?*)
SINGLE MEANING: *Because* we are without a sales manager . . .

Point of View.   Hold to one point of view, as far as possible. Avoid switching from one subject to another.

> FAULTY: *We* appreciate your order and *it* will be filled promptly.
> IMPROVED: *We* appreciate your order and will fill it promptly. (*We* is also the subject of *fill*.)

> FAULTY: After *you* enter all the amounts, *they* should be totaled in the last column.
> IMPROVED: After *you* enter all the amounts, total them in the last column. (The *you* before *total* is understood.)

> FAULTY: While [*we are*] not averse to the change, *the effects* will be felt for some time to come.
> IMPROVED: While [*we are*] not averse to the change, *we* will feel the effects for some time to come.

Parallel Structure.   Coordinate ideas should be expressed in similar grammatical fashion. Have a sound reason if you change from one type of construction to another.

> FAULTY: We will *accept* the funds, *send* receipts to the payers, and *crediting* your account at the same time.
> IMPROVED: We will *accept* the funds, *send* receipts to the payers, and *credit* your account at the same time.

> FAULTY: Sorting equipment would save *time, money,* and *provide greater control.*
> IMPROVED: Sorting equipment would *save time, reduce costs,* and *provide greater control.*
> OR: Sorting equipment would *save time and money* and *provide greater control.*

Position of Modifiers.   Words should be placed as close as possible to the words they restrict or modify.

> AMBIGUOUS: We received a *letter* from your secretary, Miss Hinchley, *dated October 16.*
> IMPROVED: We received a *letter dated October 16* from your secretary, Miss Hinchley.

> AMBIGUOUS: He would be in bad straits if he *lost* what he now has *by improvident investments.*
> IMPROVED: He would be in bad straits if he *lost by improvident investments* what he now has.

> AMBIGUOUS: Audrey and I will see you at the horse show *in any event.*
> IMPROVED: *In any event,* Audrey and I will see you at the horse show.

> COMPARE: I would suggest that you go over each of the three plans we discussed with your attorney before making a final decision.
> WITH: I would suggest that before making a final decision you go over with your attorney each of the three plans we discussed.

Sentence Completeness

Telegraphic Style.   Except in a telegram or informal note, the omission of words necessary for the completeness of a sentence is considered a mark of haste and is therefore discourteous.

> NOT: Letter received.
> BUT: *Your* letter *has been* received.

Omission of Other *and* Else. In making a comparison, use *other* or *else* when logic requires it. An exception to this rule may be made, however, in the interests of informality.

INFORMAL: This layout is better than any we've seen.
CORRECT: This layout is better than any *other* we've seen.

INFORMAL: We fly to more South American cities than anybody.
CORRECT: We fly to more South American cities than anybody *else*.

Omission of That *and* Those. In making a comparison, use *that* or *those* (or an equivalent expression) when logic requires it.

NOT: His qualifications are better than any other applicant we've seen.
BUT: His qualifications are better than *those* of any other applicant we've seen.
OR: His qualifications are better than any other *applicant's* we've seen.

NOT: The price is much lower than our competitor.
BUT: The price is much lower than *that charged by* our competitor.
OR: The price is much lower than our *competitor's*.

Mistaken Use of Other.   *Other* should not be used when it distorts the sense.

BAD: The special features of our generators justify a higher price than that charged
for *other* inferior generators.
IMPROVED: . . . justify a higher price than that charged for inferior generators.
OR: . . . justify a higher price than that charged for *other* generators.

Completeness in Paired Expressions.   When two expressions are joined by *and* (or in some similar manner) be careful about making a single word do for both.

COMPARE: *The president and chief executive officer* arrived on Tuesday. (One person)
   The president and the chief executive officer arrived on Tuesday. (Two persons)
FAULTY: *A Sheraton and Duncan Phyfe* chair . . . (One chair? Not likely.)
BETTER: *A Sheraton and a Duncan Phyfe* chair . . . (Two chairs)

FAULTY: We have no financial interest or other connection *with* that company.
BETTER: We have no financial interest *in* or other connection *with* that company.
OR: We have no financial interest *in* that company, or any other connection *with* it.

FAULTY: The truck needs *a new transmission and brakes.*
BETTER: The truck needs *a new transmission and new brakes.*

FAULTY: *The order was accepted and the goods placed* in the warehouse awaiting
shipment.
BETTER: *The order was accepted and the goods were placed* in the warehouse awaiting
shipment.

FAULTY: This is *one of the most popular numbers, if not the most popular,* in our line.
CORRECT: This is *one of the most popular numbers, if not the most popular number,*
in our line.
BETTER: This is *one of the most popular numbers in our line, if not the most popular.*
(Words may be omitted in a comparison at the end of a sentence. Here the omitted
word is *number*. See rule below.)

Omissions in Comparisons.   Words may be omitted in expressions of comparison.

CORRECT: We are sure we can do the job as well as they $\wedge$. (*Can* is understood.)
CORRECT: Better that the business should benefit us than $\wedge$ them. (*It should benefit*
is understood.)

Subject-Verb Agreement. *Agreement in Number.* A verb agrees in number with its subject—singular subject, singular verb; plural subject, plural verb.

the customer says	our customers say
Mr. Teller works	our employees work
no one believes	we believe
a discount is given	discounts are given

Intervening Words. When words come between the subject and its verb, do not let the intervening words affect the number of the verb.

WRONG: *Mr. Farmer,* not the salesmen, *were* entitled to the commission.
RIGHT: *Mr. Farmer . . . was* entitled to the commission.

WRONG: The *full order,* consisting of an assortment of sizes and colors, *were shipped* by express.
RIGHT: The *full order . . . was shipped* by express.

Together with, as Well as, and So On. A singular subject followed by a phrase beginning with the words *with, together with, as well as,* and *in addition to* takes a singular verb.

Mr. Ray, with his two assistants, is expected to attend the hearing. (Compare: *Mr. Ray and his two assistants are expected* to attend the hearing.)
The Federal Government, as well as the state and city, has a stake in this measure.

Compound Subjects. Any subjects joined by *and* take a plural verb. (For exception, see "Plural Subjects as Singular Units," in this section.)

The three workers and their supervisor have been told . . .
The desk and the file are obstructing access to the door.

Plural Words Following Verb. A singular subject takes a singular verb even when the verb is followed by a plural complement.

The *limit was three boxes* per customer.
A good time to do it *is the first two weeks* in September.
A satisfactory proportion is two spoonfuls to a glass of water.

Collective Nouns as Subjects. A singular subject, representing a group of similar persons or things, takes either a singular or plural verb, depending on the sense. Collective nouns include such words as *company, committee, group, jury, staff, management, team, crowd,* and *faculty.*

The *committee has reported* favorably on the proposal. (Here the committee is acting as a unit.)
The *committee have submitted their reports.* (Here the individual members of the committee are acting separately.)
The *jury has been out* five hours.
The *jury are* hopelessly *divided.*

Subject Following Verb. When the subject follows the verb, be sure the two agree in number.

WRONG: There *is* still *three copies* to be accounted for. (*Copies,* not *there,* is the subject.)
RIGHT: There *are* still *three copies* to be accounted for.

WRONG: Attached to the table *was a price tag and instructions* for assembling.
RIGHT: Attached to the table *were a price tag and instructions* for assembling.

Alternative Subjects.   When two or more subjects are joined by *or* or *nor*, the verb should agree with the nearer subject.

> Neither Mr. Jones nor his *associates wish* to participate.
> Either you or *I am* in the lead. (But: "You and I are in the lead.")
> A catalogue or some descriptive *folders are needed.* (Preferred to "Some descriptive folders or a *catalogue is needed.*")

Singular with Each, Every, *and So On.*   Words like *each, every, someone, somebody, everyone, everybody, anyone, anybody, no one, either,* and *neither* are followed by singular verbs.

> *Each manager is* responsible for his own department.
> *Everybody* we invited *was* there.
> *Anyone is* eligible to enter the contest.
> *Either* of the models *is* acceptable.
> *No one was* more surprised than Mr. Lee.

NOTE: Although *no one* is always singular, *none* is singular or plural depending on the sense.

> Of all the clerks in his department, *none is* better able to do the job than Bob Loring. (Only one person is indicated.)
> *None of our customers live* outside Chicago. (More than one are indicated.)

A Number, the Number.   The subject *the number* takes a singular verb, but *a number* takes a plural verb.

> *The number* of exceptions *is* increasing.
> *A number* of good buys *are* currently available.

Subjects Expressing Part of a Whole.   Subjects like *some, part, half,* and so on are followed by either a singular or plural verb depending on the sense.

> *Part of the trouble is* that no one will take the responsibility.
> *Some of the rules are* not being followed.
> *Two thirds of our quota has* been met.
> *Two thirds of our sales force are* college graduates.

One of Those Who.   The verb following *who, which,* or *that* in a construction similar to "one of those who" is invariably plural.

> He is *one of those executives who are never satisfied* with things as they are.
> This is *one of the most beautiful properties that have come* our way.

Plural Subjects as Singular Units.   When a plural subject represents a singular concept, it takes a singular verb.

> *Fifty dollars seems* like a fair price.
> *Kellogg's Corn Flakes is* probably the most popular of the cold cereals.
> *Dip and dry is* all you do.

Pronouns

Nominative and Objective Forms.   Some pronouns have different forms for the nominative case and the objective case.

Nominative	Objective
I	me
he	him
she	her
we	us
they	them
who	whom

1. Use the nominative case pronouns as follows:
   (a) Subject of the verb.

We wanted to know *who* would be there.
We secretaries are in the best position to know.
They approved the plan.

   (b) Complement of forms of the verb *to be* (*is, am, are, was, were, been*).

It is *I.*
How would you feel if you were *he?*
It was *they* who should have taken the responsibility.
If I were *she*, I would not have permitted it.

NOTE: Rule (b) is ignored in speech and informal writing by many literate persons.

Acceptable: It's *me;* that's *her;* if I were *him.*

2. Use the objective case pronouns as follows.
   (a) Object of verb or verbal (infinitive, participle, or gerund).

    He can have *whomever* he wants. (Object of *wants*)
    I asked Mr. Day to give *me* the total cost. (Object of infinitive *to give*)

   (b) Object of preposition.

    The quarrel is between *him* and *me.* (Objects of the preposition *between.*)
    You can trust the information to Mr. Gray and *us.* (Object of preposition *to.*)

   (c) Subject of an infinitive.

    You would expect *him* to respond promptly. (Subject of the infinitive *to respond;* the object of the verb *would expect* is the whole phrase, *him to respond promptly.*)

Pronoun After As *or* Than.   In a construction beginning with *as* or *than,* part of the sentence is often omitted. Determine the correct form of the pronoun by completing the sentence in your mind.

He is far more expert than *I* [am expert].
Better that we should get the credit than [that] *they* [should get it].
Please give it to me rather than [to] *him.*

Agreement in Number and Gender.   A pronoun agrees with its antecedent (the word or words it stands for) in number and gender (masculine, feminine, or neuter).

As soon as we know what *media* you have chosen, we will schedule our advertisements in *them*.

When *Miss Ray* calls, tell *her* I will be able to see *her* on Friday.

Please inspect the *shipment* carefully when *it* arrives.

Every worker should do the job for which *he is* (not *they are*) best suited.

1. When referring to a collective noun, a pronoun will be singular or plural depending on whether the noun is treated as singular or plural. An exception is occasionally made when consistency would be awkward.

CORRECT: The *management are doing* all *they* can.
CORRECT: The *management is doing* all *it* can.
ACCEPTABLE: Now that the *company is well established, they* have decided to limit *their* sales to authorized dealers.

2. A pronoun referring to two or more antecedents connected by *and* is usually plural.

CORRECT: The *foreman and the night watchman* took *their* break at the same time.
EXCEPTION: As *a father and a citizen, he* favored stricter control. (The antecedents *a father* and *a citizen* represent the same person.)

3. A pronoun referring to two antecedents connected by *or* or *nor* will be singular if both antecedents are singular, plural if one of the antecedents is plural.

Either *Bill or Joe* will have *his* car with *him*.
Neither *Mr. Jones nor his sisters* need worry about *their* lease.

See also "Subject-Verb Agreement," in this section.

Reference of Pronouns.   Be sure that the word or words the pronoun stands for are absolutely clear to the reader.

1. Do not use a pronoun—especially *it, this,* or *which*—unless it clearly refers to a specific word or idea.

BAD: Retooling is very expensive, *which* we will consider when designing a new model.
BETTER: Retooling is very expensive—a fact that we will consider when we design a new model.
ALSO GOOD: We will consider the expense of retooling before we design a new model.

2. Do not use a pronoun that may refer to more than one word or idea. If necessary, repeat the word or rephrase the sentence.

DOUBLE MEANING: Mr. Wells said that Mr. Carter would write the report after *he* had assembled the data. (Is *he* Mr. Wells or Mr. Carter?)
IMPROVED: Mr. Wells said Mr. Carter would write the report after assembling the data.
ALSO (ANOTHER MEANING): Mr. Wells said that Mr. Carter would write the report after he, Mr. Wells, had assembled the data.

Possessive.   The possessive forms of nouns and pronouns are used to show ownership. They are usually, but not always, signified by the apostrophe (').
For example: *man's, Smith's, the company's.*

Possessive Pronouns. The possessive form of personal pronouns is written without the apostrophe.

my, mine   our, ours
your, yours   their, theirs
his, her, hers
its (*it's* is the contraction of *it is* or *it has*)
whose (*who's* is the contraction of *who is* or *who has*)

Other pronouns form their possessive with the apostrophe.

one's
someone's   somebody's
anyone's   anybody's
no one's   nobody's
everyone's   everybody's

Possessive Nouns (Singular). Singular nouns regularly form their possessive by the addition of the apostrophe and *s* (*'s*). When it would be awkward to add the *s* because the word already ends in *s* or the sound of *s*, only the apostrophe need be added.

the President's advisers   the boss's daughter
the bell captain's station   the *Times's* correspondent or
an executive's privilege   the *Times'* correspondent
the shipper's terms   Mr. Willis's office or
the department's rules   Mr. Willis' office
                    for his conscience' sake
                    Los Angeles' airport
                    Jesus' teachings

Possessive Nouns (Plural). If a plural noun ends in *s,* add only the apostrophe. Otherwise, add the apostrophe and *s.*

the Smiths' dinner party   our accountants' recommendation
ladies' wear   men's clothing
boys' camps   women's markets
clients' problems   children's playthings

Double Possessive. In certain constructions, especially after *this* and *that,* the word *of* and the possessive noun or pronoun are used together.

CORRECT: that car of mine
           a customer of ours
           those photographs of Mr. Brown's (Compare with "those photographs
              of Mr. Brown.")

Idiomatic Possessive. In certain constructions, where possession is not involved, the possessive is nevertheless used.

CORRECT: a day's pay, in a month's time, a week's delay

Compound Possessive. When the expression showing possession consists of several words or a hyphenated word, the possessive is added to the last word only.

CORRECT: B. Altman & Co.'s Fifth Avenue store
Bill Blake and Ed Conway's suggestion (Compare with "Bill Blake's and Ed Conway's suggestions.")
General Motors' stock
somebody else's responsibility
his mother-in-law's heirs
Fort Worth's centennial
the branch office manager George Fry's records (But, "the branch office manager's, George Fry's, records.")

Possessive Before Understood Word.   The possessive is used even when the thing possessed is not expressed.

CORRECT: at Macy's [department store]
at your grocer's [shop]. (Also, "at your grocer")
January's output exceeded February's [output].

Possessive Before Gerund.   When a verb form ending in -*ing* is used as a noun (but not as an adjective), a noun or pronoun before it takes the possessive form.

CORRECT: Mr. *Gray's* coming was not anticipated.
Their talking disturbed the operator.
We were shocked at *his* leaving. (Not *him; leaving* is a noun, object of the preposition *at*.)
We saw *him* leaving. (Correct because *leaving* is an adjective, describing the pronoun *him*.)

NOTE: The practice is growing of omitting the apostrophe in store and company names. Follow the style adopted by the organization itself.

Gimbels	Mays	Schraffts	Wallachs
Sears	Harpers (magazine)	Merchants Bank	

Verbs.   Verbs are words that help us make a statement about a person, place, or thing. The italicized words in the following sentences are verbs.

We *sent* the order to you yesterday.
The two companies *were* not able to reach an agreement.
The package *was returned* because of insufficient postage.
Mr. Jones *will arrive* soon.
Miss Strum *is* forty-five years old.

Tense.   The form of the verb changes to show time. Note the forms of the verb *walk*.

PRESENT: I walk, we walk (*also* am walking, does walk, do walk)
PAST: I walked, we walked, (*also* did walk)
FUTURE: I will (*or* shall) walk, we will (*or* shall) walk

PRESENT PERFECT: I have walked, we have walked
PAST PERFECT: I had walked, we had walked
FUTURE PERFECT: I will (*or* shall) have walked, we will (*or* shall) have walked

Irregular Verbs.   Verbs that follow the preceding patterns are called *regular verbs*. Verbs that do not are called *irregular verbs*. The irregular verb forms are given in the dictionary. Some examples:

(I) begin	began	have begun	am beginning
(it) bursts	burst	has burst	is bursting
(I) do	did	have done	am doing

Agreement with Subject.   The form of the verb must be consistent with the form of the subject. (See also "Subject-Verb Agreement" in this section.) Examples:

I go (BUT he goes)
I am (BUT you are, he is)
I have (BUT he has)
We say (BUT the customer says)

Time Relationships.   The various tense forms are used to show time relationships between verbs. Examples:

We *are shipping* your order today. (Present)
We *have shipped* your order. (Indefinite past)
We *shipped* your order on May 12. (Definite past)
We *will ship* your order promptly. (Future)
By August 1, we *will have completed* the shipment. (Time before some time in the future)
By August 1, *we had completed* the shipment. (Time before some time in the past)

Active and Passive Verbs.   Many statements can be made in two ways, depending on whether the active or passive form of the verb is used. Example:

ACTIVE: Mr. Benson signed the check.
PASSIVE: The check was signed by Mr. Benson.

When the active form of the verb is used, the subject invariably names the performer of the action of the verb—in this instance, Mr. Benson. When the passive form of the verb is used, the subject names the thing acted upon—in this instance, the check. The active form is generally preferred because it is simpler, more direct, and more concise than the passive form. The passive form is useful, however, when the writer wants to stress the thing acted upon rather than the performer, especially for reasons of tact.

TACTLESS (ACTIVE):   You failed to sign the check.
IMPROVED (PASSIVE):   The check was not signed.

Subjunctive.   The subjunctive forms of the verb omit the *s* in the present tense (*he go,* not *he goes*) and substitute *be* for *am, is, was,* or *were,* and *were* for *was* in some constructions. Examples:

He asked that the case *be* dismissed. (Not *is*)
I wish I *were* going with you. (Not *was*)
I demand that Harry *go* with us. (Not *goes*)

Use the subjunctive:

(1) to express a request, command, motion, or resolution following the word *that.*

He requested that I *be* included on the committee.
Mr. Gordon insisted that Mr. Klein *withdraw* his petition.
I move that the meeting *be* adjourned.
Resolved, that the new training program *be* put into effect on September 1 of this year.

(2) to indicate an impossible condition following the word *if*.

He would be easier to deal with if he *were* not so stubborn. (He *is* stubborn.)
I would go if I *were* younger. (I am *not* younger.)
BUT: Mr. Starr wanted to know if I *was* coming. (I might come: so the condition is
not impossible.)

(3) to express a formal wish.

We wish he *were* able to handle the job.
I wish I *were* going with you.
BUT (informal):   I wish I *was* going with you.

Words Formed from Verbs.   Some words, called verbals, are formed from
verbs but have the characteristics of other parts of speech. For a description
of these forms, see "Infinitives," "Participles," and "Gerunds," following in
that order.

Infinitives.   An infinitive is a verb form usually preceded by the word *to*.

He likes *to work*.
What are they going *to do* about it?
We would like *to have gone* with you.
We can help you *learn* a trade. (The *to* before *learn* is omitted.)

Split Infinitive.   Splitting an infinitive is putting a word between the *to* and
the verb, for example, *to slowly walk, to eventually return*. When the split
infinitive is awkward, you should avoid it either by finding another place for
the intervening word or by recasting the sentence. In many instances, the
split infinitive is not awkward or is less awkward than the revised construction, and it should be retained.

AWKWARD: It is easy *to convincingly talk* about your own product.
IMPROVED: It is easy *to talk convincingly* about your own product.

AWKWARD: If you tried *to conscientiously apply yourself* to the problem, you would
undoubtedly be able to solve it.
IMPROVED: If you tried *to apply yourself conscientiously* . . .

NOT AWKWARD: The proposal was *to ultimately abandon* the old mine.

Tense of Infinitive.   The infinitive changes its form to show time relationships.
However, the present infinitive (*to go, to be, to do, to see,* and so on) is used
whenever the action of the infinitive takes place at the same time as the action
of the verb.

I want *to go*. (Present)
I seem *to have misplaced* the key. (Time before present)
BUT: I wanted *to go*. (Past)
I would have liked *to go* with you. (Time before present)

Participles.   A participle is a verb form that usually, but not always, ends in
-*ing* or -*ed*, and has the characteristics of an adjective; that is, it is used to
modify or describe a noun or pronoun.

Deprived of additional funds, he had to go out of business. (Modifies *he*)
The new man was seen *smoking* in the prohibited area. (Modifies *man*)

Dangling Participle. A participle that does not logically relate to the word it modifies is called a dangling participle. To correct the error, recast the sentence.

DANGLING: *Walking* across the aisle, *a hand truck* hit Mr. Haynes. (Seems as if the hand truck walked across the aisle)

IMPROVED: *Walking* across the aisle, *Mr. Haynes* was hit by a hand truck.

ALSO IMPROVED: A hand truck hit Mr. Haynes while he was walking across the aisle.

Gerunds. A gerund is a verb form ending in *-ing* and having the characteristics of a noun, that is, it may be used as a subject or object.

Typing is a valuable skill. (Subject)
We objected to his *leaving* so early. (Object of preposition *to*)
He liked *working* for us. (Object of verb *liked*)

Possessive with Gerund. A pronoun modifying a gerund should be in the possessive form. (See also "Possessive," in this section.)

We will appreciate *your* keeping a close watch on expenditures.
His talking disturbed the others.

Clear Reference. A prepositional phrase containing a gerund should clearly relate to some other word in the sentence. (See also "Dangling Participle," in this section.)

AMBIGUOUS: You have been most helpful to us in advising our customer. (Who did the advising—"you" or "us"?)

IMPROVED: The information you gave us helped us in advising our customer.

Adjectives. Adjectives are words that describe nouns. They include the articles *a, an,* and *the* and can sometimes be identified by the endings *-able, -al, -ed, -ful, -ish, -less, -ous,* and *-y.*

a good day	*a large blue* box
the genuine article	*electronic filtering* system
working women	*leather* soles
used car	*a plentiful* supply
a harmless additive	*automatic* shift
stylish clothes	*callous* treatment

Use of Comparative and Superlative. In formal English, the comparative is used when two units are being compared, and the superlative when the comparison involves more than two units.

This is the *better* of the two.
We make this shoe in a half dozen colors, but brown is the *most popular.*

NOTE: In formal English, the superlative form is sometimes used in a comparison of two. Example:

Between the sweet and the unsugared variety, our customers like the sweet *best.*

Comparison of Adjectives.   Adjectives change their degree of intensity by the addition of *-er* and *-est,* or by the words *more, most, less,* or *least* placed before them.

Simple	*Comparative*	*Superlative*
kind	kinder	kindest
	more kind	most kind
	less kind	least kind
early	earlier	earliest
competent	more competent	most competent

Irregular Adjectives.   Some adjectives do not follow the rules in their forms of comparison. When in doubt, consult the dictionary.

good	better	best
much	more	most
little	less	least

Adjectives After Certain Verbs.   Certain verbs, including *be,* (*is, was,* and so on), *feel, taste, smell,* and *turn* are followed by adjective complements that describe the subjects of the verbs.

The day was *hectic.*
The weather turned *warm.*
The new cream smells *good.*
I feel *great.*
I feel *good.**
I feel *well.**

*NOTE: In the last two examples, both *good* and *well* are adjectives, but *good* suggests a general state of well-being while *well* seems to refer to health alone.

Absolute Adjectives.   Some adjectives, like *unique, complete, perfect,* and *impossible,* already express the ultimate degree and therefore cannot logically be compared.

QUESTIONABLE: It has a *very unique* design.
CORRECT: It has a *unique* design.

QUESTIONABLE: The situation is becoming *more impossible* every day.
CORRECT: The situation is becoming *worse* every day.
OR: The situation is becoming *impossible.*

Adverbs.   Adverbs are words that limit or describe verbs, adjectives, or other adverbs. An identifying feature of many adverbs is the ending *-ly.* Some adverbs have two forms, for example, *slow* or *slowly, quick* or *quickly.*

worked *strenuously*	met *secretly*
a *very* likeable person	a *clearly* understood condition
very often mistaken	*too* soft
really unusual	*much* appreciated

Comparison of Adverbs.   Like adjectives, adverbs have degrees of comparison signified by the addition of *-er* and *-est,* or by the words *more* and *most* (or *less* and *least*) before them.

Simple	*Comparative*	*Superlative*
slow or	slower	slowest
slowly	more slowly	most slowly
	less slowly	least slowly
often	oftener	oftenest
	more often	most often
intelligently	more intelligently	most intelligently

Irregular Adverbs. Some adverbs form their degrees of comparison without regard to the preceding rule. When in doubt, consult your dictionary.

badly	worse	worst
well	better	best
far	farther, further	farthest, furthest

Double Negative. Using two negative adverbs to express a single negative idea is incorrect.

BAD: We can't see no advantage.
BETTER: We can't see any advantage.
OR: We can see no advantage.

BAD: We don't hardly go there.
BETTER: We hardly go there.

Prepositions. A preposition is a word that links a noun or pronoun with some other part of the sentence. Prepositions include such words as *in, at, to, by, for, after, before, above,* and *behind.*

Preposition at End of Sentence. There is some prejudice against the use of a preposition at the end of a sentence. However, a preposition may end a sentence when it would be awkward in another position.

AWKWARD AT END OF SENTENCE: Please let us know what conditions you will sell the property on Front Street *under.*
IMPROVED: Please let us know *under* what conditions you will sell the property on Front Street.

AWKWARD IN MIDDLE OF SENTENCE: It's a condition *with* which we will have to put up.
IMPROVED: It's a condition we will have to put up *with.*

Idiomatic Prepositions. Certain verbs characteristically take certain prepositions after them. Some verbs may be followed by one of several prepositions depending on the meaning.

We both *agree on* the need for improvement.
We *agree to* their stipulation.
I *agree with* you.

He *compared* the device *to* a thermostat. (Expresses similarity.)
The new model does not *compare with* the old in attractiveness. (Expresses dissimilarity.)

NOTE: If you are in doubt about the preposition following any verb, look up the verb in your dictionary.

8.5 DICTIONARY OF ENGLISH USAGE

The correct use of words is determined by the consensus of educated people as revealed in their speech and writing. Some guidance is provided by dictionaries and books on usage, but even with these aids you have to depend to a great extent on your own judgment of what is appropriate in any given circumstance (Figure 8-3). In this listing you will find words about which

---

ACCEPTABLE

Formal. The language of documentary writing and of statements delivered on very dignified or state occasions.

General. The predominant language of the journalist, business writer, and public speaker.

Informal. The language characteristic of the everyday speech of educated persons and of writing that imitates such speech. Also called colloquial.

ACCEPTABLE WITH RESERVATIONS

Jargon. The specialized language of a particular trade or profession, useful in technical papers. Also, in an undesirable sense, unintelligible language or language marked by the use of pretentious words.

Slang. Language that has its origins in the streets and shops and often in the underworld. Many slang terms gain wide use and respectability and may, when used with discrimination, add color and force to otherwise dignified English.

UNDESIRABLE BUT TOLERATED

Archaic. Old-fashioned; outmoded. Occasionally found in legal writing and some business letters and memorandums.

Stilted. Stiff. Used especially to denote language that is too formal for the occasion.

Stereotyped. Applied especially to phrases that are fixed in form and have lost their vigor through overuse. Also called hackneyed.

NOT ACCEPTABLE

Illiterate. Characteristic of the uneducated. Includes distortions, misuses, and misspellings of acceptable words.

Obscene. Words that offend the sensibilities.

Figure 8-3 Levels of usage. This table is designed to help determine whether a word is acceptable and appropriate in business usage.

questions are most likely to be raised and some helpful advice on their proper use.

For questions of usage involving grammar, see "Glossary of Common Grammatical Terms," Section 8.3, and "Grammar Review," Section 8.4.

abeyance, as in "held in *abeyance*" Often used in legal papers, it is considered stilted in ordinary correspondence.

> NOT: We are holding our decision *in abeyance*
> BUT: We are holding *up* our decision.

above Correct as a noun ("the *above*") and adjective ("the *above* facts"), as well as in its traditional role as an adverb ("the date shown *above*," "the *above*-mentioned procedure"). However, more informality can be achieved with a substitute expression, for example, "these facts," "this date," "the procedure we mentioned."

above-captioned Because *captioned* refers to the heading or subject line, the word *above* seems superfluous. Thus, one might refer to "the captioned account" when the name of the account is shown as a subject line above the body of a letter. This language, however, is more suited to legal correspondence than to less formal letters and memorandums. (See also *subject*.)

administrate Misused for *administer*. Correct: Mr. Treadwell will *administer* the program.

advise Well used in the sense of "counsel," but stilted and overworked in the sense of "inform."

> GOOD: I would *advise* you to sell the property.
> STILTED: If you want us to go ahead with the order, please *advise*.
> BETTER: If you want us to go ahead with the order, please *let us know*.
> AVOID: kindly advise, please be advised, we wish to advise you.

affect, effect *Affect* is a verb meaning "to influence" or "to feign." *Effect*, as a verb, means "to bring about." As a noun, it means "result."

> His decision was *affected* by personal bias. (Influenced)
> How will the reorganization *affect* the workers. (Influence)
> He *affected* an English accent. (Feigned)
> He *effected* many changes in procedure. (Brought about)
> The *effect* of the price rise will not be known for some time. (Result)

aforementioned, aforesaid Except in legal papers, these expressions are somewhat stilted. If possible, use *this, that,* or some other expression. (See also **above.**)

> STILTED: the *aforesaid* company
> IMPROVED: *this* company, *that* company
>
> STILTED: the *aforementioned* circumstances
> IMPROVED: the circumstances *we mentioned earlier*

agenda   A list of topics to be taken up at a meeting, *agenda* is the plural of the Latin word *agendum*. However, it is usually construed as singular.

> CORRECT: The *agenda* for the meeting *has been drawn up.*

all-around, all-round   Use either word in the sense of versatile.

> CORRECT: He is a good *all-around* [or *all-round*] assistant.

alright.   Not in good usage. Use *all right* (two words).

> If Mr. Gross wants to come along, it's *all right* [not *alright*] with me.

among, between   Custom still favors the use of *between* when there are two alternatives; *among,* when the number of choices is more than two.

> We'll divide the luncheon tab *between* us. (The two of us)
> The estate was divided *between* the brother and the sister.
> The dispute *among* them was settled amicably. (More than two)

amongst   Better use *among.*

> NOT: We are looking for new markets *amongst* teen-agers.
> BUT: We are looking for new markets *among* teen-agers.

amount, number   Use *amount* to signify a sum or a quantity that cannot be measured in units; use *number* to refer to a quantity of units.

> The *amount* of the sale was $456.30.
> There is a negligible *amount* of waste in the process.
> A small *number* of passengers were stranded.

and etc.   Because *etc.* is the abbreviation for the Latin term *et cetera,* meaning "and the rest," the use of *and* with *etc.* is superfluous.

> NOT: booklets, pamphlets, circulars, *and etc.*
> BUT: booklets, pamphlets, circulars, *etc.*

anyways, anywheres   Misused for *anyway, anywhere.*

> CORRECT: We'll allow the discount *anyway.* (Not *anyways*)
>   He would be welcome *anywhere.* (Not *anywheres*)

and/or   Useful and correct in indicating "either of two, or both."

> CORRECT: The system employs videotape *and/or* film.

apt, liable, likely   *Apt* means suitable, tending (to), or quick to learn. *Liable* suggests exposure to something disadvantageous or responsibility for consequences. *Likely* refers to what is probable.

> It is an *apt* phrase. He is an *apt* pupil.
> If he breaks any more sales records, his success is *apt* to go to his head.
> It is *likely* that we will need more storage space soon.
> He is legally *liable* for his actions.
> If he insists on speculating, he is *liable* to get hurt.

as, that   Do not misuse *as* for *that* or *whether.*

> WRONG: We do not know for sure *as* we can meet the deadline.
> RIGHT: We do not know for sure *that* [or *whether*] we can meet the deadline.

as how Do not misuse for *how* or *that.*

NOT: We don't see *as how* our intervention will do any good.
BUT: We don't see *that* [or *how*] our intervention will do any good.

as, like *Like* is used for *as, as if,* or *as though* only in very informal English, and even then is often subject to criticism. *Like* is correctly used as a preposition.

CORRECT: It looks *as if* [or *as though*] your prediction was right.
QUESTIONABLE: It looks *like* your prediction was right.

CORRECT: We shipped it in brown, *as* the order specified.
QUESTIONABLE: We shipped it in brown, *like* the order specified.

CORRECT: The report is bound *like* a book.

as per, per Used in the sense of *as, in accordance with,* or *following,* these expressions are stilted and should be avoided in ordinary writing.

STILTED: *As per* your request, we are sending you . . .
BETTER: *In accordance with* your request, we are sending you . . .

OR: *Following* your request, we are sending you . . .

STILTED: We are sending you the booklet *per* your request.
BETTER: We are sending you the booklet *as* you requested.

at about The *at* is unnecessary.

CORRECT: I'll call you *about* 10 o'clock. (Not *at about*)

awful, awfully Although often used informally in speech, both words are best avoided in writing.

QUESTIONABLE: He gave us an *awful* time.
BETTER: He gave us a *hard* time.

QUESTIONABLE: His performance was *awfully* good.
BETTER: His performance was *very* good. (Or *first-rate, topnotch, lively, exciting,* and so on)

bad, badly The correct expression is "looks *bad,*" "seems *bad,*" "feels *bad.*" It is also acceptable to say "feel *badly,*" as in "I feel *badly* (for *distressed, sorry*) about her misfortune." Otherwise *badly* is used in the sense of "in a faulty manner"; *bad,* in the sense of "faulty" or "not good."

The copying machine is working *badly* again.
The service is *bad.* (Not *good*)

balance, remainder *Balance* is always correct in reference to accounts, but it is considered colloquial in the sense of *remainder.*

CORRECT: We would appreciate receiving the *balance* of your account soon.
CORRECT: We will ship the *remainder* (or *rest*) of the order on June 15.
COLLOQUIAL: We will ship the *balance* of the order on June 15.

bank on Colloquial for *depend on.*

based on This construction is often used when *on the basis of* or *from* would be better. (See "Dangling Participle," in Section 8.3.)

CORRECT: Our estimate is *based* on last year's experience. (*Based* is used as an adjective modifying *estimate*.)

QUESTIONABLE: *Based on* last year's experience, we expect increasing foreign competition. (*Based on* is used as a preposition; this usage is not sanctioned in formal grammar, but is quite common in business.)

CORRECT: *On the basis of* [or *from*] last year's experience, we expect increasing foreign competition.

beg Should never be used in such business-letter phrases as "*beg* to advise" and "*beg* to remain," in which it is considered stilted and antiquated.

being that Incorrectly used for *since* or *because.*

NOT: *Being that* you are leaving for Los Angeles tomorrow . . .
BUT: [*Since*] you are leaving for Los Angeles tomorrow . . .

beside, besides Often confused. *Beside* means "by the side of"; *besides* means "in addition to" or "furthermore."

Please put the carton *beside* the desk. (Not *besides*)
Who *besides* Mr. Grant and Mr. Fellows said they would come?
Besides, we didn't want to disturb the present arrangement.

NOTE: *Beside* is also used idiomatically in such expressions as "*beside* the point" and "*beside* oneself with fear."

best of any. Used informally only. Expressions in better use are *best one* and *best of those.*

QUESTIONABLE: It's the *best of any* we've tried.
CORRECT: It's the *best one* we've tried.
CORRECT: It's the *best of those* we've tried.

between you and I Common but ungrammatical. The correct expression is *between you and me.* (*Between* is a preposition and a pronoun that follows must be in the objective case.)

bi-, semi- *Bi-* means "occurring every two" or "occurring twice." Thus *biweekly* means either "coming every two weeks," or "coming twice a week." To relieve the ambiguity, *semi-* is often used in the sense of "occurring twice," as in *semiweekly, semimonthly, semiannually* (every six months). *Biannual* means "occurring twice a year"; *biennial* means "occurring every two years."

bring, take Careful writers and speakers use *bring* to indicate action toward them, and *take* to indicate action away from them.

Bring the report with you when you come.
Please *take* the finished copies back with you.

but Like *and, but* may be used informally at the beginning of a sentence. *However* is generally preferred in more formal written work.

We tried to get Joe to work for us. *But* you know how temperamental plumbers are.

but what Colloquial for *but that.*

COLLOQUIAL: I don't know *but what* you are right.
MORE FORMAL: I don't know *but that* you are right.

can, may   In strict usage, *can* is used to denote ability, and *may* to indicate permission. In ordinary usage, however, *can* is almost invariably used in both senses.

> You *may* have both sizes if you want them. (Denotes permission)
> You *can* have both sizes if you want them. (Also denotes permission)
> Your application says you *can* write advertising copy. (Denotes ability)

can not, cannot   Both forms are correct although the latter is generally preferred.

cannot help but   In informal English, the better expression is *can't help;* in formal English, *cannot but.*

> QUESTIONABLE: You *can't help but* like a man like that.
> IMPROVED: You *can't help* liking a man like that.
> FORMAL: You *cannot but* like a man like that.

can't hardly   Misused for *can hardly.*

> We *can hardly* wait for the spring fashion opening.

can't seem   Informal for *doesn't seem able* or *seems unable.*

> INFORMAL: He *can't seem* to understand his responsibilities.
> FORMAL: He *seems unable* (or *doesn't seem able*) to understand his responsibilities.

compose, comprise   These words are often confused. *Compose* means "to constitute"; *comprise* means "to include or consist of."

> The set *comprises* three leatherbound volumes.
> Three leatherbound volumes *compose* the set.

contact   Although there are still some objections to the word in the sense of "get in touch with," *contact* is commonly and acceptably used in business when such words as *write, call on,* or *telephone* would be too specific.

> ACCEPTABLE: Please *contact* the customer as soon as you can.
> SOMETIMES PREFERRED: Please *get in touch with* the customer as soon as you can.

could of   Illiterate for *could have.*

> He *could have* had any territory he wanted.

data   Although it is the plural form of the Latin *datum, data* is acceptably used as a singular noun.

> CORRECT: the *data* show, or the *data* shows

deal   Informal for such more specific words as *transaction, arrangement,* and *bargain.*

> INFORMAL: They offered a pretty good *deal.*
> FORMAL: They offered a *bargain.*
>
> INFORMAL: He refused to go through with the *deal.*
> FORMAL: He refused to complete the *transaction.*

deem   Overformal for *think, believe,* or *consider.*

STIFF: We *deem* it advisable . . .
BETTER: We *think* it advisable . . .

different than   Now generally acceptable, although *different from* is sometimes preferred in formal usage.

CORRECT: The present plan is much *different than* the one originally proposed.
MORE FORMAL: The present plan is much *different from* the one originally proposed.

disinterested, uninterested   Although careful users of English still distinguish
between *disinterested* (impartial) and *uninterested* (not interested), the
former is commonly substituted for the latter.

QUESTIONABLE: He seemed *disinterested* in our proposal.
CORRECT: He seemed *uninterested* in our proposal.
CORRECT: He was completely *disinterested* as to the outcome. (Impartial)

due to   There is some lingering objection to the use of *due to* in the sense of
"because of," though not to its use in the sense of "caused by" or "owing
to." Few in business would care to maintain the distinction in informal
usage.

INFORMAL: *Due to* a power failure, we were forced to suspend operations for a
day. (Because of)
CORRECT WITHOUT QUESTION: The shutdown was *due to* a power plant failure.
(Caused by)

duly   This stilted expression, meaning "in a proper manner," should not be
used except in legal writing.

NOT: We have *duly* entered your order.
BUT: We have entered your order.

effect   See **affect.**

enthuse   Informally, this word is used with *is*, *was*, and so on in the sense of
"enthusiastic." It is better not used at all, however, when the meaning is
"to express enthusiasm."

CORRECT: Mr. Carmen was *enthusiastic* about the plan.
INFORMAL: Mr. Carmen *was enthused* about the plan.
DISAPPROVED: Mr. Carmen *enthused* about the plan.

Esq., Esquire   An archaic British expression still occasionally used in the
United States to address attorneys; for example, Joseph Manners, *Esq.*,
not *Mr.* Joseph Manners, *Esq.*

farther, further   In formal usage, *farther* is used to express distance; *further*,
to express degree. In informal usage, including most business practice,
further is used in both senses.

FORMAL: The new plant should be located *farther* north.
INFORMAL: The new plant should be located *further* north.
CORRECT ON ALL LEVELS: The *further* you look into the story, the more con-
vincing it is.
They must not go *further* into debt.

favor Archaic when used in the sense of "letter."

NOT: We have your *favor* of February 16.
BUT: We have your *letter* of February 16.

NOTE: If you consider the letter a favor, say, "Thank you for your letter."

fewer, less In strict usage, *fewer* refers to number, *less* to degree or amount.

He made *fewer* changes than we expected. (Not *less*)
They offered *less* than we asked.
The files contain *fewer* papers, *less* superfluous material, than they did a year ago.

figuratively See **literally.**

finalize Despite criticism, this word seems to have found a place for itself in the sense of "make final," "put the finishing touches on."

INFORMAL: If you will let us hear from you, we will be able to *finalize* the language of the contract.

flammable Correctly and advantageously used as a synonym of *inflammable,* which is sometimes mistaken for "not flammable." Both words mean "easily set on fire."

CORRECT: If we store *flammable* materials, we will have to pay higher insurance premiums.

focalize Better say *focus.*

NOT: We will *focalize* all our attention on this campaign.
BUT: We will *focus* all our attention on this campaign.

former, first Use *first,* not *former,* to indicate the first of more than two. (See also **latter, last.**)

NOT: We received bids from Allied, Murphy, and Consolidated, but we gave the order to the *former.*
BUT: . . . we gave the order to the *first.*
CORRECT: We received bids from Allied and Murphy, but we gave the order to the *former.* (Or, better, to "*Allied*")

forward Strictly speaking, to *forward* a letter is to send it from an intermediate station to its destination. Thus if one receives a misaddressed letter, he may *forward* it to the addressee. In other circumstances, the word *send* is simpler and more common.

CORRECT: When the statement arrives, I will *forward* it to you.
CORRECT: We will *send* you the statement as soon as it is ready.
QUESTIONABLE: We will *forward* the statement to you as soon as it is ready.

forward on *Forward* alone conveys the idea. The *on* is superfluous.
guess Informal for *suppose.*

INFORMAL: If he asks for the day off, I *guess* we will have to let him have it.
FORMAL: . . . I *suppose* we will have to let him have it.

hand you herewith To be used only when something is delivered with the letter in person. Otherwise, write "we are enclosing," "you will find enclosed," or "enclosed is."

hanged, hung Criminals may be *hanged,* but pictures are *hung.*

happenstance Informal for "accidental happening." In formal usage, the word should be *accident* or *circumstance.*

irregardless Illiterate for *regardless.*

> NOT: *Irregardless* of what you say . . .
> BUT: *Regardless* of what you say . . .

kind of a, sort of a The *a* is better omitted.

> CORRECT: What *kind of* [or *sort of*] credit risk is he?
> QUESTIONABLE: What *kind of a* credit risk is he?

NOTE 1: In formal usage do not use *kind of* or *sort of* for *somewhat.*

> INFORMAL: She acted *kind of* helpless.
> FORMAL: She acted *somewhat* helpless.

NOTE 2: Say *this kind* or *these kinds,* but not *these kind.*

> NOT: I like *these kind* of finishes.
> BUT: I like *this kind* of finish.
> OR: I like *these kinds* of finishes.

kind enough to, so kind as to The first expression is preferred, though both often imply some sarcasm.

> NOT: Please be *so kind as to* return our deposit.
> BUT: Please be *kind enough to* return our deposit.
> USUALLY PREFERRED: We would appreciate it if you would return our deposit.

kindly Correct when used in the sense of "with kindness," for example, "He *kindly* returned our deposit." It is a bit stiff when used in the sense of "please."

> NOT: *Kindly* sign and return the carbon copy of this letter.
> BETTER: *Please* sign and return . . .

latter, last Use *latter* to indicate the second of two; *last,* to indicate the last of three or more.

> NOT: We received bids from Allied, Murphy, and Consolidated, but we gave the order to the *latter.*
> BUT: . . . we gave the order to the *last.*
> CORRECT: We received bids from Allied and Murphy, but we gave the order to the *latter.* (Or, better, "to *Murphy*")

lay, lie *Lay* means "to place" and always takes an object. *Lie* means "to recline" and does not take an object. Confusion occurs because *lay* is also the past tense of *lie,* whereas *laid* is the past tense of *lay.* Note these forms.

> He always *lies* down in the afternoon.
> He *lay* down yesterday afternoon.
> He *has lain* down every afternoon this week.

Lay the carton on the floor.
He *laid* the carton on the floor.
He *has laid* the carton on the floor.

leave, let   Leave means "to allow to remain" ("He *left* the charts behind."); *let* means "to allow."

NOT: *Leave* the customer have the discount.
BUT: *Let* the customer have the discount.

NOT: *Leave* him go when he wants to.
BUT: *Let* him go when he wants to.

lieu, in lieu of   *In lieu of* means "in place of." It is sometimes mistakenly used for "in view of" or "because of."

NOT: *In lieu of* the defect, we are recalling all new models.
BUT: *In view of* [or *because of*] the defect, we are recalling all new models.
CORRECT: We'll take the discount *in lieu of* the bonus in merchandise.

like   See **as, like.**

literally, figuratively   *Literally* means "exactly what the words say"; *figuratively* means "not in the exact sense." Do not use one when you mean the other.

DO NOT SAY: When he objected, he was *literally* chewed up alive.
WHEN YOU MEAN: When he objected, he was *figuratively* chewed up alive.
OR (BETTER):   When he objected, he was violently shouted down.

meantime   Better say "in the meantime," or "meanwhile."

NOT: *Meantime,* we will look around for substitutes.
BUT: *Meanwhile,* we will look around for substitutes.
OR: *In the meantime,* we will look around for substitutes.

media   Plural of *medium* and should be treated as a plural.

NOT: The outdoor *media has* not been especially effective.
BUT: The outdoor *media have* not ...
CORRECT: As a *medium* for classified advertising, newspapers cannot be equaled.

moneys, monies   The first appears to be preferred for currencies, the second for amounts of money.

CORRECT: The Chase Museum has a collection of *moneys* of the world.
CORRECT: The *monies* have yet to be collected. (Amounts from several sources)

most   Do not use for *almost.*

NOT: *Most* everybody came.
BUT: *Almost* everybody came.

NOT: *Most all* of us agreed.
BUT: *Almost all* of us agreed.

myself   Sometimes used incorrectly for *me.* Myself is correctly used as an intensifier of *I* or to refer reflexively to the subject *I.*

NOT: ... between him and *myself.*
BUT: ... between him and *me.*

CORRECT: I myself will do it. (Intensifier)
CORRECT: I bought one for *myself.* (Reflexive)

not as, not so   In a negative comparison, the *not so* is more formal than *not as,* but both are correct.

CORRECT: The new design is *not so* simple as the old one.
CORRECT: The new design is *not as* simple as the old one.

noted   Sometimes misused for *marked.*

NOT: We have *noted* our records accordingly.
BUT: We have *marked* our records accordingly.
CORRECT: We have *noted on* our records that . . .

of   Illiterate when used for *have,* following *would, could,* or *should.*

NOT: He *could of* gone yesterday.
BUT: He *could have* gone yesterday.

off of   The *of* is superfluous.

NOT: We'll try to keep them *off of* the property.
BUT: We'll try to keep them *off* the property.

only   The position of *only* depends on the sense. Compare:

He *only* delivered the package. (He did not have anything else to do with it.)
He delivered *only* the package. (He delivered nothing else.)
Only he delivered the package. (He had no helper.)
He delivered the package *only.* (He delivered nothing else.)

NOTE: In informal use, when there is no chance of misunderstanding, the position of *only* is often shifted.

CORRECT: He *only talks* that way to customers. (For *only to customers*)

our, as in "*our* Miss Jones"   Considered by some not to be in good taste. Better to say only "Miss Jones" or, if further identification is needed, use some phrase like "Miss Jones in our bookkeeping department."

party   Correctly used in legal phrases and in reference to a telephone caller, but otherwise considered slang as a substitute for *person.*

QUESTIONABLE: Are you the *party* who called yesterday?
BETTER: Are you the *person* [or *lady* or *gentleman*] who called yesterday?
CORRECT: I have your *party* now. (Person telephoned to)
CORRECT: One of the *parties* to the contract raised a question about the language.

per   Correctly used in such Latin expressions as *per* capita, *per* annum, and *per* diem, and in other formal expressions like "thirty hours *per* week," "$3.60 *per* hour," "ninety miles *per* hour." In informal expression, however, *a* or *an* seems more natural.

FORMAL: The rate of pay is now two dollars *per* hour for unskilled labor.
INFORMAL: We pay two dollars *an* hour for unskilled help.

per, as per See **as per.**

percent, per cent Both spellings are correct, but usage seems to favor the first.

percent, percentage *Percent* means "per hundred"; *percentage* means "rate per hundred," or a share or portion.

> CORRECT: They pay 4 *percent* interest.
> The *percentage* of loss is really quite small.
> The producer receives a *percentage* of the gross.

percentage Slang when used in the sense of "advantage."

> SLANG: There's no *percentage* in mistreating customers.
> MORE FORMAL: There's no *advantage* in mistreating customers.

practical, practicable *Practical* means "useful," "not theoretical," or "experienced through practice"; *practicable* means "feasible" or "capable of being put into practice, but not yet tried." *Practical* may be used as descriptive of a person, but *practicable* may not.

> The plan you propose seems *practicable*.
> We are looking for a *practical* solution to the problem.
> A *practical* person is needed for the job.

prefer rather than Better say *prefer to.*

> NOT: I *prefer* staying late *rather than* working on Saturday.
> BUT: I *prefer* staying late *to* working on Saturday.
> OR: I would *rather* stay late *than* work on Saturday.

> NOT: We *prefer* the rectangular model *rather than* the square one.
> BUT: We *prefer* the rectangular model *to* the square one.

prior to Too formal for most uses. Say *before.*

> NOT: They are offering 10 percent off *prior to* their official opening.
> BUT: ... *before* their official opening.

proposition Correctly used for *plan* or *proposal,* but slang in some other senses.

> SLANG: That's a pretty good *proposition you have on.* (Suit you're wearing)
> SLANG: She's a *neat proposition.* (Attractive girl)
> CORRECT: The *proposition* struck me as very fair. (Proposal)

proved, proven Both are correct, though *proven* may sound better as a pure adjective (not part of a verb).

> He has *proved* [or *proven*] his point.
> The success of the device has yet to be *proved* [or *proven*].
> A *proven* fact (better than "a proved fact"); their *proven* ability (better than "their *proved* ability").

provided, providing Both are correct as conjunctions, but the first is generally preferred.

> CORRECT: We will come into the plan *providing* we get a satisfactory advertising allowance.
> PREFERRED: We will come into the plan *provided* ...

pursuant to   Very formal. Except in legal papers, it is better to use *in accordance with, following,* or a similar construction. (See also **as per, per.**)

> OVERFORMAL: *Pursuant to your request,* we are glad to send you . . .
> BETTER: *As you requested . . .*
>   *Following your request . . .*
>   *In accordance with your request . . .*
> BETTER STILL: We are glad to send you the booklet *you requested.*

raise, rise   To *raise* is to lift (something); to *rise* is to get up or to go up. Note these correct forms.

> We *raise* their pay every six months.
> We *have raised* their pay.
> We *raised* their pay.
> He *rises* at six in the morning.
> He *has risen* at six.
> He *rose* at six.
> Prices *are rising.*
> Prices *have risen.*
> Prices *rose.*

re, in re   Latin for "subject," "regarding," or "in the matter of," it is best avoided in ordinary correspondence.

> NOT: your letter *re* (or *in re*) the damaged carton
> BUT: your letter *about* the damaged carton

> NOTE: When a subject line is used in a letter, the word *Subject* or no prefix at all is more modern than *Re.* Compare:

> *Re:* Your letter of October 14
> *Subject:* Your letter of October 14
> Your letter of October 14

reason is that   *Reason is that* is preferred; avoid using such words as *because* and *why* with *reason.*

> QUESTIONABLE: The *reason* he declined *was because* he had already committed himself to another company.
> BETTER: The *reason* he declined *was that* he had . . .

refer to   Use *refer to* with past events.

> NOT: Please *refer back* to our order No. 16757.
> BUT: Please *refer* to our order No. 16757.

regard, regards   The correct expression is "in [or with] regard to," not "in [or with] regards to." *As regards* is somewhat stiff, but may be used correctly in the sense of "with regard to."

> NOT: your inquiry *in regards to*
> BUT: your inquiry *in regard to*
> CORRECT: *as regards* your inquiry

reimburse, reimbursement   These words refer to the repayment of money spent or compensation for damages, time lost, and so on. They should not be used in the simple sense of *pay* or *payment.*

NOT: We will *reimburse* you for the chairs.
BUT: We will *pay* you for the chairs.
CORRECT: The check enclosed is *reimbursement* for the expenses you incurred.
CORRECT: We expect to be *reimbursed* for the loss.

said   Except in legal writing, do not use *said* for *this* or *these*.

NOT: the *said* client, the *said* goods
BUT: *this* client, *these* goods

same   Considered stereotyped in the sense of *it* or *they*.

NOT: Please let us know the charges and we will send you a check for *same*.
BUT: . . . and we will send you a check to cover *them*.

NOT: We have your order and thank you for *same*.
BUT: We have your order and thank you for *it*.
BETTER STILL: Thank you for your order.

seldom ever, rarely ever   Informal for *seldom if ever, rarely if ever*.

INFORMAL: We *seldom ever* [or *rarely ever*] buy anything without getting a receipt.
USUALLY BETTER: We *seldom if ever* [or *rarely if ever*] buy anything without getting a receipt.
ALSO GOOD: We *seldom* [or *rarely*] buy anything without getting a receipt.

shall, will   The debate over *shall* and *will* never had much substance and has happily run its course. If in doubt, use *will* and don't worry about it. For a more precise guide to usage, follow these rules.

1. In formal statements, the following forms are correct:

Singular	*Plural*
I shall	we shall
you will	you will
he [she, it] will	they will

EXAMPLES:
I *shall* appreciate your prompt reply.
You *will,* of course, send us a confirmation.
The order *will* be ready when you call.

2. To express determination, the forms *shall* and *will* are reversed.

Singular	*Plural*
I will	we will
you shall	you shall
he [she, it] shall	they shall

EXAMPLES:
I *will* go. (That is, I am determined to go.)
You *shall* go. (That is, I am determined that you will go.)
He *shall* go. (That is, I am determined that he will go.)

3. In informal usage, *will* is used exclusively in all the instances already cited.

CORRECT: I *will* call you tomorrow.
We *will* look forward to hearing from you.
It *will* be good to hear from you.
You *will* pay the bill; I'll see that you do. (Determination)

4. Use *shall* with *I* and *we* (but not with *you, he, she, it,* or *they*) in questions.

CORRECT: *Shall I* [or *we*] send you a copy?
CORRECT: *Will you* please send us a copy? *Will they* send us a copy?

5. Use *shall* in formally stated rules and regulations.

EXAMPLES:
The president *shall* be the chief executive officer.
Smoking *shall* not be permitted except in designated areas.
Tools *shall* be returned to the supply room at the end of each day.

should, would   Most questions regarding *should* and *would* relate to their use with *I* or *we*. Both forms are correct, though *should* is considered more formal than *would*.

FORMAL: *I* [*we*] *should* be glad to fill your request.
INFORMAL: *I* [*we*] *would* be glad to fill your request.

1. Many writers prefer the *would* to *should* in the construction shown here because they feel the *should* implies obligation, although that is not the intent of the word.

2. Except to express obligation (see point 3), *would* is always used with all subjects other than *I* or *we*.

They would be glad to fill your request.
I am sure *you would* not object.

3. *Should* is correctly used in all constructions to express obligation. It is considered somewhat milder than *ought*.

We should follow the instructions.
They should try to meet their obligations more promptly.
It should be an interesting performance.

4. The difference between *shall* and *should* is that *should* expresses more hesitancy and is less emphatic and more polite. The same distinction holds for *will* and *would*. Compare:

Would you please let us have . . .
Will you please let us have . . .

I *should* [or *would*] be glad to . . .
I *shall* [or *will*] be glad to . . .

sick, ill   *Ill* is considered less crude than *sick,* which many people associate with nausea. Nevertheless, *sick* is a good informal word to denote any indisposition.

Mary was out *sick* yesterday.
Mr. Grimes has been *ill* for the past week.

-size, -sized   One may say "a *small-size* glass" or a "*a small-sized* glass." The latter is somewhat more formal.

someplace, somewhere, somewheres   *Somewhere* is preferred to *someplace*. *Somewheres* is incorrect.

BAD: We were looking for *somewheres* to go.
BETTER: We were looking for *someplace* to go.
MORE FORMAL: We were looking for *somewhere* to go.

subject   When a letter has a caption or subject line, references to the caption are sometimes made by such a phrase as "the *subject file*," "the *subject* account," "the *subject* letter," and so on. Such writing becomes rather stilted and is best avoided, except in fairly routine correspondence.

ROUTINE: The value of the *subject* account as of October 31, 19—, was as follows:
INFORMAL: The value of *this* (that is, the *subject*) account as of October 31, 19—, was as follows.

subsequent to   An overformal expression for *after* or *following*.

STIFF: *Subsequent to* his arrival . . .
BETTER: *Following* his arrival . . .
        After he arrived . . .

therefor, therein, thereon   Used in legal or other official papers, but considered stilted in ordinary letters and reports and should be avoided. *Therefor* means "for it" and should not be confused with *therefore*.

STIFF: The order is enclosed, with payment *therefor*.
BETTER: The order is enclosed with our check in payment.

STIFF: The drawings were kept *therein*.
BETTER: The drawings were kept *in it* [or *inside*].

STIFF: The electric coffee-maker consists of a separate heating element with a chrome urn *placed thereon*.
BETTER: The electric coffeemaker consists of a separate heating element with a chrome urn *on top of it*.

this here, these here   Omit the *here*.

NOT: *This here* style is the one we prefer.
BUT: *This* style is the one we prefer.

till, until   Both are correct, although the second often sounds better at the beginning of a sentence.

CORRECT: *Until* [or *till*] he came, we didn't know what to do.
CORRECT: Please don't do anything *till* [or *until*] you hear from us.

try and   Less formal than *try to*, but both are correct.

Try and stop me.
Try to find out when the shipment will arrive.

undersigned, the writer   Considered awkward and impersonal. Use the appropriate personal pronoun.

NOT: Please return it to *the undersigned*.
BUT: Please return it to *me* [or *us*].

unique   Because this is a superlative in a class with *most unusual* and *unequalled*, it seems illogical to modify it with such words as *very* or *most*.

NOT: This is our *most unique* design.
BUT: This is our *most unusual* design.
OR: This design is *unique*. (The only one of its kind)

verbal   This word means literally "in words," but is often used for *oral* (that is, not written) in such an expression as, "We had a *verbal* agreement." The word is now considered correct in this sense.

where   Used informally for *that*.

> QUESTIONABLE: I see *where* the Adams Company has moved again.
> BETTER: I see *that* the Adams Company has moved again.

who, which, that   *Who* usually refers to persons, *which* to things, and *that* to persons or things.

> Anyone *who* is willing to pay the price can have it.
> The table, *which* was more than six feet square, could not fit through the door.
> It's a problem *that* [or *which*] calls for the most careful consideration.
> The number of people *that* [or *who*] entered the contest was staggering.

who, whom   *Who* is usually used as a subject, *whom* as an object. In speech, however, especially when the word comes at the beginning of a sentence, it is often difficult to figure out in advance what form is called for. In such circumstances, it is recommended that *who* be used in preference to *whom*.

> CORRECT: *Who* will be responsible for the charges? (Subject)
> CORRECT: He is not the man with *whom* we were dealing. (Object of preposition *with*)
> CORRECT: I don't know *whom* he saw. (Object of verb *saw*)
> ACCEPTABLE IN SPEECH: I don't know *who* he saw.
> CORRECT: To *whom* shall I give the keys? (Object of preposition *to*)
> ACCEPTABLE IN SPEECH: *Who* shall I give the keys to?

whose   Despite some minor objections, *whose* may be used for *of which*.

> CORRECT BUT AWKWARD: We don't want a typewriter *of which* the type bars are made of plastic.
> BETTER: We don't want a typewriter *whose* type bars are made of plastic.
> BETTER STILL: We don't want a typewriter with plastic type bars.

-wise   Somewhat overworked in such words as *sales-wise, budget-wise, profit-wise, construction-wise*.

> QUESTIONABLE: We expect to show an increase *sales-wise*.
> BETTER: We expect to show an increase *in sales*.

9

Punctuation

The purpose of punctuation is to help communicate clearly the sense intended in a particular passage. At the same time, everyone connected with the flow of communications is expected to be guided by established customs. The modern tendency is to use the fewest marks of punctuation consistent with clarity and reading ease.

Grammatical terms used in this chapter are defined in "Glossary of Common Grammatical Terms," Section 8.3.

CONTENTS

9.1 APOSTROPHE [']

To Form the Possessive. Use the apostrophe to indicate the possessive case of nouns and indefinite pronouns. (See also the section on the possessive in "Grammar Review," Section 8.4.)

Mr. David's proposal   everybody's business
Tom's arrival   a month's work
a sale at Altman's   the Smiths' reception

For Omitted Letters.   The apostrophe shows the omission of letters in contractions and shortened words. It is also used in abbreviated dates.

can't   I'll   we've
isn't   he's   you're (you are)

o'clock (of the clock)
M'Grath (McGrath)

'tis   Gifts 'n' Things   Class of '68

To Form Certain Plurals.   The apostrophe is used to form the plural of letters of the alphabet, figures, and words named as words. (See also "Numbers," Section 10.3.)

dot the *i*'s
the *x*'s do not count
bundled in *10*'s and *20*'s
   (BUT: bundled in *tens* and *twenties*)
too many *and*'s and *but*'s

With Coined Verbs.   The endings of some coined verbs are preceded by an apostrophe.

x'd out
O.K.'ing the copy (OR: *okaying* the copy)

9.2   BRACKETS   [ ]

Brackets are formed on the typewriter by the diagonal and the underline keys.

For Parentheses.   Use brackets instead of parentheses within a passage already enclosed by parentheses.

In another work (*The Elements of Style* [Macmillan]), the point is treated . . .
According to the new law (Section IV [I-b]), the county . . .

Within Quotations.   An editor or transcriber uses brackets, not parentheses, to explain, amplify, question, or correct copied or quoted material.

The contract says that "the vendor [Shepherd and Stern] agrees to bear 50 percent of the advertising cost."
Part II applies these [principles] to the everyday realities of commercial life.
I quote: "Today [August 17] we fly to Brazil."
"In this contect [sic] it can be seen that . . . (*Sic*, meaning "thus," is used to show that the apparent misspelling was in the original material.)
OR: "In this contect [context?] it can be seen that . . ."

9.3   COLON   [:]

After a Formal Introduction.   A colon may be used after a formal introduction to a quotation, enumeration, or explanation.

The telegram read: "Arrive Thursday . . ."

The following steps are involved:
1. Preparation of plate
2. Transfer of copy
3. Printing

Here is the plan we have adopted: Beginning April 2, the four o'clock shift will . . .

For Emphasis.   Use a colon in place of a comma (or of no punctuation) in order to emphasize the word or words that follow. Do not use the colon, however, unless the words to which the colon applies end the sentence.

In a word: No. (COMPARE: In a word, no.)
You can reach him by telephone at: (212) 588-7606.
BUT NOT: You can reach him by telephone at: (212) 588-7606 after 10 a.m. (Omit colon.)

Amplification.   Use a colon before a word, phrase, or sentence that interprets or amplifies. It is somewhat less emphatic than a dash, which may be used for the same purpose.

He was absent one day: Friday.
It's a popular plan: 98 percent of our employees elect it.
We have several models: manual, battery, and electric.
Two courses are open to you: to invest your savings or to fritter them away.

After a Salutation.   A colon is generally used after the salutation of a business letter, and after the salutation in any context in which the attention of the reader is desired.

Dear Mr. Jones:
Gourmets: Feast on passion fruit in the Arawak Dining Room.

Clock Time.   Use a colon to separate hours and minutes and minutes and seconds.

12:45 p.m.
He ran the mile in 4:3.5. (4 minutes, 3½ seconds)
The blast was registered at 4:16:23 a.m. EST.

Capital After Colon.   As a rule, capitalize the first word of a complete sentence following a colon. An exception may be made when the sentence is short and an informal effect is desired. When the words following a colon do not form a complete sentence, do not capitalize the first word unless it is a proper name.

Here is how we see the situation: The President is determined to have his tax increase.
You can't win: stock up for hot weather and you get snow.
Many types of businesses are affected: manufacturing, retail, service.

9.4 COMMA   [,]

Between Independent Clauses. A comma is usually used before *and, but, for, or,* or *nor* when they join independent clauses (complete statements).

> We are most impressed with the performance you describe, and we will include a reference to it in the report we make.
> The building was scheduled for completion in July, but shortages of material caused a two-month delay.

NOTE: The comma is often omitted when the clauses are short.

> Mail the tape to your secretary and she'll type it up before you return.
> You have to be satisfied or you won't owe us a cent.

After Introductory Subordinate Clauses. A subordinate clause at the beginning of a sentence is followed by a comma. Usually, no comma is needed when the subordinate clause follows the main clause.

> If you want an extra supply, please let us know.
> Although we did not foresee the rise, we are prepared for it.
> After the floor is cleared, the carpenters can get to work.

BUT:

> The carpenters can get to work after the floor is cleared. (No comma because subordinate clause follows main clause.)

After Initial Verbal Phrases. An introductory phrase containing part of a verb (participle, gerund, or infinitive) is followed by a comma.

> Having watched his performance, we feel he is well qualified for the job. (Participle)
> To ensure good condition of contents, store in cool place. (Infinitive)
> On learning what had happened, they immediately got in touch with their insurance agents. (Gerund)

1. No comma follows an infinitive or gerund phrase that is the subject of the sentence.

> To know him is a pleasure.
> Dealing in speculative stocks is risky.

2. No comma follows an introductory element consisting of a simple prepositional phrase closely related to the meaning of the rest of the sentence.

In many ways he was an excellent accountant.
For the next 12 months our hands will be tied.

After Initial Connectives.   Put a comma after an initial word or phrase used as a connective, a mild interjection, or a sentence modifier.

However, we are not prepared for the consequences.
For example, every stitch is sewn by hand.
Still, you should have foreseen the possibility of a price rise.
Naturally, we would be interested in such a plan.
In any event, Mr. Greer says his decision is final.
No, we couldn't think of it.
Well, what can we do?

In a Series of Words or Phrases.   Use commas to separate sentence elements arranged in a series. In journalistic practice, the comma is omitted before the *and* or *or* preceding the last member of the series. However, the comma is often included in other writing, especially when its omission may confuse the sense.

Procedures for preparing invoices, handling accounts receivable, and reporting balances will all need to be changed.
He wrote, he telephoned, he telegraphed—but he could get no answer.
The departments affected are Accounting, Marketing and Advertising, and Personnel. (Omission of last comma would cause confusion.)

NOTE: A series of adjectives modifying the same noun are separated by commas when each adjective has a direct reference to the noun. However, no comma is used when each adjective modifies the whole phrase that follows. *Hint:* Try substituting *and* for the comma. If the phrase makes sense, the comma is necessary; if not, the comma should be omitted.

The job required a strong, healthy, cheerful individual. (That is, "strong *and* healthy *and* cheerful.")
It was a cold, rainy April. (That is, "cold *and* rainy.")

But (no comma):

Featured in the sale was a short belted white coat.
They put up 24 two-story red brick houses.

To Set Off Interrupting Elements.   Use commas to set off words and phrases that interrupt the sense or the grammatical structure of the sentence. Do not use commas where no interruption exists.

1. Connecting words.

In these circumstances, therefore, we are waiving the deposit.
We are committed, nevertheless, to this course of action.
Every stitch, for example, was sewn by hand.
It was, in fact, the model we were looking for.

But (no interruption—no comma):

We are therefore waiving the deposit.
You are nevertheless entitled to the refund.

2. *Such as, namely, that is, e.g., i.e.*

Some energy fuels, such as wood and coal, have had sharp declines.
The prime contractor, that is, the company we are dealing with, could provide the
   specifications.
Use a street name or the equivalent, e.g., R.D. 4 or Box 45.

But (no interruption—no comma):

Such energy fuels as wood and coal have had sharp declines.

3. Appositives.

The old adding machine, an Addex 505, should be replaced.
Please address the letter to Mr. Grayson, the sales manager.
Bond & Co., their advertising agency, is now preparing the campaign.

But (no interruption—no comma):

My son George will enter the business next year.
The word *profit* sometimes has a negative connotation.
The call came from their Aunt Martha.
Thank the architect Gropius for the striking design.

4. Words in direct address.

Mr. Hanley, you are to be congratulated.
We are going to ask you, Mary, to order the flowers.

5. Contrasting elements.

The high interest rates, rather than the sales decline, caused our undoing.
I want an answer from the president, not his assistant.

To Set Off Nonrestrictive Elements. Phrases and clauses that cannot be
separated from the rest of the sentence without changing the meaning are
called restrictive. Those that may be left out are called nonrestrictive. The
nonrestrictive elements are set off by commas; the others take no punctuation.
Compare:

Miss Thomas, *who has had some advanced mathematics,* is ideal for the job. (The
   italicized phrase is nonrestrictive because it can be left out without altering the
   sense.)
A girl *who has had some advanced mathematics* is ideal for the job. (The italicized
   phrase is restrictive because it cannot be left out without altering the sense.)
The Garry Duplicator, *with its strong guarantee,* should prove to be a good investment. (Nonrestrictive.)
A duplicator *with a strong guarantee* should prove to be a good investment. (Restrictive.)
The typewriter, which is now 10 years old, should be replaced. (Nonrestrictive.)
Any typewriter that is 10 years old should be replaced. (Restrictive.)

To Set Off Quotations.   A quotation is set off by commas from the words
that introduce and follow it.

> He retorted, "What other motive could I have?"
> "Yes," he said, "we have just the size you want."
> "Staying another week," read the telegram.

See also "Quotation Marks," Section 9.12.

To Signal Omitted Words.   Use a comma as a substitute for words omitted.

> This is a stationary model; the other, a portable one.

To Separate Balanced Statements.   Use a comma between statements closely
related in thought and structure.

> The more we pressed for the sale, the more he resisted.
> Once a deceiver, always a deceiver.

With Proper Names.   Use commas to set off the parts of dates and the names
of persons and places.

   1. Dates.

> On March 9, 197–, we brought suit against . . . (Also written with no comma after
>   the year.)
> The record shows that March 1970 marked the turning point.

   2. *Jr., II., Inc., Ltd.,* and other name suffixes.

> Mr. David Green, Jr., is our executive secretary.
> Robert Finch, Sr.'s account . . . (No comma after possessive.)
> Stephen Farnsworth II has accepted the invitation. (No comma if individual uses
>   none.)
> We gave B. F. Hardy, Inc., a full line of credit. (Also, preferably, without the second
>   comma.)

   3. Inverted names.

> Smith, John A.
> Fairfield, William S., Jr.
> Deere, John, & Co.

   4. Geographical names and addresses.

> He resides in London, Ontario.
> Our office in Paris, France, could be of great help to you.
> Please write to Dayton Forwarding Co., 765 South Third Street, Los Angeles,
>   California 90028. (No comma before ZIP Code.)
> Mr. James McGrory of 1765 Creston Avenue, Bronx, New York, was one of the
>   cosigners.

For Clarity or Emphasis.   Use a comma whenever it seems desirable to aid
the reader's interpretation of a passage.

   1. To prevent misreading.

> NOT: Ever since we have refused to do business with them.
> BUT: Ever since, we have refused to do business with them.

2. To break up a long passage.

Moreover, because smaller families are understandably reluctant to leave large, controlled apartments, these newer families, which tend to be fairly large, are denied access to the more spacious apartments they might find more easily in a free housing market.

3. To give emphasis. Compare:

We'll be glad to do it if that is your wish.
We'll be glad to do it, if that is your wish.

9.5 DASH [—]

A dash is typewritten with the hyphen in any of the following ways. The last form is used in printers' copy and appears to be preferred for general office use.

This is a - dash.
This is a -- dash.
This is a--dash.

Because the dash loses its effect when overused, it should be used sparingly.

To Show a Break in Thought.   A dash is used to show a sudden break in thought.

Our most recent experience—I can't remember the exact date—occurred within the last several months.
What would you do if—there's that *if* again.
More efficiency in production, a larger pool of manpower, and quicker delivery— these are the advantages of the new location.
You know, the bigger they are—.

In Quoted Speech.   The dash shows hesitation or unfinished thought in quoted remarks. It may also serve as a substitute for words too impolite or obscene to quote.

"Would you—would you consent to such a plan?"
"He didn't—?"
"I don't give a —!"

To Set Off a Parenthetical Remark.   Dashes may be used to give emphasis to a parenthetical remark for which commas or parentheses are considered too mild.

The Fair—which eventually grossed millions—attracted few backers.
If he understood the terms—and I'm sure he did—he'll live up to them.
He got out of the market—but not before he had seen a rise of ten points in his stock.

Between Parallel Elements.   Dashes may be used to emphasize parallel or balanced sentence elements.

You do your part—we'll do ours.
We waited—one hour—two hours—three hours—still no quotation appeared on the board.
That's our formula—win or lose—give or take a little.

To Emphasize Succeeding Words. A dash is sometimes used before a final word or phrase to give it emphasis. Phrases beginning with *for example, namely,* and *that is* are included in this rule.

If you're in doubt—ask.
Will you please mail your check now—before you forget.
It's yours and it's—free.
Three officers were elected—namely, the president, the secretary, and the treasurer. (The dash takes the place of a comma.)
A plan to suit you is available—for example, you can pay one third down and the balance in twelve monthly payments. (The dash takes the place of a comma, semicolon, or period.)

9.6 ELLIPSIS | ... |

To Show Omissions. In quoted material, use *three* spaced periods to show an omission at the beginning or in the middle of a sentence. *Four* periods should be used when the omission occurs at the end of a sentence.

"... the proliferation of distinctly undervalued stocks ... can be expected to brighten the depressing investment climate during the next few months."
"The effectiveness of television is unchallenged. ... Even in Germany, where commercials are run in clusters of 20 minutes, there is a waiting line for time. ..."

For Stylistic Pauses. In establishing a mood, ellipses may be used in place of other punctuation to slow up reading. This device is common in advertising copy.

Chromacolor ... a revolutionary new color television system ... that outcolors ... outbrightens ... outdetails ... and outperforms ... every other giant-screen color TV.

To Mark an Unfinished Statement. Ellipses may be used instead of a dash after an unfinished statement.

I was wondering ... Oh, let me come back to this point later.

9.7 EXCLAMATION POINT | ! |

To Show Strong Feeling. The exclamation point is placed after an expression of strong feeling. It should be used sparingly. (For punctuation after a mild exclamation, see "Comma," Section 9.4.)

Don't delay. Mail the order card at once!
How could they be so insensitive!
Sale! Bargains for Everyone! Come and Get Them!

9.8 HYPHEN   -

General Usage.   The hyphen should be used only where required by custom or for reasons of clarity or consistency. Beyond these uses, variations in hyphenating are considerable. Dictionaries themselves do not always agree. The modern tendency, however, is to do with fewer hyphens, rather than more, and to join compounds into solid words, as *housewarming, sandpaper, tradespeople.* If in doubt about the hyphenation of a particular word or common compound, use the style recommended by your dictionary.

The principal uses of the hyphen are as follows.

1. To show the division of a word at the end of a line. (See "Word Division," Section 10.5.)

2. To separate the parts of certain compound words. A compound word is a combination of two or more words that form a single unit of thought. The words are sometimes hyphenated, sometimes separated, and sometimes written as one word.

even-tempered   census taker   bookseller

3. To avoid doubling a vowel or tripling a consonant, except after a short prefix.

anti-intellectual
shell-like BUT: preemptive
                  cooperative

4. As a substitute for *to* in such expressions as

1980–1985   pp. 21–23   2:30–3:30 p.m.
the Boston-Washington air corridor

5. To spell out a word.

spelled *d-e-s-i-c-c-a-t-e*

Improvised Compounds.   Hyphenate the parts of an improvised compound phrase.

a once-in-a-lifetime opportunity
a johnny-come-lately
blue-penciled copy
bread-and-butter merchandise
apple-pie order

Modifiers.   Hyphenate the elements of the compound expression modifying a following noun.

first-class service   built-in furniture
self-made man   would-be dictator
clear-cut issue   small-town business
well-known retailer   many-faceted career

1. The presence of three words in the compound, including especially a preposition, increases the probability that hyphens are to be used.

house-to-house salesman	happy-go-lucky attitude
portal-to-portal pay	rough-and-tumble tactics
up-to-date records	a five-day-a-week schedule
a pig-in-the-poke deal	no wage-and-hour provisions

2. Hyphenate modifying phrases that might otherwise be misinterpreted.

former-partner's wife
common-stock holdings
terrible-tempered clerk
new-car buyer

3. Do not hyphenate a modifying foreign phrase.

per diem employees	laissez faire theory
ex officio member	per annum interest

4. Do not use hyphens when the first two words of a compound modifier are adverbs or when one of the words ends in -*ly*.

a very well developed plan
a not too obvious ploy
a highly regarded source
a necessarily risky adventure

5. Do not hyphenate a compound phrase when it follows the word it modifies.

The company is well known.
He thought the service was first class.
The gesture was heavy handed.

6. Noun phrases used as modifiers are generally not hyphenated as long as no confusion is likely.

a civil service job
family planning advice
Eastern District Headquarters

COMPARE: a personal loan service (confusing)
                a personal-loan service
                a personal loan-service

CONFUSING: blue gray walls
IMPROVED: blue-gray walls

Noun Compounds.   When two or more words form a noun expression:
1. Hyphenate the expression when it has the force of a single word.

trade-in   close-up   right-of-way

NOTE: This rule is not consistently observed (for example, *makeup, setup, buildup*). When in doubt, consult your dictionary.
2. Hyphenate the expression when the words show combined responsibility, participation, or constituency.

secretary-treasurer	AFL-CIO
plumber-electrician	Latin-American
artist-writer	Warner-7 Arts

NOTE: Ordinary compound titles are not hyphenated.

lieutenant colonel	BUT:	president-elect
vice president		principal-in-charge
attorney general		minister-delegate

3. Hyphenate certain compounds showing family relationship.

mother-in-law	BUT:	stepson
great-grandfather		foster mother
great-aunt		half brother

4. Do not hyphenate chemical and scientific terms.

sulfur dioxide	sodium chloride	methyl bromide
beta decay	angle of refraction	photomicrograph

Numerals.   Hyphenate compound numerals as follows. (See also "Hyphenated Numbers" in Section 10.3.)

1. Compound numerals under one hundred.

eighty-four
one hundred and sixty-five
nineteen hundred and seventy-one

2. Numerals compounded with other words to form adjectives.

a 20-year-old building
easy 12-payment plan
fourth-grade pupil
280-page book
Twenty-third Street

3. Between the numerator and denominator of fractions written as words, unless either one is already hyphenated.

a one-third interest	twelve one-hundredths
one-half a point	twenty-one hundredths
two and seven-eighths	fourteen thirty-seconds

NOTE: When the fraction is used as a noun, the hyphen is sometimes omitted.

one half a point
three fourths of the total

4. Decades expressed in words.

the nineteen-twenties
the eighteen-forties

Prefix-Root Compounds.   Do not hyphenate a word beginning with a prefix except for a good reason.

1. To prevent confusion between similar words.

re-cover (cover again)   re-creation (creating again)
recover (regain)   recreation (play)

2. To prevent mispronunciation, especially when a vowel at the end of a prefix is the same as the vowel at the beginning of the root.

co-worker (not coworker)   semi-equal
intra-agency (not intraagency) pro-urban
co-op (not coop)
  BUT: cooperate

3. When a capital letter follows the prefix.

pre-Revolutionary   pro-British
ex-President Johnson   mid-Atlantic

4. When the prefix is a single letter.

T-square
L-shaped
U-turn

5. After *ex-, quasi-,* and *self-*.

ex-wife, ex-president, ex-councilman
quasi-judicial, quasi-public, quasi-military
self-made, self-incriminating, self-sealing

NOTE: Words beginning with the following prefixes are not usually hyphenated, for example:

ante-   antechamber, antedate, anteroom. BUT: ante-bellum
anti-   anticlimax, antiknock, antisocial. BUT: anti-intellectual
bi-   biennial, bifocal, bilateral, bivalve
circum-   circumnavigate, circumscribe, circumvent
co-   coauthor, coefficient, coexist, coinsurer
extra-   extramarital, extrasensory, extraterritorial
fore-   foreclose, foreknowledge, forerunner, foreshorten
hyper-   hypercorrect, hypersensitive, hyperthyroid
infra-   infrared, infrasonic, infrastructure
inter-   intercompany, interdependent, interurban
meta-   metaethics, metaphysical, metapsychology
micro-   microanalysis, microeconomics, microprint
mono-   monoculture, monomolecular, monosyllabic
multi-   multicolored, multilingual, multimedia, multivalve
neo-   neoclassic, neomycin. BUT: neo-Darwinism
non-   noncommunicative, noninterference, nonparticipation
over-   overanxious, overelaborate, overrun, oversubscribe
para-   paraesthesia, parasympathetic, paratyphoid
poly-   polyclinic, polystyrene, polyunsaturated
post-   postdate, posthaste, postnasal. BUT: post-impressionism
pre-   preassumption, predesignate, preinclination
pro-   prodemocratic, prounion, prowar. BUT: pro-American
pseudo-   pseudoclassical, pseudoliberal. BUT: pseudo-intellectual
semi-   semifinal, semimonthly, semiskilled
sub-   subcontractor, subfreezing, subparagraph

super- superconductivity, supermarket, supersaturate
trans- transcontinental, transoceanic, transatlantic. BUT: trans-Canadian
tri- tricornered, triennial, tripartite, triweekly
ultra- ultramodern, ultrahigh frequency, ultraviolet
under- underachieve, underemployed, underwrite

Suspension Hyphen. When two or more compound words have a common base, put a hyphen after each "suspended" part of the compound.

20- and 30-year debentures
5- and 10-dollar bills
odd- and even-lot trades
8-, 12-, and 16-ounce bottles

9.9 PARENTHESES   ( )

Around Incidental Remarks. Use parentheses to enclose explanatory or supplementary remarks. (See also "Brackets," Section 9.2.)

1. To set off parts of a sentence that might otherwise be punctuated by a colon, commas, or dashes.

The accident insurance provision is terminated upon retirement (age 65 for men, 62 for women).
Your kind remarks (especially your reference to Miss Greer) are very much appreciated.
The next step (I believe it's submitting copy for the client's approval) will have to be taken in my absence.

2. To enclose synonymous abbreviations and terms.

Magnetic ink character recognition (MICR) is part of all check processing.
Open-item accounts receivable procedures are usually followed by businesses that sell to other businesses (mercantile credit), whereas balance-forward procedures are usually followed by companies dealing with consumers (individual credit).

3. To show alternate terms and omissions in form letters.

Will you please verify the specimen signature(s) on the enclosed form(s) and return (it, them) to us.
On (date) we returned to you a check for (amount) drawn to your order by (name).

4. To enclose numeric amounts in some legal documents.

... declare a dividend of One Dollar ($1.00) per share

5. To enclose editorial references.

These functions are performed by the collator (Figure 4).

In Enumerations. Use parentheses to set off the letters or numbers enumerating the items in a series.

The parties most concerned are (a) the manufacturer, (b) the supplier, and (c) the supplier's salesman.

Operating procedure
  (1) Location of units
  (2) Handling of invoices
  (3) Disbursement
  (4) Reconciliation

With Other Punctuation.   For the use of other punctuation marks with parentheses, use these guidelines.

1. Put no punctuation before an opening parenthesis within a sentence. If the sentence requires punctuation at that point, put it after the closing parenthesis.

NOT: _____, (_____) _____.
BUT: _____ (_____), _____.

2. Put no mark inside the closing parenthesis within a sentence unless the sense calls for a quotation mark, an exclamation point, or a question mark. Any marks outside the closing parenthesis should belong to the rest of the sentence.

The rate paid on Systematic Savings Accounts is the same (5 percent).
We know what concessions he wants (he told us); however, we can't give in on every point.
The new heading ("Options")—it's at the top of page 4—has a penciled correction.
His continual promises (I'm so bored with them!) have been continually broken.
Do you care for the larger size (8″ by 14″)?

3. When a statement in parentheses is placed outside a sentence, the end punctuation (period, question mark, or exclamation point) belongs inside the closing parenthesis, not outside.

NOT: _____. (_____).
BUT: _____. (_____.)

Capitals with Parentheses.   When parentheses are outside a sentence, capitalize the first word. When parentheses are inside a sentence, do not capitalize the first word unless it is a proper noun or begins a formal quotation.

Sale items are not returnable. (No exceptions.)
He agreed to the creditors' proposal (what else could he do?).
The free booklet (Professor Cramer recommends it highly) may be obtained by writing . . .
The very first statement ("Men are interdependent") states the theme of the booklet.

Parentheses Within Parentheses.   Parentheses may be used within parentheses, but it is better to use brackets within the parentheses or vice versa. (See "Brackets," Section 9.2.)

ACCEPTABLE: _____ (_____ (_____) _____).
BETTER: _____ [_____ (_____) _____].
OR: _____ (_____ [_____] _____).

9.10   PERIOD   ⟦ . ⟧

Sentence Stop.   Use a period at the end of a declarative sentence, a mild command, an indirect question, or a request phrased as a question. (See also "Question Mark," Section 9.11, and "Exclamation Point," Section 9.7.)

1. Declarative sentence.

We will write for the catalogue.
The luncheon is planned for next Thursday.
You are to be congratulated on your enterprise.
Thank you for your check.

2. Mild command.

Please send your check at once.
Have a good time.
Order now and have the goods in time for Christmas.

3. Indirect question.

He asked what he should do.
The customer wanted to know if we would extend the guarantee two years.

4. Request phrased as question ("question of courtesy").

Will you please let us know your wishes.
May we ask you to return the application as soon as possible.

Abbreviations.   The period is required after most abbreviations, but is optional after some and omitted after others. (See also "Abbreviations," Section 10.1.)

1. Period required.

| Mr. | a.m. | St. | Sec. | A.D. | Calif. |
| Mrs. | p.m. | Ave. | Gen. | B.C. | U.K. |

2. No period.

WNBC   SEATO   MOPAC   NAACP

3. Period optional.

| r.p.m. | A.M.A. | A.F.L.-C.I.O. | U.S.C. |
| rpm | AMA | AFL-CIO | USC |

Misuses.   Do *not* use a period in the following instances.

1. After a signature.
2. After shortened words and contractions.

ad (*for* advertisement)
tab (*for* tabulator)
Sam or Sam'l (*But:* Jos.)
sec'y (*But:* secy.)
cont'd (*But:* contd.)
Phil (*for* Philip)

3. After words or phrases in a list or topical outline.

Be sure to include:
 Date
 Payee
 Amount

Preparation for canning
 (1) Cleaning
 (2) Sorting and grading
   (a) By quality
   (b) By size

4. After parenthesized letters or numbers forming an enumeration.

Checking accounts are classified as (1) regular and (2) special.
The controller's major functions are (a) accounting, (b) credit, (c) systems and research, and (d) financial budgeting.

(See also the example of an outline in Rule 3 immediately preceding.)

9.11 QUESTION MARK | ? |

After Direct Question.   Place a question mark at the end of a direct question.

Have you received our letter of March 13?
When did you wish delivery?
What trade-in allowance do you offer?

1. Sometimes the question mark comes inside the sentence instead of at the end.

Will we participate? is not the question.

2. A period, not a question mark, is used after an indirect question and after a question phrased as a command. (See "Period," Section 9.10.)

Rhetorical Question.   Place a question mark at the end of a question to which an answer is not expected ("rhetorical question").

How should we have known the truck had broken down?
Who could ask for a better deal?

To Express Doubt.   The question mark is used in parentheses to indicate doubt about a preceding figure or statement.

Last June (?) he came into the office to ask . . .

To Express Irony.   The question mark is sometimes used to express irony, but the practice is debatable.

We're expecting a message from the great man (?) momentarily.

9.12 QUOTATION MARKS « »

Common Uses. Use quotation marks to enclose:
  1. A direct quotation.

> The contract says, "The buyer will provide transportation from the warehouse to the destination."

  (a) Do not use quotation marks for words indirectly quoted.

> The contract says that the buyer will provide transportation from the warehouse to the destination.

  (b) Even in an indirect quotation, however, quotation marks may be used to enclose a fragment that is quoted exactly from the original.

> The contract said that the buyer must "provide transportation from the warehouse to the destination."

  2. Literary titles: article, chapter, short story, poem.

> Have you read "The New Elite" in this month's *Atlantic?*
> Chapter 3, "The Language of Business," should be of special interest.
> "Favorite Sons" is the first story in the collection.

  NOTE: Except in journalistic practice, which often prescribes the use of quotation marks, the names of books and magazines are underlined. (See "Underlining," Section 10.4.) In publishers' correspondence, the names of books are regularly set in full capitals.

> The quotation is from Peter Drucker's "The Practice of Management."
> The quotation is from Peter Drucker's The Practice of Management.
> The quotation is from Peter Drucker's THE PRACTICE OF MANAGEMENT.

  3. Distinctive names and technical terms, on first use only.

> Flip the "Conference" button and this portable will pick up normal voices 30 feet away. The Conference feature is exclusive with Stenotalk.
> A "check-credit" account is the answer. Check-credit enables you . . .

  4. Unusual word uses, especially when a word is not to be taken at face value.

> The result is that when the tire goes into service, the cord isn't forced to "grow" back to service dimensions.
> A distinction is made between telegraphic messages covering "free" deliveries of coupon bonds and those covering delivery against payment.
> Such "windfalls" could eventually lead to bankruptcy.

  5. Slang expressions in formal writing.

> FORMAL: The safety slogan was regarded by some officials as "corny," but it apparently contributed to the sharp drop in the accident rate.
> INFORMAL: Let's not have any corny slogans to embarrass us.

6. Words used as words. (See also "Underlining," Section 10.4.)

The word "convenience" was misspelled.
The now respectable musical term "rock and roll" had its beginning on the other side
   of the tracks.
By "gross" we mean what the exhibitors pay to the distributors.

Quotation Within Quotation. Use single quotation marks (') to enclose a quotation within a quotation.

The chairman instructed, "Please answer 'Present' when your name is called."

Long Quotations. A long quotation is one that exceeds four or five typed lines or contains the full text of a letter or telegram.

1. Separation from text. A long quotation is best set off from the unquoted text. This can be done by leaving a space before and after the quotation, single-spacing the quotation even when the rest of the copy is double-spaced, and indenting the whole quotation five spaces from the left margin and, if desired, an equal amount on the right. Quoted copy set off as indicated does not require quotation marks, although they may be used if there is likely to be some question that the material is quoted. (Figure 9-1.)

2. Paragraph punctuation. When quotation marks are used for quoted copy extending for more than a single paragraph, place a quotation mark at the beginning of each paragraph, but at the end of only the last paragraph. (Figure 9-1.)

3. Letters and telegrams. With modern copying methods, it is now seldom necessary to type quoted letters and telegrams in full. When a letter or telegram is retyped as an independent unit, however, the notation "Copy" at the top of each page makes the use of quotation marks unnecessary. When a letter or telegram is incorporated into a report, a legal brief, or another letter, the method of indention described in Rule 1 here is recommended. (See also "Incoming Wires," Section 12.3.)

Capitalization. In a formal quotation, capitalize the first word and any other words that are capitalized in the original copy. If the quotation is run informally into the text, do not capitalize the first word unless it takes a capital anyway. (For capitalization in a broken quotation, see "Mixed Punctuation," in this section.)

As the advertisement says, "Let the man at Reynolds do the job."
In his own words, the statement caused "consternation among my friends and
   jubilation among my enemies."

Mixed Punctuation. The prevailing practice is to put a comma or period inside a final quotation mark, a semicolon or colon outside the quotation mark, and other punctuation marks either inside or outside, depending on whether they belong to the quotation or to the whole sentence.

the safeguarding and profitable utilization of the

assets of the whole enterprise. The American Insti-

tute of Accountants defines internal control as

follows:

> Internal control comprises the plan of
> organization and all of the coordinate methods
> and measures adopted within a business to
> safeguard its assets, check the accuracy and
> reliability of its accounting data, promote
> additional efficiency, and encourage adherence
> to prescribed managerial policies.

A satisfactory system of internal control should

include (1) a plan of organization which provides ap-

propriate segregation of functional responsibilities;

- -

Under the title, "Award of Merit Presented to
Ninth Street Office," the following story appeared in
MHT Topics:

"MHT's recently constructed Ninth Street Brooklyn
Office has been awarded the Award of Merit of the Concrete Industry Board, Inc. of N.Y.

"The award was given for excellence in design and
execution of materials.

"The architect for the building is William Milo
Barnum Associates. The exterior and the interior of
the building are constructed of reinforced and cast-
in-place concrete. Tellers' counter top is granite
as is the floor."

Figure 9-1   Two methods of handling long quotations.

"The Creative Revolution," an article by Grant Wilson, author also of "The Over-50 Job Hunter" . . .
From "The Creative Revolution": "You can't be brilliant in 30 seconds."
We resented his use of the term "sharp dealings"; still, there was little we could do but . . .
"Boom!" is the title of the movie.
He called us "victims"!
"What profits?" he wanted to know.
Did he say "profits"?
"Oh—," he blurted in frustration, "forget it."
"Beg pardon"—that's the term he used.

1. When a question is quoted within a question, use a single question mark at the end.

Why did he say, "What's new"?

2. In legal work and other copy requiring the utmost accuracy, place any necessary punctuation marks inside the final quotation mark when they are part of the quoted matter; outside, when they are not.

The date should follow the style, "May, 1981,".
Please append the words "zealous" and "zither".

3. When quotations are used with expressions like "he said," use the punctuation that the sentence structure would ordinarily require.

He wrote, "If this isn't the longest trip I've taken, it seems like it." (Comma following introduction to short formal quotation; see Section 9.4. Also see "Colon," Section 9.3.)
"Please," he said, "I couldn't stand another 'favor' like that one." (Commas to enclose interrupting element; see Section 9.4.)
"We have been filling orders as they are received," the company replied; "however, we will consider giving priority on the basis of need." (Semicolon between two complete statements not joined by a simple conjunction. See "Semicolon," Section 9.13.)

OR:

"We have been filling orders as they are received," the company replied. "However, we will consider . . ." (Period used as sentence stop. See "Period," Section 9.10.)

9.13 SEMICOLON   ;

Instead of Period. A semicolon may be used instead of a period when two complete statements, closely related in thought, are not joined by a simple conjunction like *and, but, for, or,* or *nor.*

The colored seal on genuine bills has sharp sawtooth points; on bogus money the points are usually broken off.
The agent works on a contingent basis; he collects a fee only if the client is pleased.

Before Connecting Adverbs. Use a semicolon (or period) between main clauses connected by words in the class of *therefore, however, nevertheless, furthermore, accordingly, still, then, hence, thus,* and *consequently.*

The engine is made of aluminum; therefore it is very light.
His credit was excellent; still, he insisted on paying cash.
Our survey confirms the need for rented computer services; however, we disagree
that banks lack the flexibility to provide such services.

Instead of Comma.   Use a semicolon as a substitute for a comma to separate
coordinate (grammatically equivalent) elements within a sentence when they
are already broken up by commas. The semicolon will ease reading by signify-
ing a longer pause.

They will discuss such topics as labor-management relations and labor standards;
the importance of communication, consultation, and the resolution of problems;
the responsibility of labor, management, and the government to the public; and
the role of member countries, especially Canada, in external aid programs.
New electrode capacity was brought on-stream in Mobile, Alabama, as well as at
Welland, Ontario, and Liverpool and Sheffield, England; and construction was
planned or begun on facilities in Italy, Spain, and Sweden.

10

Mechanical Style[1]

In addition to the customary punctuation, writing employs other signs and devices to prevent the reader from stumbling and to help him interpret a particular word or passage. These signs and devices are dealt with in this chapter.

CONTENTS

10.1 ABBREVIATIONS

For a list of standard abbreviations see Chapter 17.

General Usage

1. Abbreviations are used to save space in technical documents and in footnotes, charts, and statistical work. They should be used sparingly in letters and the narrative parts of business reports.

2. As a rule, the greater the formality desired, the fewer the abbreviations.

3. When there are alternative abbreviations (*sec., sect.; m.p.h., mph; a.m., P.M.*) adopt a single form and use it throughout the manuscript.

---

[1] Additional material on mechanical style will be found elsewhere in this book as follows: "Letter Form and Style," Section 3.1; "Letters to Government and the Military," Section 3.2; "Forms of Address," Section 3.4; "Footnotes and Bibliographies," Section 5.3; "Tabular Presentation," Section 5.4; "Graphic Presentation," Section 5.5; "The Report in Finished Form," Section 6.3; "Memorandums," Section 6.4; "The Press Release," Section 7.1; "Editing," Section 7.2; "Preparing Copy for the Printer," Section 7.3; "Proofreading," Section 7.4; "Word Processing and Typing Pointers," Chapter 11.

4. In preparing copy for the printer, do not abbreviate any word that you want the printer to spell out.

5. Use the standard abbreviations that you will find in Chapter 17 or in any other approved list. Note carefully the use of capitals, spaces, and periods.

Capitalization.   Ordinarily, you do not capitalize an abbreviation unless the word it stands for would be capitalized. However, some abbreviations are customarily capitalized even though they stand for common nouns.

in.	agt.	Ill.	M.I.T.
ft.	cap.	CBS	Ger.

BUT: C (centigrade)
        EST (eastern standard time)
        CPA (certified public accountant)
        NE (northeast)

Spacing

1. Abbreviations are usually not spaced when all capitals are used or when periods are supplied.

a.m.	e.g.	HOLC	M.D.
sq.ft.	cpm	U.S.	B.W.I.

2. A space is usually observed in the following state abbreviations.

N. Dak.	N. Car.	N. Mex.
S. Dak.	S. Car.	W. Va.

3. The initials of persons are spaced, though an exception may be made when three initials are used.

F. S. Anderson   R.L.A. Perry

4. Put a space between the abbreviated parts of a title preceding a name.

Maj. Gen. Thomas S. Preston
Lt. Gov. David Haines

Periods

1. Though there are many exceptions, a period customarily follows each part of an abbreviation that stands for a word.

e.o.m.	B.C.	fl.oz.
i.e.	LL.D.	Br.

et al. (*et alii*, "and others"; no period after the *et* because it is not an abbreviation)

2. Periods and spaces are usually omitted from abbreviations used as the shortened names of organizations.

FBI	NLRB	ROTC	FHA	
WNBC	AFTRA	FDIC	RCA	(*but* A.T.&T.)

3. Shortened names of persons (as opposed to abbreviations) are generally not followed by a period.

Art (*but* Arth.) Ed (*but* Edw.)
Ben (*but* Benj.) Will (*but* Wm.)

4. Contractions are not considered abbreviations and are not followed by periods.

Int'l Sam'l Ass'n Inc'd

Slant. A slant (diagonal line) is sometimes used to show the omission of a word like *of* or *per* in an abbreviation. At other times it takes the place of the period between two abbreviations.

C/D (certificate of deposit)
B/L (bill of lading)
n/o (in the name of)
bbls/day (barrels per day)
gal/min (gallons per minute)

Mr/Mrs.
M/Sgt.

Plurals

1. The plural of an abbreviation is usually formed by the addition of a small *s*.

qts. yrs. C.P.A.s
yds. bbls. Ph.D.s
mos. rpms YMCAs

2. An apostrophe is used in forming the plural of uncapitalized abbreviations internally punctuated by periods.

a.m.'s r.s.v.p.'s (but RSVPs) c.o.d.'s (*but* C.O.D.s)

3. Some abbreviations are the same in the singular and plural.

in. (inch or inches) mi. (mile or miles)
ft. (foot or feet) oz. (ounce or ounces)

4. Some plural abbreviations are formed by doubling a single letter.

v. (verse) p. (page) f. (folio)
vv. (verses) pp. (pages) ff. (folios)

Titles

1. Do not abbreviate a business title in the text or inside address of a letter.

the chairman of the board
Mr. Samuel Gore, Vice President

2. In formal usage, professional, religious, and military titles should always be spelled out; but in less formal usage, including letter addresses, the titles may be abbreviated if they are followed by a first name or initials.

the lieutenant colonel	professor of American history
Lieutenant Colonel Spanner	Professor Jameson
Lt. Col. Walter G. Spanner	Prof. H. R. Jameson
OR (MORE FORMAL):	OR (MORE FORMAL)
Lieutenant Colonel Walter G. Spanner	Professor Henry R. Jameson
NOT: Lt. Col. Spanner	NOT: Prof. Jameson

3. The titles *Reverend* and *Honorable* should be spelled out when they follow the article *the*.

the Honorable Lester T. Brooks (BUT: Hon. Lester T. Brooks)
the Reverend Mr. Chestnut (BUT: Rev. Paul Chestnut)

Company Names. Follow the company's own style with respect to abbreviations in its name.

Tiffany & Co.
Empire Scientific Corp.
U.S. News & World Report
TAP Portuguese Airways

Names of Individuals. In addressing an individual, use any initials or abbreviations used in the printed letterhead or official listing regardless of the style used in the signature. For example, a man who signs *J. F. Murphy* would still be addressed *John F. Murphy* if that is how his letterhead or company directory carries his name.

Misuses. Except in telegrams and technical and reference matter, spell out:
1. Names of weights and dimensions.

NOT:	5 ft. 10 in.	BUT:	5 feet 10 inches
	8 × 10 ft.		8 by 10 feet
	10 ts.		10 tons
	weighed out in lbs. and oz.		weighed out in pounds and ounces

2. Names of months and days.

NOT:	Feb. 17	BUT:	February 17
	last Wed.		last Wednesday
	on Thurs. and Sats.		on Thursdays and Saturdays

3. Names of streets, states, and other geographical divisions; also points of the compass except when they follow street names. (See also "Letter Form and Style," Section 3.1.)

1865 South Kensington Avenue, Delmar, New Jersey
Mount Royal, Montreal, Canada
1045 Fourteenth Street, NW

10.2 CAPITALS

General Usage. Some capitalization is decreed by custom; other capitalization is a matter of individual or corporate preference. Avoid capitalization without good reason. Do capitalize:

The first word of every sentence.
The distinctive name of a person, place, or thing.
The first word of a formal quotation.
The first word of every line of verse, unless the author has done otherwise.
The important words in the title of a book, magazine, chapter, or heading.

These and other uses of capitalization are explained and illustrated in the sections that follow.

Calendar Periods.   Capitalization is necessary for the names of days and months, but not for other calendar periods. (See also "Historical Periods and Events" in this section.)

> the third Thursday in November
> Monday, May 16
> in July 1980
>
> BUT: spring, summer, autumn, winter
>   in nineteen seventy-five
>   the eighteen-eighties
>   the mid-fifties
>   first-quarter earnings

Compound Proper Names.   Capitalize a common noun or adjective forming an essential part of a proper name, but—with the exceptions noted in "Shortened Names" in this section—do not capitalize the common noun when it is used alone as a substitute for the whole name.

George Washington Bridge	the bridge
the Union Carbide Corporation	the corporation
Jersey City	the city
Allegheny County	the county
Canal Street	the street
Sinclair Building	the building

Departments in a Company.   The name of an organized group within a business need not be capitalized, though it is customary to capitalize the name if it applies to one's own organization. (See also "Shortened Names.")

the sales department	OR	the Sales Department
the computer section	OR	the Computer Section
the legal division	OR	the Legal Division
the executive committee	OR	the Executive Committee

Derivatives of Proper Names

1. Capitalize the derivative of a proper name. (See also "Proper Names" in this section.)

American	Orwellian	Elizabethan
New Yorker	Christian	Asiatic
Romanesque	Princetonian	Manhattanite

2. Do not capitalize the derivative of a proper name when the derivative has acquired a common meaning.

pasteurize (after Pasteur)	china (porcelainware)
roman candle (after Rome)	morocco (leather)
macadam road (after J. L. McAdam)	utopia (after a fictional place)

Emphasis. A word or phrase that would otherwise not be capitalized may be capitalized for emphasis, especially in a sales or advertising presentation.

Every advertisement should have a Central Idea.
See your Travel Agent.
Your policy complies with the Financial Responsibility Laws in all states.
Only Mobil gives you an engine Detergent in Premium and Regular Blends.

Geographic Names

1. Capitalize the distinctive names of geographic subdivisions and topographical features.

the Western Hemisphere	Lake Michigan
the West	the Mississippi River
the Plains States	the Mojave Desert
the Rockies	the Isthmus of Panama
the Corn Belt	the Gulf of Mexico

2. Do not capitalize generic names, even when associated with specific places.

the western plains
the southern states
the California coast
the deepest South (But: the Deep South)

3. Do not capitalize points of the compass when used to signify direction.

travel north on Route 6
walking east
a southeast breeze
a northerly route

Governmental Units. The names of government departments, boards, commissions, judiciaries, and so on, are capitalized without exception.

the Civil Service Commission
the Board of Health
the Appellate Division
the President's Commission on Civil Disorders

Headings and Titles

1. Capitalize the important words (including always the first and last) in titles of books, magazines, newspapers, reports, and the titles or headings naming the parts of such works. The important words consist of the first and last words and all other words *except* articles, the "to" before infinitives, and short prepositions and conjunctions (usually four letters or fewer). The abbreviations *etc.* and *et al.* are not capitalized even when they appear at the end of a title.

Comments on the Minutes of the Previous Meeting
The Facts About Employment with Con Edison
Suggestions for Using the Dictaphone

2. In a running text, do not capitalize the article *the* before the name of a newspaper or magazine. Exceptions to this rule may be made by publications in the use of their own name. Also do not capitalize the word *magazine* unless it is an official part of the title.

advertisement in the *Saturday Review*
a story in the *New York Times* (common usage)
a story in *The New York Times* (publisher's usage)
in *Life* magazine (or *Life*—not *Life Magazine*)
Time magazine (or *Time*)

NOTE: When the name of the periodical follows a quotation and a dash, the *the* is capitalized.

"Profits at Bank Show Increase"—*The New York Times*

3. When a title is split by a colon or dash, any word following the split should be capitalized.

The Business Research Paper: A Style Manual
Education for Today—And Tomorrow

Historical Periods and Events.   Capitalize the distinctive name of a period or event in history.

the Renaissance   the Crucifixion
the Second World War   the Panic of 1907
the Great Depression   the Era of Good Feeling
the Roaring Twenties   the Reign of Terror
the Ice Age   the Flood (biblical)

Hyphenated Words

1. Capitalize the parts of hyphenated words that would be capitalized anyway.

the Army-Navy game   the Lincoln-Douglas debates
Afro-American   Inter-American Industries, Inc.
anti-American slogan   Fifty-ninth Street
pre-Columbian art   the President-elect

2. In a title or heading, capitalize any part of a hyphenated word that would be capitalized anyway according to the rules for "Headings and Titles" in this section.

Fifty-Ninth Street Restaurant
"Chicken-in-a-Jiffy Is Infra-Red Triumph"
"Rules for Out-of-Pocket Expenses"
"Sit-In Workers Return to Jobs" (*In* is capitalized here because it is an adverb, not a preposition.)

Legal References. Capitalize the important words in the names of laws, cases at law, statutes, and official reports. Do not capitalize *versus* or its abbreviations *vs.* and *v.*

United States Code, Vol. 28, Sec. 2201 (Suppl. IV, 1957)
Bank Holding Act
New York State Constitution
Economic Report of the President
Amazon Cotton Mill Co. v. *Textile Workers Union*

Letter Parts. Only certain parts of the salutation and complimentary close of a letter are capitalized. (See also "Letter Form and Style," Section 3.1.)

Dear Mr. Henderson:
Dear Professor Marvin:
My dear Professor Marvin:
Dear Ray:

Very truly yours,
Sincerely yours,

Literary Usage. A noun standing for some abstract quality is sometimes capitalized in literary usage.

He paid homage to Truth and Beauty.
. . . in his search for the Good Life.
No one has a monopoly on Wisdom.

Numerical and Alphabetical References. Capitalize the descriptive word before a number or letter of the alphabet used for reference. Exceptions are commonly made in the instance of small literary subdivisions such as *page, line, paragraph, verse, note,* and so on. Do not capitalize the descriptive word when it is separated from the number or follows it.

page 4	Volume 2	Figure 3	Room 435
line 8	Chapter 6	Exhibit C	Conference Room F
note 1	Article IV	Appendix I	Public School 6
par. 2	Table VI	Form Y	Catalog No. 1238B

BUT: the third volume
the sixth chapter
the second part

The room number is 435.
The public school he went to is No. 12.
In the catalog the number is given as 1238B.

Prefixed Names

1. When a name begins with *de, du, della,* or the like, the prefix is not ordinarily capitalized unless it begins a sentence or stands without a first name or title. The German *von* and *van* are usually not capitalized except at the beginning of a sentence. As with the spelling and capitalization of all names, the usage of their owners should prevail.

E. I. du Pont de Nemours & Co.	Du Pont
Raimundo de Larrain	De Larrain
Jacques d'Arcy	D'Arcy
the Duke d'Uzes	D'Uzes
Werner von Braun	von Braun
Erich Von Stroheim (an exception)	Von Stroheim

2. When a prefixed name is set in all capitals, the prefix should also be in capitals unless there is no space between the prefix and the name. In that case, appearance is improved if only the initial letter of the prefix is capitalized.

MAC INTOSH but MacINTOSH	McKEE
McNAMARA	MacGREGOR

Proper Names.   Capitalize the distinctive name of a person, place, or thing. (See also "Derivatives of Proper Names," in this section.)

Walter Bigelow	Seagram Building	Bufferin
Suffolk County	General Electric	Tide (the detergent)
Lake Michigan	Fifth Avenue	Chevrolet

Publications.   Capitalize the names of books, newspapers, magazines, and technical and professional journals. (See "Titles and Headings" in this section.)

Quotations.   Capitalize the first word of a formal quotation, but not of a quoted fragment unless it begins with a proper name.

In his testimony, he said, "The contract was made in good faith, but . . ."
When he said the contract was made in "good faith," he really meant . . .

Religious Names
1. Capitalize the names of the Deity, of the Holy Trinity, and of the Scriptures and other sacred writings of whatever religion. Also capitalize the names of religious figures and particular references to sacred works.

God (but godlike)	the Virgin Mary
the Messiah	the Son of Man
Moses	the Bible (but biblical)
the Almighty	the Talmud (but talmudic)
Muhammed	the Koran
Jesus	the Ten Commandments
Leviticus	the Psalms

2. Capitalize pronouns standing for the name of the Deity, but not if they occur within a few words of the name.

We believe in Him and all that He commands.
God is not dead, but he apparently does not show himself to everyone.

Shortened Names
1. It is customary to capitalize the shortened form for the name of one's own company or its departments. (See also "Departments in a Business" and "Titles" in this section.)

the Methods and Systems Department	the Department
Manufacturers Hanover Trust Company	the Bank
International Business Machines Corporation	the Company (*or* Corporation)
the Shipping Department	the Department*

*or Shipping, as in "We'll see that Shipping is notified."

2. Capitalize a common noun generally acknowledged as the short form of a specific proper noun.

Fifth Avenue	the Avenue
Wall Street	the Street
New York Stock Exchange	the Exchange
Lake Shore Drive	the Drive
West Point	the Point

3. Capitalize the shortened form of a specific government agency.

the Supreme Court	the Court
the Board of Standards and Appeals	the Board
the Commission on Human Rights	the Commission

The.   Do not capitalize the article *the* before a company name unless it begins a sentence or is an official part of the title.

for The Texas Company
at The Custom Shop
from The White House (a department store)

BUT: the National Cash Register Company
the Four Seasons (a restaurant)

Titles (Individuals)

1. Capitalize a title preceding a name.

Chairman Smith
Dean Harrison
General Westmoreland
Professor Edwards
Vice President Cluny

2. A title following a name or used alone is generally not capitalized unless it forms part of a letter address or belongs to an individual in one's own organization. (See also "Letter Form and Styles," Section 3.1.)

to Mr. Smith, chairman of the board, who
to Mr. Smith, Chairman of the Board, who (an official of the writer's company)
to Dr. Harrison, dean of the school, who
to Dr. Harrison, Dean of the School, who (dean of the writer's school)
the executive vice president of another company
our Executive Vice President

3. Capitalize any title to signify special distinction or deference.

William Westmoreland, Chief of Staff
the President of the United States (BUT: When a president is elected . . .)
the Chief Justice
the senior Senator from California (BUT: a senator's duty)
the Archbishop of London
the Mayor of Chicago

Trade Names.   Capitalize the distinctive name of the product of a single manufacturer, but not of a trade name that has come into popular generic use.

Munsonwear	BUT:	nylon
Acrilon		dacron
Fritos		vaseline
Del Monte		mimeograph (but Mimeograph for the particular
Kodak Instamatic		machine of that name)

10.3   NUMBERS

General Usage.   As a rule, spell out exact numbers of ten or less and use figures for higher numbers. However, in tabular and financial work, and whenever ready reference is desired, use figures for all numbers. (See also "Mixed Words and Figures" and "Round Numbers" in this section.)

three dozen	14 dozen
five dollars	$28
eight men	25 men
10 percent	16 percent

ALSO: priced at $2 each
          a three-year contract
          interest at 8.5 percent
          a six-months' delay

Abbreviations with Numbers.   Always use figures with abbreviations.

3 doz. (*not* three doz.)
4 in. (*not* four in.)
Fig. 3 (*not* Fig. Three)

Alignment.   Align whole numbers on the right and decimals on the decimal point. Fractions, ordinal endings, and parentheses are allowed to overhang. (See also "Typing Statistical Material," Section 11.3.)

23	$356	10.25	655	I	23rd
9½	5	4.00	(26)	II	24th
411	85	3.375	455	VIII	25th

Cents

1. Use the sign ¢, but not the abbreviation *cts.* for *cents*. For a more formal effect, especially in writing for publication, spell out *cents*.

CORRECT: 1¢   7¢   23¢   75¢
MORE FORMAL: one cent   seven cents (*or* 7 cents)
                    23 cents   75 cents

2. Do not use the $ sign with cents alone except (a) in a series of mixed amounts, (b) in a tabulation, and (c) before cents expressed in more than two figures. In a mixed series and whenever the possibility of error otherwise

exists, use a cipher and a decimal before amounts of less than one dollar. In a mixed series also add a decimal and two ciphers after even dollar amounts.

NOT: at $.49 each
BUT: at 49¢ (or 49 cents) each
CORRECT: earning $0.90, $1.50, and $2.00 an hour
            comes to a price of $0.375 each

3. Do not use the decimal and *cents* except to express hundredths of a cent. For example, *.40 cents* is not the same as *40 cents; .40 cents* means 40/100 (or two-fifths) of a cent.

Commas with Figures

1. Place a comma between each set of three figures counting from right to left, except for serial numbers, policy numbers, room numbers, dates, and the like (Figure 10-1).

23,465,322   BUT: Invoice No. 32258
    31,400   Policy No. 4526859
     2,655   Catalog No. 4302-S
                        Room 2305
                        projected for 1985

NOTE: Social Security numbers, credit card numbers, and the like employ spaces or hyphens between sets of numbers of varying length.

Social Security No. 085-26-4754
Credit Card No. 030 381 361 5

2. Numbers of four digits that would ordinarily be punctuated by a comma are often written without the comma.

sold 3600 shares
an order for 1200 dozen

3. Figures representing patent numbers customarily use commas.

U.S. Patents 2,278,731
             2,248,410
             2,244,845

Trillions	Hundred billions	Ten billions	Billions	Hundred millions	Ten millions	Millions	Hundred thousands	Ten thousands	Thousands	Hundreds	Tens	Units
1,	3	4	7,	2	8	9,	5	6	4,	1	2	4

Figure 10-1 Reading numbers.

Dates

1. Use the endings *-st, -nd, -rd, -d,* and *-th* only when the day precedes the month or month and year.

the 24th of January the 24th of January, 1980
BUT: January 24   BUT: January 24, 1980

2. Spell out the date only in formal invitations and some legal documents.

FORMAL: on the fifth day of November, nineteen hundred and seventy-two
MORE FORMAL: on the fifth day of November, A.D. nineteen hundred and seventy-two
MOST FORMAL: on the fifth day of November, in the year of our Lord one thousand nine hundred and seventy-two

3. When the abbreviated form of a year or period is written in words, use capital initials for emphasis, but no apostrophe.

back in Sixty-eight the Roaring Twenties
 (NOT 'Sixty-eight) a Seventy-nine Buick (OR, CLEARER:
the Gay Nineties   a 1979 Buick)

4. Note the following usages in representing dates.

back in '68
Class of 1985
the year 1985 (no capital)
1980–1981 or 1980–81 (*but not* 1980–1)

4/16/81 (American style) BUT: 16/4/81 (European style)
April 16, 1981 (American style)
16 April 1981 (U.S. military and British style)

the April, 1981, tax installment, *or*
the April 1981 tax installment

the April 15, 1981, tax installment, *or*
the April 15, 1981 tax installment

Decimals. In the interests of precision, a cipher may be placed before a decimal point that is not preceded by a whole number, though there is a tendency to leave out the extra cipher when the decimal begins with a cipher. (See also "Cents" in this section.)

.12 milligrams
a specific gravity of 0.4325
.015 of an inch, *or* 0.015 of an inch

Dollars

1. Omit the decimal point and ciphers after even dollar amounts except (a) in bank practice or other writing requiring great exactness, and (b) in a series containing mixed amounts.

$29 $340 $12,000
A balance of $2,345.00 (*or* $2,345.) remained in the account.
available at $2.00, $4.50, and $6.25

2. Use the dollar sign before each figure amount; do not use the word *dollars* after a figure amount.

NOT: 76 dollars
BUT: $76 (*or* seventy-six dollars)

3. Repeat the dollar sign before each figure amount in a series.

three payments of $25, $50, and $100, respectively
a deposit of $25 or $50 (*not* of 25 or $50, *or* of $25 or 50)

Double Representation.   Except in legal documents and formal price quotations, where the practice is divided, do not spell out an amount that is also represented in figures.

LEGAL DOCUMENT: promise to pay the sum of Four Hundred Thirty-two and
50/100ths dollars ($432.50) [Capitals are customary in this use.]
ORDINARY USE: my check for $432.50

Dual Sets of Numbers.   When two sets of numbers occur in the same passage, use figures for one set, words for the other, if convenient.

NOT: Three girls worked four hours, two worked seven hours, and twelve worked
         fourteen hours.
BUT: Three girls worked 4 hours, two worked 7 hours, and twelve worked 14 hours.

Fractions
1. Use full figures to express fractions. Use of the fractions on your typewriter keyboard is discouraged because they are sometimes illegible on multiple carbon copies. Note the following styles.

12 1/2   6 5/32   1/16   5/8 share (*not* 5/8ths share)
INCONSISTENT: $2\frac{1}{2} \times 5\frac{1}{2} \times 7 1/8$
BETTER: 2 1/2 $\times$ 5 1/2 $\times$ 7 1/8

2. Isolated fractions may be spelled out. (See also "Numerals" in "Hyphens," Section 9.8.)

bought a one-half interest
you pay two thirds of the regular price

Hyphenated Numbers.   See also "Numerals" in Section 9.8.
1. Hyphenate spelled-out number compounds under one hundred, and hyphenate any number that becomes part of an adjective compound.

twenty-two   five hundred miles, *but*
thirty-five hundred   a five-hundred-mile trip
fourteen by twenty-six   thirty-two thousand, *but*
two and three-eighths   a thirty-two-thousand-dollar house

2. Use a hyphen to indicate the omission of intermediate figures, and carry over at least two digits of figures having two digits or more. Repeat the

initial digits, if necessary, for clarity. Telephone numbers are usually excepted from this rule.

1978–80 (*or* 1978–1980)
1900–09 (*not* 1900–9)
pp. 32–39 (*not* pp. 32–9)
pp. 126–132 (*or* pp. 126–32)

Nos. 36248–36253 (*better than* 36248–53)

in the period 1977–1981
from 1977 to 1981 (*not* from 1977–1981)
Telephone: 598-2231-2-3 (*but* 598-2208-09-10)

3. Repeat the symbols used with hyphenated figures.

32°–77°F. (*not*: 32–77°F.)
$10–$20 (*but*: 10 to 20 dollars)
3¢–5¢ (*but*: 3 to 5 cents)

Measurements.   Use figures to express dimensions, weights, and capacities.

2′ × 3′	3 square miles	5 quarts
2 × 3 ft.	120 horsepower	16 barrels
2 by 3 feet	8 cylinders	26 tons

Ciphers and a decimal point are used in exact or scientific work.

a volume of 0.67 cubic inches

Mixed Words and Figures.   When several coordinate numbers are used, do not mix words and figures.

NOT: maturities of five, 15, and 25 years
BUT: maturities of 5, 15, and 25 years

Ordinal Numbers

1. Ordinal numbers expressed in figures are written as follows.

1st, 2d or 2nd, 3d or 3rd, 4th, 5th, 6th, 7th, and so on.
2d and 3d are now generally preferred to 2nd and 3rd.

2. Ordinal figures are used with dates only when the day precedes the name of the month or when the name of the month is omitted.

on the 23d of May
on May 23 (*not* May 23d)
your letter of the 23d

BUT: May twenty-third (*not* May twenty-three)

3. Ordinal endings are generally omitted after street numbers expressed in figures, but are retained when the street number is spelled out.

220 West 45 Street
30 East Fourteenth Street
30 East 14 Street

ACCEPTABLE: 30 East 14th Street

Percentages

1. Percentage is written in the following styles.

% (use with figures only)
        6%   10%   25%   100%
per cent (use with words or figures)
        six per cent   6 per cent
percent (use with words or figures; now generally preferred to *per cent*)
        six percent   6 percent

2. Repeat the percent sign, but not the word *percent* (or *per cent*) after each figure in a series.

NOT: paying 4, 5, and 6% interest
BUT: paying 4%, 5%, and 6% interest
OR: paying 4, 5, and 6 percent interest

NOT: 10 to 25% off
BUT: 10% to 25% off
OR: 10 to 25 percent off

Plural Usage

1. The use of the singular and plural with numbers is demonstrated in this table.

Numbered amounts	two hundred, twelve thousand, five million 2 billion dollars, 2 billions of dollars 2.5 billion (*or* 2.5 billions) in foreign aid
With *several*	several hundred, several thousand several thousand dollars, several thousands of dollars
With *many*	many hundreds, many thousands, many millions many millions of people
With *by the*	by the yard (unit of measurement) Buy them by the dozen. (unit of sale) Buy them by the dozens. (in large numbers) Buy them by the hundred. (unit of sale) They came by the hundreds. (in large numbers)
With *by* or *in*	They come in pairs. sold by dozens multiplied by millions

2. Figures form their plurals by the addition of *s* or *'s;* the apostrophe is usually omitted in market quotations. When numbers are spelled out, the usual rules for plurals apply. (See "Spelling Guide," Section 8.1.)

in 2's and 3's	in 2s and 3s	in twos and threes
Treasury 4 3/4s	Alcoa 6s	Mexico 6 1/2s
the 5%'s	the 5%s	the five percents
the 1980's	the 1980s	the nineteen-eighties

the 2″ × 3″s are out of stock (*or* the 2″ by 3″'s)
the two by three inches' are out of stock
the two by threes are out of stock

Roman Numerals (Figure 10-2). Roman numerals are currently used as follows.

1. To list important topics in an outline.

I. Causes
II. Effects

2. To number chapters and volumes of books.

Chapter XII
Volume III

3. To number the pages in prefaces and other material preceding the main text. Small Roman numerals are used for this purpose.

i iv x xiii xix xxii

4. To indicate the year on cornerstones and other architectural features.

MCMLXXX (1980)

5. To identify individuals, historic and otherwise.

Louis XIV
Henry Ford II

Round Numbers

1. Round numbers should be expressed in words except where quick identification is desired.

about six hundred residents
not in a thousand years

employ 2,500 workers, *or*
employ twenty-five hundred workers (*not* two thousand five hundred)

1	I	14	XIV	90	XC
2	II	15	XV	100	C
3	III	16	XVI	200	CC
4	IV	17	XVII	300	CCC
5	V	18	XVIII	400	CCCC or CD
6	VI	19	XIX	500	D
7	VII	20	XX	600	DC
8	VIII	30	XXX	700	DCC
9	IX	40	XL	800	DCCC
10	X	50	L	900	CM
11	XI	60	LX	1,000	M
12	XII	70	LXX	2,000	MM
13	XIII	80	LXXX or XXC	1,000,000	$\overline{\text{M}}$

Figure 10-2 Forming Roman numerals.

2. For ease of reading, use the words *million* and *billion* with figures.

$30 million for improvements
a $2 billion budget
spent 2 millions
a population of 200 million

Sentence Beginning.   Try to avoid using figures at the beginning of a sentence. If you cannot recast the sentence to put the figure inside, spell out the number.

BAD: 231 employees were added to our payroll last year.
BETTER: Two hundred and thirty-one employees were added to our payroll last year.
BETTER STILL: Last year 231 employees were added to our payroll.

Successive Numbers

1. Use a comma to separate two figures following each other. Or, if the numbers are not part of the same series, spell out one of the numbers. In other instances, rephrase the sentence to separate the figures.

BAD: In 1979, 250 new apprentices were hired.
BETTER: In 1979, two hundred and fifty new apprentices were hired.
BETTER STILL: In 1979 we hired 250 new apprentices.

2. When a number precedes a numeral adjective, spell out one of the numbers if it can be conveniently expressed in one or two words.

ten 5-pound boxes (*not* ten five-pound boxes)
three $100 bills (*not* three one-hundred-dollar bills)
twenty-five 50-cent cigars, *or*
25 fifty-cent cigars
BUT: a development consisting of 126 $30,500 homes (no comma)

10.4   UNDERLINING

General Usage.   Underlining is used to emphasize particular words or phrases and, in some instances, to take the place of quotation marks. Solid underlining (including spaces and punctuation marks) makes a better appearance than broken underlining, but the latter is better for emphasizing particular words. Do not underline punctuation marks at the beginning or end of an underline. (For exception, see "Italics" in this section.)

"Happy's" Almanac. or "Happy's" Almanac.

For the use of underlining in footnotes and bibliography, see Section 5.3.

Titles.   Underlining may be used for the titles of books and other long literary works, periodicals, newspapers, musical compositions, and the distinctive names of ships, trains, or planes; however, underlining is sometimes omitted altogether. Underlining is never used for the word *Bible* or for the books of the Bible.

> the New York Times (*or* the New York Times)
> the musical play Annie
> copy of Time
> the Golden Arrow flies to Chicago at 12 noon every day
> sailed on Queen Elizabeth 2
> BUT: the Bible, Proverbs xx, the Book of Job

Italics.   Use underlining to indicate any copy you wish the printer to set in italics. In copying printed matter, use underlining whenever you see italics.

NOTE: Because commas, semicolons, colons, exclamation points, and question marks following italics are also set in italics, these punctuation marks should be underlined in preparing printer's copy or in typewriting transcripts of such copy.

Words and Symbols.   In formal writing it is customary to underline words, numbers, letters, and other symbols when they are used for identification only.

> The word receive was misspelled.
> The 2 was written like a 7.
> The % was missing after the figure.
> There are two s's in misspelled.

Misuse.   It is bad form to underline words indiscriminately for emphasis. An occasional underlined word gets attention, but when many words are underlined, the attention is divided. The appearance of the page also suffers.

> BAD: With your gift you will receive details of a plan that can help you achieve the financial security you want and need for your family.

10.5 WORD DIVISION

General Usage

1. Divide words at the ends of lines in order to avoid a jagged right-hand margin. Such division should be kept to a minimum. All word divisions must be made between syllables with due regard for appearance and pronunciation. If in doubt about where a syllable ends, consult your dictionary.

2. Do not divide a word of one syllable or one of less than six letters. Note that word endings do not always create extra syllables.

thought	exit	dropped	(one syllable)
made	refer	passed	(,, ,,)
freight	delay	warned	(,, ,,)

3. Do not divide after a single letter, and preferably not after two. Do not carry over less than three letters, and preferably not less than four.

BAD:	a/go	BETTER:	ed/itor	BEST:	con/sume
	e/merge		re/verse		nec/essary
	imprompt/u		nar/row		fore/cast
	want/ed		tun/nel		oppo/nent

Abbreviations.   Do not divide an abbreviation.

UNICEF   m.p.h.   approx.   IC4A   entomol.

Affixes

1. Divide a word, if possible, after a prefix or before a suffix.

re/gain	ad/junct	discern/ible	happi/ness
pre/pare	dis/cuss	rebel/lion	astonish/ment

2. Do not divide a prefix or suffix.

under/lying (not un/derlying)
accept/able (not accepta/ble)

3. When a suffix is added to a word ending in two consonants, the division is usually made after the consonants.

tell/ing   impress/ive   remark/able   prevent/ive
BUT: instal/lation (*not* install/ation)

4. The word endings that follow form complete syllables and should not be divided except at the point indicated:

/cal	/cious	/gious	/tient
/cent	/cism	/nous	/tion
/ceous	/dant	/sion	/tious
/cial	/dure	/sive	/tive
/cian	/geon	/tent	/tude
/cient	/geous	/tial	/ture
/cion	/gion	/tian	

5. Do not divide a word before a suffix if a new syllable is not created.

dis/barred (*not* disbar/red)

Contractions.   Do not divide a contraction.

wouldn't (*not* would/n't)
haven't (*not* have/n't)

Dates.   Avoid dividing a date. If a division must be made, follow these styles:

June 27,/19—
September 6,/19—
Septem/ber 6,/19—
Sep/tember 6, 19—

Double Consonants. A word containing a double consonant or two adjoining consonants flanked by vowels can usually be divided between the consonants if the division preserves the normal syllabication.

> begin/ning   accom/modate   occur/rence
> construc/tion   conser/vatory   cul/tural
> BUT: remark/able (*not* remar/kable)

Figures. Do not divide a figure or separate a figure from an accompanying word, symbol, abbreviation, or letter.

> 1975   page 36   23,455,865
> $10 million   12 by 20 ft.   Sec. 255(b)(3)

Foreign Words. Avoid dividing words that retain their foreign pronunciation.

> mademoiselle (not mademoi/selle)
> raconteur (not racon/teur)

Headings. Do not divide a word in a title or heading.

> NOT: Communication and Organi-
>   zational Behavior
> BUT: Communication and
>   Organizational Behavior

Hyphenated Words. Do not divide a hyphenated word anywhere but at the hyphen. Correct:

> secretary-/treasurer   hard-/of-hearing,   *or*   hard-of-/hearing

Last Words. Do not divide the last word in a paragraph or the last word on a page.

Mispronunciation. Do not divide a word in such a way that mispronunciation may result.

> BAD: cauti/ous   moth/er   ear/nest   read/just
> BETTER: cau/tious   mother   earn/est   re/adjust

Proper Names

1. Avoid dividing a proper name. In any case, do not separate the title from the initials, or a middle initial from the first name. Correct:

> Dr. R. T./Swanson   Lieutenant Colonel/Henderson
> Mrs. Elsie D./Traynor   Lt. Col./John Henderson

2. Degrees and the designations *Jr., Sr., II,* and so on, should not be separated from the last name. Correct:

> Frederick/Mason, D.D.S.   Mr. Samuel E./Krey, M.E.E.
>   Mr. Irvin C./Hale, Jr.

Solid Compounds.   Do not divide a solid (unhyphenated) compound word anywhere but between the elements of the compound. Correct:

under/cover   multi/million   business/man

Successive Lines.   Avoid dividing words at the end of more than two successive lines.

BAD: .   .   .   .   work-
       .   .   .   .   .   .   debat-
       .   .   .   .   .   .   fore-

Vowels.   Divide a word after a single vowel forming a syllable or between vowels that are separately pronounced.

prevari/cate (*not* prevar/icate)   legi/bility (*not* leg/ibility)
innocu/ous (*not* innoc/uous)   notori/ety (*not* notor/iety)

11

Word Processing and Typing Pointers

Properly used, the typewriter is one of the most important machines in the office. Now linked with the computer for faster and more accurate word processing, it can store information for retrieval when needed for editing, push-button copying, and transmission to distant points. It is also capable of interchanging a large variety of type styles and sizes and can be programmed for the automatic formatting of various types of material. (See also "Word Processing" in Section 5.1.)

CONTENTS

11.1 WORD PROCESSING AND MEDIA TYPEWRITERS

Word processing centers have brought many changes to today's automated offices. Word processing is defined as the improvement of traditional secretarial/clerical functions through a managed system of people, procedures, and modern office equipment. In such a system each executive or professional staff person is supported by teams of two kinds of specialized secretaries: *correspondence secretaries*, who do most of the transcribing; and *administrative secretaries*, who handle the files, phone, mail, and numerous analytical and administrative functions, usually without use of the typewriter. The assignment of secretaries is determined not by executive status, but by analysis of the secretarial work requirements of each executive. The number and the placement of secretaries depend on the individual skill level; the volume, complexity, and nature of the work load; and the needs of the

364

organization as a whole. The work load determines the keyboard used—a stand-alone electric typewriter, a stand-alone magnetic keyboard, or a communicating keyboard that inputs work to a computer.

Correspondence and Administrative Secretaries.   In relatively large, centralized word processing (WP) centers, correspondence secretaries work under the direction of supervisors who make assignments according to the skills and work load involved. Modern dictation and automatic editing equipment with a capability for fast correction of errors and change of text permit the WP staff to produce a large quantity of work accurately and efficiently. Peak loads become less of a problem and work quality improves.

Administrative secretaries work in smaller, decentralized administrative support centers near the executives they assist. Each secretary is part of the staff of one or more executives or professionals for day-to-day work. As a staff person, the secretary also independently performs additional specialized, departmental administrative functions, such as recordkeeping, research, or itinerary planning. Work supervision and task-to-talent matching provide better support to the professional executive than does the assignment of individual private secretaries. Word processing is flexible. Procedures and personnel can be quickly adapted to company or individual needs.

Many firms have as many as six grades each of administrative and correspondence secretaries. A highly skilled person can move through those levels into managerial positions. Now appearing on organization charts are such titles as Manager of WP and Administrative Secretarial Services, Supervisor of Administrative Secretaries, Supervisor of the WP Center, WP Center Coordinator, WP Proofreader, Manager of Word Processing, WP Correspondence Manager, and Manager of Support Services.

Benefits of Word Processing.   Experience has shown that the word processing system provides several major benefits:
  1. Improved secretarial support for executives and other staff members.
  2. Controlled and supervised development of human resources.
  3. Greater career opportunities with more management positions for secretaries.
  4. Consistent service with higher quality.
  5. Optimum use of systems and equipment.
  6. Savings in secretarial/clerical payroll.

Skills Needed by Word Processors.   All persons who work in an organization with a WP system should possess some knowledge of word processing in order to utilize the system effectively. Some personnel will need training in specific WP skills in order to operate the automated typewriters, computers, and dictation systems that comprise the WP center.

Typewriting Skills.   Correspondence secretaries should possess high rough-draft speeds on automated typewriters, because these machines permit error correction by a simple backspacing and strikeover procedure. First-time accuracy in typing is not a requirement, but accuracy should still be a goal for the typist. Error correction results in wasted time regardless of the correction method used. The typist will, however, feel freer to type rapidly with assurance of sufficient control to eliminate most errors.

The correspondence secretary also needs to be adept in making author changes. These changes in text must be placed correctly in the finished document. Automatic editing machines eliminate the chore of retyping those parts of the text that already have been typed correctly. A further skill involves the assembly of business letters from pre-recorded texts stored on magnetic or paper media, thus producing an original document by automatic typing. If new material is to be interspersed into the document, it is essential to know the coding system for stored retrieval in order to obtain accurate playback. The mechanical functioning of the media typewriter and its application to specific work must be mastered by the correspondence secretary.

Proofreading Skills.   Both the correspondence secretary and the word originator should develop proofreading skills to the highest accuracy possible. Proofreading requires a person to be alert when reading copy for misspelled words or names, punctuation omitted or misplaced, transposed or incorrect figures, omitted material, poor sentence structure, confusing statements, and other items that cause a document to be less than perfect.

The secretary proofreads the text while it is in the machine or on the computer viewing screen. The word originator notes changes when editing the first draft off the typewriter. With at least two persons proofreading and with error corrections made carefully, the final copy should reflect a high standard of accuracy. (See Section 7.4, "Proofreading.")

Transcription Skills.   The correspondence secretary must develop high-level transcription skills to be able to type rapidly from hearing a voice rather than reading words or symbols. This skill calls for a strong background in spelling, grammar, punctuation, sentence structure, and paragraphing. The secretary should possess a large working vocabulary in the company's technical field. Also important is complete familiarity with the correspondence formats preferred by the company for setting up documents. (See Section 4.3, "Taking and Transcribing Dictation.")

Dictating Skills.   Personnel using the WP center need effective communication skills. The efficiency of the center depends on the ability of the word originator to dictate proficiently into a dictation machine or a telephone hookup. Familiarity with the operation of the equipment and the techniques of machine dictation will produce copy more efficiently than writing in longhand or dictating to a person. (See Section 4.2, "Dictation Techniques.")

Composition Skills.   All persons who are involved in correspondence, reports, and other documents should develop their composition skills. Effective composition must be unambiguous, supply needed information, answer all pertinent questions in the mind of the receiver, and obtain the desired understanding and action. To become a good business writer requires study and practice in situation analysis and the ability to foresee what the receiver will need to know. In today's office, letter writing is no longer handled solely by management. More and more professional employees, including the administrative secretary, dictate letters, memorandums, and reports. (See Section 4.1, "Effective Letters"; Chapter 6, "Report Preparation"; and Chapter 7, "Publicity and Editorial Work.")

Media Typewriters. A media typewriter is an electric typewriter that is combined with a magnetic tape, a magnetic card, a diskette, a cassette, or computer memory to store everything typed (Figure 11.1). The machine either types the document as nonmedia machines do or is part of a

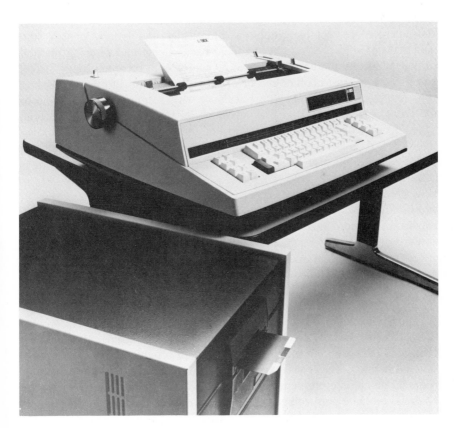

Figure 11-1   A. B. Dick Magna 1 Electronic Typewriter with Communications Option.

computer/copier that produces copy. Most models include automatic settings, immediately the machine is turned on, of left and right margins and
tab stops every five spaces. The automatic typing line is six inches, but margins can be easily reset for documents that require a different length of
typing line. Tab stops can also be reset if necessary. Margin and tab settings
are recorded electronically and reproduced automatically on future play-
backs. On many machines it is possible to change from 10- to 12-pitch type
and to justify the right hand margin. With all machines it is possible to store
for later recall words, lines, sentences, or entire paragraphs without manual
typing. An entire document, regardless of the number of pages, can be
reproduced within minutes. With electronic typewriters, material can be
typed into memory, recorded out of memory, read into memory, revised in
memory, and played back from memory—all at high speeds. For example,
some machines type a full-page letter in 45 seconds. Whereas a standard
electric typewriter may produce 12 repetitive letters an hour, an electronic
typewriter can turn out as many as 36 letters.

A time-saving feature of media typewriters is an ability to correct typing
errors and to make editing changes with the automatic adjustment of margins
and lines. A correctable ribbon automatically lifts letters, figures, and
punctuation from the page by a simple backspacing and retyping method
so that additions and corrections can be made. With these machines, strike-
overs, erasures, and blanked out errors are all problems of the past. Edited
copy can easily be inserted in a document with automatic resequencing to
the point of change so that previous material is deleted and new material
added. The automatic typing of the rest of the document resumes by activa-
ting a key. Also, when typing at rough draft speeds, the operator is relieved
of the responsibility of line-ending decisions because the carrier return is
automatic.

Keyboards on media typewriters vary from 86 to 96 print characters. In
addition to the conventional keyboard, keys have been added for correction,
playback, revision, raising and lowering the typing line, as well as those
necessary for computer adaptation. Some machines also add symbols that
are useful in legal and accounting applications. Most machines have automatic decimal tabulation and half and reverse index for typing the superscripts and subscripts used in mathematical and chemical formulas.

The operation of a media typewriter can be learned in a short time by
anyone familiar with an ordinary typewriter. Most manufacturers provide
self-pace instructional manuals for their machines. Some also conduct
classroom instruction in principal cities, and all provide on-the-spot instruction to operators when the equipment is installed. Besides providing operator
training, manufacturers' representatives assist customers in paper work flow
analysis, evaluate performance of new or improved systems, and implement
systems of their own design to solve a customer's unique problem. Usually,
manufacturers provide programs to acquaint upper management with the

advantages of electronic typewriters and companion equipment, because a considerable investment must be made when setting up a word processing center. (See Section 5.1, "Information Processing.")

11.2 IMPROVING TYPING EFFICIENCY

A person who types several hours a day should first arrange the work station so that physical aches and tensions are minimized. Next, the typist should review copying and transcription techniques, experiment with new ways to handle repetitive typing tasks, and practice more difficult copy work in preparation for advanced assignments. In fact, all those who type should review techniques on turning out copy more rapidly, setting up copy accurately, or inserting additional material in a finished document. These and other topics are treated in this section.

Care of the Machine.   A typewriter in excellent working condition produces neat, readable copy. Keep dirt out of the mechanism by covering the machine at night. If using a nonmedia typewriter, move the carriage to the extreme right or left when you erase. Dust easy-to-reach parts with a soft brush, and use a stiffer brush or a plastic cleaner to clean the keys at the beginning of each day. Refrain from poking about in the parts with makeshift tools or bending key levers when trying to unhook jammed keys. Call the service representative immediately. Arrange for a maintenance contract to have machines checked and cleaned at least once a year.

Posture and Chair Height.   For faster, easier typing at a considerable saving in energy, attempt to maintain a posture in which your arms are held parallel to the slope of the keyboard. For the average person, the typewriter should be about 28 to 30 inches from the floor. Chair seat height should be between 16 and 18 inches. If you feel eyestrain, back ache, or stiff neck, the typewriter is probably at the wrong height for you. Try experimenting with other heights.

Using a Copyholder.   A copyholder that supports the copy at eye level directly behind the typewriter permits fast, easy reading and reduces eye and neck strain. Most holders have a hand lever that raises the copy line by line to eye-level position. A ruler attachment helps to keep the place and, if you are interrupted, to locate easily where you left off.

Writing Between Lines. To type slightly above or below the original typing line, for example, when double-underscoring ($145.82) or writing subscripts (H_2O) and exponents ($90°$), use the automatic line-finder on nonmedia typewriters. This lever, at the left of the platen, releases the platen so that it may be rotated to the desired position. The platen will return to the exact typing line when the line finder is back in place. Move the line-finder lever forward *before* leaving the writing line. Rotate the platen to the new typing position and type in the information. To return to the original typing line, slide the line finder back to its stationary position and rotate the platen to lock it at the typing line. Media typewriters have special keys for raising or lowering type.

Correcting Originals and Carbon Copies. *With a Typewriter Eraser.* Before making an erasure, move the typewriter carriage to the extreme right or left to prevent crumbs from falling into the mechanism. Use a good eraser, such as Rubacore by Dixon, and an erasing shield, such as the metal Norco Steno-Shield or a stiff card. Place the erasing shield behind the original copy and on top of the first carbon. A light circular motion of the white eraser on the letter(s) to be corrected will remove the ink. Be careful not to scrape off any paper fibers. Next, move the shield or card to the back of the first carbon copy and, with the pink eraser, carefully remove the error on this copy. Correct succeeding carbon copies in the same manner. Then return the carriage to typing position and insert the correct letter(s), being careful to match the intensity of the stroke in the other words. A skillful correction will not be noticeable.

With Special Carbon Papers. The use of special carbon papers, such as Ko-Rec-Type products or Dixon Taperaser, eliminates erasing. Special carbons are available for correcting errors on originals, carbon copies, mylar-poly-paper, and colored and light-weight bond papers. Simply place these carbons *face down* on all copies over the word(s) to be corrected and *retype the error*. This process covers the black ink with white or another color, and leaves a blank space to be filled with the correct letter(s). Now, remove the correction carbons from *all* copies and strike the correct key(s). This procedure usually makes a neat, clean correction, but you may have to strike the keys harder in order to match the intensity of the other letters.

With Correction Fluid. An opaquing fluid, such as Snopake, may be painted over the typographical error on the original and all carbons. After it dries, the correction is typed over a smooth, hard, white surface. Be careful to wait a few seconds for the fluid to dry before typing over it. If the liquid dries on carbon paper, that area of the carbon will not print when used the next time.

Do not allow the liquid in the bottle to become too thick; a thin coat, merely enough to cover the error, should be used. A thinner is available for use with the correction fluid.

Correction fluid is especially effective for correcting material for photocopying, photo-offset, xerography, and similar copying and reproducing processes. These undetectable corrections are also excellent for blocking out large areas and for use in graphic art work because the fluid may be ruled, drawn on, or lettered over.

With Automatic Typewriter Equipment.   Some standard electric typewriters and most media typewriters have the capability for error correction using a simple backspace and retyping sequence. The typist should review the instructions in the manual for the particular typewriter to find the proper procedure to use. The correction operation varies from typewriter to typewriter.

Correcting Bound Manuscripts.   You need not take apart a manuscript bound at the top to make corrections on inside pages. Insert a sheet of blank paper into the typewriter until approximately one-quarter inch of the top page appears above the writing point. Next, make the erasure(s) or apply correction fluid to the pages in the manuscript to be retyped. Then slip the *bottom* edge of the page to be corrected *under* the *top* edge of the blank sheet (against the platen). Now roll the manuscript page down to the correct line and type.

Locating Original Typing Line.   Once a paper is removed from the typewriter it is difficult to align the letters perfectly when you make corrections or insertions. Because all machines are slightly different in alignment, become familiar with the construction of your own machine by practicing the following technique. Insert the typed page and disengage the ratchet release or paper release lever, permitting the paper to move freely. Align the typed line to be corrected with the aligning scale. The aligning scale is behind the ribbon at the point where the keys strike the paper. See that the typed line is parallel to and immediately above (or sitting on) the aligning scale. Engage the ratchet release lever and examine the typed line clear across the page. If the typed line has shifted anywhere across the page and is not parallel to or is too far above or below the scale, disengage the lever and reposition. Next, find an *I, i, t,* or *l* in one of the words and move the carriage so that one of the white lines on the aligning scale bisects the letter. You may have to release the ratchet lever again to move the letter directly over the line. Be sure to recheck the typed line to see that it is parallel to the scale. Place the color control lever on *stencil* or disengage the ribbon and type over a few letters or a word to ascertain whether you have perfect alignment. If you do not have alignment, reposition and test. If you have, proceed to erase and make the correction or insert the new copy.

Uniform Bottom Margin.   There are several ways to make sure that each page will end on the same line. One method is to type vertically the numbers 1 through 66 (or 66 through 1) on the right edge of an $8\frac{1}{2}''$ × $11''$ sheet of bond. Place this page behind the sheets to be typed so that the numbers extend beyond the right edge. Using the scale of six lines to a vertical inch, stop typing at line 59 (or line 7) for a one-inch bottom margin.

Some typewriters have an end-of-page indicator that is a vertical slide-up scale at the top of the typewriter to show how many lines remain on the page. As you type, the paper moves up the scale and you can easily read off the number of lines remaining.

Another common practice is to draw a light pencil line in the right margin slightly above the point where you want to stop typing, before inserting the paper into the machine. Your eye will see this line as you approach the bottom of the page and warn you that you may type only one or two more lines. All copy should have at least a one-inch bottom margin. When adding footnotes, be sure to allow one-half inch for each one when marking the pencil line.

Ruled Lines.   You can make ruled lines on cards, stencils, ditto masters, or typing paper either vertically or horizontally by simply holding a sharply pointed pencil, ballpoint pen, or stylus at some notch or angle on the paper holder that allows you to hold the pencil or pen firmly. Rotate the platen forward for a vertical line, and move the carriage left to right for a horizontal one. The lines will be as straight as if drawn with a ruler.

Chain Feeding.   *From the Front of the Platen.*   When feeding small cards into the typewriter, chain-feed from the front of the platen. Position the first card and type the copy. Do not remove it, but backfeed it into the machine so that one-half inch of the top edge remains above the writing point. Insert the next card in front of the platen so that its bottom edge is underneath and held firmly by the top edge of the card still in the machine. Turn the platen back to position the new card. The completed cards will stack up against the paper rest in the order typed.

For an exceptionally small item, first make a pocket in a sheet of $8\frac{1}{2}''$ × $11''$ bond. To do this, make a 1/4- to 1/2-inch horizontal fold in the upper third of the sheet. Roll the pocketed sheet into the machine so that the pocket faces upward at the typing point. Drop each item into this pocket and type it.

From the Back of the Platen.   When addressing envelopes and other large items, such as $5''$ × $8''$ cards, chain feed from the back. Insert each new envelope or card so that its top edge is overlapped and held in place by the bottom edge of the preceding one. Put at least two or three envelopes or cards in position before starting to type. When the first item is typed, twirl the platen knob with the left hand and pick up with the right hand another envelope or card (stacked face up at the right of the machine) and insert it. A single twirl of the platen will release the completed item and bring the new one into typing position. With an electric typewriter, the left hand is used to remove completed items for stacking at the left of the machine. If items are not to be kept in a particular order, they may be allowed to flip over the back of the machine into a box.

Typing Individual Labels.   Small individual labels may be typed with the following backfeeding technique. First, insert a sheet of paper so that the edge is one-half inch above the aligning scale. Place the label behind the paper, and roll the cylinder toward you until the label is in typing position. When it has been typed, remove it and insert another one. Labels may also be purchased in perforated sheets with self-adhesive or in gummed rolls. These may be typed in the conventional manner.

Carbon Paper Hints.   *Feeding Carbon Packs.*   An envelope or short piece of paper folded over the top of several sheets of bond interleaved with carbons will help feed the pack evenly into the typewriter. Or a sheet of bond paper may be wrapped completely around the platen and the carbon pack slipped in between the platen and the open flap of this sheet of paper.
Removing Carbons.   Use carbon paper with the upper left corner cut off. Hold the original and all copies at this point and shake out the carbon papers. Carbon paper with an extended tissue edge also allows you to pull the carbons out of the pack easily.
Inserting Color.   To insert red figures or letters in the carbon copies without removing the pack from the typewriter, place a small piece of red carbon paper (red side down) in the desired position behind each one of the regular carbons. Type with the red ribbon, and then remove the red carbons before typing with black again.
Keeping Copies Clean.   To prevent onionskin paper from creasing or *treeing* with carbon lines, add a sheet of bond or heavy paper to the back of the carbon pack before inserting it in the typewriter.
Typing on Carbon Copies Only.   You may place a special message only on the carbon copies by moving the original copy away from the typing line. If the message is to appear at the top of the carbons, use the ratchet or paper release lever to free the paper and move the carbon pack an inch or so *above* the original and the first sheet of carbon paper. If for some reason it is important that all material on the copies be in carbon, it will be necessary to type the message on the first sheet of carbon paper. Otherwise, type it on the first onionskin copy. After the message is inserted, realign all pages of the carbon pack by using the paper release lever. Be careful to lock the release lever in position before beginning to type. If typing on the first sheet of carbon paper, remember to position the machine at the spot for typing on the carbon copies *before* removing the original. It is your guide to the copy beneath the carbons.

If a message, such as a postscript or a notation about the distribution of carbon copies, is to go at the bottom of carbon copies only, first type in all the information that should appear on the original. Then release the paper by pulling the ratchet release lever toward you, and carefully slip the original out without disturbing the rest of the pack. Push the lever back to lock it, and type. If the message should appear on only one or two carbons, insert a small slip of paper behind each of the other carbons. These slips can be destroyed when the pack is removed from the machine.

Word Substitutions.   *On Machines with Backspace Key Only.*   To substitute a longer word (one or two letters longer) for a shorter word, such as *have* for *had,* first erase the incorrect word. Then position the carriage of a manual machine where the first letter of the word had been and press the backspacer halfway down while striking the first letter. Release it. After the machine spaces automatically, hold the key down halfway again and strike the next letter. Continue until the new word is typed. On an electric machine, the carriage must be held with the left hand and moved into position.

To substitute a shorter word for a longer word, position the machine where the first letter was and space forward once. Hold the backspacer halfway down and type the first letter of the shorter word. Spread the word to fill as much of the available space as possible. On an electric machine, use the carriage release button on the left to position the typing point to give the spread you want, as you hold the carriage firmly with the left hand.

On Machines with a Fractional Backspacer.   After erasing the incorrect word, position the carriage where the first letter of the shorter word had been and press the fractional backspacer. Hold it down as you type the first letter of the new, longer word. Space forward once and again press the fractional backspacer. Hold it down as you type the second letter. Proceed in this way until the new, longer word has been typed.

To substitute a shorter for a longer word, return the carriage to where the first letter had been. Space forward once and then press the fractional backspacer. Hold it down as you type the first letter of the new word. Forward space once again, press the special backspacer, and again hold it down as you type the second letter. Finish the word in the same manner.

Last-Line Corrections.   The following procedure will enable you to correct errors on the last few lines of a page without moving it out of line or having it slip from the feed rolls. Insert a sheet of bond paper between the feed roller and your last sheet of paper when the paper pack is within three inches of the bottom of the page. It will then be easy to reverse-feed the pack back into the typewriter to make corrections in the event any mistakes are made on the last few lines.

Typing Even Right Margins.   Make a copy of the text, using normal word breaks to end all lines at approximately the same place. Note the shortest and the longest lines. Determine the difference—usually from four to five characters. Add half the difference to the shortest line. Use this length for all lines in the text. As needed, contract and spread words, add extra spaces, or space once only after the period so that each line ends at the same point. If a line needs two characters to extend it, spread two words or spread one word and leave an extra space after a mark of punctuation. If another line is two spaces too long, contract one word near the beginning and one word near the end. If spreading and contracting are carefully done, the typing will appear uniform and the even right margin will make the copy more attractive.

Changing Ribbons.   Methods of changing typewriter ribbons vary for different makes of machines. Consult the manual that comes with your typewriter. In general, however, you should lift the top cover and study the course of travel of the old ribbon before removing it. Next, wind the remaining ribbon onto one spool and remove it. Set the new ribbon spool in place. Unreel 8 to 10 inches of the new ribbon and attach the end to the empty reel. Lock the carriage in upper case so as to lift the two ribbon guides at the typing point and make them more accessible. Thread the new ribbon through the guides. After unlocking the carriage, proceed to type. Check back to see that the ribbon is moving correctly.

Using Special Keys and Levers.   In addition to using the tabulator for statistical and columnar typing, use it for placing the date at the upper right side of letters; making paragraph indentations; placing the complimentary close and signature lines; typing addresses or other information on envelopes, cards, and labels; and adding other miscellaneous information, such as page numbers. Learn to clear margin and tabulator stops and to reset them rapidly. Use other special keys and levers in these ways to speed up output:

1. Use the paper release lever to remove paper rapidly.
2. Twirl (a faster motion than *turn*) paper into and out of the machine.
3. To type in the left margin or to add a letter or quotation mark to the first word on a line, press the margin release key and backspace.
4. Use the carriage release levers (not the space bar) to move the carriage to the extreme right of the paper.
5. Use both the upper and lower portions of an all-black ribbon by changing the color control lever so that the keys will strike the unused portion.
6. Plan each job in order to use as many special keys and levers of the typewriter as possible.
7. Arrange to type at one time all jobs using the same margin stops.

Selecting Carbon and Copy Paper.   *General Types.*   Carbon paper has been designed for each of the three kinds of typewriters—electric, standard, and noiseless. To determine whether your manual machine has standard or noiseless action, press one of the keys slowly and watch the movement of the type bar. If the bar swings like a golf club, you have a regular or standard-action machine. If it pushes forward like a billiard cue, it is a noiseless machine. The type on a standard-action machine hits fairly hard, whereas that on the noiseless hits lightly. Therefore, use electric carbon, regular carbon, or noiseless carbon, as the case may be.

Weight.   To select the correct *carbon weight* for the number of copies to be made, follow these guides for an electric machine or a manual with standard action.

Number of Copies at a Time	Carbon Weight for the Job
1 to 5	Standard weight
1 to 10	Light weight
6 to 16	Extra-light weight

When using a noiseless-action machine, use standard weight for one to four copies, light weight for one to six copies, and extra-light weight for one to eight copies. The lighter-weight carbons produce many copies at a time, but they do not wear as long as the heavier-weight carbons. For economy, use the heaviest-weight carbon that will produce the desired number of copies.

Copy paper comes in several weights. With a standard-action or electric typewriter, use copy paper as follows.

Number of Copies at a Time	Copy Paper for the Job
1 to 3	20 lb.
1 to 6	16 lb.
1 to 12	13 lb.
6 to 20	9 lb.

When using a noiseless machine, use any weight copy paper for one copy and nine-pound copy paper for more than one copy.

Finish.   Type size affects the readability of copies. Pica type (10 characters to the inch) makes good readable copies with all kinds of carbon. Elite type (12 characters to the inch) and smaller type produce clearer carbon copies if the carbon paper used is extra-hard, hard, or medium finish. If intense or extra-intense-finish carbons are used, the *a*'s, *b*'s, *d*'s, *e*'s, *g*'s, *o*'s, *p*'s, *q*'s, and most *figures* fill in. These softer (intense or extra-intense) finishes should be used only with large type.

Carbon paper finishes give a range of impressions. Select the best weight and finish for each job. Hard or extra-hard-finish carbons (like hard pencils) produce a gray impression. Medium-finish carbons produce a medium tone. Intense and extra-intense carbons produce an extreme black. If the platen on your typewriter is new and soft, use a soft-finish (extra-intense, intense, or medium) carbon. Typing on a hard platen is like writing with a pencil on a paper laid over a hard surface, such as glass. Use medium-, hard-, or extra-hard-finish carbon with an old, hard platen. If your touch on the keys is strong and you hit them quite hard, use one of the harder finishes. If you hit the keys lightly, use a softer finish to get good, readable copies. When making a number of copies at a time, use a light-weight carbon with a softer finish so that the last copies will be distinct.

The Right Ribbon.   Be sure to select the correct ribbon for the make and model of your machine. For instance, electric machines use an extra-heavy fabric ribbon to withstand the heavy blow of the keys. A typewriter ribbon pads the type, thus reducing the sharpness of the imprint that has to carry through the entire paper pack. The thinner the ribbon, the less padding, and the sharper and more readable the copies. The use of nylon, silk, or fine cotton ribbons, which are tougher than plain cotton, will make better carbon copies. These ribbons wear longer, too. A typewriter equipped with both fabric and carbon-paper ribbons may be switched to carbon-paper ribbon when several copies are to be made.

The size of type is also important when choosing a ribbon. Larger type can use any inking on the ribbon, but smaller type should not be used with medium-heavy and heavy inkings because the type fills in and makes a blurred impression. The heavier the ribbon inking, the blacker the impression. Choices range from light, expert, and medium to medium-heavy and heavy inking. The harder the platen, the lighter the inked ribbon that is needed. If your touch is average, you should use a ribbon in medium inking. If your touch is light, swing toward heavier inking; and if heavy, swing toward lighter inking. Also, use the special touch-control setting on your machine to produce more readable copies.

Typing on Printed Forms.   Whether typing one copy or several of a printed form, first position it so that you will be typing slightly above lines and within boxes. Check the vertical line spacing also to find out if it corresponds to the single- or double-line spacing on your machine. If it does not, disengage the ratchet release lever and position each entry by hand.

When typing several copies of a printed form, check the alignment of these copies by holding them up to the light before inserting them in the machine. Attempt to use copies that are as closely aligned as possible. After aligning the copies, insert them in the typewriter *without* the carbons, just far enough to hold them securely. Now place the carbons with the shiny side toward you between each one of the copies. Roll the pack into position and type.

Proofreading Typed Copy.   Accurate proofreading is a skill. By being interested, alert, and particular, you can develop a high degree of skill in detecting errors in format and typography, including omissions and transpositions. Proofread your own work before removing it from the machine. Always check the accuracy of numbers, especially addresses, amounts owed, estimates, bids, and dates. Two people other than the typist should proofread statistical work, if possible. When the typist must proofread her work with a second person, the typist should read the rough copy, phrase by phrase. If an error is discovered on the finished copy, place a small *pencil* mark in the margin opposite the error to allow the correction to be made without retyping the page.

See also "Proofreading," Section 7.4.

Typing Two-Column Copy.   To type a two-column page similar to newspaper or handbook copy, draw a guide sheet with India ink on your heaviest bond paper. A heavy black line should be drawn around the outer margins (one-inch margins on all sides except for one and one-half inches on the side to be bound). Next, draw a line down the center of the typing space. If heads are to be used over each column, draw a horizontal line at least one inch below the top margin line. Type the numbers 1 to 10 in reverse order at the bottom of the left column (Figure 11-2) to indicate the number of remaining lines. Place this guide sheet behind a lighter weight bond sheet or a stencil when typing the two-column material.

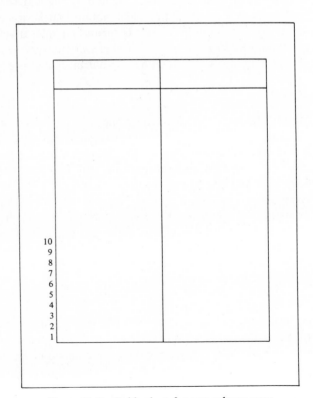

Figure 11-2   Guide sheet for two-column copy.

11.3   TYPING STATISTICAL MATERIAL

The centering of headings and the placement of material in rows and columns that are neat, attractive, and easy to read are important tasks of the typist. By preplanning the setup and following a few easy steps, anyone can turn out an attractive table. Procedures for both the vertical and the horizontal spacing of tabulated data on single sheets or within paragraphs are described in this section.

See also "Tabular Presentation," Section 5.4.

Headings.   *Centering.*   Table titles, subtitles, and columnar headings are easy to center by use of the backspace centering method. Find the *center of the typing line* and backspace *once* for every *two* letters, spaces, and marks of punctuation. For material bound at the left, allowance must be made for the wider left margin (usually one and one-half inches). Thus, by finding the *center of the typing line,* you need never be concerned with the differences in margin widths. For example, if the margin stops are at 30 and 100, the typing line is 70 spaces—one half that is 35, and added to the left margin stop at 30, places the *center of the typing line* at 65. Find the center of the typing line or the space allotted to the column in all instances.

Underscoring and Spacing.   Underscoring is usually optional, but should be used when necessary to highlight headings or important columnar items that might be lost in the copy. When the main title of a table is typed in capitals and lower case, underscoring is optional. If the title is in all capitals, however, it is preferably not underscored because it has already been highlighted. A subtitle is always in capitals and lower case, and may be underscored if the main title is in capitals or has been underscored. Columnar heads are typed in capitals and lower case and should be underscored if the table is unruled. If the columnar heading is pyramided, only the bottom line need be underscored. The underscoring should extend the length of the longest line in the pyramid. A *total* line is a single underscore under the last item in an addition of numbers and must extend the same length as the longest item (including the $ sign) in the series. A double line may be used after the total to separate it from succeeding figures. (Figure 11-3.) Any other use of single or double underscoring with other representative figures, such as averages, percentages, or the last figure in the column, is at the discretion of the designer of the table, who may desire to call the attention of the reader to important figures.

Horizontal and vertical spacing depends mainly on the need to display the

| | Number of Men | | |
	Present Work Force	Proposed Work Force	Reduction
Personnel reductions:			
Yard crews (five men to a crew)	40	35	5
Track maintenance gang	13	8	5
Locomotive maintenance:			
Shop men	6	5	1
Hostlers	3	1	2
Total	62	49	13

Figure 11-3 Spacing and underscoring in a typed table.

statistical material attractively. A slightly wider bottom than top margin and even left and right margins—except for the bound side, which is one-half inch wider on documents to be bound—are general rules to follow. Usually a subtitle is double-spaced after the main title, and columnar heads follow the subtitle after a triple space. The first column item is usually double-spaced after the head but may be singlespaced if it is necessary to compress a long table. Single- or double-spacing of items depends on the space available. Horizontal spacing must be carefully worked out to maintain adequate left and right margins and assure easy reading of the material in the columns. The following step-by-step directions should assist a typist to achieve attractive placement of statistical material.

Vertical Placement. Basic to the figuring of vertical placement is the fact that there are six line spaces to a vertical inch on most typewriters. For instance, if three inches or 18 line spaces are left on a page, you have 12 line spaces on which to type plus 6 for a one-inch bottom margin. If the table is longer than 12 lines, consider adding more paragraph material to that page and place the table on the next page. An $8\frac{1}{2} \times 11$ inch sheet of paper has 66 lines. When double-spacing, you leave one blank line and type on the second line. If triple-spacing, you leave two blank lines and type on the third line. To leave a one-inch top margin, space down seven times from the top edge of the paper so as to leave six blank lines and begin typing on the seventh line.

Spot Table. To place a short table attractively with paragraph material, determine first the number of vertical lines available. Then count the number of lines needed for the table.

1. Leave two or three line spaces between the last line in the paragraph and the main heading or the first line of the table.

2. Leave one line space between the main heading and the subhead.

3. Leave two lines between the main heading or subhead and the columnar headings.

4. Leave at least one line between the columnar heading and the first item in the column.

5. Keep all items in the table on one page. If space allows, you may double-space the items in a short table.

6. Triple-space, if space permits, before continuing paragraph typing.

Reference Table.   To center a table vertically on a separate page, first determine the number of lines available—32 on a half sheet, 66 on an 11-inch sheet, 84 on a 14-inch sheet, 96 on a 16-inch sheet. Then follow these steps.

1. Add the number of lines in the tabulation. Watch for longer items that will need to be carried over to a second line.

2. Add to this total the number of blank lines. Be sure to count the headings and the blank lines between them. (See rules 2, 3, and 4 under "Spot Table.")

3. Subtract the total number of lines to be used from the total available.

4. Divide the answer by two for the number of line spaces for the top and bottom margins for exact centering. To have the table slightly above the center of the page, subtract three line spaces from the number of lines to be left at the top. In any case, be sure to leave at least a one-and-one-half-inch top margin and a one-inch bottom margin.

5. If the table continues to a second page, plan the first page so that four to six entries will be carried over. Always retype the columnar headings on the second page. A table of more than two pages should adhere to these general principles.

Horizontal Placement.   It is necessary to know the number of horizontal spaces on a sheet of paper when planning the placement of columns. An easy way to learn the exact number is to determine the number of units your paper scans on the typewriter scale. If the left edge is at 12 on the scale and the right edge at 114, you have 102 spaces to work with. Another way is to know the type size. Pica type has 10 spaces to an inch and elite has 12. On paper 8½ inches wide there are 85 pica and 102 elite spaces. Electric typewriters have a variety of special type faces with individual spacing characteristics. When using one of these, consult the operating manual.

Because all typed work should have at least one-inch margins on all sides, allow for these when figuring stops for tabulation. Also, remember that bound materials require a wider margin on the bound side.

Centering Method.   To place a table attractively on the page, center it. Use the following five easy steps if your typewriter scale begins at zero at the left.

1. Count the number of strokes in the longest item in each column. Write these numbers on the rough copy or on a sheet of paper.

$$\boxed{12} \qquad \boxed{8} \qquad \boxed{19} \qquad \boxed{14}$$

2. Determine the number of spaces to be allowed between columns, remembering that they are easier to read if close together—at least five and no more than ten spaces.

$$\boxed{12} \quad 7 \quad \boxed{8} \quad 7 \quad \boxed{19} \quad 7 \quad \boxed{14} \quad = 74$$

3. Clear all tabulator stops from the machine. Insert the paper with the left edge at zero and move the carriage so that the writing point is at the center of the paper. The center on pica machines is 42 and on elite 50. Or, if the left edge will be at some point other than zero, you may make a slight crease at the center of the paper before inserting it in the machine, and move the carriage to this spot.

4. Add the total number of strokes in the tabulation and backspace half the total. Set the left marginal stop at this point.

5. Now tap out on the space bar the number of strokes in the first column plus the number of spaces to be left between columns, and set a tab stop. Then space over the number of strokes in the second column plus the spaces between columns, and set a second tab stop. Proceed in a similar manner until all the necessary stops are in the machine.

If the typewriter has a zero-center scale, do steps 1 and 2 and set the left margin stop at half the total spaces. Now proceed with step 5.

Columnar Headings. A columnar heading that is shorter than the longest item in the column should be centered over the column. If it is longer, place it attractively on two or three lines and center each line. To do this, count the number of spaces in the heading, subtract from the number reserved for the column, divide by two, and space over or backspace that number before typing the heading. If the spaces between columns permit, a heading no more than eight spaces longer than the longest item in the column may be extended one half the difference into the spaces allowed between columns.

1979	1982	% Change 1979–1982
$24,358,635	$29,199,520	+19.9

Underline the last line of a heading unless the table is to be ruled. The last line of all columnar heads must be on the same plane no matter how many lines are pyramided in any one column.

A *spanner heading* is a primary columnar head that extends over two or more secondary columnar heads. If it is long, it may be placed on two or more lines. If it is shorter than the space needed by the secondary heads, it should be centered over them. The secondary head under the spanner may also take two (no more than three) lines. The spacing of these heads in relation to those of other columns calls for preplanning. The last line of the longest secondary head establishes the horizontal plane for all columns. For clarity, the underscoring of the last line of each spanner head should be extended to the full width of all columns covered by the heading.

	Actual Time		Number of Freight Cars	
Assignment	Start	Complete	Placed	Removed

Tables requiring elaborate headings are often ruled. Columnar headings are then centered vertically as well as horizontally in the space provided. (See "Tabular Presentation," Section 5.4, Figure 5-13.)

Columnar Entries. When the descriptive words in the first column (the stub) must be typed on two or three lines in order to fit the space given to the column, be sure to align the corresponding entries across all columns with the last line of the stub entry. Second and succeeding lines of a stub entry may be in block form (if double-spacing follows each entry) or may be indented one or two spaces. Subtopics under a stub entry are usually indented three to five spaces. The word *Total* after an addition of figures is indented five, ten, or more spaces, depending on the arrangement of the material or the preference of the typist (see Figure 11-3).

Plant and Equipment	$12,000	$14,000	$9,750	$11,950

Align columns of whole numbers on the right.

15
550
3,500
115,954

Figures with decimal points are aligned by the decimal point.

.16
1.4
42.5
5.498
.7

Columns of dissimilar figures may be aligned on the left or centered.

515	$85
4231	35 ounces
39½	18 gross
$80	44.8%
55 lbs.	$1.95

Dollar signs, plus and minus signs, percent symbols, and the like are always aligned in a column. The dollar sign is placed in front of the first figure in the column and in front of totals and subtotals in columns containing only dollar figures. Align the dollar mark with the longest figure in the column, regardless of whether it is the first one.

$ 24.00	−24.1%
987.50	+ 8.6
1,032.24	+10.2
7.98	− 3.0
$2,051.72	

Place the dollar sign before the first number in the column when you have a column of dollar figures and the first spaces of the column are blank. Never put the dollar sign at the top of such a column.

——	——
——	——
——	$ 138.75
$5,845.00	——
462.58	——
——	1,588.25

A double column of figures in a single money column has the dollar sign before both figures in the first line.

Repair Expense	$1,000–$1,500
Replacement Expense	2,200– 3,500

In a column of numbers in which some are monetary figures and some are not, place a dollar sign before each monetary figure. The dollar signs are aligned with the longest dollar figure.

$$
\begin{array}{r}
1,772 \\
\$\quad 11,100 \\
69\% \\
+10\% \\
6,000 \\
\$11,840,000
\end{array}
$$

In a mixed list of numbers in which there are percentages to a tenth or a hundredth and dollars and cents, the items should either be aligned at the left or centered. A guiding rule is to present the material as clearly as possible.

Use of Leaders.   Periods that connect the stub to the first column in the field are known as *leaders*. They are typed at *every other* space. In order to keep leaders vertically aligned, notice on the typewriter scale whether the first one starts on an odd or even number. In the first item of the stub, the initial period is placed immediately after the last letter. If the initial leader starts on an odd number, space to the first odd number after typing the second item and strike the first period for that row of leaders. If the initial leader begins at an even number, space over to the first even number.

All leaders end at the same point, at least two or three spaces before the start of the longest item in the next column. They are never used between columns of figures, but only between the stub and the first column in the field. When the first item in the stub takes more than one line, use leaders only after the last line in the item. Hyphens are never substituted for leaders because they can be mistaken for minus signs when figures are involved.

An index, however, may be set up as follows.

Abbott Smith Assoc., Inc.	60
Chartmakers, Inc.	54
Dale Carnegie & Assoc., Inc.	102
Eastman Kodak Co.	8
Methods Research Corp.	22
Readers Service Card	3, 4, 63, 64
Telex	18
Wilson Corp., H.	2nd Cover

11.4   TYPING SPECIAL CHARACTERS, FORMULAS, AND EQUATIONS

Special Characters.   The usual characters on standard typewriter keyboards may be used as they are or combined to form special characters. For example, the following symbols may be made by the use of two or three keys or a single key.

¶	Paragraph mark	Lower case *l* typed over capital *P*.
[ ]	Brackets	For left bracket: type diagonal, backspace *once,* type underscore, roll paper back one line, type underscore.
		For right bracket: type diagonal, backspace *twice,* type underscore, roll paper back one line, type underscore.
÷	Division sign	*Colon* and *hyphen* typed in same space.
=	Equals sign	Two *hyphens*—one slightly below other.
✚	Plus sign	Type *diagonal,* backspace, strike *hyphen.*
x	Multiplication sign	Use capital *X*.
√‾	Root or radical sign	Type *diagonal,* roll platen back one line, strike underscore key as many times as necessary. Draw in first short line.
£	Pound Sterling sign	Either lower case *f* typed over lower case *t* or capital *L* typed over lower case *f*.
ç	Cedilla beneath *c*	Lower case *c* and *comma* typed in same space.
′	Accent mark	Use *apostrophe* one-half line above accented letter.
78°F	Degree sign	Roll platen back one-half line and type lower case *o*.
o ′ ″	Degrees, minutes, seconds	Roll platen back one-half line and type lower case *o*, apostrophe, and quotation mark.
!	Exclamation point	*Apostrophe* and *period* in same space.

Equations and Formulas.   The typing of reports, speeches, manuscripts, and other material containing technical material is often difficult because of the presence of equations and formulas in the copy. Of first importance is a clear rough draft from which the typist may accurately copy the information. The typist should ask the mathematician, engineer, or scientist for a handwritten copy of frequently used symbols and the Greek alphabet in order to eliminate guesswork while copying the handwriting. It is also wise to type all equations or formulas on a practice sheet before placing them in the final copy. Because the position of each sign and symbol is of vital importance, this trial spacing will assure correct and meaningful placement.

Several aids for typing equations are available, such as the IBM Selectric typewriter with the Universal Element that contains the Greek alphabet and mathematical symbols. Technical keys are also obtainable for some machines either as interchangeable keys or as a bank of additional keys. Templates may be purchased at local stationery stores. Rapidesign No. 50 (Pocket Pal) and No. 17 with the Greek alphabet, mathematical symbols, and the chemist's triangle are especially useful. Adhesive transfers such as Prestype may also be used for time-saving and artistic application in the final copy. Hand-drawn symbols with pen and India ink should be made when the symbols cannot be typed or special aids are not available (Figure 11-4).

Spacing Rules. In technical typing, equations and formulas are set up in two ways. Many times they are merely part of the sentence. At other times, they are set off and displayed in the copy. Displayed equations are usually complicated with numerous aggregates containing several superscripts (exponents)

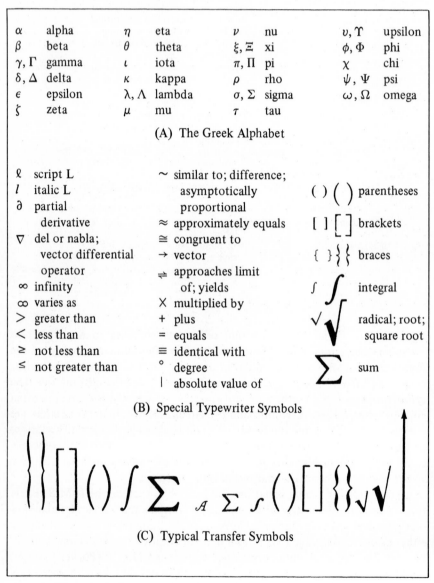

α	alpha	η	eta	ν	nu	υ, Υ	upsilon
β	beta	θ	theta	ξ, Ξ	xi	ϕ, Φ	phi
γ, Γ	gamma	ι	iota	π, Π	pi	χ	chi
δ, Δ	delta	κ	kappa	ρ	rho	ψ, Ψ	psi
ϵ	epsilon	λ, Λ	lambda	σ, Σ	sigma	ω, Ω	omega
ζ	zeta	μ	mu	τ	tau		

(A) The Greek Alphabet

ℓ	script L	$\sim$	similar to; difference; asymptotically proportional	( )	parentheses
l	italic L				
∂	partial derivative	$\approx$	approximately equals	[ ]	brackets
∇	del or nabla; vector differential operator	$\cong$	congruent to		
		$\rightarrow$	vector	{ }	braces
∞	infinity	$\rightleftharpoons$	approaches limit of; yields	$\int$	integral
∞	varies as	$\times$	multiplied by		
$>$	greater than	$+$	plus	$\sqrt{}$	radical; root; square root
$<$	less than	$=$	equals		
$\geq$	not less than	$\equiv$	identical with	Σ	sum
$\leq$	not greater than	$\circ$	degree		
		$\vert$	absolute value of		

(B) Special Typewriter Symbols

(C) Typical Transfer Symbols

Figure 11-4 Letters and symbols available for mathematical copy.

and subscripts (inferiors). The following format rules for typing both in-text and displayed equations give the horizontal and vertical spacing for standard typewriters and the IBM Executive with Bold Face No. 2 type. *Spacing for the IBM Executive is given in units in parentheses.*

In-Text Equations and Formulas.   Read all the following suggestions before attempting to type any equations.

   1. Leave 2 spaces (4 units) *before* and *after* a mathematical symbol, expression, equation, or formula that is part of a sentence.

   2. Leave 1 space (2 units) *between* such symbols and expressions and a punctuation mark that follows.

   3. Leave 2 spaces (4 units) between a comma (following a symbol or an expression) and whatever follows. Leave 2 spaces (6 units) between a period and the next sentence.

EXAMPLES   ...corresponding to $\bar{k}^T$, which equals...

       ...the term $\bar{k}^T$. Then the ...

   4. Leave 1 space (3 units) before and after $=$, $>$, $<$, $\geq$, and $\leq$.

EXAMPLE: ...in $2xy = b$ we find...

   5. Leave 1 space (2 units) before and after $+$, $-$, $\pm$, $\times$, and $\cdot$ (a soft-rolled period).

   6. Leave no space (1 unit) after $+$, $-$, and $\pm$ when these indicate the sign of a single term in the text.

EXAMPLE: ...within ± 4 cm ...

   7. When a mathematical expression is followed by a unit of measurement, leave 1 space (2 units) between it and the unit of measurement.

EXAMPLE: ...the interval of $\Delta t = 0.04$ sec. used in the...

   8. Fractions in the text should be typed with the diagonal (slash) fraction bar.

EXAMPLE: ...to the resultant $\underline{P}$ is $(1 \neq \bar{x})/2$ ...

   9. Leave no space (1 unit) before, after, or between a group of three dots (ellipses) indicating an omission. Type the dots on the line as if they were periods.

   10. Type chemical formulas without spaces (1 unit) between symbols and numbers.

EXAMPLES: $C_x(H_2O)_y$, $2C_2H_5OH$, $_nC_6H_{12}O_6$

   11. Align reaction equations on the arrow or plus sign.

EXAMPLE: $C_6H_{12}O_6 \rightarrow 2\ CO_2 + 2\ C_2H_5OH$

Displayed Equations and Formulas.   These hints will be helpful when you are typing equations and formulas within paragraphs.

1. Center displayed equations or formulas on a line or lines by themselves.

2. Triple-space before and after the entire expression. A trial typing should be made in order to allow sufficient space for all superscripts, subscripts, and aggregates.

3. Use the horizontal bar (underscore) for most displayed fractions and the diagonal (slash) key occasionally where appropriate.

EXAMPLE: $s_t = \frac{10,000}{12} = 834$ lb./sq. in.

4. Leave 1 space (3 units) before and after the operational signs $+$, $-$, $\pm$, $\times$, and $\cdot$ (a soft-rolled period) when these signs indicate that a quantity is being added to, subtracted from, added to or subtracted from, or multiplied by another quantity.

5. Leave 2 spaces (4 units) before and after $=$, $>$, $<$, $\geq$, and $\leq$.

6. Center material above and below a summation sign.

EXAMPLE: $\sum\limits_{\infty-0}^{0}$

7. Make parallel lines long enough to extend to the top and bottom of the material between them.

EXAMPLE: $\left| E_{x_0}^2 \right|$

8. Use signs of aggregation large enough to enclose all material. Center them relative to the equals sign. Leave no space (1 unit) between adjacent signs of aggregation (Figure 11-5).

9. Align the bar of a built-up fraction with the center of the equals sign. Center the numerator and denominator relative to the horizontal bar in a built-up fraction, allowing a small space above and below the bar.

EXAMPLE: I_0 about $CD = \frac{1}{12}bh^3 = \frac{10 \times 6^3}{12} = 180$ in.

10. Leave no more than 1 space (1 unit) between the single-line elements of a product, and no space (1 unit) before punctuation within such material.

EXAMPLE: $I_0^2 \left(A_0^2, N \right)$

11. Leave 1 space (2 units) between double-line (built-up) elements of a product and 2 spaces (3 units) between elements of a product that exceed a double line.

EXAMPLES: $\dfrac{1}{2m}\dfrac{(j \neq m)!}{(j-m)!}$, $\dfrac{1 + \dfrac{\gamma-1}{2}M_0^2}{\eta_c}\left[\varsigma_{2,3}^{(\gamma-1)}\Big/\gamma_{-1} \right]$

Placement of Subscripts and Superscripts.   The correct placement of these mathematical symbols follows a few general rules.

$$\frac{1}{2\pi} \int_{-\infty}^{\infty} \frac{\exp\,(-itw_1)}{2\sigma_{11}\,\sigma_{12}\,\sin\theta_{12}}$$

$$\frac{dt}{\left\{\left[\frac{1}{4}\left(\frac{1}{\sigma_{11}^2\,\sin^2\theta_{12}} - \frac{1}{\sigma_{12}^2}\right)\right]^2 + \left[\frac{1}{4}\left(\frac{1}{\sigma_{11}^2\,\sin^2\theta_{12}} + \frac{1}{\sigma_{12}^2}\right) - it\right]^2\right\}^{1/2}}$$

$$= \frac{1}{2\pi} \int_{-\infty}^{\infty} \exp\,(-itw_1) \left\{\frac{1}{2\sigma_{11}\,\sigma_{12}\,\sin\theta_{12}} \int_0^{\infty} \exp\left[-\frac{1}{4}\left(\frac{1}{\sigma_{11}^2\,\sin^2\theta_{12}} + \frac{1}{\sigma_{12}^2}\right)s\right]\right.$$

$$J_0\left[\frac{1}{4}\left(\frac{1}{\sigma_{11}^2\,\sin^2\theta_{12}} - \frac{1}{\sigma_{12}^2}\right)s\right]e^{ist}ds\Bigg\}\,dt'$$

$$\frac{(-)^n}{n!}\,y^{2n}\left[(2 + 3 + 4 \cdots + n) + 2(3 + 4 \cdots + n) \cdots + i(i + 1 + \cdots + n) \cdots \right.$$
$$\left. + (n - 1)n\right]$$

$$= \frac{(-)^n}{n!}\,y^{2n}\left[\frac{(n - 1)(n + 2)}{2} + \frac{2(n - 2)(n + 3)}{2} \cdots + i\,\frac{(n - i)(n + i + 1)}{2} \cdots\right]$$

$$= \frac{(-)^n}{n!}\,y^{2n}\sum_{i=1}^{n}\left[(n^2 + n)\,i - i^2 - i^3\right]$$

Figure 11-5 Examples of stacked right-hand and left-hand members and use of signs of aggregation.

1. Type all superscripts and subscripts for a given line at one time so that they will be even.

2. Place subscripts and superscripts, respectively, half a line below and above the lowest and highest characters in the related material.

EXAMPLES: R_1 , $2\left(\frac{N\phi_1}{Eh}\right)^{1/2}$

3. Align subscripts with superscripts.

EXAMPLES: P_n^2 , $F^{(p,q)}$

4. Place sub-subscripts half a line below the subscript.

EXAMPLE: E_{x_0}

5. Use lowercase o's for both subscript and superscript zeros, except in juxtaposition to other superscript or subscript numbers.

EXAMPLES: K_o^2 , $f_2(t_0) = f_2(t_1)$, $n^{0.15}$

6. Raise *th* to a superscript position.

EXAMPLES: n^{th} , i^{th}

7. Do not leave any spaces before and after $+$, $-$, $\pm$, $\times$, and $\cdot$ (a soft-rolled period) in subscripts and superscripts.

EXAMPLES: na^{n-1} , $\displaystyle\sum_{x=0}$

8. Leave no space (1 unit) before and after $=$, $>$, $<$, $\geq$, and $\leq$ in subscripts and superscripts.

9. Use the standard-size typewriter keys for aggregation signs when the material contains only simple superscripts or simple subscripts (but not both).

EXAMPLES: $(K^2 \not> A)$, $\left(K^2 \not> A_1 \not> K_2 \not> B^2\right)$

10. Type the number preceding the sign for more than three plus or minus signs to a superscript.

EXAMPLE: $p^{5\not+}$ (<u>not</u> $p^{\not+\not+\not+\not+\not+}$)

11. Type the degree sign (lower case letter *o*) as the superscript and *zero* as the subscript when typing thermodynamic symbols.

EXAMPLE: s_0^o

Placement of Arrows. Horizontal arrows may be typed by the use of either the underscore or the hyphen. When using the underscore, raise the line almost two thirds of a space and type two underscores (or as many as needed). Draw the arrowhead with pen and ink using the *less than* or *more than* ($< >$) signs, which can be found on a template, or finish freehand.

When using the hyphen, type two hyphens and backspace once. Then use the half-backspace key or hold the cylinder by hand to type a hyphen that fills the space between the other two. Draw the arrowhead.

To type double arrows, use the underscore. Type the bottom arrow a quarter line above the main-line character, backspace twice (or more if the arrows are to be longer), and roll the platen one-half line above the first arrow. Type the line. Make the arrowheads with pen and ink.

EXAMPLE: $SO_2 \not> H_2O \rightleftarrows H_2SO_3 \rightleftarrows H^+ \not> HSO_3^- \rightleftarrows 2H^+ \not> SO_3^=$

When explanatory material appears in equations above or below an arrow, make the arrow as long as necessary to fit the explanation.

General Spacing Rules. The following practices should be observed when you are setting up both in-text and displayed material.

1. Break an equation at the arrow or equals sign when it must be carried over to the next line. Do not break short equations. If there is no equals or arrow sign in the formula, you may break it at an operational sign. Type the arrow, equals, or operational sign as the last character on the line and indent the next line.

2. Use the sequence {[()]} for signs of aggregation, except where conventional notation specifies brackets or braces.

3. Use parentheses to enclose an argument that contains a plus or minus sign ($\ldots$ cos $(\omega t - \beta x)$).

4. Make a solidus extend from the top to the bottom of the values it separates.

EXAMPLE: $\kappa^2/2c_1$

5. Type any required bar or dot immediately above the mathematical symbol so that it is obvious that either one and the symbol constitute a unit. Make the bar over a capital letter by rolling the underscore back one line; roll up the hyphen for the bar over a lower case letter. For lower case *i*, roll the platen back one full line to raise the bar or the dot a little higher.

EXAMPLES: $\bar{\kappa}$, $\bar{k}$, $\bar{i}$, $\dot{r}$

If bars are used over both capital and lower case letters in a report, the rolled-up underscore is used throughout.

6. Leave 1 space (2 units) before and after trigonometric, logarithmic, or exponential functions, and leave 1 space (2 units) between the parts of such functions. If these functions must be divided, divide them after an appropriate operational sign.

EXAMPLES: $v \cos \theta$, $Y \ln x$, $2 \log y \log z$, $\frac{1}{2} \exp \left(a \neq \frac{h}{2} \right)$

7. Leave 1 space (1 unit) before and after differentials and 1 space (1 unit) between differentials.

EXAMPLES: $x \, dx$, $(x^2 \neq y^2) dx \, dy$

8. Often symbols in an equation must be identified. The equation is centered on the next typing line, and each symbol is typed at the left margin in vertical alignment as illustrated here.

$$s = v_o t \pm \frac{1}{2} at^2$$

where

s = distance

v_o = velocity

t = time

a = acceleration

When only a few symbols are to be identified, the identifications may be given in horizontal alignment. For example,

$$E = mc^2$$

where E is the intrinsic energy, m the mass, and c the velocity of light.

Inserting Line Bonds.   Horizontal line bonds may be made by the typing of two underscores, raised one half a line. No space is left before or after the line.

Na–Cl

Vertical line bonds are drawn in by hand with pen and India ink, if interchangeable keys are not available.

To type a formula with vertical and horizontal line bonds, type the letters in the top line first, double-space and type the letters for the second and subsequent lines. Type all horizontal bonds. Remove the paper and draw in the vertical bonds.

H H
| |
H —— C–C —— H
| |
H H

To type a formula with diagonal line bonds, type the *central* letter on the *main* line first, then any other letters on that line. Space forward three times from the central letter, roll the platen back two lines, type the *upper right* bond. Return the carriage to the central letter, backspace three times plus one for each letter or number, roll the platen back two lines and type in the *upper left* bond. Return again to the central letter and type the lower left and right bonds, if necessary, in the same way. Draw diagonal line bonds with pen and ink.

$\begin{bmatrix} NH_3 & & NH_3 \\ & Cu & \\ NH_3 & & NH_3 \end{bmatrix}^{+2}$ H   NH_2   R —— C —— COOH

Double and triple horizontal line bonds may be typed with the underscore key when the ratchet lever is disengaged to allow the platen to move freely. Double and triple vertical and diagonal line bonds should be drawn with pen and ink.

Office Services

Skillful management of the office provides a solid foundation for the successful operation of any business. The person in charge, therefore, should possess practical knowledge of current office procedures and standards and should be familiar with office equipment and its efficient use. A person who is capable of managing people and who has had experience in handling the paper work, using the office machines, and following the office routines would be a good choice. In some large companies, the office manager is hired mainly for proved management skills, even though he has had little experience with office routines and machines. In such cases, the manager will need to become familiar with office systems and procedures. Even managers who have been in the field for several years find it necessary to study new developments and to apply new techniques to old procedures when appropriate. Information on four important operating functions of the office is given in this section to assist the person in charge to initiate the functions, to perform or direct their performance, and to control them.

CONTENTS

12.1 RECORDS MANAGEMENT

Because the creation, protection, storage, and disposition of records are vital functions in every office, information about these functions should be readily available for reference purposes. The application of the principles explained here will assist a department or a company in the systematic organization of its initial filing functions or in the reorganization of the existing system for greater efficiency. Administrative personnel and other workers who need a working knowledge of filing and the filing system in use in their company will find valuable information in this section on records management.

Storage of Records.   The systematic arrangement of records so that they may be quickly found can be a simple problem. The first step is to determine the specific purposes of your files, the manner in which they are to be controlled, the equipment you have on hand, the different kinds of material to be filed, and the way the stored information is to be used by members of the organization. Often you find that your problem presents peculiarities that call for an individual application of a basic filing principle. Therefore, the next step is to combine the various methods of filing to fit the particular needs of your company for the retrieval of specific information.

The different methods may be illustrated in this way. Let us suppose you wish to file incoming orders. If you refer to these by the names of the people who order, use the *alphabetical* method. If the orders are numbered, you will want a duplicate file in which they are arranged numerically. On the other hand, your company may be interested primarily in the territories that generated the orders. In this case, the *geographical* method should be used. The *subject* method is used if you refer to orders by subject (the kind of goods ordered), and the *chronological* method if you refer to orders by the dates on which they were received or were filled. As can be seen, the material may be filed by a number of basic methods. Before deciding to adopt any one or a combination of methods, you should study the advantages of each.

Alphabetical Filing Systems (Figure 12-1)

1. Filing by name. The majority of firms file correspondence alphabetically according to the client's or supplier's name whether it be a firm or an individual. In card filing, the alphabetical method is used for cross-reference work and the indexing of names. In paper filing, it is best adapted to correspondence, invoices, purchase orders, and similar records. With this method, papers are found by direct reference; no card index is required as is true of some other systems. The method is flexible for small or large filing needs— any number of divisions can be created.

2. Filing by subject. Subject files are set up in much the same way as name

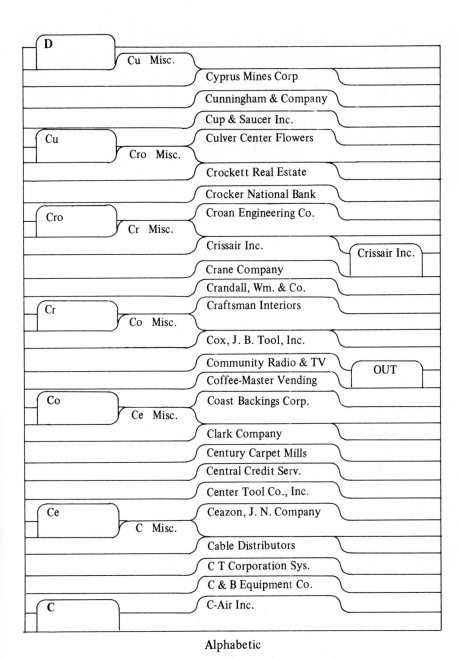

Alphabetic

Figure 12-1 Alphabetic, subject, geographic, and numeric filing systems. (Continued on pages 396–98.)

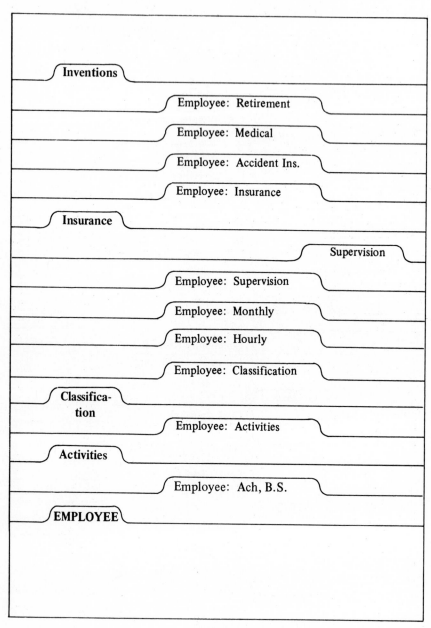

Subject

Figure 12-1 (continued).

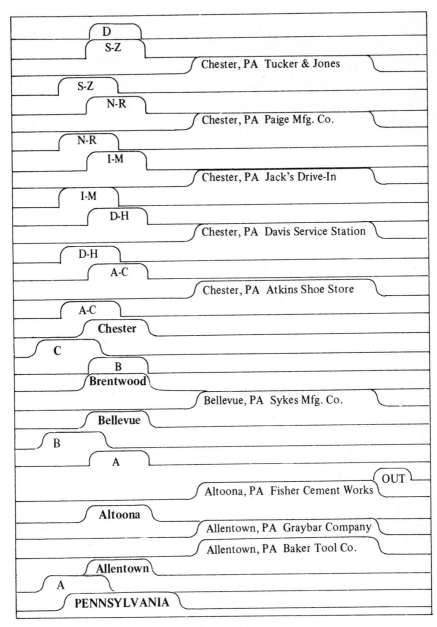

Geographic

Figure 12-1   (continued).

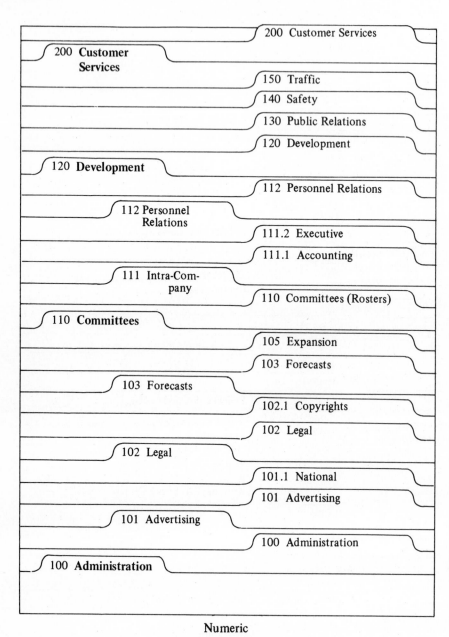

Numeric

Figure 12-1   (continued).

files. Instead of the names of people or organizations, however, the captions are concrete subjects. The subject method of filing meets a need in those offices that have a large quantity of related papers from different sources to file under one heading, for example, typewritten data, news clippings, catalogs, and so on. Records should be organized by subject in the following situations.

(a) When the records do not refer to the name of a person or an organization, e.g., inventory records.

(b) When it is likely that the records will be called for by subject.

(c) When all the records about one product or activity are likely to be needed at one time.

(d) When records might otherwise become unnecessarily subdivided.

Subject filing is accompanied by a card index that lists alphabetically all the headings, divisions, and subdivisions of the file. It should list also all topics related to the actual captions used. For instance, the subject of advertising might be subdivided into budget, 10-year plans, direct mail, sources of mailing lists, magazine, radio/TV, contests, promotional schemes, previous campaigns, competitors' campaigns, advertising agencies, and so forth. In this same case, budget information might be kept under the general headings of "Administration"; division: "Budgets"; subdivision: "Advertising Budget." Perhaps also under "Advertising Contests" there might be a subdivision for "Budget." Because individuals tend to differ in their selection of *the* filing subject for a piece of correspondence, all possible cross-references should be given in the card index to direct the search as quickly as possible to the needed document.

3. Filing by geographical area. Businesses that use *geographical* filing include sales organizations, mail-order houses, and public utilities. Where records are of a territorial nature, the geographical method is unquestionably the system of filing to adopt. The equipment consists of country guides in one color, state or province guides in another, county guides in a third, and city and town guides in a fourth color. If this system is used for a letter file in sales work, customers' folders may be tabbed on the left and prospects' folders on the right.

Nonalphabetical Filing Systems. *Numerical Index.* Records may be arranged according to serial numbers that are assigned arbitrarily and consecutively, or according to code numbers (Figure 12-1). The code number represents a topic or subject. Numerical filing systems are indirect. That is, the file clerk must first consult an alphabetical index to determine the code number of a record. Even though numerical filing may appear to require duplication of effort, many firms find that it has definite advantages over alphabetical filing.

1. Numerical systems make possible the quick sequential identification of records.

2. They aid efficient sorting and handling and result in fewer misfiles.

3. They provide for unlimited expansion.

4. They make possible permanent and extensive cross-referencing.

5. The card index for the numerical file provides a compact list of the names and addresses of correspondents and of subjects. It may also list various useful facts about clients.

Lawyers, architects, contractors, engineers, and scientists find a serial numbering system convenient for classifying cases and projects. The usual arrangement is in consecutive order from lowest to highest. The simplest system uses three-digit numbers in hundreds and tens. The first major alphabetical division is assigned 000 and each subdivision within the subject is assigned a ten, i.e., 010, 020, 030, 040, and so on. If more subdivisions are needed, the decimal-numeric system may be used. With the addition of more digits to the right of the decimal point, the subject may be divided into more and more parts, for example, 241 may be subdivided into 241.1, 241.2, 241.21, 241.22, and so on. The simple numerical system is limited to ten main headings 000 to 900 and nine main divisions under any one heading 010 to 090.

Public utilities find that the numerical system combined with letters allows them to use more headings and subheadings. One utility company, for instance, uses the letter *E* for "Equipment and Facilities" with numbered subdivisions as follows.

```
E7   Trunking
     E7.1   Assignments
     E7.2   Design Planning and Coordination
            E7.2A   Alternate Routing
            E7.2B   Extended Service
            E7.2C   Local
            E7.2D   Multimessage Unit
            E7.2E   Route Advance
            E7.2F   Special
            E7.2G   Tandem
            E7.2H   Toll
     E7.3   Leased Channels
     E7.4   Facility Relief
            E7.4A   Connecting Company
            E7.4B   Trunk Cable
     E7.5   Trunking Forecasts
            E7.5A   Interoffice Trunk Estimates
            E7.5B   Toll Circuit Estimates
     E7.6   Usage and Requirements
```

Bank checks, invoices, sales slips, and other prenumbered office forms are often filed by the terminal or the middle digit. Users of terminal-digit indexes claim a substantial reduction in misfiles, an unlimited expansion ability, and more efficient sorting and handling. In this system, numbers are read from right to left, and the end digits are considered in pairs or in groups of three:

Usual Sequence	Terminal-Digit Twos	Terminal-Digit Threes
10015	130 08	13 008
13008	100 15	10 015
22021	220 21	22 021
24589	357 21	24 589
35721	245 89	35 721

Those who use the middle-digit index find that it spreads items more evenly than does the terminal-digit system. The sequence in this system is based on the middle row of digits as follows.

$$1 \ 00 \ 15$$
$$2 \ 20 \ 21$$
$$1 \ 30 \ 08$$
$$2 \ 45 \ 89$$
$$3 \ 57 \ 21$$

Chronological Index.   This method of filing is used mainly in connection with other basic methods. For instance, correspondence from a firm is placed in an alphabetical or subject folder by date with the latest date on top. When a folder becomes congested with letters, these are then subdivided according to years or months and placed in several folders. Chronological filing as a method in itself, however, is often used for daily reports, deposit tickets, freight bills, statements, order sheets, and other material that you may want to keep together by dates.

Another important use of chronological filing is for follow-up information in a card index. In the follow-up system, all cards that need attention on the 26th of January are filed behind the "26" guide, which in turn is behind the "January" guide. The card then turns up automatically on the proper date. After each card is given attention, it is refiled behind the guide that indicates the date on which it should again have attention—January 30, for example— or behind the monthly guide for the month in which it is to receive attention. At the beginning of the month, the cards are divided by days. Such a card file is an example of a follow-up system called a "tickler" file (Figure 12-2).

Phonetic Index.   In this system, filing is done by sound rather than by actual spelling. Names that sound alike are grouped together. Such a system helps in the detection of duplications and minimizes the effects of transcribing and typing errors. In the several phonetic indexes, vowel sounds are omitted and the basic consonant sounds are stressed. The names are eventually filed by number. A phonetic index is most useful in large name files. One phonetic code is as follows.

Code numbers	Letter equivalents
1	b, f, p, v
2	c, g, j, k, q, s, x, z
3	d, t
4	l
5	m, n
6	r

Information-action card
(filed by month and then
by day action is to be taken)

Subject	Tickler Date
MONTHLY INVENTORY	11/16
Action: Distribute tally sheets to	
stock clerks - Form #I-5a	
J. Bone-12-01, H. Thomas-33-10	
S. Smith-12-05, B. Williams-16-01	
Signed	

Month guides (current
month in front)

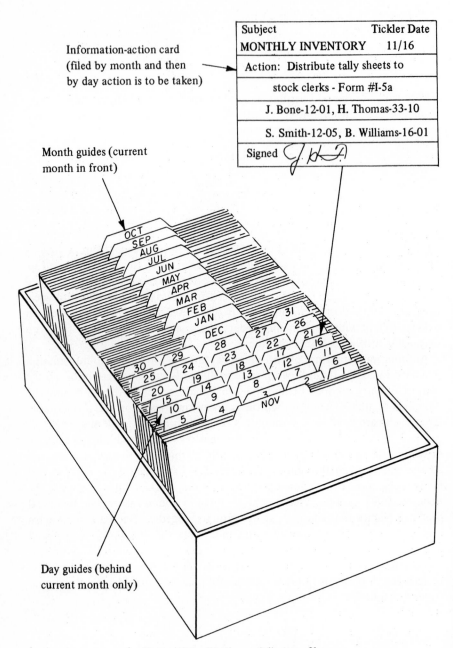

Day guides (behind
current month only)

Figure 12-2 Tickler or follow-up file.

Each code is made up of the first letter of the name and three numbers from the code. Vowels and *w, h,* and *y* are not coded. Double key letters are treated as a single unit. A key letter and its equivalent, such as *ch* or *mn,* are coded as one unit. If a name cannot be coded into three numbers, zeros are added. To illustrate, Thomsen, Thompson, Tompson are all coded *T525.* Within each section of the file, names are arranged alphabetically by the second indexing unit—the given name or first initial.

Filing Equipment Needs. Careful consideration should be given to the extent of equipment necessary to carry out a filing plan. A sufficient amount of the correct supplies will eliminate congestion. These guides are helpful in setting up efficient, orderly, and money-saving files using conventional 4-drawer file cabinets.

1. A vertical 26-inch letter drawer holds approximately 4,500 papers plus the average number of guides and folders.

2. No more than 50 papers should be placed in one folder. More papers will expand the folder until the tab is buried, and will cause mistakes in filing and lost time in hunting for misplaced papers.

3. When there are more than 50 papers for a folder, they should be subdivided into additional folders. This sorting may be done chronologically.

4. Folders marked "Miscellaneous" should be used sparingly. Inspect them periodically to see if there are enough papers on any one subject or from any one account to warrant a separate folder. When there are as many as five papers in a single group (for instance, five letters from one correspondent), they should be put in a separately labeled folder.

If the above guidelines are observed, one drawer for correspondence will need 25 alphabetical guides with a miscellaneous folder for each and about 75 separate folders. Then if you have approximately 18,000 papers in your current files, you will want four drawers or one four-drawer cabinet. Assuming that you are filing letters of a general run, you will need a 100-division set of alphabetical guides with accompanying folders. However, if your papers are confined to a few correspondents, you will want more folders, some of them subdivided perhaps, and a smaller division of guides.

Open Shelf Filing. The use of open shelves for filing is increasing rapidly. Approximately 62 percent less floor space is required with this type of equipment, and retrieval is 50 percent faster than with conventional file cabinets. Open shelving is available in a wide variety of sizes and colors. It requires fixed aisles of at least 36 inches for efficient filing and retrieval of material. However, the latest concept in shelving, mobile track-mounted shelving, requires only one fixed aisle. Access to other aisles is by push button, which activates motors to roll the shelving on tracks to open the aisle where and when it is needed. Models of open shelving are available in letter, legal, X-ray film, book, and computer reel sizes. Mobile track-mounted shelving saves 50 percent of the floor space required by open shelving equipment.

Modern Mechanized Files. With modern mechanized housing, records come to the operator without the need to stoop, stretch, or squat constantly to retrieve or refile. According to Sperry Univac, a company that specializes in office equipment, fatigue is reduced substantially and more work is accomplished with the use of automated filing equipment. Greater capacity is also achieved with substantial floor space savings by the use of equipment that takes advantage of space up to ceiling limits. It is possible to file to 10-foot heights without the need for stools, ladders, or other injury-prone items.

Planning the File System. *Office-Planned.* Many offices set up their own filing system to fit their special needs. If the person in charge of records management knows exactly what arrangement of guides and folders is best for the filing procedures of the company, an office-planned system functions satisfactorily. But such systems are often found to be unsatisfactory because they are oversimplified and quickly become obsolete. Usually the advice of a records management or office systems expert should be sought early so that the firm's needs may be studied and a satisfactory system worked out.

Commercial. Most large office equipment companies manufacture patented filing systems that are complete with the exception of captions or individual folders. These systems represent the most modern thinking about record-keeping and may be tailored to meet any specific need. Special features of these systems include (1) use of color as a double check against misfiling, (2) numerical captions combined with alphabetical captions for a filing double-check, and (3) use of special guides to highlight important names or subdivide major alphabetical sections. Listed here are the names of a few commercial systems.

Filing System	*Manufacturing Company*
Variadex Alphabetic	Sperry Rand Corporation
Colorscan Indexing	Sperry Rand Corporation
Amberg Nual Alphabet Index	Amberg File & Index Company
F. E. Bee Line	Filing Equipment Bureau
Safeguard Index	Globe-Wernicke
Super-Ideal	Shaw-Walker
Tell-I-Vision	Smead Manufacturing Company
Director Line	Wabash Filing Supplies, Inc.

Steps in the Filing Process. When material reaches the filing area, it should be scanned first for a release mark and/or date. Many firms use a *FILE* stamp with a line for the initials of the person authorizing release and the date of authorization. If a paper reaches the files without the release mark, it is customary to return it to the person to whom it was assigned. Having a document properly released to the files assures that any needed action has been taken.

Indexing. The paper should be read quickly for determination of the name, subject, or other caption under which it is to be filed. In compliance with the indexing system(s) used by the firm, the paper may be classified by (1) the name in the letterhead, (2) the name of the person or organization addressed, (3) the signature name, (4) the subject discussed, (5) the project title, (6) the geographical location about which the correspondence is concerned, or (7) the date on the document. It should be determined at this point whether any other subordinate or related subjects should be cross-referenced. Because too many cross-references are a waste of time and file space, they should be limited to those absolutely essential to finding the paper.

Coding.   The paper should now be coded. The pinpointing of the captions (name, subject, geographical location, date, and so forth) selected for filing is called coding. Several methods may be used to highlight the main and secondary captions.

1. The main caption under which the paper is to be filed can be underlined with a colored pencil.

2. If the main caption is not identical to the one in the correspondence, as often occurs in subject or numerical filing, it should be written in the upper right-hand corner. The words in the correspondence that lead to the selection of the caption should be underlined.

3. If the correspondence is to be cross-referenced, the cross-reference caption should be underlined and followed by an X in the margin. It is helpful to write the cross-reference caption in the upper right corner under the main reference.

4. Make follow-up notations if future action is needed. A simple method of doing this is to prepare a chronological file. Special folders (which bear across the top edge a printed range of dates from 1 to 31) may be used. To pinpoint the date on which action must be taken, metal clips or other signals are slipped over the date. This folder is then placed in the follow-up (tickler) file behind the correct month guide. When the date arrives, the folder is sent to the person responsible for taking action. Upon the folder's return, the material in it is placed in the regular files.

Sorting.   After coding, the captions are arranged in alphabetical order. At this time, a cross-reference sheet, usually of a distinctive color, is made up under the subordinate subject to show where the original correspondence is filed. Sometimes a card index is preferable as the cross-reference index.

If a numerical filing system is used, numerical coding follows alphabetical sorting. The card index containing all the classifications in alphabetical order is consulted for the file number. The number is written in the upper right corner, and the papers are then placed in numerical sequence.

Storing.   The papers are now ready to be placed in the files. Before being taken to the file cabinets, papers should be stapled together, if necessary, and torn ones mended. File carefully and accurately. Make a double check to see that each paper is filed in the correct folder. Besides checking the folder tab, check the caption on the paper to be filed against the caption on the latest paper already in the folder.

Indexing. The basic rules for indexing have been rather firmly established by business firms over the years. Each part of the name is an indexing unit; thus *Carlin, John G.* consists of three units, of which *Carlin* is the first. Generally, in determining the sequence of two or more names, you compare the first unit of each name, and if they are identical, proceed to compare the second unit to determine the alphabetical order. Another rule of thumb is that "nothing precedes something." For example, *Carlin* precedes *Carlins* because the *n* in *Carlin* is not followed by another letter whereas the *n* in *Carlins* is. Difficulty occurs, however, when you must determine what are the first, second, and third units. The following rules will help you solve indexing problems.

1. Transpose and alphabetize the names of individuals by last, first, middle. For example, "Kayton, Elmer T."

2. Compare the first unit in each name, letter by letter. The second units are considered only when the first units are identical.

3. A surname prefix is NOT a separate indexing unit but is considered part of the surname (*d', D', Da, de, De, Del, Des, Di, Du, Le, M', Mc, O', Van, Von,* and so on). The prefix *St.* is indexed as though spelled out—*Saint.* *M', Mac,* and *Mc* should be alphabetized in regular order as part of the complete surname, in spite of the existence of a *Mc* divider in many alphabetical card sets.

4. Titles or degrees are NOT units and are disregarded in indexing. Terms that designate seniority, such as *Jr., Sr.,* and *II,* ARE indexing units.

5. Firm names containing complete individual names are transposed as in names of individuals.

Clarkson	William	Securities	Incorporated
Williams	R.	J.	Co.

6. Firm names are considered in the same sequence as written when they do not contain the complete name of an individual. (See Rule 14 about the indexing of foreign company names.)

Abbott	Orthopedic	Supply
Burt	Plumbing	Co.

7. Articles *a, an, the,* and conjunctions and prepositions, such as *and, &, for, in,* and *of,* are not units and are disregarded in indexing, regardless of where they appear in the firm name or the caption.

8. Hyphenated words in firm names are indexed as *separate* units. Hyphenated surnames of individuals are considered as *one* indexing unit.

9. Abbreviations are indexed as though the represented words were spelled out in full. Single letters other than abbreviations are considered as separate indexing units.

AMB Carpet Co.	A	M	B	Carpet
Abbott Labs	Abbott	Laboratories		
Gen. Elec. Co.	General	Electric	Company	
Internat'l Trucking Inc.	International	Trucking	Incorporated	
St. George Hotel	Saint	George	Hotel	
Thomas Bros. Mfg. Co.	Thomas	Brothers	Manufacturing	Company
UP	United	Parcel		

10. Firm endings, such as *Bros., Co., Corp., Inc., Ltd., Mfg.,* and *Son,* are indexing units.

11. Names that may be written either as one or two words are indexed as one unit.

Inter State Bus Co.	Inter State	Bus	Company
Interstate Funding Co.	Interstate	Funding	Company

12. The parts of compound geographical names are separate units, except when the first part of the name is not an English word, such as *Los* in Los Angeles.

Des Moines	Tire	Company	
New	Jersey	Chemical	Company

13. Possessives. When a word ends with apostrophe *s,* the *s* is disregarded in indexing. When a word ends in *s* apostrophe, however, the *s* that is part of the original word *is* considered. In other words, consider everything up to the apostrophe.

Nelson's	Management	Services
Nelson	Thomas	B.
Nelsons' (The)	Decorating	Shop

14. Names of foreign companies should be indexed exactly as written even though the words may be articles, conjunctions, or prepositions; foreign words for *company* or type of business; or names that are not distinguishable as either surnames or given names.

Banco	de	Acapulco (Mexico)	
Compania	Molinera	de	Alamos (Brazil)
Les	Parfums	Importers	

If the firm is engaged extensively in foreign trade, it may be more efficient to set up a geographical file by country, separate the folders by the type of business, and then alphabetize the companies by the name in the title most familiar to those working on the account.

15. Names pertaining to the Federal Government are indexed under "United States Government" and subdivided, first by department title, followed by bureau, division, commission, or board. For example, "Social Security Administration" would be

United	States	Government	Social	Security	Administration

The U.S. Department of Commerce, Bureau of The Census, would be

United	States	Government	Commerce	Census
			(Dept. of)	(Bureau of)

16. Other political divisions are indexed under the name of the chief governing body, followed by its classification, such as *state, county,* or *city,* and then subdivided by the title of the department, bureau, division, commission, or board.

Board of Education, Atlanta Georgia:

Atlanta	City	Education
		(Board of)

Bureau of Weights and Measures, State of Wisconsin:

Wisconsin	State	Weights	Measures
		and	(Bureau of)

Water and Power Department, Austin, Texas:

Austin	City	Water	Power
		and	(Department of)

17. A number in a name is considered as though it were written in words and is indexed as *one* unit. Numbers over 1,000, such as 1,435, should be indexed as *fourteen hundred thirty-five* and not as *one thousand four hundred thirty-five.*

18. When the same name appears with different addresses, it should be alphabetized according to city or town. The state is considered only when there is a duplication of both individual or company name and city name. If the same correspondent is located at different addresses within the same city, then the correspondence should be alphabetized by streets. If the same correspondent is located at several addresses on the same street, the alphabetizing should be from the lowest to the highest street number.

Firestone	Stores	Newark	Delaware	
Firestone	Stores	Newark	Ohio	
Firestone	Stores	Providence	Main, 20	Street
			(20 Main St.)	
Firestone	Stores	Providence	Main, 520	Street
			(520 Main St.)	
Firestone	Stores	Providence	Maple	Avenue
Firestone	Stores	Tulsa		

19. Banks, churches, societies, associations, clubs, and so on, are indexed under the full name as written. If there are several branches, subalphabetize by the names of cities.

American Business Communication Association
American National Red Cross
   Albany Chapter, American National Red Cross
   Mobile Chapter, American National Red Cross
   New Orleans Chapter, American National Red Cross
   Pittsburgh Chapter, American National Red Cross

Bank of America
   Dallas, Bank of America
   Oakland, Bank of America
   Salinas, Bank of America
   Salt Lake City, Bank of America
   Tucson, Bank of America
English-Speaking Union
Society of Automotive Engineers, Inc.
United Presbyterian Church, USA
   Topeka, United Presbyterian Church
   Seattle, University Presbyterian Church
   Washington, D.C., Fourth Presbyterian Church
United Way
University Club (The)
   Chicago, University Club (The)
   St. Louis, University Club (The)

20. Universities, schools, and colleges are filed under the principal part of the name. A cross-index file may be kept under the full name, if needed.

California, University of (Berkeley)
John Marshall High School (Los Angeles)
New York University (New York City)
Notre Dame, University of (South Bend, Indiana)
Pennsylvania State University (University Park)
Stanford University (California)
Virginia, University of (Roanoke)
William and Mary, College of (Williamsburg, Virginia)

21. Married Women. The legal name of a married woman is the one used for indexing. Legally, the surname is the only part of a husband's name that a woman assumes upon marriage. A married woman's legal name could be either (a) her own first and middle names together with her husband's surname, or (b) her first name and maiden surname together with her husband's surname. The name should be written on filing cards or folders as shown here:

Pollock, Lorna Jane (Mrs.)
(James G.)

McCarroll, Mary Parker (Mrs.)
(Neil C.)

Charge-Out and Control of Records. In order that file-section personnel have information at all times about the location of files, a record of all material loaned or removed should be maintained. Substitution cards with *Out* tabs at the top take the place of the folder or document in the file drawer. The card should contain the description of the document or the file caption or code, the date of removal, and the name and extension number of the borrower.

It is the responsibility of the file section to make periodic checks of charged-out records and, if they have been retained for more than 15 days, to contact the user and request the return of them. In some instances the user to whom records have been charged may need to send them to another person or department for action. Notification of the rerouting of records should be given the file section so that the *Out* card may be updated.

A valuable control, established by a majority of companies, is to dissuade everyone from removing papers or folders from the file cabinets or from placing any material in them, except for members of the file section.

Training File Personnel. It is important that employees who work with files either in the central file department or in departmental offices be well trained in filing procedures. Refresher training can be handled within the company by using this office handbook. For employees with little or no background in business, the multi-media program, *Business Filing and Records Management*, offered by WESTERN TAPE, 2761 Marine Way, P.O. Box 69, Mountain View, CA 94042, will provide thorough training in the methods of filing. The complete package consists of ten audio recordings, a student handbook, and a teacher's manual with answers.

Centralized Versus Decentralized Files. Records are usually located in (1) centralized files in which records for the entire organization are merged together and kept in a central location; (2) departmental files that are kept in the offices of the separate departments and contain only the records of those departments, such as corporate offices, sales, or advertising; and (3) a combination of centralized and departmental files.

Departmental Files. Records should be located in the files of the various departments when:

1. They are confidential and should be available only to the department needing them.

2. Copies of the same records are filed differently according to how the using department calls for them.

3. Space for an adequate, well-staffed and well-equipped, centrally located file room is not available.

4. Fast, immediate reference to records is necessary.

5. It is more economical to locate records nearest the point of most frequent use.

Centralized File System. A centralized file system should be used when:

1. Records need to be well protected and controlled.

2. Records are used by more than one department and need to be easily accessible.

3. Duplication of records, space, equipment, and supplies must be eliminated in order to lower overhead.

4. Filing can be handled by full-time professional file clerks who can apply the latest filing techniques on a production basis.

5. Procedures can be standardized, making it easier to file, find, request, deliver, and return records to the files.

Combination of Decentralized and Centralized Files.   Many large companies maintain a centralized file system for the protection of vital records. At the same time certain departments are permitted to maintain their own files under the supervision of the central file department or a records manager. Under this system departmental files are checked periodically to avoid costly duplication or proliferation of records.

Importance of a Retention Schedule.   The needless filing of every piece of paper received by a company or generated within its doors should be scrupulously avoided. A records manager or another executive should determine the relative value of the various classes of company records and establish a retention schedule that complies with State and Federal laws. The rules and regulations of the Federal Communications Commission regarding the preservation of the records of communication common carriers might be used as a guideline (Figure 12-3). Copies of FCC's *Rules and Regulations, Part 42, Preservation of Records of Communication Common Carriers* may be found in the government periodicals section of most libraries or may be secured from the Superintendent of Documents, who also has other excellent bulletins on records retention.

Vital records that are essential to the existence of the organization are kept permanently in a safe place because they are irreplaceable. Such documents as legal papers of incorporation, titles to ownership, deeds, major contracts, property plans, reports to stockholders, and insurance policies are considered vital records. Other important documents that should be kept permanently are

Accounting Records, such as ledgers, balance sheets, trial balances, and accountants' and auditors' reports.
Drafts, checks, and receipts for cash payments plus the correspondence relating thereto.
Inventory records of plant facilities.
Invoices and related records.
Mortgages.
Payroll records.
Stock certificate records.
Tax records.
Vouchers.

The following records may be kept for shorter periods.

Seven to Ten Years	*Two to Three Years*
Accounts receivable ledgers.	Assignments, attachments, and garnishments.
Contracts and agreements for other than purchase or sale of materials.	Contracts for purchase or sale of materials.
Deposit books and records of checks.	Employees' fidelity bonds records.
Documents substantiating claims.	Purchase orders.
Insurance records.	Reconciliation papers.
Inventories of merchandise, materials, and supplies.	
Lists of proxies and voting stockholders.	
Sales records.	

Item No.	Description of records	Period to be retained
	Corporate and General	
1	Corporate organization:	
	a. Charter or certificate of incorporation and amendments thereto......................	Permanently.
	b. Legal documents in connection with mergers, consolidations, reorganizations, receiverships, and similar actions which affect the identity or organization of the company.....	Do.
	c. By-laws	Do.
2	Corporate elections and stockholders' votes:	
	a. Notices of meetings, proxy statements, and proxy solicitation material	10 years.
	b. Voting lists	3 years.
	c. Proxies.......................................	Do.
	d. Ballots and tabulations of votes	Do.
	e. Judges' or inspectors' reports of results	Do.
3	Minutes of meetings:	
	a. Meetings of stockholders and directors........	Permanently
	b. Meetings of executive committee and other directors' committees......................	Do.
	c Meetings of employees' benefit committee	Do.
4	Securities issued or assumed:	
	a. Applications to governmental bodies and authorizations therefrom to issue securities or assume debt issued by others.	Do.
	b. Registration statements and amend thereto ...	Do.
	c. Bids and contracts for sale of securities, including underwriting agreements, except as provided in item 4-1-(4).	Do.
	d. Agreements with trustees of security issues....	Do.

Figure 12-3 Extract from FCC's *Preservation of Records of Communication Common Carriers, Rules and Regulations.*

Transfer and Disposal of Records. The systematic transfer of records that have future worth or value includes transfer from active to inactive files, and from inactive files to the storage area. At each move in the transfer process, the retention schedule should be checked and obsolete or useless records destroyed. Many times entire files are transferred to inactive status at some predetermined time, such as the beginning of the calendar year, the fiscal year, or the busy season. The material remains in the original folders and is moved intact to an adjacent file cabinet or to the bottom drawers of the cabinet. New folders are prepared for the new active files before transfer is made. *Periodic transfer,* as this method is called, operates most effectively if the inactive files are close to the new files for convenient reference.

Transfer of these recent files to another floor or building would result in wasted time because of the frequent need to check past records at the beginning of the new period.

The *perpetual transfer* method places time limits on individual papers by appropriate marks on the folders. The files may be checked at intervals of two or three months or perpetually at irregular intervals for materials that should be placed in the inactive files, sent to storage, or destroyed. In situations where a transaction, such as a job or a case, is completed, all records generated by the transaction are transferred immediately.

Material in the inactive files is removed periodically and sorted by classification as either *important* or *vital*. *Important* material may be handled in three ways: (1) records placed in storage and eventually destroyed; (2) records microfilmed and then destroyed, films placed in storage and ultimately destroyed; (3) records destroyed, having outlived their span of importance. If the material is classified as *vital*, it is a permanent record and may be placed in storage or microfilmed, the record itself destroyed, and the film kept permanently. The destruction date of material should be placed on it at the time of transfer to storage. A separate card file should indicate the contents of transfer files and the destruction dates of papers.

Micrographics.   The various methods of print-to-film transference are known by the generic term *micrographics*. Included in the group are microfilm, opaque microcard, and transparent microcard known as microfiche.

Microfilm.   Through microfilming, documents may be photographed at reduced sizes with the developed film serving as the record. Companies using this method of storing documents find that it saves approximately 98 percent of storage space. One to two file cabinets of film hold the equivalent of hundreds of drawers of original records. The chances of losing a document are minimized because documents are photographed in sequence on a roll of film. The retained materials do not wear out, remain clean, and are easily handled. Because microfilm is of a noncombustible type, the hazard of fire is reduced. In addition to placing images on a roll of film, another microfilm process mounts a single frame on a punched card that carries the identification of the record. Even large engineering drawings, blueprints, specifications, and photographs may be reduced on film and, through a punched card system, quickly found and consulted.

A reading machine or viewer is used when there is need to consult a document. The document is magnified to readable size, or may even be enlarged further for projection on a screen. Some readers will make a full-sized photocopy of the filmed record. One machine, the FileSearch, automatically scans 6,400 microfilmed pages a minute in the search for a particular document.

A complete unit of microfilm equipment may be purchased or leased on an operational basis. The process of filming documents is relatively simple.

The most difficult types of records to photograph, however, are green tissue carbon copies, faint hectograph and mimeograph material, negative photostats, deep shades of colored papers, and blurred carbon copies on white paper. Exposed film should be checked to see that every image is clearly legible; and, if not, the document should be rephotographed. Outside concerns that specialize in microfilm work will photograph a company's records either on its premises or at the company's plant. Usually the cost for this service, including film and developing, varies for each 1,000 pieces. A cost analysis should be made before a decision is made to purchase or lease equipment.

Microcard and Microfiche. *Microcard* is a flat sheet or film "card" that contains, on the average, sixty book pages. The cards can be opaque or transparent, the latter being known as *microfiche*. The advantage of this process is that the reader-printer that enlarges the card will also supply, at the press of a button, a copy of the page being read. (Figure 12-4.)

Microfiche reduces the original document from one fifth to one twentieth of its original size, enabling the equivalent of 10,000 pages to be stored in

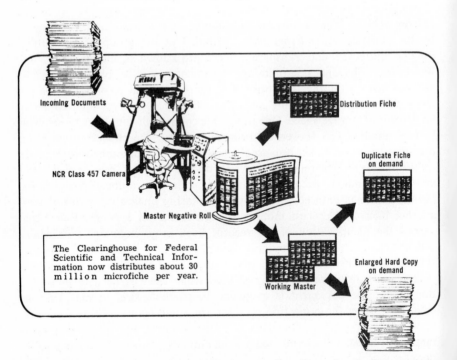

Figure 12-4 A typical microfiche system in operation. (Reproduced with permission from "Microfiche Fact File" published by the Industrial Products Division of the National Cash Register Company, Dayton, Ohio.)

less than two inches of drawer space. It is especially valuable when one is filing and retrieving information in such documents as technical reports, scientific and research data, industrial catalogs, or maintenance manuals. Most standard systems of classification and indexing can be applied to microfiche. The standard fiche established by COSATI, the President's Committee on Scientific and Technical Information, measures approximately 4″ × 6″ (105 mm × 148 mm) and contains up to sixty $8\frac{1}{2}$″ × 11″ pages (30 frames) filmed at $18 \times -20 \times$ reduction. An eye-legible heading on the fiche contains the classification or identifying number, the document title, its source, its author, and other basic information. For documents more than 60 pages in length, "trailer" fiche are used. These have an abbreviated heading and a maximum capacity of 72 pages. The exact method of filing is largely determined by the type of information, the frequency of updating, the frequency of reference, and related factors.

Companies engaged in providing tailor-made microfiche systems to businesses or in handling all production from master negative to hard copy at their own production sites are

National Cash Register
Bell & Howell
3M (Minneapolis)
Leasco Data Processing
Xerox Corporation

Legality of Microfilmed Documents. Microfilm may cause some legal problems. Courts prefer original records. If these have been destroyed, the company must establish that the destruction was in the natural course of business. To be free from suspicion, the film of controversial records should be verified as to their authenticity by the insertion of a target on the film bearing the signature of an officer of the company. The Bureau of Internal Revenue advises against microfilming general books of account, such as cash books, journals, voucher registers, and ledgers. Taxpayers may, however, use microfilm reproductions for supporting records of details, such as payroll records, canceled checks, invoices, and vouchers, provided the following conditions are met: (1) microfilmed copies are retained as long as the contents may be needed as evidence in the administration of any internal revenue law; (2) appropriate facilities are provided for the safekeeping of the films and are open for inspection and review on a company machine at all times; and (3) transcriptions will be made from the microfilm when required.

12.2 REPROGRAPHICS

Business papers are produced in quantity; rarely is a single copy adequate. The major need of a company is to produce as economically as possible the desired number of clear copies. Reprographics is the term used to define all the processes, techniques, and equipment employed for copying, photo-typesetting, and printing. Consequently, a knowledge of available processes will ensure selection of the right type of duplicating and copying equipment to meet reproduction needs. The following material includes information on the most popular and most modern reproduction equipment in use in today's business offices.

The Reproduction Department. Most large firms establish a photographic and reproduction department in order to obtain more efficient use of special equipment and to capitalize on the skills of trained personnel. Some duplicating methods, however, can easily be handled by semiskilled operators. The most common of these methods are carbon paper, automatic typewriters, spirit and stencil duplicators, and copying machines such as Thermofax and Xerox.

The selection of a reproduction process should be based on cost, appearance, and reproduction time. (For a comparison of processes, see Figure 12-5.) *Cost* is determined by the number of copies needed and the process used. The *appearance* desired must be determined by ultimate use. *Reproduction time* may overrule other considerations because some processes are faster than others. If possible, use the least expensive process that reconciles cost, appearance, and speed.

When a company has a graphic production department, requests for reproduction are made on a work order similar to the one in Figure 12-6. Fill in this form accurately and completely to get the quantity and quality of reproduction desired. Even page sequence should be stated on the work order. The originator, for instance, should specify whether page 1 is to be *backed up* with page 2, and so on, and whether the *backer* is to be *head-to-head* (the heading of the back copy directly opposite the heading of the front copy, so that the pages can be turned right to left) or *tumblehead* (the heading of the back copy at the bottom of the front copy, so that the pages can be turned bottom to top). Choice of *head-to-head* or *tumblehead* depends on whether copies will be bound on the left or along the top. If the job is complicated, it is advisable to prepare a dummy or mock-up.

Duplicating Processes. *Carbon Paper.* When two to eight copies of a rough or final draft are needed, one typing with an original and carbon copies is the most economical process. Carbon paper is available in sheets (for insertion) and in rolls (for continuous feeding of forms). One-time carbon paper is used in snap-out forms and with second-sheet sets. Approximately 20 readable copies can be made on an electric typewriter with electric carbon paper. Eight to ten copies is the maximum that can be produced on a manual typewriter with the correct intensity of carbon, weight of paper, hardness of platen, and the right touch control on the machine.

PROCESS	Approximate Single-Copy Cost	Maximum Size (inches)	Economical Run	Remarks
Ditto. Black, purple, red, or green line on white or colored paper or on card stock. Fair appearance. Makes 50 to 60 copies a minute.	$.007–8½ x 11 $.012–11 x 17 $.03–Ditto master	11 x 17	10 to 150	Cheapest method up to 300 copies. Copies are of solid color becoming progressively fainter. Master may be reused once. Good for one-sided copy only. Not recommended when copy permanency is essential. Black ditto should not be used if runs of more than 100 copies are needed.
Mimeograph. Good copy appearance on white or colored 20# mimeograph paper or on card stock.	$.009	8½ x 13	50 to 5000	Typewritten or hand-drawn stencils produce a neat, sharp, legible copy. Both sides of paper may be used, if slipsheeted. Several colors of ink are available. Stencil may be rerun if properly stored.
Thermofax. Makes four copies a minute on lightweight paper. Several colors of paper are available.	$.05–8½ x 11 $.29–8½ x 11 transparency	11 x 17	Up to 10	Cannot enlarge or reduce. Extremely difficult to make additional copies from a Thermofax print. Will copy either opaque or translucent copy. Will not reproduce aniline dye inks, such as Ditto and ball point pen. Not recommended for filing.
Copytron. Black line on white background. Same size as original.	$.05–8½ x 11 $.10–11 x 17	11 by any length	15 copies	Reproduces any translucent or opaque copy.

Figure 12-5 Comparative features of reproduction processes.

(continued)

417

PROCESS	Approximate Single-Copy Cost	Maximum Size (inches)	Economical Run	Remarks
Xerography. Copies reproduced in 3 minutes; takes longer if cleanup needed after use of color. Produces finished copies from a paper plate in several colors or with an overlay of print, if desired.	Fraction of a cent to 5¢ a copy depending on type of material.	11 x 17	Subject to method used for subsequent reproduction. U s u a l l y 15-500.	Can make masters for offset printing or vellum copies for Diazo reproduction. Can enlarge and reduce. Reproduces opaque copy and/or originals printed on both sides. Quicker and less expensive than photo-offset printing. No negative needed. Both sides of paper may be used.
Xerox. Black line on white or colored stock. Same size as original. Books may be copied without being disassembled. Rapid process up to 40 copies a minute.	$.03 to $.10 a copy	9 x 14		Will reproduce almost any original. Not good for half-tones. Reproduces from opaque and two-sided originals onto bond paper, cardstock, vellum, and a transparency.
Copyflo Xerox. Black line on white background. Reduction to 50 per cent from 22″ maximum width. Produces 15 to 20 copies a minute.	$.09–8½ x 11 $.17–multilith plate	11 by any length		Will reproduce almost any original. Not good for half-tones. Least expensive way to make multilith plates and to reproduce opaque and two-sided originals. Quality not as good as flat Xerox equipment.
Blueline. Duplicates transparent or translucent material onto sensitized paper which produces a blue-on-white copy. Same size as original. A roll may be run at 12 feet a minute, and an 8½″ x 11″ sheet is produced in one minute.	$.03 sq. ft. –roll $.01–8½ x 11	36 by any length	Up to 15	Recommended for duplicates of drawings or layouts prepared on vellum. A fast, inexpensive method of reproducing large prints needing wide distribution.

Process	Cost	Size	Quantity	Remarks
Ozalid or Diazo. Letter-size equipment produces 200 copies an hour. Other equipment takes copy up to 42" wide, at speeds averaging 20 to 30 feet a minute. Makes a positive print from positive copy.	$.017 sq. ft. ½₄–8½ x 11	8½ to 42 in width by any length	1 to 25 originals, 25 copies each; 25 to 50 originals, 15 copies each; 50 to 100 originals, 10 copies each.	Masters can be prepared by pencil, ink, typing, printing, Xerography, etc., on translucent paper, cloth, or film. All prints are of equal clarity. Masters are good indefinitely. Fast, inexpensive method of reproducing large prints for small distribution. Economical method of reproducing half-tone prints where photo quality is not needed.
Multilith (Offset Printing). Black or colored ink on white or colored paper or on cardstock. Same size as image on offset plate, usually a paper master.	$.02–.05 a copy	Paper size 11 x 17 Printing area 10½ x 17	500 with paper masters	Used to produce forms, manuals, etc., when large volume is required. Makes better copies than other methods of reproduction. Since plates can be re-run, excellent process for repetitive work.
Photo Offset. Excellent appearance. Printing may be made in several colors on various grades and weights of white or colored paper, or on cardstock. Uses a metal master.	$.02–100 copies Fraction of a cent in longer runs.	3 x 5 to 17 x 22	50 to unlimited	Not recommended for one-time printing or short runs, except where excellent quality or exactness of reproduction is absolutely necessary.
Photostat. Black line on white background in positive. White line on black background in negative. May be reproduced in half scale or double size of copy.	$.20—18 x 24 negative $.40—18 x 24 positive	18 x 24 Sections can be spliced to make larger sizes.	Up to 5	Either negative or positive is an exact copy. Reasonable cost where few copies are needed. Recommended for legal documents. Advantage in being able to reproduce pages of bound books and magazines.

Note: Labor and equipment costs vary considerably and are not included in this table.

Figure 12-5 (continued).

419

SPECIAL INSTRUCTIONS | RUSH ☐ | TITLE OF DOCUMENT | NO.
PAGES

PROCESS	QUANTITY	PRICE	PROCESS	QUANTITY	PRICE
Ditto			Set-up		
Stencil			Typeset		
Multilith			Photo print		
Xerox			Vellum		
Offset					
			Collate		
			Staple		
			Punch		
			Bind		
Covers			Padding		
			Cutting		
			Folding		
Sub Total			Sub Total		

INSTRUCTIONS BY: _____ Dept. _____ Ext. _____

Copies _____
Collate ☐
Staple ☐
Punch ☐
Bind ☐
Pad - 25 ☐
50 ☐
100 ☐

Date Submitted _____
Date Due _____
Distribution List: _____

Cut ☐
Fold ☐
Covers ☐
Color Paper: ☐
Color Ink: _____

Submitted Size _____ X _____
Finish Size _____ X _____
Copies to Author _____

DUPLICATING SECTION
Rec. Order: _____

Name _____ Date _____
Dept. Costs $ _____
Distribution Costs $ _____
Date Distributed _____

Figure 12-6 Reproduction work order.

Media Typewriters. Media typewriters rapidly reproduce stored information without error. A single operator can handle a bank of ten or more machines, manually typing the date, inside address, salutation, and any personalized fill-ins in the body of the message. These machines may be programmed to type certain portions of the message, stop, and continue when signaled to do so by the operator. Through the use of magnetic tape, stored information is located and combined automatically with material stored on a second tape to provide new combinations of typewritten material. Whenever changes are made in the copy or margins are reset, the machine respaces sentences, adjusts line lengths, even drops hyphens, and automatically checks itself to ensure accuracy of retyping. Any number of form letters and envelopes may be reproduced, depending on the number of machines and operators available. (See Sections 5.1 and 11.1.)

Spirit Process. Ditto is the name commonly associated with the spirit process, but the terms *liquid* and *hectograph* are also used. Ditto is a quick, low-cost process and should be used when 10 to 150 copies are needed. It is possible to make up to 500 copies with a fresh, new Ditto master, freshly cleaned typewriter keys, and a plastic backing sheet, which provides a hard, even surface that sharpens the typewritten copy. With skilled operation to control the flow of the alcohol-base liquid that moistens the copy paper, a spirit duplicator can produce up to 500 copies. Ditto masters are reusable. The carbon backing, from which the impression is transferred to the master, comes in purple, blue, red, green, and black. Various sizes of masters and carbons, as well as single sheets or sets, are available. Lines and letters may be ruled on a Ditto master with a 6, 7, or 8H pencil or a stylus, provided the master is placed over a hard surface. Certain office forms are available on preprinted masters to which you may add your own data. Many stationers and specialized companies, such as Moore Business Forms, Inc., maintain a supply of these forms and will work with a company to develop new ones that meet individual needs.

Stencil Duplicating. The mimeograph process uses a stencil master on which the image may be cut by typewriter, stylus, or special machines. Lettering, handwriting, and art work can be imprinted on the stencil. Special pens, punches, and shaders are available for ruling, shading, drawing, and lettering. Tint plates and a shader are used to apply textures and patterns to drawings that have been made with the wheel or stylus pen. Preimprinted stencils of your letterhead or routine forms and art work may be obtained from stationers or manufacturers' outlets. Stencil duplicating is an inexpensive process when you are preparing more than 200 and up to 5,000 copies. Stencils may be filed, then altered or added to, and rerun. The copy may be produced in a wide color range that includes red, green, blue, brown, purple, yellow, and black.

A drawing and tracing desk is an important companion piece to the duplicator. The stencil is placed over a translucent, movable glass drawing surface, illuminated from beneath. A detachable lightweight T-square can be used either horizontally or vertically while the stencil is held firmly. A suspended stencil filing system is available to store, protect, and index up to 240 stencils in one unit. An electronic stencil cutter is a valuable addition to stencil duplicating. Such a machine automatically produces perfect stencils direct from line or wash drawings, heavy solids, half-tones or full-tone photographs. It cuts high definition stencils even when the original is in pastel colors or has very faint lines.

Copying Processes.   There are a variety of copying machines on the market today from the small table models to the large floor consoles. Some process single sheets only, whereas others are able to duplicate pages from bound books and periodicals. Some produce copy on thin white or beige paper, and others turn out copies on a heavier weight of white paper, which itself may be used to make additional copies. Usually the larger models may be leased from the supplier, who also provides maintenance service. The office manager must control the use of these machines. Most companies find that once a copying machine is installed, employees tend to copy material indiscriminately and to make too many copies without regard to the cost involved.

Copying Machines.   *Thermofax* and *Readyprint*, desk-model office copiers, use an exposure-by-heat process to reproduce single pages up to $8\frac{1}{2}'' \times 14''$. They are economical to use if five or less copies are needed. Copies are printed on opaque tissue or thin paper, usually light beige in color. Thermofax requires a strong carbon definition on the material to be copied, such as a clear, black typewritten or pencil copy. It is not capable of copying originals that have been written with a red or blue pencil or pen nor of copying Multilith masters or one of its own copies. The Readyprint produces exact copies of letters and other papers, including the letterhead and signature.

Copytron prints copies from any opaque or translucent master (bond, carbon copy, Ditto copy, and so on). The machine uses a dry, electrostatic process that places a charge on special Copytron paper as it enters the machine. The photosensitive image is then projected into a mirror, which, in turn, is reflected on sensitized paper. A developer is applied to the sheet to produce an image of the master, and finally the image is fused to the paper by heat. The finished print is highly legible and permanent. Use of Copytron is recommended when a few quick copies of important or complicated printed material are needed. The paper stock comes in several sizes: $8\frac{1}{2}'' \times 11''$, $8\frac{1}{2}'' \times 14''$, and $11'' \times 17''$.

Xerography is a method of electrostatically reproducing an image directly on ordinary letter paper without the need for an intermediate master. Xerox office copying machines, which employ the xerographic process, can be operated by anyone in the office. The 720 and 914 reproduce written, printed, or typed originals up to $9'' \times 14''$ maximum size. The 2400, 3600, 813, and

660 reproduce originals up to $8\frac{1}{2}''$ × 14″. All colors are copied with black-on-white fidelity; however, the larger solid black or colored areas fade to a light gray toward the center. Ditto or Thermofax originals do not reproduce satisfactorily. Photographs are copied with usable legibility. Either single sheets or pages from bound publications may be copied in their original size.

To operate the Xerox, you simply place the original document face down on the scanning glass, dial the number of copies desired, and push the button. The machine operates by itself, rapidly printing copies automatically, and turns itself off when the desired quantity is reached. The Xerox 2400 makes 40 copies a minute. The cost of reproduction by xerography is relatively high, especially for large quantities. Paper Multilith masters can be made on the Xerox, but the quality of printed material from the Xerox-produced masters is not generally equal to that produced by copy camera photography with subsequent printing from a metal master. Legibility is good to excellent.

Through adjustment of the Xerox camera, copy can be enlarged or reduced. The Xerox 7000 Reduction Duplicator, for instance, will reduce a 14″ × 18″ original to $8\frac{1}{2}''$ × 11″, $8\frac{1}{2}''$ × 13″, or $8\frac{1}{2}''$ × 14″ size.

Copyflo Xerox is used to make full-scale copies of any original up to 11 inches wide by any length. Half-scale reproductions can be made of originals up to 22 inches wide by any length. The material to be copied must first be microfilmed, preferably on 35-mm film. Copies are made on bond paper, card stock, vellum, or any such material that comes on a roll. Multilith plates of adequate quality for internal use can also be made on this equipment at a cost saving over plates produced on flat Xerography equipment.

The *Blueline* process duplicates transparent or translucent material by exposing it onto sensitized paper. The sensitized paper then goes through an ammonia developing process that produces a blue-on-white copy. Blueline is recommended when you need duplicates of drawings or layouts prepared on vellum, or up to 15 copies of any transparent or translucent material. The master is typed or drawn on transparent or translucent paper (vellum, smooth onionskin, and so on) and backed with orange carbon or typewriter carbon for an especially dark, legible copy. The only corrections on the master that prove satisfactory are extremely neat erasures. Paper stock comes in several sizes: $8\frac{1}{2}''$ × 11″, 11″ × 14″, 11″ × 17″, 17″ × 22″, and 22″ × 34″. The paper stock also comes in rolls 18″ and 36″ wide × 500′ long. The maximum size of the original is 36″ wide by any length. Yellow or blue writing will not reproduce, and cockled onionskin produces a fuzzy image because of irregularity of the paper surface.

Ozalid is a method of exact reproduction from an original of highly translucent or transparent material up to 42 inches wide and any length. This process, more expensive than Ditto, should be used only when the original is on translucent paper, and one or more of the following conditions prevail.

Cost of retyping or copying to another form such as Direct Image Multilith master is excessive.

Time is limited and copy of existing record or document must be obtained immediately.

Handwritten notations or drawings must be reproduced exactly.

Number of copies required is less than 25.

Size of original exceeds maximum width and length of paper used on other processes.

The quality of reproduction is fairly good; however, the paper on which the final copy appears is sometimes slightly gray rather than pure white. Reproduction time on the machine is much longer than that of the Multilith process. Letter-size equipment produces copies at a rate of 200 copies per hour, whereas larger equipment produces copies up to 42 inches wide at a rate of 20 to 30 feet per minute. The preparation of the master consists of typing or drawing on highly translucent paper, such as vellum, which is backed with a piece of orange carbon paper for sharper copies. Overhead projection transparencies of $8'' \times 10''$ inches may be prepared by the Ozalid process. Masters may be rerun indefinitely with no decrease in quality of the copies and will last indefinitely providing they do not become damaged.

The *Direct Image Multilith* process, a simplified method of offset printing, may be used for production runs from 10 copies to as many as 5,000. Direct image plates can be procured in varying qualities, depending on the volume of the desired run—short-, medium-, or long-run plates. In this process typing, drawing, writing, or printing is placed directly onto the Multilith paper master, which reproduces the copies in the Multilith duplicating machine. The quality is less than, but nearly equal to, that of photo-offset reproduction. There is practically no decrease of image sharpness or density up to the recommended limit. Legibility is good to excellent if the master is carefully prepared. The following suggestions will assist you in preparing a good master.

1. Use an electric typewriter with any type face except a fine one that will not photograph well.

2. Use a ribbon suitable for Multilith duplication and a plastic backing sheet.

3. Locate the image properly on the master. Position the master in the machine so that the typewritten message will be in the same position as you would like to have it on the finished copies.

4. Select a paper master that is clean and in good condition without being cracked or dried because of long or improper storage. Handle the master on the edges to avoid the reproduction of smudges.

5. Make corrections carefully with a special Multilith eraser while the master is in the typewriter.

6. Use a Multilith reproducing pencil or pen for signatures, underscores, drawings, and sketches.

7. Allow an aging period of at least one-half hour for the image to set between typing and running.

Photographic Processes.   The *photo-offset* process should be used when more than 500 high-quality copies are required. This process is basically the same as direct-image offset except that in the photo-offset method all typing, drawing, writing, or printing is on a piece of hard, smooth white paper that is then photographed. Ditto master paper produces excellent copy. Photo-offset allows enlargement or reduction in the finished copy. Paper or metal masters are then prepared for use on the Multilith duplicating machine. The quality is less than, but nearly equal to, that of typeset printing. It is superior to the direct-image process. There is no decrease in image sharpness or density, and practically no limit to the number of copies a Multilith metal master can reproduce. Reproduction time is short; copies may be reproduced at the rate of 4,500 to 6,000 an hour. In preparing the master it is important to make corrections carefully with Snopake correction fluid or with correction tape because a poor correction will show on the reproduction. A carbon type-writer ribbon should be used; or if a fabric ribbon is used, it should be new and bright. The maximum size of the original master may be $17'' \times 22''$ with the maximum finished size $11'' \times 17''$. Usually the original can be enlarged up to 10 percent or reduced by 50 percent.

Photostats are exact photographic reproductions of the original document. They may be the same size as the original, smaller, or larger. Either a negative photostat (white on black background) or a positive photostat (black on white background) may be obtained. This method is used only when an exact copy of an original document is needed; for example, for legal or tax purposes. If more than one copy is required, the first copy will be a photostat negative and the other copies will be made up as positives. Photostat negatives should be saved for reuse, if additional copies might be required, as this is a relatively expensive process. Use for up to five copies is considered economical. If more than five are necessary, another type of reproduction should be considered.

Microfilm is a process by which documents may be photographed in reduced size on 16-mm or 35-mm film. Usually the use of microfilm is confined to corporate records of such importance that destruction would prove a hardship on the company. However, the use of microfilming to conserve filing space is increasing rapidly, as explained in the records management section of this chapter.

Combination Copier/Duplicators.   Plain paper copying machines that combine the convenience features of a copier with the productivity of a duplicator are on the market. For instance, the IBM Series III Copier/Duplicators, Model 10 and Model 20, feature an advanced document feed, completely automatic duplexing, and a rated speed of 4,500 copies per hour. In addition, the Model 20 offers reduction capability. One or two 20-bin collator modules are optional with both models. Both Series III models produce high-quality copies of line documents, solids and half-tones (photographs), low-contrast originals, drawings, and bound volumes. The automatic duplexing system makes it possible to copy on both sides of either letter- or legal-size sheets simply by pushing a button. The Model 20 features two reduction modes— 26 or 35 percent—and will accept an original of up to $12'' \times 17''$. A 26 percent reduction reduces an $11'' \times 14''$ computer printout to $8.5'' \times 11''$. The 35 percent reduction mode reduces a $12'' \times 17''$ document to $8.5'' \times 11''$. Or, two $8.5'' \times 11''$ originals could be copied side by side onto a single $8.5'' \times 11''$ sheet. Convenience features for both machines include letter- or legal-size copies at the touch of a button, easy paper changing and misfeed clearing procedures, a push button 1-to-999-copy quantity selector that returns automatically to one, large top cover work space, and a 400-copy exit tray. Each bin of the optional collator holds up to 100 sheets. Copies made on one or both sides of a sheet can be collated.

Auxiliary Equipment for Reprographic Work.   An *electric paper drill* can drill slits or holes either one-quarter inch or three-eighths inch in diameter. It usually accommodates any size paper and up to 500 sheets at one time.

An *electric collator* accommodates paper up to $8\frac{1}{2}'' \times 14''$. Approximately 20 pages can be collated at one time.

An *electric stapler* will staple up to 32 pages at one time.

A *paper cutter* may be purchased that accommodates paper up to 19 inches and can cut 500 sheets at one time.

A *padding machine* provides for the application of padding compound, which is an adhesive substance similar to that on scratch pads. It can accommodate up to $8\frac{1}{2}'' \times 11''$ paper.

A *binding machine* is useful, such as the kind that makes tubular plastic bindings one-quarter inch to one inch in diameter for $8\frac{1}{2}'' \times 11''$ paper.

An *electric folding machine* can fold a packet containing up to three or more pages. Paper $8\frac{1}{2}'' \times 14''$ can usually be accommodated and the following folds made: (1) single, (2) parallel, (3) double parallel, (4) accordion, (5) french (6) horizontal, and (7) double vertical.

Addressing machines make it possible to address envelopes rapidly for an active mailing list that is used periodically. The least expensive process appears to be the machine that uses stencil address plates. These stencil plates can be prepared by the typewriter on special fiber stencil masters designed for the addressing machine. The Addressograph machine uses metal plates prepared on a Graphotype, which embosses the names, addresses, dates, and any other needed information on the plates. These can also be notched or tabbed so that the Addressograph will select or reject plates automatically according to a predetermined pattern.

Magnetic tape and magnetic card word processing machines also have the capability of preparing envelopes from stored address lists. (See Sections 5.1 and 5.11.)

The *VariTyper 1010,* with the usual media typewriter keyboard plus additional characters, prepares copy for reproduction by the offset process. The type is removable, thus making it possible to use different sets of keys in various type styles and sizes on the same page. Type sizes vary from the small 6-point type to 16-point type; approximately 400 styles are available. The VariTyper makes it possible to vary spacing between lines and letters. The right-hand margin of copy can be justified or made even. Statistical material may be condensed into a small space by the use of very small type. All strokes of the keys are uniform, which guarantees sharp master copies resembling printing. The machine is especially useful in preparing newspapers; catalogs; small booklets, such as employee handbooks; financial reports; sales literature; office forms; charts; and spec sheets.

The *Justowriter,* used to prepare material for offset or stencil duplicating, turns out even right margin copy. Two units, a recorder and a reproducer, are needed. As the copy is typed on the recorder, a punched paper tape is produced plus a visible copy for proofreading. Corrections may be made on the tape. The tape is inserted in the reproducer, which automatically types the justified copy at 100 words a minute on stencils, offset plates, or special paper for transfer by photographic processes.

12.3   TELECOMMUNICATION SYSTEMS

In a way, the organization's nervous system is its communication network. This includes its telephone and telegraph facilities. The administrator and the secretary are deeply involved in these systems not only because they use them, but also because they often have to decide, among the many alternatives available, which systems should be employed and in what manner. These vital links in the successful functioning of a company connect the home office with suppliers, customers, salesmen, branch offices, and the like. The office manager, therefore, should be aware of the types of available equipment and their advantages for the most efficient transfer of information between these groups. For helpful information on the telephone, see Section 1.3.

Special Telephone Services.   Besides the regular service whereby a company is assigned a single telephone number, there are other special telephone hookups for small and large companies.

Centrex.   In many companies where the PBX switchboard is overloaded, it has been found to be more economical to install Centrex than to enlarge the switchboard. Through the use of Centrex, every person requiring out-side service is assigned an individual telephone number from the city ex-change. By dialing this number, an outside caller is connected to the inside party without the delay of going through an operator. One makes out-going local and long-distance calls by simply dialing the desired number. In fact, only the calls to the listed company number go through the switch-board attendant. If the phone is manipulated correctly, one can have outside calls transferred quickly and easily by slowly depressing the cradle button all the way down once only to get a dial tone. Then the four digits of the station to which the call is being transferred are dialed. If the station number is not known, the call may be transferred to a company information four-digit number. One may also have a call transferred to a company building or unit serviced by a manual board by dialing "0" after receiving the dial tone. The call is then transferred manually within the company. As long as a call remains in the Centrex system, there is no limit to the number of times it may be transferred. One makes intercom calls by simply dialing a three- or four-digit number. Conference, consultation, and other automatic dial services are available.

A Centrex feature is individual number billing for long-distance calls. The telephone company keeps an itemized statement that identifies and lists every long-distance call by the individual telephone number. Thus your com-pany knows exactly what department or person to charge for the call.

Wide Area Telecommunications Service (WATS). WATS is a telephone service offered to companies having a high volume of station-to-station long-distance or toll calls. Only calls originated by the company use the WATS lines. Interstate (within the United States and including Alaska and Hawaii) service is offered.

Interstate WATS users have a choice of two types of service, Full Business Day and Measured Time.

1. Full Business Day service enables the user to make an unlimited num-ber of calls to all telephones within a designated calling area for a flat monthly charge.

2. Measured Time service enables the user to make calls totaling ten hours of conversation per month to a chosen service area. If this usage time is exceeded, a fixed charge is assessed for each additional hour or major fraction of an hour.

A WATS user may subscribe to any of five calling areas or terminating zones across the United States. These zones are usually numbered consecu-tively from 1 through 5. Subscription to a higher-numbered zone includes service to all lower-numbered zones; for example, service to Zone 4 includes service to Zones 1, 2, and 3, as well. Assistance calls and calls to nondialable points are placed on a station basis by dialing "Operator" over a WATS line.

Because WATS service is offered only on a station-to-station basis, the operator will turn back all person-to-person, collect, and special instruction calls (e.g., bill to a third number, credit card, requests for time and charges, notify at a specific time). If a nondialable number has been placed with the operator and a busy, no answer, or out-of-order condition exists, the customer will be requested to place the call later. The operator is not able to call back on a WATS service line.

Inward WATS is available through the "800" area code whereby shoppers and buyers can call from any place in the United States.

Telephone Equipment. The telephone equipment manufacturers are continually improving their equipment. Your local telephone company representative will gladly demonstrate the latest models and will advise you on how to combine certain pieces in order to get the most efficient and economical system for your office or company. Some of the most useful and efficient pieces of equipment are described here.

Operator-Controlled PBX. The PBX system has been popular for many years because it provides control over all outgoing, incoming, and intercom calls. Calls are completed quickly with easy-to-handle push buttons. A minimum of training is needed for efficient operation. The equipment allows for conference tie-lines, selected station night services, connection to the company paging system, WATS lines, dial dictation, toll restriction, conference trunks, and other communication features. Many sizes of advanced communication systems are available that use attractive, cordless consoles with push-button call-handling in gracefully styled desk-top units. The accompanying cabinet that accommodates 100 lines occupies less than 10 square feet of floor space and can be located anywhere in the office. A telephone systems expert will study the telecommunications needs of a company and recommend the type and size of equipment needed for a cost-saving, highly efficient package.

The Electronic Secretary. The Electronic Secretary Telephone Answering Set is a fast, money-saving way to increase the efficiency of your telephone system. It answers the phone with your announcement message and then receives up to two hours of incoming messages with excellent fidelity. The announcement can be changed at any time. The machine may be used during the day to take customers' orders and, with a change of the announcement, to record out-of-town salesmen's reports in the evening.

Speakerphone. The Speakerphone frees both hands during a conversation. You may look up a file, check a blueprint, even write an order while you carry on a conversation with the called person. It is also usable during a conference if you need to call for additional information or have a question answered. The entire group in your office can listen and talk. It is also a private phone when the attached handset is used.

Portable Conference Telephone. A portable push-button conference telephone, weighing less than 20 pounds, may be plugged into regular telephone lines when two-way communication is desired between a distant speaker and a group. The device amplifies the voice of the speaker so that it can be clearly heard by the audience. Members of the audience can speak directly to the person, to ask or answer questions, exchange views, and develop meaningful interaction. It can be connected to a public address system for larger audiences. Stored information resources and computer programs providing voice answerback may be provided over the nationwide telephone network by an optional Touch-Tone phone that plugs into the rear of the unit.

Automatic Call Distributor. An efficient way to handle a high volume of incoming calls is to install the automatic call distributor, a high-performance high-capacity, flexible-response system. It can accommodate a maximum of 68 trunks (central office, associated PBX, WATS, Foreign Exchange, tie lines) plus intercom, transfer, overflow, and night-service trunks. Incoming calls are automatically distributed to attendants in the order of their arrival. When all attendants' positions are "busy," calls are stored and released individually to attendants as they become available to take calls. The system is designed to produce the most effective use of the answering force and thus to control associated administrative costs.

Card Dialer Telephone. The Card Dialer Telephone quickly, effortlessly, and automatically dials calls for you. Cards for frequently dialed numbers (maximum 40) are filed alphabetically right in the telephone. Additional cards may be coded and kept ready for use for such tasks as periodic calls at the end of the month or calls to groups of persons, such as salesmen. The machine is so flexible that it may be used for all kinds of calls—local, long distance, and intercom. You may add new numbers easily by merely punching the desired number on a new card with the point of a pencil or a ball-point pen.

Magicall *Electronic Dialer.* The *Magicall* Electronic Dialer is a compact desk-top companion to any telephone. It automatically dials up to 400 numbers with a standard tape cartridge or 1,000 with a special tape. You can record numbers quickly and accurately by writing or typing the names on tape and recording the numbers with the dial-in unit. Erase old numbers simply by dialing in new ones. Local, long-distance, and intercom calls— including access, area, and special codes—can be placed automatically. It is usable with any dial-telephone equipment. Such a machine saves time by eliminating a search for numbers, by cutting calling time, and by completing all calls quickly and accurately.

Electrowriter. The Electrowriter Communication System transmits handwritten messages or sketches to any number of receiving stations—over any distance (50 yards, 5 miles, 5,000 miles). Messages are transmitted the instant you write them, exactly as you write them. Printed Electrowriter forms may be used to get specific needed information. The unit is powered by ordinary electrical outlets and operates over private wire, leased or company owned, as well as over regular local and long-distance telephone networks. An

Electrowriter installed with a Data-Phone allows you to write and to receive any message, sketch, or graphic information and alternately talk as you write and receive. In addition, the flexibility of the Data-Phone permits you to call any third party to verify information.

Data-Phone.   Besides providing direct communications between telewriting and facsimile business machines, the Data-Phone makes possible direct computer-to-computer operation. It accepts data signals from business machines that use punched cards, paper tape, or magnetic tape. Data-Phone service is provided on regular telephone lines for local or long-distance data communications at normal telephone rates, and operates in the same manner on private line service or WATS service at a fixed monthly charge. It offers automatic answering and appropriate terminating controls for unattended receiving stations. This tie-up with your computer offers an economical means of expanding data communications between the production plant and company headquarters, the warehouse and the distributing outlets, the regional sales offices and headquarters, and the purchasing department and production.

Dataspeed. The Bell System Dataspeed service is designed to meet the need for communicating information at high speed, high volume, and low cost. Information collected on paper tape by any of the coding schemes can be transmitted by Dataspeed equipment. A five-thousand-word message can be sent via the regular telephone network with accuracy and reliability in approximately five minutes. Transmission can be one-way or two-way at the same time over regular telephone lines (Data-Phone Service) or private line service. Units can be left unattended for automatic transmission. They can send and receive information at prearranged times, often at low-cost after-hours rates. Voice communications are usually an integral part of the service to allow voice contact with other stations and to check on transmissions.

Tie Line Service.   A direct and private telephone line connecting two locations. The locations can be across town or across the country. Tie Line provides two-way service between any type of telephone equipment—dial systems, PBX switchboard—for unlimited calling at a fixed monthly rate. It allows fast, direct business communications between the head office and any of its departments, such as the production plant, warehouse, sales office, and engineering.

Call Director.   The Call Director is a key phone for larger offices. It provides up to 29 outside lines with a hold feature. Employees may answer and hold calls at the push of a button. They can pick up calls on other lines, transfer calls, and dial other phones in the key system. A pre-set conference service may be added to the Call Director that allows groups of up to six pre-selected telephones to be called simultaneously by the dialing of an intercom code or by the push of a button. An add-on feature makes it possible to add another person (associated with your dial intercom) to an outside call.

Telephone Economies. In the constant vigil to cut overhead costs, the office administrator needs to establish control over the placing of local and long distance calls, determine the most economical equipment to install, and investigate ways to maximize use of telephone equipment. Consider these ways of significantly reducing telephone costs:

Limit Personal and Nonbusiness Calls. Management should issue guidelines to employees stating company policies regulating the use of the company telecommunication system for personal and nonbusiness calls. These policies will be readily accepted if presented to new employees when hired. They are more difficult to apply if employees over a long period of time have considered the free use of company phones a perquisite of their job.

Install Restrictors on Telephone Equipment. The telephone company has several devices that will control the indiscriminate use of company phones. The Call Controller is a simple restrictor for Key Telephone or PBX services. It controls calls to specific calling areas. One Call Controller will work with up to 20 telephone lines and is capable of prohibiting calls to any combination of 800 possible three-digit prefix or area codes. The first three digits dialed are compared to the specified codes; then the call is allowed or disallowed.

The Call Restrictor Phonemaster 1040 is a solid state toll and message unit restriction system. It restricts calls to specific area codes, prefixes within your area code, and, with six-digit programming, prefixes within other area codes. The service provides effective control of direct dialed calls over specified lines or trunks including local, WATS, Tie Lines, and foreign exchange.

Through One-Number Dialing, an optional feature on single- and multi-line rotary and TOUCH-TONE phones automatically dials any programmed number of up to 14 digits. For a company using private lines, the feature offers the opportunity to cut costs through the alternative of automatic point-to-point connection over the regular telephone network. Single-line phones may provide one-number dialing at the touch of an auxiliary pushbutton. These phones may also be used to dial other numbers in the regular way. However, where desired, single-line dial-less phones may be programmed to dial only one telephone number automatically when the handset is lifted. This feature effectively protects such phones against unauthorized use.

Multi-line pushbutton phones may be programmed to dial several different numbers. One remotely located one-number dialing module is required for each programmed number. Each phone may have precisely the ideal mix of programmed numbers that it needs to function most efficiently as part of your voice-and-data communication system, whether for dialing frequently called numbers or transmitting terminal identification to a computer, or both. One non-locking pushbutton is provided for automated dialing of each number.

Use Pay Phones. With pay phones available in the lobby, reception area, certain factory areas, or the cafeteria, both employees and visitors can be directed to them for personal calls.

Add Timing Devices.   A device can be added to telephones that will indicate to the user by an audio sound that a certain time period has elapsed. This aid is especially helpful when making message-unit and long distance calls. For instance, a signal indicating that there is one minute to go on a minimum three-minute call will motivate the caller to wind up the conversation immediately, if possible.

Arrange for Locked Phones and Night Lines.   A special lock for dial phones can be attached to prevent the making of outgoing calls (incoming calls can still be received). Companies use these locks at night, over the weekend, and at other times when an office is unoccupied. For phones with up to six buttons, a bar attachment is available to lock down the two hangup buttons under the receiver. Both locks can be purchased at stationery or hardware stores.

To lock phones with more than six buttons, it is possible to install a switch inside a desk or cabinet to disconnect as many lines as wanted. The desk or cabinet can then be locked overnight. Some phones can be unplugged and stored in locked cabinets.

PBX night lines should be carefully selected by location and number of open lines and made available only to authorized personnel after office hours. A marketing consultant from the phone company will explain ways to set up night lines for the company's PBX equipment. Fixed Night Transfer, Flexible Night Transfer, and Trunk Answer from Any Station are three ways of handling incoming and outgoing calls. Together with phone restrictors, one of these options will provide the most economical service.

Contract for Automatic Logging of Telephone Calls.   Automatic message accounting systems may be used to record outgoing calls on magnetic tape by Centrex or extension numbers in order to obtain cost summary information. Calls may be identified by origin and destination and summarized by state, area code, WATS zone, and foreign exchange area. With such information, a company can identify actual call expense, make efficient use of toll and message unit calling, design or modify networks, evaluate alternative services, pinpoint misuse, and justify usage control systems. For further information, contact Account-A-Call Corporation, 4450 Lakeside Drive, Burbank, California 91505, (213) 846-3340. Account-A-Call, a large telecommunications service bureau, offers advanced data processing concepts in telephone usage management.

Telegraph Service: Domestic.   Before sending a message by telegraph, you should consider carefully the alternative ways to get a message to the receiver as quickly as possible at the least cost (Figure 12-7). A letter is definitely cheaper than a telegram and allows the sender to include a great deal more

---

Be Brief—Avoid "Rush" Teletype Service—Use the Mails

Eliminate wordiness; use simple, clear language and construction in the message.

Check time difference at destination.

Use mail service when time permits.

Deliver teletype messages to company communication center early in day to avoid overloads in late afternoon.

Use "night letter" service on telegrams or mailgrams whenever possible.

Use standard teletype punctuation marks only—the period, slash, and dash.

Figure 12-7   Ways to cut telegram and teletype expense.

information. Will the time saved compensate for the extra cost of a telegram? Or will a telegram actually save time? If you are sending a message late Friday afternoon, it will not be delivered until the next business day— Monday morning. A letter posted Friday afternoon should arrive at most destinations on Monday also. Another question to ask yourself is "Would a telephone call be more economical?" A message that calls for an immediate answer might be cheaper if transmitted as one long-distance call than if two telegrams were exchanged. Besides saving money, the telephone call would save time.

To assure economy, companies having a large volume of wire messages assign one person or an office service department the task of determining the type of service to be used when sending wire messages. Thus, the burden of choosing the most economical use of wire services is removed from the originator. The explanation of domestic and international wire services that follows will aid in setting up efficient practices for these special messages.

Classes of Service.   Through the use of domestic telegraph service, Western Union, you can connect with all points served by wire in the continental United States, Mexico, Canada, Alaska, and Saint Pierre–Miquelon islands. It is possible to send two classes of telegrams, which differ in speed and cost. No charge is made for the first address and the signature, which may include the company name and the code. The message can be telephoned to the nearest Western Union office and the charges billed by the telephone company. Telegrams may also be transmitted from a business office over its teletype equipment.

Telegram. The telegram is the fastest and most expensive service available on a cost-per-word basis. A minimum flat rate is charged for the first 15 words or less, and you are charged extra for each word over 15.

Night letter. The night letter is the least expensive service, transmitted to its destination during the night and delivered in the morning of the next business day (no deliveries on Saturday or Sunday). A night letter may be filed with the telegraph office until 2 a.m. An extra charge is made for each group of five or less words over the minimum 50 words.

Special Telegraph Services.   In addition to the two basic services mentioned, the telegraph company provides a variety of other useful communication aids.

1. Telegraphic money orders. These may be used to transmit money, delivered to the Western Union office, to any point in the United States. Two classes of service are available—the fast or full-rate telegram service, which is the more expensive, and the night letter service. Supplementary messages, either business or personal, may be included with the money order at the additional word rates, except that in an overnight money order no charge is made for the first ten words. The fee is determined by the distance and the amount of money being transferred.

The telegraph office provides a special form for telegraphic money orders. Besides including the name and address of the person who is to receive the money, you may indicate whether or not you waive identification when the recipient calls for the money. The usual practice is to ask for identification before relinquishing money.

2. Errand service. Business errands may be handled by telegraph company messengers, who will pick up and deliver documents, blueprints, press releases, and any envelope or package. A messenger will call for personal articles at the home, office, cleaners, drugstore, gift shop, and so on, and deliver them to a designated address. Gifts, such as flowers and candy, may be ordered and delivered through Western Union. Errand service is available in most large cities on either a trip or an hourly basis.

3. Mailgram service. Western Union's computerized network speeds letters electronically to distant post offices. If the copy arrives at the receiving post office before 7 p.m., mailgrams are delivered the next business day in distinctively designed envelopes to any address in 50 states. One text may be sent to hundreds of addresses. The messages may be transmitted over a company's Telex or TWX teleprinter between 8 a.m. and 11 p.m. EST Monday through Friday. Mailgrams may also be sent by INFOCOM, Tie Line, Telephone, and at Western Union offices. They provide (1) the impact of a telegram at much lower cost, (2) a copy for the files, and (3) the opportunity to send a minimum message of almost 100 words.

By using the company computer for input, it is possible to take advantage of the Computer Originated Mailgram service that offers unlimited ways to deliver high-impact messages for credit and collection, new product and service announcements, market surveys, sales leads, and more. (See page 449.)

Factors to Be Considered.   In choosing the class of domestic telegram to send, consider the factors of time, number of words, and cost.

Time. The four time zones in the United States—Eastern, Central, Mountain, and Pacific—are each separated by a one-hour time differential. If you are in New York City at twelve o'clock noon, the time in each of the zones is as follows.

Eastern Time	Noon
Central Time	11:00 a.m.
Mountain Time	10:00 a.m.
Pacific Time	9:00 a.m.

In other words, if you start at New York City and move west, the time is one hour earlier in Chicago, two hours earlier in Denver, and three hours earlier in Los Angeles. Or if you start at Los Angeles and move east, the time is one hour later in Denver, two hours later in Chicago, and three hours later in New York City. (See Figure 12-8 for a map of United States showing the time zones.)

Daylight Saving Time, as set forth in the Federal Uniform Time Act of 1967, is observed by all states, except Kentucky and Alaska, which have temporary exclusion, and Hawaii. By this plan clocks are set ahead one hour on the last Sunday in April and set back one hour on the last Sunday in October.

Number of words. A clear message using the least number of words should be written. Because a telegram is expensive if many words are used, you may have to sacrifice speed for economy in a long message and consider the use of a night letter or mailgram. When attempting to be as concise as possible, remember that common words not essential to the meaning may be omitted, for example, *I, we, the, a,* and *to.* The following message contains many unnecessary words.

AM ATTENDING AMERICAN MANAGEMENT ASSOCIATION CONFERENCE UNTIL FRIDAY STOP WILL BE BACK IN THE OFFICE ON TUESDAY STOP PLEASE SET UP COMMITTEE MEETING WITH TAYLOR AND JONES FOR TEN A.M. STOP   (Total words: 31)

Now read the same message, which has been rewritten within the 15-word limit without any loss of meaning:

ATTENDING AMA CONFERENCE. RETURN TUESDAY FOR TEN A.M. MEETING WITH TAYLOR AND JONES. PLEASE ARRANGE
                                             (Total words: 15)

Nouns, verbs, and adjectives are the important words in a message. Standard punctuation—period, comma, quotation marks, parentheses, hyphen—may be used without charge. Domestic wire messages should be punctuated. *Stop* is no longer necessary and a charge is made for it, if used.

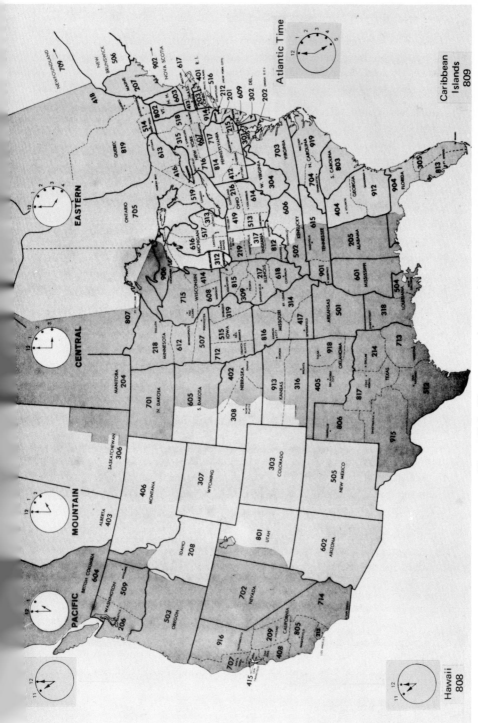

Figure 12-8 Time zone and area code map.

437

Cost. The cost of a telegram may be determined with the aid of a rate chart supplied by Western Union. Clarification of the following points, however, is needed for an accurate estimate.

1. Addresses. No charge is made for essential material in the address. "Personal" and "Will Call" are free notations. You will be charged for additional or alternate names or addresses.

2. Signature and address of sender. No charge is made for the name of the sender and the city and state (included in the date line). The company name may accompany the name of the sender, but the department and title are charged for, if included. The telegraph company also charges for the sender's street address.

3. Word count. In general, each dictionary word up to and including fifteen characters counts as one word. Words of more than fifteen characters or combinations of dictionary words are divided and counted as two or more words. Hyphenated words are counted as one word for each part, unless the compound word is hyphenated in the dictionary. Words must be used in the same sense as conveyed by the definition in a standard dictionary.

The names of states, counties, and cities are counted according to the number of words they contain. For example, Las Vegas is two words; New York City is three. Running the names together as in *Newyorkcity* will not affect the count; it is still three words. Abbreviated city names, such as LA, NYC, and KC, count as one word.

Some abbreviations are permissible. Be sure before abbreviating that the result will be understandable. Do not abbreviate unless the length of the word is such that a shortening of the word count will result.

EXAMPLES: parts catalog . . . . 2 words
parts cat . . . . 2 words
District of Columbia . . . . 3 words
D.C. . . . . 1 word
Certified Public Accountant . . . . 3 words
CPA . . . . 1 word

Common combinations of abbreviations are permissible and are counted as five characters to a word. Arbitrary misuse of abbreviations and words is not permitted by the telegraph company.

EXAMPLES: National Association of Manufacturers . . 4 words
NAM . . . . 1 word
Retel . . . . 1 word (5 characters)
Reurtel . . . . 2 words (7 characters)
Federal Bureau of Investigation . . . . 4 words
FBI . . . . 1 word

Proper names are counted as they are normally written: Van de Kamp is three words.

A group of five figures or a combination of not more than five figures and letters will count as one word. Any more than five characters will add to the word count. Code numbers containing all figures or figures and letters may be hyphenated, because the hyphen is considered a mark of punctuation.

EXAMPLES:
72192	1 word (5 characters)
T5437	1 word (5 characters)
F-376-2	1 word (5 characters)
AN-904	1 word (5 characters)
P-129875	2 words (7 characters)

The diagonal (/) or slash mark with figures or letters is counted as one character.

EXAMPLES:
T/5437	2 words (6 characters)
1/2	1 word (3 characters)
one-half	2 words
B/L	1 word (3 characters)
bill of lading	3 words

The decimal point in figures is not counted, but the dollar sign ($) or the English pound sterling sign (£) counts as one character.

EXAMPLES:
$22.50	1 word (5 characters)
$220.50	2 words (6 characters)
£118.50	2 words (6 characters)

The percent sign (%) is transmitted as 0/0 and counts as one word in the United States, Alaska, and Mexico and as three words in Canada and Saint Pierre–Miquelon islands. The symbol @ is not transmitted by wire; therefore, "at" should be used. The signs for pound, number, feet, inches, and minute are charged for as words. In a message to Canada or Saint Pierre–Miquelon islands, each figure or "other character" is counted as one word.

Instructions for Typing Domestic Telegrams.   Telegraph blanks are provided free by Western Union. Regular office stationery may also be used (Figure 12-9).

1. Decide on the number of copies to make. Four copies of a telegraphic message are usual—the original for pickup by the messenger, a copy sent by mail to the recipient for confirmation purposes, a general file copy, and a copy for the telegraph account file for bookkeeping purposes.

Mail the confirmation copy immediately in case the addressee fails to receive the telegram and to ensure that he has an exact copy of the message for his records.

2. Double-space the message and triple-space between paragraphs. Paragraphs may or may not be indented, as desired.

3. Type in caps and lower case, allowing at least one-inch margins. Use caps for code words.

4. Type *Domestic Service* or *International Service* and the class of service *(Telegram, Night Letter, Mailgram)* at the left margin two spaces above the address. Single-space the address; be sure to use a street number and not a post office box. Addresses must be complete and accurate.

```
Domestic Service - Mailgram                          Charge: OMC 95

Report Delivery
Mr. James A. Webster
United Shippers
Pier 105B
New York, New York 10068           April 15, 19--   9:35 a.m.

Shipment 10578 of 86 two-by-three foot wooden boxes lost in tran-

sit. Tracer initiated. Word of whereabouts expected in 12 hours.

Request you hold space on African Star bound for Nigeria on

April 18. When shipment located will telegraph day and hour it

will reach docks.

                                        H. T. Snyder

Oklahoma Manufacturing Co.
143 Factory Road
Oklahoma City, Oklahoma 73105

mt
```

Figure 12-9   Sample of typewritten telegram on company stationery.

5. Type the date and hour at the right margin on the same line as city and state or on the appropriate line provided in a telegram blank.

6. Never divide a word at the end of a line.

7. Indicate in the appropriate space on the blank either *Paid* or *Collect*. If the telegram is to be charged, type the name of the charge account in the space provided on the blank.

8. Type the address and phone number of the sender in the lower left-hand corner of the blank. The reference initials may be placed one space below.

9. To indicate that an answer is requested, type *AR* in the space provided for payment information.

10. To confirm delivery, type the words *Report Delivery* for which you will be charged as part of the address. A collect telegram will be sent to your company indicating when and to whom the telegram was delivered.

11. To send the same message to a number of people, list the names and addresses on the special Western Union form for this purpose or type them on a separate sheet of paper. Usually, as many as four addressees may be typed in two columns on a telegraph form.

Telegraph Service: International.   Messages to foreign countries are sent over cable or radio facilities. Basic procedures are similar to those for sending telegrams. You may file cablegrams and radiograms with your local Western

Union office. Or you may file directly via your teletype equipment or make a long-distance call to New York, San Francisco, or Washington, D.C., with ITT World Communications, RCA Communications, or Western Union International. To place a cable with Tropical Radio (TRT) for Bermuda or other points in the Caribbean, you may contact their offices in Miami or Fort Lauderdale. Because the four international carriers are not linked to the same cities overseas, it is helpful to check the routing chart *Pocket Guide to International Telecommunication,* distributed free of charge by ITT World Communications, for the most direct route.

Your cablegram will reach its destination faster if you indicate to Western Union the desired route. For instance, simply type *VIA WUI* after the destination in the address, if you find that Western Union International has a link to the city to which you are sending a message. If you do not indicate a routing, the domestic telegraph company cannot do it for you. Instead the message must go to a *pool* from which it is distributed to a carrier without regard to the most direct routing.

Classes of Service. Two classes of international telegraph service are provided.

1. *Full rate cablegram (FR)* is the fastest service for international use. The distance traveled determines the rate per word. The FR charge per word from all points in the United States ranges from 21 cents for a cable to the Hawaiian Islands to 34 cents for one to Taiwan. A minimum charge is assessed for seven words. Any message wholly or partly in code must be sent FR.

2. *Letter cable (LT)* is an overnight service for longer messages. The minimum charge is for 22 words. An extra charge is made for each additional word. It would be delivered after eight o'clock local time on the morning after the date of filing. An LT telegram after midnight would be delivered the morning of the next calendar day, at least 32 hours later. An LT message sent from the Western Hemisphere to the Southwest Pacific and Far East might be delayed as long as two days because of the time differential.

Factors to Be Considered. As with domestic telegrams, international telegraph services are used more efficiently when one considers the time differences around the world and the cost per word. Of importance also is the need to specify delivery and handling instructions.

Time. Consider the time difference between the city of origin and the destination to decide whether a fast cable is justified. A message reaching its destination after 10 p.m. will not be delivered until the following morning unless special delivery is requested. Request night delivery by inserting the word *NUIT* before the name of the addressee. The ITT international time chart that follows will help you determine the approximate time at the destination of the cable. When using this chart, remember that it is based on Eastern Standard Time and that in crossing the International Dateline, your computation may take you into yesterday and tomorrow. Each new day starts at the International Dateline in the Pacific Ocean, and moves west across Auckland, Wake Island, Tokyo, Saigon, Moscow, Accra, London, Rio de Janeiro, New York, Lima, San Francisco, and Honolulu. Here is an example of how to use the chart

At 10 a.m. in your office in Denver, you decide to cable Geneva, Switzerland. Because you are in the Mountain Time Zone, the time in New York (Eastern Time) is twelve noon. Opposite Switzerland on the chart you see + 6, which means to add six hours to Eastern Standard Time. At 10 a.m. in Denver, the time is 6 p.m. in Geneva. A fast cable is transmitted in approximately one hour; therefore, your message would arrive about 7 p.m. It is doubtful that the office in Switzerland would still be open; therefore, a cable letter would be the more economical service to use.

To determine STANDARD TIME overseas, add (+) to or subtract (−) from EASTERN STANDARD TIME as indicated:

Afghanistan	+ 9½	France	+ 6	Pakistan	+ 10
Albania	+ 6	Germany	+ 6	Panama	0
Algeria	+ 6	Ghana	+ 5	Paraguay	+ 1
Argentina	+ 2	Great Britain	+ 5	Peru	0
Aruba	+ ½	Greece	+ 7	Philippines	+ 13
Australia	+ 15	Guatemala	− 1	Poland	+ 6
Austria	+ 6	Haiti	0	Portugal	+ 5
Azores	+ 3	Hawaii	− 5	Puerto Rico	+ 1
Belgium	+ 6	Hungary	+ 6	Rhodesia	+ 7
Bermuda	+ 1	Iceland	+ 4	Romania	+ 7
Bolivia	+ 1	India	+ 10½	Salvador, El	− 1
Borneo	+ 13	Indonesia	+ 12½	Saudi Arabia	+ 8
Brazil	+ 2	Iran	+ 8½	Singapore	+ 12½
Bulgaria	+ 7	Iraq	+ 8	So. Africa, Rep. of	+ 7
Burma	+ 11½	Ireland	+ 5	Spain	+ 6
Canal Zone	0	Israel	+ 7	Sri Lanka	+ 10½
Chile	+ 1	Italy	+ 6	Surinam	+ 1½
China	+ 13	Japan	+ 14	Sweden	+ 6
Colombia	0	Korea	+ 13½	Switzerland	+ 6
Congo	+ 6	Lebanon	+ 7	Syria	+ 7
Costa Rica	− 1	Luxembourg	+ 6	Taiwan	+ 13
Cuba	0	Madagascar	+ 8	Thailand	+ 12
Curaçao	+ ½	Malaya	+ 12½	Tunisia	+ 6
Czechoslovakia	+ 6	Morocco	+ 5	Turkey	+ 7
Denmark	+ 6	Netherlands	+ 6	USSR	+ 8
Dominican Rep.	0	Neth. Antilles	+ ½	Uruguay	+ 2
Ecuador	0	Newfoundland	+ 1½	Venezuela	+ ½
Egypt	+ 7	New Zealand	+ 17	Vietnam	+ 12
Ethiopia	+ 8	Nicaragua	− 1	Virgin Islands	+ 1
Finland	+ 7	Norway	+ 6	Yugoslavia	+ 6

Other time factors must be considered, too. For instance, office hours move with the day and follow individual local patterns. Holidays vary from country to country. Almost every day is a holiday somewhere on earth. Midday closing in some cities may mean that afternoon office hours extend to 7 p.m., or offices may open at 7 a.m. and close for the day in the early afternoon. Working days do not coincide all around the world. As the day advances, weekends start and stop at different times; on Friday morning in New York the weekend has already begun in Manila. All weekends do not necessarily fall on Saturday and Sunday; the business week in Saudi Arabia and Egypt, for example, runs Saturday through Thursday. A telegram sent late Friday from Honolulu to Jidda could be acted upon within a few hours, whereas one sent the next day in the opposite direction could not. Telegraph offices themselves observe varying work weeks and business hours around the world, both for message delivery service and for the actual operation of the circuits. Major communication distribution points like Buenos Aires, London, New York, or Vienna operate seven days a week, 24 hours a day, but in smaller stations this is not so. If you are cabling Arica, Chile, for example, on September 18, it will help to know that September 18 and 19 are holidays in Chile and that on holidays the Arica telegraph office closes from 1 p.m. to 4 p.m. and from 8 p.m. to 9 a.m. Similar circumstances may hold true for a provincial French town or a holiday resort in Hawaii.

Cost. Determination of the cost of a cable may be made from a rate chart furnished by any one of the international carriers. Here are a few points to remember when estimating cable charges.

(1) Every word is charged for in a cable including name, address, and signature. Therefore, all unnecessary words should be omitted. The name of the country of destination, when enclosed in parentheses, is not included in the charges, but it must be part of the address. You may use a registered code address and a code signature.

(2) Punctuation marks are not transmitted in cables unless specifically requested by the sender. When punctuation is required to retain the meaning of the text, type at the beginning of the message *count punctuation*. Punctuation marks are counted as additional words except when used in groups of figures or letters. A punctuation mark used with figures is counted as one character. To give an example, 1,575 and 16/40 are each counted as one word. The parentheses and quotation marks are counted as one word when used in pairs to enclose one or more words. Other acceptable marks counted as one word *each* are the period, comma, colon, question mark, apostrophe, dash, and diagonal. The percent sign (%) is transmitted as 0/0 (3 characters), and the ¢ sign, $ sign, and £ sign are spelled out—*cents, dollars, pounds*—and each letter is counted as one character. For example, $50 is transmitted as *dollars 50* (2 words); $98.50 and 87¢ are also two words each.

(3) Word count is based on dictionary words. Each dictionary word up to and including 15 letters is counted as one word. Words with more than 15 letters are divided and counted as one additional word for each group of 15 letters or less. The same general rules for abbreviations in other wire messages apply to cables except that charges will vary depending on the type of service (full-rate or letter cable). Well-known commercial terms or trademarks that are familiar to the general public or are published in catalogs are counted in the same manner as figures (five characters per word). Word combinations are not allowed. If used they will be divided and counted separately, *except* as follows.

Compound words appearing in a standard dictionary of the admitted language (WU Tariff Book 5.501).
EXAMPLE: closefisted

Names of places, squares, streets, and other public roads.
EXAMPLES: Hollywoodway   for Hollywood Way
          Losangeles   for Los Angeles
          Ruedelapaix   for Rue de la Paix

Family names.
EXAMPLE: Vandegrift   for Van de Grift

Numbers written out as words. See paragraph 4, following.

Groups of figures and letters used as reference or identifying numbers. See paragraph 4, following.

(4) A group of five figures counts as one word. Each additional five characters or less count as another word. If more than one third of the text is in figures, full rates apply unless the figures are known to be reference or identifying numbers. Under this rule of counting, combinations of letters and figures are not permitted. When such information (figures plus letters) must be transmitted, the figures must be spelled out. Figures that require 15 or less characters when spelled are counted as one word.

EXAMPLES: *AN736* will be transmitted by the carrier as *AN seven thirty-six* (four words), unless the number is spelled or instructions are given that this is a reference number. You may write *AN seventhirtysix* (two words).
              sevenhundredthirtysix (21 characters): 2 words.
              eleventhousand (14 characters): 1 word.
              11,000 (6 characters): 2 words.

The exception to this rule of counting concerns reference or identifying numbers, such as file numbers or contract numbers. These numbers will be transmitted without spelling if you identify and list them on the original copy delivered to the international carrier or Western Union.

(5) Code may be used in the FR message and is usually counted as five characters or fraction thereof to the word.

Registered code addresses for overseas companies you contact may be secured from any regional office of the four international carriers. Because charges are assessed on each word in an address on wires sent to other countries, the use of one-word code addresses saves considerable money. Examples of code addresses are *BARCLADOM* for Barclay's Bank in London, *MENARDS* for Menards Custom Tailors in Hong Kong, *ORIENTRA* for Toyo International Corporation in Yokohama, and *BANKAMERICA* for Bank of America National Trust and Savings Association in San Francisco.

A code address for your company may be secured from the local Western Union Office, who will suggest a one-word address that is significantly different from other local code addresses. The registration fee is approximately $17.50 a year or almost half that for six months. Because the code address is a point-of-destination address, you should send it to your foreign contacts for their use in sending messages to your company.

Delivery and handling instructions.   It is possible to specify exactly how you want your telegram handled. Instructions can cover details of payment, time or method of delivery, and forwarding or holding information. Operators experienced in handling international telegrams will code your verbal instructions, but domestic operators unfamiliar with international practice may not know how to forward your requests. The following coded instructions, which cost the price of one word each unless otherwise noted, will assist you in indicating exact international delivery instructions.

Specifying Place of Delivery

Instruction	Code	Example
Care of	CHEZ	JOHN SMITH CHEZ TURNER CHAMPS ELYSEES 117 PARIS FRANCE VIA ITT
Forward	FS (request of sender)	FS JOHN SMITH CHAMPS ELYSEES 117 PARIS FRANCE VIA ITT
		VIA VENETO 32 ROME ITALY VIA ITT
or	REEXPEDIE DE (request of addressee)	REEXPEDIE DE JOHN SMITH CHAMPS ELYSEES 117 PARIS FRANCE VIA ITT
		VIA VENETO 32 ROME ITALY VIA ITT
General delivery	GP	GP JOHN SMITH HELSINKI FINLAND VIA WUI
General delivery registered	GPR	GPR JOHN SMITH HELSINKI FINLAND VIA WUI
Hold for	TR	TR JOHN SMITH COPENHAGEN DENMARK VIA RCA
Personal delivery	MP	MP JOHN SMITH CUMBERLAND HOTEL LONDON ENGLAND VIA RCA
Post office box	BOITE POSTALE (2 words)	JOHN SMITH BOITE POSTALE 1098 BONN GERMANY VIA ITT

Specifying Time of Delivery

Daytime hours	JOUR	JOUR JOHN SMITH JONESMIT JOHORE MALAYSIA VIA RCA
Nighttime hours	NUIT	REMETTRE 24 DEC. NUIT
Specified date	REMETTRE (date)	JOHN SMITH HOTEL OKURA TOYKO JAPAN VIA ITT

Specifying Method of Delivery

Instruction	Code	Example
Shore/ship message (Number of days at sea-denoting when ship is to be called)	J(number)	J4 JOHN SMITH SS QUEEN ELIZABETH 2 NORTH ATLANTIC WSL VIA ITT

Specifying Method of Delivery

Instruction	Code	Example
Airmail or	PAV	PAV JOHN JONES 158 WILLIWAW SPRINGSIDE NEW SOUTH WALES
Airmail, registered	PAVR	AUSTRALIA VIA ITT
Mail	POSTE	POSTE JOHN SMITH 124 MADRID SPANISH TOWN, JAMAICA VIA TRT
Mail, registered	PR	PR JOHN SMITH 124 MADRID SPANISH TOWN, JAMAICA VIA TRT
Any method faster than mail	EXPRES (addressee pays delivery charges)	EXPRES JOHN SMITH PETITE ANSE HAITI VIA TRT
	XP (sender pays delivery charges)	XP JOHN SMITH MAMBALI TANGANYIKA VIA ITT
Telephone	TF (number)	TF PASSY 5283—JOHN SMITH PAULI PARIS VIA ITT
Telex	TLX (number)	TLX 84213465 JOHN SMITH LISBON PORTUGAL VIA RCA
Delivery confirmation	PC (sender pays for a seven-word minimum charge)	PC JOHN SMITH CALLE FLORIDA 194 BUENOS AIRES ARGENTINA VIA WUI

Specifying Rates and Other Details of Payment

Instruction	Code	Example
Full Rate	FR (No charge for the symbol. FR service provided if no indication appears.)	
Letter Rate	LT	LT JOHN SMITH 215 CALLE JUAN LUNA MANILA PHILIPPINES VIA RCA
European Letter Rate	ELT	
Press Rate Deferred Press Urgent Press	PRESSE LCPS URGENT PRESSE	} Reserved for bona fide press representatives sending messages to publishers.
Reply prepaid	RP (Amount)	RP $4.50 JOHN SMITH 116 RUE DU RHONE GENEVA SWITZERLAND VIA ITT

The difference between LT and ELT is that LT service applies to traffic outside Europe or between Europe and another point. LT messages are delivered the day after the calendar date on which they are sent. ELT, Europe-to-Europe international deferred service, may be delivered five hours or more after being sent.

Payment for cables must be arranged for in advance with one or more of the international carriers. There is no blanket arrangement for collect service on international telegrams. It is covered by transferred and credit account agreements that differ according to the countries involved. Each carrier issues credit cards and is ready to handle credit applications and to furnish a credit card directory.

Incoming Wires.   Most companies establish a policy concerning receipt and opening of incoming wires. Often the wire is delivered to the mail room where it is logged in and then taken to the addressee. At other times the wire is delivered unopened to the addressee, who is responsible for noting the time of receipt and seeing that sufficient copies are made for the files and other personnel who need to know the contents of the wire. Copies may be made on a copying machine, or if one is not available, they may be typed on a printed form such as the one in Figure 12-10.

Wires Concerning Government Information.   Security regulations prohibit the transmittal of classified information by standard wire. Special facilities are available, however, for sending coded messages by wire as explained in the *Industrial Security Manual for Safeguarding Classified Information* and the *Cryptographic Supplement* to the manual, issued by the Department of Defense. In general, the same security measures are followed as for the preparation of classified letters (see Section 3.2). The message is given a classified control number, typed on a telegraph form with the correct number of copies, labeled with the proper classification, signed by an authorized person, placed in the correct number of envelopes with an attached secret information receipt form, and delivered by the document control office to the proper communications message center. All copies and the supplies used in the preparation are safeguarded and destroyed in the same manner as for other classified material.

Unclassified teletypes and telegrams may contain either technical or administrative information. They may also contain statements of company policy, but most companies forbid the transmittal of proprietary or sensitive information by wire. Wires to federal agencies, such as NASA, the Air Force, or the Navy, use the format in Figure 12-11. The subject line in these wires may be omitted if its use will require an otherwise unclassified message to be classified or will noticeably increase the length of an otherwise brief message. A one-paragraph message need not be numbered, and where there are only one or two references, the identification may be included in the message. The wire to the Air Force in Figure 12-12 has no subject and lists the references

COMPANY NAME

Copy of

INCOMING TELEGRAM (or CABLE)

Date and Time
of Receipt: 3:34 p.m.
                  March 4, 19--

Copies to: B. B. Bias - for reply
           J. M. Sinson - for preparation
                          of quotation
           E. G. Timm - for information
           General Files

THIS FORM MAY BE USED WHEN COPYING INCOMING WIRES FOR DISTRIBUTION

UNLESS SO MANY COPIES ARE TO BE PREPARED THAT A DITTO MASTER WOULD

BE MORE PRACTICAL. IN SUCH EVENT USE DITTO MASTER IN PLACE OF

THIS FORM BUT USE SAME HEADING. THE WIRE SHOULD BE COPIED EXACTLY

AS RECEIVED WITH ALL DISTINGUISHING MARKS. IF MISTAKES ARE MADE

IN SPELLING, UNDERLINE THE ERROR.

SIGNATURE

rr (Initials of person who made the copy should be shown.)

Figure 12-10 Form used for copy of incoming wire.

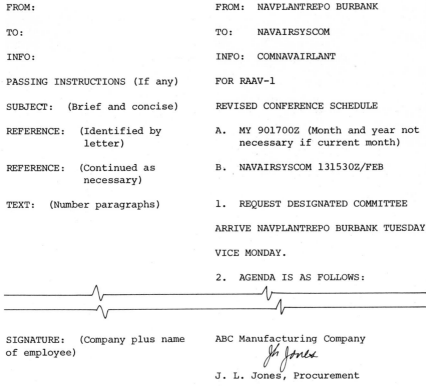

FROM:	FROM: NAVPLANTREPO BURBANK
TO:	TO: NAVAIRSYSCOM
INFO:	INFO: COMNAVAIRLANT
PASSING INSTRUCTIONS (If any)	FOR RAAV-1
SUBJECT: (Brief and concise)	REVISED CONFERENCE SCHEDULE
REFERENCE: (Identified by letter)	A. MY 901700Z (Month and year not necessary if current month)
REFERENCE: (Continued as necessary)	B. NAVAIRSYSCOM 131530Z/FEB
TEXT: (Number paragraphs)	1. REQUEST DESIGNATED COMMITTEE ARRIVE NAVPLANTREPO BURBANK TUESDAY VICE MONDAY.
	2. AGENDA IS AS FOLLOWS:

SIGNATURE: (Company plus name of employee)

ABC Manufacturing Company

Jh Jones

J. L. Jones, Procurement

Figure 12-11   Recommended format for wires to Defense and other Federal service agencies.

with the text. If you send a wire of two or more pages, it is customary to head the second and subsequent pages with the complete address (Figure 12-13).

Telex and TWX.   New automated equipment makes it possible for a company to use its Telex/TWX terminal for faster, more efficient everyday business communications. Companies with such teletypewriters should study ways to use the equipment to advantage, and those companies with a high volume of communications that do not have the equipment should investigate adding Telex/TWX teletypewriters to their offices.

Telex.   This service connects a teleprinter with any one of thousands in the United States and around the world. You pay for this direct subscriber-to-subscriber service by time and distance. At the standard international speed of 66 words per minute you can transmit more information for less money than a telegram the same length will cost. Either tape or manual transmission is available. A teleprinter in your office may connect you directly with one of the international telegraph carriers, or may connect you with

```
21 February 19--

Dept. 898

Ext. 3456

TO:  AIR FORCE PLANT REPRESENTATIVE, FORT WORTH

     IN TURN TO: AFLC PLANS OFFICE
                 DIRECTORATE OF PLANS AND PROGRAMS
                 HQ., AIR FORCE LOGISTICS COMMAND
                 WRIGHT-PATTERSON AIR FORCE BASE,
                 OHIO

                 ATTENTION: COLONEL J. JENSEN, MCFD

(Leave four blank spaces for insertion of reference
number by teletype operator.)

AFLC LETTER MCFD/AJ, AF04(647)599, DATED 18 DECEMBER

19--. REURLETTER DATED 27 JANUARY 19--. REQUESTED

REPORTS WILL BE FORWARDED ON OR BEFORE 1 MARCH 19--.

PLATT-WHITNEY, INC.

    C.C. Jones

C. C. JONES, MANAGER
CONTRACTS & PROPOSALS

aa
```

Figure 12-12   Modified format of short wire to Air Force.

TWX through a computer interface. If your office is in New York City, San Francisco, or Washington, D.C., you may subscribe to a direct Tie Line with an automatic switch to one of the international or marine traffic operations. The local representatives of the four international telegraph services will give you details.

Time and money are saved if you work your own international circuit, which delivers your message as fast as it can be typed and eliminates handling en route. Calling abroad by Telex is as convenient as calling by phone:

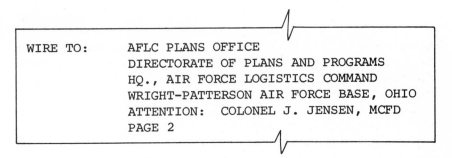

Figure 12-13   Heading of second page of wire.

you type instead of talk, read instead of listen. Unfamiliar accents and languages are less important than when you use the spoken word. Also, you have immediate written confirmation of what transpired.

Automatic operation is available through the use of prepunched tapes. Manual operation, though slower, allows you to converse in writing with the person at the other end of the circuit. To determine whether to use the manual mode, you must balance the value of immediate conversational contact with the possibility of slower speeds, unused circuit time, and a higher cost per word. Telex conversations are possible only when both ends of the circuit are manned, which limits their usefulness to coincidental office hours or to prearrangements. Calls to a public Telex booth must be prearranged. Manual installations are available within the United States for an annual minimum billing. Both national and international installations will receive on an unattended basis so long as the teleprinter is plugged in and there is plenty of paper on the roll.

The international carriers—ITT World Communications, Inc., RCA Global Communications, Inc., and Western Union International, Inc.— have communication analysts who will study your total communications needs and recommend the right service for your firm. They offer guidance in the choice of proper terminal equipment, arrange for its installation, work out the necessary agreements with the foreign administration that handles the overseas portion of the circuit, see you through inauguration of service, and remain on call thereafter.

TWX.   The code name TWX stands for the teletypewriter exchange service that permits the sending and receiving of *written* communication between two or more locations within the United States by use of telephone circuits. The teletypewriter used by the Bell System TWX is similar to an ordinary typewriter. Messages typed on one machine are instantly and exactly reproduced on any other teletypewriter to which it is connected. Each teletypewriter has its own number just as with telephones. All teletypewriter numbers and listings in the United States appear in *Telex/TWX Directory &*

Buyers Guide. The white-page section of the directory is arranged alphabetically by state, then cities within each state. The businesses are listed alphabetically by name under each city heading. The yellow-page section lists TWX users alphabetically by classified heading and by company name under each heading. To call another TWX give the teletypewriter operator the distant teletypewriter number. Connection is established as rapidly as though it were a person-to-person call. Local and long-distance communications are two-way, and as many as six copies may be typed simultaneously. TWX charges are by the time used, with a one-minute minimum rather than by the word. A company may use its own business forms. Special equipment may be added to send pre-recorded messages automatically.

Efficient Telex/TWX Utilization. With a Telex/TWX terminal, you have direct access to Western Union's InfoMaster computer, an advanced message-switching computer center. InfoMaster can transmit Mailgram messages, telegrams, and cablegrams directly from the Telex/TWX terminal. You may write and/or address multiple messages without repetitive typing and with complete communication flexibility, 24 hours a day, seven days a week.

International telegrams (*cablegrams*) to overseas correspondents not on the Telex/TWX network can be sent more economically by using the Info-Master computer. The telegram will be sent electronically, toll free, to an international carrier for prompt delivery. You pay only the cost of the telegram.

Mailgram messages can be sent overnight to addressees in the 48 contiguous states or Hawaii via Telex or TWX for up to 50 percent less than the same message filed by phone or in person. The InfoMaster will electronically transmit the message to a post office nearest each addressee.

Telegrams can be sent by dialing InfoMaster from your Telex/TWX terminal to just about anywhere in North America, any time of the day or night for approximately 30 percent less than a typical 15-word message. Western Union arranges delivery by phone within two hours, or by messenger within five hours.

Datagram provides sales representatives, distributors, and other authorized persons 24-hour telephone-to-teletypewriter access for automatic transmission and delivery of orders, data, and miscellaneous information. Telex/TWX Datagram service allows tighter control of sales, distribution, payroll, inventory, production, and financial data; speeds and simplifies order entry from sales personnel and authorized customers; collects field sales reports and travel plans from on-the-road personnel; and extends customer-service hours without adding staff operators or attendants.

RediList and NiteCast are computer addressing services that store address lists in the InfoMaster computer for instant access by code. You dial the computer, enter your seven-character list code, and type the text. You can send a message to as few as seven or as many as 250 addresses per list via TWX, Telex, International Telex, Telegram, International Telegram, Mailgram, or any combination of these. NiteCast offers automatic addressing of messages for delivery at low rates to Telex/TWX terminals at night, when lines are free. Messages can be sent to from 35 to 250 addresses per list anytime during the business day and until 5 a.m. the day following for delivery to your correspondents' terminals between 8 p.m. and 8 a.m. There is no telegram, mailgram, or international service with NiteCast.

Other services that can be used with your Telex/TWX terminals are Collect Service, FYI News Service and Stock Quote, Commercial Money Order, and the addition of computer interface equipment to your Telex/TWX terminal. A maintenance plan structured to the company's needs on a continuing basis can be arranged with Western Union, which has a corps of experienced technicians at 400 service centers coast to coast.

12.4 TRAVEL ARRANGEMENTS

Making arrangements for either business or personal travel involves collecting specific information about the type of transportation to use, time schedules, costs, the location of terminals, the availability of terminal transportation to parts of the city, baggage handling, insurance, hotel and motel accommodations, and many other features that contribute to the success of any trip. In some instances, companies maintain a transportation or travel reservation department that handles the details for business trips. A travel authorization form is filled out and approved before the trip is made (Figure 12-14). In other instances, the secretary or administrative assistant makes all arrangements or gathers the necessary information to pass on to the transportation department.

Use of Travel Agents.   Because the travel industry today is highly specialized, a professional travel agent will provide expert guidance in the choice of transportation alternatives, accommodations, and other travel services. The members of the American Society of Travel Agents, Inc., who display the ASTA insignia in their advertisements and offices, support high ethical standards of conduct in the sale of travel. There is no extra charge for their services, unless you ask for extraordinary service or cancel a trip after funds have been expended for long-distance calls or telegrams. An ASTA member will notify you in writing if you will be required to pay any charge in the event a booking is changed or canceled. The agent will help plan the itinerary,

TRAVEL ORDER

T.O. No. _____
Issued _____
Date _____

Employee no. _____ Name _____

Department _____

Is authorized to proceed from (origin) _____

to _____

via commercial air( )   rail( )   personal car( )   other( )   One way _____   Round trip _____

From _____   To _____   Per Diem Rate _____

Rented car authorized at _____

Total	Distribution of Costs		
	Dept.	Work & %	W.O. & %

Travel advance

Cash $ _____   Checks _____ @ $ _____

Personal transportation costs
Company transportation costs
Estimated total advance
Estimated car rental
Total Estimated Trip Costs

Approved signatures _____

Traveler   Department   Administration

Places to Be Visited	Purpose of Visit	Dates	Persons to Be Visited

Miscellaneous Information

Figure 12-14   Travel authorization form.

Something

will secure the necessary tickets, make hotel and motel arrangements, arrange for car hire, and often extend credit for end-of-the-month billing. Commissions are paid the agent by airlines, railroads, steamship companies, hotels, motels, and car hire agencies. Some companies find it more efficient to work through a travel agent exclusively, especially for foreign travel.

Trip Information to Collect. Before contacting the company travel reservations office, a travel agent, or the transportation carriers and hotels direct, compile the following information.

1. Destination plus any intermediate stops.

2. Probable date of departure, specific date(s) of arrival at business appointment(s), and date of return.

3. Desired method of travel.

(a) Type of service: by airplane, first-class or tourist; by train, roomette (one person), bedroom (two or more) or coach; by ship, first-class or tourist and type of stateroom.

(b) Drive-yourself or chauffeur-driven car.

(c) Company-owned or chartered airplane.

4. Mode of transportation desired at each stop on the trip.

(a) Automobile rental: make of car, standard or automatic shift (especially important for one driving in a strange city or country), insurance coverage, credit cards available, need for maps of city or country, and desired delivery and return site(s).

(b) Local taxis, buses, or chauffeur-driven cars.

(c) Helicopter service, if available.

5. Overnight accommodations desired.

(a) Hotel: preference or location in city, type and number of rooms, floor preference, room location (proximity to conference attendees, travelers in same party, or exhibit rooms), special furnishings or telephones.

(b) Motel: location in or near city, type and number of rooms, floor and room location preference, special furnishings or telephones, motel facilities preferred (restaurant, bar, entertainment, swimming pool), proximity to other businesses (banks, telegraph office, pharmacy, and so on).

Itinerary. From the trip information compiled and from schedule and accommodation information received from the travel reservations office or some other source, a tentative itinerary is drawn up and approval secured, if necessary. The items and notes on the trip plans should be sorted in chronological sequence by the day and time each will occur. List and describe each item in order. The usual itinerary covers *when* the traveler will go, *where,* and *how.* It may also serve as a daily appointment calendar and contain helpful reminders. Include transportation and hotel reservations; appointments and personal appearances; and reminders of any details to be carried out by the traveler during the trip, such as last-minute ticket validations, confirmation of reservations, and appointments that must be reconfirmed on arrival. Sufficient copies of the approved itinerary should be made for supervision, the traveler's family, and any other person who might need to contact him while he is away. The itinerary format in Figure 12-15 is suggested.

Other Preparations for the Trip.   To assure a pleasant trip, a travel package should be made that contains the following items.

1. Copy of ITINERARY.

2. TICKETS (check for conformance to itinerary).

3. MONEY (cash and/or traveler's checks).

4. Copies of WIRES OR LETTERS CONFIRMING HOTEL RESERVATIONS.

5. Blank TRAVEL EXPENSE WORK SHEETS.

6. Copies of PERTINENT CORRESPONDENCE and other material needed for the transaction of business, placed in clearly marked folders.

7. If applicable, INVENTORY OF HAND-CARRIED CLASSIFIED MATERIAL.

8. A briefcase or portfolio large enough to hold the material accompanying the traveler and additional items to be picked up during the trip.

9. Stamps and stationery items.

10. Company telephone directory or list of key personnel and company sales or product brochures and annual report, if needed for distribution.

Expense Reports.   *Government Requirements.*   The Internal Revenue Service requires that complete and accurate records be submitted to support tax-deductible items in an expense account. Adequate records and substantiation are both necessary. For a full explanation of the U.S. Treasury Department laws, see the Internal Revenue Service Publication #463, "Rules for Deducting Travel, Entertainment and Gift Expenses." The following records must be collected by the business traveler.

1. A diary, account book, or similar summary of travel and entertainment expenses.

2. Receipts, itemized paid bills, and similar statements for single items exceeding $25. Exceptions:

(a) Receipts for travel expenses over $25 are required only when readily available, as for air travel.

(b) A canceled check is not acceptable. If a bill or voucher is not available, other evidence may have to be presented.

(c) Receipts for lodgings are required regardless of the amount unless their cost is covered by a per diem allowance of $25 or less.

Each receipted bill should contain the following data: (a) the amount of the expense; (b) the date the expense was incurred; (c) the place the expense was incurred; and (d) the nature of the expense. The diary and supporting

```
          Itinerary for Mr. Clarence C. Dotson
                   March 18-26, 19--
  Los Angeles--Dayton--Washington, D.C.--Los Angeles


Monday, March 18 (Los Angeles to Dayton)

    8:45 a.m.      Leave Los Angeles on TWA, Flight 24
                   International Airport.

    3:35 p.m.      Arrive Dayton Airport. Hourly air-
                   port limousine service available
                   ($1.50). Reservations at Stratford
                   Motel. Single with bath, TV, and
                   typewriter. Address: 1012 Express-
                   way West.

                   Call Major Dodger (326-6666) to re-
                   confirm 8 a.m. Tuesday appointment
                   and pick-up by Government car at
                   7 a.m.

    6:30 p.m.      Dinner meeting with Mr. Alpha and
                   other officials of ABC Corporation
                   at Nikabob Restaurant. Company car
                   will call at motel at 6:10 p.m.


Tuesday, March 19 (Dayton-Wright-Patterson)

    7:00 a.m.      Government car will arrive at motel
                   for trip to WPAFB.

    (Complete in detail)
```

Figure 12-15 Suggested form of itinerary.

records must be kept for three years after the due date for the tax return that the records support. Records must show the business reason for travel or the nature of the business benefit derived or expected as a result of the travel. The daily cost of breakfast, lunch, dinner, and other incidental travel expenses can be listed together as "meals, gasoline, and taxi fares." If the firm pays directly for transportation, such costs do not have to be included in the record. If the trip, however, is charged to the firm through a credit card, transportation costs must be reported.

Entertainment expense records for business or tax purposes should include the following information.

1. The cost of each entertainment.

2. The cost of incidental items, such as taxi fares and phone calls, which may be aggregated on a daily basis.

3. The date of entertainment. If it directly precedes or follows a business discussion, include the place, nature, and duration of the discussion.

4. The name, address or location, and description of the type of entertainment, such as dinner and/or theater, if these facts are not apparent.

5. The business reason or business benefit derived or expected.

6. The name, title, and occupation of the person entertained to establish his business relation to the host company.

7. When entertaining a group of associates, refer to the group as "five officials of ABC Corp." instead of listing each name.

The record of business gifts should include the cost of the gift to the taxpayer, the date of the gift, and the business reason for the gift or the nature of the business benefit derived or expected from it. The recipient's occupation, title, or other data showing his business relation to the donor must be given. Names are not needed for relatively inexpensive sports tickets given to many people—only a general description of the recipients. For season tickets, each use should be treated as a separate gift and the cost of the ticket prorated.

Company Travel Policies.   Most companies establish travel policies for control purposes. Travel orders (Figure 12-14) are usually required as authorization for all business trips in excess of 100 miles from the traveler's work location, and for any trip that requires overnight accommodations. Other policies concern class of carrier or hotel accommodations, per diem allowance, reimbursable expenses, classified trips, removal of company property, attendance at professional meetings, and foreign travel.

Class of carrier or hotel accommodations policies are established partly to uphold the company image and partly to control costs. Usually a first-class flight is arranged if any part of the flight will be during nonworking hours. A tourist flight is normally arranged if the complete flight will take place between eight and five o'clock. When travel is by train, a first-class roomette accommodation is normally arranged. Many companies patronize hotels in cities around the nation with whom efficient working relationships have been established. In order to establish this long-term association, the hotels may offer special prices and services.

A per diem allowance is normally paid to the traveler on company business to cover expenses for hotels, meals, and tips. The traveler receives full per diem for all days between the first and the last day of the trip. On the day of departure and the day of return, per diem is figured by dividing the day into quarters. Figure 12-16 shows how to determine the amount of per diem to

Day of Departure

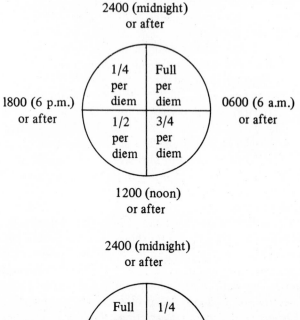

2400 (midnight)
or after

1800 (6 p.m.)
or after

0600 (6 a.m.)
or after

1200 (noon)
or after

Day of Return

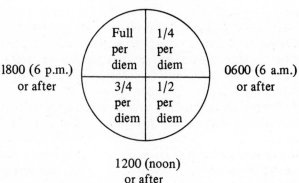

2400 (midnight)
or after

1800 (6 p.m.)
or after

0600 (6 a.m.)
or after

1200 (noon)
or after

Figure 12-16 Determining per diem allowance.

allow. A time allowance to and from the airport or terminal should be added to departure and arrival times.

All reimbursable expenses are entered on the expense report (Figure 12-17), which is normally due within five working days after the traveler returns. A statement of expenses incurred by the traveler is an authorization to credit those expenses to the travel funds advanced to him. The following expenses are normally allowed by most firms.

1. Excess hotel. Half of the traveler's per diem is allotted for the hotel. A reasonable hotel charge in excess of this amount is reimbursable, unless the room is shared by any member of the traveler's family.

2. Communications. Business phone calls or telegrams are reimbursable

TRAVEL EXPENSE REPORT

Audited by: _____
Approved by: _____

NAME _____ No. ___ Page _____

DEPARTMENT _____ Ext._____

Purpose of trip _____

Method of travel (be specific) _____

Transportation furnished by _____

Departures and arrivals (date and hour) _____

Date									Total
Room plus tax (attach receipt)									
Breakfast plus tip									
Lunch plus tip									
Dinner plus tip									

Additional Expenses   **TOTAL** _____

Date	Expense Description	Amount	Date	Expense Description	Amount
	Total Room and Meals			Total Forward	
	Total Forward			Total Expenses	

Traveler Account Balance

Due Co. from last report _____   Due Emp. from last report _____
Cash received _____   Expenses paid _____
Due Emp. at end of period _____   Cash returned to Co. _____
_____ _____   Due Co. at end of period _____
Total _____   Total _____

I Hereby Certify That All Expenditures Were Necessary Expenses.

Signature _____
Department _____
Employee No. _____

Accounting Department Use Account Distribution	Amount

Subject to Withholding Tax   Yes ☐   No ☐

Approved _____   _____
Department Head   Company Executive

Figure 12-17   Travel expense report.

461

and are itemized if charges are $1 or more. Tolls less than $1 are noted without explanation.

3. Auto expenses. Parking fees, bridge or road tolls, and so on may be included on expense records.

4. Gas for a rented car. Normally receipts for gasoline are turned in to the car rental agency and a cash refund is obtained. If, however, they have not been given to the car rental agency, the receipts are attached to the expense report and the amounts entered and itemized.

5. Excess baggage. Charges for excess baggage required for business are reimbursable.

6. Registration fees. Most companies pay the fees for attendance at professional meetings.

7. Traveler's checks. When traveler's checks are purchased by the traveler, reimbursement is allowed for the charge covering the amount of the original travel advance. Receipts are asked for.

8. Luncheon or banquet. Normally, the cost of a scheduled luncheon or banquet in connection with a professional meeting is reimbursable in the amount that exceeds the traveler's per diem allowance for that meal.

9. Valet and laundry service. Reasonable costs of laundry and valet service incurred on a trip are allowed by many companies. If the charges are not shown on the hotel bill, a separate receipt is required.

10. Purchase of technical material. Many times the purchase of technical material pertinent to the company's business is reimbursable.

11. Shipping documents. If it is not possible to use the mailing facilities of one of the company's offices, the cost of shipping documents or materials is reimbursable if a receipt is obtained.

12. Secretarial services. The costs of secretarial services are reimbursable.

13. Entertainment. The costs of entertainment are usually reimbursable only if prior approval has been obtained by the traveler. Social hours, cocktail parties, and so on are normally not reimbursable expenses.

Classified Trip Requirements. Companies that work with classified government information usually construct a special form to be completed by a traveler to a secured facility to discuss classified information (Figure 12-18). The classified-trip-information form may include a space for the name of the originator of the trip as the person best informed about the nature of and need for the trip. Clearances must be obtained for the traveler to visit secured facilities. Permission is necessary for the removal of classified documents from the company premises, if the traveler needs to take these with him. Many companies, if possible, mail the classified material to the destination beforehand. If time does not permit mailing it ahead, an inventory of hand-carried classified material is prepared and special locked containers are used for its transport.

CLASSIFIED TRIP INFORMATION

Trip originator _____ Dept. _____ Date _____

Traveler(s) name in full	Emp. No.	Type of clearance	Clearance No.	Places to be visited		
				A	B	C
1.						
2.						
3.						
4.						
5.						

	Date of visit	Places to be visited (complete address)	Persons to be visited (name and title)	Purpose of visit and project number
A			Informed of visit?__	
B			Informed of visit?__	
C			Informed of visit?__	

Approved by _____ _____
    Signature   Name and Title (Please type)

Figure 12-18 Form for trip involving discussion of classified information.

REQUEST FOR AUTHORIZATION TO ATTEND PROFESSIONAL MEETING

Name of professional organization _____ Date of request _____

Date(s) of meeting _____ thru _____ Place of meeting _____

Duration of visit at meeting, excluding travel time _____

It is requested that the following personnel be authorized to attend the above meeting for the reasons stated:

Name(s) of Personnel	Date Employed	Job Class	Emp. No.	Dept.	W. O. No.	Member?	Present Paper Yes	Present Paper No	Business Trip Info. Dates, Incl. Travel Time	Location	Acct.	Cost per Person
1.												
2.												
3.												
4.												
											Total Cost	

Justification: Originating unit

Comments: Executive office

REQUEST SHOULD BE SUBMITTED THREE WEEKS IN ADVANCE. IF TRIP IS CANCELLED, NOTIFY THE EXECUTIVE OFFICE.

Requested by: _____ Approved, with exceptions as noted above:

Department Head Executive Office _____

Return copy to: _____ Date _____

Figure 12-19 Request form for attendance at professional meetings.

Attendance at Professional Meetings. Most companies establish precise policies regarding the attendance of employees at professional meetings. A request form (Figure 12-19) is filled out and submitted well in advance of the meeting (three weeks to a month) for approval. After approval is obtained, the usual travel procedures are followed if the meeting is more than 100 miles from the company.

Use of Company or Personal Automobiles. When an employee uses either a company car or his own on company business, authorization is secured before the trip is made. A special form requesting permission is completed and approved (Figure 12-20). A complete record of trip expenses is kept. For a single trip, a record of expenses is entered on the approved request form and presented to the cashier for reimbursement. An employee using his own car over an extended period submits itemized trip expenses at the end of a specified time or at the end of each month (Figure 12-21). When employees use their own car, they are reimbursed at a flat rate, for example 15 cents a mile, plus other allowable expenses, such as parking fees and tolls. Some companies establish flat amounts for reimbursement of specific trips between company buildings and established points. Most policies state that there is no mileage reimbursement from the employee's home to the normal workplace and return, or from the home to a closer destination than the normal workplace and return. All mileage is paid for a trip from the normal workplace to any destination (except home) and return, and partial mileage is paid for a trip to a farther destination than the normal workplace and return. Compute partial mileage by subtracting the mileage between home and the normal workplace from the actual mileage.

Travel Abroad. Foreign travel policies follow rather closely those established for travel within the United States. Employees who represent the company abroad are probably more carefully chosen, but the usual forms must be prepared and approved. A foreign travel form (Figure 12-22) is used to request authorization for business travel outside the continental United States (Alaska and Hawaii are usually included). After approval is received and the pertinent information gathered, the services of a travel agent are engaged because arrangements for a trip abroad are quite involved.

The International Operations Division, Internal Revenue Service, Washington, DC 20025, supplies booklets explaining how to establish residence abroad and how to report income. Such booklets as *Tax Guide for U.S. Citizens Abroad, Fulbright Awards,* and *U.S. Income Tax: Tax Guide for Small Business* are helpful. Any local bookstore also has a wealth of published material on foreign travel and living abroad.

Passport. A passport must be secured for foreign travel to all countries except Canada, Mexico, and the Caribbean islands, which usually waive the requirements for United States citizens who have a return ticket and some

AUTOMOBILE TRAVEL ON COMPANY BUSINESS (Single trip—personal car or company car)			
Name	Dept. & Clk. No.	Date of trip	Approved by

IF A COMPANY CAR IS USED, MAKE ENTRIES HERE		
Company Car No.	Time out A.M. P.M.	Mileage in _____
		Mileage out _____
Driver's License No.	Time in A.M. P.M.	Total miles _____

IF A PERSONAL CAR IS USED, MAKE ENTRIES HERE				
Trip approval	From	To	Mileage only	Flat amount for specific trip
		☐ Round trip ☐ One way		

Other auto expense _____

PETTY CASH VOUCHER	Accounting distribution			
Received the sum of $ _____ as reimbursement for the trip shown above.	Dept.	Account	Order	Amount
Requested by _____				
Received by _____				
Approved by _____				

Figure 12-20 Reimbursement form for single trip using either company or personal car.

proof of citizenship. To secure a passport, take along a birth certificate (or notarized affidavit of birth vouched for by a relative or person who has known you for a long time), a baptismal certificate, or an expired passport. Two passport pictures should be obtained, front view, two and one-half to three inches square on a white background. A passport is valid for five years; the fee is $14. Application should be made in person at the Passport Division of the Department of State, Washington, D.C., or the Passport agencies in Miami, New Orleans, Los Angeles, San Francisco, Seattle, Chicago, Boston, New York, and Honolulu. In other cities apply at the

USE OF PERSONAL CAR EXPENSE RECORD

Use this form for more than one authorized trip a week by personal car. Use Form 000 for single authorized trips by personal or company car.

Name

Dept. & Emp. No.   Date

Social Security No. _____

Trip approval	Date	From	To	Mileage only	Flat amounts for specific trips

Total Miles @ 8¢ $

Other auto expense:

$

*Withholding tax $

GRAND TOTAL $

Petty Cash Voucher	Accounting distribution			
	Dept.	Account	Order	Amount
Received the sum of $ _____ as payment for the amount shown above.				
Requested by _____				
Received by _____				
Approved by _____				
*Subject to withholding tax. Yes ☐ No ☐				

Figure 12-21   Example of form used to reimburse employee for use of personal car on company business.

REQUEST FOR FOREIGN TRAVEL
(To be completed for all foreign visits whether classified or unclassified)

Date

1. Complete name of traveler	2. Is travel necessary and required according to terms of contract now in effect?
3. Job title	YES ☐ NO ☐
4. Current home address	(If yes, state contract no.) _____

5. Foreign languages (indicate whether you speak, read, or write)

6. Is travel for the sole or primary benefit of a foreign government?

Yes ☐   No ☐

7. Will foreign nationals be contacted? Yes ☐ No ☐	8. Will classified information be disclosed to foreign nationals? Yes ☐ No ☐

9. Mode of travel
  ☐ Commercial airline   Other _____

10. REMARKS. Include purpose of visit in detail indicating highest degree of classified discussion and additional information as required.

11. Departure date from United States:

12. Date(s) of visit.	13. Complete name and address of place(s) to be visited.	14. Person to be contacted.	15. Date appt. made.

Figure 12-22   Company form for travel abroad.

Office of the Clerk of a Federal Court or at your local post office. Many countries outside Western Europe require a visa or a tourist card. A travel agent, travel guidebooks, the consulate of the country to be visited, and the local State Department office can supply information about these. It saves time to get visas and tourist cards in the United States.

Health Documents.   For reentry to the United States and for entry to most foreign countries, a smallpox vaccination certificate is no longer needed. Yellow fever and cholera certificates are required by most countries from travelers who have come from an infected area. The following periods of validity for vaccination certificates are accepted.

> Yellow fever—not less than ten days nor more than six years old.
> Cholera—not less than six days nor more than six months old.

Typhus and typhoid-paratyphoid inoculation certificates are not required under the World Health Organization sanitary regulations as a prerequisite for admission to a country. They are recommended, however, for visits to some countries. Your physician or travel agent can advise you regarding the need for these shots. The record of inoculations must be entered by the local health authority in the official WHO certificate-of-vaccination form. Forms may be secured from a travel agent, an airline office, the steamship office, or from a doctor.

Travel Funds.   Money may be carried in several ways. Traveler's checks may be purchased in $10, $20, $50, and $100 denominations from the American Express Company, and at banks, telegraph companies, some transportation companies, and most travel agencies. A business traveler may also apply for a credit card from the American Express and VISA and Master Charge from U.S. banks that have established international credit. A traveler's letter of credit may be purchased before departure that will be honored at certain foreign banks of which the issuing bank is a correspondent. The traveler is furnished a list of these correspondent banks. Prearranged deposits may be made in foreign banks. Many foreign-based banks maintain local offices in major U.S. cities to facilitate international banking. Some of these are Barclay's Bank of London, Banco Nacional de Mexico S.A., Bank of Montreal, Royal Bank of Canada, Bank of Tokyo, Ltd., and Mitsubishi Bank, Ltd. Your local bank will also be able to help you transfer funds through its U.S. correspondent banks.

Foreign currency may be purchased before one leaves the United States, where frequently one may get a better rate of exchange. However, the traveler should note the total amount of foreign currencies that may be taken into each country. It is a good idea to familiarize oneself with the currency of countries in which one will be traveling. (See Section 14.3, "Foreign Monetary Terms.") Most travel agencies and transportation companies can supply a currency converter that describes and pictures the various coins and paper used by other countries. A few one-dollar bills should be taken along so that it is not necessary to cash a traveler's check or exchange a large bill into local currency in order to make small purchases in those countries where one plans only a short stopover between planes. They also are convenient when one is paying for baggage handling and the taxi fare upon arrival at one's destination.

The U.S. government urges American citizens to purchase foreign currency when traveling in Sri Lanka, Guinea, India, Israel, Pakistan, Tunisia, and Egypt. Purchases may be made at the U.S. embassy or consulates in those countries. Sales are made at the official rate of exchange, and no conversion fee is charged. When local currencies are purchased in this way, the dollars stay in the U.S. government accounts, and there is no outflow of dollars to foreign holders. Additional information on doing business abroad may be found in Chapter 14, "International Trade."

13

Financial and Tax Considerations

Every business, large and small, has certain financial and tax matters to handle daily, to keep records on, and to report about to government agencies. In this chapter, those areas important to the smooth functioning of a business are presented to assist the company establish reliable systems, locate additional information, and set up records that will produce adequate reports.

The material will also help individuals in solving their personal financial and tax problems. Secretaries or assistants who maintain personal business records for an executive and handle minor business transactions for the office will find the following sections invaluable.

CONTENTS

13.1 BANKING

Most business men and women are familiar with banking procedures for savings and checking accounts and the need for adequate records of the in-and-out flow of funds. In this section, the services offered customers by banks are explained, and attention is called to certain factors in handling savings and checking accounts which will minimize errors and losses. Definitions of banking terms may be found in the "Dictionary of Business Terms," Section 16.2.

Checking Accounts. A company may maintain several checking accounts for special purposes, departments, or subsidiaries. Individuals may also need two or more checking accounts, for example, personal, joint, household, travel, and so on. Accounts should be kept separate and carefully labeled so that monies in and out will not become intermingled. Besides careful labeling, the use of checks of different colors will help prevent errors in the handling of transactions.

Making Out Checks. It is important that a check be correctly written from both the payer's and the payee's standpoints. The use of check-writers simplifies the writing because the words and figures are automatically entered in the appropriate blanks. Use of check-writers is no assurance, however, that the information on the check is correct; as with all other documents, the check will need to be proofread for accuracy against the original request. A variety of check-writing machines are available that supply automatic totals of the number and amounts of checks written for a specific period—daily, weekly, monthly. There is little chance of raising amounts on machine-written checks. The only opportunities for forgery occur in the signature and the endorsement. Access to the check-writing machine should be closely supervised, and it should be placed in the safe or vault each night and removed during the day only when checks are to be made out.

More care is needed when one is making out a check on the typewriter or by hand.

1. Date. The date of writing should be used on all checks. An earlier date may be put on a check, if necessary, but usually the date of receipt is the one established for payment, so little advantage is gained. Antedating over a week is frowned on. Postdating—putting a later date on a check—is possible, and the check cannot be cashed or deposited until the date arrives. If money is inadvertently paid on a postdated check, it may be recovered. Checks may be dated for any day of the year, holidays and Sundays included. If a check is received undated, fill in the date of receipt. Cash or deposit checks as soon as possible after receipt, or they may be refused by a bank if too old (stale). It is also possible that the account will have insufficient funds at a later date.

2. Payee's name. The business or legal name of the payee should be used because this is the name to which the payment is credited and is the one that must be signed as the endorsement. If the check is made out to other than the legal signature, the payee then has to sign the name as written on the check followed by the legal signature. Companies with particularly long names should arrange with the bank for a shortened form and advise customers to use it. Most banks accept abbreviated commercial titles regardless of pre-arrangement, but it is wise to use an approved one in case there are several company names whose abbreviations could be confused.

Do not use titles preceding the name (Dr., Judge, and so on), but follow it with the title of an office (Treasurer, Secretary-Treasurer, and so on) if the person is acting in an official capacity for an organization. If the check is typed, it is recommended that the name be followed by three *** or hyphens, so that other names cannot be added.

3. Amount. The amount of the check should be in both figures and words. The figures after the dollar sign should be as close as possible to it and clearly written as to dollars and cents ($118.32). For even dollars be sure to fill in the zeros ($118.00). Spell out the amount on the next line in this manner.

One hundred eighteen and 32/100---------------Dollars
or

One hundred eighteen and thirty-two/100----Dollars
and

One hundred eighteen and no/100------------Dollars

As the examples illustrate, the line should be completely filled in to discourage the raising of the amount by a forger. The written words are considered correct, if there is a difference between them and the figures. It is also wise to spell out all cents up to nine or place a "0" before the number, e.g., "09/100" or "nine/100."

Large amounts should be written in the fewest words possible. For example, $3,256.22 may be written in the following ways.

Three thousand two hundred fifty-six and twenty-two/100---Dollars

Thirty-two hundred fifty-six and twenty-two/100-------------Dollars

Thirty-two hundred fifty-six and 22/100------------------------Dollars

The last example is preferred.

4. Signature. The signature(s) should be authorized and on file at the bank. A good ink or ball-point pen should be used for a clear, legible signature. A lead or indelible pencil should never be used.

Changes on the Check.   Corrections or changes on a check should be avoided. If a minor one must be made, erase carefully and correct; then ask the signer to initial the correction. Banks usually refuse to honor a check that has been changed, especially one in which the figures or spelled out words have been tampered with. A better practice is to cancel the incorrect check by writing "Void" across the face of both the check and the stub and filing the voided check in the check file.

Endorsements.   A check presented for cash or deposit is signed by the payee on the reverse side, preferably at the opposite end from the figures.

The name as it appears on the face must be the one signed first. If it is not the person's legal name or the one on his own account at the bank where it is being cashed or deposited, he will need to follow the first endorsement with a second one. Several types of endorsements may be used.

1. Blank. In a blank endorsement, only the payee's signature is placed on the reverse side. This type of endorsement makes the check *payable to bearer;* therefore, it should be cashed or deposited immediately because if lost it may be cashed by whoever finds it.

2. Special or full. When the payee wishes to have a record of the company or person to whom he transferred the check, he may write "Pay to the order of (name of the recipient)" at the top left of the reverse side of the check. He then signs his name immediately after this special endorsement. The designated person or company must now endorse the check before cashing, depositing, or transferring it. Usually, a bank is the only institution that will accept a check with a third-party endorsement. Merchants and other businessmen prefer to handle personal checks and occasionally might take one from the second endorser, if he is known as a good risk. The last endorser is the one who receives the amount shown on the face of the check if the maker's account has sufficient balance to cover it. If not, the last endorser might seek restitution from the endorser before him, to whom he gave credit or cash for the amount of the check.

3. Restrictive. To ensure that the money is paid to a designated person and no one else, the payee places a restrictive endorsement above his signature that states "Pay to (name of designee)".

4. Qualified. If the endorser desires to be relieved of any future liability on the check, he places the words "Without recourse" above his signature before passing it along to someone else. Attorneys frequently use this endorsement when transferring payments on judgments or claims to their clients. The client could expect payment only from the maker in such a case.

5. For deposit only. Checks sent through the mail for deposit should contain the words "For deposit only" above the payee's signature. Businesses are permitted to use a rubber stamp as the endorsement. The message includes, besides the deposit statement, the name of the bank, the company, and the account number. The stamp may be obtained from the bank for a small fee.

To Stop Payment. Commercial accounts may telephone a request for payment of a company check to be stopped. The bank will immediately initiate the necessary paper work.

Payment of a personal check may not be stopped by telephone or telegraph, but must be requested in writing by the maker, who also completes the bank's stop-order form. It may be secured by a telephone request but nothing will be done until the signed form is returned. If the stop order reaches the computer before the check is paid, the person who presented it will be notified that payment has been stopped. To speed matters, the check maker should go to the bank and fill out the form there.

Record of Account Transactions. A daily balance of cash in the checking account ought to be maintained by businesses and individuals to avoid overdrawing. Therefore, it is important that a record be kept of all checks written and of deposits made. Maintaining a continuous balance on the check stubs or other forms supplied by the bank is an easy recordkeeping method.

Careful accounting of all legitimate transactions in and out of the account will uncover any irregularities more quickly. Unfortunately, there are a vast number of check forgers here and abroad and it is imperative that companies, and small businessmen in particular, be aware of problems in processing checks. Six principal types of check fraud are used: (1) raising the amount, (2) altering the payee's name, (3) altering the date, (4) counterfeiting existing checks, (5) concocting fictitious checks, and (6) forging signatures of either the drawer or the endorser. Usually, the proof of fraud rests with the person who drew the check. Checks, therefore, should be examined closely.

The Bank Reconciliation. When the bank statement is received after the end of the month, it should be compared with the record of deposits and checks drawn so that errors or omissions on either the depositor's or the bank's books can be corrected. The balance shown on the bank statement rarely corresponds to the balance on the check stubs or the cash-in-bank account. There are always outstanding checks or deposits. In a company, an employee other than the one who makes out checks should prepare the reconciliation as a control function.

Before beginning to reconcile the bank statement, gather these materials: the bank statement with the cancelled checks and other memoranda from the bank, last month's reconciliation statement, the checkbook or register, and the record of deposits as shown by duplicate deposit slips. The following steps should then be taken.

1. Check the canceled checks and other memoranda from the bank against the statement to ascertain that none are missing.

2. Arrange the checks in numerical order and compare them with the stubs or the entries in the check register to locate those that are still outstanding.

3. Compare deposits with the bank statement to locate any that have not been credited.

4. List the information from the bank memoranda: (a) corrections for errors in deposits; (b) bank charges; (c) automatic collections or payments made by the bank for the account; and (d) other items, such as notice of stop payments or uncollectable checks that have been deposited.

5. Prepare the reconciliation statement as illustrated in Figure 13-1.

(a) Copy the balance on the checkbook or register for the given date.

(b) List the adjustments to be made to the checkbook balance. When the reconciliation is complete and the bank statement balance agrees with the

---

ABC Corporation

Bank Reconciliation as of August 31, 19___

Checkbook Balance $6,225.56

Adjustments:
  Less: Bank charges . . . . $ 1.85
          Error in deposit 7/24 . . .   2.65
          Mortgage payment . . . . <u>375.20</u>   −379.70
  Add: Automatic deposit—rentals
          from 2940 Garfield Bldg . . . . . . <u>472.50</u>   <u>92.80</u>

Adjusted Checkbook Balance $6,318.36

Add: Outstanding checks #1472 . . .   25.00
                   #1503 . . .   78.90
                   #1504 . . .   10.95
                   #1505 . . . 115.08
                   #1507 . . . <u> 34.00</u>   263.93

Less: Outstanding deposit 8/30 . . . . <u>125.00</u>   <u>138.93</u>

Adjusted Bank Balance $6,457.29

Balance on Bank Statement . . . . <u>$6,457.29</u>

Figure 13-1   Example of a bank reconciliation statement.

adjusted bank balance, these adjustments will need to be entered in the stub record and adjusting entries made, if accounting records are involved.

(c) Find the adjusted checkbook balance.

(d) List and add outstanding checks.

(e) List and subtract outstanding deposits to determine the adjusted bank balance.

(f) Copy the bank balance from the statement. If it is not the same as the adjusted bank balance, search for errors in the stubs or the register, such as additions, subtractions, items not listed or listed twice, transpositions, or items not picked up from the bank statement. The balance on the bank's statement should agree with the adjusted bank balance.

Cashing Checks. According to law enforcement agencies, care should be taken when you cash a check for anyone. Most check swindlers appear to be respectable citizens. Here are some suggestions to follow.

Ask enough questions about the check to ascertain that it is genuine before cashing it.

Get positive identification from the endorser, preferably several with signatures, because drivers' licenses and Social Security cards are easily forged.

Refuse to cash checks that show signs of alteration. Recovery can be made only for the original amount of a raised check.

Ask that the check be endorsed in your presence and compare the endorsement with the signatures offered for identification. Make sure the endorsement agrees exactly with the payee's name on the face of the check. If it is not the same name on the identification, ask for the payee's legal signature below the first endorsement. Do not cash checks with second or third endorsements nor one with a rubber-stamp endorsement.

Investigate thoroughly if you are asked to cash a check outside of business hours or on Sunday. These are favorite times for the passers of bad checks.

Out-of-town checks should be cashed only for persons whose identity and character are known. Make sure the check is from an existing concern and is drawn on an actual bank.

Be just as careful about cashing what appears to be a bank cashier's or certified check as you would a personal check.

Cash checks for only a few dollars over the price of a purchase.

Because juveniles are not legally responsible, do not cash checks for them unless they and their parents are known to you.

Report to the police forged checks that the bank refuses, and supply all the facts possible to aid them in their search for the swindler.

Deposits to Accounts. Almost any negotiable item may be deposited in checking and savings accounts. For instance, such items as the following are accepted by banking institutions.

Cash	Money orders
Checks	Promissory notes
Interest coupons	Unused portion of letters of credit
Traveler's checks	Foreign currency and checks
Drafts	

A deposit slip in duplicate listing each item should accompany the deposit. Usually, the totals of coins and currency are listed separately, then each check by its ABA bank number (see Section 16.2), and finally other items. A receipt is given upon request for hand-delivered deposits to checking accounts and to savings accounts if the depositor forgets to bring the passbook. Mail deposits to checking accounts are always acknowledged either by a receipt giving the total or a stamped acknowledgment on the duplicate list of deposits. Deposits to checking accounts are usually not listed in a passbook but are recorded on the monthly bank statement. If a bank issues a passbook for checking accounts, the deposit is entered as a total only. Deposits to savings accounts are entered in a passbook and the account balance is adjusted to reflect the new total.

Checks to be deposited must be endorsed on the back. Either a rubber stamp or a handwritten "deposit only" endorsement should be used (see "Endorsements," in this section). Peruse checks carefully to see that they are properly drawn and signed. Figures and spelled-out amounts should agree; the date should be that day's date or one that is recently past. Postdated checks or ones with discrepancies are not acceptable to the bank. Before listing a check that indicates "paid in full," refer to the customer's account balance to ascertain that it is for the full amount due.

Interest coupons are collection items negotiable without endorsement and are not deposited to an account until payment is received. A collection teller handles them and they should be entrusted to the bank about a week or ten days before the due date. Often a coupon envelope and a certificate of ownership, supplied by the bank, must be completed for their records. Promissory notes and drafts drawn by a depositor on another person are also handled as collection items and are not credited until paid. The collection teller will handle these transactions and deposit the funds upon receipt.

Unused traveler's checks may be deposited after the owner has counter-signed them. They are then endorsed on the back in the same manner as traveler's checks that have been accepted as payment on account. They are listed on the deposit slip with other items, such as bank drafts and money orders.

Deposits by mail should not include any negotiable items, such as cash or coupons. These should be taken to the bank or sent by a bonded messenger. The post office prefers not to handle letters with coins enclosed, but will register mail that carries paper money, coupons, or other negotiable paper.

Savings Accounts.   Savings accounts, called time deposits, are interest-bearing accounts in which the depositor intends or agrees to maintain a certain balance. Commercial banks, savings and loan associations, and mutual savings banks offer this service to customers.

Interest Paid.   Interest rates on deposits tend to fluctuate with movements in the economy. Generally though, commercial bank interest rates are $\frac{1}{4}$ percent lower than those of savings banks and savings and loan associations. All banks pay higher rates for term accounts, the exact rate depending on the amount deposited and the length of time for which it is committed. Early withdrawal of a term account requires the permission of the bank, which imposes a stiff penalty in loss of interest.

Insurance of Savings Accounts.   The insurance provisions of the Federal Savings and Loan Insurance Corporation and the Federal Deposit Insurance Corporation (for commercial banks) are in substantial conformity as to the insurance of accounts. All types of savings accounts in an insured institution are insured, whether regular passbook, certificate or bonus, installment or systematic savings, or other forms of withdrawable accounts. The basic insured amount for each saver is $40,000. A person may, under certain circumstances, hold or have an interest in more than one separately insured account in the same institution. As illustrated in Figure 13-2, a family of two may maintain as much as $200,000 on a fully insured basis; a family of three, $400,000; and a family of four, $560,000. Legal title to the funds in the accounts is not the determining factor of insurance coverage, but it is the interrelations of individuals and joint account ownership. Of the nine possible ownership groups, four are basically personal account ownerships and five are entity account ownerships held by corporations, partnerships, and other entities. The nine ownership groups are as follows.

Single ownerships	Corporation ownerships
Joint ownerships	Partnership ownerships
Revocable trust ownerships	Unincorporated association ownerships
Irrevocable trust ownerships	Public unit ownerships
Decedent estate ownerships	

Revocable and irrevocable trust accounts contain insurance provision for each beneficiary's interest to $40,000. The $40,000 maximum insurance for all other accounts listed here is applicable to each insured account in each insured association without regard to the accounts in any other insured association. In the case of an association having one or more branches, the main office and all branch offices are considered as one association.

Banking Services.   Most banking institutions offer their customers the following services.

Appliance and furniture financing either through the dealer or with a personal loan.

Automobile financing for the purchase of a new or used car.

Automobile loans on a car to refinance an existing contract or to buy another one.

Boat financing for boats of all kinds, outboard motors, boat-carrying trailers, and other equipment.

Business loans for large or small businesses—with sound commercial, industrial, and agricultural purposes—on a secured or unsecured basis, for short- or long-term periods.

Checking accounts.

Check reserve accounts, which protect the checking account holder up to a predetermined sum in case the account is overdrawn.

Christmas club accounts.

Collateral loans on marketable stocks and bonds, warehouse and field

FOR A FAMILY OF TWO

Individual	Husband	Individual		$ 40,000
accounts	Wife	Individual		$ 40,000
Joint	Husband and wife	Joint		$ 40,000
account				
Revocable	Husband	Trustee	Wife	$ 40,000
trusts	Wife	Trustee	Husband	$ 40,000
		Total		$200,000

FOR A FAMILY OF THREE

Individual	Husband	Individual		$ 40,000
accounts	Wife	Individual		$ 40,000
	Child	Individual		$ 40,000
Joint	Husband and wife	Joint		$ 40,000
accounts	Husband and child	Joint		$ 40,000
	Wife and child	Joint		$ 40,000
Revocable	Husband	Trustee	Wife	$ 40,000
trusts	Husband	Trustee	Child	$ 40,000
	Wife	Trustee	Husband	$ 40,000
	Wife	Trustee	Child	$ 40,000
		Total		$400,000

FOR A FAMILY OF FOUR

Individual	Husband	Individual		$ 40,000
accounts	Wife	Individual		$ 40,000
	Child #1	Individual		$ 40,000
	Child #2	Individual		$ 40,000
Joint	Husband and wife	Joint		$ 40,000
accounts	Husband and child #1	Joint		$ 40,000
	Wife and child #2	Joint		$ 40,000
	Child #1 and #2	Joint		$ 40,000
Revocable	Husband	Trustee	Wife	$ 40,000
trusts	Wife	Trustee	Husband	$ 40,000
	Husband	Trustee	Child #1	$ 40,000
	Wife	Trustee	Child #1	$ 40,000
	Husband	Trustee	Child #2	$ 40,000
	Wife	Trustee	Child #2	$ 40,000
		Total		$560,000

Figure 13-2   Savings account ownerships that qualify for maximum insured savings.

warehouse receipts covering readily saleable merchandise, assigned accounts receivable, or other security.

Collection services, such as interest and principal collected for customers on notes and other obligations. Drafts collected for shippers, and documentary drafts discounted.

Data-processing services for small businesses and professional people, such as doctors, dentists, and lawyers. The data-processing department of the bank is able to take care of professional billing, customer billing, payroll, accounts payable, installment loans, and many other collection and accounting chores.

Escrow service, in which the bank acts as impartial intermediary between buyer and seller to hold funds and documents under instructions pending completion of a real estate or other transaction.

Farm loans, such as those for crop and livestock production and marketing, and the purchase of farm lands, buildings, machinery, and other equipment.

Insurance premium financing, which eliminates the paying of insurance premiums in a lump sum and enables one to take advantage of reduced premiums on longer-term policies. Monthly payments are arranged.

International banking services, which include the buying and selling of exchange, sending remittances abroad, issuing commercial and travelers' letters of credit, handling and financing of import and export transactions, and maintaining overseas offices to assist the American businessman.

Investment services, which include the buying and selling of federal, state, and municipal bonds; the executing of customers' orders for the purchase or sale of other securities; and the supplying of monthly records of transactions.

Mail banking for both savings and checking accounts with postage-paid envelopes provided.

Money orders for a fee and cashier's checks issued for large amounts.

Personal loans arranged for depositors and nondepositors for almost any purpose, repayable in easy-to-budget monthly installments.

Property improvement loans to modernize, enlarge, or repair homes, apartment houses, stores, farm buildings, or any other property. Usually no collateral, endorsers, or down payment is required, and persons in all types of jobs are eligible. In many cases, repayment is extended to three years or longer.

Real estate loans for buying, building, or refinancing homes, apartment buildings, and other income property.

Safe-deposit boxes for the safekeeping of valuables in a guarded, fireproof vault. Only persons whose signatures are on file have access to the box. A yearly fee may be charged or the use may be a free service of the bank or association.

Savings accounts paying interest rates, which are compounded either daily or quarterly.

Traveler's checks available for purchase.

Trust services in which the bank acts as executor, guardian, trustee, transfer agent, registrar, and in other fiduciary capacities for individuals and corporations, and the management of securities and properties as required in estate matters.

Vacation club accounts.

Office Cash. A petty cash fund is set up in most offices and entrusted to a cashier, a receptionist, or a secretary to administer. This fund allows for payments in cash for small items such as messenger service, stamps, postage-due mail, supplies, and other incidental expenses. A voucher system is used to process these transactions. A form such as the one in Figure 13-3 is prepared and signed by the person in the office who is authorized to approve the expenditure and the person receiving payment. Any bill, receipt, or other paper pertaining to the transaction is attached to the voucher. The petty cash fund also operates as an emergency loan fund for employees. Whenever cash is borrowed, an IOU for the amount should be placed in the petty cash box, and the keeper of the box should see that it is reclaimed within a reasonable time.

The worker handling petty cash should always have cash and vouchers totaling the amount of the fund for which he or she is responsible. In a small office the sum may be $10 and in large offices as much as $100. When the cash is depleted, the worker takes the signed vouchers to the accounting department or the bookkeeper and receives in return for them a check or cash to replenish the fund to its maximum amount. The accounting records for the petty cash account are maintained by the accounting department from the vouchers.

SAMUEL H. JONES COMPANY

Petty Cash Voucher

Date _____   No. _____

Paid to _____ , $ _____

For _____

_____

Approved _____   _____

                                          Payment Received

Figure 13-3   Petty cash voucher.

13.2   CREDIT

Credit purchases by 50 million or more Americans using approximately 3,000 different types of credit cards present certain problems to both the consumer and the retailer. Each one should understand how the government attempts to protect the consumer by requiring a meaningful disclosure of credit terms. The following credit areas are discussed in this section.

Responsibility of Businesses Under the Consumer Credit Protection Act.   Any company or merchant that does not collect the full amount of a sale in cash is considered a lender. Thus he is required to comply with the law if he charges the customer for credit. However, he is excluded from compliance if payment in full is required in four or less installments and there is no finance or other charge for using the deferred payment plan. Under the Truth-in-Lending Act, the merchant must inform customers of all direct and indirect costs they have to pay when buying on credit. Also, customers are to be told the terms and conditions of credit arrangements. The customer will then be able to compare the cost of credit among different sources and shop more effectively for the best buy.

Truth-in-Lending Act.   A detailed explanation of the Truth-in-Lending Act and Regulation Z, which implements it and covers exactly what must be disclosed in writing to the customer when credit is extended, arranged, or just offered, may be found in *What You Ought to Know About Federal Reserve Regulation Z—Truth-in-Lending.* To secure a free copy, write to the Board of Governors of the Federal Reserve System, Washington, DC 20551. Additional references that should be consulted are

Understanding Truth in Lending. Small Marketers Aids No. 139, Small Business Administration. Free, Washington, DC 20416.

Truth in Lending, Regulation Z: Annual Percentage Rate Tables. Board of Governors of the Federal Reserve System, Washington, DC 20551.

What You Ought to Know About Truth in Lending. International Consumer Credit Association, 375 Jackson Ave., St. Louis, MO 63130.

Truth in Lending: Understanding the New Consumer Credit Rules. Commerce Clearinghouse, Inc., 4025 W. Peterson Ave., Chicago, IL 60646.

Truth in Lending: Regulation Z: Annual Percentage Rate Tables. Commerce Clearinghouse, Inc., 4025 W. Peterson Ave., Chicago, IL 60646.

The two most important items to be disclosed to the consumer are the finance charge and the annual percentage rate. The finance charge is the total of all the costs that must be paid for obtaining credit, either direct or indirect. Included are interest, carrying charges, costs of insurance premiums (under certain circumstances), and the cost of the appraisal or investigation reports required to complete the sale, as well as similar fees. Costs that would be paid even if credit was not granted can be excluded. The annual percentage rate (APR) must be stated as a percentage to the nearest quarter of 1 percent. Figuring the APR for closed-end sales transactions may be greatly simplified by the use of the booklet published by the Federal Reserve Board, *Annual Percentage Rate Tables*. It contains four tables for closed-end credit sales with payment ranging from 1 to 60 months, 61 to 120 months, 121 to 480 months, and 1 to 104 weeks. It may be purchased for $1 from the nearest Federal Reserve Bank or by written request to the Federal Reserve System in Washington.

Open-End Accounts.   Purchases of relatively small value at such outlets as department stores and service stations are usually charged to an open-end account. A two-step disclosure procedure is involved. First, before the new account is opened, the customer is shown a written or printed form that states:

1. The conditions under which a finance charge may be made and the period within which, if payment is made, there is no finance charge (such as "30 days without interest").

2. The method of determining the balance upon which a finance charge may be imposed.

3. How the actual finance charge is calculated.

4. The periodic rates used and the range of balances to which each applies as well as the corresponding annual percentage rate—for instance, a monthly rate of 1 1/2 percent (APR, 18 percent) on the first $500, and 1 percent (APR, 12 percent) on amounts over $500.

5. The conditions under which additional charges may be made, along with the details of how they are calculated. (This applies to new purchases, when charges are added to the account.)

6. A description of any lien (secured interest) that may be acquired on the customer's property—for instance, rights to repossession of a household appliance.

7. The minimum periodic payment required.

Second, the periodic statement (usually monthly) on any account with an unpaid balance of more than $1.00, or one on which a finance charge is made, must include certain information as illustrated in Figure 13-4, a typical statement in use by department stores. It is possible to use other formats as shown in *What You Ought to Know About Federal Reserve Regulation Z*.

Closed-End Credit.   Installment contracts for the purchase of larger items, such as appliances, television sets, and furniture, must also provide the customer with written information. A typical retail installment contract as shown in Figure 13-4 must include certain information on the face of the

ANY STORE U.S.A.
MAIN STREET–ANY CITY, U.S.A.

(Customer's name and address)

AMT. PAID $ _____

TO INSURE PROPER CREDIT RETURN THIS PORTION WITH YOUR PAYMENT

Transaction Date	Store	Reference Number	Dept. Number	Description		Purchases	Payments & Credits

Previous Balance	Minus Payments and Credits	Balance subject to FINANCE CHARGE	Plus FINANCE CHARGE	Plus Purchases	New Balance

Regular account terms—Full payment is due upon receipt of statement.

Next Closing Date Is:

YOU MAY ELECT TO PAY YOUR ACCOUNT IN FULL AT ANY TIME. THERE WILL BE NO FINANCE CHARGE IF THE NEW BALANCE IS RECEIVED BY YOUR NEXT CLOSING DATE. IF YOU ELECT TO PAY THE MINIMUM PAYMENT SHOWN ABOVE, A SMALL *FINANCE CHARGE* WILL BE ADDED, COMPUTED ON THE PREVIOUS BALANCE, AFTER DEDUCTING PAYMENTS AND CREDITS, AT PERIODIC RATES OF *1 1/2% (AN ANNUAL PERCENTAGE RATE OF 18%)* ON BALANCES OF *$1000.00* OR LESS AND *1%* PER MONTH (AN *ANNUAL PERCENTAGE RATE OF 12%*) ON THAT PORTION OF THE BALANCE OVER *$1000.00.*

Figure 13-4 Example of open-end account billing statement designed to conform with Truth-In-Lending Act.

sales contract above or adjacent to the customer's signature or on one side of a separate sheet that identifies the transaction. In particularly large sales, such as home improvements requiring installation, the customer has the right of rescission or cancellation of the sale within three days. The merchant must be notified by mail, telegram, or any other form of writing by midnight of the third business day following (1) the date the sale was made, or (2) the date the merchant supplied the required disclosures, whichever is later. The merchant should give the customer along with the disclosure two copies of a notice of the right to rescission and should wait to start installation work, if required, until the cancellation period has expired.

Advertising Limitations and Penalties.   Under the Act, advertising is limited to such terms as "Use our easy payment plan" and "We welcome credit accounts." A specific down payment, installment plan, or amount of credit that can be arranged may be stated only when such terms are *usually* arranged. No specific credit terms may be spelled out unless *all* other terms are stated clearly and conspicuously. Such terms as "No money down" or "Thirty-six months to pay" may not be used unless all other related terms are given.

The Act provides for both civil and criminal penalties. The consumer has the right to sue a merchant who fails to disclose credit information. Anyone who willfully disregards the law is subject to criminal penalties of a maximum fine of $5,000 and maximum imprisonment of one year, or both.

Business and Personal Use of Credit.   Sources of loan money are (1) banks, (2) savings and loan associations, (3) consumer finance and small loan companies, (4) credit unions, (5) pawnbrokers, (6) retail stores and automobile dealers when purchases are made, and (7) life insurance companies that make loans on life insurance policies. Most of these sources are readily available to the borrower, but some depend on a person's individual circumstances. Everyone, however, should know how they differ and be able to determine how much a loan from any one of these sources will cost him.

Determining the Cost of Credit.   One method of identifying the cost of a loan is to compute the *dollar cost*—merely the difference between the total amount paid back and the amount borrowed or the original price of the purchased item.

Another method is to find the *true interest* rate. Under the Truth-in-Lending Act, lenders may no longer mislead the borrower when quoting interest rates or the conditions for borrowing or making purchases on time. Even so, the majority of borrowers generally underestimate finance costs by a large margin. For instance, if you borrow $100 at 6 percent, keep it a year and then repay $106, the true interest rate is 6 percent. But if finance charges are deducted immediately (discounted) and you receive $94 but pay back $100 at the end of the year, the actual annual interest rate is higher than 6 percent because you had the use of only $94 for the year. Or if, in addition, monthly payments are made on the discounted loan, the borrower has the use of only half the total amount over the course of the loan. In this latter case, the true interest rate would be almost double the quoted rate, or 12 percent instead of 6 percent.

The following formula may be used to compute true interest when one is checking the finance charges quoted by the lender. Most loans or purchases on time are presented as a total number of monthly payments of a specified sum of money. Suppose in shopping for a $1,000 loan, you are offered the following alternatives.

	Monthly Payments	Number of Payments
Loan 1	$89.40	12
Loan 2	52.75	24
Loan 3	38.40	36

Using the formula $R = \dfrac{2\ PC}{T(N + 1)}$ where R = the annual interest rate.

P = the payment period in the *year*.

C = the cost in dollars: the total in payments minus the amount borrowed. (In the case of a credit purchase, subtract the cash price of the merchandise from the total you pay—down payment plus all payments.)

T = the total amount borrowed or, on a credit purchase, the *balance due* after the down payment.

N = the total number of installments or payment periods.

to compute the *true interest* rate for Loan 2 where, $1,000 is to be repaid in 24 months at $52.75 a month, P is 12; C is $266 (24 times $52.75 or $1,266 minus $1,000, leaving $266); T is $1,000, and N is 24.

$$R = \frac{2 \text{ times } 12 \text{ times } \$266}{\$1,000 \text{ times } (24 + 1)}$$

$$R = \frac{6,384}{25,000}$$

$$R = .255 \text{ or } 25.5\%$$

A borrower under Loan 2 would pay 25.5 percent annual interest. Of the three alternatives, Loan 1 offers the lowest interest rate (13.4 percent).

A helpful interest-calculating chart is available from *Changing Times* Reprint Service, 1729 H Street NW, Washington, D.C. 20006.

Banks and Savings and Loan Associations. Banks and savings and loan associations are anxious to loan to customers and other people who are good credit risks. Most personal loan departments collect their charges as discounts (a certain percentage of the amount collected in advance) or add-ons (a certain percentage added to the sum owed). A depositor of one of these institutions is usually not required to furnish references nor is a credit investigation made. A person not having an account would have to furnish references and submit to a credit investigation. The minimum repayment period for other than a mortgage loan is usually six months, and the maximum five years. A monthly repayment plan is often used with the balance payable at any time without a prepayment penalty. Many institutions have eliminated late charges, fees or service charges, relying on the interest to cover the expenses of handling loans. Figure 13-5 shows a typical repayment schedule. True annual interest rates run between 8 percent and 18 percent, averaging about 12 percent.

Many banks offer preferred checking-account customers a ready-reserve account from which a predetermined sum may be drawn upon automatically in case the balance in the checking account is depleted. The loan terms for use of this ready credit are similar to the following.

1. A finance charge is imposed on the account consisting of (a) a transfer fee in the amount of 1 percent of each advance made to the account and added to the ready-reserve account balance at the time it is made, and (b) periodic interest as of each monthly statement date in an amount equal to $1\frac{1}{2}$ percent (annual rate, 18 percent) of the balance of the account at the end of the previous cycle date, less all payments made and credits applied during the statement period. Payments of the amount transferred and the 1 percent fee must be made within 25 days of the end of the statement period if the borrower is to avoid the imposition of the finance charge mentioned in (b).

2. A minimum payment based on the balance of the account must be made within 10 days after the statement cycle date as follows.

Account Balance at Statement Cycle Date	Minimum Periodic Payment
$ 0.01 to $ 25.00	Balance due
$ 25.01 to $ 600.00	$ 25.00
$ 600.01 to $1200.00	$ 50.00
$1200.01 to $1800.00	$ 75.00
$1800.01 to $2400.00	$100.00

3. In the event the minimum payment is not paid prior to the next succeeding statement date, a late charge is made at the rate of five cents per dollar on the past-due amount, but not exceeding $5.00 per statement date.

4. As security for payment of the balance of the ready-reserve account, security interest, called a banker's lien, is acquired on any property which at any time is in the possession of the bank or on which the bank carries a mortgage or a loan.

Consumer Finance and Small Loan Companies.   Consumer finance companies specialize in small loans to the family. They generally want to know how the applicant for a loan pays his bills, how much he earns, and whether he has a steady income. The local credit exchange is contacted for the applicant's

| Borrow | And repay this monthly amount | | |
up to	In 60 months	In 30 months	In 12 months
$ 300	$ 6.50	$ 11.50	$ 26.50
500	11.00	19.50	44.50
1,000	22.00	38.50	88.50
1,500	32.50	57.50	132.50
2,000	43.50	77.00	177.00
2,500	54.50	96.00	221.00
3,000	65.00	115.00	265.00
5,000	108.50	192.00	442.00
10,000	217.00	383.50	883.50

Figure 13-5   Typical repayment schedule for a loan from a savings and loan association.

record for prompt payment, which follows a person from community to community. The applicant himself should gather the following information.

1. Is the loan agency licensed by the state?
2. What is the total amount to be repaid?
3. What is the total dollar cost or true annual percentage rate?
4. Are there penalties for late or missed payments? If so, how much are they?
5. What is the amount of the rebate for early repayment?

The contract should be read carefully, and amounts, dates, and terms checked for agreement with the applicant's understanding of the terms. Never sign a blank contract or one with any blank spaces. Obtain a copy of the contract and file it with personal papers for future reference.

Small loan companies are able to negotiate a loan quickly because most of them grant loans on a person's signature alone, not requiring collateral or a cosigner. True interest on the amount owed during the month is quoted. The range is from less than 2 percent a month to $3\frac{1}{2}$ percent, with the majority of companies charging $2\frac{1}{2}$ percent to 3 percent. Thus, the true interest rate varies from slightly less than 24 percent to over 36 percent a year, which must be stated according to Regulation Z. A sliding scale is used: the larger the loan, the lower the interest rate.

Credit Unions.   If the employees at your company or the members of an organization to which you belong have formed a credit union, you may borrow from it. A credit union may loan to members only. Members deposit money, drawing interest in the form of dividends, and are eligible to borrow from the fund at a fixed rate, usually 1 percent a month. The highest rate that any credit union may charge according to the 1968 Truth-in-Lending Act is 1 percent a month, which under this regulation must be quoted as 12 percent per annum.

Pawnbrokers. A pawnbroker specializes in small loans that other loan sources wouldn't consider. An item of value, such as jewelry, a watch, or a musical instrument, is given as security until the loan is repaid. The borrower is charged a true interest rate from 2 percent to 10 percent a month (24 percent to 120 percent a year). These loans are not repayable in installments. Approximately, 20 cents to $1 a month is charged for each $10 owed. The pawnbroker has the right to sell the article left with him if the loan is not repaid with interest and charges within a certain time after the debt becomes due. The loan is limited to the resale value of the article, which is often considerably lower than its worth to the borrower.

Retail Stores. Sales or purchase credit is available at many retail outlets through several types of accounts. The regular charge account calls for payment on receipt of the monthly bill or, in a few cases, within 30 days of the date of the bill. If the customer fails to pay on time, service charges may be added (see the terms in Figure 13-4).

Budget accounts are available at some stores. Equal monthly payments are made of the total of the purchases plus finance or carrying charges. A similar type is the revolving purchase account, wherein the customer may make purchases each month up to a certain amount. A specific sum or percentage of the balance of the account plus carrying charges must be paid each month to keep the account revolving. No carrying charge is made if the account is paid in full each month.

Installment purchase contracts, such as conditional sales contracts, are also available for the purchase of appliances, television sets, and other expensive items (Figure 13-6). A down payment is required and the customer agrees to pay off the balance plus finance charges, usually in equal amounts, every month over a period of time. Chattel mortgages, bailment leases, and rental contracts are also available.

Department store revolving credit and revolving car-credit accounts cost approximately $1\frac{1}{2}$ percent a month or about 18 percent a year.

Automobile Dealers. Most automobile dealers prefer to sell cars on the installment purchase plan in order to take advantage of increased revenue through credit financing. Hidden costs in the purchase of automobiles on time should be assessed carefully. The true interest rate on the installment purchase of a new or used car has been known to be as high as 36 percent. The selling of automobiles at big-volume outlets is done on the *shuffle system* by a team made up of a *liner*, a salesperson who meets the prospect, sizes him up, and gathers certain information; a *T-O person*, who builds up the deal with more extras, more insurance, longer terms, and so on; a *finance person*, who figures up the take on one deal as opposed to another and adjusts the terms to make up for the trade-in; and a *closer*, who winds up the deal. It may become so complicated that the prospective buyer is unable to assess clearly the terms and actual cost over the life of the contract or the life of the car. The new disclosure laws ensure the customer the receipt of a written

Seller's Name _____ Contract # _____

_____

RETAIL INSTALLMENT CONTRACT AND SECURITY AGREEMENT

The undersigned (herein called Purchaser, whether one or more) purchases from _____ (seller) and grants to _____ _____ a security interest, in, subject to the terms and conditions hereof, the following described property.

Quantity	Description	Amount

Description of Trade-in: _____

_____

_____

	Sales Tax	
	Total	

Purchaser's Name _____
Purchaser's Address _____
City _____
State _____ Zip _____

1. Cash Price $ _____
2. Less: Cash Down Payment $ _____
3.   Trade-in $ _____
4.   Total Down Payment $ _____ $ _____
5. Unpaid Balance of Cash Price $ _____
6. Other Charges:
   _____ $ _____
   _____ $ _____
7. Amount Financed $ _____
8. Finance Charge $ _____
9. Total of Payments $ _____
10. Deferred Payment Price (1 + 6 + 8) $ _____
11. Annual Percentage Rate _____ %

Insurance Agreement

The purchase of insurance coverage is voluntary and not required for credit. ____(Type of Ins.)____ insurance coverage is available at a cost of $_____ for the term of credit.

I desire insurance coverage

Signed _____
Date _____

I do not desire insurance coverage

Signed _____
Date _____

Purchaser hereby agrees to pay to

_____

at their offices shown above the "TOTAL OF PAYMENTS" shown above in _____ monthly installments of $_____ (final payment to be $ _____) the first installment being payable _____ 19__, and all subsequent installments on the same day of each consecutive month until paid in full. The finance charge applies from (date) _____.

Signed _____

Notice to Buyer: You are entitled to a copy of the contract you sign. You have the right to pay in advance the unpaid balance of this contract and obtain a partial refund of the finance charge based on the "Actuarial Method." [Any other method of computation may be so identified, for example, "Rule of 78's," "Sum of the Digits," etc.]

Figure 13-6 Example of retail installment contract and security agreement.

contract that may be taken home so that a study can be made of the terms. The actual cost of the purchase can be computed before closing the deal. A decision to contact other sources for an automobile loan can also be made at this time. Some insurance companies, some credit unions, and most banks make automobile loans.

Insurance Companies. Cash loans to holders of certain types of insurance policies are available from insurance companies. These loans are based on the total or part of the cash value of the insurance, as explained in the policy. Many companies loan up to 95 percent of the cash value of a straight life policy. True interest rates are from 5 percent to 9 percent and about 4 percent on GI policies. The advantages of a loan on an insurance policy are its low cost and the fact that as long as the policy remains in force the principal need not be repaid until the borrower desires to repay it. The disadvantage is that protection for the beneficiaries is seriously jeopardized while the loan is in effect. Borrowing against an insurance policy, until the loan is repaid, reduces the insurance protection unless term insurance is taken out to maintain the insurance program. Life insurance policies having cash or loan value may be used as security for cash loans from various agencies.

Additional Credit Charges. Many lenders make additional charges on loans for a variety of reasons. A borrower should recognize these as cost factors for the privilege of borrowing money.

1. Investigation fee. Many loan companies charge an investigation fee of $3 to $10. When a lender agrees to lend you $100 at 6 percent plus an investigation fee of $5, the cost of the loan is $11 or 11 percent, if the interest is paid with the principal at the end of the year. If the interest is deducted in advance and the total principal is paid at the end of the year, the cost of the loan is slightly more than $11 or 11+ percent. If the loan is to be paid back in twelve monthly installments, the true interest rate is twice 11 percent or about 22 percent.

2. Delinquency charge. Another hidden cost when one borrows money involves penalties for failing to make payments within the required time. Credit unions rarely assess such penalties because payments are usually deducted from the member's paycheck. Some states have strict laws that prohibit small loan companies from making such charges. In most states, however, lenders can exact penalties if payments are not made promptly.

3. Repayment allowance. Should a person repay a loan early, prepaid interest due as a refund may be forfeited. Some states do not require lenders to refund any of the prepaid interest. Some banks will voluntarily make refunds; others do not. Some companies refund the prepaid interest but make a special charge for retiring a loan before its due date. Policies regarding repayment of a loan should be understood before one signs any loan papers.

4. Insurance cost. Small loan companies and installment sales dealers, unless prohibited by law, may require the borrower to buy health, accident, or life insurance in order to secure a loan. Therefore, a careful analysis of the insurance policy and its cost should be made before one accepts the loan. It may be possible to arrange for the loan and/or insurance coverage at more favorable rates.

The use of credit life insurance is increasing, especially in connection with mortgages. Credit life insurance insures the life of the time purchaser (borrower) for the unpaid balance in the event of death. Many states require that credit life insurance be described and listed separately with its cost in the contract. In some cases, lenders or creditors provide such insurance without extra charge. The person insured by credit life insurance should be the one whose income is paying for the mortgage, the credit purchase, or the loan.

Pointers on the Wise Use of Credit. Obtain a written statement of all terms and conditions of the credit transaction. Find out exactly what you are paying for the time purchase or the loan in dollars and in true annual interest.

Before using credit make certain that the extra cost is offset by the advantages of that specific purchase or situation. Be sure that the immediate possession and use of what you acquire is worth the additional cost.

Report at once to your creditor if you are unable to make a payment on time, so that you may make arrangements to protect your credit rating and save penalty costs.

Make the use of credit a part of long-range financial planning in order to maintain a sound relationship between income, investments, and expenditures.

Consult a lawyer if the finance charges and interest rate are more than those stated on the contract. You have the right to sue.

Members of the legal profession, such as the Chicago Bar Association, suggest that a person using credit observe the following policies.

1. Read carefully every paper *before* you sign it.
2. Be sure *all* blank spaces are filled in before signing.
3. Total all the charges and compare them with the *cash* price.
4. Rely on the written word in the contract or note, not on sales talk.
5. Remember that a signed promissory note or conditional sales contract calls for prompt payment. Business reversals, sickness, accident, the loss of your job—these events do not excuse delay in payment.
6. Do not sign anything that is not clear. If the amount is substantial, consult a lawyer, who can be of more help *before* than *after* the document is signed.
7. Check monthly statements for errors, such as overcharges, uncredited payments, irregular finance charges. Computer errors do occur and when discovered should be reported in writing to the company with a clear explanation of the error. Overcharges may be the result of an unauthorized person's using your credit card or of a charge from another account with a similar name or account number. Arithmetical errors are not common, but often

credits to the account arrive after the machine billing date and are not picked up by the computer until the next month. Sometimes interest charges are figured by a certain method when in reality another one should be used. For example, the count of the number of days for which interest is to be charged might not agree with the original terms. Any discrepancy between your figures and those on the statement should be checked immediately.

Credit Information. *Collecting Credit Ratings.* There are several sources of information regarding a person's or a firm's credit standing that should be consulted and their reports checked against each other before credit is advanced. The best known credit agency for company ratings is Dun & Bradstreet, Inc., which provides information to subscribers on businesses around the world. Dun & Bradstreet rates each firm, indicates the amount of working capital and the net worth, and supplies a credit rating of "High," "Good," "Fair," or "Limited," based on such things as experience of owners, pay record, and location. International credit information is available for Latin America and Continental Europe. Dun & Bradstreet also provides national and international collection services on past-due accounts as a separate service.

Many firms specialize in local credit reporting for subscribers on a yearly or case fee basis. Their addresses and telephone numbers may be found in the yellow pages of the telephone directory under "Credit Reporting Agencies." Other sources of local information are banks that give information on the credit standing of their customers; wholesale firms, which often supply information to competitors in return for similar favors; and the customer's own statement of assets, liabilities, and sales for the past year. Credit agencies will secure for a client registered information of recent bankruptcies, assignments, compositions, mortgages and other preferential claims, and court judgments as they are recorded.

Several directories of manufacturers are available, and you should consult them to ascertain that the prospective creditor is actually a going concern and also to locate firms in certain trades with whom you desire to do business. One of the most complete is *Thomas' Register of American Manufacturers,* published annually by Thomas Publishing Company, New York. It contains a list of over 75,000 products with manufacturers' names under each product, arranged by state and city, and a list of the trade names and the trademarks of widely advertised products. *MacRae's Bluebook* (Chicago) is more complete as far as addresses of local distributors and branch offices are concerned than *Thomas' Register* but less complete in detailed information on the company. A classified-materials section and a list of trade names are part of the *Bluebook*. An international source of the names and addresses of merchants and manufacturers in each city within a country is *Kelley's Directory of Merchants, Manufacturers and Shippers of the World—A*

Guide to the Export, Import, Shipping and Manufacturing Industries, published by Kelley's Directory, Ltd., London.

Supplying Credit Information.   Policies regarding the supplying of customer credit information to other firms should be established by a company and certain personnel delegated to handle all such inquiries.

An employee's credit standing is a personal matter and any inquiries regarding it, including telephone requests, should be directed to the employee. If this is not possible, the personnel manager or someone else with delegated authority, possibly the employee's supervisor, should supply only certain routine facts, for instance, length of employment and job title, after first determining who the caller is and why there is a need to know. In some cases, the request may have to be denied.

A secretary should never divulge personal information about a superior (or any other worker) unless permission has been given to do so.

Fair Credit Reporting Act.   The Fair Credit Reporting Act guarantees certain rights to the consumer who is the subject of credit reports. All the information in the credit file, including its source, is available. The consumer may find out the names of those who have received employment reports within the past two years and the names of all others who have received credit reports within the past six months. The credit record may be reviewed at the local credit bureau(s) by furnishing proper identification or by written request for a telephone interview. During a personal interview, the consumer may be accompanied by another person (in addition to his/her spouse). This other person must furnish reasonable identification, and a signed statement may be required granting permission to the credit bureau to review the file in the presence of someone other than a husband or wife.

Contents of a Credit File.   Information accumulated in a credit file includes identity facts (name, address, marital status, social security number), present employment (position held, length of employment, and salary), personal history (date of birth, number of dependents, previous address, previous employment record), credit history (credit experiences with credit granters), and other facts of public record.

Correction of Errors in a Credit File.   A re-investigation of questionable items may be requested by a consumer. If an item is found to be inaccurate or can no longer be verified, it will be deleted. If the re-investigation does not resolve the question, a brief statement of about one hundred words may be filed that reports the consumer's side of the issue. The statement, or a summary of it, will be included in any future reports of the file. The credit bureau may be requested to notify those who have received employment reports within the past two years and all others who have received regular credit reports within the past six months of any deletions, changes, or additions of explanatory statements.

Cost to Review a Credit File. The Act provides that a consumer cannot be charged for an interview if within the past 30 days credit has been denied because of a credit report from a credit bureau or a notice has been received from a collection department affiliated with the credit bureau. The bureau may, however, make a reasonable charge for a consumer interview (plus a charge not to exceed that which is charged to its own customers for furnishing notifications and statements) if a consumer has *not* been denied credit or received a notice from a collection department of the credit bureau. The amount of the charges must be stated in advance.

A consumer is not charged for notifications to previous recipients of a deleted item that is found to be inaccurate or can no longer be verified. Also, charges cannot be levied for notification to previous recipients of the addition of an explanatory statement if credit has been denied within the past 30 days.

Locating a Credit File. The credit granter who refuses credit must provide the name and address of the credit bureau supplying the report on which the decision was based. If credit references have been contacted directly, the person or company refusing credit must inform the consumer at the time the credit application is rejected that the consumer has the right to request in writing within 60 days the nature of the information on which the credit decision was based. The credit granter need not disclose the source of information but must supply sufficient facts with which the accuracy of the information can be refuted or challenged.

File Life of Adverse Information. Credit and employment records report adverse information on the following situations for a limit of seven or fourteen years:

7 years	*14 Years*
Suits and judgments (or until statute of limitations expires)	Straight bankruptcies
Wage earner plans	
Paid tax liens	
Collection accounts	
Accounts changed to bad debts	
Records of arrests, indictments, convictions, or other adverse information	

None of these limitations apply on credit reports in connection with credit or life insurance transactions over $50,000 or an employment report involving an annual salary over $20,000.

Qualified Recipients of Credit Reports. A credit report on a consumer may be obtained if it is to be used in one of the following ways:

1. To consider a person for credit.
2. To review or to collect an account.
3. To consider a person for employment.

4. To consider a person for insurance.

5. To comply with a court order.

6. To fulfill a legitimate business need, such as a potential partnership, investment, or lease.

7. To comply with the written instructions of a consumer to a credit bureau to issue a credit report for a legitimate purpose.

8. To satisfy the requirements of a governmental agency that is proposing to extend credit, to collect or review an account, to employ or to insure a person, to make a military security clearance, or to comply with a law that states a person's financial responsibility must be checked.

In all other instances, individuals, companies, and governmental agencies may secure only identifying information from a credit bureau. Such information is limited to name, address, former addresses, place of employment, and former places of employment. Anyone who willfully obtains a credit report under false pretenses can be fined up to $5,000 or imprisoned for one year, or both.

Equal Credit Opportunity Act. Discrimination in any aspect of a credit transaction because of sex, marital status, race, national origin, religion, or age (with limited exceptions) is prohibited by the Equal Credit Opportunity Act. According to the Federal Trade Commission, the Act helps creditworthy persons obtain charge accounts, loans, mortgages, and other kinds of credit by not allowing creditors to treat applicants unequally because of the characteristics mentioned. It does not, however, guarantee a person credit; and creditors may still determine creditworthiness by considering such factors as income, expenses, debts, and reliability of the applicant. Institutions that regularly extend credit, such as banks, small loan and finance companies, retail and department stores, credit card companies, and credit unions, are covered by the Act.

Women in particular are assisted through the Act to build a good credit history (a record of how bills have been paid in the past) and thus be able to obtain credit on their own. One provision states that creditors who report histories to credit bureaus must report information on accounts shared by a husband and wife in both their names. Another requires that a creditor must not use unfavorable information about an account shared with a spouse or former spouse if it can be shown that the bad credit rating does not accurately reflect the applicant's willingness or ability to repay. Also, a creditor must not refuse to consider the credit history of any account held in a spouse's or former spouse's name that the applicant can show is an accurate picture of willingness and ability to repay. Thus, a woman who is married, divorced, separated, or widowed and seeks to establish a credit history should make a special point to call or visit the local credit bureau(s) to make sure that all relevant information usually carried by the credit bureau is in a credit file under her own name.

If you believe you have been discriminated against, you can complain to the creditor, you can sue the creditor, and you can file a complaint with the government. General questions about the Equal Credit Opportunity Act will be answered in writing by the Federal Trade Commission, Equal Credit Opportunity, Washington, DC 20580, or one of the regional offices in Atlanta, Boston, Chicago, Cleveland, Dallas, Denver, Los Angeles, New York, San Francisco, and Seattle. Consult your local telephone directory for the address and telephone number. You may also secure copies of the Equal Credit Opportunity Act or copies of a pamphlet giving highlights of the Act by writing to Federal Trade Commission, Legal and Public Records, Room 130, Washington, DC 20580. The American Express Company makes available single copies of "The Credit Handbook for Women" upon request in writing to American Express Card Division, American Express Plaza, New York, NY 10004.

Fair Credit Billing Act. This Act allows a borrower to challenge and correct billing information and prohibits creditors from sending adverse credit reports until the rules covering disputes have been followed.

Fair Collection Practices Act. Under this Act, a borrower is protected from abusive, deceptive and unfair debt collection practices by debt collection agencies. The Federal Trade Commission in Washington can supply detailed information on the federal laws that protect a person who buys on credit.

13.3 INSURANCE

Insurance is a means of limiting economic losses by sharing risks with others who face similar risks. Today, it is possible to insure a company against almost any disaster or loss. A company should work with an insurance agent when attempting to select adequate coverage so that the firm and its employees are fully insured at every possible moment. Shifts in inventory, merchandise on hand, construction in process, and the perils of doing business may change from day to day.

In this section the descriptive list of available insurance illustrates how extensive is the coverage. No attempt has been made, however, to present costs because premiums are based on the options selected when the policy is tailored to company or individual needs. Suggestions for safeguarding policies and maintaining records are included. An agent or broker will keep the businessman informed as to insurance needs, will check changes in company circumstances that require added or reduced coverage, will place insurance, will advise on renewals before expiration dates, will send bills for premiums, will cancel policies, will secure returns on prepaid premiums, and will report claims under the policies to the insurance company. But the company will need to maintain its own records of premium due-dates, expiration dates, and claims for loss; to receive and check policies for accuracy and safeguard them during their life; and to review the insurance program periodically to make certain that it includes recent changes in personnel, plant, equipment, or other conditions of doing business.

Treated in this section are the insurance topics listed below. Additional insurance options and terms can be found in the "Dictionary of Business Terms," Section 16.6.

Insurance Coverage for Businesses.   Practically any risk may be covered by insurance. Usually, a company purchases a general policy to cover common risks, and adds certain options according to the nature and location of the business. The newer types of policies are portfolio or package plans that extend basic protection against property damage losses on buildings and business personal property and include general liability coverage. Options are added as needed to complete the portfolio or package, which costs less than individual policies providing the same coverages. According to insurance companies, one agent, one company, one policy, and one premium mean better service with flexible premium payments either monthly or quarterly. The following list of business insurance illustrates the extent of available protection against risks.

The basic policy usually provides property coverage for loss or damage by:

Civil commotion	Riot
Explosion	Smoke
Fire	Vehicles or aircraft
Lightning	Windstorm and hail

Broader coverage that may be added as options to the basic policy includes:

Accounts receivable lost or damaged	Property being transported in motor vehicles leased or operated by the insured
Burglary, theft, or robbery while closed	
Collapse of building	
Expense of continuing normal operations	Property temporarily off premises
	Signs coverage
Falling objects	Sprinkler leakage
Glass breakage or damage	Valuable papers and records loss or damage
Interruption of business	
Loss of rents	Water damage
Malicious mischief	Weight of ice, snow, sleet
Premises burglary and robbery	

The property coverage of buildings also applies to:

All additions and extensions attached to the insured buildings, except outdoor signs

Materials and supplies intended for use in the construction, alteration, or repair of the buildings

All permanent service equipment, machinery, and fixtures on the premises

Yard fixtures

Personal property of the insured used in maintaining or servicing the buildings, including floor coverings; fire extinguishing apparatus; refrigerating, ventilating, cooking, dishwashing, and laundering equipment; shades and outdoor furniture (but excluding other furnishings)

Business personal property coverage includes:

Furniture, fixtures, equipment, merchandise, and supplies on the premises and usual to occupancy of the buildings

Property belonging to others for which the insured is liable

Improvements and betterments to a rented office of the building

Basic general liability coverage insures against the following up to a policy limit.

Bodily injury to others

Damage to the property of others

Liability arising out of the operation of elevators, warehouses, parking areas, restaurants, swimming pools, gift shops, and private garages

The payment of expenses for defending the insured, including lawyer's fees and court costs, if a lawsuit results

The cost of premiums for appeal bonds and bonds to release attachment in such a suit

First aid expenses for others at the time of an accident

Any reasonable expense incurred at the request of the insurance company to attend hearings and trials

Any of the following liability options may be added to the basic general liability policy.

Cameras and musical instruments	Fine arts
Comprehensive general liability	Garage keepers' legal liability
Comprehensive personal liability	Guests' property–innkeeper's liability
Contractual liability	Medical payments
Elevator collision	Personal injury
Employer's nonownership automobile liability	Radium

Businesses may add the following comprehensive crime coverage to the insurance package.

Employee dishonesty—loss of money, securities, or other property.

Loss inside premises—loss of money and securities by destruction, disappearance, or wrongful abstraction within the premises, bank premises, or similar recognized places of safe deposit.

Loss outside the premises—destruction, disappearance, or wrongful abstraction of
money and securities outside the premises while being conveyed by a messenger
or armored car company, or while in the living quarters in the home of a messenger. Covers other property against loss or damage by robbery while being conveyed
by a messenger or armored car company, and against robbery and theft while in
the living quarters in the home of a messenger.

Loss due to counterfeit currency—covers counterfeit postal money orders, express
money orders, and U.S. or Canadian paper currency.

Depositors' forgery—losses sustained through forgery or alteration of checks, drafts,
notes, or similar written instruments drawn by or upon the insured. Coverage
applies to the insured's instruments only—NOT incoming drafts, checks, and so
on.

The following boiler and machinery coverage is available as an option.

Loss to property arising out of accidents to boilers and certain types of pressure
vessels. After payment for damages to property, the remaining limit of liability
is applied to expedite the repair and to pay for damages to the property of others.

Extended coverage includes additional types of pressure vessels, machinery, electrical
equipment, extra expense, use and occupancy (daily or weekly indemnity), con-
sequential damage, and prevention of occupancy.

It is also possible to take out an umbrella liability policy. This is an extra-
high, single-limit protection against catastrophe-type losses. It fills many
coverage gaps in basic policies. Liability limits of $1 million or more are
provided, subject to a deductible.

Protection of Policies. All insurance policies should be examined upon
receipt to see that the names of the insured and the beneficiaries are correct.
If the coverage is on jointly owned property, both owners' names must be
listed. The face value, the terms, and any other typed information should be
checked against the original application. The details of coverage and exclusions should be examined to determine that they meet the needs of the
insured. Much of this checking can be handled by the secretary, but some of
the finer points of coverage should be the responsibility of an officer of the
company or the proprietor of the business.

After it is ascertained that all details are in order and that records have been
made, the policy should be placed in a safe and readily accessible spot. A
safe-deposit box at the bank is the safest storage for these valuable documents.
The office safe or locked (fireproof) file cabinet, however, may be used, if the
policies must be close at hand for frequent reference.

When the policy has expired or been canceled, it should be placed in
storage according to a predetermined retention schedule (see Section 12.1).
An old policy may be needed for reference or evidence if claims or possible
claims covered by it are pending. Clip to the old policy the form on which a
summary of the details of coverage was made when it was issued (Figure
13-7). The information on this sheet will save time when one is hunting for a
particular policy; otherwise, each one might have to be unfolded and read.

INSURANCE POLICY FOR (Name of company or person)

Type	Issuing Company	Amount	Date of Issue	Expiration Date	Details of Coverage	Beneficiary	Amount of Premium— Due Dates	Agent
				Cancellation date:	Exclusions:			

Figure 13-7 Form for recording information about insurance policies.

Insurance Records.   The keeping of insurance records cannot be left entirely in the hands of the insurance company or its agent. Even though an insurance agent can usually be counted on to handle most aspects of a client's business, a change in the office personnel, a breakdown in the billing system, or his own prolonged absence from the office due to illness, travel, or emergency could result in oversights and delays in the mailing out of important notices. Consequently, a businessman, company, or individual must keep records of payment and expiration dates. If a policy expires or is canceled on the last day of the grace period, insurance coverage ceases. Premiums must be in the office of the insurance company or its agent prior to the due date for assurance of continuation of coverage. Even if a policy has been carried for years with the same company, that company has no obligation to underwrite a loss that occurs after the policy has expired or has lapsed because of nonpayment of the premium.

Tickler File Record.   When the policy is first received, a card for the tickler file should be prepared. The two important entries on it are the premium due dates and the expiration date. It should be placed in the file so that it automatically receives attention a week to ten days before the due date and approximately one month before the expiration date. It may be necessary for the insured to arrange a loan to cover the premium, or the company management might wish to discuss changes in the coverage, the agent, or the issuing company. One need not wait until the expiration date, however, to make an important change. There are many ways to modify an existing policy during its life, and it may be canceled at any time, with prepaid premiums being returned or applied to a new policy.

The card should also contain sufficient information to identify the policy—type, number, issuing company, insured, amount of premium, and where to pay. A typical setup for such a card may be seen in Figure 13-8.

Insurance File Record.   A record of each insurance policy should be maintained on a form similar to the one in Figure 13-7. All pertinent details regarding the policy and its coverage can be listed on an 8 1/2″ × 11″ sheet that will allow interested persons to review the total coverage for that policy. It is important to include a summary of the details of coverage and the exclusions. If the coverage is extensive and it is desired to restrict the information to one page, the executive responsible for the insurance program should indicate to the secretary the features of the coverage that should be listed. These records should be separated in the files by the company, the subsidiary, or the person insured. Later, the sheet should be attached to the canceled, lapsed, or expired policy when it is placed in storage.

Claims Records.   A loss covered by an insurance policy should be reported immediately to the agent or the insurance company. A claim form or proof of loss will need to be filled out and a duplicate filed with the other insurance records. A detailed explanation of the events leading up to the loss and a description of the items damaged, lost, or whatever should be prepared.

Premium Due Dates:	Expiration Date:

Jan. 1, Apr. 1, July 1, Oct. 1   December 31, 19_
(15 days grace)

Amount $165.00

Payable to: Houser Insurance Agency

3000 West Eighth Street

Los Angeles, California 90005

Type of policy Business Pak   Policy # 1654208

Name of issuing company Hartford Insurance Group

Insured   Acme Hardware, Inc.

Figure 13-8 Tickler card for payment of company or personal insurance premiums.

This record should be as detailed as possible and probably will contain more facts than the insurance company wants. But writing down this material when it is fresh means that the facts will be more accurate than if one waits until the insurance company requests the information. File the description of loss with the other insurance records and use it when filling out proof of loss and other required insurance forms.

Additional Insurance Records.   Often it is helpful to see the total insurance program at a glance. A list of policies according to type, amount, issuing company, policy number, and yearly premium should be compiled. It could be organized by the type of coverage with sufficient space left between types to allow the addition of new policies under their categories. Canceled, lapsed, or expired policies could be crossed out, and a new list typed only when necessary, such as for a special meeting or when the sheet becomes hard to read.

Another worthwhile grouping of insurance information is a yearly schedule of premiums due. It may be a list by the month or a calendar chart. With many companies and individuals carrying several policies, premiums might all become due within a few weeks or be scattered throughout the year. Perhaps the seasonal flow of cash does not coincide with the required cash premium payments. If the payment of premiums as they automatically fall due results in hardship or the need to borrow, the insured should arrange with the agent for a distribution of payments that allows due dates to be met easily.

Personal Insurance Coverage.   Insurance on individual's, families, and personal property is available for almost every conceivable purpose.
Personal Insurance to Cover Business Risks.   Coverage may be purchased by a professional person to protect against major lawsuits. An excess indemnity policy written around coverage in primary policies provides high-limit personal (and professional, where applicable) liability insurance up to $1 million, $2 million, or $5 million. Merchants, office building owners, processing and servicing firms, doctors, lawyers, and motel and apartment house owners are a few of the types of people who might find such coverage worthwhile.

Corporations, individual businessmen, and partnerships have found it profitable to insure themselves or key members of the firm when death or prolonged illness would create hardships for the firm. For instance, if one of two partners dies, the surviving partner would need funds to buy the partner's share of the business, or might need to hire someone to take over the duties of the employee who died. The death of a key person could be a major problem for a small company, and a life insurance policy would provide money while a new one is being trained.

Business health insurance benefits business and professional persons who are unable to work because of illness or accident. Called business overhead or professional overhead insurance, the policy pays overhead expenses, such as salaries, rent, utilities, and other expenses, for a year or more, until the insured is able to return to work or arrangements are made to close the office.

13.4   SECURITIES TRANSACTIONS

Some organizations and many business persons invest in stocks, bonds, and mutual funds. Familiarity with the operation of the securities market will assist them to function more efficiently in it. Equally important is adequate recordkeeping to comply with Internal Revenue Service regulations about reporting profits and losses on income tax forms. Secretaries and administrative personnel should understand these financial transactions because they are usually delegated much of the recordkeeping and the contacts with brokerage firms. This section contains information about the types of securities, the function of the securities market, and the records needed. Other financial terms are defined in the "Dictionary of Business Terms," Section 16.10.

Bonds.   Bonds rank ahead of preferred or common stocks in a corporation's capital structure, with prior claim to earnings and assets. Payment is guaranteed of (1) a stated amount at a definite future date, and (2) a series of interest payments at a fixed rate, usually semiannually.

The *face value,* sometimes called *par value,* the amount printed on the bond, is the sum of money the borrower promises to pay the holder. The *coupon rate* is the percentage of the face value that the borrower promises to pay in two interest payments each year. The *date of maturity* is the date when the bond becomes due and at which time the borrower pays the holder the face value of the bond.

Bonds may be purchased through banks and brokerage firms that trade on regulated exchanges and over-the-counter. The market price of a bond is frequently different from its face value. Some bonds trade at a premium, or more than their face value (which is usually $1,000); others trade at a discount, or less than face value. Current yield on a bond is the ratio of its interest to its market value and may be different from the coupon yield.

Bond quotations are listed at a percentage of face value. A bond that trades for "100" may be bought for 100 percent of par, or $1,000. One that trades at "84" is priced at 84 percent of par, or $840. The price of a bond quoted at "$108\frac{1}{2}$" is $1,085. To compute the current yield on an 8-percent $1,000 bond purchased at "95," divide the price paid into the yearly interest ($80 ÷ $950). The interest on a *registered bond* is sent by the issuing company directly to the holder on payment dates. The holder of a *coupon bond* detaches the interest coupon and deposits it in the bank for collection.

Preferred and Common Stocks.   Companies having preferred stock give certain preferential treatment, except the voting privilege, over the common shareholder to the preferred shareholder. Preferred stocks receive a fixed dividend before any payment can be made on the common stock and also have prior claim against assets in the event that the company is liquidated. Dividends are usually cumulative. Preferred stocks seem, however, to lack the growth element found in common stocks, and do not appear to be a good hedge against inflation. Yet, they are noted for their price stability, and they rank between bonds and common stocks from the standpoint of safety. Market movements in preferred stock are influenced more by factors governing the bond market than by those affecting common stocks. The yields are usually moderately higher than those on bonds.

Common stocks also represent ownership in a company, and the shareholder is entitled to elect directors, to vote on certain other matters, and to participate in the distribution of earnings after all prior claims (bond interest, preferred-stock dividends, and so on), if any, have been met. Common stock shareowners bear the greatest risk but are in a position to reap the largest profits. Most companies reinvest about 40 percent of their earnings into the business; the remainder is available for distribution to shareowners.

A regular dividend rate in good years may be increased or extra dividends declared, and in poor years it may be cut or omitted.

Listed in "Dictionary of Business Terms," Section 16.10, are additional terms that explain many features of preferred and common stock and define the technical terms used by traders in the securities and commodities markets.

Mutual Funds. A mutual fund is an investment company that buys and sells shares of stocks and bonds of many different corporations. Its business is investing, instead of manufacturing or merchandising, and it operates just like any other company, with officers and directors responsible to the shareholders. An investor may buy and sell shares of a mutual fund and thus have money invested in a variety of companies. In effect, the mutual fund is a kind of middleman who receives the investor's money and buys securities with it. Each mutual fund shareholder owns a tiny part of each security that the fund has purchased. Specialists select, supervise, buy, and sell the securities for mutual fund investors.

The following tasks are performed by the staff of a mutual fund.

Constant surveillance of the market to determine when certain securities are attractively priced.

Analysis of the financial reports of all industries and individual companies within an industry.

Purchase of high-quality securities when their market prices are low.

Sale of securities when they are overpriced or when market prices are about to fall.

Receipt of dividends and interest on the securities and bonds owned by the fund.

Distribution of the proportional share of the fund's income and capital gains to each shareholder.

Sale of new shares of the fund to prospective investors.

Repurchase of shares from owners who wish to sell.

Preparation of periodic reports of the activities of the company for shareholders.

Preparation and filing of reports required by governmental agencies.

Characteristics of the Securities Market. A stock exchange provides a meeting place for buyers and sellers of securities. Brokers and commission houses who are members of the exchange do the actual buying and selling of shares of listed securities for their customers. Exchanges do not trade in securities nor do they fix prices. Prices are determined by a two-way auction system. Federal and state controls regulate the functioning of securities markets and the use of credit therein. The exchanges see that these regulations are followed.

The unlisted, off-board, or over-the-counter market does not provide a meeting place for buyers and sellers in the same manner as the exchanges. A complex network of trading rooms linked by telephone, teletype, and telegraph facilitates the meeting of buyer and seller. A much larger volume is handled on the over-the-counter market than on the listed or exchange market. Prices are arrived at by negotiation. Many times the dealers buy the securities or sell from their own holdings. Over-the-counter brokers and dealers are subject to federal and state regulations, as well as to the rules of their trade association, the National Association of Securities Dealers, Inc. Investors may not borrow on unlisted securities from a broker, although there is no legal limitation on borrowing from a bank.

Orders to buy or sell are placed with a broker in a brokerage or commission house who acts as an agent in the execution of orders and receives a commission for services. Commissions are competitive and vary with the services offered. Most firms furnish investment information; accept and execute orders; report transactions to customers; and receive, store, or deliver securities.

Persons who invest in stocks and bonds should be familiar with the vocabulary of the securities market. Terms commonly used in trading are the following.

Bid and Asked.   The bid price is the amount a prospective buyer will pay for a share. The asked price (also called an *offer*) is the price at which a holder offers to sell.

Eighth Stocks.   Stocks in which odd-lot orders (less than 100 shares) are executed at one-eighth point from the next full-lot price are eighth stocks.

Even Lot.   A round or even lot consists of 100 shares or multiples thereof.

Ex-Dividend.   A stock that is quoted ex-dividend reserves the right to the pending or accrued dividend to the seller. The ex-dividend date is the first day that the stock sells without the dividend, usually the fourth full business day before the date the stockholder's name must be on record in order to qualify for the dividend. The opening price that day shows a decline from the previous day equal to the value of the dividend.

Ex-Rights.   Ex-rights is similar to ex-dividend in that the seller retains ownership of the rights.

Margin.   Margin refers to a credit transaction in which the security buyer pays a portion of the purchase price and borrows the remaining amount from the broker. The margin requirement is the difference between the market value and the maximum loan value. A buyer of stock worth $1,000 must make a minimum cash payment of $700 if the margin requirement is 70 percent; he may borrow only $300. The stock certificate is held by the broker until paid for in full.

Margin Call.   Should the price of a stock bought on margin decline, the broker would call for additional funds in order to maintain the margin requirement. If a margin call is not satisfactorily answered, the broker has the right to sell the securities to satisfy the loan.

Odd Lot.   A transaction of less than 100 shares is called an odd lot.

Odd-Lot Differential.   The prices of odd-lot transactions are determined by the prices of round-lot trades made on the floor of the exchange, modified by a differential. On a purchase, the odd-lot differential is added to the next round-lot sale price or the best offer, if no sale takes place. On a sale, the differential is subtracted from the next round-lot price or the best bid if there is no transaction.

Point.   One point, the unit of measurement for changes in stocks, bonds, or commodity quotations, is equal to $1 a share for stocks or commodities and $10 for a bond of $1,000 denomination.

Quarter Stocks.   Stocks in which odd-lot orders are executed at one-quarter point from the next full-lot sales price are the higher-priced listed stocks.

Spread.   The difference between the bid and the asked price of a security is the spread.

At the Opening.   At opening is an order left with a broker for execution at the best price obtainable at the opening of the market.

At the Close.   At the close is an odd-lot order executed on the basis of the final bid and asked prices.

Day Order.   A day order is good only for the day on which it is received, after which it is automatically canceled.

Discretionary Order.   A discretionary order permits the broker to use his own judgment in executing it.

G.T.C.   A *good till canceled* order may be carried over for several days until the market reaches the price stipulated or the order is canceled. Other time limits may be designated, such as *good this week* or *good this month.*

Limited Order.   A limited order is executed at a specific price or at a price more favorable to the customer, if possible. In the case of odd lots a limited order to buy at "26" will not be executed until the price for round-lot sales reaches "25 7/8."

Market Order.   A market order is executed at the best price obtainable immediately after its receipt by a broker. If no price is stated, an order is always understood to be *at the market.*

Seller 30.   The seller contracts to deliver securities 30 days after sale. Other delivery periods may be specified.

Stop Order.   A stop order does not go into effect until the market price reaches the price specified on the order. It changes from a stop order to a market order at that moment. Execution does not necessarily take place at the stop-order price. Stop orders to buy are usually placed above the current market, whereas stop orders to sell are placed below the current price. A buy stop-order protects the buyer against a sudden advance in price, whereas a sell stop-order limits the loss of a stockholder against a sudden decline in price.

Stop and Limit.   A stop-and-limit order, similar in one aspect to a stop order, limits the price at which it may be executed after going through the stop. The limit price may be the same as the stop price, or a different price may be set.

An investor can keep track of fluctuations in the price of securities through the financial pages of local newspapers, the *Wall Street Journal,* or the *New*

York Times in which daily quotations from the following sources can be found.

- New York Stock Exchange-Composite*
- American Stock Exchange-Composite*
- Local or regional exchange
- National over-the-counter prices
- Regional over-the-counter prices
- Commodity Market
- Investment funds (Mutual funds)
- Treasury bonds
- U.S. and foreign bond markets

* Figures include trades on other exchanges.

All these tables give at least the bid and asked prices and the net change from the previous day's closing price for each listed item. The stock exchanges include additional information in their lists. On a specific day, for example, quotes from the New York Stock Exchange-Composite stock table appeared as follows.

52 Weeks					*Sales*				Net
High	Low		*Yld.*	P-E	(in *100s*)	*High*	*Low*	*Close*	*Chg.*
$63\frac{5}{8}$	$56\frac{7}{8}$	ATT 4.60	7.5	8	1199	$61\frac{3}{4}$	61	$61\frac{1}{2}$	$+\frac{1}{8}$
$41\frac{3}{8}$	$30\frac{3}{8}$	Fluor 1.20	3.1	9	479	$39\frac{1}{4}$	38	$38\frac{5}{8}$	$+\frac{3}{8}$
295	$234\frac{3}{4}$	IBM 11.52	4.0	15	1121	$291\frac{1}{4}$	$286\frac{3}{4}$	$287\frac{1}{2}$	$-1\frac{1}{4}$
$25\frac{3}{8}$	$16\frac{3}{8}$	McGrH 1	4.1	—	2070	25	$24\frac{1}{8}$	$24\frac{1}{4}$	$-\frac{5}{8}$

The highest price of American Telephone & Telegraph common stock in the prior 52-week period was $63\frac{5}{8}$; the lowest $56\frac{7}{8}$. ATT common pays $4.60 per share as an annual dividend. The stock's yield is 7.5 percent based on the annual dividend payment computed from the latest dividend declared. Its price-earnings ratio is 8. The number of shares sold on that particular day were 119,900. The price fluctuated during trading from a high of $61\frac{3}{4}$ to a low of 61 and closed at $61\frac{1}{2}$. The stock advanced $\frac{1}{8}$ of a point or $0.125 from the previous day's close.

Symbols following the abbreviation for the company or the dividend rate are explained in a "How to Read Stock Tables" box at the bottom of the financial page. For instance, the letters *pf* immediately following the abbreviation indicates preferred stock of that company.

Sources of Security Information. Information on all phases of security investment may be secured from two leading services—Moody or Standard & Poor. Each service assembles comprehensive data on individual companies and maintains current figures through loose-leaf periodic cumulations. Also, many brokerage firms publish brochures and newsletters that explain how and where to invest and also list the advantages and the disadvantages of investing in certain securities or commodities. Some brochures offer advice on total investment programs for professionals, single persons, the self-employed, and the retired or soon-to-be retired. A great deal of material is available, but for helpful statistics one should consult the publications of the independent security services.

Moody's Investors Service, 99 Church Street, New York City, issues a semi-weekly cumulative record of dividend payments and corporate meetings, called *Moody's Dividend Record. Moody's Bond Record* is a pocket guide to all types of information on bonds. The American and foreign annual volumes of *Moody's Manual of Investments* contain full information about the following types of issuers of securities: governments and municipalities; banks; insurance companies; real estate enterprises; investment trusts; industrial firms; public utilities; and transportation companies.

Standard & Poor's Corporation, 345 Hudson Street, New York City, supplies complete factual information on major American, Canadian, and foreign corporations and their securities through its *Corporation Records.* Six loose-leaf volumes, revised bimonthly, supply the bulk of the data on balance sheets, earnings, and market prices. Standard & Poor's Trade and Securities Service includes (1) a weekly *Outlook* for securities markets, (2) a monthly earnings and ratings *Stock Guide,* and (3) a monthly loose-leaf *Statistical Section.* Their pocket-size *Bond Guide* lists information for each security on one line. A *Daily Stock Price Index* supplies the price range of a stock for any day beginning with January 1, 1962, up to the current day. It is brought up-to-date four times a year. Their capsule stock sheets list companies traded on the New York Stock Exchange and the American Stock Exchange and over-the-counter, together with the high and low for the year and Standard & Poor's opinion on each company and its future performance. See also "Economic and Financial Services," p. 199.

Records to Be Maintained. A list of all investments in securities should be compiled. It should be brought up to date weekly, biweekly, or monthly, as desired by the investor, in order to incorporate all changes during the period and to indicate the current market value of each item and the total value of securities investments. The use of the suggested form in Figure 13-9 will allow the investor to see the market position at a glance.

A record of all purchases and sales should be kept and should include the information required by the Internal Revenue Service when one is accounting for short- and long-term capital gains and losses. Without detailed records, the taxpayer will find it difficult to explain figures in this area to the Internal Revenue Service during an audit. A chart similar to the one in Figure 13-10 should be completed for each company, fund, or governmental agency. Notice how much detailed information is required by Internal Revenue Service regulations.

In order to make an accurate declaration of yearly income, an investor should record interest and dividend income as it is received. Figures 13-11 and 13-12 illustrate charts that are useful for recording income information.

Besides these personal records, which summarize securities transactions, the Internal Revenue Service requires that the facts be supported by brokers' transaction slips of purchases and sales, brokers' monthly statements, and

LIST OF INVESTMENTS IN SECURITIES

as of _____

No. shares or face value	Name	Maturity date (if applicable)	Purchase price	Current market price

Stocks:

Bonds:

Investment Funds (Mutual):

Miscellaneous:

Total amount originally invested _____

Current value of investments—(Date) _____

Figure 13-9   Chart for listing investments in securities.

RECORD OF SECURITY OR MUTUAL FUND TRANSACTIONS

Name of Security or Fund _____

Exchange on which listed _____

Broker _____ Phone _____

PURCHASES:

No. of Shares	Kind	Date of Purchase	Price per Share	Broker's Commission	Total Purchase Price	Certificate Number	Registered Name(s)	Location of Certificate

SALES:

No. of Shares	Kind	Certificate Number	Date of Sale	Price per Share	Total Sales Price	Commission	Taxes and Other Charges	Capital Gain or Loss (in red)	
								Short Term	Long Term

Figure 13-10   Chart for recording purchases and sales of securities and mutual fund shares.

INTEREST INCOME

January 1, 19___ – December 31, 19___

for _____(Owner(s))

Tax Exempt Bonds

Name	Date	Amount	Total
Nontaxable Interest Income for 19___			

Taxable Interest

Name	Date	Amount	Total
Taxable Interest Income for 19___			

Figure 13-11 Chart for recording interest income.

DIVIDEND INCOME
January 1, 19 ___ - December 31, 19 ___
for _____(Owner(s))

Security	Quarter				Year's Total
	1st	2nd	3rd	4th	
Total for Quarter					
Total Dividend Income for 19 ___					

Figure 13-12   Chart for recording dividend income.

yearly dividend or interest statements from the issuing companies. These supporting documents should be carefully filed by appropriate subject headings and retained at least three years *after* a security is sold. The year of a security sale is the one in which the outcome of the investment is explained on the investor's income tax form. Income tax declarations may be audited three years after their filing date.

Safeguarding Security Certificates.   Stock certificates should be kept in a safe place, preferably in the safe deposit vault of a bank. All nonregistered certificates, those not registered as to the owner's name, should always be kept in a safe deposit box. Often registered certificates are left with the broker so that delivery may be made easily when the security is sold. Some investors keep their certificates in the office safe or in a locked file cabinet. There is some risk in this practice, however, because the certificates may become mixed with company documents, and proof of ownership might become a problem later on. Other investors keep their certificates at home in a "safe place." The dangers here, as in an office building, are of fire or theft. Nonregistered certificates may be irretrievably lost, and the reissue of registered certificates takes considerable time. (See Section 13.8 on replacing lost documents.) While waiting for a reissue, the investor is unable to take advantage of stock market movements. Other certificates may be held as security for a loan by a bank. Regardless of where certificates are kept, it is important that their whereabouts be noted on a chart such as the one in Figure 13-10. A simple code may be developed for use in the "Location" column, for example:

SD	Safe deposit box
B	Broker's office
H	Home
O	Office (indicate the location and the file number or subject)
M–( )	Miscellaneous (state the place)

Certificate numbers should be carefully checked before anyone forwards the document to the broker to complete a sale. If certificates are kept at the broker's office, check the certificate number on the transaction slip to see that the first one acquired is the first one sold. This is the general practice in taking advantage of a long-term capital gain or loss. If there is a discrepancy in either the certificate number or the date of acquisition, call the broker for clarification.

13.5 ESTATE PLANNING—THE WILL

The single most important document in an estate plan is a person's will. It guarantees one's wishes, conserves the estate, and protects beneficiaries. If it is properly drawn and up to date, a will is a binding document. A person whose financial matters are complicated, encumbered, or extensive should select an attorney to draw up the will. A professionally prepared document will contain the correct legal terminology and will be properly witnessed and notarized.

Holographic Wills.　A person may write entirely in longhand a holographic will. To avoid any problems it should be written on a blank sheet of paper, dated, and signed by the testator. The intentions of the writer must be absolutely clear in order to avoid misinterpretation later. This need alone indicates that the services of an attorney should be considered. If the holographic will is ruled invalid for any reason, no matter how minor, the court will step in and distribute the estate as if there were no will. An example of a temporary will that might be used in a special situation for a short period of time is shown in Figure 13-13.

Division of an Estate in the Absence of a Will.   If a person does not leave a will, the property will be distributed to certain related persons in accordance with state law. The right to intestate succession is not an inherent right, but exists only because the state legislatures have so provided. The legislatures of the individual states have the right to change, modify, or destroy the right to inherit property.

Last Will and Testament of

I, _____ of _____,

City of _____, State of _____,
do hereby make, publish, and declare this to be my last will and testament and I do hereby revoke all former wills and codicils thereto by me at any time made.

First: I desire that my just debts, including the expenses of my last illness and funeral, be paid as soon as may be practical after my death.

Second: All of the residue of my estate, whether real, personal, or mixed, wheresoever situate, and whether now owned or hereafter acquired, I give, devise   and   bequeath   unto   my   beloved   wife   (husband),

_____, for her (his) own use and benefit forever.

Note: If there are children, they should be specifically mentioned, or the will
may be set aside.

Third: I appoint as executrix (executor) of my will my wife (husband); I request that she (he) be permitted to serve without sureties on her (his) bond and that, without application to or order of courts, she (he) have full power and authority to sell, transfer, grant, convey, exchange, lease, mortgage, pledge, or otherwise encumber or dispose of, any or all of the real and personal property of my estate
In   Witness   Whereof,   I   have   hereunto   subscribed   my   name   this

_____ day of _____, 19_____.

_____ (Signature)

Figure 13-13   Example of the wording of a temporary holographic will.

Although intestate distribution varies from state to state, current state laws do exhibit general patterns as follows.

1. Spouses. The surviving spouse, whether husband or wife, will share in the estate. The extent of the share generally depends upon the number of children and other specified heirs (except in the eight community property states [Idaho, Washington, New Mexico, California, Nevada, Arizona, Texas and Louisiana] where the surviving spouse is entitled to 50 percent of the estate). In the absence of surviving blood relations, the surviving spouse usually takes the entire estate.

2. Lineals. Lineals or lineal descendants are blood descendants of the decedent. The major portion of an estate not distributed to the surviving spouse is generally distributed to lineals, although sometimes parents also have a claim to part of it.

3. Parents. If there are still assets in the estate, the remainder is commonly distributed to the decedent's parents.

4. Collateral heirs. These are persons who are not descendants of the decedent but who are related through a common ancestor. Generally, they include brothers and sisters, and they are next in line after parents, although in some states they have equal claim with the parents.

Information Needed by Your Attorney and Your Executor. To simplify the administration of the estate and to avoid delay in its distribution, file a copy of the following information in a safe place with your will. Be sure the information is correct and up to date.

Date on which compiled or updated
Your full name
Legal address and temporary addresses
Date of birth
Place of birth
If a naturalized citizen, date and place of naturalization
Date you became a resident of your state
Former residences
Name of present spouse
Date of marriage
Children—names and birth dates
Previous marriage, if any:
    Date
    Name of spouse
    Date marriage terminated
    Reason
    Children—names and birth dates
Social Security number
Name and address of any company having funeral arrangement contract
Mortuary preference
Other remarks or instructions regarding funeral
Persons to be notified at death—names and addresses

Attorney—name, address, and phone number
Physician—name, address, and phone number
Life insurance agent
Accountant
Bank accounts—name and address of bank, account number
Safe deposit boxes—name and address of bank and name under which registered
Brokers' accounts—names and addresses
Location of personal property (securities, automobiles, jewelry, furniture, mortgages, contracts, and so on)
Employer
Description of any employment contracts, compensation due, or other benefits
Names of business associates
Liabilities (describe any debts, including loan or contract payments)
Property in storage—name and address of storage company
Gifts made prior to death
  To whom
  Amount
Tax return—where filed
Interest in trust—name and address of trustee
Armed services information
  Location of discharge and other related documents
  Veterans' organization memberships
Miscellaneous information that might be helpful

Periodic Review of the Will. A will should be reviewed every year and brought up to date. Do not make changes by scratching out, adding to, or writing over something. Changes and amendments should be made by an attorney and properly witnessed in the same manner as the original will. Here are some items that should definitely be reviewed.

Death of a beneficiary named in the will
Change of residence to another state
Birth of a child after the making of the will
Extreme rise or drop in the value of the estate
Payment of debts that were listed as collectable
Major changes in tax laws
Sale of stock or other property bequeathed to someone in the will
Change of status of a beneficiary (such as reaching majority), making a change in a trust necessary
Change in purchasing power of the dollar, which may necessitate change in support allowance under a Trust

The Executor of a Will. Banks through their trust departments can act as the executor of a will, or an individual may be named by the testator as the executor. Co-executors may be named, such as a bank and an individual. Naming an individual poses certain problems: the person is subject to illnesses, travel, the press of personal business; an individual must post a bond, unless it is specifically waived by the terms of the will; if the individual is also a beneficiary, it may be difficult to convince others of impartiality in handling the estate; an individual may lack management skills and the facilities to perform all the required duties of an executor.

Duties of an Executor. Some of the duties an executor must perform in handling the probate of a will are to

Employ an attorney to represent the estate.

Locate and analyze the will with his help.

Apply for appointment as executor.

Arrange living allowances for the decedent's immediate family.

Collect the life insurance payable to the estate.

Assemble and inventory all the assets of the estate.

Have each asset properly appraised.

Provide protection for all property in the estate and maintain adequate insurance on all insurable property.

Keep real property in good repair, maintain the rental of income property, and collect rents.

Pay all real and personal property taxes when due.

Collect dividends and any other income from security or bond investments and attend to all investment matters.

Operate, liquidate, or sell the interest in any business owned by the estate.

File notice to creditors and approve or reject any claims filed against the estate; defend actions on rejected claims; obtain approval from the court to pay claims and pay those so approved.

Sell property in the estate, as necessary, to pay taxes and claims, and pay those so approved.

Prepare Federal Estate Tax and State Inheritance Tax returns; file and pay such taxes at the proper time. Prepare and file final income tax returns and negotiate any audits of prior income tax returns. Obtain clearance of all tax items.

Keep the family informed of all estate matters and consult with beneficiaries on personal matters pertinent to the estate.

Account for all monies received and disbursed and submit a detailed report thereof to the court when the estate is ready to close.

Make final distribution of the estate as directed by the court.

Executor's Fees. There are established statutory fees for acting as an executor whether as an individual, a bank, or a court-appointed administrator. The court may also make such further allowances as are just and reasonable for extraordinary services. All these charges are tax-deductible to the estate.

Estate, Inheritance, and Gift Taxes. The Federal Estate Tax and the State Inheritance Tax must be paid or provided for before an estate can be distributed. The Federal Estate Tax must be paid within fifteen months after the testator's death. States usually allow more time for payment of the Inheritance Tax. California, for instance, asks for payment within two years. Discounts are often allowed for prepayment of the Inheritance Tax before the due date. Penalties and interest are added to all delinquencies.

Property that is given away during a person's lifetime is subject to both federal and state gift taxes. However, if the gift is made in *contemplation of death* (to keep the property out of an estate), the transfer is not subject to regular gift-tax treatment, but instead will be taxed as part of the estate.

The Internal Revenue Service Publication 559, "Federal Tax Guide for Survivors, Executors, and Administrators," is designed to assist the person charged with the responsibility for settling an estate to understand the federal government requirements in reporting and paying the proper income and estate taxes. Also, the trust office of your bank is ready to advise you and your attorney of their trust services that will help reduce estate tax liability and assure protection for you and for your family in the future.

The federal estate tax is based on the value of your taxable estate and taxable gifts made after December 31, 1976. If a tax is due, it is paid by your executor from the estate. However, the government does not require an estate tax return if the sum of the gross estate and taxable gifts made after December 31, 1976 is less than $147,000 during 1979, $161,000 during 1980, or $175,625 after December 31, 1980. A decedent may pass a minimum of $250,000 worth of cash and property to his or her surviving spouse without estate taxation. Under the tax credit system, the exempted part of an estate may be added to the marital deduction.

13.6.   TAXES

Local, state and federal taxes are payable by all U.S. businesses and citizens and also by aliens who receive income from U.S. sources. The Internal Revenue Service at the federal level, as well as state and local revenue services, stand ready to help individuals and businesses to complete tax forms so that they comply with tax laws. Personnel at local tax offices will advise taxpayers and assist them to complete the necessary tax forms. Published information and instructions are available, free or at a small fee, from the local IRS office or the Superintendent of Documents in Washington, D.C.

A study of the information in this section will clarify many tax issues and will assist you in complying with regulations.

Arrangements for Paying Taxes.   The three governments agree that the businessperson must take the responsibility to pay taxes owed. It is necessary to locate the most recent tax laws that concern the business enterprise and to comply with them. When starting a business, a person should immediately contact the tax and permit division of the city government, the tax collector of the county government, and the franchise tax board of the state government to secure tax publications that explain the tax laws. An employer will need an employer's identification number from the Internal Revenue Service and will be required to file numerous forms and/or make deposits on specific dates. Compliance is mandatory and ignorance unexcused.

Most cities require one to have a permit to operate a business within their city limits; many have established sales taxes that are collected for them by the retailer; and some have assessed income taxes on individuals and businesses. County governments usually levy property taxes on personal property, real estate, merchandise inventory, office and trade machinery, and other items, such as signs and permanent fixtures. State governments levy income taxes and special taxes on saleable items, such as gasoline. Then there are such things as Social Security taxes, excise taxes, federal and state unemployment taxes, and workmen's compensation premiums that must be collected.

Tax Publications.   Because tax laws change from year to year, current regulations, rates, and due dates should be secured from the local, state, and federal revenue services. The local and state tax laws in each of the fifty states are all slightly different. The businessperson therefore, should investigate these in all the states in which business is transacted and secure explanatory material. The federal tax requirements are the same for everyone and are discussed in some detail in this section.

The Internal Revenue Service publishes pamphlets that answer practically any tax question that might be raised. They may be secured from any one of the 58 IRS field offices or from the nearest Superintendent of Documents office. These offices are listed in the telephone book under "United States Government." A complete list of informative IRS publications may be found in Publication 552.

A *Mr. Businessman's Kit* may be secured free of charge from any IRS office. It contains instructions and samples of forms that indicate when and where to file returns and pay taxes, and it gives answers to commonly asked questions. Two publications in it are of particular value—Publication 15, Circular E (*Employer's Tax Guide*) and Publication 552 (*Recordkeeping Requirements and a Guide to Tax Publications*). Circular E contains definitions of *employer* and *employee*; instructions for securing an employer identification number; explanation of Social Security regulations, taxable wages and tips, withholding regulations, the reporting and payment of quarterly returns, adjustments, and other important regulations. Most importantly, it contains both the percentage and the wage-bracket table method of income tax withholding so that regardless of the payroll period, the paymaster can quickly ascertain the correct sum to withhold. Social Security employee tax tables are also part of the booklet. Publication 552 lists the records that every taxpayer must keep in order to prepare accurate income tax returns or to answer questions for the IRS in case the return is audited. Ordinarily, the statute of limitations for an income tax return expires three years after the return is due to be filed. However, the following records should be retained indefinitely.

Transactions affecting the basis of an asset
Changes in the method of accounting or the adoption of the LIFO method of inventory
The basis of property received by gift
An auxiliary record of depreciation for tax purposes

Tax Guide for Small Business, Publication 334, explains, among other things, how income, excise, Social Security, and withholding taxes apply to sole proprietorships, partnerships, and corporations. It answers questions about starting, operating, and disposing of a business. A checklist of business activities shows the kinds of federal taxes to be paid for each, what forms to use, and the page on which each kind of tax is explained.

Your Federal Income Tax, Publication 17, explains such things as, how to prepare a return, what exemptions and deductions are allowed, what income is taxable, how to determine income and deductions from investment property, and how to determine capital gains and losses. Publications 334 and 17 are obtainable from the Superintendent of Documents in Washington or the local IRS office.

Farmer's Tax Guide explains the income tax rules as they apply to farming and may be secured free from county farm agents or IRS offices.

Tax Calendar.   *Tax Calendar and Checklist for 19__,* Publication 509, supplies the dates on which required deposits of income tax withheld, Social Security taxes, federal unemployment taxes, and excise taxes must be deposited with an authorized commercial bank or a Federal Reserve bank. Local and state governments also require that taxes be paid and deposits made by specific dates. Penalties are assessed by the three governments for late returns. It is necessary, therefore, for the office person who is responsible for payment to add these dates to the tickler file. Individuals should also make notes on their calendars of due dates and should allow ample time to complete forms.

Taxable Income and Nontaxable Income, Publication 525, discusses wages, salaries, and other compensation received for services as an employee. In addition, it discusses items of miscellaneous income, items exempt from tax, the minimum tax on tax preference income, the maximum tax on personal service income, the earned income credit, and the general tax credit.

Tax Information on Depreciation, Publication 534, which explains the depreciation of property used in trade or a business for the production of income, should be followed in conjunction with Publication 553, *Highlights of 1977 Changes in the Tax Law,* and any other subsequent publications that explain changes in the law.

Travel, Entertainment, and Gift Expenses, Publication 463, explains the conditions under which expenditures for travel, entertainment, and gifts that arise from your business or employment are deductible on your federal income tax return. The reporting and recordkeeping requirements of these expenses are included for both employers and employees.

Keeping Adequate Tax Records. Every taxpayer, individual or corporate, must maintain records and keep supporting documents that substantiate entries in these records. The law does not require any particular kinds of records, but they must be permanent, accurate, and complete, and clearly establish income, deductions, credits, inventories, employee information, sales of items subject to excise taxes, and so on. Memorandums or sketchy records that merely approximate income, deductions, or other pertinent items affecting tax liability are not considered adequate for compliance with the law. Paid bills, canceled checks, sales slips, invoices, receipts, and other documents should be filed in an orderly manner and stored in a safe place. Records supporting items on a tax return should be retained until the expiration of the statute of limitations for that return. Ordinarily, the statute of limitations for an income tax return expires three years after the return is due to be filed. However, there are many cases in which all or some records should be retained indefinitely. (See "Importance of a Retention Schedule" in Section 12.1).

Microfilm records containing reproductions of general books of account, such as cash books, journals, voucher registers, ledgers, and so on, do *not* meet the recordkeeping requirements of the law. You need maintain, however, only the microfilm reproductions of supporting records, such as payroll records, canceled checks, invoices, vouchers, and so on, provided the following conditions are met.

1. Microfilmed copies are retained as long as their contents may become material in the administration of any Internal Revenue Service law.

2. Appropriate facilities are provided for preservation of the films and for the ready inspection and location of the particular records, including a projector for viewing the records in the event inspection is necessary for tax purposes.

3. Transcriptions of the information contained on the microfilm may be made when required.

If the records are maintained within an automatic data processing system, the system must include a method for producing from the punched cards or tapes visible and legible records that provide adequate information for the verification of the tax liability.

Tax-Deductible Business Expenses. To claim tax deductions for certain business expenses, the company or an individual must submit adequate records and substantiation to the Internal Revenue Service. For example, a diary, account book, or similar summary of travel and entertainment expenses is required, plus receipts, itemized paid bills, and similar statements for single items exceeding $25. The only possible exception to a receipt for travel expenses over $25 is a canceled check made out to an air, rail, car rental, or steamship transportation company. However, if a paid receipt is available for transportation costs, the IRS prefers such a receipt. Canceled checks are not acceptable for expense items over $25. If a bill or a voucher isn't available, other evidence may have to be presented. Receipts for lodgings are required regardless of amount unless their cost is covered by a per diem allowance of $25 or less.

For travel, entertainment, and gift expenses, a chart similar to the one in Figure 13-14 should be completed as these expenses occur. This procedure plus the filing of supporting documents will ensure compliance with the regulations that are spelled out by the IRS in Publication 463 (Figure 13-15).

Most business expense items are handled by the accountant or bookkeeper, who sets up accounts for all the normal costs of operation. The IRS is concerned that only ordinary and necessary expenses directly connected with or related to the trade, business, or profession be deducted. Not all business expenditures are deductible even though they may be ordinary and necessary. For further information, the following IRS pamphlets, which discuss, list, and supply examples of deductible and nondeductible business expenses, should be consulted.

Travel, Entertainment, and Gift Expenses	#463
Tax Information on Depreciation	#534
Tax Information on Business Expenses	#535
Tax Information on Partnership Income & Losses	#541
Tax Information on Deductions for Bad Debts	#548

Tax Information for Individuals.   The Internal Revenue Service publishes many pamphlets that explain how to fill out Form 1040 and its supplementary schedules. These are available at the local IRS office or through the Superintendent of Documents in Washington.

For complete information and examples, *Your Federal Income Tax,* provided by the Internal Revenue Service, should be consulted for the pertinent year. You may secure it by writing the Superintendent of Documents, or by visiting the nearest IRS office. Another good outline, *Your Income Tax,* by J. K. Lasser, published by Simon & Schuster, may be purchased at most bookstores for about $4.

An individual is required to maintain adequate records to substantiate income and deductions. A diary record that gives the details of each transaction is acceptable, if supported by documents. It is especially important to keep separate records on medical expenses, charitable contributions, deductible taxes, and household worker(s) expenses. The secretary who is assigned the task of maintaining these records for an employer should

RECORD OF TRAVEL, ENTERTAINMENT, OR GIFT EXPENSES

January 1, 19 _____ –December 31, 19 _____

Dates (Event, Gift, Departure and Return)	Place	Business Purpose or Benefit Derived	Names and Business Relationship	COSTS				
				Trans-portation	Gas & Oil	Lodging	Meals	Miscellaneous (Phone, Taxi, etc.)

Figure 13-14 Chart for recording travel, entertainment, or gift expense information to comply with IRS regulations.

Factors to be Proved in Substantiating Elements in Column 1—

Elements to be substantiated (1)	For expenditures for travel away from home (2)	For expenditures for entertainment (3)	For expenditures for gifts (4)
Amount	Amount of each separate expenditure for transportation, lodging, and meals. Permissible to total incidental expenses in reasonable categories, such as gasoline and oil, taxis, daily meals for traveler, etc.	Amount of each separate expenditure. Incidental items such as taxis, telephones, etc., may be totaled on a daily basis.	Cost of gift.
Time	Dates of departure and return for each trip, and number of days attributable to business activities.	Date of entertainment or use of a facility for entertainment. (Duration of business discussion.)	Date of gift.
Place	Destination by name of city or other appropriate designation.	Name and address or similar designation of place of entertainment, or place of use of a facility in connection with entertainment. Type of entertainment if not otherwise apparent. (Place of business discussion).	Not applicable.
Description ... Business purpose.	Not applicable. Business reason for travel or nature of business benefit derived or expected to be derived.	Not applicable. Business reason or nature of business benefit derived or expected to be derived. Nature of business discussion or activity, if entertainment is other than "business meals,"	Description of gift. Business reason for making the gift or nature of business benefit derived or expected to be derived.
Business relationship......	Not applicable.	Occupations or other information—such as names or other designations—about persons entertained which establishes their business relationship to taxpayer. (Identification of persons entertained who participated in business discussion.)	Occupation or other information—such as name or other designation—about recipient which establishes business relationship to taxpayer.

Figure 13-15 Elements of travel, entertainment, and gift expenses that must be substantiated to Internal Revenue.

collect the pertinent IRS publications and then construct charts on which to collect the information in chronological order from January 1 to December 31. Files should be set up in which to collect the supporting documents. A systematic approach to the collection of income tax information will eliminate much frustration and work at the end of the year.

13.7. SOCIAL SECURITY

During working years employees, their employers, and self-employed persons pay Social Security contributions into special trust funds. When earnings stop or are reduced because the worker retires, dies, or becomes disabled, monthly cash benefits are paid from these trust funds to replace part of the earnings the person has lost. Also, part of the contributions goes into a separate hospital insurance trust fund so that workers and their dependents, upon reaching age 65, will have help in paying hospital bills. Voluntary medical insurance is available in addition for those 65 or over to help pay doctors' bills and other medical expenses. This latter program is financed out of premiums shared equally by the older people who sign up and the federal government (see "Medicare—Hospital and Medical Insurance" in this section).

A list of the main topics covered in this section follows.

How to Qualify for Benefits. *Credits—Quarters of Coverage.* To qualify for monthly cash payments, a worker must first have credit for a certain amount of work under Social Security. Social Security credits are called *quarters of coverage.*

Calendar Quarters

January	April
February	May
March	June

July	October
August	November
September	December

A worker receives one quarter of coverage for each $250 of earnings in a year, up to a total of four quarters, based on annual earnings of $1,000 or more. The $250 measure increases automatically (beginning in 1979) as average wages increase. The new system applies to all workers and self-employed persons.

Minimum Number of Credits Needed. To be fully insured, one needs a minimum number of credits—at least one and one-half and no more than ten years of work. A fully insured status means only that certain kinds of cash benefits may be payable—it does not determine the amount.

1. For retirement. The number of years of credit needed to qualify for retirement benefits is shown in Figure 13-16. No earnings credits are needed for the medical insurance part of Medicare.

2. For survivors. Benefits may also be available for survivors of a worker under Social Security. If the worker dies before age 62, monthly benefits can go to certain members of the family if the worker has adequate years (Figure 13-16) of coverage. Regardless of a worker's birth date, monthly payments can be made to surviving dependent children if the person worked one and one-half years (six quarters) in the three years before death. A parent may also be eligible if caring for children entitled to benefits based on the worker's earnings.

3. For disability. Disability benefits depend upon the worker's age when disabled. If the person is under 24, credit is needed for one and one-half years of work (six quarters) out of the three-year period ending when the disability begins. If the worker is 24 to 30 years of age, credit is needed for half the time between 21 and disablement. A person 31 or older needs credit for five years of work out of the ten years ending with disability—in other words, twenty quarters of coverage out of the previous forty quarters.

How to Figure Monthly Benefits. The amount of benefit depends on average earnings, not on how many years of coverage a worker has. Under the present Social Security law, actual earnings for past years will be adjusted to take account of changes in average wages since 1951. These adjusted earnings will be averaged together and a formula will be applied to the average to determine the benefit amount. This method will ensure that benefits reflect changes in wage levels over your working lifetime and will have a relatively constant relationship to pre-retirement earnings. In addition, Social Security benefits will increase automatically in future years as the cost of living rises. Each year, living costs will be compared with those of the year before. If living costs have increased 3 percent or more, benefits will be increased by the same amount and will be included in checks issued the following July unless Congress has already acted to raise benefits.

While you are working, Social Security contributions are taken out of your wages. The maximum earnings creditable for Social Security for past and future years can be found in Figure 13-17. As an employed person, you

Work credit for retirement benefits

If you reach 62 in	Years you need
1979	7
1981	7½
1983	8
1987	9
1991 or later	10

Work credit for survivors benefits

Born after 1929, die at	Bore before 1930, die before age 62	Years you need
28 or younger		1½
30		2
32		2½
34		3
36		3½
38		4
40		4½
42		5
44		5½
46	1975	6
47	1976	6¼
48	1977	6½
50	1979	7
52	1981	7½
54	1983	8
56	1985	8½
58	1987	9
60	1989	9½
62 or older	1991 or later	10

Figure 13-16 Work credit requirements for retirement and survivors benefits under Social Security.

Year	Maximum wage creditable
1951–54	$ 3,600
1955–58	4,200
1959–65	4,800
1966–67	6,600
1968–71	7,800
1972	9,000
1973	10,800
1974	13,200
1975	14,100
1976	15,300
1977	16,500
1978	17,700
1979	22,900
1980	25,900
1981	29,700
1982 on	Adjusted automatically as earnings levels rise.

Figure 13-17   Maximum amount of wages covered by Social Security.

and your employer each pay an equal share of Social Security contributions. A self-employed person pays contributions for retirement, survivors, and disability insurance at a rate about equal to $1\frac{1}{2}$ times the employer/employee rate. The hospital insurance contribution rate is the same for the employer, the employee, and the self-employed person. As long as you have earnings that are covered by the law, you continue to pay contributions regardless of your age and even if you are receiving Social Security benefits. In 1979 and 1980, the contribution rate for the combined retirement, survivors, and hospital insurance coverage is 6.13 percent; in 1981, 6.65 percent; in 1982, 6.70 percent; in 1985, 7.05 percent; in 1986, 7.15 percent; and in 1990, 7.65 percent.

Approximate monthly Social Security payments to eligible persons can be found in Figure 13-18. Because payments are based on average earnings over a period of years, maximum payments cannot be reached because accredited earnings for all workers were lower in past years. Those years of

APPROXIMATE MONTHLY SOCIAL SECURITY PAYMENTS (Effective June 1979)

	Average Yearly Earnings after 1950 Covered by Social Security						
	$920 or less	$3,000	$4,000	$5,000	$6,000	$8,000*	$10,000*
Retired Worker 65 or older Disabled Worker under 65 Widow or Widower at 65 of worker never received reduced benefits	$121	$252	$296	$343	$388	$483	$535
Wife or Husband at 65	61	126	148	172	194	241	267
Retired Worker at 62	97	201	237	275	311	386	428
Wife or Husband at 62	46	94	111	129	146	181	201
Widow or Widower at 60, sole survivor	87	180	212	246	278	345	382
Disabled Widow or Widower at 50, sole survivor	61	126	148	172	194	241	267
Wife under 65, one child	61	133	210	290	324	362	401
Widow or Widower, one child	183	378	444	515	582	724	802
Maximum Family Payment	**183**	**385**	**506**	**634**	**712**	**844**	**936**

*Because maximum earnings covered by social security were lower in past years, the average yearly earnings shown in the last two columns will not be payable until future years. The maximum retirement benefit generally payable to a worker who is 65 in 1979 is $553.

Figure 13-18 Examples of monthly cash payments under Social Security.

lower limits must be counted in with the higher ones of recent years to figure the average covered yearly earnings. That average determines the amount of a retiree's, survivor's, or disabled worker's check.

How to Apply for Benefits.   Before one can receive payments from Social Security, an application must be filed with the nearest Social Security office. It is to your advantage to apply before reaching retirement age, even if you do not plan to retire. If you have high earnings that would increase the amount of your benefit in the year you are 65 or later, your benefit amount will be refigured.

When a person who has worked under the Social Security law dies, a member of the family should get in touch with the Social Security office.

A person who is unable to come to the Social Security office should write or telephone and arrange for a representative to visit the home.

Delays in filing an application can cause loss of some benefits, because back payments for monthly cash benefits can be made for no more than 12 months. An application for a lump-sum death payment must be made within two years of the worker's death.

Proofs Needed.   The following documents must be produced, whether you are applying for your own Social Security benefits or for benefits based on the earnings of another person.

1. The Social Security card or a record of the number.

2. Proof of age—a birth certificate or a baptismal certificate made at or shortly after birth for the insured and spouse, a widow, a widower, or eligible children.

3. If applying for wife's, widow's, divorced wife's, or widower's benefits, a marriage certificate and divorce papers.

4. If available, the insured worker's Form W-2, "Wage and Tax Statement," from the previous year. If the person was self-employed, a copy of the last federal income tax return.

5. Proof of support by a parent.

Apply immediately for benefits even if all the proofs are not available. The Social Security office will advise you about other proofs that may be used.

Lump-Sum Payment at Death.   The lump-sum payment at a worker's death is ordinarily three times the amount of the monthly retirement benefit at age 65, or $255, whichever is less.

How to Question or Appeal the Decision on a Claim.   If a worker covered by Social Security feels that the decision on his/her rights under the Social Security law is not correct, the worker may take the following steps within specified time limits to have the claim reconsidered.

Reconsideration.   A request for reconsideration must be made within sixty days of the date of the mailing of the notice of the initial determination. A thorough examination of all the evidence submitted when the original decision was made plus any additional evidence will be made by persons other than those who made the original determination to ensure a new and independent decision. If agreement is not reached, the worker may take the next step.

Hearing Before a Hearing Examiner. Within sixty days of the date of the mailing of the notice of reconsidered determination, the worker may request a personal appearance before a hearing examiner at the nearest Social Security district office. Appearance in person may be waived, if desired. A copy of the examiner's written decision is sent to the worker. If this decision is not acceptable, a review by the Appeals Council may be requested.

Appeals Council Review. The worker may make a request within thirty days of the date of mailing of the hearing examiner's decision or the dismissal of the hearing request. The Appeals Council may or may not decide to review the case. If the case is to be reviewed, the worker has the right to appear (in Washington, D.C.) and present new evidence and/or to file a written statement. The council sends a copy of its written decision to the worker. If the decision is not correct or if the Appeals Council has declined to review the hearing examiner's decision, the worker may bring suit in a federal district court.

Court Action. The worker may file a complaint in a district court of the United States within thirty days of the date of the mailing of the notice of the Appeals Council's decision or its denial of review.

When the last day of the period for requesting any of the actions falls on a nonworkday (Saturday, Sunday, or a national holiday), the period is extended to the next full workday. Failure to request the appropriate review within the time specified may result in loss of the right to that review and ineligibility to take advantage of the next step in the review process. However, for good cause, such time limits may be extended.

A worker may be represented by a qualified person in dealing with the Social Security Administration at any stage of the claim. All Social Security offices have qualified personnel who are willing to discuss a claim and answer questions. All inquiries should start at the local office.

A Disabled Person. A person is considered disabled only for severe physical or mental condition, including blindness, that prevents working and if this condition is expected to last (or has lasted) for at least 12 months or is expected to result in death. A person with a severe medical condition could be eligible even if some parttime work is possible.

Disability protection is provided in three different situations.

1. Disabled workers under age 65 and their families.

2. Persons disabled in childhood (before the age of 18) who continue to be disabled. These benefits are payable as early as the age of 18 when a parent receives Social Security retirement or disability benefits.

3. Disabled widows, disabled dependent widowers, and (under certain conditions) disabled surviving divorced wives of workers who were insured at death. These benefits are payable to those as young as fifty.

There are special provisions for the blind. A person whose vision is no better than 20/200 even with glasses (or who has a limited visual field of 20 degrees or less) is considered "blind" under Social Security law. A person who meets this test of blindness and who has worked long enough and recently enough under Social Security is eligible for a disability "freeze" even if actually working. Under the "freeze," the years in which there were low earnings (or no earnings) because of disability will not reduce the amount of future benefits, which are figured from average earnings. A person 55 to 65 years old who meets the test of blindness and who has worked long enough and recently enough under Social Security can get cash disability benefits if unable to perform work requiring skills or abilities comparable to the work done regularly before reaching 55 or becoming blind, whichever is later. Benefits are not paid, however, for any month in which the person actually performs substantial gainful work. A blind worker under 55 can become entitled to cash benefits only if unable to engage in *any* substantial gainful work.

Vocational rehabilitation is available to disabled persons. Everyone who applies for Social Security disability benefits is referred for possible services to the state rehabilitation agency. These services help many people to return to productive employment. Social Security often helps to pay the cost of such services.

Social Security for the Self-Employed.   A person who engages in a trade, a business, or a profession, either individually or as a partner, is self-employed. Almost all self-employment is covered by Social Security.

Ministers, Christian Science practitioners, and members of religious orders are automatically covered unless exempted by the Internal Revenue Service.

A self-employed person receives Social Security credit if net earnings are at least $400 or more a year, unless wages are from covered employment. If wages are also received, the worker will receive credit only for a sufficient amount of net earnings from self-employment to bring the combined total up to the maximum covered wage.

Gross income from trade or business, less allowable business deductions and depreciation, is considered net income. If the worker is self-employed in more than one activity, the profits or losses from each of the activities must be taken into account when figuring total net earnings. Therefore, a net loss in one business will affect the amount of credit received from net earnings in another.

The following kinds of income do *not* count for Social Security credit.

1. Dividends from shares of stock and interest on bonds or other interest-bearing instruments issued by corporations, *unless* received in the course of business as a dealer in stocks and securities.

2. Interest from loans, *unless* the person is engaged in the business of lending money.

3. Rentals from real estate, *unless* the person acts as a real estate dealer (real estate dealers should exclude income from properties held for investment rather than as stock-in-trade) or when furnishing services primarily for the convenience of the occupant. For information on farm rental income, secure *Farmers Are Asking About Farm Rental Income* at the nearest Social Security office.

At the end of the year, earnings of $400 or more should be reported on Form 1040 ("U.S. Individual Income Tax Return"), Schedule C ("Profit (or Loss) from Business or Profession"), and Schedule C-3 ("Computation of Social Security Self-Employment Tax"). The income tax return and schedules, along with the self-employment contribution, should be sent to the Internal Revenue Service on or before April 15 of the following year. Also, on or before April 15 of any year for which a self-employed person expects to owe income tax and self-employment contributions (see p. 531 for rates) of $40 or more, a declaration of estimated tax on Form 1040-ES must be filed along with the estimated tax or the first installment of the tax.

A man and wife who operate a business as a *true* partnership or a joint venture should each report their respective shares of the business profits as net earnings from self-employment on separate schedules even though they file a joint tax return. The amount of net earnings each should report depends on the terms of the partnership agreement regarding the division of the profits of the business. Each one will receive Social Security credit if each has net earnings of $400 or more.

If a man and wife are not actual business partners, net earnings go only to the one who manages and controls the business. Usually this is the husband, and the net earnings for Social Security purposes should be reported for him alone, even though a joint income tax return is filed. In a community-property state, the earnings are considered the husband's unless the wife exercises practically all management and control of the business.

A parent and child may work together to conduct a business as partners or joint venturers. In either case, both are self-employed, and each should report a share of the profits of the business as net earnings.

Social Security for Citizens Employed by a Foreign Agency in the U.S.A. A United States citizen who works for a foreign government, an international organization, or an instrumentality wholly owned by a foreign government within the fifty states and U.S. territories should report earnings from these employers as though self-employed. See "Social Security for the Self-Employed" in this section.

Reporting Cash Tips.   Earnings in the form of tips are covered by Social Security. Cash tips that add up to $20 or more a month in the course of work for *one* employer must be reported. If the tips are split or shared with other workers, only the amount finally received counts. If the employer requires customers to pay a service charge and this charge is divided among the employees, the part the employee receives is considered a regular wage and *not* a tip.

The employee must give the employer a written report of tips within ten days after the end of the month if they add up to $20 or more in a month. If the person works for more than one employer during the month, the $20 limit applies separately to the tips received while working for each employer. The Internal Revenue Service provides Form 4070 ("Employee's Report of Tips") to use in making tip reports. Document 5635, in which to keep a record of tips and reports, can be obtained from the IRS. These records of daily and monthly tips should become a part of the worker's personal tax papers.
Non-Cash Tips or Gifts.   Tips received in any form other than cash, such as passes, tickets, or merchandise, should not be included with cash tips. Their value must be reported by the employee, however, on the income tax return.
Payment of Social Security Contribution on Tips.   The employer collects Social Security tax contributions on tips. The money may be deducted either from regular wages owed the employee or from funds given by the employee for the purpose of paying contributions. The employer matches the employee's contribution on tips that are considered part of regular wages. The employee pays the same tax rate on tips as paid on regular wages. (See p. 531.)

An employer reports tips and regular wages to the Internal Revenue Service every three months on Form 941(IRS). These returns are later sent to the Social Security Administration, where wages and tips are credited to the employee's record. Tips reported to the employer on Form W-2 ("Wage and Tax Statement") are also reported. Any uncollected Social Security tax contributions due on tips are reported to the IRS by the employer and must be paid by the employee with the income tax return for that year.

How to Check Social Security Earnings Record.   Persons may check their earnings record by sending a post card to the Social Security Administration, P.O. Box 57, Baltimore, Maryland 21203, or by securing from the local Social Security office a post card form to use in requesting a copy of the record.

If the amounts on the statement received from the SSA do not agree with the worker's records, he/she should get in touch with the local Social Security office immediately. If this is not feasible, a letter should be mailed to the local office, giving the Social Security number, the periods of work in question, the pay in each period, and the employer's name and address. If the earnings in question were from self-employment, the date of the filing of the tax return and the address of the IRS office to which the return was sent should be included.

Medicare—Hospital and Medical Insurance.   The two parts of Medicare—hospital insurance and medical insurance—protect people 65 and over from the high costs of health care. Disabled people under 65 who have been entitled to Social Security disability benefits for 24 or more consecutive months and insured workers and their dependents who need dialysis treatment or a kidney transplant also have Medicare protection.

Hospital Insurance.   Everyone who is 65 or older and is entitled to monthly cash Social Security or railroad retirement benefits gets hospital insurance automatically. Even if a person is still working for substantial earnings and does not plan to retire, he/she still receives hospital insurance protection.

To receive hospital protection starting the month in which one reaches 65, a worker must apply three months before the 65th birth date. The cost of inpatient hospital care and certain kinds of follow-up care are provided. Detailed information about Medicare can be found in *Your Medicare Handbook*, which can be secured from your local Social Security office.

Medical Insurance.   Everyone who is 65 or older may sign up for voluntary medical insurance under Medicare, which helps pay for a wide range of health care services and supplies that your doctor may prescribe. It covers doctors' medical and surgical services, outpatient hospital services, outpatient physical therapy and speech pathology services, durable medical equipment services from independent laboratories, ambulance services, home health care, and a number of other health services and supplies. It does not pay for all health care services. For example, it does not pay for routine physical checkups, routine eye or hearing examinations, eyeglasses, or hearing aids, routine dental care and dentures, or prescription drugs or other medicines you buy yourself.

Medical insurance pays 80 percent of reasonable charges for all covered services for the year above a $60 deductible. For this coverage, participants pay a premium of $8.20 a month, which may be increased each year by the government if the current rate is not enough to cover the program's expenses.

Benefits of Workers over 65.   *General Rule.*   The conditions under which benefits are paid to people who work after age 65 are as follows:

   1. You may earn in 1979 $4,500 or less and receive all the benefits.
                    in 1980 $5,000 or less
                    in 1981 $5,500 or less
                    in 1982 $6,000 or less
                    After 1982, the amount will increase automatically as wages go up.

2. If you are under age 72, earnings over the maximum allowable call for a deduction of $1 in benefits for each $2 earned above the maximum. Starting in 1982, there will be no limit on earnings for people 70 or older. Until then, benefits to persons 72 or older are payable for all months regardless of the amount of earnings.

Earnings to Be Counted.   Earnings from work of any kind must be counted, whether or not the work is covered by Social Security. Tips amounting to less than $20 a month with any one employer, however, are not counted. Total wages (not just take-home pay) and all net earnings from self-employment must be added together. Income from savings, investments, pensions, insurance, or royalties received after age 65 because of copyrights or patents obtained before age 65, should *not* be counted as earnings.

Reasons for Discontinuation of Payments.   Once monthly Social Security payments are started, they continue until stopped for one of the following reasons.

1. Marriage. Benefits for a child, an aged dependent parent, a disabled dependent widower, a divorced wife or husband, a disabled widow, or a parent receiving benefits generally stop when the beneficiary marries a person who is not also getting Social Security dependent's or survivor's benefits. However, widows, widowers, or surviving divorced wives who remarry after age 60 may continue to be eligible for benefits.

2. Divorce. Payments to a wife or a dependent husband generally end if a divorce is granted. However, a divorced wife of 62 or older may qualify for benefits if the marriage lasted at least ten continuous years before the divorce.

3. No child "in his/her care." Payment to a parent under age 62 or to a widow, widower, or surviving divorced wife under age 60 will generally stop when a child in the parent's care marries before age 18 or an unmarried child reaches age 18. A widow, widower, or surviving divorced wife who is age 50 or over and is severely disabled should get in touch with the Social Security office for information about any benefits that may be payable.

4. Child reaches age 18. When a child reaches age 18, payments stop unless the child is disabled or is a full-time, unmarried student. A student is eligible for benefits until age 22.

5. Adoption. An adopted child's payments end unless adopted by a step-parent, grandparent, aunt, uncle, brother, or sister after the death of the person on whose record benefits are received.

6. Death. When any person receiving monthly benefits dies, his or her payments end.

7. Disability benefits. When the benefits stop because a person is no longer disabled, the benefits payable to dependents also stop.

If payments end for any of these reasons, the last check due is the one for the month *before* the event.

13.8 PROTECTION AND REPLACEMENT OF IMPORTANT DOCUMENTS

To alleviate any future problems, it is wise to know at all times where important documents are located and that they are properly secured. As explained in Section 3.2, the security of classified government documents must conform to government regulations. Important company papers, such as those of incorporation or partnership agreements, must be retained for the life of the company. The proper filing and retention of these types of documents is fully explained in Section 12.1, "Records Management."

Protection of Important Personal Documents. Personal documents require the same careful attention as that given to important papers belonging to a company. Accurate and detailed records should be kept in several places— dates, names, numbers, and so on, of all valuable papers, such as birth, marriage, divorce, stock certificates; insurance policies; deeds; credit and charge-account cards; banking records; tax and estate records; all papers having to do with security transactions; employment and Social Security information. A list of the facts pertinent to the personal papers should be kept at home, another copy at the office, and a third copy in a safe deposit box along with irreplaceable documents. This list should be updated every year. Trying to recall or collect information after papers are lost, stolen, or destroyed is difficult and time-consuming. The documents themselves should be kept in the safest place available to the individual—home, office, or bank. The Social Security card, the driver's license, and credit cards are usually carried on one's person. If they are not, they should be filed carefully or locked away until needed. For some documents, you should consider having duplicate copies made and then should store each one in a different place. Hidden items often cause frustration as one hunts for them. Therefore, resist the temptation to bury documents and their copies but merely place them in logical places or file them systematically by cross-referencing.

Replacement of Documents. If documents are lost, stolen, burned, or damaged in any other way, the following suggestions on how to replace them will help you secure copies without too much difficulty.

Birth, Marriage, and Divorce Certificates. Write the bureau of vital statistics, or similar office, in the city where you were born, married, or divorced. Be sure to supply detailed information to assist them in locating the correct record—your name; your present and previous addresses; your parents' names; your maiden name, if necessary; the date of the event; the hospital or church; the doctor, minister, or attorney; and so on. In a large city, there are so many identical names that it is often difficult to isolate the correct person. Most cities charge a fee, which must be paid in advance, for a photostat or copy of the requested certificate.

A person lacking a birth certificate can secure proof of age from the Census

Bureau. A letter should be sent to Bureau of the Census, Personal Census Service Branch, Pittsburg, Kansas 66762, asking for an "Age Search Application Form." The form contains instructions for its completion and must be returned with a fee of approximately $4.

Checks.   If a check you sent someone does not arrive, ask the bank to stop payment. A telephone request must be followed by a letter or a completed bank form for stopping payment. Banks usually levy a small charge for this service. Next, notify the payee not to cash or deposit the check if it does turn up later, but to return it to you. Give the number and the date of the lost check for identification. Then issue a new one.

Commercial Checkbook.   If you lose blank checks or your entire checkbook, notify the bank immediately of the missing check numbers. A caution card will be attached to your records in the bank, and thereafter the bank assumes responsibility in case someone attempts to present one of your checks for payment. Most banks recommend closing the account and opening a new one.

Credit and Charge-Account Cards.   Notify immediately by telephone or telegraph the nearest business office of the company issuing the particular credit card. Give your complete name and address; the account or card number; the location and the date when it was lost, stolen, or damaged. If you reported the loss to the police, include this fact. Follow up the verbal contact with a letter giving the same information. You are usually not held responsible for charges made by others to your account after you have properly notified the issuer of the card. By federal law, an individual's maximum liability for the fraudulent use of any kind of credit card is limited to $50 per card.

Keep a separate record of all credit and charge-account cards in your possession so that you will have the number and be able to report the loss immediately. A card case with transparent sections will remind you visually of a missing card.

Deeds to Real Property.   If a deed to property is lost or destroyed, a copy may be secured for a small fee from the county recorder where the property is located. Sometimes a deed is not necessary when one is transferring property that has been sold. Sales of real estate that go through escrow do not require a copy of the deed because title to the property is searched by a title company and a new deed issued to the new owner.

Driver's License and Car Registration or Pink Slip.   Go to the nearest office of the Department of Motor Vehicles and apply for a duplicate of your driver's license. If you have proper identification, you will receive a duplicate permit immediately. If not, you will be mailed one in a few days. There is a small fee for this service.

If the pink slip for your automobile is lost, take the original registration slip to the Department of Motor Vehicles. They will issue a duplicate pink slip. If the registration slip is lost, take the pink slip in for a new white registration slip. It is best to take care of these losses immediately for your own protection. Also, if you are cited for a traffic violation, there is usually an additional fine for driving without a license.

Government Savings Bonds. Write the Bureau of Public Debt, Division of Loan and Currency, 536 South Clark Street, Chicago, Illinois 60605, for Form PD 1048. List the serial numbers of the bonds, dates issued, and persons to whom issued. Duplicate bonds are forthcoming in about six months and carry the same issue dates as the old ones. In cases of hardship, when prompt replacement is important, a letter should be sent with the completed form explaining the circumstances. Every effort will be made to replace the bonds as quickly as possible.

Income Tax Returns. You may secure a copy of an old tax return by writing the Internal Revenue Service office where the original return was filed. Send adequate identifying information, such as the year of the return, the Social Security number(s), the name(s), and the address. A copy of the return should be forthcoming in about two months for a small fee.

Insurance Policies. Notify your agent or the headquarters of the insurance company by telephone or in writing of the loss of the policy. Include as much pertinent data as possible—the kind, the names in which issued, the number, the dates, and so on. Insurance coverage continues without interruption while a duplicate policy is being processed. The important point here is that the policy or record of it be among the personal papers of a deceased person so that his estate may make claim for any proceeds that may be due.

Mortgage and Other Loan Papers. Notify the company, the bank, or the other institution that loaned the money by telephone or in writing. A photocopy of the agreement will be sent you. If your payment book has been lost, the bank or collecting agent will replace it.

Passport. If you lose your passport abroad, notify the nearest United States embassy or consulate. A duplicate will be issued within a week. Passports lost in this country should be reported to the local passport agency, if there is one, or the local police station. It is important to be able to supply your passport number. For those cities without an office (even though the loss has been reported to the police), write the Passport Agency, Department of State, Washington, DC 20520, giving the number, the date of issue, the name(s) in which issued, and other pertinent facts.

Savings Passbook or Receipt Book. The savings receipt book that has been used since 1967 records only the total of the deposit or the withdrawal. The customer must keep a record of the current balance in the pages provided at the back of the book. If the savings passbook in which the bank continues to maintain a running balance for the customer or the receipt book is lost, a restriction is placed on the account for thirty days. A new book using the same account number is issued after that time. A new account number may be secured if desired. Usually, the customer is allowed to withdraw some of the funds on deposit before the new book is issued.

Social Security Card. Take the duplicate card given you when you first obtained your Social Security card to the post office or the nearest Social Security office. If you are unable to find the duplicate, secure your Social Security number from your list of important documents, a paycheck receipt, or a copy of last year's income tax form. At the Social Security office you will be given a replacement application to complete. A new card will be processed within ten days. To find the address of the local Social Security office, look in the phone book under "United States Government, Department of Health, Education and Welfare."

Stock Certificates. Notify the transfer agent immediately. If you do not have a record of the agent, write the company or call a local broker or stock exchange if there is one in your area. The company will alert the transfer agent for the stock or tell you to. The agent, in turn, will put a *stop* against your stock.

Most companies require that you purchase an indemnity bond from a surety company before a replacement certificate is processed. The issuing company is then protected against the sale of the missing certificate by someone else. An indemnity bond premium costs approximately $40 per $1,000 of a stock's current market value. The premium is not returnable.

If you lose the record of the purchase or sale of stock, which information is needed for income tax accounting, contact your broker (who need not be the one through whom you purchased or sold the stock). The broker will contact the exchanges for prices and will also supply the brokerage fees paid on each transaction.

Traveler's Checks. The numbers of traveler's checks should be kept separately from the checks themselves. If any checks are lost, go to the issuing company's branch office or its local representative, such as a bank or travel agent. You will be asked to sign an affidavit listing the numbers of the missing checks and the date and place of their loss. Replacement checks are issued immediately. If you do not have the numbers, you may be given a partial refund only; and the balance will be paid as soon as the agent receives confirmation of your purchase from the issuing office or bank. When traveling abroad, take precautions to safeguard traveler's checks, even though representatives of issuing companies are extremely helpful in cases of emergency.

14

International Trade

The world has become a one-market, low-tariff area, and most countries have entered an era of tremendously expanded international trade. With stepped-up competition in all markets, at home and abroad, U.S. firms need to compete aggressively in protecting and strengthening both their domestic and overseas markets. Those who limit their horizons to the U.S. market may soon find themselves in trouble from foreign competitors. Consequently, the government has called upon American businesses to step up export activity and to increase income from overseas trade. The information in this chapter provides valuable reference material for the exporter and the business person interested in becoming an exporter.

CONTENTS

14.1 DOING BUSINESS ABROAD

Any company interested in entering the export market or in increasing the worldwide market for its products should work closely with the Industry and Trade Administration of the Department of Commerce. The prime objective of ITA is to increase U.S. exports through these means.

Providing services and information that make it easier for American businessmen to trade abroad.

Operating trade centers, organizing and sponsoring trade missions, and running trade fair exhibits and other marketing devices to promote U.S. goods in markets abroad.

Working with other government agencies and international organizations to create a climate in which international trade and investment can flourish.

544

Presenting the views of traders and investors in governmental councils.
Working out policies and procedures that make it simpler and more profitable to do
  business abroad.

Following is an index to topics dealt with in this section. You may secure
further information by visiting or writing the U.S. Department of Commerce,
Industry and Trade Administration, Fourteenth Street between Constitution
Avenue and E Street NW, Washington, DC 20230, or the nearest Department
of Commerce field office. (See Figure 14-1 for the addresses of field offices.)

Department of Commerce Services.   *Registration with the Bureau of Export
Development.*   Businesses that register with the Commercial Intelligence
Division of the Bureau of Export Development (BED) are placed on the
Department's mailing list ("American International Traders Index") to
receive information about export trade opportunities applicable to U.S.
firms. A company will also be notified of future program activities covering
its products. Through this service an exporter may keep up to date on specific
assistance offered by the Department of Commerce.

Export Counseling Service.   All inquiries received by the Department of
Commerce in Washington concerning questions or problems that involve
exporting are directed to the Industry and Trade Administration (ITA) for
initial discussions to ensure that all relevant governmental resources are
brought to bear in each case. In addition to special guidance for firms new
to export and continual aid to established exporters, ITA works closely
with other divisions of the Commerce Department, the Departments of
Agriculture and Interior, the Agency for International Development, the
Small Business Administration, and the Export-Import Bank. It will arrange
appointments for the exporter throughout these agencies.

The Office of International Marketing (OIM) is a central source of information on nongovernment-sponsored foreign fairs and exhibitions, maintaining files of pertinent foreign service despatches, official fair catalogs,
pamphlets, and other materials concerning international trade shows that
may offer U.S. firms a means of displaying their products and thereby increasing their export sales. It operates an export information office in
Washington, located in the lobby of the Commerce Department building on
the Fourteenth Street side, between Constitution Avenue and E Street.

Albuquerque, NM   87102
505 Marquette Ave. NW, #1015
(505) 766-2386

Anchorage, AK   99501
412 Hill Bldg., 632 6th Ave.
(907) 265-5307

Atlanta, GA   30309
Suite 600, 1365 Peachtree St. NE
(404) 881-7000

Baltimore, MD   21202
415 U.S. Customhouse
Gay and Lombard Sts.
(301) 962-3560

Birmingham, AL   35205
Suite 200-201
908 S. 20th St.
(205) 254-1331

Boston, MA   02116
10th Floor, 441 Stuart St.
(617) 223-2312

Buffalo, NY   14202
1312 Federal Bldg.
111 W. Huron St.
(716) 842-3208

Charleston, WV   25301
3000 New Federal Office Bldg.
500 Quarrier St.
(304) 343-6181

Cheyenne, WY   82001
6022 O'Mahoney Federal Center
2120 Capitol Avenue
(307) 778-2220

Chicago, IL   60603
1406 Mid-Continental Plaza Bldg.
55 E. Monroe St.
(312) 353-4450

Cincinnati, OH   45205
10504 Federal Office Bldg.
550 Main Street
(513) 684-2944

Cleveland, OH   44114
Room 600, 666 Euclid Ave.
(216) 522-4750

Columbia, SC   29204
2611 Forest Drive
(803) 765-5345

Dallas, TX   75242
Room 7A5, 1100 Commerce St.
(214) 749-1515

Denver, CO   80202
Room 165, New Customhouse
19th and Stout Sts.
(303) 837-3246

Des Moines, IA   50309
609 Federal Bldg.
210 Walnut Street
(515) 284-4222

Detroit, MI   48226
445 Federal Bldg.
231 W. Lafayette
(313) 226-3650

Greensboro, NC   27402
203 Federal Bldg., W. Market St.
P.O. Box 1950
(919) 378-5345

Hartford, CT   06103
Room 610-B, Federal Office Bldg.
450 Main St.
(203) 244-3530

Honolulu, HI   96813
286 Alexander Young Bldg.
1015 Bishop Street
(808) 546-8694

Houston, TX   77002
2625 Federal Bldg., Courthouse
515 Rusk Street
(713) 226-4231

Indianapolis, IN   46204
357 U.S. Courthouse and
    Federal Office Bldg.
46 E. Ohio Street
(317) 269-6214

Los Angeles, CA   90049
Room 800, 11777 San Vincente Blvd.
(213) 824-7591

Memphis, TN   38103
Room 710, 147 Jefferson Ave.
(901) 521-3213

Figure 14-1 Locations of Field Offices of the United States Department of Commerce.

Miami, FL   33130
Room 821, City National Bank Bldg.
25 W. Flagler St.
(305) 350-5267

Milwaukee, WI   53202
Federal Bldg./U.S. Courthouse
517 E. Wisconsin Avenue
(414) 224-3473

Minneapolis, MN   55401
218 Federal Bldg.,
110 S. 4th Street
(612) 725-2133

Newark, NJ   07102
4th Floor, Gateway Bldg.
Market St. and Penn Plaza
(201) 645-6214

New Orleans, LA   70130
432 International Trade Mart
No. 2 Canal St.
(504) 589-6546

New York, NY   10007
37th Floor, Federal Office Bldg.
26 Federal Plaza, Foley Square
(212) 264-0634

Omaha, NB   68102
Capitol Plaza, Suite 703A
1815 Capitol Avenue
(402) 221-3665

Philadelphia, PA   19106
9448 Federal Bldg.
600 Arch Street
(215) 597-2850

Phoenix, AZ   85037
Suite 2950 Valley Bank Center
201 N. Central Avenue
(602) 261-3285

Pittsburgh, PA   15222
2002 Federal Bldg.
1000 Liberty Avenue
(412) 644-2850

Portland, OR   97204
Room 618, 1220 SW 3rd Avenue
(503) 221-3001

Reno, NV   89509
2028 Federal Bldg.
300 Booth Street
(702) 784-5203

Richmond, VA   23240
8010 Federal Bldg.
400 North 8th Street
(804) 782-2246

St. Louis, MO   63105
120 S. Central Avenue
(314) 425-3302

Salt Lake City, UT   84138
1203 Federal Bldg.
125 S. State Street
(801) 524-5116

San Francisco, CA   94102
Federal Bldg., Box 36013
450 Golden Gate Avenue
(415) 556-5860

San Juan, PR   00918
Room 659, Federal Bldg.
(809) 763-6363

Savannah, GA   31402
235 U.S. Courthouse and P.O. Bldg.
125-29 Bull St.
(912) 232-4321

Seattle, WA   98109
Rm. 706, Lake Union Bldg.
1700 Westlake Avenue N.
(206) 442-5615

Figure 14-1   (continued).

Export Market Identification.   The Overseas Business Opportunities Division of OIM identifies specific export opportunities, by product and country, that have immediate and long-term sales potential. These product/market opportunities are determined by the pulling together and analyzing of market research data from a multitude of sources. The results are disseminated to the U.S. business community in the form of regularly issued publications.

They are designed to motivate the new exporter or nonexporter to undertake positive action to capitalize on export potentials identified in the studies.

Concurrently, OIM develops, on a highly selective basis, several long-term global marketing plans. Each of these plans covers a product or a product category and projects maximum export sales growth on a worldwide basis over a two- to five-year period. The implementation of each global plan is the dual responsibility of industry and government, and industry is encouraged to participate in Commerce Department trade promotional activities in those markets that offer the best sales potential and optimum profit return.

Joint Export Promotions. The Joint Export Establishment Promotions (JEEPs) offer cooperation and financial assistance from the U.S. government to groups of manufacturers joining together to sell abroad. Under JEEPs, the government shares specified costs of overseas market development activities with cooperating groups on a contract basis. JEEPs provide the means for planned, long-term development of selected export markets by joint industry/ government action. Industry groups seeking support are required to prepare detailed proposals for promotional activities for which they desire the government to share the costs. They have operational responsibility; the government, through the Industry and Trade Administration, provides planning and other assistance related to trade expansion programs and maintains the degree of supervision necessary to assure fulfillment of the contracts.

The following promotional activities are illustrative of those eligible for government assistance.

Advertising and publicity
Participation in trade exhibitions
Market research
Supplying samples and technical data
Preparing and submitting bids
Overseas promotional visits
Training of sales and service personnel
Product-use familiarization programs
Operation abroad of sales offices, showrooms, warehouses, and service centers

Four general types of business organizations are most adaptable to this program: (1) trade associations or subsidiaries or components thereof; (2) groups of firms operating under the leadership of export management companies; (3) export trade associations organized under the Webb-Pomerene Export Trade Act of 1918; (4) groups of firms specially organized to participate in this program; (5) piggyback arrangements, whereby one manufacturer represents a group of companies with related products.

Publications of Interest.   *Department of Commerce.*   The following publications of the Department of Commerce are helpful to any company engaged in worldwide trade. Most of them may be secured from the field offices or from the U.S. Department of Commerce, Industry and Trade Administration, Export Information Division, Room 1033, Washington, DC 20230.

1. "EXPORT, Contact List Services" is a pamphlet that describes the Export Mailing List Service and provides guidelines on how to take advantage of it. The Foreign Traders Index (FTI) from which the Export Mailing Lists are retrieved is an automated file of foreign importers and some exporters. It contains data on more than 138,000 firms in 130 countries and is designed to produce lists of potential foreign business contacts; efforts are made to continually expand the file and update information on the firms listed. Much of the material is available in magnetic tape form so that users of FTI can retrieve various segments of the data through their own computer facilities.

2. "Product Marketing Service" explains the office-away-from-the-office facilities provided by the Department of Commerce in international business centers around the world.

3. "The Agent/Distributor Service" contains specific information on how the U.S. Foreign Service, Department of State, assists the business person to find interested and qualified agents or distributors overseas.

4. "U.S. Trade Center Facilities Abroad" and its companion publication, "Overseas Export Promotion Calendar," are designed to help U.S. manufacturers sell their products in the expanding world market and to take advantage of the extensive opportunities for profits in international trade. The first-named publication describes trade center facilities in major cities in Europe, Asia, Australia, and Latin America. These trade centers serve as excellent vehicles for showing products to thousands of buyers throughout the world.

5. *American Business*, a biweekly journal of industry and trade published by the Department of Commerce, offers practical, authoritative, and concise international marketing information, news, and reports. It carries feature articles and timetables on significant developments in the United States export expansion program. Twice each year an issue is devoted to the world trade outlook. In each issue, export trade opportunities are presented in a semi-classified advertisement style and listed by SIC code numbers. SIC code numbers refer to specific commodities as classified in the *Standard Industrial Classification (SIC) Manual*, which is available from the Superintendent of Documents, U.S. Government Printing Office, Washington, DC 20402. *American Business* keeps an exporter, or potential exporter, constantly informed on what the Department is doing to help the U.S. business community in its international trade activities. A subscription to the magazine can be obtained from the Superintendent of Documents.

6. The Export Mailing List Service issues periodically a checklist of international publications of the Industry and Trade Administration. It also gives a detailed listing by country of the economic and commercial reports available for a particular country. Recent reports of the Bureau of the

Census concerning imports and exports are included along with a list of applicable labor law and practice monographs issued by the Department of Labor. A company or business person involved in exporting and importing may ask to be placed on the mailing list.

7. Information about a particular foreign firm mentioned in *American Business* is obtainable in the form of "World Traders Data Reports" (WTDR). These reports indicate the type of organization, the sales territory, the size of the business, its sales volume, its trade and financial reputation, and other factors supplied by the U.S. Foreign Service. WTDR reports may be ordered from Export Information Division, Room 1033, Industry and Trade Administration, U.S. Department of Commerce, Washington, DC 20230.

8. The *TOP Bulletin*—Trade Opportunities for Exporters—is a weekly announcement of new business leads overseas. It includes weekly news of direct export sales opportunities, overseas representation opportunities, and foreign government tenders. Multinational firms will find it helpful for original, conveniently packaged export leads on their diverse product lines and services. Senior export executives, export management companies, engineering firms, consultants, bank officials, trade associations, and transportation and freight-forwarding firms will find the bulletin a quality information service. A subscription may be placed with the Industry and Trade Administration, Trade Opportunities Program.

9. The best sources of country information of value to exporters are the Overseas Business Reports (OBR) of ITA. Several types of information are available. The "Basic Data" series are the broadest of the group and should be studied first by the prospective exporter. Such basic data on a country as geography, population, government, economic structure, markets, national income, industries, commercial crops, mineral resources, manufacturing, power, transportation, communications, labor force, finance, banking system, foreign trade, import regulations and restrictions, and development plans of the government are included in each report.

The "Foreign Trade Regulations" series of OBR include topics such as the country's trade policy, tariff system, customs provisions, shipping documents, marking and labeling requirements, nontariff import trade controls, export controls, and representation in the United States. These reports also include any import or export controls set up by the United States in regard to the particular country.

The third informational series of the Overseas Business Reports are designed for the firm wishing to open a local plant or office in a foreign country. The "Establishing a Business" series supply current information on the investment climate; the trade factors affecting investment; the extent of foreign investment; the regulations governing investment; patents; trademarks and copyrights; employment; taxation; the availability of capital; and investment information services. Other OBR series, "Market Profiles for

(Region)," "Selling in *(Country),*" and "Market Factors in *(Country),*" are helpful in finding and analyzing the market.

A subscription to the Overseas Business Reports may be ordered from any Department of Commerce field office or from the Superintendent of Documents.

Miscellaneous Sources.   Other publications of help to exporters are available from the following agencies.

1. The Small Business Administration. Of special importance to owner-managers of smaller firms who seek sales in foreign markets is the booklet *Export Marketing for Smaller Firms.* This manual, issued by the SBA, outlines for the management of smaller firms the sequence of steps necessary to determine whether and how to utilize foreign markets as a source of immediate and future profits. It describes the problems facing smaller firms engaged in, or seeking to enter, foreign trade and the many types of assistance available to help them cope with these problems. A step-by-step guide to the appraisal of the sales potential of foreign markets is included. The requirements of local marketing practices and procedures are explained. A copy of the manual may be secured from the Superintendent of Documents.

2. The International Monetary Fund. Another good source of financial information for a country that is a member of the International Monetary Fund is IMF's annual report series entitled *Exchange Restrictions.* The yearly report is an excellent summary of monetary regulations as they pertain to trade and capital transfers. A current copy should be available at large public or university libraries, or may be obtained from the Fund in Washington, D.C.

3. The Department of State. United States personnel stationed at foreign service posts will perform a variety of services for the business person engaged in international trade. For instance, the primary responsibility of the Commercial Officer is to promote trade, travel, and private investment interests of the United States. The Commercial Officer helps to develop trade contacts and export opportunities; arrange appointments for U.S. business travelers and assist in contacts with local government officials; support special overseas activities of the Department of Commerce, such as trade centers, trade missions, and trade fairs; and report on business trends, market potentials, and laws and customs that affect U.S. commercial interests. Efforts are also made toward eliminating any discriminatory treatment of U.S. business interests. The Labor Attaché is responsible for following the political and economic activities of the national labor organizations. The Attaché is ready to supply information regarding labor and social attitudes and trends, wages, non-wage costs, Social Security regulations, government labor policies and regulations, and labor attitudes toward U.S. business investments. The Department of State Publication 7877, *Key Officers of Foreign Service Posts Guide for Businessmen,* lists the addresses and the telephone numbers of foreign service posts. The names of key officers at these posts are included in the publication, which is brought up to date four times a year. It may be secured from the Superintendent of Documents by subscription.

4. Chambers of Commerce. Many local chambers of commerce provide world trade information for members who are interested in importing and exporting. For instance, the Los Angeles Area Chamber of Commerce publishes a monthly *World Trade Bulletin,* which lists both import and export business opportunities. Overseas companies may subscribe on a yearly basis and members of the Los Angeles Chamber receive copies. However, the publication is not sold domestically to non-Chamber members. Contact your own Chamber of Commerce for similar world trade information.

Stateside (Private) Assistance. Regional Export Expansion councils are established in the same areas served by the Department of Commerce field offices. The council members are local business leaders appointed by the Secretary of Commerce to work with the Department in promoting world trade. As a group and as individuals, they give advice and guidance to fellow businessmen interested in foreign markets but not yet exporting. These councils, in cooperation with the Department's field offices, work closely with chambers of commerce, trade associations, banks, schools, and the Small Business Administration in arranging courses, seminars, and clinics dealing with exporting procedures. They also provide private consultations between experienced and prospective exporters. Each local field office, as well as the Washington-based Bureau of Field Operations, has a list of members.

Many banks in the United States maintain large international departments that make available to their customers a wide range of services and information. The following New York banks have well-established international departments:

Bankers Trust Company
Chase Manhattan Bank
Chemical Bank
First National City Bank
Manufacturers Hanover Trust Company
Morgan Guaranty Trust Company

If your local bank does not have an international department, it will be able to arrange for one of its correspondent banks either in your city or in New York to help you.

Several foreign banks have stateside branches in the larger cities and are willing to assist the U.S. exporter/importer. A check of the banks listed in the yellow pages of the local telephone directory will indicate where they may be located.

Many airlines and steamship companies offer more extensive services and information to businessmen and representatives of firms than those usually available to ordinary passengers. Special services are available if there is a possibility of joint publicity arrangements and/or substantial freight contracts.

Both Pan American Airways and Trans World Airlines maintain departments in international trade to assist the exporter. To obtain help, direct a letter on company letterhead to the Manager-Marketing Services, Pan American World Airways, Pan Am Building, New York, NY 10017, or telephone your nearest Pan Am district sales or cargo office. When writing, indicate whether you're interested in importing or exporting. Include a description of the products you wish to buy or sell and the kind of outlets you're looking for— wholesalers, retailers, processors, sales agents, and so on. Indicate your preference in the market areas also. A brief description of any previous experience in international marketing should be included. A Pan Am marketing specialist will, if possible, suggest likely markets for your product or promising sources of supply. Pan Am has more than 900 offices around the world and wide business contacts in 122 major markets overseas. You should also write to Pan Am, Publication Department, Pan Am Building, New York, NY 10017, for a list of materials for the importer/exporter. Two informative booklets distributed by Pan Am are *Trade With China* and *Strategies for Penetrating Markets of Eastern Europe and Russia.*

Trans World Airlines provides similar services for the international business firm. A letter addressed to the Manager, MarketAir Planning, 605 Third Avenue, New York, NY 10016, should include the same information suggested for the letter to Pan Am. TWA's marketing services are explained in its "MarketAir Newsletter," which will be sent to interested persons upon request.

Steamship companies, through their freight sales departments, assist the importer/exporter with marketing problems. Worldwide coverage is offered by seven American steamship lines through the Council of American Flag Ship Operators (CASO). These companies have approximately 300 ships visiting 450 major ports regularly. Figure 14-2 lists the principal countries where you will find offices and agents around the world. For the names and addresses of representatives in any city or port in any of the countries listed write, wire, or phone one of the steamship companies shown opposite the country. The trade expansion program of the Council offers the exporter/ importer overseas marketing information in such areas as finding new customers overseas, increasing exports, developing new markets, locating new sources of supply, packaging, licensing, and advertising abroad. A "Trade Assistance Request" to the Council or any one of the lines listed in Figure 14-3 will bring a prompt reply.

United States port authorities are also anxious to help the exporter/importer who uses their facilities. For instance, the Massachusetts Port Authority has prepared a directory of sea and air services between Boston and major world points. The booklet contains the names of customs brokers and forwarders in Boston, a glossary of shipping terms, air trade routes, steamship trade routes, cargo ship lines and their agents serving the world from the Port of Boston, and important government addresses and telephone numbers in

Algeria (Lykes)
Angola (Farrell)
Argentina (Moore-McCormack)
Aruba (Farrell, Prudential, Lykes, Moore-McCormack)
Ascension (Farrell, Moore-McCormack)
Australia (Farrell)
Austria (Lykes, U.S. Lines)
Azores (Farrell, Lykes)

Bahamas (Moore-McCormack)
Barbados (Moore-McCormack)
Basutoland (Farrell, Moore-McCormack)
Bechuanaland (Farrell, Moore-McCormack)
Belgium (Farrell, Lykes, Moore-McCormack, U.S. Lines)
Bermuda (Farrell, Lykes)
Bolivia (Prudential, Moore-McCormack)
Brazil (Moore-McCormack)
Burma (American President)
Burundi (Farrell, Moore-McCormack)

Cambodia (American President, U.S. Lines, States Line)
Cameroon (Farrell)
Canal Zone (Farrell, Prudential, Lykes, Moore-McCormack)
Canary Islands (Farrell, Lykes)
Cape Verde Islands (Farrell)
Chile (Prudential)
Colombia (Prudential, Lykes, Moore-McCormack)
Congo-Leopoldville (Farrell, Moore-McCormack)
Congo-Brazzaville (Farrell)
Costa Rica (Prudential)
Curacao (Farrell, Prudential, Lykes, Moore-McCormack)
Czechoslovakia (Lykes, Moore-McCormack, U.S. Lines)

Dahomey (Farrell)
Denmark (Lykes, Moore-McCormack, U.S. Lines)
Dominican Republic (Prudential, Lykes)

Ecuador (Prudential)
Egypt (Lykes)
El Salvador (Prudential)

Fiji (Farrell)
Finland (Lykes, Moore-McCormack, U.S. Lines)
France (American President, Farrell, Lykes, U.S. Lines)

Gabon (Farrell)
Gambia (Farrell)
Germany (Farrell, Lykes, Moore-McCormack, U.S. Lines)
Ghana (Farrell)
Great Britain (Farrell, Lykes, U.S. Lines)
Greece (Lykes, Prudential)
Guam (American President)
Guatemala (Prudential)
Guinea (Farrell)
Guinea–Bissau (Farrell)

Haiti (Prudential, Lykes)
Honduras (Prudential)
Hong Kong (American President, Lykes, States Line, U.S. Lines)
Hungary (Moore-McCormack, U.S. Lines)

Iceland (Moore-McCormack)
India (American President)
Indonesia (American President, Lykes)
Ireland (Lykes, U.S. Lines)
Israel (Lykes)
Italy (American President, Lykes, Prudential)
Ivory Coast (Farrell)

Jamaica (Prudential, Lykes, Moore-McCormack)
Japan (American President, Lykes, States Line, U.S. Lines)

Kenya (Farrell, Lykes, Moore-McCormack)
Korea (American President, Lykes, States Line, U.S. Lines)

Laos (American President, States Line, U.S. Lines)
Lebanon (Lykes)
Liberia (Farrell)
Libya (Lykes)
Luxembourg (Moore-McCormack, U.S. Lines)

Figure 14-2 Council of American Flag Ship Operators (CASO) offices and agents in principal countries around the world.

Malagasy Republic (Madagascar)
(Farrell, Lykes, Moore-
McCormack)
Malawi Republic (Farrell, Moore-
McCormack)
Malaysia (American President,
Lykes)
Malta (Lykes)
Martinique (Prudential)
Mauretania (Farrell)
Mauritius (Farrell, Lykes, Moore-
McCormack)
Midway (States Line)
Mexico (Farrell, Prudential, Lykes,
Moore-McCormack)
Morocco (Lykes)
Mozambique (Farrell, Lykes,
Moore-McCormack)

Netherlands (Farrell, Lykes, Moore-
McCormack, U.S. Lines)
New Britain (Farrell)
New Caledonia (Farrell)
New Guinea (Farrell)
New Zealand (Farrell)
Nicaragua (Prudential)
Nigeria (Farrell)
Norway (Lykes, Moore-McCormack,
U.S. Lines)

Okinawa (American President, Lykes,
States Line, U.S. Lines)

Pakistan (American President)
Panama (Farrell, Prudential,
Lykes, Moore-McCormack)
Paraguay (Moore-McCormack)
Pemba Island (Farrell, Moore-
McCormack)
Peru (Prudential, Moore-
McCormack)
Philippine Islands (American Presi-
dent, Lykes, States Line, U.S.
Lines)
Poland (Lykes, Moore-McCormack,
U.S. Lines)
Portugal (Farrell, Lykes,
U.S. Lines)
Portuguese West Africa (Farrell)
Puerto Rico (Lykes)

Reunion Island (Farrell, Lykes,
Moore-McCormack)
Rhodesia (Farrell, Moore-McCormack,
Lykes)

Rwanda (Farrell, Moore-
McCormack)

Sarawak (American President,
States Line)
Senegal (Farrell)
Sierra Leone (Farrell)
Singapore (American President;
Lykes, U.S. Lines)
Somalia (Farrell, Lykes, Moore-
McCormack)
South Africa (Farrell, Lykes,
Moore-McCormack)
South West Africa (Farrell, Lykes,
Moore-McCormack)
Spain (American President, Farrell,
Lykes, Prudential, U.S. Lines)
Spanish Guinea (Farrell)
St. Helena (Farrell, Moore-
McCormack)
Sri Lanka (American President)
Swaziland (Farrell, Moore-
McCormack)
Sweden (Lykes, Moore-McCormack,
U.S. Lines)
Switzerland (Farrell, Lykes, Moore-
McCormack, U.S. Lines)

Tahiti (Farrell)
Taiwan (Formosa) (American Presi-
dent, Lykes, States Line, U.S. Lines)
Tanzania (Farrell, Lykes, Moore-
McCormack)
Tasmania (Farrell)
Thailand (American President, Lykes,
States Line, U.S. Lines)
Togo (Farrell)
Trinidad (Farrell, Lykes, Moore-
McCormack)
Tunisia (Lykes)
Turkey (Lykes, Prudential)

U.A.R. (Lykes)
Uganda (Farrell, Lykes, Moore-
McCormack)
Uruguay (Moore-McCormack)

Venezuela (Prudential, Lykes,
Moore-McCormack)
Vietnam (American President, Lykes,
States Line, U.S. Lines)

Yugoslavia (Lykes)

Zambia (Farrell, Moore-McCormack)

Figure 14-2   (continued).

American President Lines, Ltd. 1950 Franklin Street Oakland, CA 94612 415/271–8000	Moore-McCormack Lines, Inc. Two Broadway New York, NY 10004 212/363–6628
Farrell Lines Incorporated One Whitehall Street New York, NY 10004 212/425–6300 (Note: Includes American Export Services)	Prudential Lines, Inc. One World Trade Center Suite 3601 New York, NY 10048 212/775–0550 States Steamship Company 320 California Street San Francisco, CA 94104 415/982–6221
Lykes Bros. Steamship Co., Inc. Lykes Center 300 Poydras Street New Orleans, LA 70130 504/523–6611	United States Lines, Inc. One Broadway New York, NY 10004 212/344–5800

Figure 14-3   Names and addresses of CASO members.

the Boston area. You may secure one of these booklets by writing the Massachusetts Port Authority, 470 Atlantic Avenue, Boston, MA 02110. Contact the port authorities of the ports listed in Figure 14-4 for information or assistance when using their facilities.

Assistance Abroad.   When abroad the U.S. businessman may contact Foreign Service officers at the U.S. embassies or consulates for assistance. Commercial officers are assigned to embassies in countries that are major trading partners of the United States. In other countries, officers assigned to the economic section perform similar functions. Reports prepared by these officers furnish the Department of Commerce with a good part of its country information. Assistance is given to visiting U.S. businessmen and representatives of U.S. firms in a variety of ways. Direct correspondence from the United States is discouraged because the information requested is usually already available at the Department of Commerce.

In some foreign cities, local chambers of commerce actively assist the visiting businessman. In others, there are associations of resident U.S. businessmen or joint U.S.-foreign groups that welcome visitors and accord them facilities. For example, there are almost fifty U.S. chambers of commerce abroad (AmChams). These voluntary associations of businessmen and host-country nationals operate in concert with host-country business firms, affiliates, individuals, and governments. Through a wide spectrum of activities, AmChams work (a) to develop mutually prosperous and amicable economic, social, and commercial relations between United States business and industrial interests and those of host countries, (b) to foster and communicate abroad the beneficial concepts of U.S. private enterprise, and (c) to promote local economic and social contributions for the benefit of host countries. AmChams represent their members before the governments, the business communities, and the general publics of host countries.

Besides offering translation services, AmChams frequently provide letters of introduction for U.S. and host-country members planning to visit the United States. They also assist, generally at early stages and on an informal basis, in mitigating or remedying trade disputes between (a) members, (b) members and nonmembers, or (c) U.S. and foreign firms. When the desired solution is not achieved, difficulties are frequently referred to the American Arbitration Association and its affiliates, to the International Chamber of Commerce, or to foreign boards of arbitration. Visiting U.S. businessmen may use AmCham headquarters as bases of operations during

OCEAN AND RIVER PORTS	GREAT LAKES PORTS
Port of New York, New York	Duluth-Superior, Minn., Wis.
New Orleans, Louisiana	Toledo, Ohio
Houston, Texas	Chicago, Illinois
Philadelphia, Pennsylvania	Detroit, Michigan
Norfolk Harbor, Virginia	Indiana Harbor, Indiana
Baltimore, Maryland	Cleveland, Ohio
Beaumont, Texas	Buffalo, New York
Baton Rouge, Louisiana	Calcite, Michigan
Port Arthur, Texas	Ashtabula, Ohio
Los Angeles, California	Gary, Indiana
Boston, Massachusetts	
Corpus Christi, Texas	
Mobile, Alabama	
Texas City, Texas	
Portland, Maine	
Lake Charles, Louisiana	
Richmond, California	
Portland, Oregon	
Tampa, Florida	
Huntington, West Virginia	
Newport News, Virginia	
Seattle, Washington	
Long Beach, California	

Figure 14-4   Major United States ports in order of total tonnage.

visits. AmChams assist in arranging meetings, luncheons, receptions, and business appointments for members of visiting trade missions. Chapters may be found in the following countries.

Far East and Pacific	*Europe*
Melbourne, Australia	Brussels, Belgium
Sydney, Australia	London, England
Tokyo, Japan	Paris, France
Seoul, Korea	Berlin, Germany
Koza, Okinawa	Bremen, Germany
Manila, Philippine Islands	Dusseldorf, Germany
Taipei, Taiwan	Frankfurt/Main, Germany
Bangkok, Thailand	Hamburg, Germany
Saigon, Vietnam	Munich, Germany
	Dublin, Ireland
	Florence, Italy
Latin America	Milan, Italy
Buenos Aires, Argentina	Rome, Italy
Pôrto Alegre, Brazil	The Hague, The Netherlands
Recife, Brazil	Barcelona, Spain
Rio de Janeiro, Brazil	Bilbao, Spain
São Paulo, Brazil	Madrid, Spain
Santiago, Chile	Oviedo, Spain
Santo Domingo, Dominican Republic	Seville, Spain
Guatemala City, Guatemala	Valencia, Spain
Guadalajara, Mexico	Zaragoza, Spain
Mexico City, Mexico	Zurich, Switzerland
Lima, Peru	
Montevideo, Uruguay	*Africa*
Caracas, Venezuela	Casablanca, Morocco

Foreign Market Reports. Up-to-date information of activity in foreign markets is of paramount importance to the exporter/importer. Several agencies make studies of countries and their industries and gather other economic facts that influence the flow of goods and services. These studies are published in reports and statistical charts that are made available to the U.S. businessman.

Foreign Market Report Service. This service provides the businessman with copies of unclassified Foreign Service reports covering useful marketing information on the status of certain industries in a country plus recent economic developments in that country. A listing of these reports is compiled each month and sent to the Department of Commerce field offices, which perform secondary distribution to interested firms. The Bureau of Export Development, which does the compiling, maintains copies of all reports and files them by Standard Industrial Classification code by country or general subject matter. An interested firm can subscribe for the monthly compilations through the National Technical Information Service (NTIS), U.S. Department of Commerce, 5285 Port Royal Road, Springfield, VA 22161.

Share of Market Statistical Studies. These statistics show the U.S. share of the world market for 1,127 commodities (products) and provide a comparison of the value of U.S. trade with that of competing countries. The figures given are the U.S. share of imports into ninety different countries. Also given is the export figure of each of the countries for a particular commodity.

The purpose of these studies is to identify product groups in which the U.S. share of particular foreign markets appears unduly low in relation to the possibilities and to indicate the opportunities for significant increases. These studies also enable the businessman to:

1. Pinpoint the source and strength of foreign competition in world markets.

2. Determine where specific products sell best, thus ranking the markets so that the most important get prime attention.

3. Identify markets where U.S. exporters are already doing well, thus recognizing the competition and necessitating the determination as to whether more intense market development is worthwhile.

4. Determine whether a company's share is increasing or decreasing relative to comparative U.S. performance. For example, if the U.S. share is increasing but a company's showing is contrary to the trend, it will be useful to the management to know this fact so that corrective action may be taken.

These trade statistics are reported in terms of the Standard International Trade Classification (SITC) system of the United Nations and are currently available at the four- and five-digit levels.

In addition to all the above benefits, these studies provide two of the three elements necessary to determine what a country's current market for a given product is. The total existing market is simply imports plus domestic production less exports. Thus, any U.S. company interested in finding out what is the statistical market for its product in a particular country would need only to ascertain the production figures within that country in order to determine the total consumption of the product. In many cases the applicable industry division of the Bureau of International Economic Policy and Research will be able to furnish such production figures.

NTIS has available domestic and foreign market share reports for countries and commodities. These are listed in a Market Share Reports Catalog, which is sent free to companies on its mailing list or may be secured at the nearest Commerce field office. The address is National Technical Information Service, U.S. Department of Commerce, Springfield, VA 22161.

World Trade Annual. A publication of the International Trade Statistics Centre of the United Nations, the *World Trade Annual,* contains detailed trade statistics. The purpose of the Centre is to collect, verify, and standardize trade statistics from as many countries as possible. Data are collected from approximately fifty countries, mostly on a quarterly basis and in terms of the 1,312 items of the United Nations Standard International Trade Classification (SITC). These figures go to a five-digit classification, and are stored on tape in standard units of value (the U.S. dollar) and of quantity (metric units). The Centre arranges for certain publications in printed form and supplies at cost selections and rearrangements of the figures in the form of machine tabulations, punched cards, or magnetic tape.

United Nations statistical publications are available throughout the United States at all United Nations depository libraries, which include the principal public and university libraries. A set for 19 industrial countries is available for reference purposes at the Bureau of Export Development in Washington.

Other Export Considerations. *C.I.F. Price Determination.* Foreign business-men prefer to have prices quoted as c.i.f. rather than f.o.b. The U.S. exporter can figure more accurately the total costs of shipment to the port of embarka-tion and the means and routing to use to get the goods there and to the port of debarkation. Many factors beside cost (net amount required by exporter), insurance (marine), and freight (inland plus overseas) have to be considered in determining the final market price. Cost elements listed here should also be determined.

> Export packing
> Special marking and labeling
> Shipping registration, documentation, and other fees
> Financing and credit insurance costs, where applicable
> Wharfage and pier handling charges
> Warehousing, if necessary
> Customs clearance, consular, or purchasing fees
> Distributor/dealer markups
> Duties and taxes

General information on duties (tariffs) and taxes may be found in the Over-seas Business Reports series "Foreign Trade Regulations of *(Country)*."

Nontariff barriers may need to be considered also when determining mar-ket price. Barriers of a broad scope such as electrical, plumbing, and safety standards; pharmaceutical or pharmacopoeia standards; container sizes; customs surcharges; internal taxes; licensing; and exchange control systems (some countries require import licensing in order to entitle the importer to an exchange permit that allows payment for the goods in dollars) are dis-cussed in the OBR country series.

Electric Current Characteristics. Because most overseas markets operate on different electric current than that in the United States, design and engineering changes in the product may be necessary. A booklet entitled *Electric Current Abroad* may be secured from the Superintendent of Documents or consulted at any of the Department of Commerce field offices.

Selection of an Overseas Outlet. Trade lists are available that contain the names and addresses of firms handling a specific commodity in a particular foreign country. By consulting these lists, U.S. companies may locate agents, distributors, and in some instances potential customers for the particular overseas market. These automated trade lists include also a numerical busi-ness code, the type of organization, the year it was established, its size, its number of employees, whether it has U.S. representation, the languages of correspondence, and the date of the source information. Lists are available for country and commodity from the Export Mailing List Service or from any Department of Commerce field office. After selecting the names of a few firms whose brief description makes them appealing, the businessman may request a "World Trade Directory Report" (WTDR) on each specific company.

Upon special application through the Department of Commerce, an exporter may ask a Foreign Service officer at an overseas post to make an on-the-spot trade contact survey to find two or three, and sometimes more, qualified local firms who are specifically interested in the exporter's product. Applications for trade contact surveys, however, will be accepted only after all other efforts to locate a foreign distributor have failed.

Export Distributors.   A number of private export agents in this country and abroad are willing to function as exclusive distributors on a worldwide basis or in a certain locale. Many of these firms have a network of foreign representatives, salesmen, and/or distributors. As independent representatives, they generally handle a number of related but noncompetitive lines for several exporters. Most of them work on a commission basis, but many request a retaining fee to develop markets for new products. A directory of the available export agents is available for review in the Bureau of Export Development (BED) or at the Department of Commerce field offices.

The functions of an exporter manager closely parallel those of the export agent. The combination export manager prefers to act as the export department for the exporter, doing business in the exporter's name and on the exporter's letterhead. Similarly to the export agent, the combination export manager usually handles a number of related but noncompetitive lines and sells through a network of foreign representatives, salesmen, and/or distributors. These firms generally operate on a minimum retainer plus a commission basis. A directory of these firms is available at the Department of Commerce field offices.

Legislation Favorable to Exporters.   A U.S. firm that incorporates under the China Trade Act to do business in Hong Kong or Taiwan may be fully exempted from U.S. corporate income tax on dividends distributed to qualified stockholders. Moreover, if the stockholders of a CTA corporation are resident in Hong Kong or Taiwan, they, too, are exempted from U.S. personal income tax on the dividends distributed to them. The articles of incorporation are required to state that a major portion of the corporation's business will be in developing markets for goods produced in the United States. Three or more persons, a majority of whom are U.S. citizens, may apply for CTA incorporation. The company's president, its treasurer, and a majority of the board of directors must be U.S. citizens residing in either Hong Kong or Taiwan. Application forms and additional information may be obtained from the Acting Registrar of the China Trade Act in the Commerce Department.

Under the Internal Revenue Act of 1971, a Domestic International Sales Corporation (DISC) is entitled to defer federal income taxes on 50 percent of its export income. The deferral is limited to 25 percent of export income for sales of military property. A DISC is a domestic corporation that meets certain minimal organizational requirements and limits itself almost exclusively to export sales activities. A DISC can operate as a principal, buying and selling for its own account, or as a commission agent. It can be related to a manufacturer or be an independent merchant or broker. A DISC also can maintain sales and service facilities abroad to enhance its foreign promotional and marketing efforts. A corporation that wishes to be treated as a DISC must file a statement of election (IRS Form 4876) with the Internal Revenue Service within 90 days preceding the beginning of the year for which it seeks DISC status, or if newly formed, within 90 days after the date of incorporation. For further information write U.S. Department of Commerce, Foreign Business Practices Division, Office of International Finance and Investment, Washington, DC 20230.

Trade Fair Participation.   Two types of international trade fairs are used by the United States. Commercial exhibitions are held in the more developed areas, which have been selected entirely for their sales potential. Specific market research has been made to pinpoint product classification and the models thereof that are the most saleable. BED conducts an extensive promotional campaign to attract buyers and prospective agents for the exhibited products. It designs, constructs, and installs the exhibits; and U.S. businessmen are encouraged to participate. Participation agreements are handled by the Office of International Marketing, and a telephone call to the Project Officer will elicit the going fee for space charges and other information. Only products of at least 50 percent American origin may be displayed.

United States national exhibitions are put on by BED in conjunction with the State Department and the U.S. Information Agency and are primarily designed to portray the American way of life under the free-enterprise system. Most of these fairs are now concentrated behind the Iron Curtain. The cost of participating in this type of fair is generally nominal. Display space for U.S. products is free, and except where there are commercial overtones for the product on display, there is no charge to an exhibitor for transporting products from the U.S. dockside to the fair site—and back, in the event that the goods are not sold at the fair. A real effort is made, however, to make sales at the fair, although this is the secondary purpose of the presentation. "How to Get the Most from Overseas Exhibitions" is an informative Department of Commerce pamphlet.

Trade Centers.   Permanent trade centers have been established by BED in London, Frankfurt, Paris, Milan, Tokyo, Sydney, Bangkok, and Stockholm. The trade centers are permanent merchandise marts where groups of related U.S. products are placed on exhibition for two to three weeks and then replaced by another exhibit of different U.S. products. A permanent U.S.

staff operates each trade center, handles all the necessary advance promotion and publicity, and helps to find agents, distributors, and dealers for the products exhibited.

Trade Missions.   There are three categories of missions, all with the common objective of assisting the American businessman to initiate or expand trade with overseas markets.

1. Government-organized and -sponsored trade missions are composed of business specialists, selected by the Department of Commerce, and sent abroad at government expense. In this type of mission, business proposals for the products or industries represented may be submitted by a company anywhere in the United States in advance of the mission's departure. Such a business proposal, after having been screened for validity, is discussed in conferences overseas by one businessman talking to another—one from the United States and the other a national of the host country. Mission members agree not to undertake business on behalf of their own interests while in the country.

2. An "industry-organized, government-approved trade mission" may represent a state, a city, a chamber of commerce, a trade association, a group of industries, or a single industry. The selection of the membership is the responsibility of the organizers. The members pay all expenses of the mission and may do business on their own behalf. Department of Commerce approval and sponsorship is granted provided the mission adheres to the criteria set up by the Department.

3. Other privately organized and financed business groups traveling abroad are invited to avail themselves of the services offered.

Mobile Trade Fairs.   BED, through its Office of International Marketing, offers technical and limited financial support to private operators of mobile trade fairs. These fairs are designed to show and sell products of U.S. business and agriculture at foreign ports and other commercial centers throughout the world.

Shipping to the Market.   The procedures for effecting and protecting foreign shipments are more complicated than for domestic shipments. Complete information for handling this particular marketing element can be secured through the Industry and Trade Administration of the Department of Commerce.

Use of Freight Forwarders.   Many firms are equipped to perform a variety of services for the exporter, including the handling of paper work involved in shipping to and collecting from the market. A freight forwarder can package the items; is familiar with the necessary marking and labeling; can arrange for marine insurance; can prepare any necessary shipping, consular, and other documents; can arrange customs clearances; can handle the inland transportation of the products both here and abroad; can book the necessary freight space; and can oversee the placement of the goods aboard ship. The forwarder can also help prepare and will forward banking collection papers. A list of customhouse brokers and foreign freight forwarders can be obtained from the Custom Brokers and Forwarders Association of America, Inc., 8 Bridge Street, New York, NY 10004.

Necessary Documentation.   Export sales may require the following documents:

1. A bill of lading.
2. A commercial invoice.
3. A Consular Invoice describing the merchandise being exported and used to clear the goods through the customs office of the importing country.
4. A certificate of, or the actual policy covering, marine insurance and war risk.
5. Certificates of origin, packing lists, health certificates for certain types of food products, and certificates of quality.
6. The shipper's export declaration.
7. Marine insurance and freight.

Foreign-Trade Zones.   A foreign-trade zone is a controlled area into which may be brought domestic and foreign merchandise without such goods being subject to the U.S. customs laws governing entry or payment of duties. In such a zone a broad range of business activities may be conducted, including manufacturing, assembling, processing, packaging, exhibiting, storing, and other activities. These goods, or the products derived therefrom, may be exported, imported, or transshipped from the zone. Foreign merchandise sent from a zone into U.S. customs territory for consumption is subject to the laws and regulations affecting imports.

The business advantages inherent in a foreign-trade zone operation include opportunities for:

1. Duty-free and quota-free manufacturing for export using foreign materials or components in the production of goods.
2. The employment of U.S. labor, technology, and management at a duty-free U.S. site.
3. A reduction in volume of the outlay of working capital for the payment of customs duties on foreign goods or components destined for U.S. markets. (These are paid only when and if goods enter U.S. customs territory and apply only to the quantity of imported goods that actually enter.)
4. The establishment of production facilities in the United States as an alternative to establishing similar facilities abroad.
5. Immediate export status for U.S. exports placed in a zone solely for export. Such a classification permits prompt customs drawback and refund or exemption from liability for Internal Revenue taxes.
6. The possibility of a saving in ultimate customs duties, particularly on that merchandise shipped abroad from a trade zone.

Foreign-trade zones are listed in Figure 14-5. General inquiries pertaining to their use by business firms should be referred to the Executive Secretary of the Foreign-Trade Zones Board, headquartered at the Bureau of Trade Regulation, U.S. Department of Commerce.

Collecting from the Market. Knowledgeable domestic banking facilities, the Export-Import Bank, and the Foreign Credit Insurance Association aid the U.S. businessman in collecting from the foreign market.

Foreign Credit Insurance. Several types of credit insurance are available for export sales under programs administered by the Foreign Credit Insurance Association (FCIA). Insurance can be obtained covering comprehensive risks (credit and political), or political risk alone for short-term (up to six months) transactions and medium-term (six months to five years) transactions. In the case of short-term insurance, the exporter retains from 5 percent to 15 percent of the political risk (the percentage varying according to the country and to the terms of the credit extended) and 10 percent of the credit risk. In the case of medium-term insurance, the customer generally makes a down payment of 20 percent and the exporter carries at least 10 percent of the remainder. Member insurance companies are listed in a booklet issued by the

Zone Number	City	Zone Number	City
1	New York City, New York	21	Dorchester County, South Carolina
2	New Orleans, Louisiana		
3	San Francisco, California	22	Chicago, Illinois
4		23	Buffalo, New York
5	Seattle, Washington	24	Pittston, Pennsylvania
6		25	Port Everglades, Florida
7	Mayaguez, Puerto Rico	26	Shenandoah, Georgia
8	Toledo, Ohio	27	Boston, Massachusetts
9	Honolulu, Hawaii	28	New Bedford, Massachusetts
10	Bay County, Michigan	29	Louisville, Kentucky
11		30	Salt Lake City, Utah
12	McAllen, Texas	31	Granite City, Illinois
13		32	Miami, Florida
14	Little Rock, Arkansas	33	Pittsburgh, Pennsylvania
15	Kansas City, Missouri	34	Niagra County, New York
16	Sault Ste. Marie, Michigan	35	Philadelphia, Pennsylvania
17	Kansas City, Kansas	36	Galveston, Texas
18	San Jose, California	37	Orange County, New York
19	Omaha, Nebraska	38	Spartenburg, South Carolina
20	Portsmouth, Virginia	39	Dallas/Fort Worth, Texas

Figure 14-5 Foreign-trade zones in the United States.

Foreign Credit Insurance Association, 250 Broadway, New York, NY 10007. Policies are available from any insurance broker or agent.

Export-Import Bank.   The Export-Import Bank will guarantee medium-term (six months to five years) export transactions to commercial banks or other financial institutions. In the event the exporter cannot get financing through the commercial bank or credit insurance through the Foreign Credit Insurance Association, application may be made directly to the Export-Import Bank for either a guarantee or a direct credit. The exporter is required generally to obtain a 20 percent cash down-payment from the customer and to carry not less than 10 percent of the balance to be financed. Further details on this program, as well as on the FCIA, can be obtained from the International Finance Division of the Office of Commercial and Financial Policy or from any commercial bank with a foreign department.

United States and International Lending Agencies.   Two U.S. agencies and several international institutions provide loans that help U.S. exporters and investors. United States exporters and investors seeking financing should become familiar with the differences in purposes and facilities of these lending agencies, as they vary considerably. Generally, however, the company should turn first to the two U.S. government agencies (the EX-IM Bank and the Agency for International Development), as they are more closely concerned with U.S. business operations, and procurement under these programs must— with some exceptions—be in the United States.

Use of Commercial Banks' International Departments.   Most of the large banks have active international departments, which are becoming more and more familiar with details involved in getting paid for exports. If your local bank does not have an international department, or does not handle import or export papers, it is in all probability a correspondent of a large metropolitan bank that does and can provide assistance in helping to arrange financing for sound export business transactions.

Small Business Administration Loans.   In the interest of making an effective contribution to the National Export Expansion Program and of assisting small concerns and individuals in the United States, as defined in the Small Business Act, to enter into and to expand export trade and international commerce, the SBA considers applications for loans, including working capital, to defray the costs of:

1. Professional foreign marketing advice and service.
2. Foreign business travel.
3. Shopping foreign markets.
4. Ocean freight and the insurance of sample merchandise shipped abroad.
5. Participation in U.S. trade center shows and exhibits at international trade fairs.
6. Foreign advertising and the preparation of promotional material.
7. Other related purposes not otherwise described.

The prime collateral required to secure such a loan is a lien on real and/or personal property, inventory, assignments of accounts receivables, and/or monies due under a contractual obligation, all of which are subject to foreclosure, enforcement, and collection in the United States or its possessions.

Other Market Information.   *Export Control.*   No special license is needed to engage in export trade. The U.S. government does, however, control the export of U.S. goods to all foreign countries. With the exception of certain specialized commodities and implements of war, export licensing is handled by the Office of Export Development.

The vast majority of goods can move to free world countries under what is called a *general license.* No formal license application is required, and the shipper's export declaration is all that is required.

The necessity for a *validated license* depends on *what* you are shipping *where.* Validated licenses are necessary for certain types of strategic goods regardless of destination and for all except a select list of *peaceful* items intended for the European Soviet Bloc. To all intents and purposes there is a total embargo on U.S. trade either directly or indirectly with North Korea, Cambodia, Vietnam, Rhodesia, and Cuba. The Office of Export Development or a Department of Commerce field office can give the exporter the necessary information on the status of a particular shipment. In addition, the *Comprehensive Exports Schedule*, an annual publication kept up to date with supplementary bulletins, is a compilation of U.S. export-control regulations and policies. It includes complete instructions, interpretations, and explanatory material.

Foreign Business Practices.   An exporter might have problems with foreign business customs and practices stemming either from discriminatory action by trade associations or cartels or from any other form of private, restrictive trade barrier. Any such cases should be reported to the Foreign Business Practices Division of BED, which will give the proper information and seek corrective action.

Patents and Trademarks.   Information on foreign patent, trademark, and copyright laws and practices, and international treaties concerned therewith, is available from the Foreign Business Practices Division of the Office of International Trade Policy.

Imitation and Copying Complaints.   Product imitation, trademark piracy, and design copying can be a scourge to the exporter. Instances of this nature should be reported to the Foreign Business Practices Division.

Licensing and Exchange Control.   Certain countries require import licensing in order to entitle the importer to an exchange permit to allow payment for the goods in dollars.

Trade Dispute Resolutions.   Business practice complaints are handled by the Foreign Business Practices Division and involve the areas of collections, discriminatory practices, patents and trademarks, and imitation and copying.

Disputes with foreign government agencies as well as cases involving the apparent violation of U.S. businessmen's rights and privileges under the terms of treaties and international agreements are handled by the Office of International Trade Policy.

Choice of Language. Seven-eighths of the world's population do not understand English. If you are able to correspond with the foreign businessman in his own language, greater understanding will result. In cases where the foreign businessman requests an answer in his own language, do all you can to oblige. The Department of Commerce field offices can help with translations or can direct you to a linguist competent in the business vocabulary and practices of the foreign nation in which you are interested.

Answering a Foreign Advertisement. When answering a foreign advertisement or selling abroad through correspondence, give the whole story the first time: the metric or other unit of sale; the details of the various price lines available if you have such distinctions as *utility, standard,* or *deluxe*; the c.i.f. price including discounts for quantity and for prompt payment; and the delivery schedule and the payment terms. Copies of catalogs and other literature should be sent also.

Use of the Metric System. Most countries use, or are changing to, the metric system for measurements. When corresponding with foreign importers, quote in metric measurements to facilitate understanding. (See Chapter 18, "Weights and Measures," for an explanation of the metric system.)

Export Reference Guides. An indispensable reference guide for firms actively engaged in importing and exporting is the *Custom House Guide, Foreign Traders' Encyclopedia*. Published yearly, it contains up-to-date information on United States customs ports, customs tariffs, customs regulations, the Revenue Act, and trade agreements. The addresses of United States ports, foreign consuls, steamship companies, surety companies, warehouses, customhouse brokers, and freight forwarders are listed also. The *Custom House Guide* is published by Budd Publications, Inc., 26 Beaver Street, New York, NY 10004.

The Exporters' Encyclopedia, published by Dun & Bradstreet, is another guide for exporters worthy of their attention. Besides a comprehensive 850 pages of facts and figures on every facet of foreign trade, the subscriber is offered free consultation on export problems by letter, telegram, or telephone as often as needed and is sent the *World Marketing Newsletter,* a twice-monthly publication. The basic encyclopedia is updated during the year with twice-monthly revisions. Exporters desiring additional information about this guide and its supplemental services should write Dun's Exporters' Encyclopedia, International Business Information Service, P.O. Box 3088, Grand Central Station, New York, NY 10017.

14.2 FOREIGN COUNTRIES, THEIR CAPITALS, AND DESCRIPTIVE NATIONAL TERMS

Country	Capital	Nationality	
		Noun	*Adjective*
Afghanistan	Kabul	Afghan(s)	Afghan
Albania	Tirana	Albanian(s)	Albanian
Algeria	Algiers	Algerian(s)	Algerian
Andorra	Andorra la Vella	Andorran(s)	Andorran
Argentina	Buenos Aires	Argentine(s)	Argentine
Australia	Canberra	Australian(s)	Australian
Austria	Vienna (Wien)	Austrian(s)	Austrian
Barbados	Bridgetown	Barbadian(s)	Barbadian
Belgium	Brussels	Belgian(s)	Belgian
Bhutan	Thimphu	Bhutanese	Bhutanese
Bolivia	Sucre; La Paz, seat of government	Bolivian(s)	Bolivian
Botswana	Gaberone	Botswana	Botswana
Brazil	Brasília	Brazilian(s)	Brazilian
Bulgaria	Sofia	Bulgarian(s)	Bulgarian
Burma	Rangoon	Burman(s)	Burmese
Burundi	Bujumbura	Burundian(s)	Burundian
Cambodia (see Kampuchea)			
Cameroon	Yaoundé	Cameroonian(s)	Cameroonian
Canada	Ottawa	Canadian(s)	Canadian
Central African Empire	Bangui	Central African(s)	Central African
Chad	Fort-Lamy	Chadian(s)	Chadian
Chile	Santiago	Chilean(s)	Chilean
China, People's Republic of	Beijing	Chinese	Chinese
China, Republic of	Taipei, Taiwan	Chinese	Chinese, Taiwanese
Colombia	Bogotá	Colombian(s)	Colombian
Congo, People's Republic of	Brazzaville	Congolese	Congolese or Congo
Costa Rica	San José	Costa Rican(s)	Costa Rican
Cuba	Havana	Cuban(s)	Cuban
Cyprus	Nicosia	Cypriot(s)	Cypriot
Czechoslovakia	Prague	Czechoslovak(s)	Czechoslovak
Dahomey	Porto Novo	Dahomean(s)	Dahomean
Denmark	Copenhagen	Dane(s)	Danish
Dominican Republic	Santo Domingo	Dominican(s)	Dominican
Ecuador	Quito	Ecuadorean(s)	Ecuadorean
Egypt	Cairo	Egyptian(s)	Egyptian
El Salvador	San Salvador	Salvadoran(s)	Salvadoran
Equatorial Guinea	Santa Isabel	Guinean(s)	Guinean
Estonia	Tallinn	Estonian(s)	Estonian
Ethiopia	Addis Ababa	Ethiopian(s)	Ethiopian
Fiji	Suva	Fiji(s)	Fiji
Finland	Helsinki	Finn(s)	Finnish
France	Paris	Frenchman(men)	French
Gabon	Libreville	Gabonese	Gabonese

Country	Capital	Nationality	
		Noun	*Adjective*
Gambia	Bathurst	Gambian(s)	Gambian
German Democratic Republic	East Berlin	German(s)	German
Germany, Federal Republic of	Bonn	German(s)	German
Ghana	Accra	Ghanaian(s)	Ghanaian
Greece	Athens	Greek(s)	Greek
Guatemala	Guatemala City	Guatemalan(s)	Guatemalan
Guinea	Conakry	Guinean(s)	Guinean
Guyana	Georgetown	Guyanese	Guyanese
Haiti	Port-au-Prince	Haitian(s)	Haitian
Honduras	Tegucigalpa	Honduran(s)	Honduran
Hungary	Budapest	Hungarian(s)	Hungarian
Iceland	Reykjavik	Icelander(s)	Icelandic
India	New Delhi	Indian(s)	Indian
Indonesia	Djakarta	Indonesian(s)	Indonesian
Iran	Tehran	Iranian(s)	Iranian
Iraq	Baghdad	Iraqi(s)	Iraqi
Ireland	Dublin	Irishman(men), Irish (collective plural)	Irish
Israel	Jerusalem	Israeli(s)	Israeli
Italy	Rome	Italian(s)	Italian
Ivory Coast	Abidjan	Ivoirian(s)	Ivoirian
Jamaica	Kingston	Jamaican(s)	Jamaican
Japan	Tokyo	Japanese	Japanese
Jordan	Amman	Jordanian(s)	Jordanian
Kampuchea (Cambodia)	Phnom Penh	Kampuchean(s)	Kampuchean
Kenya	Nairobi	Kenyan(s)	Kenyan
Korea, Democratic People's Republic of (North)	Pyongyang	Korean(s)	Korean
Korea, Republic of (South)	Seoul	Korean(s)	Korean
Kuwait	Kuwait City	Kuwaiti(s)	Kuwaiti
Laos	Vientiane	Lao	Lao or Laotian
Latvia	Riga	Latvian(s)	Latvian
Lebanon	Beirut	Lebanese	Lebanese
Lesotho	Maseru	Basuto(s)	Basuto
Liberia	Monrovia	Liberian(s)	Liberian
Libya	Benghazi and Tripoli	Libyan(s)	Libyan
Liechtenstein	Vaduz	Liechtensteiner(s)	Liechtenstein
Lithuania	Vilnyus	Lithuanian(s)	Lithuanian
Luxembourg	Luxembourg	Luxembourger(s)	Luxembourg
Malagasy Republic (Madagascar)	Tananarive	Malagasy	Malagasy
Malawi	Zomba	Malawian(s)	Malawian
Malaysia	Kuala Lumpur	Malaysian(s)	Malaysian
Maldives, Republic of	Male	Maldivian(s)	Maldivian
Mali	Bamako	Malian(s)	Malian

Country	Capital	Nationality	
		Noun	*Adjective*
Malta	Valletta	Maltese	Maltese
Mauritania	Nouakchott	Mauritanian(s)	Mauritanian
Mauritius	Port Louis	Mauritian(s)	Mauritian
Mexico	Mexico City	Mexican(s)	Mexican
Monaco	Monaco	Monacan(s), Monegasque(s)	Monacan or Monegasque
Mongolian People's Republic	Ulan Bator	Mongol(s)	Mongol
Morocco	Rabat	Moroccan(s)	Moroccan
Nepal	Katmandu	Nepalese	Nepalese
Netherlands	Amsterdam; The Hague, seat of government	Netherlander(s)	Netherlands
New Zealand	Wellington	New Zealander(s)	New Zealand
Nicaragua	Managua	Nicaraguan(s)	Nicaraguan
Niger	Niamey	Nigerois	Niger
Nigeria	Lagos	Nigerian(s)	Nigerian
Norway	Oslo	Norwegian(s)	Norwegian
Oman	Muscat	Omani(s)	Omani
Pakistan	Islamabad	Pakistani(s)	Pakistani
Panama	Panama City	Panamanian(s)	Panamanian
Paraguay	Asunción	Paraguayan(s)	Paraguayan
Peru	Lima	Peruvian(s)	Peruvian
Philippines	Quezon City; Manila, seat of government	Filipino(s)	Philippine
Poland	Warsaw	Pole(s)	Polish
Portugal	Lisbon	Portuguese	Portuguese
Rhodesia	Salisbury	Rhodesian(s)	Rhodesian
Romania	Bucharest	Romanian(s)	Romanian
Rwanda	Kigali	Rwandan(s)	Rwandan
San Marino	San Marino	Sanmarinese	Sanmarinese
Saudi Arabia	Riyadh; Jidda, diplomatic center	Saudi	Saudi Arabian or Saudi
Senegal	Dakar	Senegalese	Senegalese
Sierra Leone	Freetown	Sierra Leonean(s)	Sierra Leonean
Singapore	Singapore	Singaporan(s)	Singaporan
Somalia	Mogadishu	Somali(s)	Somali
South Africa, Republic of	Pretoria; Capetown, legislative capital	South African(s)	South African
Spain	Madrid	Spaniard(s)	Spanish
Sri Lanka	Colombo	Sri Lankan(s)	Sri Lankan
Sudan	Khartoum	Sudanese	Sudanese
Swaziland	Mbabane	Swazi(s)	Swazi
Sweden	Stockholm	Swede(s)	Swedish
Switzerland	Bern	Swiss	Swiss
Syria	Damascus	Syrian(s)	Syrian
Tanzania	Dar es Salaam	Tanzanian(s)	Tanzanian
Thailand	Bangkok	Thai	Thai
Togo	Lomé	Togolese	Togolese
Tonga	Nukualofa	Tongan(s)	Tongan
Trinidad and Tobago	Port of Spain	Trinidadian(s), Tobagan(s)	Trinidadian, Tobagan

| Country | Capital | Nationality | |
		Noun	Adjective
Tunisia	Tunis	Tunisian(s)	Tunisian
Turkey	Ankara	Turk(s)	Turkish
Uganda	Kampala	Ugandan(s)	Ugandan
Union of Soviet Socialist Republics	Moscow	Soviet(s)	Soviet
United Arab Emirates	Abu Dhabi	Arabian(s)	Arabian
United Kingdom	London	Briton(s), British (collective plural) Irishman(men) Scot(s) Welshman(men)	British Irish Scottish Welsh
United States of America	Washington, D.C.	American(s)	American
Upper Volta	Ouagadougou	Upper Voltan(s)	Upper Voltan
Uruguay	Montevideo	Uruguayan(s)	Uruguayan
Venezuela	Caracas	Venezuelan(s)	Venezuelan
Vietnam, Democratic Republic of	Hanoi	Vietnamese	Vietnamese
Western Samoa	Apia	Western Samoan(s)	Western Samoan
Yemen Arab Republic	San'a	Yemeni(s)	Yemeni
Yemen, People's Dem. Republic of	Aden	Yemeni(s)	Yemeni
Yugoslavia	Belgrade	Yugoslav(s)	Yugoslav
Zaire	Kinasha	Zairean(s)	Zairean
Zambia	Lusaka	Zambian(s)	Zambian

14.3   FOREIGN MONETARY TERMS[1]

| Country or Area | Basic Monetary Units | | Name and Number of Principal Fractional Units in Basic Unit |
	Name	Symbol	
Afghanistan	Afghani	Afg	100 Puls
Albania	Lek	L	100 Quintars
Algeria	Dinar	Da	100 Centimes
Andorra	French Franc	Fr	100 Centimes
	Spanish Peseta	Pta	100 Centimos
Argentina	Peso	M$N	100 Centavos
Australia	Dollar	$A	100 Cents
Austria	Schilling	S	100 Groschen
Bahamas	Dollar	$	100 Cents

[1] Dollar values of foreign currencies fluctuate widely. Current rates of exchange for leading world currencies are listed daily in most metropolitan newspapers, such as the *Wall Street Journal*, the *New York Times*, the *Washington Post* and the *Los Angeles Times*. Currency rates are also quoted by commercial banks and foreign exchange dealers.

| Country or Area | Basic Monetary Units | | Name and Number of Principal Fractional Units in Basic Unit |
	Name	Symbol	
Bahrain	Dinar	BD	1,000 Fils
Barbados	Dollar	WI$	100 Cents
Belgium	Franc	BF	100 Centimes
Bhutan	Indian Rupee	R	100 Naya Paisa
Bolivia	Peso Boliviano	$b	100 Centavos
Botswana	S. African Rand	R	100 Cents
Brazil	Cruzeiro	Cr$	100 Centavos
British Honduras	Lempira	L	100 Cents
Bulgaria	Lev	LV	100 Stotinki
Burma	Kyat	K	100 Pyas
Burundi	Franc	FBu	100 Centimes
Cameroon	CFA Franc[2]	CFAF	100 Centimes
Canada	Dollar	Can$	100 Cents
Canary Islands	Peseta	Pta	100 Centimos
Central African Empire	CFA Franc	CFAF	100 Centimes
Chad	CFA Franc	CFAF	100 Centimes
Chile	Escudo	Esc	100 Centesimos
China, People's Republic of	Yuan	$	100 Fen
China, Republic of (Taiwan)	New Taiwan Dollar	NT$	100 Cents
Colombia	Peso	Col$	100 Centavos
Congo, People's Republic of	CFA Franc	CFAF	100 Centimes
Costa Rica	Colón	₡	100 Centimos
Cuba	Peso	$	100 Centavos
Cyprus	Pound	C£	1,000 Mils
Czechoslovakia	Koruna	Kč	100 Halers
Dahomey	CFA Franc	CFAF	100 Centimes
Denmark	Krone	DKr	100 Øre
Dominican Republic	Peso	RD$	100 Centavos
Ecuador	Sucre	S/	100 Centavos
Egypt	Pound	LE	100 Piasters
El Salvador	Colón	₡	100 Centavos
Equatorial Guinea	Peseta	Pta	100 Centimos
Estonia	Ruble	Rbl	100 Kopecks
Ethiopia	Dollar	Eth$	100 Cents
Fiji	Dollar	F$	100 Cents
Finland	Markka	Fmk	100 Pennis
France	Franc	Fr	100 Centimes
Gabon Republic	CFA Franc	CFAF	100 Centimes
Gambia, The	Dalasi	£G	100 Batut
German Democratic Republic	Ostmark	M	100 Pfennigs
Germany, Federal Republic of	Deutsche Mark	DM	100 Pfennigs
Ghana	Cedi	N¢	100 Pesewa
Greece	Drachma	Dr	100 Lepta

[2] Currency of the African Financial Community.

| Country or Area | Basic Monetary Units | | Name and Number of Principal Fractional Units in Basic Unit |
	Name	Symbol	
Guatemala	Quetzal(es)	Q	100 Centavos
Guinea	Franc	GF	100 Centimes
Guyana	Dollar	G$ or G	100 Cents
Haiti	Gourde	G	100 Centimes
Honduras	Lempira	L	100 Centavos
Hong Kong	Dollar	HK$	100 Cents
Hungary	Forint	Ft	100 Fillér
Iceland, Republic of	Króna	IKr	100 Aurar
India	Rupee	R	100 Paise
Indonesia	Rupiah	Rp	100 Sen
Iran	Rial	Rl	100 Dinars
Iraq	Dinar	ID	1,000 Fils
Ireland, Republic of	Pound	£Ir	100 Pence
Israel	Pound	I£	100 Agorot
Italy	Lira (Lire)	Lit	100 Centesimi
Ivory Coast	CFA Franc	CFAF	100 Centimes
Jamaica	Dollar	J$	100 Cents
Japan	Yen	Y	100 Sen
Jordan	Dinar	JD	1,000 Fils
Kampuchea (Cambodia)	Riel	CR	100 Sen
Kenya	Shilling	KSh	100 Cents
Korea, People's Republic of	Won	W	100 Jun
Korea, Republic of	Won	W	100 Chon
Kuwait	Dinar	KD	1,000 Fils
Laos	Kip	K	100 At
Latvia	Ruble	Rbl	100 Kopecks
Lebanon	Pound	LL	100 Piasters
Lesotho	S. African Rand	R	100 Cents
Liberia	Dollar	Lib$	100 Cents
Libya	Dinar	D	1,000 Dirhams
Liechtenstein	Swiss Franc	Sw Fr	100 Centimes
Lithuania	Ruble	Rbl	100 Kopecks
Luxembourg	Franc	Lux Fr	100 Centimes
Macao	Escudo	Esc	100 Centavos
Madeira	Escudo	Esc	100 Centavos
Malagasy Republic (Madagascar)	Ringgit Dollar	M$	100 Centimes
Malawi	Kwacha	£M	100 Tambala
Malaysia	Dollar	M$	100 Cents
Maldives, Republic of	Rupee	MRp	100 Larees
Mali	Franc	MF	100 Centimes
Malta	Pound	£	100 cents
Marshall Islands	US Dollar	$	100 Cents
Martinique	Franc	Fr	100 Centimes
Mauritania	CFA Franc	CFAF	100 Centimes
Mauritius	Rupee	MRp	100 Cents
Mexico	Peso	Mex$	100 Centavos
Monaco	Franc	Fr	100 Centimes

Country or Area	Basic Monetary Units		Name and Number of Principal Fractional Units in Basic Unit
	Name	Symbol	
Mongolian People's Republic	Tughrik	Tu	100 Mongo
Montserrat	Dollar	$	100 Cents
Morocco	Dirham	DH	100 Francs
Nepal	Rupee	NR	100 Pice
Netherlands	Guilder	gld	100 Cents
Netherlands Antilles	Guilder	Ant gld	100 Cents
New Caledonia	Franc	CFP Fr	100 Centimes
New Zealand	Dollar	$NZ	100 Cents
Nicaragua	Cordoba	C$	100 Centavos
Niger	CFA Franc	CFAF	100 Centimes
Nigeria	Niara	N	100 Kobes
Norway	Krone	NKr	100 Öre
Oman	Riyal	RS	1,000 Baiza
Pakistan	Rupee	PR	100 Paisas
Panama	Balboa	B	100 Centesimos
Paraguay	Guarani	₲	100 Centimos
Peru	Sol(es)	S/	100 Centavos
Philippines	Peso	P	100 Centavos
Poland	Zloty	Zl	100 Groszy
Portugal	Escudo	Esc	100 Centavos
Puerto Rico	US Dollar	$	100 Cents
Qatar	Riyal	R	100 Dirhams
Reunion Island	Franc	CFA Fr	100 Centimes
Rhodesia	Dollar	R$	100 Cents
Romania	Leu	L	100 Bani
Rwanda	Franc	RF	100 Centimes
Ryukyu Islands	US Dollar	$	100 Cents
Samoa	Dollar	S$	100 Cents
San Marino	Italian Lira	Lit	100 Centesimi
Saudi Arabia	Riyal	SRl	20 Qurush
Senegal	CFA Franc	CFAF	100 Centimes
Sierra Leone	Leone	Le	100 Cents
Singapore	Dollar	S$	100 Cents
Somalia	Shilling	SSh	100 Centesimi
South Africa, Republic of	Rand	R	100 Cents
Spain	Peseta	Pta	100 Centimos
Sri Lanka	Rupee	cR	100 Cents
Sudan	Pound	Sd	100 Piasters
Surinam	Guilder	Sur gld	100 Cents
Swaziland	Rand	R	100 Cents
Sweden	Krona	SKr	100 Öre
Switzerland	Franc	SwF	100 Centimes
Syria	Pound	LS	100 Piasters
Tanzania	Shilling	TSh	100 Cents
Thailand	Baht	B	100 Satangs
Togo	CFA Franc	CFAF	100 Centimes
Trinidad and Tobago	Dollar	TT$	100 Cents
Tunisia	Dinar	D	1,000 Milliemes

	Basic Monetary Units		Name and Number of Principal Fractional Units in Basic Unit
Country or Area	*Name*	*Symbol*	
Turkey	Lira	LT	100 Kurus
Uganda	Shilling	USh	100 Cents
Union of Soviet Socialist Republics	Ruble	R	100 Kopecks
United Arab Emirates	UAE Dirham	DH	1,000 Fils
United Kingdom	Pound	£	100 Pence
United States	Dollar	$	100 Cents
Upper Volta	CFA Franc	CFAF	100 Centimes
Uruguay	Peso	Ur$	100 Centesimos
Venezuela	Bolivar	B	100 Centimos
Vietnam, Democratic Republic of	Dong	D	100 Xu
Virgin Islands (US)	US Dollar	$	100 Cents
Western Samoa	Tala	WS$	100 Cents
Yemen Arab Republic	Yemeni Riyal		40 Bugshas
Yemen Democratic People's Republic	Dinar	SYD	1,000 Fils
Yugoslavia	Dinar	Din	100 Paras
Zaire	Zaire	Z	100 Makuta
Zambia	Kwacha	ZK	100 Ngwee

14.4   CUSTOMS REGULATIONS

The U.S. government has established the Customs Service to enforce the customs regulations passed by the Congress. Anyone intending to travel outside the boundaries of the United States or any company intending to import materials should be familiar with these rather precise regulations. This chapter outlines a few of them, such as exemptions for travelers, declaration procedures, and prohibited or restricted items for importation. You may obtain additional information from your local customs officer or by writing to the Bureau of Customs, Department of the Treasury, Washington, DC 20226.

Customs Exemptions. Exemptions may be applied only to articles you bring with you at the time of your return to the United States if you are a returning resident who has not abandoned permanent residence in the United States and taken up permanent residence abroad.

Three-Hundred Dollar Exemption. This exemption applies if you are returning from a stay abroad of at least 48 hours (an exact computation). Exception: If you return from Mexico, there is no minimum time requirement, unless you have used this $300 exemption, or part of it, within the preceding thirty-day period.

Articles totaling $300 (based on the fair *retail* value of each item in the country where it was acquired) may be entered free of duty, subject to limitations on liquors and cigars, if:
1. They accompany you at the time of your return.
2. They were acquired as an incident of your trip.
3. They are for your personal or household use.
4. They are properly declared to customs.

Cigars and Cigarettes.   There is no limitation on the number of cigarettes that may be imported for personal use. However, not more than 100 cigars may be included. This exemption is available to each person regardless of age.
Liquor.   One quart of alcoholic beverages may be included in this exemption if you are 21 years of age or older, subject to state and federal restrictions.
Ten-Dollar Exemption.   If you are not entitled to the $300 exemption because of the 30-day or 48-hour minimum limitations, you may bring in free of duty and tax articles acquired abroad for your personal or household use if the total fair retail value does not exceed $10. This is an individual exemption and may not be grouped with articles brought in by other members of your family on one customs declaration. Any of the following may be included: 50 cigarettes, 10 cigars, one-half pound of manufactured tobacco, 4 ounces of alcoholic beverages, or 4 ounces of alcoholic perfume. CAUTION: If any article is subject to duty or tax, or if the total value of all articles exceeds $10, no article may be exempted from duty or tax.
Importation in Excess of Exemption.   Articles in excess of your customs exemption may be imported unless they are prohibited from entering the United States (see "Prohibited and Restricted Articles" in this section). Items not entitled to free entry will be subject to customs duty. An abbreviated list of the usual rates of duty on popular tourist items appears in Figure 14-6.
Traveling Back and Forth Across Borders.   After you have crossed the U.S. boundary at one point and swing back into the U.S. to travel to another point in the foreign country, you run the risk of losing your customs exemption unless you meet certain requirements. If you make a *swingback*, be sure to ask the nearest customs officer about these requirements.
Virgin Islands of United States, American Samoa, Guam.   If returning directly or indirectly from the Virgin Islands, American Samoa, or Guam, you may receive a customs exemption of $600, based on the fair retail value of the articles in the country where they were acquired, *provided* not more than $300 of this exemption is applied to merchandise obtained elsewhere than in these islands. The Virgin Islands are excepted from the 48-hour minimum-time requirement. Residents 21 years of age or older may enter one U.S. gallon of alcoholic beverages free of duty and tax, *provided* not more than one quart of this amount is acquired elsewhere than in these islands.
Duty-free GSP Items.   Approximately 2,700 items can be brought into the United States free of duty under the Generalized System of Preferences (GSP). This program is designed to help developing nations improve their

DESCRIPTION	RATE	DESCRIPTION	RATE
Alcoholic beverages (See Fig. 14–7.)		Dolls and parts	17.5%
Antiques:		Drawings (works of art) originals and copies	
over 100 years old	Free	(entirely by hand)	Free
Automobiles, passenger	3%		
		Earthenware tableware, available in 77-piece sets:	
Bags, hand, leather	8.5 to 10%	valued not over $3.30/set	5¢ doz. + 14%
Bamboo, manufacturers of	12.5%		
Beads:		value over $3.30 but not	10¢ doz.
imitation precious and semi-precious stones	to 25%	over $22/set	+ 21%
ivory	10%	valued over $22/set	5¢ doz. + 10.5%
Binoculars, prism	20%		
Books:			
foreign author or foreign language	Free	Figurines, china	12 to 22.5%
		Flowers, artificial, plastic	21%
		Fruit, prepared	35% or under
Cameras:		Fur:	
motion picture, over $50	6%	wearing apparel and	8.5 to
still, over $10	7.5%	other manufactures of	18.5%
cases, leather	8.5 to 10%	Furniture:	
lenses	12.5%	wood, chairs	8.5%
Candy:		wood, other than chairs	5%
sweetened chocolate bars	5%		
other	7%	Glass tableware valued not	
Chess Sets	10%	over $1 ea.	20–50%
China:		Gloves:	
bone	17.5%	not lace or net, plain, vegetable fibers, woven	25%
nonbone, other than tableware	22.5%	wool, over $4/doz.	37.5¢ lb. + 18.5%
nonbone, available in 77-piece sets:		fur	10%
valued not over $10/set	10¢ doz. + 48%	horsehide or cowhide	15%
		Golf balls	6%
value over $10 but not over $24/set	10¢ doz. + 55%		
valued over $24/set but not over $56	10¢ doz. + 36%	Handkerchiefs:	
Cigarette lighters:		cotton, hand embroidered	4¢ ea. + 40%
pocket, valued over 42¢ ea.	22.5%	cotton, plain	2.5%
table	12%	other vegetable fiber, plain	9%
Clocks:			
valued over $5 but not	75¢ + 16%	Iron, travel type, electric	5.5%
over $10 each	+ 6¼¢ ea jewel	Ivory, manufactures of	6%
valued over $10 each	$1.12 + 16% + 6¼¢ ea jewel	Jade, cut but not set	2.5%
Cork, manufacturers of	18%	other articles	21%

Figure 14-6 Advisory guide of tariff rates for imported items.

DESCRIPTION	RATE	DESCRIPTION	RATE
Jewelry, precious metal or stone:		Sterling flatware and tableware:	
silver chief value, valued not over $18/doz.	27.5%	knives and forks	4¢ ea. + 8.5%
other	12%	spoons and tableware	12.5%
		Stones, cut but not set:	
Leather		diamonds not over 1/2 carat	4%
pocketbooks, bags	8.5 to 10%	diamonds over 1/2 carat	5%
other	4 to 14%	other	Free to 5%
		Sweaters, wool, over $5/lb.	37.5¢ lb. + 20%
Mah jong sets	10%		
Motorcycles	5%	Tape recorders	5.5 to 7.5%
Musical instruments:		Toilet preparations:	
music boxes, wood	8%	not containing alcohol	7.5%
woodwind	7.5%	containing alcohol	8¢ lb. + 7.5%
bag pipes	Free	Toys	17.5%
		Truffles	Free
Paintings (works of art):			
original and copies entirely by hand	Free	Vegetables prepared	17.5%
Paper, manufactures of	8.5%	Watches, on $100 watch duty varies from	$6 to $13
Pearls:		Wearing apparel:	
loose or temporarily strung:		embroidered or ornamented	21 to 42.5%
genuine	Free	not embroidered, not ornamented:	
cultured	2.5%	cotton, knit	21%
imitation	20%	cotton, not knit	8 to 21%
permanently strung	12 to 27.5%	linen, not knit	7.5%
Perfume	8¢ lb. + 7.5%	manmade fiber, knit	25¢ lb. + 32.5%
Postage stamps	Free		
Printed matter	2 to 7%	manmade fiber, not knit	25¢ lb. + 27.5%
Radios			
transistors	10 2/5%	silk knit	10%
other	6%	silk, not knit	16%
Rattan:		wool, knit	37.5¢ lb. + 15.5 to 32%
furniture	16%		
other manufactures of	12.5%	wool, not knit	25 to 37.5¢ lb. + 21%
Records, phonograph	5%	Wood: carvings	8%
Rubber, manufacturers of	6%	manufactures	8%
Shaver, electric	6.5%		
Shell, manufacturers of	8.5%		
Shoes, leather	2.5 to 20%		

Figure 14-6   (continued).

financial condition by allowing their exports to enter this country without duty. The U.S. Customs Service booklet *GSP and the Traveler* lists many of the duty-free items and all the nations and territories from which these goods may be brought into the United States free.

Customs Declaration.   You must declare to U.S. Customs, either orally or in writing, ALL articles acquired abroad and in your possession at the time of return. Include also:

1. Items another person requested you to bring home.
2. Any article you intend to sell or use in your business.
3. Alterations or repairs made to articles taken abroad.
4. Gifts presented to you while abroad, such as wedding or birthday presents.

The wearing or use of an article acquired abroad does not exempt it from duty, and it must be declared at the price you paid for it. The customs officer will make an appropriate reduction in its value for wear and use.

Written Declaration.   All articles acquired abroad must be declared to customs in writing when:

1. Their total fair retail value (including alterations and repairs) exceeds $300.
2. More than one quart of alcoholic beverages or more than 100 cigars are included.
3. Some of the items are not intended for your personal or household use, such as commercial samples, items for sale or use in your business, or articles you are bringing home for another person.
4. A customs duty or Internal Revenue tax is collectible on any article in your possession.

Family Declaration.   The head of a family may make a joint declaration for all members residing in the same household and returning with him to the United States as a group. A family of four, for instance, may bring in articles free of duty valued up to $1,200 fair retail value on one declaration, even if the articles acquired by one member of the family exceed the personal $300 exemption. Infants and children returning to the United States are entitled to the same exemption as adults (except for alcoholic beverages). Children born abroad, who have never resided in the United States, are not eligible for the exemption.

How to Avoid Customs Penalties.   Do not rely on advice given by persons outside the Customs Service. It is well known that some merchants abroad offer travelers invoices or bills of sale showing false and understated values. This practice only delays your customs examination and may prove costly. Current commercial prices on foreign items are available at all times and on-the-spot comparisons of these values are made.

Listing, Packing, and Opening Your Baggage.   Make a list of the articles acquired before you reach the port of entry. Retain sales slips and purchase orders covering these items and have them available for ready examination by the customs officer. Pack your baggage in a manner that will make inspection easy. Pack separately articles acquired abroad. If asked to open your luggage or the trunk of your car, comply without hesitation.

Other Customs Exemptions.   *Foreign-Made Articles Taken Abroad.*   Articles of foreign origin, such as cameras, watches, jewelry, and plumage, are dutiable upon each importation into the United States unless you can *prove* to the customs officer that you possessed the items in this country before your departure. Bills of sale or receipts for purchase, repair, or cleaning will be reasonable proof of prior possession. Register valuable articles of foreign origin before your departure by taking them to any customs office in the United States for identification. This may also be done when you leave the country at the port of embarkation.

Gifts.   Gifts accompanying you are considered to be for your personal use and may be included within your exemption. Included are those given you by others while you were abroad and those you intend to give to others after your return. Gifts intended for business or promotional purposes may not be included.

While you are abroad you may send gifts totaling $10 fair retail value to friends or relatives in the United States without payment of duty and tax, provided the addressee does not receive in a single day gift parcels exceeding the $10 limitation. Write GIFT ENCLOSED in large letters and the fair retail value of the contents on the outside of the package. Alcoholic beverages and tobacco products are not included in this privilege, nor are perfumes valued at more than $1.

Personal Belongings Sent Home.   Personal effects of United States origin are entitled to entry free of duty. They may be sent home by mail before you return and receive free entry if a statement is placed on the outside wrapper or enclosed in the package explaining that the articles were taken out of the United States as personal effects and are being returned without having been altered or repaired while abroad.

Automobiles, Boats, Airplanes.   Automobiles, boats, planes, or other vehicles taken abroad for noncommercial use may be returned duty free if you can prove to the customs officer that they were taken out of the United States. This proof may be the state registration card for an automobile, the Department of Commerce certificate for an aircraft, a yacht license or motorboat identification certificate for a pleasure boat, or a customs certificate of registration obtained before departure. Dutiable repairs or accessories acquired abroad for these vehicles must be declared on your return.

A leaflet, *Imported Automobiles,* may be obtained from a customs office near you or from the Bureau of Customs, Treasury Department, Washington,

DC 20226, if you are considering the purchase of a foreign-made car during your travel abroad.

Antiques. Antiques are free of duty if they were made at least 100 years ago. Antique furniture, unless brought in as personal and household effects, must be inspected for free entry by the antique examiners located at most of the major ports of entry.

Household Effects. Household effects, professional books, or tools of trade or occupation that you prove were taken out of the United States are duty free at the time you return, if properly declared and entered.

Books, furniture, carpets, paintings, tableware, linens, and similar household furnishings acquired abroad may be imported free of duty if:

1. They are not imported for another person.
2. They are not imported for sale.
3. They have been used abroad by you for not less than one year, or were available for use in a household in which you were a resident member for one year. This privilege does not include articles placed in storage outside the home.

The year of use need not be continuous, nor does it need to be the year immediately preceding the date of importation. Vehicles, consumable supplies, and office furniture cannot be passed free of duty as household effects.

A customs declaration must be made by the owner to avoid the posting of an entry bond to secure release of the goods without a deposit of duties. This declaration may be made only at the time of, or after, your arrival in the United States. To keep broker charges to a minimum, arrive home before your shipment so that you can mail your customs declaration to the carrier to speed clearance of your goods through customs. Otherwise, the broker must furnish a bond to produce the declaration of the owner. There are times when the carrier is unable to obtain the services of a broker willing to furnish the bond. When this happens, the goods must either be held at the port of arrival, where storage and handling fees accrue, or be shipped in bond to an interior port where customs clearance must be arranged.

Prohibited and Restricted Articles. Articles considered injurious or detrimental to the general welfare of the United States are prohibited entry by law. Among these are narcotics, drugs containing narcotics in any amount (including prescriptions and preparations such as cough and headache remedies), obscene articles and publications, lottery tickets, wild birds, and the feathers and eggs of wild birds.

Special Requirements for Specific Items. Other items must meet the special requirements described here before they can be released by a customs officer.

1. Trademarked articles. Any foreign article bearing a trademark recorded in the Treasury Department, e.g., perfumes, cameras, watches, musical instruments, and so on, cannot be brought into the United States without the consent of the trademark owner. If the trademark is removed or obliterated,

there is no restriction. A list of trademarked articles may be obtained from the nearest U.S. consular officer or from the Commissioner of Customs, Washington, DC 20226.

2. Fruits, vegetables, plants, and plant products. The Department of Agriculture is responsible for preventing the entry of injurious pests and plant diseases into the United States. Fruits, vegetables, plants, cuttings, seeds, and unprocessed plant products are the hosts for these pests and diseases. Consequently, these items either are prohibited from entering the country or require an import permit. Permits should be obtained in advance of importation. Applications for import permits or information should be addressed to the Import and Permit Section, Plant Quarantine Division, 209 River Street, Hoboken, NJ 07030.

3. Livestock, meats, and poultry. The customs officer also enforces for the Department of Agriculture the rules and regulations that prevent the importation of animal diseases into the United States—including rinderpest and foot-and-mouth disease, a threat to our livestock industry. Because animal diseases exist in most countries of the world, for all practical purposes the following animals, animal products, and poultry are prohibited from entering the United States.

(a) Fresh, chilled, frozen, or dried meat.

(b) Cured and cooked meats, such as bacon, hams, sausages, bologna, salami, and similar products.

(c) Organs, glands, extracts, secretions, untanned hides and skins, wool, hair, and so on.

(d) Cattle, sheep, goats, swine, deer, horses, mules and burros, and dogs for use around livestock.

(e) Chickens, ducks, geese, swans, pheasants, grouse, partridges, quail, guinea fowl, and pea fowl, including eggs for hatching purposes.

If you are considering either bringing or sending any of the above items to the United States, write for detailed requirements to the Animal Inspection and Quarantine Division, Agricultural Research Service, Department of Agriculture, Washington, DC 20250.

4. Books protected by American copyright cannot be brought into the United States if they are unauthorized foreign reprints. Books bearing a notice falsely claiming copyright in the United States are similarly prohibited. Also, for some books by American authors, or first published in this country, copyright law prohibits or restricts importations of foreign-made editions unless accompanying the traveler and for personal use.

Fish, Wildlife, and Pets.   The leaflet *Pets, Wildlife, U.S. Customs* explains the general import requirements for cats, dogs, monkeys, psittacine birds, and wildlife. A copy may be secured from the customs field office near you or the Commissioner of Customs, Washington, DC 20226. For more specific information, write to the Division of Foreign Quarantine, U.S. Public Health

Service, Silver Spring, MD 20910. Questions on fish, wild birds, migratory game birds, and other wildlife should be addressed to the Bureau of Sport Fisheries and Wildlife, Department of Interior, Washington, DC 20240.

Biological Materials. Biological materials of public health importance (disease organisms and vectors for research and educational purposes) require import permits. Write to the Foreign Quarantine Program, U.S. Public Health Service, Center for Disease Control, Atlanta, Georgia 30333.

Merchandise Prohibited by Foreign Assets Control Regulations. The importation (as well as the purchase abroad) of all merchandise originating in Cambodia, North Korea, Vietnam, Rhodesia, or Cuba and all goods containing Cuban components is prohibited without a Treasury license. These licenses are strictly controlled and, for all practical purposes, may be considered unavailable to tourists.

Copies of Foreign Assets Control Regulations, Cuban Assets Control Regulations, and Rhodesian Sanction Regulations, listing the commodities affected and explaining the certification procedures, may be obtained from the Office of Foreign Assets Control, Department of the Treasury, Washington, DC 20220.

Gold Coins and Medals. The Treasury Department gold regulations permit the importation of gold bullion, gold medals, and gold coins.

	Internal Revenue Tax Per U.S. Gallon[1]	Customs Duty Per Gallon
Beer	$ 9 bbl. (31 gal.)	6¢
Brandy	$10.50	50¢ to $5.00
Gin	$10.50	50¢
Liqueurs	$10.50	50¢
Rum	$10.50	1.75
Whisky[1]		
Scotch	$10.50	51¢
Irish	$10.50	57¢
Other	$10.50	62¢
Wine		
Sparkling	$ 2.40 to $3.40	1.17
Still	$ .17 to $2.25	.31½ to $1

[1] Proof gallon if 100 proof or over

Figure 14-7 Rates of duty and tax on alcoholic beverages.

Firearms and Ammunition. Firearms and ammunition are subject to restrictions and import permits. Travelers entering and leaving the United States are permitted for personal use three firearms (nonautomatic rifles, carbines, revolvers, and pistols) and 1,000 rounds of ammunition as part of their accompanied or unaccompanied baggage. These firearms must be declared with customs at the time of departure from the U.S. A special license from the Office of Munitions Control, Department of State, Washington, DC 20520, is required for additional firearms and ammunition. Pistols, revolvers, and other firearms capable of being concealed on the person, and all types of ammunition are prohibited by law from being shipped in the mails.

Importation of Alcoholic Beverages. Liquor may not be imported into a state of the United States in violation of its laws. Information on state restrictions and state taxes should be obtained from the state government.

United States postal laws prohibit the shipment of alcoholic beverages by mail.

Alcoholic beverages forwarded to persons in the United States are not entitled to free entry under the $10 gift exemption, and any carried in by travelers in excess of the one-quart limitation are subject to duty and Internal Revenue Tax. The usual rates of duty and tax are shown in Figure 14-7.

14.5 UNITED STATES FOREIGN SERVICE POSTS

To assist U.S. business interests abroad, the Department of State provides key officers at all foreign service posts around the world who act as liaison between the particular country and the businessman. The following description of the variety of services offered by the officers at these posts will aid the businessman in selecting the correct person to contact for assistance. When seeking information, write directly to the officer responsible for the area of endeavor in which you are interested.

Key Officers at Foreign Service Posts

Chief of Mission, with the title of "Ambassador" or "Minister," and *Deputy Chief of Mission* are responsible for the entire U.S. mission within a country, including all consular posts as well as the embassy.

Political officers participate in negotiations to further U.S. political objectives. They analyze and report on political developments of internal or international significance.

Economic officers take part in negotiations relating to our economic policy objectives and analyze and report on economic matters. At the smaller posts they also perform the functions of the commercial officer.

The *commercial officer's* primary responsibility is to promote trade, travel, and the private investment interests of the United States. He helps to develop trade contacts and export opportunities; arrange appointments for U.S.

businessmen and assist in contacts with local government officials; support special overseas activities of the Department of Commerce, such as trade centers, trade missions, and trade fairs; and report on business trends, market potentials, and laws and customs that affect U.S. commercial interests. He also works toward eliminating any discriminatory treatment of U.S. business interests.

The *labor attaché,* or labor officer, is responsible for following the political and economic activities of the national labor organizations. The officer is able to supply information regarding labor and social attitudes and trends, wages, nonwage costs, Social Security regulations, government labor policies and regulations, and labor attitudes toward American business investments.

Consular officers extend to U.S. citizens and their property abroad the protection of the U.S. government; maintain lists of local attorneys; and act as a liaison with customs, tax, and policy officials. Consular officers have the authority to notarize documents and authenticate the signatures and seals of foreign officials. In troubled areas, the U.S. businessman is advised to register with the consular officer.

The *administrative officer* is responsible for the management of the post, including such matters as personnel, budget, operations, and so on. This

ACM	Assistant chief of mission	L	Legation
ADM	Administrative section	LAB	Labor officer
AGR	Agricultural section	M	Mission
AID	Agency for International Development	MIN	Minister
		NATO	North Atlantic Treaty Organization
AMB	Ambassador		
BO	Branch office of embassy	OAS	Organization of American States
C	Consulate		
CAO	Cultural affairs officer	OIC	Officer in charge
CG	Consul general, consulate general	PAO	Public affairs officer (USIA)
COM	Commercial section		
CON	Consul, consular section	PO	Principal officer
COUN	Counselor	POL	Political section
CRD	Mission coordinator	USEC	US Mission to European Communities
DCM	Deputy chief of mission		
DEP	Deputy	USIA	US Information Agency
DPO	Deputy principal officer	USRO	US Mission to North Atlantic Treaty Organization and European Regional Organizations
E	Embassy		
ECO	Economic section		
FAO	Food and Agriculture Organization		
IAEA	International Atomic Energy Agency	USUN	US Mission to United Nations
ICAO	International Civil Aviation Organization		
		VC	Vice consul

Figure 14-8   Foreign service abbreviations.

officer is in charge of purchasing for the post and would be the individual to contact regarding sales to the post, its commissary, or its personnel.

The *agricultural attaché,* the officer of the U.S. Department of Agriculture attached to the post, reports on agricultural production, trade policy, and market developments in the area and promotes U.S. agricultural exports.

The *AID Mission Director* is responsible for the Agency for International Development programs, including dollar and local currency loans to governments and private enterprises, grants, investment guaranties, technical assistance, and fellowships.

The *public affairs officer,* an officer of the U.S. Information Agency, is responsible for U.S. informational and cultural programs in the host country. Although not specifically charged with assisting U.S. business abroad, this officer is ready to advise American companies on general public relations programs.

Foreign service abbreviations are listed in Figure 14-8.

Directory of Foreign Service Posts.   A list of addresses and telephone numbers of foreign service posts may be found in the Department of State Publication 7877, *Key Officers of Foreign Service Posts Guide for Businessmen.* This publication includes the names of key officers at these posts and is brought up to date four times a year. A single copy or a yearly subscription may be secured from the Superintendent of Documents.

15

Postal Regulations

Postal rates and regulations change frequently. That is why every office should have for ready reference the latest directives of the U.S. Postal Service. Two handy leaflets, *Domestic Postage Rates, Fees, and Information*, and *International Postage Rates and Fees*, are free and can usually be obtained at local post offices. Indispensable to every large-volume user of the mails are two other post office publications. The *Postal Service Manual* is available on a subscription basis, under which new pages are sent to owners of the manual as changes are made. The *National ZIP Code Directory* offers an up-to-date listing of ZIP code information by state and post office and includes instructions for quickly finding a ZIP code when an address is known. Both publications can be purchased from the Superintendent of Documents, U.S. Government Printing Office, Washington, DC 20402.

Many companies issue their own regulations for the handling of outgoing letters and parcels. These regulations are designed to speed the mail, ensure its arrival in good condition, and save money. (See Figure 15-1.)

This chapter provides information from Post Office sources for all companies engaged in domestic or foreign trade.

CONTENTS

15.1 CLASSES OF DOMESTIC MAIL

The class of mail determines the rate and the kind of handling it receives. Basic rates for first-, third-, and fourth-class mail are given in Figure 15-2. Restrictions on size and weight are noted on pages 592–94.

First-Class. Letters, bills and statements of account, and other matter wholly or partially in handwriting or typewriting, including carbons and

MAILING TIPS

1. Do not let mail accumulate to the end of the day. Dispatch it several times a day, or as it becomes ready for mailing. This practice relieves the end-of-day pile-up in your own office and improves the chances for early delivery.
2. Remember that the first-class rate is higher for the first ounce than it is for the second and additional ounces; so apply postage accordingly.
3. For first-class mail weighing over 13 ounces, use priority mail, which receives first-class treatment at considerable savings in postage.
4. When addressing a large envelope with first-class matter, mark it *First Class Mail* just below the postage area to ensure that it receives first-class handling.
5. First-class mail can be forwarded without payment of additional postage. Simply change the address and remail; do not enclose in another envelope.
6. When third- and fourth-class matter is sent with a letter, mark the package *First Class Mail Enclosed.* Postage is then computed separately for each class. To speed delivery, you may specify special handling, but first compare with the first-class or priority rate (whichever applies) for the whole package.
7. To save postage, use fourth-class mail (parcel post) for printed matter weighing over 16 ounces.
8. To save postage on third-class printed matter weighing over 12 ounces, use the fourth-class zone rate, if lower.
9. Use special delivery sparingly. It travels no faster than ordinary first-class mail to the addressee's post office, and is then delivered during working hours only.
10. Use special handling to speed the delivery of fourth-class mail. As much as two days can be saved, and costs are less than airmail.
11. Ask for a return receipt on certified, insured, or registered mail only when proof of delivery is vital.
12. If proof of mailing is sufficient for mail of little or no intrinsic value, a *Certificate of Mailing* offers a low-cost alternative to certified, insured, or registered mail. Fill out the Certificate of Mailing and have it stamped by the postal clerk when the letter or package is presented for mailing.
13. Consider the use of post cards instead of letters for routine acknowledgments and announcements.
14. When preparing multiple pieces of mail, use a single size envelope to eliminate the need for sorting and meter adjustments for different sizes. Also flap envelopes by opening the flaps slightly and folding them one inside the other. This arrangement speeds them through the stamping machine and ensures that none goes unsealed.
15. International mail, unlike domestic letters which travel by air without extra labeling or cost, will go by air only if it is so designated and paid for. Also keep in mind that airmail letter rates are charged for by the half ounce. If aerogrammes are not adequate, use thin-paper airmail envelopes and tissue sheets. Within the half-ounce basic limit, three full 8 1/2- by 11-inch tissue sheets may be enclosed in the airmail envelope. Place a paper clip where the stamp should be to alert the mailroom to the need for foreign postage.

Figure 15-1 Some thrifty and efficient ways to handle outgoing mail.

FIRST CLASS

Letter Rates

1st ounce	$0.15
Each add'l ounce	0.13
Over 12 ounces	Priority mail (heavy pieces) rates apply.
Single postal cards sold by the post office	10¢ each.
Double postal cards sold by the post office	10¢ each.
Single post cards	10¢ each.
Double post cards (reply half of double post card does not have to bear postage when originally mailed)	10¢ each half.
Presort rate	Consult Postmaster
Business reply mail	Consult Postmaster

SECOND CLASS

(Newspapers and periodicals with second-class mail privileges).

Copies mailed by public: 10¢ for first 2 ounces, 6¢ each additional ounce or fraction thereof, or the applicable fourth-class rate, whichever is lower.

THIRD CLASS

Circulars, books, catalogs, and other printed matter; merchandise, seeds, cuttings, bulbs, roots, scions, and plants, weighing less than 16 ounces.

SINGLE PIECE RATE*

0 to 2 ozs.	$0.20
Over 2 to 4 ozs.	0.40
Over 4 to 6 ozs.	0.53
Over 6 to 8 ozs.	0.66
Over 8 to 10 ozs.	0.79
Over 10 to 12 ozs.	0.92
Over 12 to 14 ozs.	1.05
Over 14 to 15.99 ozs.	1.18

BULK RATE CONSULT POSTMASTER

*Over 14 ounces, use the 4th class zone if lower.

Rates effective June 1978

FOURTH CLASS (PARCEL POST) ZONE RATES CONSULT POSTMASTER FOR WEIGHT AND SIZE LIMITS

Weight 1 pound and not exceeding (pounds)	Zones							
	Local	1 & 2	3	4	5	6	7	8
2	$1.15	$1.35	$1.39	$1.56	$1.72	$1.84	$1.98	$2.22
3	1.23	1.45	1.53	1.73	1.86	2.04	2.24	2.61
4	1.29	1.56	1.65	1.82	2.00	2.23	2.50	3.00
5	1.36	1.66	1.77	1.92	2.24	2.43	2.77	3.39
6	1.42	1.71	1.84	2.01	2.28	2.62	3.03	3.78
7	1.47	1.76	1.90	2.11	2.41	2.82	3.29	4.17
8	1.51	1.80	1.97	2.20	2.55	2.99	3.56	4.56
9	1.54	1.85	2.03	2.29	2.69	3.21	3.81	4.95
10	1.57	1.89	2.10	2.39	2.83	3.41	4.08	5.34
11	1.60	1.94	2.17	2.50	3.00	3.65	4.42	5.73
12	1.64	1.98	2.22	2.56	3.09	3.77	4.57	6.12
13	1.67	2.02	2.27	2.63	3.17	3.89	4.72	6.41
14	1.70	2.05	2.32	2.69	3.25	3.99	4.86	6.62
15	1.73	2.09	2.36	2.74	3.33	4.09	4.99	6.80
16	1.76	2.13	2.41	2.80	3.40	4.19	5.11	6.98
17	1.79	2.16	2.45	2.85	3.47	4.28	5.23	7.15
18	1.82	2.20	2.49	2.91	3.54	4.37	5.34	7.31
19	1.86	2.23	2.53	2.96	3.61	4.46	5.45	7.47
20	1.89	2.27	2.58	3.01	3.67	4.54	5.55	7.62
21	1.92	2.30	2.62	3.06	3.74	4.62	5.66	7.76
22	1.95	2.34	2.66	3.14	3.85	4.78	5.80	7.90
23	1.98	2.37	2.72	3.25	3.99	4.96	6.02	8.03
24	2.01	2.44	2.80	3.35	4.12	5.13	6.24	8.16
25	2.04	2.51	2.89	3.46	4.26	5.31	6.46	8.28
26	2.07	2.58	2.97	3.56	4.39	5.48	6.68	8.40
27	2.11	2.65	3.06	3.67	4.53	5.66	6.90	8.52
28	2.14	2.72	3.14	3.77	4.66	5.83	7.12	8.63
29	2.17	2.79	3.23	3.88	4.80	6.01	7.34	8.75
30	2.20	2.86	3.31	3.98	4.93	6.18	7.56	8.85
31	2.68	3.09	3.46	4.09	5.07	6.36	7.78	9.41
32	2.71	3.12	3.49	4.19	5.20	6.53	8.00	9.51
33	2.74	3.16	3.57	4.30	5.34	6.71	8.22	9.61
34	2.77	3.19	3.65	4.40	5.47	6.88	8.44	9.80
35	2.80	3.22	3.74	4.51	5.61	7.06	8.66	10.06

Weight 1 pound and not exceeding (pounds)	Zones							
	Local	1 & 2	3	4	5	6	7	8
36	2.83	3.28	3.82	4.61	5.74	7.23	8.88	10.32
37	2.86	3.35	3.91	4.72	5.88	7.41	9.10	10.58
38	2.89	3.42	3.99	4.82	6.01	7.58	9.32	10.84
39	2.93	3.49	4.08	4.93	6.15	7.76	9.54	11.10
40	2.96	3.56	4.16	5.03	6.28	7.93	9.76	11.36
41	2.99	3.63	4.25	5.14	6.42	8.11	9.98	11.62
42	3.02	3.70	4.33	5.24	6.55	8.28	10.20	11.88
43	3.05	3.77	4.42	5.35	6.69	8.46	10.42	12.14
44	3.08	3.84	4.50	5.45	6.82	8.63	10.64	12.40
45	3.11	3.91	4.59	5.56	6.96	8.81	10.86	12.66
46	3.14	3.98	4.67	5.66	7.09	8.98	11.08	12.92
47	3.17	4.05	4.76	5.77	7.23	9.16	11.30	13.18
48	3.20	4.12	4.84	5.87	7.36	9.33	11.52	13.44
49	3.23	4.19	4.93	5.98	7.50	9.51	11.74	13.70
50	3.27	4.26	5.01	6.08	7.63	9.68	11.96	13.96
51	3.30	4.33	5.10	6.19	7.77	9.86	12.18	14.22
52	3.33	4.40	5.18	6.29	7.90	10.03	12.40	14.48
53	3.36	4.47	5.27	6.40	8.04	10.21	12.62	14.74
54	3.39	4.54	5.35	6.50	8.17	10.38	12.84	15.00
55	3.42	4.61	5.44	6.61	8.31	10.56	13.06	15.26
56	3.45	4.68	5.52	6.71	8.44	10.73	13.28	15.52
57	3.48	4.75	5.61	6.82	8.58	10.91	13.50	15.78
58	3.51	4.82	5.69	6.93	8.71	11.08	13.72	16.04
59	3.54	4.89	5.78	7.03	8.85	11.26	13.94	16.30
60	3.57	4.96	5.86	7.13	8.98	11.43	14.16	16.56
61	3.60	5.03	5.95	7.24	9.12	11.61	14.38	16.82
62	3.64	5.10	6.03	7.34	9.25	11.78	14.60	17.08
63	3.67	5.17	6.12	7.45	9.39	11.96	14.82	17.34
64	3.70	5.24	6.20	7.55	9.52	12.13	15.04	17.60
65	3.73	5.31	6.29	7.66	9.66	12.31	15.26	17.86
66	3.76	5.38	6.37	7.76	9.79	12.48	15.48	18.12
67	3.79	5.45	6.46	7.87	9.93	12.66	15.70	18.38
68	3.82	5.52	6.54	7.97	10.06	12.83	15.92	18.64
69	3.85	5.59	6.63	8.08	10.20	13.01	16.14	18.90
70	3.88	5.66	6.71	8.18	10.33	13.18	16.36	19.16

Consult postmaster for rates on bound printed matter and other exceptions.

Exception: Parcels weighing less than 15 pounds, and measuring more than 84 inches but not exceeding 100 inches in length and girth combined, are chargeable with a minimum rate equal to that for a 15 pound parcel for the zone to which addressed. See Postal Service Manual section 135.3 for size and weight restrictions.

Figure 15-2 Basic rates for the various classes of mail. Parcel post rates are scaled to the relative distance a package must travel.

machine copies; private post cards, postal cards (stamped cards sold by the post office), and business reply mail (that is, cards and letters on which postage is paid by the addressee upon their return) comprise first-class mail. Wherever feasible, domestic first-class mail travels by air; there is no extra charge. First-class mail that weighs more than 13 ounces is treated as Priority Mail, for which special zoned rates apply (Figure 15-3).

Second-Class. Newspapers, magazines, and other periodicals for which second-class mail privileges have been obtained by the publisher are second-class mail. Rates for copies mailed by the public are shown in Figure 15-2.

Third-Class. Circulars, books, catalogs, and other printed matter; merchandise, seeds, cuttings, bulbs, roots, scions, and plants that weigh less

PRIORITY MAIL (HEAVY PIECES)

Weight over 12 oz but not exceeding (pounds)	Local 1 2 & 3	4	5	6	7	8
1.0	$1.71	$1.81	$1.88	$1.97	$2.06	$2.25
1.5	1.86	1.96	2.07	2.21	2.34	2.50
2.0	1.99	2.12	2.27	2.44	2.61	2.83
2.5	2.11	2.27	2.46	2.68	2.89	3.16
3.0	2.23	2.42	2.65	2.91	3.17	3.50
3.5	2.35	2.58	2.84	3.15	3.45	3.83
4.0	2.47	2.73	3.03	3.38	3.73	4.16
4.5	2.59	2.89	3.22	3.62	4.01	4.50
5	2.72	3.04	3.42	3.85	4.29	4.83
6	2.96	3.35	3.80	4.32	4.84	5.50
7	3.20	3.66	4.18	4.79	5.40	6.16
8	3.44	3.96	4.56	5.26	5.96	6.83
9	3.69	4.27	4.95	5.73	6.51	7.49
10	3.93	4.58	5.33	6.20	7.07	8.16
11	4.17	4.89	5.71	6.67	7.63	8.83
12	4.42	5.20	6.10	7.14	8.18	9.49
13	4.66	5.50	6.48	7.61	8.74	10.16
14	4.90	5.81	6.86	8.08	9.30	10.82
15	5.15	6.12	7.25	8.55	9.86	11.49
16	5.39	6.43	7.63	9.02	10.41	12.16
17	5.63	6.74	8.01	9.49	10.97	12.82
18	5.87	7.04	8.39	9.96	11.53	13.49
19	6.12	7.35	8.78	10.43	12.08	14.15
20	6.36	7.66	9.16	10.90	12.64	14.82
21	6.60	7.97	9.54	11.37	13.20	15.49
22	6.85	8.28	9.93	11.84	13.75	16.15
23	7.09	8.58	10.31	12.31	14.31	16.82
24	7.33	8.89	10.69	12.78	14.87	17.48
25	7.58	9.20	11.08	13.25	15.43	18.15
26	7.82	9.51	11.46	13.72	15.98	18.82
27	8.06	9.82	11.84	14.19	16.54	19.48
28	8.30	10.12	12.22	14.66	17.10	20.15
29	8.55	10.43	12.61	15.13	17.65	20.81
30	8.79	10.74	12.99	15.60	18.21	21.48
31	9.03	11.05	13.37	16.07	18.77	22.15
32	9.28	11.36	13.76	16.54	19.32	22.81
33	9.52	11.66	14.14	17.01	19.88	23.48
34	9.76	11.97	14.52	17.48	20.44	24.14
35	10.01	12.28	14.91	17.95	21.00	24.81

Weight over 12 oz but not exceeding (pounds)	Local 1 2 & 3	4	5	6	7	8
36	10.25	12.59	15.29	18.42	21.55	25.48
37	10.49	12.90	15.67	18.89	22.11	26.14
38	10.73	13.20	16.05	19.36	22.67	26.81
39	10.98	13.51	16.44	19.83	23.22	27.47
40	11.22	13.82	16.82	20.30	23.78	28.14
41	11.46	14.13	17.20	20.77	24.34	28.81
42	11.71	14.44	17.59	21.24	24.89	29.47
43	11.95	14.74	17.97	21.71	25.45	30.14
44	12.19	15.05	18.35	22.18	26.01	30.80
45	12.44	15.36	18.74	22.65	26.57	31.47
46	12.68	15.67	19.12	23.12	27.12	32.14
47	12.92	15.98	19.50	23.59	27.68	32.80
48	13.16	16.28	19.88	24.06	28.24	33.47
49	13.41	16.59	20.27	24.53	28.79	34.13
50	13.65	16.90	20.65	25.00	29.35	34.80
51	13.89	17.21	21.03	25.47	29.91	35.47
52	14.14	17.52	21.42	25.94	30.46	36.13
53	14.38	17.82	21.80	26.41	31.02	36.80
54	14.62	18.13	22.18	26.88	31.58	37.46
55	14.87	18.44	22.57	27.35	32.14	38.13
56	15.11	18.75	22.95	27.82	32.69	38.80
57	15.35	19.06	23.33	28.29	33.25	39.46
58	15.59	19.36	23.71	28.76	33.81	40.13
59	15.84	19.67	24.10	29.23	34.36	40.79
60	16.08	19.98	24.48	29.70	34.92	41.46
61	16.32	20.29	24.86	30.17	35.48	42.13
62	16.57	20.60	25.25	30.64	36.03	42.79
63	16.81	20.90	25.63	31.11	36.59	43.46
64	17.05	21.21	26.01	31.58	37.15	44.12
65	17.30	21.52	26.40	32.05	37.71	44.79
66	17.54	21.83	26.78	32.52	38.26	45.46
67	17.78	22.14	27.16	32.99	38.82	46.12
68	18.02	22.44	27.54	33.46	39.38	46.79
69	18.27	22.75	27.93	33.93	39.93	47.45
70	18.51	23.06	28.31	34.40	40.49	48.12

Exception: Parcels weighing less than 15 pounds, and measuring over 84 inches but not exceeding 100 inches in length and girth combined, are chargeable with a minimum rate equal to that for a 15-pound parcel for the zone to which addressed.

Rates effective June 1978

Figure 15-3   Rates for priority mail.

than 16 ounces are third-class mail. Packages weighing 16 ounces or more are classified as fourth-class mail.

Fourth-Class (Parcel Post).   Merchandise, books, printed matter, and so on, weighing more than 16 ounces, are fourth-class mail. Educational materials, including books, films, sound recordings, printed music, and manuscripts, are entitled to *Special Fourth-Class Rates* (consult post office). The *Library Rate* applies to specific items loaned or exchanged between schools, colleges, public libraries, museums, and nonprofit organizations and associations, and between libraries, organizations, and associations, and their members, readers, or borrowers.

Mixed Classes.   A letter may be enclosed with second-, third-, or fourth-class mail provided first-class postage is added for the letter. The legend *First Class Mail Enclosed* should be written on the outside of the parcel. Or the sealed letter may be securely fastened to the outside (Figure 15-4).

Restrictions on Size and Weight.   All mail must be at least .007 of an inch thick; and all mail that is one-quarter inch or less in thickness must be rectangular in shape and at least $3\frac{1}{2}$ inches high and five inches long. Exempted from all but the minimum thickness standard are keys, identification cards, and tags.

First-class mail weighing an ounce or less and single-piece third-class mail weighing two ounces or less will be considered nonstandard and subject to a surcharge if (1) it exceeds $6\frac{1}{8}$ inches in height or $11\frac{1}{2}$ inches in length or

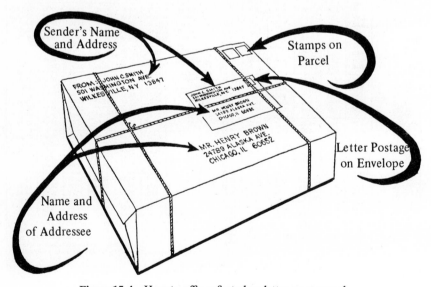

Figure 15-4   How to affix a first-class letter on a parcel.

¼ inch in thickness, and (2) it has a height to length ratio that does not fall between 1:1.3 and 1:2.5 inclusive.

With the exceptions noted on page 594, parcel post within the contiguous 48 states is limited to packages weighing not more than 40 pounds and measuring not more than 84 inches in combined length and girth (see Figure 15-5).

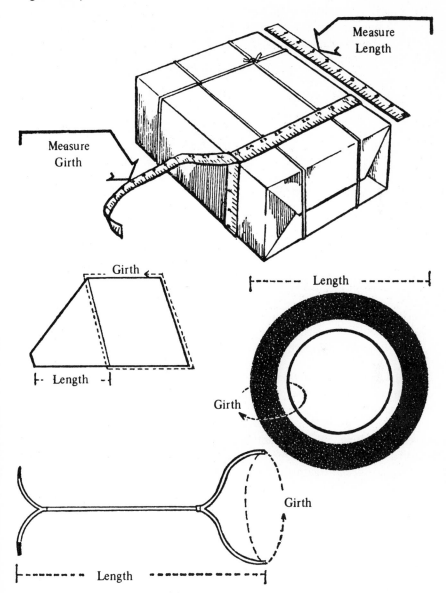

Figure 15-5   How to measure the size of a package.

Packages up to 70 pounds and 100 inches in combined length and girth are permitted when mailed to certain smaller post offices (those unstarred in the National ZIP Code Directory); to any Army, Air Force, or Fleet post office; and to any post office in Alaska, Hawaii, Puerto Rico, or any territory or possession of the United States. These maximums also apply to certain classes of goods, including books, appliances for the blind, and agricultural commodities, shipped to any domestic post office. Packages up to 70 pounds and 100 inches in length and girth combined that do not qualify as fourth-class mail under the exceptions stated, may be sent at the higher priority-mail rate.

15.2 SPECIAL POSTAL SERVICES

Rates and fees for many of the services listed here are given in Figure 15-6.

Priority Mail.   Priority mail ensures first-class service, including air mail where feasible, for letters and packages weighing more than 13 ounces. Rates are shown in Figure 15-3.

Special Delivery.   Available for all classes of mail, special delivery assures prompt delivery from the post office of destination to the receiver, usually by messenger.

Special Handling.   Special handling assures expeditious in-transit handling of third- and fourth-class mail. It is cheaper than special delivery, but mail receives no special treatment after it reaches the post office of destination.

Registered Mail.   The safest way to send valuables is by registered mail. All mailable matter with prepaid postage at the first-class rate may be registered. The sender is required to declare the full value of the item, which in turn determines the registration fee. When the value of the item sent exceeds the maximum liability of the post office, added insurance may be obtained from a private insurance broker. All items must be securely sealed; transparent tape and masking tape may not be used.

SPECIAL HANDLING
Third and Fourth-Class Only
(Fees shown are in addition to required postage)

Weight	Fee
Not more than 2 pounds	$0.70
More than 2 pounds but not more than 10 pounds	0.70
More than 10 pounds	1.25

MONEY ORDERS
For Safe Transmission of Money

Amount of money order	Amount of fee Domestic
$0.01 to $10	$0.55
$10.01 to $50	0.80
$50.01 to $400.00	1.10

SPECIAL DELIVERY
(Fees shown are in addition to required postage)

Class of Mail	Not more than 2 pounds	More than 2 pounds but not more than 10 pounds	More than 10 pounds
First class and priority mail	$2.00	$2.25	$2.85
All other classes	2.25	2.85	3.25

COD
Consult Postmaster for fees and conditions of mailing

CERTIFIED MAIL
For Proof of Mailing and Delivery

Fee (in addition to postage)	$0.80
Restricted delivery	0.80

RETURN RECEIPTS*
(Fees in addition to postage)

Insured Certified and Registered Mail

Requested at time of mailing:
Showing to whom and when delivered $0.45
Showing to whom, when, and address where delivered 0.55

Requested after mailing:
Showing to whom and when delivered 2.10

*Not available for mail insured for $15 or less

INSURANCE
For Coverage Against Loss or Damage
(Fees in addition to postage)

LIABILITY	FEE
$0.01 to $15	$0.50
15.01 to 50	0.85
50.01 to 100	1.10
100.01 to 150	1.40
150.01 to 200	1.75
200.01 to 300	2.25
300.01 to 400	2.75

REGISTRY
For Maximum Protection and Security
FEES (in addition to postage)

Value	For articles not covered by commercial or other insurance	For articles also covered by commercial or other insurance
$0.00 to $100	$3.00	$3.00
$100.01 to $200	3.30	3.30
$200.01 to $400	3.70	3.70
$400.01 to $600	4.10	4.10
$600.01 to $800	4.50	4.50
$800.01 to $1,000	4.90	4.90
$1,000.01 to $2,000	5.30	$4.90 plus handling charge of 35¢ per $1,000 or fraction over first $1,000

For higher values— Consult Postmaster

STAMPS, ENVELOPES, AND POSTAL CARDS
ADHESIVE STAMPS AVAILABLE

Purpose	Form	Denomination and prices
Regular postage	Single or sheet	1, 2, 3, 4, 5, 9, 10, 11, 12, 13, 14, 15, 16, 18, 20, 21, 24, 25, 29, 30, 40, & 50 cents; $1 and $5.
	Book	8—15¢ = $1.20 24—15¢ = $3.60
	Coil of 100	13 and 15 cents (Dispenser to hold coils of 100 Stamps may be purchased for 5¢ additional.)
	Coils of 500	1, 2, 3, 5, 9, 10, 13, 15 & 16 cents and $1
	Coil of 3,000	1, 2, 3, 5, 9, 10, 13, 15, 16, and 25¢
International Airmail postage	Single or sheet	21, 25, 26, and 31¢

ENVELOPES AVAILABLE

Kind	Denomination	Selling Price each
		Less than 500
Regular	15¢	18¢

POSTAL CARDS AVAILABLE

Kind	Selling price each
Single	10¢
Reply (10¢ each half)	20¢

Figure 15-6 Rates for special postal services (domestic).

595

Insured Mail.   Third- and fourth-class mail may be insured up to a limit of $400. For mail insured for $15.01 or more, a return receipt can be requested for an additional fee. Not acceptable for insurance are extremely fragile articles and those not adequately packaged to withstand customary handling in the mail.

Businesses that send out quantities of insured mail may apply to the post office for a mailing book that simplifies the preparation of receipts.

Express Mail.   Next-day delivery of packages is guaranteed with Express Mail, a service that links more than 1,000 post offices in more than 400 U.S. cities. Anything mailable, up to 70 pounds, is acceptable. It must be delivered to a designated Express Mail Post Office by 5 p.m. to be ready for pickup at the destination Express Mail Post Office as early as 10 a.m. the next day. For an extra fee, the mail will be delivered to the door by 3 p.m., including weekends and holidays. The Postal service is also experimenting with same-day delivery service within selected metropolitan areas. The fee compares favorably with that of private messenger services. Ask your post office for details.

Note: Overnight air delivery of small packages is also available, often more conveniently and at lower cost, from a number of so-called courier services, which operate in competition with the Postal Service. Among them are Federal Express, Emery Express, and Purolator Courier Service. Fast overground express services are provided by Greyhound and Trailways over their regular routes. For information about these and other carriers, see the Yellow Pages under "Courier Service," "Air Cargo Service," and "Express and Transfer Service."

Mailgram and Electronic Mail.   Offered jointly by Western Union and the Postal Service, a mailgram provides next-day delivery for messages to almost any destination within the United States (see page 435). For companies already using computers, Western Union lines transmit computer-originated messages direct to post offices in major cities. There, the messages are printed, inserted in envelopes, and then delivered with the regular mail. Service is guaranteed anywhere in the country within two days and, in most instances, within a day. The service is especially suited to big-volume mailings.

COD Mail.   First-, third-, and fourth-class matter may be sent COD, that is, collect on delivery. Acceptance of COD mail is limited to merchandise the addressee has ordered on terms agreed to in advance with the sender. Arrangements may be made to have the postman collect not only the amount due on the merchandise, but also the postage and the COD fee. The fee includes insurance against loss or damage and failure to receive payment, as well as the cost of a postal money order needed to return the amount collected to the mailer.

Certified Mail.   Certified mail provides a receipt to the sender and a record of delivery at the addressee's post office. Any mailable matter of no intrinsic value on which postage at the first-class rate has been paid will be accepted as certified mail. Insurance is not available.

Return Receipts.   A postal card verifying receipt by the addressee of certified, insured, and registered mail may be secured for an additional fee.

Certificate of Mailing.   For a small fee, the post office will provide a Certificate of Mailing for any class of mail. Filled in by the sender, it is presented with the letter or package to the postal clerk, who stamps it as proof that the item was mailed.

Stamps, Envelopes, and Postal Cards.   Postage stamps in various denominations are available singly or in sheets. Coils in three sizes (100, 500, and 3,000 stamps) are available in several popular denominations; and small, wallet-size books of stamps are available for letter postage.

Envelopes with imprinted first-class postage may be purchased in either the small size, $6\frac{3}{4}$ inches long, or the large size, 10 inches long.

Single postal cards and double reply cards are also available.

Precanceled Stamps.   Precanceling means the cancellation of postage stamps, stamped envelopes, or postal cards in advance of mailing. Adhesive postage stamps may be precanceled only by the post office. The use of precanceled postage reduces the time and costs of mail handling. Precanceled mail, sorted and tied in packages by the mailer, requires less processing time in the post office and is therefore dispatched more quickly.

Precanceled stamps may be used to pay postage on post cards, but on no other first-class mail, unless specifically authorized by the postmaster on Form 3620; and on second-, third-, and fourth-class mail. Any number of pieces may be mailed at one time, regardless of whether they are identical, except for third-class bulk mailings. Matter bearing precanceled stamps may be mailed only at the post office that sold the stamps.

Metered Mail.   Postage on any class of mail may be printed with a postage meter machine. Such machines make it easy to purchase, control, and affix postage. The same machines can also seal and stack letters. Metered mail does not require canceling and postmarking in the post office and can therefore be dispatched more quickly than other mail.

Postage meter machines contain in one sealed unit the printing mechanism and two recording counters, one that keeps a total of postage printed and another that shows the balance of postage in the meter. From time to time, before the paid-for postage is used up, mailers must take the meter to the post office to have the counter set for additional postage. For a fee, a postal representative will be sent to set the counter in the office.

In addition to the postage, the meter machine will print a brief advertising message. Some models also print the postage on gummed tape for use on large envelopes and packages.

A license to use a postage meter machine may be obtained at the post office where the metered mail will be deposited. No fee is charged. The application must specify the make and model of the machine.

Permit Imprints.   Under certain conditions, the post office will issue a permit allowing bulk mail of any class to bear a printed substitute for stamps or cancellations (Figure 15-7). Postage is paid at the time of mailing. Your local post office can provide full information and Form 3601, "Application to Mail Without Affixing Postage Stamp." See also "Bulk Mail."

Bulk Mail.   Special bulk rates are available for identical pieces mailed to different addresses. The rates are figured by the pound, with a minimum rate for each piece. Lower rates govern the mailings of nonprofit organizations. Postage must be prepaid by meter stamps, precanceled stamps or precanceled stamped envelopes, or by permit imprints. An annual bulk mailing fee is charged.

Presorted First-Class Mail.   Mailers who send out a minimum of 500 items at a time and pay an annual fee may qualify for a special first-class rate provided they sort the mail by ZIP code, pack it in special containers, and deliver it to designated locations at specific times. Any postmaster can give details.

Undeliverable Mail.   First-class mail, except postal and post cards, is returned to the sender without charge if it bears a request for return. If postal and post cards bearing a request for return are returned to the sender, postage at the card rate is collected. Undeliverable third- and fourth-class mail that have obvious value or bear the words *Return Requested* will be returned and a charge at the applicable rate collected.

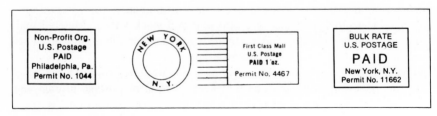

Figure 15-7   Examples of authorized permit imprints.

When registered, certified, insured, and COD mail is undeliverable as addressed and cannot be forwarded, a notice is sent to the mailer on Form 3858, "Notice of Undeliverable or Abandoned Mail," showing the reason. By completing the form and returning it immediately in an envelope bearing first-class postage, the mailer may tell the postmaster what to do with the mail. Mail will be returned to the mailer if there is no response.

Forwarding of Mail.   When mail is forwarded, the address should be changed and any required postage affixed before remailing. The original envelope or wrapper should be used. (See also "Change of Address.")

First-class mail requires no additional postage.

Second-, third-, and fourth-class mail requires the applicable postage except when it is forwarded within the same postal district.

Special delivery mail will be forwarded as ordinary mail without charge, but it will not receive special-delivery treatment unless a second special-delivery fee is paid.

Registered, insured, special handling, and COD mail will be forwarded without a second payment of the fees for those services but, with the exceptions previously noted, ordinary postage must be paid.

Change of Address.   To have mail delivered to a new address, file Form 3375, "Change of Address Order," which is available at any post office or from any carrier. A written and signed order or a telegram is acceptable and must be sent by the patron, the patron's agent, or the person in whose care mail will be addressed. The old and new addresses must always be furnished, including the ZIP code numbers, if known. Mail received at the post office of the old address will be handled as follows.

1. All first-class mail, all official mail, and all third- and fourth-class parcels of obvious value will be forwarded.

2. Second-class, other fourth-class, and other third-class mail of obvious value will be forwarded only when specifically requested by the order.

3. Third-class matter of no obvious value and mail addressed to "Occupant" or "Postal Patron" will NOT be forwarded.

4. Mail bearing specific instructions of the sender *DO NOT FORWARD* will not be forwarded.

The order to forward mail constitutes the pledge of the addressee to pay forwarding postage if required. The order to forward also covers registered, certified, insured, and COD mail unless the sender has given other instructions or unless the addressee has moved outside the United States.

Recall of Mail.   If for any reason it is necessary to recall an already mailed letter before delivery, file immediately with your local post office Form 1509, "Sender's Application for Return of Mail." The mailer pays all the expenses of recalling mail, including the cost of any necessary telegrams or telephone calls, and the regular rate of return postage (except for first-class mail, which is returned without additional postage). If the mail has been delivered before receipt of the recall application, the mailer is notified. The addressee is not informed that recall has been requested.

Lost Mail. Letters and packages that have become lost in the mails may be traced by the sender or the addressee by the filing of a request form with the post office. The form must be filed within a year from the date of mailing.

15.3 INTERNATIONAL MAIL

International mail consists of letters, aerogrammes, post cards, printed matter, small packets, and parcel post for delivery to foreign countries. The aerogramme is a form of prestamped stationery, sold at post offices, that can be folded and sealed to make its own envelope. The price of the postage includes the stationery. The regulations for international mail do not apply to overseas military mail addressed to APO (Army Post Office) or FPO (Fleet Post Office).

Postal Union Mail (Rates in Figures 15-8 and 15-11). International mail is either postal union mail or parcel post. Parcel post will be discussed later. Postal union mail, regulated by international agreement, is divided into LC mail and AO mail. LC mail (letters and cards) comprises letters, letter packages, aerogrammes, and post cards. AO mail (other articles) includes printed matter, matter for the blind, and small packets of merchandise or samples. *Preparing and Addressing.* Articles must be securely sealed or wrapped. Use strong envelopes and wrapping papers and stout twine for tying packages. Reserve at least the entire right half of the front side for the addressee's address, the stamps, and the service labels and notations. Make out the address legibly and completely, using *roman* letters and *arabic* figures placed lengthwise on *one* side of the article only. Give the house number and the street or box number when mail is for towns or cities. Show the names of the post office and the country of destination in *capital* letters and include the postal code if known. Foreign postal codes are to *precede* the name of the country of destination. The country name should not be abbreviated and must be the last item in the address. An address in a foreign language is permissible *provided* the names of the post office, the province, and the country are in English; or, if the English form is not known, are in *roman* characters. Addressing international mail to "Boxholder" or "Householder" is not permissible. The sender's name and complete address should be shown in the upper left corner of the address side.

INTERNATIONAL LETTER CLASS MAIL

Canada and Mexico*

Post Cards $0.10

Letters and Letter Packages

First Ounce $0.15
each additional ounce or
fraction thereof through 12
ounces $0.13

*letter class mail to Canada and Mexico receives air service

Use Eighth-Zone PRIORITY Mail Rates For Letter Class Mail Weighing More Than 12 Ounces.

Maximum Weights

Canada   60 pounds
Mexico   4 pounds

All Other Countries

SURFACE MAIL RATES

Post Cards $0.14

WEIGHT		LETTERS AND LETTER PACKAGES	Printed Matter	Small Packets
pounds	ounces	Rate	Rate	Rate
0	1	$0.20	$0.20	$0.20
0	2	0.36	0.20	0.20
0	4	0.48	0.40	0.40
0	8	0.96	0.66	0.66
1	0	1.84	1.05	1.05
2	0	3.20	1.26	1.26
4	0	5.20	1.68	. . . . .
Each additional 2 lbs.		. . . . .	0.84	. . . . .

AIRMAIL RATES TO: Central America, Colombia, Venezuela, Caribbean Islands, Bahamas, Bermuda, St. Pierre and Miquelon. Also from American Samoa to Western Samoa and from Guam to the Philippines:

$0.25 per HALF ounce through 2 ounces
$0.21 each additional HALF ounce or fraction

AIRMAIL RATES TO ALL OTHER COUNTRIES:

$0.31 per HALF ounce through 2 ounces
$0.26 each additional HALF ounce or fraction

AEROGRAMMES.. $0.22
AIRMAIL POST CARDS $0.21

Rates effective June 1978

Figure 15-8   Rates for international letter class mail, including surface rates for printed matter and small packets.

Dimensions.   Requirements are as follows: (a) For articles not in the form of a roll, the maximum length is 24 inches and the maximum size is 36 inches in combined length, breadth, and thickness; at a minimum, one surface must measure at least $5\frac{1}{2}$ by $3\frac{1}{2}$ inches; (b) For articles in the form of a roll, the maximum permissible size is 36 inches in length or 42 inches in length plus twice the diameter; the minimum is 4 inches in length or $6\frac{3}{4}$ inches in length plus twice the diameter; (c) For post cards, the maximum size is 6 by $4\frac{1}{2}$ inches, and the minimum is $5\frac{1}{2}$ by $3\frac{1}{2}$ inches.

Sealing.   Registered letters and registered letter packages must be sealed. Ordinary letters and small packets may be sealed; and printed matter may be sealed if postage is paid by permit imprint, postage meter stamps, precanceled stamps, second-class or controlled circulation indicia. Matter for the blind must be left unsealed.

Endorsements.   The envelopes or wrappers of postal union articles, except letters and cards, must be endorsed to show the classification under which they are mailed, for instance, *Small Packet*. Endorse envelopes or wrappers *Printed Matter* when mailing prints at regular printed matter rates, and *Printed Matter—Books* or *Printed Matter—Sheet Music* when mailing at the special rates prescribed for these categories. The words *Letter (lettre)* should be added on the address side of letters or letter packages that, because of their size or manner of preparation, may be mistaken for matter of another classification. When mailing small packets, endorse the envelopes or wrappers *Small Packet* or its equivalent in a language known in the country of destination, for example, *Petit Paquet* (French) or *Pequeno Paquette* (Spanish). In addition, airmail articles should be plainly endorsed *Par Avion* or have a *Par Avion* label affixed. Articles intended for special delivery should have a red international *Exprès* label or be marked boldly in red *Exprès* (*Special Delivery*).

Customs Forms.   Small packets, letters and letter packages containing dutiable merchandise, and dutiable printed matter must have the green customs label, Form 2976, affixed. If the sender prefers, or if the contents exceed $120 in value, customs declaration, Form 2976-A, must be completed and enclosed and only the upper portion of the green label affixed to the cover of the package. The forms are furnished free at post offices.

Prohibited Articles.   Articles of a dangerous or objectionable nature are generally prohibited. These include matches, most live or dead creatures, poisons, narcotics, firearms capable of being concealed on the person, flammable liquids, and radioactive materials. Each country prohibits or restricts the importation of various articles in addition to those generally prohibited. Information on these special country prohibitions or restrictions appears in Appendix B of the Postal Service Publication 42, "International Mail," or may be secured at a local post office. Failure to investigate these limitations before you mail may result in the seizure of packages in the country of address.

SPECIAL SERVICES FOR POSTAL UNION MAIL

1. Registration

   All countries except Canada, maximum indemnity $15.76* $3.00

   Canada, maximum indemnity $100   3.00

   Canada, maximum indemnity $200   3.30

   *Registration not available to Kampuchea (Cambodia) and Socialist Republic of Vietnam (North and South)

2. Return Receipt $0.45

3. Special Delivery

	Through 2 pounds	Through 10 pounds	Over 10 pounds
Letters, letter packages, post cards, and airmail other articles	$2.00	$2.25	$2.85
Surface other articles	2.25	2.85	3.25

4. Special Handling

	Through 10 lbs.	Over 10 lbs.
AO surface packages only	$0.70	$1.25

5. Insurance, Certified Mail, and COD

   Not available

SPECIAL SERVICES FOR PARCEL POST

1. Registration

   Available to only a few countries. Consult post office.

2. Insurance

   For availability, consult Figure 15-11. Ask post office about fee.

3. Air Service

   Available to countries for which rates are shown in Figure 15-11.

4. Special Handling

   Through 10 pounds $0.70

   Over 10 pounds   1.25

5. COD, Special Delivery, and Certified Mail

   Not available

Rates effective June 1978

Figure 15-9   Rates for special services—international mail.

Prepayment of Replies from Other Countries. A mailer who wishes to prepay a reply by letter from another country may do so by sending the correspondent one or more international reply coupons, which may be purchased in U.S. post offices. One coupon is exchangeable in any country for a stamp or stamps of the country sufficient to prepay a surface letter of the first unit of weight (usually one ounce or 20 grams) to the United States. If prepayment of a reply by airmail is desired, a sufficient number of coupons for the anticipated charge should be obtained.

Business reply mail and reply-paid cards, applicable in the U.S. domestic service, are not accepted in international mail.

Undeliverable Articles. Postal union mail is generally returned to the sender if delivery cannot be made. However, post cards that do not bear the return address of the sender are not returned. Neither are undeliverable, unregistered printed-matter articles (other than books) returned unless they bear the sender's request for return.

Special Services Available (Rates in Figure 15-9). Letters and letter packets may be registered to practically all countries, but insurance, available for parcel post, is not available for postal union mail. Return receipts, which must be requested at the time of mailing, are returned by air mail. Special delivery and special handling are available to most countries, and air mail to practically all. Special handling entitles AO surface packages to priority handling only between the mailing point and the U.S. point of dispatch. There is no certified mail to foreign countries.

Parcel Post (Rates in Figures 15-10 and 15-11). Packages in international mail must adhere to most of the regulations for postal union mail. With few exceptions, the weight limit is either 22 or 44 pounds. Special regulations for parcel post include those listed on page 611.

	First 2 pounds	Each additional pound or fraction*
Canada, Mexico, Central America, Caribbean Islands, Bahamas, Bermuda, St. Pierre and Miquelon	$2.19	$0.52
All other countries	2.34	0.59
*For weight limits, see Figure 15–11.		

Rates effective June 1978

Figure 15-10 Surface rates for international parcel post.

COUNTRY INFORMATION TABLE

Country	Mer-chan-dise admit-ted in letter pack-ages	Spec-cial deliv-ery service avail-able	Air Rates				Parcel post insur-ance avail-able	Max. weight for parcel post (sur-face and air)
			AO Mail (4)		Parcel Post (5)			
			First 2 oz.	Each addi-tional 2 oz. or frac-tion	First 4 oz.	Each addi-tional 4-oz. or frac-tion		
(1)	(2)	(3)					(6)	(7)

								Lbs.
Afghanistan	No	Yes	$0.86	$0.42	$3.14	$1.20	No	22
Albania	No	Yes	.73	.29	3.33	.79	No	22
Algeria	Yes	Yes	.73	.29	2.71	.80	No	44
Andorra	Yes	No	.73	.29	2.79	.70	$395	44
Angola	Yes	Yes	.86	.42	2.93	1.01	20	22
Anguilla (Leeward Is.) (Caribbean)	Yes	No	.60	.16	1.78	.36	100	22
Antigua (Leeward Is.) (Caribbean)	Yes	No	.60	.16	1.78	.36	100	22
Argentina	Yes[1]	Yes	.73	.29	2.46	1.07	200	44
Aruba (Neth. Antilles) (Caribbean)	Yes	No	.60	.16	2.08	.45	200	44
Ascension	Yes	No	.73	.29	(4)	...	No	22
Australia (3)	Yes	Yes	.86	.42	2.62	1.21	225	44
Austria	Yes	Yes	.73	.29	2.70	.74	395	44
Azores	Yes	Yes	.73	.29	1.95	.56	395	22
Bahamas	Yes	Yes	.60	.16	2.19	.27	120	22
Bahrain	Yes	No	.86	.42	2.42	1.03	100	22
Bangladesh	Yes	Yes[1]	.86	.42	3.46	1.22	200	22
Barbados (Caribbean)	Yes	No	.60	.16	1.90	.51	100	22
Barbuda (Leeward Is.) (Caribbean)	Yes	No	.60	.16	1.78	.36	100	22
Belgium	Yes	Yes	.73	.29	2.41	.66	200	44
Belize (Central America)	Yes	Yes[1]	.60	.16	1.89	.48	No	22
Benin (Dahomey)	Yes	Yes	.86	.42	2.36	.85	No	44
Bermuda	Yes	No	.60	.16	1.77	.35	No	33
Bhutan	No	Yes	.86	.42	(4)	...	No	(5)
Bolivia (3)	No	No	.73	.29	2.47	.69	No	44
Bonaire (Neth. Ant.) (Caribbean)	Yes	No	.60	.16	2.08	.45	200	44
Botswana	Yes	Yes	.86	.42	2.66	1.27	No	22
Brazil	No	Yes	.73	.29	2.94	.79	No	44
British Virgin Is. (Lee-ward Is.) (Caribbean)	Yes	No	.60	.16	1.78	.36	100	22
Brunei	Yes	No	.86	.42	3.01	1.47	No	22
Bulgaria	No	Yes	.73	.29	2.15	.75	No	22
Burma (3)	Yes	No	.86	.42	3.30	1.43	No	22
Burundi	Yes	Yes	.86	.42	2.76	1.07	No	22
Cameroon	Yes	Yes	.86	.42	2.79	.92	No	22
Canada (3)	Yes	Yes[1]	(6)	...	(6)	...	400	35
Cape Verde	Yes	Yes	.86	.42	2.72	.81	20	22
Cayman (Caribbean)	Yes	No	.60	.16	2.36	.33	No	22
Central African Empire	No	No	.86	.42	2.76	1.07	No	44
Chad	Yes	No	.86	.42	2.76	1.07	No	44

See footnotes at end of table.

Figure 15-11 Air rates and other conditions for international AO mail and parcel post.

Country	Merchandise admitted in letter packages	Special delivery service available	Air Rates				Parcel post insurance available	Max. weight for parcel post (surface and air)
			AO Mail (4)		Parcel Post (5)			
			First 2 oz.	Each additional 2 oz. or fraction	First 4 oz.	Each additional 4 oz. or fraction		
(1)	(2)	(3)					(6)	(7)
								l.bs.
Chile ([3])	No ...	Yes ..	$0.73	$0.29	$2.92	$0.89	No	22
China, People's Republic of ([7])	No ...	No ...	.86	.42	3.08	1.37	No	44
China, Republic of (Taiwan, Penghu, Quemoy and Matsu Islands)	No ...	Yes ..	.86	.42	2.46	1.05	200	44
Colombia ([3])	No ...	Yes[1]..	.60	.16	2.86	.50	200	44
Comoro, State of	Yes ..	No ...	.86	.42	3.13	1.43	No	44
Congo (People's Rep) (Brazzaville)	Yes ..	No ...	.86	.42	2.76	1.07	No	44
Corsica	Yes ..	Yes ..	.73	.29	2.98	.66	395	44
Costa Rica (Central America)	Yes ..	Yes ..	.60	.16	2.06	.43	No	44
Cuba (Caribbean)	No ...	No ...	[1].60	.16	([4])	...	No	([5])
Curacao (Neth. Ant.) (Caribbean)	Yes ..	No ...	.60	.16	2.08	.45	200	44
Cyprus	Yes ..	Yes[1]..	.73	.29	2.88	.85	200	44
Czechoslovakia	Yes ..	Yes ..	.73	.29	2.17	.76	200	44
Denmark	Yes ..	Yes ..	.73	.29	2.14	.72	395	44
Dominica (Windward Is.) (Caribbean)	Yes ..	No ...	.60	.16	2.39	48	100	22
Dominican Republic (Caribbean)	No ...	Yes ..	.60	.16	2.24	.36	No	44
Djibouti	Yes ..	Yes ..	.86	.42	2.89	1.03	395	44
East Timor	Yes ..	Yes ..	.86	.42	3.64	1.72	No	22
Ecuador	Yes[1]..	Yes[1]..	.73	.29	2.78	.48	50	44
Egypt	Yes ..	Yes ..	.73	.29	2.32	.92	200	44
El Salvador (Central America)	No ...	No ...	.60	.16	2.21	.44	No	44
Equatorial Guinea	No ...	Yes ..	.86	.42	2.82	1.22	No	44
Estonia ([2])	No ...	Yes ..	.86	.42	2.84	.95	200	44
Ethiopia (incl. Eritrea) .	No ...	Yes ..	.86	.42	2.83	1.10	200	44
Faeroe Islands	Yes ..	No ...	.73	.29	2.14	.72	395	44
Falkland Islands	Yes ..	No ...	.73	.29	2.99	.85	No	22
Fiji	Yes ..	No ...	.86	.42	2.79	.90	120	22
Finland	Yes ..	Yes ..	.73	.29	2.17	.79	395	44
France	Yes ..	Yes ..	.73	.29	2.98	.66	395	44
French Guiana	Yes ..	Yes ..	.73	.29	2.19	.56	No	44
French Polynesia	Yes ..	Yes ..	.86	.42	2.70	.76	395	44
Gabon	Yes ..	No ...	.86	.42	2.76	1.07	No	44
Gambia	Yes ..	Yes ..	.86	.42	2.39	.76	No	22
German Democratic Rep. (East Germany) ..	No ...	Yes ..	.73	.29	2.10	.70	No	22
Germany, Federal Rep. (West Germany)	Yes ..	Yes ..	.73	.29	2.10	.70	395	44
Ghana	Yes ..	Yes ..	.86	.42	2.92	.92	80	22
Gibraltar	Yes ..	Yes ..	.73	.29	2.16	.75	50	22
Gilbert Islands	Yes ..	No ...	.86	.42	2.66	1.00	No	44
Great Britain & Northern Ireland	Yes ..	Yes ..	.73	.29	2.08	.66	1200	44

See footnotes at end of table.

Figure 15-11 (continued).

Country	Merchandise admitted in letter packages	Special delivery service available	Air Rates AO Mail (4) First 2 oz.	Each additional 2 oz. or fraction	Parcel Post (5) First 4 oz.	Each additional 4 oz. or fraction	Parcel post insurance available	Max. weight for parcel post (surface and air)
(1)	(2)	(3)					(6)	(7)
								l.bs.
Greece, incl. Crete and Dodecanese Is.	Yes	Yes	.73	.29	2.62	.84	200	44
Greenland	Yes	No	.73	.29	2.35	.93	395	44
Grenada and The Grenadines (Windward Islands) (Caribbean)	Yes	No	.60	.16	2.39	.48	100	22
Guadeloupe (Caribbean)	Yes	Yes	.60	.16	2.00	.36	No	44
Guatemala (Central America)	Yes[1]	Yes	.60	.16	2.51	.46	100	44
Guernsey (Channel Islands) (Great Britain)	Yes	Yes	.73	.29	2.08	.66	1200	44
Guinea, Rep of	Yes	No	.86	.42	2.46	.96	No	44
Guinea Bissau	Yes	Yes	.86	.42	2.93	1.01	20	22
Guyana	Yes	Yes	.73	.29	2.42	.50	200	22
Haiti (Caribbean)	Yes	No	.60	.16	2.25	.35	No	44
Honduras (Rep.) (Central America)	Yes	Yes	.60	.16	2.14	.46	No	[1]44
Hong Kong	Yes	Yes	.86	.42	2.65	1.24	395	22
Hungary	Yes	Yes	.73	.29	2.16	.76	100	44
Iceland	Yes	Yes	.73	.29	2.66	.56	395	44
India	Yes	No	.86	.42	2.67	1.27	200	[1]44
Indonesia	Yes	Yes	.86	.42	3.48	1.52	No	22
Iran	Yes	Yes[1]	.86	.42	2.67	.96	200	44
Iraq	Yes	No	.86	.42	2.98	.95	No	44
Ireland	Yes	Yes	.73	.29	2.06	.66	1000	22
Isle of Man (Great Britain)	Yes	Yes	.73	.29	2.08	.66	1200	44
Israel	Yes	Yes	.86	.42	2.93	.91	No	33
Italy	No	Yes	.73	.29	2.63	.79	120	44
Ivory Coast	Yes	Yes	.86	.42	2.46	.95	No	44
Jamaica (Caribbean)	Yes	No	.60	.16	2.36	.33	No	22
Japan, incl Ryukyu Islands–Okinawa	Yes	Yes	.86	.42	2.19	.80	395	22
Jersey (Channel Islands (Great Britain)	Yes	Yes	.73	.29	2.08	.66	1200	44
Jordan	Yes	Yes	.86	.42	2.72	.90	No	22
Kampuchea (Khmer Republic) (Cambodia)	No	No	(1)	...	(4)	...	No	(5)
Kenya	Yes	Yes	.86	.42	2.93	1.10	No	22
Korea: Republic of (South)	Yes[1]	Yes[1]	.86	.42	2.25	.85	200	22
Democratic People's Rep. (North)	No	No	.86	.42	(4)	...	No	(5)
Kuwait	Yes	Yes	.86	.42	2.39	1.00	200	44
Lao	Yes	Yes	.86	.42	3.35	1.37	No	22
Latvia (2)	No	Yes	.86	.42	2.84	.95	200	44
Lebanon	Yes	No	.86	.42	2.72	.90	No	[1]44

See footnotes at end of table.

Figure 15-11 (continued).

Country	Merchandise admitted in letter packages	Special delivery service available	AO Mail (4) First 2 oz.	Each additional 2 oz. or fraction	Parcel Post (5) First 4 oz.	Each additional 4 oz. or fraction	Parcel post insurance available	Max., weight for parcel post (surface and air)
(1)	(2)	(3)					(6)	(7)
								Lbs.
Leeward Islands (Caribbean)	Yes ..	No ...	$0.60	$0.16	$ 1.78	$0 .36	100	22
Lesotho	Yes ..	Yes ..	.86	.42	2.66	1.27	No	22
Liberia	Yes ..	Yes ..	.86	.42	2.24	.84	100	22
Libya	Yes! ..	Yes ..	.73	.29	2.70	.85	No	44
Liechtenstein	Yes ..	Yes ..	.73	.29	2.39	.67	395	44
Lithuania²	No ...	Yes ..	.86	.42	2.84	.95	200	44
Luxembourg	Yes ..	Yes ..	.73	.29	2.47	.65	200	44
Macao	Yes ..	Yes ..	.86	.42	3.20	1.24	120	22
Madagascar (Malagasy Rep.)	Yes ..	No ...	.86	.42	3.09	1.22	No	44
Madeira Islands	Yes ..	Yes ..	.73	.29	2.10	.72	395	22
Malawi	Yes ..	No ...	.86	.42	2.66	1.24	No	22
Malaysia	Yes ..	No ...	.86	.42	3.23	1.42	100	22
Maldives, Rep. of	No ...	No ...	.86	.42	3.59	1.29	No	22
Mali	Yes ..	Yes ..	.86	.42	3.46	.82	No	44
Malta	Yes ..	Yes ..	.73	.29	2.61	.79	No	22
Martinique (Caribbean)	Yes ..	Yes ..	.60	.16	2.00	.36	No	44
Mauritania	Yes ..	Yes ..	.86	.42	2.36	.79	No	44
Mauritius	Yes ..	No ...	.86	.42	3.01	1.29	No	22
Mexico	Yes ..	Yes ..	.60	.16	1.77	.35	No	44
Monaco (France)	Yes ..	Yes ..	.73	.29	2.98	.66	395	44
Mongolian People's Republic	No ...	No ...	.86	.42	(⁴)	...	No	(⁵)
Montserrat (Leeward Islands) (Caribbean) ..	Yes ..	No ...	.60	.16	1.78	.36	100	44
Morocco, incl. Ifni Territory	Yes ..	Yes ..	.73	.29	2.63	.79	No	44
Mozambique	Yes ..	Yes ..	.86	.42	3.43	1.28	100	22
Namibia (South West Africa) (South Africa)	Yes ..	Yes ..	.86	.42	2.66	1.27	No	22
Nauru	Yes ..	Yes ..	.86	.42	2.62	1.21	200	22
Nepal	No ...	No ...	.86	.42	2.66	1.27	No	22
Netherlands	Yes ..	Yes ..	.73	.29	2.36	.66	395	44
Netherlands Antilles (Caribbean)	Yes ..	No ...	.60	.16	2.08	.45	200	44
Nevis (Leeward Is.) (Caribbean)	Yes ..	No ...	.60	.16	1.78	.36	100	22
New Caledonia	Yes ..	Yes ..	.86	.42	2.81	.93	395	44
New Hebrides	Yes ..	No ...	.86	.42	2.65	.93	No	44
New Zealand	Yes ..	No ...	.86	.42	2.98	1.07	200	22
Nicaragua (Central America)	Yes ..	No ...	.60	.16	2.08	.43	200	44
Niger	Yes ..	Yes ..	.86	.42	3.45	.80	No	44
Nigeria	Yes ..	Yes ..	.86	.42	3.14	.93	No	22
Norway, incl. Spitzbergen	Yes ..	Yes ..	.73	.29	2.14	.72	395	44

See footnotes at end of table.

Figure 15-11 (continued).

608

Country	Merchandise admitted in letter packages	Special delivery service available	Air Rates				Parcel post insurance available	Max. weight for parcel post (surface and air)
			AO Mail (4)		Parcel Post (5)			
			First 2 oz.	Each additional 2 oz. or fraction	First 4 oz.	Each additional 4 oz. or fraction		
(1)	(2)	(3)					(6)	(7)
								l.bs.
Oman	Yes	No	$0.86	$0.42	$2.42	$1.03	100	22
Pakistan	Yes	Yes!	.86	.42	3.46	1.22	200	22
Panama (Rep.) (Central America)	No	Yes	.60	.16	2.50	.45	No	¹70
Papua-New Guinea	Yes	No	.86	.42	2.72	1.32	100	22
Paraguay	Yes	Yes	.73	.29	2.47	.67	No	44
Peru	No	No	.73	.29	2.88	.60	No	44
Philippines	Yes	Yes	.86	.42	3.03	1.17	200	¹44
Pitcairn Islands	Yes	No	.86	.42	2.89	1.03	No	22
Poland	Yes	Yes	.73	.29	2.61	.75	No	44
Portugal	Yes	Yes	.73	.29	2.05	.64	395	22
Qatar	Yes	No	.86	.42	2.42	1.03	100	22
Reunion	Yes	Yes	.86	.42	2.89	1.27	No	44
Rhodesia	Yes	No	.86	.42	2.66	1.24	No	22
Rumania	No¹	Yes	.73	.29	2.42	.79	No	22
Rwanda	Yes	Yes	.86	.42	2.76	1.07	No	22
Saba (Neth. Antilles) (Caribbean)	Yes	No	.60	.16	2.08	.45	200	44
St. Christopher (St. Kitts) (Leeward Is.) (Caribbean)	Yes	No	.60	.16	2.39	.48	100	22
St. Eustatius (Neth. Antilles) (Carribbean)	Yes	No	.60	.16	2.08	.45	200	44
St. Helena	Yes	No	.86	.42	3.01	1.22	No	22
St. Lucia (Windward Is.) (Caribbean)	Yes	No	.60	.16	2.39	.48	100	22
St. Pierre & Miquelon	Yes	Yes	.60	.16	1.72	.35	No	44
St. Thomas and Principe (Dem. Rep.)	Yes	Yes	.86	.42	2.93	1.01	20	22
St. Vincent (Windward Is.) (Caribbean)	Yes	No	.60	.16	2.39	.48	100	22
San Marino (Italy)	No	Yes	.73	.29	2.63	.79	120	44
Santa Cruz Islands	Yes	No	.86	.42	3.10	1.39	No	22
Saudi Arabia	No	No	.86	.42	3.10	1.00	No	22
Senegal	Yes	Yes	.86	.42	2.34	.75	No	44
Seychelles	Yes	No	.86	.42	2.53	1.12	No	22
Sierra Leone	Yes	Yes	.86	.42	3.09	.81	No	22
Singapore	Yes	No	.86	.42	3.23	1.42	100	22
Solomon Islands	Yes	No	.86	.42	3.12	1.39	No	22
Somalia	Yes	Yes	.86	.42	3.23	1.13	No	22
South Africa (Rep.)	Yes	Yes	.86	.42	2.66	1.27	No	22
Spain, incl. Canary and Balearic Islands)	Yes	Yes	.73	.29	2.79	.70	200	¹44
Sri Lanka (Ceylon)	Yes	Yes	.86	.42	3.33	1.28	200	22
Sudan	Yes	No	.86	.42	3.13	1.01	No	22
Surinam	Yes	No	.73	.29	2.24	.53	100	44
Swaziland	Yes	Yes	.86	.42	2.66	1.27	No	22
Sweden	Yes	Yes	.73	.29	2.14	.72	395	44

See footnotes at end of table.

Figure 15-11 (continued).

Country	Merchandise admitted in letter packages	Special delivery service available	Air Rates				Parcel post insurance available	Max. weight for parcel post (surface and air)
			AO Mail (4)		Parcel Post (5)			
			First 2 oz.	Each additional 2 oz. or fraction	First 4 oz.	Each additional 4 oz. or fraction		
(1)	(2)	(3)					(6)	(7)
								Lbs.
Switzerland	Yes ..	Yes ..	.73	.29	2.39	.67	395	44
Syria	Yes ..	No ...	.86	.42	2.47	.92	200	¹ 44
Tanzania	Yes ..	Yes ..	.86	.42	2.99	1.15	No	22
Thailand	Yes ..	Yes ..	.86	.42	3.28	1.17	120	22
Togo	Yes ..	Yes¹..	.86	.42	2.57	.95	No	44
Tonga	Yes ..	No ...	.86	.42	2.34	.93	No	22
Trinidad & Tobago (Caribbean)	Yes ..	No ...	.60	.16	2.37	.45	145	22
Tristan da Cunha	Yes ..	No ...	.86	.42	2.83	1.21	No	22
Tunisia	Yes ..	Yes ..	.73	.29	2.62	.75	No	44
Turkey	Yes ..	Yes ..	.73	.29	2.26	.85	200	44
Turks and Caicos Islands (Caribbean) ..	Yes ..	No ...	.60	.16	2.25	.33	No	22
Tuvalu (Ellice Islands) .	Yes ..	No ...	.86	.42	2.66	1.00	No	22
Uganda	Yes ..	Yes ..	.86	.42	2.93	1.10	No	22
Union of Soviet Socialist Republics² ..	No ...	Yes ..	.86	.42	2.84	.95	200	44
United Arab Emirates .	Yes ..	No ...	.86	.42	2.42	1.03	100	22
Upper Volta	Yes ..	Yes ..	.86	.42	2.72	.89	No	44
Uruguay	Yes ..	No ...	.73	.29	2.93	.90	No	44
Vatican City State	Yes ..	Yes ..	.73	.29	2.42	.74	No	44
Venezuela	No ...	Yes ..	.60	.16	2.71	.43	No	44
Vietnam, Socialist Republic of¹ (North and South) ...	No ...	No ...	.86	.42	(⁴)	...	No	(⁵)
Wallis and Fortuna Islands (New Caledonia)	Yes ..	Yes ..	.86	.42	2.81	.93	395	44
Western Samoa	Yes ..	No ...	.86	.42	2.71	.80	200	22
Windward Islands (Caribbean)	Yes ..	No ...	.60	.16	2.39	.48	100	22
Yemen Arab Republic (Sanaa)	Yes¹..	Yes¹..	.86	.42	3.04	1.55	No	44
Yemen, People's Dem. Rep. of (Aden)	Yes ..	Yes ..	.86	.42	2.81	1.10	No	44
Yugoslavia	No ...	Yes ..	.73	.29	2.17	.79	200	44
Zaire	Yes ..	Yes ..	.86	.42	2.76	1.07	No	44
Zambia	Yes ..	No ...	.86	.42	2.66	1.24	No	22

¹ Restrictions apply. Consult post office.
² To facilitate distribution and delivery, include "Union of Soviet Socialist Republics" or "U.S.S.R." as part of the address.
³ Small packets weight limit 1 pound.
⁴ No air parcel post service.
⁵ No surface parcel post service.
⁶ No airmail AO or air parcel post to Canada. Prepare and prepay all airmail packages as letter mail.
⁷ Mail must be addressed to show name of the country as "People's Republic of China;" also acceptable spelling of capital is "Peking."

Figure 15-11　(continued).

Dimension Limits.   Greatest length, 3½ feet; greatest length and girth combined, 6 feet. To some countries parcels may measure 4 feet in length if not more than 16 inches in girth. Consult the post office.

Packing.   Containers should be used that are strong enough to protect the contents from the weight of other mail, pressure and friction, climatic changes, and the repeated handlings to which parcels are subjected. When using fiberboard or double-faced corrugated boxes, use only those made of good-quality material. Containers of 275-pound test, with contents solidly packed, are preferred. Cushioning material should be used. When sending liquids or easily liquefiable substances, place sufficient absorbent material between the inner and outer containers to absorb all the liquid contents in case of breakage.

Sealing.   Registered or insured parcels must be sealed. The sealing of ordinary parcels is optional to some countries and compulsory to others. Consult the post office.

Customs Forms.   At least one customs declaration, Form 2966-A, is required for parcel post packages (surface or air) mailed to another country. To some countries Form 2966 and/or a dispatch note, Form 2972, may be required. The forms may be obtained at post offices.

Special Parcel Post Services (Figure 15-9).   Registration is available to only a few countries, insurance is available to many countries, and air service is possible to most countries. COD and certified mail are not available. Special handling, for which a fee is charged, entitles surface parcels to priority handling only between the mailing point and the United States point of dispatch.

15.4   NONMAIL POSTAL SERVICES

Among other services, the post office issues money orders and documentary internal revenue stamps and rents post office boxes that hold mail for pickup by the renter.

Money Orders.   Domestic money orders may be purchased at all post offices and branches. The maximum amount for a single money order is $400 (see rates in Figure 15-6).

International money orders will be issued at many post offices to addresses in those countries that have agreed with the United States to conduct such business. The amount is written in United States dollars and converted into foreign currency in the country where payable. The payee's address should include the name of the canton, department, or district in which the city, town, or village is located. Also, if the payee is a woman, her marital status (single, married, or widowed) should appear after her name.

Documentary Internal Revenue Stamps.   Documentary Internal Revenue stamps are sold at all first- and second-class post offices, and at third- and fourth-class offices located in county seats. These stamps are used for the payment of taxes on the following documents: (a) issuance of capital stock and certificates of indebtedness of a corporation; (b) sales or transfers of capital stock and certificates of indebtedness of a corporation; (c) real estate conveyances, deeds, and so on; (d) steamship passage tickets; and (e) policies by foreign insurers.

Box Rental. Boxes and drawers are provided at most post offices for the convenience of individuals and companies. The service provides privacy and permits the pickup of mail during the hours the lobby is kept open. To rent a box the patron submits Form 1093, "Application for Post Office Box." A box is assigned immediately to a known qualified applicant upon payment of rent. An unknown applicant must present a driver's license, Social Security card, military identification card, or some other identification document. After the postmaster verifies that the applicant resides or conducts business at the addresses shown and is served by the telephone number shown, the application is approved.

Box rents vary according to the classification of the post office and are payable quarterly in advance.

16

Dictionary of Business Terms

Definitions of selected terms in ten important fields are listed here. **Bold-face** terms in the definitions can be located in the alphabetical listing.

CONTENTS

16.1 ACCOUNTING

account   A ledger record of a specific transaction or series of related transactions entered as money or some other appropriate unit.

accountancy   Theoretical and practical accounting; its purpose, conventional standards, and general applications.

accountant   An accounting specialist. A public accountant serves the public. A Certified Public Accountant meets the statutory requirements of a state or other political subdivision of the United States and is registered or licensed to practice public accounting and use the initials *CPA* after his name. A private accountant is employed by a single organization.

accounting   The recording and reporting of transactions, including design of systems, bookkeeping, and auditing.

accrue   To increase in worth; to accumulate.

adjusting entry   An accounting transaction recorded to correct an error or to enter supplementary information, such as accruals, write-offs, depreciation, and bad debts.

allowance for bad debts   A valuation account set up to reduce the recorded amount of notes and accounts receivable to that considered collectable. Also called *allowance for credit losses* or *reserve for bad debts*.

allowance for depreciation   The credit derived from net depreciation provisions; the account in which these items appear. See **depreciation**.

asset   Any physical object (tangible) or right (intangible) having value, expressed in terms of its cost, depreciated cost, or as it benefits present or future worth.

auditing   An exploratory review by a public accountant of the internal controls and accounting records of a business or economic unit, before he gives an opinion of the propriety of its financial statements.

auditor   Either a regular employee or an outside professional, who audits accounting records kept by others.

bad debt   An uncollectable receivable.

balance sheet   A business financial position statement disclosing assets, liabilities, and the equity of owners.

bank reconciliation   A statement of the items of difference between an account balance reported by a bank and the account being kept by the bank's customer. Such items include outstanding checks and deposits in transit.

bank service charge   A bank charge to a customer for collection, protest fees, exchange, checks drawn, or other services, exclusive of interest and discount.

bank statement   A deposit and withdrawal statement (usually monthly) sent by a bank to the holder of a checking account.

bond   A written certificate of indebtedness. Bonds may be in the form of coupon or bearer instruments, or registered in the name of the owner as to principal only (registered coupon bonds) or as to both principal and interest (registered bonds).

bookkeeping   Analyzing, classifying, and recording transactions in accordance with an accounting plan.

budget   A periodic financial plan to estimate and control expenditures.

canceled check   A check paid by the bank and returned to the writer. It supports the bank's charge against the account and is the depositor's receipt of payment.

capital   Invested amount plus retained income (or earned surplus); net worth; net assets; stockholders' equity.

capital stock   Shares representing ownership in a corporation.

cash discount   An amount allowed for the prompt cash payment of a purchase.

closing entry   At the end of an accounting period, a final entry eliminating the year's revenue and expense accounts, their net total being carried to **earned surplus** or other proprietorship accounts.

comparative statement   A statement of assets and liabilities, operations, or other data, giving figures in comparative form for more than one date or period or organization.

control account   An account containing the totals of a series of transactions, the details of which are kept in a subsidiary ledger. Its balance equals the sum of the balances of the detailed accounts.

controller (comptroller)   An accountant in charge, who has been given that title by the management or board of directors.

cost accountant   One skilled in cost accounting.

cost accounting   The branch of accounting dealing with the classification, recording, allocation, summarization, and reporting of current and prospective costs.

cost of goods sold   The total cost of goods sold, ascertained from invoices and other expense records.

credit   A bookkeeping entry recording the reduction in an asset or an expense, or an addition to a liability or item of net worth or revenue; an entry on the right side of an account. Compare with **debit**. The balance of a liability, net worth, revenue, or credit account.

current asset   May be any one or all of the following: cash and items that are the equivalent of cash; inventories of merchandise, raw materials, goods in process, finished goods, operating supplies, and ordinary maintenance material and parts; trade accounts, notes, and acceptances receivable; receivables from officers, employees, affiliates, and others, if collectable within a year; installment or deferred accounts and notes receivable, if payment is to be received within the year; marketable securities; and prepaid expenses.

current liability   An obligation or short-term debt that will become due in the near future.

debit   A bookkeeping entry recording the creation of or the addition to an asset or an expense, or the reduction of a liability, credit account, or item of net worth or revenue; an entry on the left side of an account. Compare with **credit**. The balance of an asset, expense, or debit valuation account.

deposit   Currency, checks, or coupons presented to a bank by or for a customer for credit to his account.

depositor   One who makes a deposit or for whom a deposit is made.

depreciation   Lost usefulness; expired utility; the diminution of service from a fixed asset that cannot be restored by repairs or by the replacement of parts, caused by wear and tear from use, disuse, poor maintenance, obsolescence, or inadequacy.

discount on purchases   An amount allowed for the prompt settlement of a debt arising out of a purchase.

dishonor   To refuse to accept a check or other commercial paper in payment.

draft   A written order drawn by one party (drawer) ordering a second party (drawee) to pay a specified amount of money to a third party (payee).

earned surplus   Accumulated net income, less distributions to stockholders. Also known as **retained earnings**.

equity   Any right or claim to assets. An equity holder may be a creditor or a proprietor.

financial statement   A balance sheet, an income statement, a statement of application of funds, or any supporting statement of financial data derived from accounting records.

fixed asset   Any tangible item of the plant held for the services it provides in the production of other goods and services.

flow chart   A graphic presentation of operational sequences in the handling of materials or documents.

freight in   Freight charges paid on incoming shipments; treated as an item of the cost of the goods received.

goodwill   An intangible asset, such as the value of the company name, its reputation, or its location. Shown only when one company purchases another.

gross profit   Sales, less the cost of the goods sold and inventory losses, and before the deduction of selling, administrative, and general expenses, and income taxes.

income   Money, or its equivalent, earned or accrued during an accounting period that increases the total of previously existing net assets.

income statement   A summary of the revenues and expenses for an accounting period.

journal   A book of original entry in which a condensed record of each transaction is entered in chronological order.

journal voucher   A filled-in form that supports a noncash transaction. A file of journal vouchers may take the place of a general journal, or vouchers may be summarized periodically in the general journal.

ledger   A book of final entry to which the sums entered in the journals are transferred under account names.

liability   An amount owed by one person (a debtor) to another (a creditor), payable in money or in goods and/or services.

liquid asset   Cash in banks and on hand or a readily marketable investment. The term is somewhat more restrictive than **cash asset** and much more restrictive than **quick asset**.

long-term liability   An obligation that will become due after a year or more has elapsed. Examples: mortgages; mortgage bonds and debentures; secured-note issues; and funded debt generally.

margin on sales   See **gross profit**.

outstanding checks   Uncollected or unpaid checks that have been sent to the payees but have not cleared the drawee's bank.

perpetual inventory   Inventory kept in continuous agreement with stock on hand by means of a detailed record that could serve as a subsidiary ledger if dollar amounts as well as physical quantities are maintained.

petty cash   A relatively small sum of money on hand or on deposit, which may be used for minor disbursements.

petty cash voucher   A document that serves as authority to disburse petty cash and as evidence of payment.

physical inventory   The actual counting, weighing, or measuring of tangible items.

posting   The bookkeeping process of transferring dollar amounts and other information from a document or book of original entry to a ledger.

profit and loss statement   See **income statement**.

quick asset   A current asset convertible into cash within a relatively short period of time. Examples: a call loan, a marketable security, a customer's account, or a commodity immediately saleable at quoted prices on the open market.

register   A record of the consecutive entry of similar transactions, with space for notations of essential information that may be needed for future reference.

reserve for bad debts   See **allowance for bad debts**.

reserve for depreciation   See **allowance for depreciation**.

retained earnings   See **earned surplus**. A more meaningful term for use on the balance sheet.

revenue   Income from the sale of products, merchandise, and services; and earnings from interest, dividends, rents, and wages.

sales returns and allowances   Goods sent back to the seller, the amount being deducted from his gross sales.

sight draft   A draft payable by the drawee upon demand or presentation; distinguished from **time draft** or *acceptance*.

sole proprietorship   A business enterprise whose net worth belongs entirely to one individual.

subsidiary ledger   A supporting ledger consisting of a group of accounts the total of which is in agreement with a control account. Examples: customers' ledger, creditors' ledger, factory ledger, expense ledger, and departmental ledger.

surplus   Stockholders' equity in a corporation in excess of the par or stated value of capital stock. Always used with a qualifying adjective in the balance sheet.

tickler   A file or record of maturing obligations or other items of interest maintained in such a manner as to call attention to each item at the proper time. Examples: in a bank, the note tickler; in an insurance office, the policy-expiration or premiums-due tickler.

time draft   A draft payable within a specified time after acceptance by the drawee, usually thirty days.

treasury stock   Fully paid capital stock reacquired by the issuing company through gift, purchase, or some other means, and available for resale or cancelation.

trial balance A list of the balances, or of total debits and total credits, of the accounts in a ledger. Its purpose is to show the equality of posted debits and credits and to provide a basic summary for financial statements.

working capital Capital in current use in the operation of a business in excess of current assets over current liabilities.

16.2 BANKING

See Section 13.1 for information on banking.

ABA number The number assigned by the American Bankers Association to a bank. The top figures designate the city and state and the number of the individual bank; the bottom figures signify the Federal Reserve district and other routing symbols, e.g., $\frac{16\text{-}5}{1220}$. Only the bank number (16-5) is written on a deposit slip.

acceleration clause A contractual clause that provides that if interest or an installment is not paid when due, the entire debt becomes payable at once.

amortization The making of periodic payments to eliminate a debt. Each payment includes interest on the outstanding debt and a repayment of part of the principal.

bank discount The interest charge made by a bank on a loan or for converting commercial paper into cash before maturity.

bank draft An order by one bank on another authorizing the latter to pay a stated sum of money to the order of the person named in the draft.

bank statement The monthly statement supplied by the bank to checking-account customers.

callable loan A bank loan that may be repaid at any time by the borrower but that must be repaid upon the lender's demand.

canceled check A check paid by the bank and returned to its depositor. It is listed on the bank statement as a withdrawal from the account, and serves as the depositor's receipt from the payee.

cashier's check A check drawn by a bank on its own funds. A customer may purchase one of these checks for a fee in order to meet the demands of a supplier for such a check. Used especially in international trade.

certificate account A depositor may place a certain sum of money with the bank to be redeemed on demand or on a specified date. A certificate in the form of a passbook is issued stating the maturity date of the account. Penalties are assessed for early withdrawals of the principal. Interest may be withdrawn at any time. Terms vary from 90 days to eight or more years.

certified check The depositor's own check, which has been guaranteed as to the amount by the bank on which it is drawn. A fee is charged; and to stop payment on it, the maker must post a bond. Because funds have been set aside to cover the check, an unused one should be endorsed by the maker with the statement "Not used for purpose intended" and deposited in his account.

clearing house   A voluntary association of banks, usually citywide, to facilitate the settlement of interbank debits and credits. Besides checks, money orders, bond coupons, and other paper are cleared.

comaker   A person who signs a note or check of another and thereby also assumes responsibility for payment.

commercial bank   A general banking business primarily engaged in financing businesses on short-term or seasonal loans. It may also have savings and trust departments depending on the state law.

commercial credit   Loans made by commercial banks to business concerns for relatively short periods of time.

commercial draft   A written order by one party directing another party to pay a sum of money to a third party.

commercial letter of credit   The importer arranges for a sufficient amount of credit to meet his obligations on a certain purchase of goods. His bank notifies a bank in the seller's city by a letter of credit that credit has been established. The seller may then draw a draft and receive his money before he ships the goods.

correspondent bank   A bank in another location with which the local bank has established a working relationship to facilitate the handling of customers' needs. Often the local bank has established a line of credit or opened an account with the correspondent bank.

days of grace   Extra days within which to meet an obligation without penalty. Usually no grace is allowed on notes and bills.

deceased account   No transactions may be made in an account of a deceased person after the bank has been notified of the death. A bank is not liable in case checks clear the account before notification.

demand deposit   A deposit in a checking account that may be withdrawn at any time without previous notice. The majority of deposits are demand deposits, and no interest is paid on them.

deposits   The following items may be deposited in either savings or checking accounts: cash, checks, interest coupons, money orders, traveler's checks, drafts, and promissory notes.

direct deposit   A system whereby a depositor may authorize checks to be mailed directly to the bank or savings and loan for deposit in checking or savings accounts.

drawee   The person named in the draft who pays its amount to the drawer.

drawer   The person who draws a draft asking for payment.

endorsements   See Section 13.1 for a description of acceptable endorsements.

escrow   The delivery of funds or other security to a third person, such as a bank, to be held until the happening of some event or the performance of some act, under the terms of an escrow agreement.

estate taxes An excise tax on the right to transfer property from the dead to the living.

exchange rate The monetary rate at which one country can exchange its money for the money of another country.

excise taxes Federal, state, and local taxes imposed on acts rather than on property.

Federal Deposit Insurance Corporation (FDIC) A federal agency that insures bank deposits.

Federal Home Loan Bank System Savings and loan associations are members of this System.

Federal Reserve System The banking system established by Congress to provide an elastic currency and to unify banking. The United States is divided into twelve districts with a Federal Reserve bank in each district. These banks deal only with member banks.

Federal Savings and Loan Insurance Corporation A federal agency that insures deposits in savings and loan associations.

fee simple The absolute ownership of real property that the owner has the right to dispose of as he wishes.

foreign bill A commercial draft drawn in one state or country on a person or business in another state or country.

forged or raised check A check on which the drawer's name, the endorser's name, or the amount has been written by another in order to defraud. A bank is liable to a depositor for payment of a forged or raised check, if the bank is notified within one year after the return to the depositor of a forged or raised paid check.

frozen account An account in which no transactions may take place because of a court order or the demise of the account holder.

gift tax A federal or state excise tax on the transfer of money or property from one person to another without a return in money or other value.

gold certificates Certificates issued by the government and held by the Treasury or Federal Reserve banks; none are used by the public.

gold standard A monetary unit expressed as a weight of gold. U.S. currency cannot be redeemed for gold, because the United States went off the gold standard in 1933.

grantee and grantor The parties to a deed are (1) the grantor, who gives his interest in the property to the grantee, and (2) the grantee, who in return gives a consideration to the grantor.

Individual Retirement Account (IRA) A pension-type savings account held by (a) working individuals not covered by a retirement plan, or (b) those who wish to reinvest a lump sum distribution from a qualified retirement plan. Individuals under (a) may tax-shelter up to 15% of compensation not to exceed $1,500 a year. Those under (b) should consult their bank for the conditions under which a tax-sheltered IRA Rollover Account may be established.

inheritance tax Excise tax levied by states on the right of the living to receive property from the dead.

interest Payment for the use of another's money.

inter vivos trust A trust created by the grantor during his lifetime, also known as a living trust. The grantor or another person may be the beneficiary, and the trust may be either irrevocable or revocable.

investment bank A firm that buys large blocks of securities and sells them to the public in small amounts, thus supplying immediate capital to businesses.

investment trust A financial organization that sells shares of the trust to the public and invests the funds thus obtained in high-grade securities.

irrevocable trust An irrevocable trust occurs when the grantor gives away assets without any right to or control over the income and without the right of repossession of the assets. There is no right to alter, amend, or revoke the trust. Because their revocable trust is in the nature of a gift, gift taxes apply. The income earned by the trust fund is taxable to the trust.

joint account A checking or savings account in the names of two or more people. See **joint tenants** and **tenants in common.**

joint tenants Depositors who open a bank account as joint tenants may each deposit or withdraw from the account. If one of the depositors dies, the other is entitled to the balance of the account (the right of survivorship). Persons may also own other types of assets as joint tenants. (See also **tenants in common.**)

kiting The illegal practice of writing checks against a bank account in which there are insufficient funds to cover them but fully expecting to deposit funds to cover the amount drawn before the checks are presented to the bank for payment.

letter of credit A letter from one bank to another, or from a company to its bank or business associates, stating that a specified amount of credit has been established by the named person or company.

liquidity The maintaining of cash reserves against unforeseeable needs and as capital for future investment.

living trust An agreement whereby the trustor, while he is alive, engages a trustee to take care of his property on behalf of beneficiaries, who may include himself, or any other person, group, or organization.

loan The temporary use of another's money at interest, with repayment usually secured by a promissory note or a mortgage on real property.

medium of exchange Anything used as the basis for the exchange of goods or services. Money is the most frequently used medium of exchange.

member bank A national or state bank or a trust company that is a member of the Federal Reserve System.

money orders The purchase of a checklike form for a certain sum at a bank, post office, or telegraph office. Money orders are used for payments under a maximum set by the issuing institution. A fee is charged according to the amount of the order.

night depository   A lock-box of a type that permits a depositor to come to the bank after it is closed and drop his deposit in it. The bank then assumes the responsibility for safekeeping until its opening the next day.

notary public   A person commissioned by the state to administer oaths, certify to the genuineness of documents, witness signatures, and take acknowledgments.

note   A written promise to pay a specified sum of money on demand or at a named future date. It may be made payable to a person's order or to the bearer and thus becomes negotiable by endorsement. The payee may deposit the note with the collection teller at his bank, who will place the collected amount in his account upon receipt.

per stirpes   The distribution of the principal of a trust fund in accordance with ancestral lines. Grandchildren would receive the prorated share to which their parents had a claim.

pour-over trust   A person who has established a living trust may make provision in his will for the assets remaining at his death to "pour over" into the living trust.

private bank   A commercial bank, privately owned, that lends money to finance international projects in addition to the usual commercial banking activities.

promissory note   See **note**

protest   A formal notification that the maker has not made payment when due on a note, a draft, or other paper. A notary public or a responsible person in the presence of two witnesses may draw up the protest certificate that lists the facts in the case. A copy is served on all parties whose names appear on the instrument as drawer and endorsers. An endorser may write "Protest waived" above his signature if he is willing to assume liability should the drawer default.

reconciliation   See Section 13.1 for instructions for the reconciliation of a bank statement.

rediscount rate   The rate charged by the Federal Reserve banks for discounting commercial paper presented by member banks. The Federal Reserve banks set their own rediscount rates, subject to review by the Federal Reserve Board. The Board often uses the rediscount rate to control credit by raising the rate to limit borrowing and lowering it to encourage borrowing.

revocable trust   A trust containing the revocable clause may be terminated at any time or at a certain specified time. No gift tax applies at the time of creation because control is retained over the assets of the trust. The income tax laws regarding revocable trusts are very strict.

revolving letter of credit   A letter of credit issued by a bank to a traveler in return for cash or established credit at the bank in the amount stated in the letter. When the traveler presents the letter of credit to any of the listed foreign banks, he is entitled to draw checks or drafts against the credit. The amount of each withdrawal is entered on the letter until the full amount has been used. Any unused portion should be returned by the traveler to his account at the bank that issued the letter.

savings and loan association   A savings institution established primarily for the deposit and investment of savings and the loaning of money to builders and buyers of homes.

Self-Employed (HR-10-Keogh) Retirement Account   Any unincorporated, self-employed person may establish this account to provide tax-sheltered retirement benefits for the employer and certain employees. Withdrawals cannot be made earlier than age $59\frac{1}{2}$ and no later than age $70\frac{1}{2}$.

sight draft   Payment on this type of draft is immediate—at sight or on demand. These payment terms are stated in the draft when drawn.

stale check   An old check, usually one with a date more than six months old. Many banks refuse to honor a stale check.

stop payment   See Section 13.1 for the stopping of payment of checks.

straight loan   A short-term loan (three to five years) on real estate for a definite number of years at a specific interest rate. It is payable in full at maturity, but interest is paid periodically during the life of the loan.

tenants in common   Depositors who open a **joint account** as tenants in common may all make deposits, but the signatures of all tenants are required for withdrawals. At the death of one of them, the survivors are entitled to their share only, and the decedent's heirs are entitled to his interest. (See also **joint tenants**.)

testamentary trust   A trust fund set up in a will that takes effect upon the death of the testator. The major reason for its creation is to protect the beneficiary from his or her own inexperience. A simple testamentary trust clause might be stated as follows.

All the rest, residue, and remainder of my estate, I give, devise and bequeath to my Trustee, hereinafter named, IN TRUST, nevertheless for the following purposes and uses: To collect and receive the income and to pay or apply the net income therefrom not less frequently than monthly, to my beloved wife, Mary Smith, during her life. Upon her death my Trustee shall pay and distribute the principal remaining, if any, of said trust, equally share and share alike to my children, and to my children's children *per stirpes* for those of my children who are deceased.

time deposits   Savings and thrift accounts are time deposits and are not subject to withdrawals by checks. The record of deposits is kept in a passbook, or certificates of deposit are issued for the amount on deposit. These accounts earn interest.

time draft   A draft ordering payment at a certain time after receipt, acceptance, or date. The drawee writes "accepted," the date, the place payable, and his signature on the face of the draft. He usually has 24 hours to examine the goods and the papers attached to the draft and to decide whether or not to accept the draft and the merchandise.

title insurance   An assurance by a title insurance company that property is clear at the time of transfer. Such a company will make good to the beneficiary any loss, up to a fixed amount, sustained through defects in the title.

traveler's checks   Checks that must be purchased from firms such as the American Express Company, the Bank of America, the First National City Bank of New York, and Thos. Cook & Son. They are available in denominations of $10, $20, $50, and $100 for a fee. When purchased they must be signed in the presence of the company representative, and when cashed they must be signed again in the presence of the person who is accepting them in lieu of cash.

traveler's letter of credit   See **revolving letter of credit**.

trust   The holding of property by a trustee (a bank, trust company, or persons) who manages it for the benefit of the named beneficiaries. See **living trust, irrevocable trust, revocable trust,** and **testamentary trust**.

voucher check   A check with a detachable stub on which are listed the items for which payment is being made. A voucher is a receipt for or a proof of a business expenditure, and the stub of the check is considered to be a voucher.

warrant   In banking, a written order to pay money.

16.3   DATA AND WORD PROCESSING

A discussion of data processing and its uses in the office will be found in Section 5.1. Information on word processing can be found in Section 11.1.

access time   The time it takes a computer to locate information in storage and transfer it to the **arithmetic unit**.

address   An identification—name, label, or number—for the location of information in storage.

ADP (automated data processing)   A system of electronic machines so interconnected and interacting that there is minimum need for human intervention.

ALGOL (algorithmic language)   A system by which numerical procedures may be precisely presented to a computer in a standard form.

algorithm   A set of finite steps or processes for the solution of a problem.

analog computer   A computer that measures physical relationships in processing data, in contrast to a **digital computer**, which represents relationships numerically.

analyzer   A routine used to analyze a program written for the same or a different computer.

arithmetic function   The computational steps involved in data processing.

arithmetic unit   The portion of the hardware of a computer in which arithmetical and logical operations are performed.

artificial language   A language specifically designed for ease of communication in a particular area of endeavor.

assembler   A computer program that translates symbolic programming language into machine language.

asynchronous computer   A computer in which each operation starts as a result of a signal indicating that the previous operation has been completed or that the parts of the computer required for the next operation are available. Also, a computer that is able to go directly to stored data at any point in storage.

audio-response unit   A device that provides verbal replies to questions directed to the computer through a dial telephone input unit.

autocoder   A **symbolic coding** system for writing instructions that must be translated into **machine language** before they can be executed by a computer.

automation   A self-regulating process in which work is done with a minimum of human effort; also, the investigation, design, development, and application of methods of rendering processes automatic.

batching or batch processing   A technique in which a number of similar programs are grouped and processed during the same machine run.

BCD (binary-coded decimal system)   A system of representing decimal digits so that each appears as a combination of four binary digits (**bits**). For example: the number *thirty-two* is represented as *0011 0010;* whereas in a pure binary system, *32* is represented as *100000.*

binary coding system   A system having only two possibilities—on or off, yes or no, go or no go, open or closed.

binary number   A number of two characters or digits (usually *1* and *0*).

bionics   Knowledge gained from analysis of living systems applied to the creation of computer circuits.

bit (binary digit)   A single digit in a binary number that represents one digit of information.

block   Set of things, such as words, characters, or digits, handled as a unit.

block diagram   A schematic chart setting forth the detailed sequence of internal operations for the computer to perform. Used as a tool in programming.

block transfer   The movement of a group of consecutive words from one place to another.

BPS   Bits per second; method of measuring machine speed.

branch   Program movement to a step that is not the next sequential one.

breakpoint   A point in a computer **program** that permits a visual check of progress or some other analysis.

buffer   A device or system used to make two other devices or systems compatible; an area of storage temporarily reserved for use in performing an input/output operation.

card column   One of the vertical areas on a **punch card** in which a digit, letter, or symbol may be recorded. A standard IBM card has 80 columns; the Univac has 80 or 90; and the IBM System 3 has 96 columns.

card-punch machine   A machine that records data by punching holes in cards.

card read-punch unit   A device that reads information punched in cards into the processing unit of the computer. It also punches data that have been processed by the computer into the same card or a new set of cards.

card-to-tape converter   A device that converts information directly from punched cards to punch or **magnetic tape**.

card verifier   A machine used to check the accuracy of holes punched into a card. It is similar in appearance to a **card-punch machine**.

cathode-ray tube (CRT)   The cathode-ray tube makes it possible to display data stored in the computer on a video screen as part of the word processing equipment.

cell   A storage unit in a computer.

cell address   The number or symbol designating the location of a cell in which information is stored.

chad   The small pieces of paper that are removed when holes are punched in cards or tape.

character density   The number of characters that can be stored per inch.

character reader   A device that converts type fonts or scripts directly into **machine language**.

check bit   A bit used by the computer in checking its own accuracy in transmitting data.

check indicator   A device that indicates that an error has been made.

classifying   The process of coding similar types of data.

COBOL (*common business oriented language*)   A language used to present a business program to a computer.

coded program   A program expressed in the code or language of a specific machine. See **computer code** and **computer program**.

collator   A device used to collate or merge sets of cards in sequence.

common machine language   Information presented in a manner common to a related group of machines.

compiler   A special computer program that translates programs written in symbolic form to machine-language form. It can generate more than one machine instruction for each symbolic statement as well as perform the functions of a processor program.

computer code   A machine language used by a given computer.

computer program   A set of instructions and/or statements used by a computer in accomplishing a specific result.

configuration   Machines interconnected and programmed to operate as a system.

console   The part of the computer that provides information to the operator about the performance of the system and that is used to put information into the system manually, to alter content when necessary, and to start and stop the machine.

constant   An item of information, such as a total, stored in the computer in a fixed location and used repeatedly during the running of the program.

control board or panel   A removable grid or plate on which wires for controlling the computer must be assembled manually.

control sequence   The order of instructions to a machine.

correction seal   A small rectangle of tape placed over an incorrect punch to correct a minor error on cards used only once or twice.

CPU (central processing unit)   An electronic machine capable of receiving and storing instructions, receiving and storing data to be processed, transferring and editing data already stored, making arithmetic computations, making decisions of logic, and directing the action of the input and output units (synonym for computer).

crosstalk   Unwanted signals in a channel that originate from other channels in the same system.

cryogenics   The field of technology dealing with the properties of elements at very low temperatures.

cybernetics   The technology involved in the comparative study of information-handling machines.

cycle   The frequency with which any given set of data is processed.

data conversion   The changing of information from one form of representation to another.

data processing (or data handling)   The processing of source material containing basic information by classifying, sorting, calculating, summarizing, and recording.

d-character   The last character in computer instructions. Its function is to ask questions—Has the last card been processed? Is the page filled on which output is being printed? or, What is the definition of the operation being performed?

debug   The location and correction of errors in a computer program.

deceleration time (or stop time)   The elapsed time between completion of the reading or the writing of a tape and the cessation of its motion.

decision symbol   A symbol denoting the need to verify the existence or non-existence of a given condition and for determining future action.

decoder   A device that interprets a set of signals and initiates appropriate computer operation.

detail printing   A printout on the final computer report of all information on each card that entered the computer.

diagnostic routine (also called malfunction routine)   A procedure for locating computer **malfunction**.

digital computer   A computer that uses numbers in processing data. Compare with **analog computer**.

disk, diskette, floppy disk   See **magnetic disk or tape.**

down time   The time during which a computer is out of service because of mechanical or electronic failure.

EBDIC (extended binary coded decimal interchange code)   A code that converts two sets of four binary digits into hexadecimal code, unique to IBM/360 computers.

EDP   Electronic data processing.

EDST   Elastic diaphragm switch technology.

11 position (or "X" position)   The position immediately below the 12 position of a standard punch card.

EOF   *End of file* or the point of completion of a quantity of data.

equal sequence   An arrangement whereby the value of a particular **field** on one card may be equal to the value of the same field on a succeeding card.

erasable storage   Data stored on magnetic tapes, drums, and cores, and subject to alteration during the course of a computation.

error-detection routine   A routine used to detect whether an error has occurred in the internal or external transfer of information.

excess-three code   A coding system derived from the **binary-coded decimal** system, in which each decimal digit is represented by its binary equivalent plus 3. A fixed number of four **bits** is used to express each digit.

execution time   The time required to do a job.

fast-access storage   The section of storage from which data may be obtained most rapidly.

field   One set of positions on a punch card, tape, or disc that is always used to record similar data.

fixed-count coding   Coding in which a fixed number of **bits** (usually two) are moved. Computers using this coding system are primarily designed for numeric processing.

fixed-data area   An area of the computer set aside for information common to all processing requirements.

fixed word-length   A term describing data treated in units of a fixed number of characters or **bits** (as contrasted with variable word-lengths).

flow chart   A graph of the physical movement of data.

FORTRAN   A programming language for problems expressed in algebraic notation.

gigo   A term used to explain what happens when incorrect information is fed to the computer. It means "garbage in, garbage out."

global replace   A feature that allows a particular item or set of items to be changed throughout a document with a single instruction.

grandfather tape   Old information (from preceding processing cycles) retained as backup in case of future need.

graph plotter   An output device capable of displaying the results of a computation in graph form.

grouping   The process of bringing together related bits of information.

hardware   The physical equipment making up a data-processing system.

heuristic   Pertaining to trial and error as applied to the solution of problems.

hexadecimal   A base of 16 that requires 16 symbols to represent 16 number values. Hexadecimal code is used on IBM/360 computers.

high-order position   The position at the extreme left of a **field**.

high sequence   An arrangement whereby the value of a particular **field** in one card may be less than the value of the same field in another card following it.

hollerith code   A system used by IBM for representing data by rectangular holes punched in an 80-column card.

housekeeping routine   The initial instructions executed only once in a program.

IDP (integrated data processing)   A sequence of data-processing steps integrated into a complete system.

immediate access   A storage device that handles input or output data in a short period of time.

incremental computer   A computer in which changes in the variables are recorded rather than the variables themselves.

information processing system   The seven-step procedure of classifying, sorting, calculating, summarizing, recording, communicating, and storing information.

information retrieval   The recovery of specified information or data from a collection of records.

input   The original placement of data in the computer.

input media   The forms on which data to be processed are recorded.

instruction format   The order in which instructions are written for the computer.

instruction time   The time required by the computer to perform on instruction.

internal storage (or internal memory)   A data storage device that is an integral part of the computer.

interpreter   A machine that prints on a punch card the data already punched in the card.

iterative process   Calculation by means of a repeating cycle of operations.

key punch   A perforating device used to put information on cards or tape.

key sort   A method of processing data that uses cards with holes punched around the four edges. Notches are made in the holes and used as codes for sorting data.

language   Any set of symbols and the rules governing interrelations between the symbols that can be used to convey or represent information.

language translator   A routine designed to convert input in one language into equivalent statements in another.

loading routine   A stored routine for bringing other information into storage from cards or tapes.

logic function   The machine process of comparing numbers and testing the data being processed to ascertain that certain conditions have been met.

loop   The repetition of a group of instructions in a routine until certain conditions are reached.

low-order position   The position at the extreme right of a word.

low sequence   An arrangement whereby the value of a particular **field** in one card may be greater than the value of the same field in a succeeding card.

LPM   "Lines per minute."

machine language   A language designed for use by a machine without translation.

macro instruction   An instruction in symbolic language that is the same as a specified sequence of machine-language instructions.

magnetic disk or tape   A storage (input and output) medium on whose magnetized surface data are recorded.

malfunction   A failure in the hardware of a computer.

mark-sensed card   A special card, having 27 vertical positions, on which information is recorded by the use of a graphite pencil. Special equipment converts the pencil marks into punched holes.

master card   A punched card containing standard information that applies to a group of cards, such as program number and customer's name, address and code number.

matching process   A process whereby two decks of punched cards arranged in sequential order are compared. Unmatched cards are removed, and the two matched decks are either kept separate or collated in order.

media code   A special coding system used in WP to indicate the location of a document on media. It is placed usually on the same line immediately following the dictator's and the typist's initials.

media typewriter   A typewriter connected to a computer terminal so that as messages are typed they are stored simultaneously on media (paper tape, magnetic tape or card, cassette, or diskette) or directly into the computer memory. Each keystroke, space, tab, and carrier return is electronically entered on the media or sent over wires to the computer.

memory   That part of the computer that stores programs, intermediate results, and various constant data.

merging process   A process whereby two decks of punched cards arranged in sequential order are brought together in one sequenced set.

microsecond   One millionth of a second.

millisecond   One thousandth of a second.

minuend   The quantity from which another quantity is subtracted.

MIT   A "master instruction tape" on which all programs for a system of runs are recorded.

mnemonic operation code   A code that abbreviates the names of operations; e.g., *CLR* for "clear storage" and *SQR* for "square root."

Modem—modulator—demodulator A device that varies the characteristics of signals transmitted via communications facilities.

Monte Carlo method Repeated trial-and-error calculations used to discover the best solution to a problem.

move-and-edit function A process that edits data as they are moved from storage to the printing area of the computer.

multiple-address instruction An instruction consisting of an operation code and two or more addresses.

multiprogramming A technique used for the simultaneous handling of a number of programs.

nanosecond One billionth of a second.

9 edge The bottom edge of a standard punch card.

no-address instruction An instruction for an operation the computer can perform without referring to its storage unit.

nonerasable storage Stored information that cannot be erased during computation.

numeric code Numerical abbreviations used to prepare **input** information.

off-line equipment The peripheral or auxiliary devices not in direct communication with the **central processing unit** of a computer.

on-line processing The passage of information to the central unit as activity occurs through the input and output devices under the direct control of the central processing unit.

operand An instruction that designates the location or **address** of the data to be processed.

operating ratio Hours of correct machine operation in relation to the hours of scheduled operation.

optical-mark page reader A machine that senses marks made by pencil or pen on a specially designed form.

optical scanner A device that photoelectrically speed-reads data from a page directly into the computer.

optical scanning The reading of data into a computer through the use of magnetic ink or optical marks.

optimize To arrange the instructions or the data in storage for a minimum of time-consuming jumps or transfers when the program is run.

output The data processed from internal storage to printed sheets, cards, tapes, or some other output media.

overpunch The addition of holes to a card column that already contains one or more holes.

parallel storage The equally available storage of data, including all **bits**, characters, or words.

parameter A quantity to which different values may be assigned, which usually remains the same throughout a particular program.

parity (or odd-even) check A process that determines whether the number of ones (or zeros) in an array of binary digits is odd or even.

perforation rate   The rate at which characters, rows, or words are punched in a paper tape.

peripheral equipment   Auxiliary machines under the control of the central computer.

permanent storage   The storage of intermediate or final results usually in the form of punched cards or magnetic tape outside the computer.

pinboard   A control panel using jacks or pins instead of wires to control the operation of a computer.

PL/1   A programming language having increased capability and combining the best aspects of COBOL and FORTRAN. It is a single language that can be effectively used by both commercial and scientific programmers.

plus zone   The coded **bit** positions that represent the algebraic plus sign.

polyvalent number   A number made up of several digits, each digit representing one of several characteristics being described.

postedit   To edit the results of a previous computation.

post-mortem routine   A routine for analyzing the cause of a failure.

predicate   To affirm or deny, using mathematical logic.

probability   The likelihood of the occurrence of an event.

problem-oriented language   A language designed for the convenience of a problem statement rather than for easy machine instruction.

processor program   A program formulated by the computer manufacturer that may be used to translate a source program into a **machine language** program.

program   A set of instructions for solving a problem that directs the computer in its operations.

program chart   The form on which the program for a computer is written.

program language   The code used by programmers to write computer programs.

programmer   A person who plans the steps and the order of the operations for the solution of the problem and who **debugs** the program, if necessary.

programming   The process of planning and writing the program.

program register   A device in which the instruction of a program is stored.

propagated error   An error in one operation that spreads through and influences later operations.

punch card   A stiff card upon which data may be stored as punched holes.

punch tape   Paper tape on which data may be stored as punched holes.

random-access storage (or RAM for "random-access memory")   A storage device in which each record with a specific **address** may be reached directly.

raw data   Facts that have not been processed and that may or may not be in **machine language**.

read-in   To transmit external information to internal storage in the computer.

reading rate   The number of characters, words, **fields, blocks,** or cards transmitted by a sensing device per unit of time.

read-out   To transmit internally stored information out of the computer.

real-time   The processing of individual transactions at the time they occur rather than collecting them for future processing.

recursive   Repetitive.

repertory instruction   The set of instructions that a computer is capable of following.

rerun routine (or rollback routine)   A set of instructions designed to be used after a computer **malfunction** to reconstitute a routine from the last rerun point.

rounding error (or round-off error)   The error that results from rounding off a quantity by deleting some significant digits, e.g., 0.3853 can be rounded to 0.385 with a rounding error of .0003.

RPG (report program generator)   A fixed-form language for simplified programming that is then translated into machine language.

scanner   An instruction that automatically samples or interrogates various processes or files and initiates action as required.

scratch date   A calendar date assigned to any group of data, after which day the stored information may be destroyed.

secondary storage   Magnetic drums and tapes that are not part of the computer but are connected to and controlled by it.

sequential operation   A series of steps or instructions in a program that the computer will perform one after the other without interruption.

serial operation   Information flow through a computer in sequence using only one digit, word, line, or channel at a time.

serial programming   A computer operation that permits only one arithmetical or logical function at a time.

serial transmission   Data movement in sequence, one character at a time.

servomechanism   A device used to monitor and control an operation as it proceeds.

seven-bit alphameric code   A coding system that is an outgrowth of the binary-coded decimal system. Four **bits** are used to express the digits and two more bits to express alphabetic and special characters. The seventh bit is a **parity check**.

signal attenuation   Reduction in the strength of electrical signals.

signal-to-noise ratio   The relationship of information signals to random signals not conveying information.

skip instructions   Directions to a computer to proceed to another instruction in the storage portion.

software   Any of the specially prepared programs or routines designed to make most efficient the operation of a computer.

sophisticated vocabulary   Advanced or elaborate instructions requiring complex mathematical processes.

sorter (or sequencer)   A machine that sorts information into a particular order or into similar groups.

source machine   The computer on which the **source program** is translated into the object program.

source program   A program coded in other than **machine language**, which must be translated into machine language before use.

SPS (symbolic programming system)   A programming language using **mnemonic** substitutes for easier programming of operation codes and storage addresses.

statement   An instruction to the computer to perform some sequence of operations.

storage allocation   The reservation of blocks of storage for specific blocks of information.

storage cycle   The sequence of occurrences when information is transferred to or from the storage unit of a computer.

store   To place data in a location in storage so that it may be retrieved for later use.

stored-program computer   A **digital computer** that, under the control of internally stored instructions, can synthesize, alter, and store instructions as though they were data and can subsequently carry out these new instructions.

subprogram   A part of a larger program that can be independently processed or compiled.

subroutine   Instructions for carrying out a well-defined mathematical or logical operation that may be included in other programs requiring the particular operation.

subroutine library   A set of **subroutine** instructions kept on file for later use.

subscript   A notation used to specify a particular member of a series of items (not necessarily arranged in a meaningful pattern) when the name for the group of items does not identify each item.

symbolic coding   Writing programs in any language other than absolute machine language.

tape-to-card converter   A device that transfers information punched into paper tape or recorded on magnetic tape to punched cards.

tape-to-tape reproducer   A device that transfers information on paper or magnetic tape to other sections of tape.

telecommunications   The transmission of information between widely separated locations by means of electrical or electromagnetic systems such as telephone or telegraph.

terminating symbol   A symbol on the tape that indicates the end of a block of information.

test routine   Instructions designed to show whether a computer is functioning properly.

throughput   Term used in WP systems to refer to time taken to process typewritten work from author's dictation (input) and final distribution (output). See **turnaround time.**

time-sharing   An arrangement whereby more than one user share the same computer.

transducer   A device that converts a signal from one form to another.

transfer   To terminate one sequence of instructions and begin another sequence.

transfer check   A test process to verify that information is transferred correctly.

transfer operation   An instruction that moves information from one storage location to another.

trouble location problem   A test problem for locating faulty equipment.

turnaround time   The time elapsed between the beginning of a project and its completion.

12 edge   The term used to designate the top edge of a punch card.

12 position (or "Y" position)   The punching position nearest the top or **12 edge** of the standard punch card.

unconditional branch   An instruction that switches or branches the computer to another instruction, regardless of conditions.

Univac   A computer system manufactured by the Univac Division of the Sperry-Rand Corporation.

uptime   The time during which equipment is available for productive work.

utility   A standard program, usually provided by the manufacturer, that performs the functions commonly required by all computer installations, such as card-to-tape and tape-to-printer programs.

variable   A symbol whose numeric value changes from one run of a program to the next or changes within each run of a program.

variable word-length   Some computers accept machine words in variable word-lengths; others can accept only a fixed number of characters in each machine word. With variable word-length, the end of each word must be indicated.

verifier   A device on which a record can be compared as to identity, character by character, with a retranscription or copy.

word   A single character or a group of characters representing a complete unit of information.

word mark   A **bit** used to signal the beginning or the end of a **word**.

word originator   Term used in WP for the person who uses a dictating machine or telephone to transmit letters, reports, and other documents to the WP center.

word processing (WP or wp)   A program for improving the efficiency and effectiveness of business communications.

write   To transfer information, usually from main storage to an **output** device.

"X" position   See **11 position**.

"Y" position   See **12 position**.

zero position   The topmost printed digit position on a standard card. A punch in this position represents the digit *zero*. When used with another punched number, the zero punch represents a letter of the alphabet or a symbol.

zero suppression   The elimination before printing of nonsignificant zeros to the left of significant digits.

zone bits   The **bits** used in combination with digit bits in a **cell** to represent the letters of the alphabet as well as some special signs and symbols.

16.4   ECONOMICS

absolute advantage   The ability to supply a product or service at a cost lower than that of a competitor.

actuary   A statistician who determines the annual retirement of plants and equipment.

affluent society   A community in which most persons enjoy an abundance of material things.

arbitrage   The act of simultaneously purchasing foreign exchange, securities, commodities, or other goods in one market and selling them in another market at a higher price.

balanced budget   The equalization of revenues and expenditures.

bankruptcy   A legal declaration of the insolvency of individuals, partnerships, or corporations, discharging the debtor from his debts and assuring creditors of an orderly process of liquidation.

basic research   Scientific investigation undertaken for the advancement of knowledge, not gain.

book value   The net value of a corporation according to its accounting records.

budget deficit   An excess of expenditures over revenues.

capital budget   A company budget that involves the planning and controlling of capital expenditures.

capital goods   Goods needed in the production of other goods; e.g., factory buildings, machinery, trucks, and so on.

circular flow   The continual movement of money and goods in the economy.

circulating capital   Goods that can be used only at one time or over a relatively short period of time.

closed corporation   A corporation in which all or almost all of the stock is owned by a small number of people.

collateral   Property pledged to secure a loan.

commercial paper   The unsecured promissory notes of companies with a high credit rating.

commodity exchange   An association of traders who buy and sell contracts for the delivery of commodities.

convenience goods   Inexpensive items that the consumer purchases frequently near his home or place of business.

credit card   A card of identification that allows the purchase of goods and services and payment for them at a later date.

creeping inflation   Slow upward movement in the general price level.

depletion allowance   A tax allowance extended to the owners of exhaustible natural resources.

direct cost   A cost that can be identified with a specific unit of output.

discount rate (or rediscount rate)   The interest a Federal Reserve bank charges a commercial bank for a loan.

econometrics   The application of statistical and mathematical techniques in testing and demonstrating economic theories.

economic analysis or economic theory   A study of the cause-and-effect relationships of economic phenomena.

economic policy   A course of action based on economic analysis and influenced by political, military, and social policies.

economics   A systematic study of matters relating to the efforts of people to satisfy their wants by the use of goods and services. Such matters as the production, distribution, and consumption of goods and services are studied.

entrepreneur   A business operator who introduces a new product, a new productive process, or an improved organization and raises the necessary capital, assembles the factors of production, and sets up the management of a business.

equity capital   The total investment in a business of all its owners.

escalator clause   A contractual provision that requires the payment of automatic increases or decreases in the event of price changes.

escrow   A deed, bond, or other written document adopted by two parties and deposited with a third party for safekeeping, to be held until the grantee fulfills specific conditions.

excess-profits tax   A tax on corporate profits above a specified normal level.

fair-trade law   A state resale price-maintenance law that permits manufacturers to set minimum retail prices for their products.

fiscal year   The accounting year, which may start at any time in the calendar year.

fringe benefit   Nonwage benefits or payments to workers in addition to their wages, e.g., pensions, travel pay, vacation pay, health insurance, and so on.

frozen asset   An asset that is not readily convertible into cash or would be sold at a loss.

funded debt   The long-term indebtedness of a corporation or a government, usually in the form of interest-bearing bonds.

garnishment   A court order requiring an employer to pay part or all of an employee's wages to a court officer for the benefit of a creditor.

goodwill   The money value of the reputation of a company.

horizontal combination   The bringing under control of one company several firms engaged in the sale of the same product or similar products.

indirect cost   Any cost not consistently identified with a specific product unit.

installment credit   Credit in which repayment, including interest charges, is made by regular periodic payments.

limited liability   Restriction of an owner's loss in his business to the amount of his invested capital.

long-term forecast   A forecast that extends at least five years ahead.

macroeconomics   A study of the problems of the economy as a whole or a general equilibrium analysis of total employment, total production, business cycles, inflation, and the effects of changes in the rate of economic growth.

Malthusian theory   "The world's population increases faster than does the means of subsistence."

marginal cost   The additional cost of making one additional unit of output.

microeconomics   The study of the problems of individuals, firms, and industries; in other words, a partial equilibrium analysis concerned with only part of the total economy.

minimum wage   The lowest wage rate allowed by law.

mixed economy   A system composed of both unplanned economy and **planned economy** by a centralized authority, either public or private.

monetary system   The kinds of money used in a nation.

mutual company   A corporation without capital stock in which profits are divided among the members in proportion to the business that each has done with the company.

net worth   The excess of assets over liabilities, representing the equity, or values, of the owners' interest in the assets.

operations research   An analytic approach by a team or group to the study of the operation of a system or an integrated set of actions. It uses the talents of different specialists, utilizes mathematical analysis, seeks underlying principles, and forms conclusions that indicate the probable results of various courses of action. It is most useful in solving complex problems involving many factors that can be measured and described in quantitative terms.

overhead   A cost that a firm incurs for general and administrative expenses.

parent company   A corporation that owns the majority of the stock of another company, called its *subsidiary*.

planned economy   An economy in which some central authority or power sets the goals for production and allocates the available productive resources to uses that are intended to result in the attainment of those goals.

price control   Government regulation of prices of goods and services designed to stabilize the cost of living.

price-earnings ratio   The current market price of a company's stock expressed as a multiple of the company's per-share earnings.

profiteering   Unreasonably large profit-taking on the sale of goods and services.

profit sharing   A bonus for workers above their regular wage, based on a certain percentage of the profits of their employer.

profit squeeze   Reduced profits due to rising costs and stable prices.

proprietorship   An organization in which one individual owns the business.

quantify   To express in terms of number, force, or weight, or some other indication of measurement.

quantitative analysis   The use of descriptive statistics—the collection, organization, and presentation of empirical data in the form of tables and charts—and analytical statistics—the formulation of general relationships or conclusions from the data.

simulation games   The acting out of real-life business situations by management trainees to provide experience in the operations of a business.

soft goods (or nondurable goods)   Consumer items that last a short time, usually under three years.

stabilizer   An economic policy designed to control rapid upward and downward movements in the economy over the long run.

statistics   The collection, classification, and use of numerical facts.

symbolic reasoning   A system in which mathematical symbols and their manipulation are used to state and solve logic problems. Just as arithmetic can be put into verbal terms, so verbal logic may be represented by mathematical symbols.

tax-free carryforward   A provision permitting businesses and individuals to use the losses of one year to offset the income of succeeding years.

technological unemployment   The displacement of labor by machinery and improved methods of production.

time study   The determination of the time required by an experienced person, working at a normal pace, to do a specified task.

trademark   Any word, name, symbol, or device used by a manufacturer or merchant to identify his goods and services.

trusts   The control by a group of trustees of corporations whose stock certificates have been exchanged for certificates of the trust.

unemployment rate   The number of jobless persons expressed as a percentage of the total labor force.

variable cost   The cost of production other than fixed costs, such as labor and materials.

vertical combination   The corporate combination of several companies engaged in different steps in manufacturing or marketing a product.

16.5 GOVERNMENT

anarchism   A political doctrine advocating the overthrow of organized authority.

authoritarian   A term used to describe a dictatorlike government.

autonomy   Self-government.

balance of payments   The difference between a country's payments for imports and its receipts for exports.

balance of power   The strength of one group of nations equal to the strength of an opposing group.

bilateral agreement   An agreement between two parties.

bipartisan foreign policy   A foreign policy on which two political parties agree.

boondoggling   Wasteful use of public funds.

bossism   Control by political bosses.

bourgeoisie   Marx so denoted the middle class—proprietors, manufacturers, merchants, and so on.

brainwashing   Systematic indoctrination that tends to change or undermine a person's political beliefs.

buffer state   A state or country situated between two other states that lessens the danger of direct conflicts between them.

bureaucracy   Government by bureaus or departments; the excessive use of bureaus.

by-election   An election to fill an unexpired term.

capitalism   An economic system in which businesses for the most part are owned and operated for private profit.

caucus   A meeting of political party members to select candidates and plan campaigns.

censure   A resolution by a legislative body disapproving the actions of a public official.

checks and balances   The division of power among the legislative, executive, and judiciary branches of government.

civil rights   The individual rights guaranteed by the Constitution.

cloture rule   A parliamentary procedure to stop debate in order to secure a vote.

common law   Law based on custom, precedent, and tradition.

Congressional Record   An official publication of proceedings in Congress.

contraband   Goods that are banned for export or import.

coup d'état   Sudden overthrow of a government by force.

de facto   Actually existing.

de jure   By legal right.

détente   The easing of strained relations between states.

due process of law   Legal method for determining guilt in a criminal or civil offense.

eminent domain   The state's right to buy private property for public use.

extradition   Surrender of a wanted person by one state to another state where the person is suspected of committing a crime.

filibuster   A delaying tactic in Congress to prevent the passage of a bill.

franchise   The right to vote.

gerrymandering   Uneven apportionment of election districts used expressly to benefit a political candidate.

grass roots   The common people or electorate.

gross national product (GNP)   The total market value of a nation's goods and services.

imperialism   The policy of a nation seeking to extend its power, territories, or dominion.

incumbent   An officeholder running for reelection.

isolationism   Opposition to national involvement in international affairs.

legislation   An enacted law or the act of making laws.

logrolling   Vote trading among legislators to obtain passage of bills in which they have an interest.

mandamus   A court order to a public official to perform his duty.

mugwump   One who votes his conviction, regardless of party.

municipality   An incorporated town, borough, or city.

national debt   The amount owed by a nation.

nationalization   The transfer of private property to the state.

naturalization   The procedure by which an alien becomes a citizen.

nihilism   A revolt against all authority.

nonaggression pact   An agreement between two nations to refrain from the use of force against each other.

nonpartisan   Not supporting any of the regularly established political parties.

partisanship   The support of a political party.

pigeonhole   To file away.

pivotal state   A state with a large electoral vote that might swing the outcome of the election from one party to another.

plebiscite   The vote of the people on an issue.

plurality   The votes one candidate receives in excess of those received by his opponent.

precinct   A voting district.

pressure group   A group influencing legislators toward its own interests.

primary election   A vote in which party members choose their candidates.

proletariat   Wage earners with little or no property.

quorum   The fewest members of a body that must be present to transact business legally.

rapprochement   The reestablishment of good relations between states.

reapportion   To change the boundaries of districts within the state so that they are more equal as to residents.

referendum   Referral of legislation to the voters.

states' rights   The rights of individual states, as opposed to the rights of the Federal Government.

subpoena   An order to appear as a witness.

16.6 INSURANCE

See Section 13.3 for a discussion of business and personal insurance.

accident and health insurance Personal insurance that pays benefits for illness, accidental injury, or accidental death.

accidental-death benefit Also known as *double indemnity*. A clause in a life insurance policy that offers an additional amount in case of accidental death.

actuary A professionally trained person who works out the technical aspects of insurance and its mathematics, such as the calculation of premiums and the determination of risks, reserves, and other values.

adjuster One who acts for an insurance company in settling claims arising out of insurance contracts, by determining the amount payable for a loss.

agent A salesman for an insurance company or a single proprietorship that sells and services insurance from one or more companies to its clients.

annuity A contract that provides a given amount of income payable for a specified number of years at regular intervals, based on the previous deposit of a certain sum of money.

assignee The person to whom the interest in a policy is transferred.

assigner The person who transfers the interest in the policy.

automatic premium loan A provision in the policy that authorizes the payment of premiums from the loan value of the policy if payment is not made by the end of the grace period.

beneficiary The person named in a policy or a trust account to receive the benefits on the death of the insured or the depositor.

binder Notification from an agent to an applicant that his insurance is in force even though the policy is still to be issued.

blanket policy The coverage of an entire group under one policy.

borrower's protective insurance Insurance in the amount of an indebtedness of a debtor, payable to a creditor as the beneficiary.

broker A sales and service representative who sells insurance for several companies and handles many insurance needs for clients. May also be known as an **agent**.

business life or health insurance Policies issued on the life and health of executives to minimize the company's loss of the services of key personnel. The company is named as beneficiary.

cancelation The termination of an insurance policy before its expiration.

cash option When certain kinds of policies mature, the policyholder may elect to take an amount in cash in lieu of some other settlement.

cash surrender value The cash amount a policyholder would receive upon the voluntary termination of a policy before maturity or death.

casualty insurance Protection against loss from injuries to a third party for which the insured is responsible, such as automobile and public liability insurance; injury or illness to the insured himself, such as accident, health, hospital, and medical expense insurance; damage or loss to certain types of property owned by the insured, such as burglary, theft, and robbery insurance, and plate glass insurance.

claimant   The policyholder who presents a claim for a loss covered by an insurance contract.

coinsurance   An arrangement whereby property is insured for a certain percentage of its cash value in case of loss. If the owner does not insure up to this value, he becomes his own insurer by assuming part of the risk. Also, in the case of extremely expensive properties, two or more insurance companies might share the risk on the same terms and conditions.

common carrier's insurance   A policy to cover the liability of transportation companies for loss of, or damage to, cargo or property being transported by them.

credit insurance   A policy to insure wholesalers, manufacturers, and jobbers against excess or abnormal loss from credit accounts.

credit life insurance   A policy issued through a lender to cover the payment of a loan, installment contract, or some other obligation in the event of death.

declination   The refusal of a life insurance company to insure a person for reasons of health or occupational hazard.

deferred group annuity   The purchase of paid-up deferred annuities for each member of the group, who will receive the total amount purchased for him at his retirement.

dividend   A share of the profit paid to a policyholder in a participating insurance company.

dividend accumulations   The adding of dividends to the cash value of a policy.

dividend additions   The use of dividends to purchase additional insurance that is added to the face value of the policy.

effective date   The date on which an insurance contract goes into effect. Later known as the *policy anniversary date.*

endorsement   An amendment that changes the original coverage in some way either by adding or subtracting some feature.

endowment policy   A policy with an investment or savings feature whereby the holder pays in a certain sum that will be repaid to him after a certain number of years as a lump sum or in periodic payments. In case of death prior to expiration of the period, his heirs would benefit.

equity   The portion or value of a policy in excess of liens or other charges against it.

exclusions   Conditions in an insurance contract excluding coverage under certain conditions or in certain situations.

expiration date   The date on which a policy matures and no longer covers the conditions for which it was taken out.

extended coverage The addition of an endorsement or rider that extends coverage to include risks not already covered in the basic policy.

fidelity bond A policy or bond that an employer may purchase to insure himself against loss through the dishonesty of an employee in a position of trust.

floater policy The insurance of property that is changeable in quantity, value, and/or location.

general average A general charge made against parties who hold an interest in a cargo or ship that has been sacrificed for the common safety.

grace period A specified number of days after the premium due date when the insured may still pay without a penalty or loss of coverage.

group insurance Insurance covering a group of persons under one policy, e.g., group life, hospital and major medical, and so on.

HR-10 (Keogh Retirement Plan) A plan, approved by federal legislation, whereby self-employed persons can set up retirement programs and receive certain tax advantages. Available through insurance companies, banks, and mutual funds.

indemnify To make good a loss.

insurable interest In order for a contract to be enforceable, a person or business must have an insurable interest by being financially injured by the occurrence of the event insured against.

insurance examiner An employee of the state insurance department who audits and examines the affairs of an insurance company.

Keogh Retirement Plans See **HR-10.**

lapsed policy A policy that has been canceled because of nonpayment of the premium.

legal reserve The portion of its assets set aside by an insurance company to meet the liabilities on its policies.

liability insurance See **casualty insurance.**

loss-of-income policy An insurance policy that provides cash income if the insured is unable to work because of sickness or injury.

major medical insurance Insurance coverage of specific medical costs in addition to hospital costs.

maturity date The date on which a policy matures or proceeds may be paid out.

mutual life insurance company An insurance company owned and operated by the policyholders, and one that issues participating insurance.

ocean marine insurance Insurance that protects the owners of ships and cargoes against losses at sea or in transit.

paid-up policy One on which premiums have been paid in full.

participating insurance A contract that entitles the policyholder to receive dividends when the actual costs are lower than the premiums paid.

pension and profit-sharing plans An incentive plan set up by employers to reward employees through the creation of a retirement plan or other kinds of profit sharing.

policy A printed document that states the terms of an insurance contract and guarantees certain kinds of protection.

policy loan A loan by the insurance company to the policyholder on the security of the cash value of a policy.

preauthorized premium payment plan The arrangement by the policyholder with his bank for the automatic payment of premiums from his checking account.

premium The regular periodic payment that a policyholder agrees to make for insurance coverage.

premium loan A loan on the cash value of the policy for the purpose of paying premiums.

property insurance Insurance that protects property against risks, such as fire, flood, theft, and collision.

rider See **endorsement.**

straight life insurance A life insurance policy on which premiums are payable for life.

underwriting The study by underwriters of each application for insurance and the determination of whether the insurance company should assume the risk. Their main principle is to scatter or diversify risks so that no single loss can endanger the company's financial stability.

waiver of premiums A provision in the policy that keeps the insurance in force without payment of premiums if such a condition as disability occurs.

workmen's compensation The payment of funds to workmen injured on the job from liability insurance purchased by their employers as required by the Workmen's Compensation Law.

16.7 LAW

abrogate To abolish or annul (a law or custom) by an authoritative act; repeal; do away with.

abscond To go away suddenly and secretly; go off and hide.

abstract A short statement giving the main information of a larger treatise.

abstract of title A written summary of important facts concerning title to land.

acceptance Agreement by a person to be bound by the terms of an offer.

accessory (before, during, after the fact) One who aids a known felon.

accommodation endorser A person who signs negotiable paper for another to allow the other to receive credit.

accroach To exercise power without due authority.

acknowledgment Affirmation before a public officer that one has executed an instrument by his free act and deed.

acquiescence   Giving consent by failing to make an objection.

adjudicate   To determine by judgment after weighing the evidence and hearing the argument.

administrator   A person appointed by the court to administer the **estate** and distribute the property of a decedent who fails to leave a will.

affidavit   A statement sworn to before a notary public.

agent   One party acts for or in the place of another, called the *principal,* in doing business with third parties.

antitrust laws   Statutes that outlaw or control business practices that restrain trade and impede free competition.

appellant   A person who takes an appeal from one court to another.

apportionment   Division or distribution of proportionate parts.

artisan's lien   A legal right of a skilled worker to retain possession of something he has made or worked on until paid.

assignment   The transfer of a right.

attachment   Legal proceeding by which a creditor acquires a **lien** against a debtor's property as security for payment of any **judgment** he may recover.

attorney at law   A person licensed to practice law.

attorney in fact   A person designated in writing as an **agent**.

bailment   The delivery of personal property by the owner to another in **trust** for a specific purpose.

bankruptcy   The state of a person who is unable to pay his debts; a legal procedure whereby a bankrupt person is permitted to have available assets distributed to creditors, thereby releasing him from further obligation.

bilateral contract   A **contract** in which there is an exchange of mutual promises.

bill of exchange   An unconditional written order from one person to another, signed by the offeror, requiring the offeree to pay on demand, or at a fixed or determinable future time, a sum of money to order or to the bearer.

bill of sale   A written agreement transferring title to personal property.

binder   A written notation that is in effect only until the execution of the formal agreement.

bogus   Counterfeit, sham. A check drawn by a person on a bank in which he has no funds is called a *bogus check.*

brief   A discussion of the facts and points of law that are to be pleaded in court when a case comes to trial.

capacity   Competence to enter into binding contractual relationships. A minor or a mentally ill person lacks legal capacity.

chattel   Any article of personal property.

chattels real   Interest in land or a building for a limited time, such as a lease.

chose in action   A person's right to recover money or property from another by judicial proceedings. Such a right arises out of **contracts**, claims for debt, or rights against property. Stock certificates and notes are examples of choses in action.

circumstantial evidence Evidence that tends to prove a fact by proving related facts and thus establishing a reasonable basis for the occurrence of the fact in question.

civil Pertaining to the private rights of individuals and the legal proceedings connected with these rights.

claimant One who voluntarily makes a claim for justice.

codicil An addition to an executed last will and testament.

collateral Security placed by a borrower with a creditor to assure performance or reimbursement of the obligation.

collusion A secret alliance between two or more persons to defraud another or to secure something forbidden by law.

common law Law based on **precedents** stemming from previous court decisions.

compensatory damage Payment for loss in direct proportion to the amount of value lost.

complaint The allegations made by one who institutes a suit at law.

condemnation Taking of private property for public use.

conditional sale A transaction whereby the seller retains title and the goods are delivered to the buyer until some condition is performed. Upon payment of the purchase price or some other act, the buyer is given title. If the buyer defaults, the possession of the goods reverts to the seller.

condition precedent Condition that must be fulfilled before one becomes entitled to some right.

confusion of goods The intermingling of the goods of two or more persons by any of the owners so that the property of an individual owner cannot be separated.

consideration An item of value given in exchange for a promise.

contract A legal agreement between two or more persons made voluntarily in good faith and with **consideration**.

conveyance A written instrument by which title or interest in land is transferred from one person to another.

copyright An author's right, upon registration with the Federal Government, to publish, use, and sell his writings exclusively for a period of twenty-eight years, with the privilege of renewal for an additional twenty-eight years.

court of appeals A court that reviews the proceedings and findings of a lower court.

court of equity A court legally qualified to hear and act in equity cases— those based on the natural law of fairness and justice.

court of law A court governed by the rules and principles of common law— hears cases based on written law and prior court decisions.

covenant An agreement in writing under seal.

damages The monetary compensation that A must pay to B under a court ruling that A, by violating a legal duty owed to B, is responsible for B's loss or suffering.

deed   A written agreement by which an owner transfers his interest in land to a new owner.

de facto **corporation**   A corporation that fails to comply with one or more requirements of the incorporation law but is still recognized as a corporation in fact if not in law.

defalcation   Both **embezzlement** and misappropriation are included, but it is a broader term than either.

defamation of character   An attack upon the good name of a person; **slander**.

defective title   Title obtained by **fraud**, force, or fear, or other unlawful means, or the negotiation of such title in breach of faith.

defendant   A person who has been sued in a court of law.

de jure   By right and just title.

de jure **corporation**   A corporation that complies fully with the incorporation laws.

demurrage   Compensation for the delay of a vessel or railroad car beyond the time allowed for loading, unloading, or transit.

demurrer   A pleading that raises a question of law. It might be a motion to dismiss for failure to state a cause of action.

deposition   Testimony taken outside the court that is written and witnessed and that will be used if the case goes to court.

discharge   A court order to cancel, dismiss, or set aside the obligation of a **contract**.

dissolution   The stage at which a company or partnership ceases to exist as a legal entity.

documentary evidence   Written documents of all kinds, as contrasted to oral **evidence**.

draft   A written request by a person to a second person for the payment of a specific sum of money to a third party on demand or at a future time.

duress   Compelling by threat or imprisonment a person to enter into a **contract** or perform some act.

earnest money   Money given by one **contracting** party to another to bind the bargain.

easement   The right to use the land of another.

ejectment   Action to recover the possession of real property.

embezzlement   Fraudulent appropriation by a person of the property entrusted to him.

eminent domain   The right of the Federal Government or a state, county, city, school, or other public body to take private property for public use upon payment of just compensation.

enjoin   To command or forbid by **injunction**.

escheat   The return of property to the state, when no one makes a claim thereto.

estate   An interest in property.

estate in fee simple An inherited **estate** in which the owner may use the entire property with unconditional power of disposition during his life and passing to his heirs upon his death intestate.

estoppel The legal principle that says a person is legally barred, because of his prior conduct, from asserting certain facts or doing certain acts.

evidence Any factual data that is presented to a trial court as a means of ascertaining the truth, such as through witnesses, objects, documents, or records.

executory contract An agreement that has not yet been executed because something still needs to be done.

exemplary damages The awarding of **damages** beyond actual loss to punish and make an example of the offender.

feasance The doing or performing of a condition or duty.

fiduciary relationship A relationship involving a high degree of trust and confidence. One who holds goods in **trust** for another or one who holds a position of trust and confidence has a fiduciary duty.

fixture Personal property that is annexed to realty and thus becomes part of it.

franchise A privilege or right granted by a government, a manufacturer, or a corporation.

fraud In contract law, the making of false and misleading statements to induce another to enter into a **contract**.

garnishee To attach a person's property or wages and hold them until the results of a law suit are known.

guarantor One that signs a guaranty that is a promise to answer for the debt, default, or miscarriage of another.

hearsay evidence Evidence given by a witness who testifies about information learned from another person and not from his own knowledge.

holder in due course The holder of a bill, note, check, or other **negotiable instrument** who is legally entitled to receive payment.

hypothecate To pledge without delivery of title or possession.

inchoate Recently begun but incomplete. **Contracts** are inchoate until they are signed.

indictment A written accusation by a grand jury charging a person with the performance of an act that by law is a public offense.

injunction A court order **enjoining** a person from doing a particular act that will be detrimental to another.

interpolation The act of inserting new words in a document.

irrevocable Unalterable.

judgment A decision by a court.

jointly and severally Pertaining to several defendants who may all be sued simultaneously or each separately as the plaintiff desires.

kite To issue or negotiate worthless paper and then redeem it with the proceeds of similar paper.

libel   Anything written, printed, or published that is intended to expose another to public hatred or ridicule.

lien   A legal right to retain the goods of another until certain conditions are satisfied.

limited liability   Under corporate law, a stockholder is liable for the debts of the corporation only to the limit of the amount he paid or agreed to pay for his shares of stock.

liquidate   To clear up the affairs of a **bankruptcy**; to close out a business.

litigate   To contest a suit in court.

malfeasance   The performance of an unlawful act.

malice aforethought   A predetermination to commit a wrongful act toward some person.

mandamus   A writ issued by a court directing the performance of specific acts.

misfeasance   Improper performance of a lawful act.

mitigation of damages   A reduction in **damages** because of extenuating circumstances.

negligence   Failure to exercise proper care.

negotiable instrument   An instrument such as a promissory note, bill of exchange, check, or security that may be transferred freely from one person to another by endorsement and delivery or, in some cases, by delivery alone.

nominal damages   A small sum given for the violation of a right where no actual loss has resulted.

nonfeasance   Omission or failure of an **agent** to perform some distinct duty or obligation that he has agreed to do.

nonsuit   Failure to establish a case in court.

offer   The communication of a proposal by the offeror (the person making the offer) to the offeree (the person receiving the offer).

overt   Open; public.

patent   A grant by the Federal Government to the inventor of a new device, not previously patented, of exclusive right to reproduce, use, and sell the device for 17 years.

pecuniary damages   Monetary **damages**.

plat   A map or drawing showing the dimensions and locations of sections of land.

pleadings   The exchange of legal documents by the parties to a lawsuit—plaintiff's complaint and **defendant**'s answer.

pledge   The offer of personal property as security for the payment of a debt or the performance of an obligation.

power of attorney   A document authorizing another to act as one's attorney.

precedent   A previous decision that may be relied on in the deciding of similar or analogous future cases.

prerogative   An exclusive or special right or privilege.

proxy   Authority to act for another in some matter.

punitive damages   More than ordinary **damages**.

quasi-legal   A matter that has some legal implications but is not genuinely legal.

quo warranto   A proceeding in court used for trying title to a corporate or other type of **franchise**, or to a public or corporate office.

ratification   The approval of an act that previously had not been binding.

recrimination   A countercharge against the accuser.

replevin   An action used to recover the possession of goods unlawfully taken or held.

rescission   The cancelation of a **contract** and the restoration of each party to his original position.

restraint of trade   Business practices that tend to interfere with free competition.

revocation   The recall of some power or thing granted.

set-off   In a suit for **damages** when both parties owe something to the other, the amount recovered is reduced by the respective debt.

slander   The speaking of defamatory words tending to prejudice.

solvent   Able to pay all that is owed.

sound and disposing mind   The normal condition of the mind. A phrase usually found in a will to indicate the testator's competency.

statute of frauds   A statute that calls for **contracts** and certain agreements to be in writing, in order to be enforced in court.

statute of limitations   A statute that imposes a time limit on when an action may be instituted in certain cases.

subpoena   A process that compels a witness to appear and give testimony.

subrogation   The substitution of one person for another, who then succeeds to the other's debt or claim.

surety   A promise to answer for the debt of another.

tort   A **civil** wrong other than a breach of contract.

transcript   An official copy of the original proceedings in a court trial.

trust   A relationship between persons by which one holds property for the use and benefit of the other.

turpitude   Anything done contrary to right, honesty, or modesty.

ultra vires   An act or **contract** that a corporation has no legal power to do or make.

undue influence   Influence that destroys free will and substitutes the will of another.

unilateral contract   A **contract** in which only one party makes an offer or promise of performance.

usury   An excess interest charge for the use of money; interest charged above the rate allowed by law.

venue   The place in which a case is to be tried.

verdict   The decision of the jury or of a judge acting without a jury.

waiver   The voluntary relinquishment of a known right.

writ of attachment   A writ issued for the seizure of property pending court action.

16.8　MARKETING

ad valorem　A term applied to duty on imports or exports based on their value.

advertising agency　A professional organization that prepares and places copy in media for an advertiser.

advertising copy　The text of an advertisement written as an attempt to influence prospective buyers.

advertising media　Newspapers, magazines, radio, television, direct mail, throwaways, and billboards that present advertising copy to potential buyers.

bill of lading (or B/L)　A receipt and contract from a **common carrier** for the transportation of goods.

brand name　Words or letters that identify a seller's product.

break-even point　The volume at which a seller covers all his costs but makes no profit.

buying habits　Recognizable patterns that indicate how people buy.

buying motives　Reasons for buying goods and services.

buying power　The total purchasing power of consumers in a particular product area.

buyer's commission　A percentage payment given to an agent for negotiating the purchase of merchandise.

carload (c.l.) rate　Freight charges for a full carload of freight; lower than the less-than-carload rate.

cartel　An agreement among foreign businesses to regulate competition and fix prices.

cash discount　A discount allowed a buyer for paying his bill within a specified period of time.

caveat emptor　"Let the buyer beware"; implies purchase at the buyer's own risk.

cease-and-desist order　Usually refers to a restraining order issued by the Federal Trade Commission to cease questionable marketing practices.

central merchandising　Chain-store buying by a central office, which then distributes the merchandise to its individual stores.

certificate of origin　A certificate attached to a draft covering the shipment of goods, testifying to the origin of the material or labor used in producing the merchandise.

c.o.d. (cash on delivery)　Upon the delivery of goods, the buyer must make immediate payment to the bearer.

commissary　A company store.

commodity exchange　A market for buyers and sellers of certain commodities.

common carriers　Transportation companies that offer services for hire to the general public.

consignee　The receiver of a shipment of goods.

consignor   The one who ships goods to a **consignee**.

consul general   The top official appointed to a foreign country to facilitate the affairs and trade of the country sending him and to look out for the commercial interests of its citizens.

consumer cooperative   An organized collective association that buys goods for resale within the group.

consumer goods   Products used by the consumer without further processing, e.g., tools.

consumer research   The analysis and classification of **buying habits, buying motives,** and other important data for the purpose of determining the consumer's willingness and ability to buy a product.

copy testing   A survey made to test the selling power of advertisements.

corporate chain   A group of branch stores that are controlled by the parent organization.

cost price   The actual price paid for a commodity or product.

customhouse   The building where customs and duties are paid and where vessels are cleared.

customs inspector   A person who inspects vessels and reports violations of neutrality laws to the customs collector of the port.

damageable   Capable of being broken or disfigured and thus being reduced in value.

declaration   A full report of goods so that duty or taxes may be determined.

demurrage   A freight charge levied against a receiver of goods when he fails to unload a freight car within a specified time.

departmentalizing   Organizing units in the company according to product lines.

depth interview   A probe into a respondent's attitudes or opinions.

discount house   A retail store where merchandise is sold below the usual price.

distribution cost-analysis   A study of the costs or the profitability of various distribution methods.

e.o.m. (end of month)   A term used in the processing of invoices.

exclusive agent   One who has the exclusive selling privileges for a product or products in a designated territory.

Federal Trade Commission (FTC)   The federal agency that deals with unfair marketing practices.

f.o.b. (free on board)   A term that indicates that the merchandise has been delivered to the carrier without extra charge to the buyer.

franchise agreement   A contract between a manufacturer and a **jobber** or a **retailer** that sets forth the responsibilities of the **exclusive agent**.

freight forwarders   **Middlemen** who consolidate **less-than-carload** shipments into full carloads, thereby taking advantage of special **mixed-car rates** and offering better service to the shippers.

futures contract A **commodity exchange** transaction that involves delivery at some specified future date.

futures trading The buying and selling of **futures contracts**.

grade labeling A letter or number placed on the product label to indicate the quality of the contents.

group buying Cooperative buying by independent stores.

hand-to-mouth buying The practice of buying only enough merchandise to serve immediate needs.

information aggregation A method of maintaining two types of detailed information in the **system** data files. Micro data maintenance is concerned with individual items whereas macro is concerned with the mass of data and what it shows as trends, share of the market, six-month reports, and so on.

information recency The time between the occurrence of an event and the inclusion of data describing that event in the **system**.

jobber (or wholesaler) A **middleman** who buys goods in bulk from a manufacturer or importer for resale to **retailers**.

less-than-carload (l.c.l.) rate The freight charge for shipping less than a carload of merchandise; usually higher than the **carload rate**.

loss leaders Items sold below cost to attract trade and increase traffic in a store.

markdown A reduction in the selling price of an item.

market analysis An investigation of the market to determine the quantity of the product that might be sold in it.

market information system A continuous arrangement for collecting market facts about operational areas, such as advertising, distribution, **market research**, product development, and sales.

marketing concept The coordination of the entire marketing process with production, finance, accounting, statistical control, and personnel.

marketing fundamentals Five interrelated marketing functions: product design, manufacturing, advertising and sales, physical distribution, and billing and collection.

marketing mix Involves the integration of product planning, pricing, distribution, and promotion.

market potential The expected sales for a particular product in a given area during a particular period of time.

market research The identification of the firm's customers, its trading area, the consumers' desires and attitudes, the sales potential for the industry and the firm, the effectiveness of a sales promotion program, and the most profitable channels of distribution.

markup The difference between the cost price of an item and its selling price.

media Includes newspapers, magazines, trade journals, radio, television, billboards, handouts, throwaways, or any other means by which a manufacturer or retailer may advertise his product to the buying public.

merchandise control   The analysis of sales, inventory, and prices in order to establish a profitable relationship between inventory and sales.

metropolitan area   A central city and its suburbs.

middlemen   The persons or organizations who buy in bulk from producers and sell to **retailers** or consumers.

mixed-car rate   The freight charge that a shipper pays for shipping a full car of several commodities to the same destination, somewhat less expensive than the combined **less-than-carload rate.**

motivation research   The study of people's behavior in order to understand their preferences, buying habits, and so on.

open system   One that receives and sends out messages, such as a business organization that interacts with customers, competitors, labor organizations, suppliers, and government agencies.

piggyback service   The practice of hauling loaded truck trailers on special railroad flatcars in order to reduce freight handling and increase speed of delivery.

premiums   Coupons, trading stamps, box tops, or gifts of merchandise or cash given with the purchase of goods.

price discrimination   An unfair trade practice in which varying prices are given to different buyers and are not based on differences in manufacturing, selling, or delivery costs.

price fixing   The agreement among competitors, a monopoly, or a government agency on a set price for a product.

private brand   A name that is owned and sponsored by a **jobber** or a **retailer.**

product line   The group of similar products that a manufacturer has for sale.

product research   The study of a product to determine if it will meet the demands of the consumer market.

promotions   Special endeavors to sell the product, such as special TV exposure, free samples, refund coupons, and demonstrations, which supplement the regular advertising campaign.

raw materials   The unprocessed products of farms, forests, or mines used in the manufacture of products.

receipt of goods (or r.o.g.)   A term that means that the **cash discount** period begins on the day the goods are received by the buyer, not on the date the goods are shipped.

resident buyer   A buying organization located in a central wholesale market to serve clients who are too far away or too small to have buyers in the market at all times.

retailer   A merchant **middleman** between the manufacturer and the customer or between the **jobber** and the customer.

retail trade A general term that includes all the activities of businesses primarily engaged in selling merchandise for personal, household, or farm consumption.

sales analysis The study of the sales records of a company.

sales forecast The prediction of the amount of sales during a particular period and/or from a given area.

sales potential The share of the total market that a company hopes to corner.

sales quota A goal set to encourage a salesman or a sales force to equal or exceed a predetermined level of activity.

sales territory A defined geographic area that is assigned to a salesman, branch office, or manufacturer's agent.

shopping center A concentration of small retail establishments outside the central business district.

short sales A contract made by a seller promising future delivery of goods he does not yet have.

specialty store An establishment that sells only one class of goods.

speculation The sale and/or purchase of inventory or **futures contracts** for the purpose of making profits from price changes.

standardization The establishment of grades for different classes of products.

stock control The maintenance of a profitable relationship between inventories and sales by the budgeting of inventories and purchases.

stock turnover The ratio of sales to average inventory.

survey method The use of questionnaires to gather market data.

system An on-going process or a set of objects with a given set of relationships between the objects and their attributes.

systems analysis A decision-making process of systematically investigating objectives; comparing the costs, the effectiveness, and the risks associated with alternative policies or the strategies for achieving them; and formulating additional alternatives, if necessary.

terms of sale The conditions of sale, excluding price, that accompany a price quotation.

trademark A name, design, or symbol used by a merchant or manufacturer to identify his goods and distinguish them from those made or sold by others.

variable-price policy A pricing policy whereby the purchase price is determined at the time of sale.

variety stores Retail stores that carry a large variety of low-cost merchandise.

vertical integration The single ownership of production and marketing facilities.

warehouse receipt A document issued to the owner of goods stored in a warehouse. Usually, the receipt may be used as collateral for a loan.

zone pricing A pricing method whereby all buyers located within a given geographic area pay the same price for goods.

16.9 PERSONNEL

ability   The capacity to perform; includes such things as attitudes, personality, configuration skill, education, and knowledge, and skills gained from experience.

accident proneness   The tendency to have more than the average number of accidents.

arbitration   The settlement by a third party of a **grievance** between an employee and his employer or between the union and the company.

attitude survey   A questionnaire survey that attempts to find out how an employee feels about his job, his **supervisor**, company policies, or the company as a whole.

authority   The right to proceed on one's own cognizance, or the power to command others in order to further departmental or company purpose.

bargaining   A meeting between a group representing the workers and a group representing management to talk things over and to make compromises in an effort to settle problems or to secure acceptance of proposed changes.

blue-collar workers   Factory workers or manual laborers.

brainstorming   The process of expressing ideas as they occur without evaluating their appropriateness as possible solutions to a problem.

bumping   The seniority principle that allows a person released in one department because of low seniority among the workers there to displace a worker in another department with less seniority.

by-passing   The process of ignoring intermediate worker or supervisory levels and going to a higher or lower level for a decision or information.

centralization   An organizational policy that states that almost every decision must go through many levels for approval.

change   The phenomenon of constant introduction of new technology, processes, ideas, and so on, which cause a shift from the present condition.

clerical workers   Those employees who work mainly with routine tasks involving forms, ledgers, and periodic reports, reproduced by hand, on the typewriter, or on some other office machine; a **white-collar worker**.

communication downward   Information passing from the top level or from some lower rung of management through all subsequent levels to the lowest **subordinate**.

communication upward   Messages from lower levels being passed up through all supervisory levels to top-level management.

conference   A meeting of persons with similar interests who come together to discuss mutual problems and who tend to contribute to the discussion. Conferees usually come from a number of companies or from different departments within a company.

decentralization   A policy whereby interrelated jobs are grouped in order to complete the total operation. The workers are given autonomy to make decisions as they coordinate the effort and cooperate in reaching the goal.

delegation of authority   The delegation by a superior to a **subordinate** of the right or freedom within specified limits to solve a problem or to proceed on an assignment.

discipline   Corrective action taken to maintain standards of performance. Progressive discipline calls for increasingly severe penalties—an oral warning followed by a written one, then disciplinary layoff, and finally discharge.

distortions downward   Messages are subject to changes or distortions as they move downward if subtle shades of meaning are involved.

downtime   The pay a worker receives when unable to earn the regular incentive pay because of a breakdown in machinery or placement on a special assignment.

fatigue   The product of chemical and physical changes in the nerves and muscles of the body that make it difficult to continue work.

featherbedding   The requirement by the union of unneeded workers or the slowdown of workers to stretch the job out.

feedback   Messages that management receives from workers about their performance, understandings, insecurities, confidence in the company, and so on. Also refers to the ability of certain systems to check on their own performance and to correct it, if necessary.

first-line supervisor   The foreman or **supervisor** whose **subordinates** are production workers, office people, engineers, and so on, who are doing the actual work of the organization.

flow charts   Charts or drawings that plot the progress of a product through the plant from raw material to finished product. They may also be used to show the progress of a piece of paper or a report.

fringe benefits   All of the employee benefits—insurance, holidays, paid vacations, overtime pay, pensions, and so on—provided by the employer in addition to direct-wage payments.

grapevine   A flexible informal system of communications among employees of a company for the passage of information by word of mouth.

grievance   A complaint by an employee who disagrees with the **supervisor**'s decision in any matter concerning him/her, personally. A **grievance** may be filed claiming that management is acting in violation of either the contract or of past practice (the equivalent of the contract).

group cohesion   Unity; a group of workers may have a greater or lesser degree of unity or cohesion in adhering to group standards.

group norm   The standards of attitudes or common points of view adopted by a group of people working closely together that are shared by each member of the group. These attitudes may have no basis in fact but are accepted by the group as facts.

group standards   The standards of behavior set up by the group to which each member is pressured to conform.

human relations   The human aspect of management that attempts to understand people and help them to work together to accomplish company objectives.

incentive pay   Payment in addition to a basic wage for production exceeding a stated quota. Used in mass-production industries where the work is standardized, the units of output are measurable, and the quantity of output is proportional to employee effort and attention.

industrial relations   The area concerned with the relations between a worker and the boss. Another term for *personnel management*.

interview   Primarily thought of as the initial meeting between a prospective employee and a member of the personnel department. A meeting between a worker and a superior for a variety of reasons, the purpose being to draw the worker out, to discover what he really wants to say, and to give him a chance to express himself fully.

job classification   Jobs with roughly similar requirements of experience, training, and skill, or with similar types of tasks, are grouped as a job classification or labor grade. Each job within the classification receives the same rate of pay.

job description   A list of the duties and responsibilities of a job.

job evaluation   A method of determining the relationship between wage rates that enables management to determine how much one job should pay relative to others.

job specification   A statement written from the job description of specific qualifications needed by the individual who will fill the job. Such things are included as knowledge, experience, judgment, initiative, manual dexterity, accuracy, physical activity, strength, and years of schooling.

management development   A continuing program of training designed to help all managers perform more adequately on their present job and to prepare for more responsible positions.

merit increases   Increases in salary above the minimum rate set by the job evaluation as recognition of outstanding performance.

merit rating   A periodic review of a worker by the **supervisor** on a merit-rating form on which are summarized the employee's strong and weak points. A merit-rating interview is usually held by the supervisor with the employee to communicate the results of the merit rating.

micromotion charts   Slow-motion film of a worker performing a task is analyzed on micromotion charts, in order to discover the number and complexity of motions.

mobility   The ability of a person to move upward in a company or to move from one job to another.

motion study   The determination of the most efficient method of production; industrial engineering. The motion study of individual workers involves an analysis of how the job is performed today, whether steps may be eliminated or combined, and how the job might be performed more quickly and easily.

motivation   An attempt to encourage **subordinates** to perform more effectively and efficiently in a situation in which they can satisfy their own **needs** while working toward the goals of the company.

needs   Every worker desires or needs certain things for his own fulfillment; he may need money, advancement, security, a sense of accomplishment, a sense of creativity, productiveness, a certain amount of autonomy, knowledge, and certain social needs.

negative transfer   The negative effect on present learning because of previous learning.

nondirective interview   An **interview** in which the interviewer encourages the interviewee to express his own thoughts with considerable freedom—contrasted to directive interviewing in which the interviewer asks questions and keeps the discussion within certain limits.

open-door policy   A policy whereby every employee may walk into the office of any manager at any level to voice his complaints.

open-end question   A question that allows and encourages a respondent to answer in his own words.

operations chart   A diagram of the manner in which an operator performs his task and that indicates what he does with each hand. An attempt to understand the motion involved in the performance of a task in order to simplify, substitute, or rearrange the motions.

organization man   A person deeply involved in the company and its goals, who intends to stay with it and work his way up.

Parkinson's Law   The tendency to expand work to fill the time available.

paternalism   A situation in which management emphasizes how much it has given its employees, thus implying that employees might lose these benefits if they fail to show proper appreciation.

pension   An allowance for past services.

perception   The perceiving of a situation according to one's prejudices, stereotypes, and past experiences or beliefs.

power test   A test designed to measure ability that is not limited in time.

process chart   An analysis of the steps taken during the progress of a product or a piece of paper by the use of special symbols to highlight the various steps.

professional   A person who has specialized and lengthy training in a recognized field and who adheres to a code of ethics advocated by his own profession or by professionals in general. Some established professional groups are engineers, doctors, lawyers, economists, accountants, and educators, who identify themselves with a national organization that promotes high standards of performance and behavior and lengthy training as a prerequisite to membership.

profit sharing   A bonus paid to workers based on a percentage of the company's profits beyond some fixed minimum.

rate busting   The outcome when a worker ignores the level of output established by the work group and produces at a level substantially above the agreed-on ceiling.

rate range   Instead of a single wage or salary rate for the job, the company establishes a wage range that is divided into a series of steps. Rate ranges normally overlap with the highest step in one **job classification,** paying more than the lowest step in the next job classification.

recruitment   The active search for employees to fill jobs and positions at all levels.

role playing   The technique of acting out parts as one would in a real business situation.

sensitivity training   A group situation in which the discussion centers on what is happening within the group itself. Each person is helped when he becomes aware of how he actually does behave so that he can decide how he should behave.

span of control   The number of workers and/or departments for which a **supervisor** is responsible.

specialization   The breaking down of a single job into several separate jobs and the restricting of an employee to a single task.

staff   The *staff* employee provides advice and information to the supervisor; the *line* makes decisions.

status   A certain standing within a company that is measured by title, pay, the type of work performed, symbols, size of office, secretarial assistance, and other factors.

subordinate   A person who is responsible to a higher level of supervision. Every company employee is subordinate to someone; the president is subordinate to the board of directors and the board of directors is answerable to the stockholders.

supervisor   The person who directs the activities of a group of workers.

symbolic meanings   Meanings attached to a word that are different from person to person; no clear-cut definition is accepted by everyone.

tests   A means of measuring the qualifications of job applicants as well as candidates for transfer or promotion.

time study   A means of determining the standard output of a worker within a given period. These standards aid the **supervisor** to allocate work fairly, to judge performance, and to estimate costs. They also serve as the basis for piece-work and incentive plans. Time studies are often made in conjunction with **motion studies**.

unemployment insurance   State insurance plans that pay the worker who has been laid off and is actively looking for another job a weekly benefit for a specified number of weeks. Most of these plans are designed in such a way that companies with an unstable employment record pay more into the fund than companies with a stable record.

union shop A company in which all employees belong to the union that has won bargaining rights. The union security agreement states that an employee who fails to join within a brief probationary period must forfeit his job.

union steward An employee who represents the union within the plant, consults with supervision about proposed changes, handles **grievances**, and conducts other union business on company time. He usually does not work on the production line although he is paid by the company.

vestibule training Off-the-job training.

wage and salary administration A systematic procedure for establishing a sound compensation structure that makes use of wage and salary surveys, job evaluations, merit ratings, and incentives.

white-collar worker An office worker below the ranks of management.

workmen's compensation A public system that provides social insurance against the costs of medical care and the loss of income arising out of industrial accidents. The employer pays the insurance premium, which is based on the average number of accidents in the plant and the type of accident prevention fostered by the company.

16.10 SECURITIES MARKET

In Section 13.4, "Securities Transactions," many terms, in addition to those listed below, are defined in the explanation of the functions of the securities field.

arrears The term used to refer to unpaid dividends on **cumulative** preferred stock or unpaid interest on cumulative income bonds.

averaging down The practice of purchasing additional shares of a security at more favorable prices than the original commitment. The purpose is to lower the average cost of the combined purchases.

bear A person who believes that security or commodity prices will decline and liquidates a **long** position or goes *short*.

blue-chip stock A stock that has a high degree of popularity or preference and commands a high price relative to its earnings because of its stature or reputation.

blue-sky laws State laws that protect the public against securities frauds.

board room A customers' room in a broker's office where quotations are electronically posted on a board while the exchanges are open.

book value The stated value of the assets of a corporation after the deduction of all liabilities and any arrears on the preferred stock. It is usually expressed in terms of dollars per common share, after the deduction of the preferred stock, if any, at its involuntary liquidating value. It does not necessarily represent the amount that would be realized in liquidation.

borrowing demand   This situation occurs when a person *short* of the market looks for stocks to borrow in order to make a needed delivery.

bull   A person who believes that prices will rise and buys on that assumption.

businessman's investment   An intrinsically sound security that is affected by business conditions and therefore should be watched closely.

call money   Loans that are good only from day to day and are subject to demand payment at any time.

capital stock   All classes of stock issued by a company. Where only one class of stock is outstanding, it is often called capital, rather than common, stock.

carrying charge   The fee charged by brokers for carrying customers' securities on margin.

cats and dogs   An expression used for highly speculative securities.

Class A and Class B stock   A labeling device used to indicate that one stock may have voting power and the other none or that one may participate in dividends to a greater extent than the other.

convertible preferred   A preferred stock that may be exchanged, at the option of the holder, before a certain time for a specified number of common shares.

cumulative   A preferred stock feature that guarantees the shareholder the receipt of full dividends regardless of how long they have not been paid. Not all preferred stocks bear this feature; some are noncumulative.

distress selling   Forced sale brought about when an owner's equity in stocks purchased on margin has been impaired or eliminated by declining prices.

Dow-Jones Averages   An average price of 65 stocks—30 industrials, 20 railroads, and 15 utilities. They are indications as to whether the market has advanced or declined since the previous day.

futures   Contracts in which the seller agrees to deliver commodities, foreign exchange, or securities at a specified future date.

growth stock   The stock of a company whose sales and profits have been rising faster than those for corporations generally.

guaranteed stocks   Stocks in which the dividends are guaranteed by a company other than the one issuing them. Railroad issues of leased lines usually contain this feature.

hedging   The process of protecting a **long** transaction by means of a *short* transaction to prevent loss through price fluctuation. It is commonly practiced in grains and foreign exchange. In the commodity markets, it takes the form of selling a futures contract in an amount equal to cash purchases.

in and out   A transaction turned over quickly—within a day, a week, or even a month.

insider   A person close to a corporation who has intimate knowledge of financial developments before they become public knowledge.

intrinsic value   The value of a security based on its underlying worth. Its market value may be either higher or lower than its intrinsic value.

loan crowd   Brokers who desire to borrow or to lend stocks in connection with **short sales**.

long   The position of a person who has bought and is holding stocks or bonds, as distinguished from one who has sold **short**.

major trend   The long-term trend of prices, even though interrupted by temporary **rallies** or reactions.

melon   A stock dividend or extraordinarily large special cash dividend. Declaration of such a dividend is called *cutting a melon*.

overbought   When a weak technical market results from active speculative buying and advanced prices, speculative holders of stock who are concerned that they have overbought tend to sell and accept the profits.

oversold   The reverse of **overbought**, particularly when a holder with short interests is anxious to cover.

overstay   A speculator is said to have overstayed his market when he has failed to accept a paper profit at its highest point.

par value   The face value assigned to a security when issued. It has nothing to do with the market value of the security. Some companies issue no par stock.

penny stocks   Those that sell for less than $1 and are quoted in cents.

portfolio   The total security holdings of an individual or an institution.

price-earnings ratio   A measure of investment values that is regarded as more reliable than straight earnings per share. Found by dividing the earnings per share into the current market price of the stock. Earnings per share are included in the company's quarterly and annual reports to stockholders.

profit taking   The realizing of profit by either the selling of a **long** holding or the covering of a **short** position.

proxy   A statement that, when signed by the registered owner, gives another person the right to vote his stock at the annual meeting.

puts and calls   Options purchased by a speculator that give him the right to decide whether to exercise them. A *put* is a right to sell 100 shares of a certain stock within a given time at a price fixed in the contract. A *call* is the right to buy 100 shares of a certain stock at a set price within a given period of time.

pyramiding   The purchase of additional securities through the use of unrealized profits as additional margin.

rally   A temporary price advance after a decline.

reaction   A temporary price decline following an advance.

rights   The privilege extended to a shareholder of subscribing to additional stock of the same or another class or to bonds, usually at a price below the market and in an amount proportional to the number of shares already held. Rights must be exercised within a time limit and may be sold if the holder does not wish to purchase additional shares.

risks   The chances taken when capital is invested. *Business risk* refers to the stability and earning power of the issuing company. *Market risk* is determined by the general market conditions that affect the saleability and market price of a security. Fluctuating interest rates create a *money rate risk.* For instance, in a period of rising interest rates, bond prices decline, and vice versa. A rise in prices of goods and services, *price level risk,* means a loss of real income to holders of bonds and preferred stock with a fixed return.

scale buying   The placing of buy orders at regular price intervals above prevailing quotations.

secondary distribution   The sale of a block of stock off the floor of an exchange by a securities firm or a group of such firms at a fixed price geared to the current market price. Firms must have the approval of their exchange to participate in a secondary distribution of a listed stock.

secular trend   The long-term trend judged to be normal.

selling against the box   Another term for a sale of stock without delivery of the certificate. As a short operation, it may be covered through the repurchase of the stock sold or delivery of certificates already owned.

short   In a declining market, a person may sell a security or commodity he does not own and buy it at a lower price later on. In the case of securities, the person borrows the securities sold to make delivery.

short covering   The purchase of securities or commodities to complete a short transaction.

special offering   A large block of stock sold in a particular market at a special time for a fixed price. Announcement is made on the exchange ticker tape of the offering at a fixed price based on the last transaction in the regular auction market. Member firms may buy the stock for customers directly from the seller's broker during trading hours. Only the seller pays a commission.

squeeze   The event that occurs when a short seller is forced to cover his contract in a rising market for fear that the advance will continue.

Standard & Poor's Index   An hourly stock market index based on the prices of five-hundred stocks, similar to the Dow-Jones Averages, that shows the movement of the market.

stock dividend   Shares of the issuing company declared in lieu of a cash dividend.

stock purchase warrant   An agreement whereby the stockholders may purchase a certain number of shares of the corporation based on the number of warrants held for a fixed price, with or without a time limit.

stock split   The division of the outstanding shares of a company that results in an increase in the number of shares, usually by some round-number multiple, such as two for one or three for one. The chief purpose of a stock split is to reduce the market value of each share to make possible a wider ownership.

street certificate   A stock certificate that has been endorsed in blank by the registered owner and guaranteed by a responsible broker. It may then be bought and sold without being transferred on the books of the company. Such certificates are used as collateral in margin accounts.

swings Movements up or down in security or commodity prices, business activity, money rates, and so forth. In stock, there are primary or major swings and secondary or minor swings.

technical position A condition of the market affected by immediate supply of and demand for stocks without regard to external factors.

trading market A market in which the range of price movements is relatively narrow for a considerable period of time. It has profit possibilities only for those who trade actively to take advantage of smaller price movements.

voting trust certificates A negotiable receipt for stock certificates deposited with a trustee. Stockholders retain all rights in the stock except voting power, which is delegated to the trustee. Many states limit the term of the voting trust agreement to five years.

17

List of Standard Abbreviations

For rules governing the use of abbreviations, see "Abbreviations," Section 10.1. Common abbreviations of government agencies are listed on pp. 708–10.

NOTE: There is considerable variation in the use of capitals and periods with abbreviations. In the list that follows, generally accepted practice is observed. Also, there does appear to be a trend in the business sector toward elimination of periods.

A

a   are (metric); ampere (see *amp.*)
@   at; to (in market reports)
A, A., A.U.   angstrom unit (of light)
A.   Army; acre(s); absolute (temperature); answer (in court writings); area
A-1   first-class
A.A.   Associate in Arts
aa   author's alterations (printing)
AAA   American Automobile Association
AAAS   American Association for the Advancement of Science
AAR   against all risks (insurance)
A.A.S.   Fellow of the American Academy (*Academiae Americanae Socius*)
AAU   Amateur Athletic Union
ab.   about; absent
A.B.   Bachelor of Arts (see *B.A.*)
ABA   American Bankers Association; American Bar Association
abbr., abbrev.   abbreviation; abbreviated
ABC   American Broadcasting Company
abr.   abridged
abs.   absolute; abstract; absent
Abs., A.   absolute (temperature)
abst.   abstract

abt., ab.   about
a.c.   alternating current
a/c, acct.   account
A/C   account current
A.C.   Air Corps
A/cs Pay.   accounts payable
A/cs Rec.   accounts receivable
accum.   accumulative
ack.   acknowledgment
act.   active; actual
Actg.   Acting (officer or official)
a/d   after date
ad   advertisement (pl. *ads*)
a.d.   before the day
A.D.   in the year of our Lord (L. *anno Domini*) (e.g., *A.D. 1972* or *1972 A.D.*)
add., ads.   address
A-D-C., ADC   Aide-de-Camp
addl.   additional
ad fin.   to the end (L. *ad finem*)
ad inf.   to infinity (L. *ad infinitum*)
ad init.   at the beginning (L. *ad initium*)
ad int., a.i.   in the meantime or meanwhile (L. *ad interim*)
adj.   adjective; adjustment (bonds)
Adj.   Adjutant
Adj. Gen., A.G.   Adjutant General
ad lib.   at one's pleasure; freely (L. *ad libitum*)
ad loc.   to or at the place (L. *ad locum*)
Adm.   Admiral, -ty
adm.   administration, -tive
Admr.   Administrator
Admx.   Administratrix
adv.   adverb
ad val.   according to value (L. *ad valorem*)
adv. chgs.   advance charges
advtg.   advertising
A.E.   Agricultural Engineer
AEC   Atomic Energy Commission
a.f., AF   audio frequency
Af., Afr.   African; Africa
aff., affd., aff'd   affirmative; affirmed
afft.   affidavit
A/1C   Airman 1st Class; A/2C; A/3C
AFL-CIO   American Federation of Labor and Congress of Industrial
  Organizations

AFRes.   Air Force Reserve
AFTR   American Federal Tax Reports
A.G., Adj. Gen.   Adjutant General
a.g.b.   a good brand
agcy.   agency
agr., ag., agri.   agriculture; agricultural
agr.   agreement
agt.   agent; against
a-h   ampere-hour
AIAA   American Institute of Aeronautics and Astronautics
AIB   American Institute of Banking
AIEE   American Institute of Electrical Engineers
AK, Alas.   Alaska
AL, Ala.   Alabama
ALA   American Library Association
alt.   altitude; alternate; alteration
Alta.   Alberta, Canada
a.m., A.M.   before noon (L. *ante meridian*)
Am.   America; American
AM   amplitude modulation (radio)
AMA   American Medical Association
Amb.   Ambassador
amp., a   ampere(s)
amp-hr.   ampere-hour
amt.   amount
AMVETS   American Veterans of World War II
a.n.   arrival notice (shipping)
anal.   analysis; analytic; analogy
anon.   anonymous
ANPA   American Newspaper Publishers Association
ans.   answer; answered
A. to O.C.   attach(ed) to other correspondence
AP   Associated Press
A/P   authority to pay or purchase; additional premium (insurance)
Apd.   assessment paid
API   American Petroleum Institute
APO   Army Post Office
app.   appendix; applied; apparatus
appd.   approved
appl.   application
approx.   approximately
appt.   appointment; appointed
Apr.   April
apt.   apartment

aq.   water; aqueous
ar., arr.   arrive
A/R   all risks; against all risks (marine insurance)
AR, Ark.   Arkansas
A.R.   Army Regulations
ARA   American Railway Association
ARC   American National Red Cross
arch.   architect; architecture
Arch.E.   Architectural Engineer
arr.   arranged
art.   article
a.s.   at sight
A.S.   Academy of Science; Apprentice Seaman
ASA   American Standards Association
A.S.A.   American Statistical Association
ASCAP   American Society of Composers, Authors, and Publishers
ASCE   American Society of Civil Engineers
asgd.   assigned
asgmt.   assignment
ASME   American Society of Mechanical Engineers
A.S.N.   Army Service Number
assn., ass'n   association
assoc.   associate
asst.   assistant
AST, AT   Atlantic Standard Time
ASTA   American Society of Travel Agents, Inc.
ASTM   American Society for Testing Materials
astr.   astronomy; astronomical
A/T   American terms (grain trade)
Atl.   Atlantic
atm.   atmosphere(s); atmospheric
at. no.   atomic number
att.   attached
attn., atten.   attention
atty.   attorney (pl. *attys.*)
Atty. Gen.   Attorney General
at. vol.   atomic volume
at. wt.   atomic weight
au.   author
Aug.   August
Aus., Austl.   Australian; Australia
AUS   Army of the United States
auth.   author; authorized
aux.   auxiliary

A.V.   Authorized Version
A/V   according to value (L. *ad valorem*)
avdp.   avoirdupois
Ave., Av.   Avenue
avg., av.   average
avn.   aviation
A/W   actual weight; all water (transportation)
A.W.G.   American wire guage
a.w.l.   absent with leave
a.w.o.l., AWOL   absent without leave
AZ, Ariz.   Arizona

B

b.   born
b7d, b10d, etc.   buyer 7 days to take up (stocks and bonds)
B.A.   Bachelor of Arts
bal.   balance
bar.   barometer; barometric
b.b.   bail bond; bill book; break bulk
BBC   British Broadcasting Corporation
bbl.   barrel(s)
bbls/day, b/d   barrels per day
B.C.   before Christ (e.g., 100 B.C.); British Columbia, Canada
B/C   bill of collection
bch.   bunch (pl. *bchs.*)
bd.   board; bond; bound
B/D   bank draft; bar draft (grain trade)
bd. ft., b. ft.   board foot or feet
Bd. of Rev.   Board of Review
bdl.   bundle
bdy.   boundary
B/E   bill of exchange; bill of entry
bet.   between
Bev.   billion electron volts
bf.   boldface
b.f.   board foot or feet
B/F   brought forward (bookkeeping)
b. hp., bhp.   brake horsepower
B/H   bill of health
bibliog.   bibliography, -er, -ical
biog.   biography, -er, -ical
biol.   biology, -ical, -ist
bk.   bank; book

bkg.   banking
bkkp.   bookkeeping
bkpt.   bankrupt
bkt, bsk.   basket(s)
B/L   bill of lading (pl. *Bs/L*)
bl.   bale(s); black
B/L Att.   bill of lading attached
Bldg.   Building
bldr.   builder
blk.   block (pl. *blks.*); black; bulk
B.L.S.   Bachelor of Library Science
Blvd.   Boulevard
b.m.   board measure
B/M   bill of material(s)
b.o.   buyer's option; back order
b/o   brought over
B.O.   branch office
Bor.   borough
bot.   bottle(s); bottom; bought
BOT   Board of Trade
bp., Bp., BP   blueprint
b.p., bp   boiling point; boiler pressure
B/P, b. pay., B. Pay.   bills payable
b.p.b.   bank post bill
b.p.d., bpd, b/d, bbls/day   barrels per day
B.Pd.   Bachelor of Pedagogy
Br.   British; Branch; Brother
B/R   bills receivable; builders' risks
b. rec.   bills receivable
Brig. Gen.   Brigadier General
Brit.   British; Britain
Bro.   Brother
Bros.   Brothers
brt. fwd., b.f.   brought forward
B.S.   Bachelor of Science
B/S   bill of sale
bsk, bkt.   basket
B/St.   bill of sight
bt.   bought; boat
BTA   Board of Tax Appeals
BTU   British Thermal Unit(s)
bu.   bushel(s)
bul.   bulletin
Bur., Bu   Bureau

bus.   business; bushels
Bus. Mgr.   Business Manager
b.v., B/v   book value
B.W.G.   Birmingham wire gauge
bx.   box (pl. *bxs.*)

C

c   carat (metric); cycle (electrical); candle
C.   Celsius; Centigrade; Congress
©, Copr.   copyright
¢, c., ct.   cent(s)
c/   case(s)
ca.   circa; about; centiare
C.A.   Chartered Accountant
C/A   capital account; credit account; current account; commercial agent
CA, Calif.   California
C a/c   current account
c.a.f.   cost, assurance, and freight
cal.   small calorie; calendar; caliber
Can.   Canadian; Canada
canc.   canceled; cancellation
cap.   capital; capacity
caps   capital letters
Capt.   Captain
cart.   cartage
cat.   catalog
C/B   cash book
c.b.d., C.B.D.   cash before delivery
CBS   Columbia Broadcasting System
cc, cc.   carbon copy; cubic centimeter
cd.   cord
cd. ft.   cord foot
c/d   carried down
C/D   certificate of deposit; consular declaration; commercial dock
c. & d.   collection and delivery
cem.   cement
cen.   center; central; century
Cen. Am., C.A.   Central America
cert., ct., ctf.   certificate, -tion; certified
cf.   compare, certificate
c/f   carried forward (bookkeeping)
c. & f.   cost and freight

C.F.C.   Consolidated Freight Classification
c.f.i.   cost, freight, and insurance
cfm (cfs)   cubic feet per minute (second)
c.f.o.   cost for orders
cg, cgm   centigram(s)
c.g.   center of gravity
C.G.   Consul General; Commanding General; Coast Guard
cge. pd.   carriage paid
ch.   chain; chapter; channel (television); chemical; chart
c.-h.   candle-hour
Ch.   Chinese; China; Chaplain; Church
CH., c.h.   customhouse; courthouse
C.H.   Clearing House
chap., chapt., ch., C. (with number)   chapter (pl. *chaps.* or *chs.*)
Ch. Clk.   Chief Clerk
Ch.E., Chem.E.   Chemical Engineer
chem., ch.   chemical, chemistry
chf.   chief
chg.   charge; change (pl. *chgs.*)
C.I.   consular invoice
c.i.f.   cost, insurance, and freight
CIR   Commissioner of Internal Revenue
cir.   circle; circular; circumference
cit.   citation; citizen
civ.   civil; civilian
ck.   check; cask
ckt.   circuit
cl   centiliter (metric)
cl.   class; classification; clause
c.l.   carload
c/l   craft loss
cld.   colored; cleared; called (bonds)
clk.   clerk
clr.   clear; clearance; color
clt.   collateral trust (bonds)
cm   centimeter (metric)
cm²   square centimeter
cm³, cc   cubic centimeter
c.m., cir. mils   circular mils (wire measure)
cml.   commercial
cm. pf.   cumulative preferred (stocks)
C/N   credit note; consignment note; circular note
cn.   consolidated (bonds)
CO   Commanding Officer

C/O   cash order; certificate of origin; case oil
CO, Colo.   Colorado
Co.   Company (pl. *Cos.*); County
c/o, %   carried over (bookkeeping); in care of
c.o.d.   certificates of deposit; cash on delivery (also *C.O.D.*)
coef.   coefficient (mathematics)
C. of C.   Chamber of Commerce
col.   column
Col.   Colonel; College
coll.   collection; collateral
colloq.   colloquial
coll. tr., clt.   collateral trust (bonds)
com., comm.   commerce; commission, -er; committee; communication
Comdr.   Commander
Comdt.   Commandant (Navy and Marine)
coml., cml.   commercial
Commo.   Commodore
Com'r, Comm.   Commissioner
con.   continued
conc.   concentrate
cond.   conductivity (electrical); condition
Cong., C.   Congress; Congressional
cons.   consolidated; consign, -ed, -ment
const.   constant; construction
Const.   Constitution
cont.   contract; contents; continent
contd., cont., con.   continued
Contl.   Continental
CONUS   Continental United States
conv.   convertible
coop, co-op   cooperative
Copr., ©   copyright
cor.   corner; correct, -ed
Corp.   Corporation
corr.   corrected; corresponding, -ence
Cor. Sec.   Corresponding Secretary
c.o.s.   cash on shipment
cp.   compare; coupon
c-p   candle power
C.P.A., CPA   Certified Public Accountant
CPFF   cost-plus-fixed-fee
CPI   Consumer Price Index
Cpl.   Corporal
c.p.m., cpm (cps)   cycles per minute (second)

cpn., cp. coupon
cp. off (on) coupon off (on) (bonds)
C.P.S. Certified Professional Secretary
cr. credit; creditor
C.R. class rate; current rate; company's risk; carrier's risk
CRP C-reactive protein
crt. crate (pl. *crts.*)
cs centistere (metric)
cs., c/s cases
csc cosecant
csch hyperbolic cosecant
CST, C.S.T. Central Standard Time
Ct. court
CT, Conn. Connecticut
CT, C.T. Central Time
ctf., ct. certificate (pl. *ctfs.*)
ctg. cartage
ctn. carton
ctr. center; counter
cu. cubic
cu. cm cubic centimeter(s)
cu. ft. cubic foot or feet
cu. in. cubic inch(es)
cu. mi. cubic mile(s)
cum., cm. cumulative
cum d., cum div. with dividend
cum. pfd., cu. pf. cumulative preferred (stock)
cur. current; currency
cust. customer
cu. yd. cubic yard(s)
cv., cvt. convertible (securities)
cv. db. convertible debentures (securities)
cv. pf. convertible preferred (securities)
C.W. commercial weight
c.w.o. cash with order
CWO Chief Warrant Officer
cwt. hundredweight
CZ, C.Z. Canal Zone

D

d dyne
d. date; died; density; distance; daughter

D. Democrat; diameter
D.A. District Attorney
d/a days after acceptance
D/A deposit account; documents against acceptance; discharge afloat
DAR Daughters of the American Revolution
db decibel (unit of sound)
dbu decibel unit
d.b.a. doing business as (company name)
d.b.h. diameter at breast height
db. rts. debenture rights (securities)
d.c. direct current
DC, D.C. District of Columbia
D/C deviation clause
D.C.L. Doctor of Civil Law
D.Cn.L. Doctor of Canon Law
dd. delivered
D.D. Doctor of Divinity (honorary)
D/D demand draft; delivered at docks; delivered at destination; dock dues
D/d days after date
d.d. in d. from day to day
D.D.S. Doctor of Dental Surgery
D.D.Sc. Doctor of Dental Science
DDT Dichlorodiphenyltrichloroethane
D.E., D.Eng. Doctor of Engineering
DE, Del. Delaware
deb. debenture
dec. decrease; deceased; decimal; declination
Dec. December
def. deferred (securities); definition; defense
deg., ° degree(s)
del. deliver, -y
Dem., D. Democrat
dep. deposit; deputy; depot; departure
dep. ctfs. deposit certificates
dept. department (pl. *depts.*)
det. detached; detachment; detective
dev. deviation
DEW distant early warning (*DEW line*)
d.f. dead freight
D.F.A. Division Freight Agent
dft., Dft. draft; defendant
dg. decigram(s)
dia., diam. diameter
diag. diagram; diagonal

dict.   dictionary
dir.   director
dis.   discount; discharge
disch.   discharge
dist.   district; distance; distribution
div.   dividend; division (pl. *divs.*)
D.J.S.   Doctor of Juridical Science
dk.   dock; deck
dkg   dekagram (metric)
dkl   dekaliter (metric)
dkm   dekameter (metric)
dks   dekastere (metric)
dkt.   docket
dl   deciliter (metric)
DL   day letter
D/L   demand loan
dld.   delivered
D.Lit., D.Litt.   Doctor of Literature or Letters
d.l.o.   dispatch loading only
D.L.O.   Dead Letter Office
dls/shr   dollars per share
dm, decim.   decimeter(s)
D.M.D.   Doctor of Dental Medicine
D. Mus., D.M.   Doctor of Music
D/N   debit note
do.   ditto *(the same)*
D/O   delivery order
D.O.   Doctor of Osteopathy
doc.   document (pl. *docs.*)
dol., dl., $ dollar (pl. *dols.* or *dls.*)
dom.   dominion; domestic
doz.   dozen
d.p.   direct port
DP   dew point
D/P   documents against payment
D.P.H.   Doctor of Public Health
D.P.Hy.   Doctor of Public Hygiene
dr.   debit; debtor; dram
Dr.   Doctor (pl. *Drs.*); Drive
dr. ap.   apothecaries' dram(s)
dr. av.   dram(s) avoirdupois
D.R.E.   Doctor of Religious Education
D/s   days after sight

ds   decistere (metric)
D.Sc., D.S.   Doctor of Science
D.S.C.   Distinguished Service Cross
D.S.M.   Distinguished Service Medal
D.S.O.   Distinguished Service Order (British)
d.s.p.   died without issue (L. *decessit sine prole*)
DST, D.S.T.   Daylight Saving Time; Doctor of Sacred Theology
dstn.   destination
dtd.   dated
D.V.M.   Doctor of Veterinary Medicine
D/W   dock warrant
d.w.   dead weight
d.w.c.   deadweight capacity
d.w.t.   deadweight tons
dwg.   drawing
dwt.   pennyweight(s)
d.w.t.f.   daily and weekly till forbidden (advertising)
D/y   delivery
dz.   dozen

E

e   erg
E.   east
ea.   each
E.A.O.N.   except as otherwise noted
ed.   editor; education; edition (pl. *eds.*)
Ed. Note   Editorial Note
EDT, E.D.T.   Eastern Daylight Time
educ.   education, -al
e.e.   errors excepted
E.E.   Electrical Engineer
eff.   effective
e.g.   for example (L. *exempli gratia*)
EHF   extremely high frequency
el.   elevation
elec.   electric, -al, -ian, -ity
E. Long.   east longitude
E.M.   Engineer of Mines (see *M.E.*)
e.m.f.   electromotive force
e.m.p.   end of month payment
enc., encl.   enclosure(s)

encyc. encyclopedia

end. endorse, -d, -ment

ENE east-northeast

eng. engine; engineer; engraved

Eng. England; English

engg. engineering

engr. engineer; engraver, -ing

Ens. Ensign

entd. entered

env. envelope(s)

e.o.d. every other day (advertising)

E. & O.E. errors and omissions excepted

e.o. ex officio

e.o.h.p. except as otherwise herein provided

e.o.m. end of month

eq. equal; equivalent; equation

equip., eqpt. equipment

ESE east-southeast

esp. especially

Esq. Esquire

est. establish, -ed, -ment; estimate; estate

EST, E.S.T. Eastern Standard Time

e.s.u. electrostatic unit

et al. and others (L. *et alii*)

etc. and so forth (L. *et cetera*)

et seq. and the following (L. *et sequens*)

et ux. and wife (L. *et uxor*)

et vir and husband (L.)

Eur. Europe; European

Euratom European Atomic Energy Community

ex out of or from (e.g., *ex warehouse, ex officio*)

ex without or not including (e.g., *ex interest, ex dividend*)

ex. example; extra

ex cp. or x/cp without the coupon

ex d. or ex div. without the dividend

exam. examination; examined

exch. exchange

exec. executive

ex. fcy. extra fancy

ex int. without the interest

exp. express; expense; export

expt. experiment, -al

ex r. ex rights or without rights

exr. executor

exrx.   executrix

ext.   exterior; extended; extension; extract; external; extinct

F

F.   Fahrenheit; franc(s); French

f.   farad; force

f., ff.   and following page(s)

f.a.a.   free of all average (insurance)

F.A.A.S.   Fellow of the American Association for the Advancement of
Science

fac.   facsimile

F.A.C.S.   Fellow of the American College of Surgeons

F.A.G.S.   Fellow of the American Geographical Society

F.A.I.A.   Fellow of the American Institute of Architects

f.a.q.   fair average quality; free at quay

f.a.s.   free alongside ship

fath., fm., f.   fathom

f.b.   freight bill

fbm   feet board measure

fcp.   foolscap

f.c. & s.   free of capture and seizure (insurance)

fcy, pks.   fancy packs

f.d.   free discharge; free delivery; free dispatch

f. & d.   freight and demurrage

fd.   fund; funding

fdg.   funding (bonds)

fdy.   foundry

Feb.   February

Fed.   Federal; Federated; Federation

fem., f.   feminine; female

ff.   and the following [pages]; folios

f.f.a.   free from alongside; free foreign agency

Fid.   Fidelity; Fiduciary

fifo   first in, first out (merchandise)

fig.   figure (pl. *figs.*)

fin.   financial; finance; finish

Fin. Sec.   Financial Secretary

f.i.o.   free in and out

f.i.t.   free of income tax; free in truck

FL, Fla.   Florida

fl.   fluid; floor

fl. dr.   fluid dram

fl. oz.   fluid ounce

flt.   flight; fleet
fm.   fathom; from; form
FM   frequency modulation
fn., ftnt.   footnote
fn. p., fnp   fusion point
f°, fol., f.   folio (pl. *ff.*)
f.o.   for orders; firm offer; full out terms (grain trade)
f.o.b.   free on board
f.o.d.   free of damage
f.o.f.   free on field (airmail)
fol.   follow, -ing; folio
f.o.q.   free on quay
f.o.r.   free on rail
for.   forward; foreign; forestry
f.o.t.   free on truck
f.p., fp   freezing point
F.P.   floating policy; fully paid
f.p.a.   free of particular average (insurance)
f. pd.   fully paid
f.p.m.   feet per minute
FPO   fleet post office
f.p.s.   feet per second; frames per second
FR   full-rate (telegram and cables)
F/R   freight release
FRB   Federal Reserve Bank
Fri.   Friday (F. in tabulations)
f.r.o.f.   fire risk on freight
FRS   Federal Reserve System
frt.   freight
Ft.   Fort
ft.   foot or feet
f.t.   full terms
ft-c   foot-candle
ft-L   foot-lambert
ft-lb.   foot-pound(s)
ft/sec.   feet per second
ft-tn   foot-ton
fur.   furlong
furn.   furnished; furniture
fut.   futures (exchange)
f.v.   on the back of the page (L. *folio verso*)
fwd.   forward
FX   foreign exchange
F.Y.I.   for your information

G

g   gram (metric)
g.   gold; gauge; gulf; gravity
g.a.   general average
GA, Ga.   Georgia
gal.   gallon(s)
GAW   guaranteed annual wage
GCA   ground control approach
g-cal   gram-calorie
GCD, g.c.d.   greatest common divisor
GCI   ground control intercept
G.C.T., GCT   Greenwich Civil Time
gds.   goods
g.f.a.   good fair average
G.F.A.   General Freight Agent
gen.   general; generator; genus or kind
Gen.   General (pl. *Gens.*)
geog.   geography, -ic, -ical, -er
geol.   geology, -ic, -ical, -ist
g. gr.   great gross (144 dozen)
GHQ   General Headquarters (military)
GI   government issue; general issue
gi.   gill(s)
gm.   gram(s) (*g* is preferred)
GMAT, G.M.A.T.   Greenwich Mean Astronomical Time
GMT, G.M.T.   Greenwich Mean Time
G.N.   Graduate Nurse
GNP   gross national product
G.O.P., GOP   Republican Party (Grand Old Party)
Gov.   Governor
govt.   government
G.P.A.   General Passenger Agent
g.p.m.   gallons per minute
GPO   Government Printing Office
g.p.s.   gallons per second
gr.   grain; gross
gr. wt.   gross weight
grad.   graduate, -ed, -tion
g.s.   ground speed (aviation)
Gt. Br.   Great Britain
GTC   good till canceled (brokerage order)
GTM   good this month (brokerage order)
GTW   good this week (becomes void on Saturday)
guar.   guarantee; guaranteed

H

h   henry (electricity); hours, as *8h* or *12h*
ha   hectare (metric)
h.c.f.   highest common factor
hd.   head
hdbk.   handbook
hdkf.   handkerchief(s)
hdqrs.   headquarters
hdw., hdwr.   hardware
H. Doc. (with number)   House of Representatives document
HE   high explosive
HEW   Department of Health, Education, and Welfare
hf.   half
h-f., HF   high frequency
H.F.M.   hold for money
hg   hectogram
hhd.   hogshead(s)
HI, Ha.   Hawaii; Hawaiian Islands
hist.   history, -ical, -ian
hl   hectoliter (metric)
hm   hectometer (metric)
Hon.   Honorable
hosp.   hospital
hp.   horsepower
h.p.   high pressure
h-p. cyl.   high-pressure cycle
hp-hr.   horsepower-hour
hq.   headquarters
hr.   hour
H.R.   House of Representatives; House bill (with number)
H.R.H.   His, or Her, Royal Highness
H.S.S.   Fellow of the Historical Society
ht.   height; heat
hund., C   hundred
H.W.   high water
H.W.M.   high water mark
Hwy., Hy.   Highway
hyp.   hypothesis

I

I.   Island(s); Isle(s)
IA, Ia.   Iowa
ib., ibid.   in the same place (footnote) (L. *ibidem*)

I.B. invoice book; in bond
I.B.I. invoice book, inwards
i.b.p., ibp initial boiling point
I.C. & C. invoice cost and charges
id. the same (L. *idem*)
ID Idaho (*also* Ida.); identification
i.e. that is (L. *id est*)
IES Illuminating Engineering Society
ign. unknown; ignition
i. hp. indicated horsepower
IL, Ill. Illinois
ill., illus. illustration; illustrated
ILO International Labor Organization
imp. improvement; implement; imperial; import, -ing, -ed, -er
imp. gal. imperial gallon(s)
in., ″ inch(es)
IN, Ind. Indiana
Inc. Incorporated
inc. increase; income, -ing
incl. inclusive; including
incog. incognito; unknown; unofficially; in secret
ind. industrial; industry; independent
Ind.E. Industrial Engineer
inf. inferior; below (L. *infra*)
init. initial
in-lb. inch-pound
in loc. in the proper place (L. *in loco*)
INP International News Photos
ins. insurance; inspector
INS International News Service
inst. instant; instrument; installment
Inst. Institute, -tion
int. interest; interior
intl., intnatl. international
inv. invoice; investment; inventor, -tion
invt. inventory
I O U I owe you
i.p. intermediate pressure; i-p (adj.)
i.p.s., ips inches per second
I.Q. Intelligence Quotient
IRC Internal Revenue Code
iss. issue
ital. italics
i.v. invoice value; increased value

J

j   joule (electricity)
J.   Judge; Justice
J.A.   Judge Advocate
J/A   joint account
J.A.G.   Judge Advocate General
Jan.   January
jato   jet-assisted takeoff
jc., jct., junc.   junction
J.C.D.   Doctor of Canon or Civil Law
J.C.L.   Licentiate in Canon Law
J.D.   Doctor of Laws
jg.   junior grade
JJ.   Justices
jnt. stk.   joint stock
jour.   journal
J.P.   Justice of the Peace
Jr.   Junior; journal
J.S.D.   Doctor of Juristic Science (law)
jt.   joint
J.U.D.   Doctor of both Canon and Civil Laws
junc., jct.   junction

K

K   karat (gold measure); kilo
K.   Kelvin (absolute scale of temperature)
kc   kilocycle
kcal   kilocalorie
kcps, kc/s   kilocycles per second
K.D.   knocked down (freight)
kg   kilogram (metric)
kg.   keg(s)
kl   kiloliter
km   kilometer
km²   square kilometer
km³   cubic kilometer
kn.   knot
KS, Kans.   Kansas
kt.   karat; kiloton
kv   kilovolt
kv-a   kilovolt-ampere
kw   kilowatt

kw-hr.   kilowatt-hour
KY, Ky.   Kentucky

L

l   liter (metric)
l.   line (pl. *ll.*); left; length; lumen (light measure)
L   listed (securities); fifty; lire
L.   Latin; law(s); ledger
£   pound sterling (British)
la., lge.   large
LA, La.   Louisiana
l.a.   law agent
L/A   letter of authority; landing account; Lloyd's agent
lab.   laboratory; labor
lang.   language
lat., ϕ latitude
lb.   pound(s)
lb. ap.   pound, apothecary's
lb. av.   pound, avoirdupois
lb-ft.   pound-foot
lb/ft²   pounds per square foot
lb-in.   pound-inch
lb/in²   pounds per square inch (see *p.s.i.*)
lbr.   lumber
lb. t.   pound, troy
lc.   lowercase
l.c.   in the place cited (see *loc. cit.*)
LC   deferred cable
L/C   letter of credit (pl. *Ls/C*)
l.c.l.   less than carload lot(s) (pl. *l.c.l.s.*)
l.c.m.   least common multiple
l.c.t.   long calcined ton
ldg.   loading
ldg. & dely.   landing and delivery
lds.   loads
L.D.S.   Licentiate in Dental Surgery
l.d.t.   long dry ton
lea.   league
L. Ed.   Lawyer's Edition (Supreme Court reports)
leg.   legal
legis.   legislature, -tion
lf.   lightface
LF   low frequency

l.f.   ledger folio
lge., la.   large
lg.tn., l.t.   long ton(s)
l.h.   left hand
L.H.D.   Doctor of the Humanities or Doctor of Humane Letters
l-hr   lumen-hour
li.   link
L.I.   Long Island
lib.   library
Lieut., Lt.   Lieutenant (pl. *Lts.*)
lifo   last in, first out (merchandise)
lin.   linear
lin. ft.   linear foot
L.I.P.   life insurance policy
liq.   liquid; liquor
lit.   literature; literally; liter
lkg. & bkg.   leakage and breakage
LL   leased line (securities)
LL.B.   Bachelor of Laws
LL.D.   Doctor of Laws
L.M.S.C.   let me see correspondence
ln.   lien; loan
loc.   location; local
loc. cit.   in the place cited (L. *loco citato*)
log   logarithm
long.   longitude
loran   long-range navigation
lox   liquid oxygen
l.p., lp   low pressure; long-playing (records)
LPG   liquefied petroleum gas
lpw, l/w   lumens per watt
l.s.   left side
L.S.   place of the seal
l.s.t., LST   local standard time
lt.   light; left
l.t.   local time; long ton
LT   letter message (cables)
Lt., Lieut.   Lieutenant (pl. *Lts.*)
Lt. Col.   Lieutenant Colonel
Lt. Comdr.   Lieutenant Commander
ltd., Ltd.   limited; Limited (British)
Lt. Gen.   Lieutenant General
Lt. Gov.   Lieutenant Governor
Lt. (jg)   Lieutenant (junior grade) (Navy)

Lt.-V light vessel
ltr. letter
lv. leave
l.w.l. load waterline
l.w.m. low watermark

M

m minutes, meter (metric)
m. noon; married; masculine; month; male
M thousand (1,000); 2M (2,000), and so on
M. Master (degree); Monday; Monsieur (pl. *MM.* or *Messrs.*)
ma milliampere
m/a my account
MA, Mass. Massachusetts
M.A. Master of Arts
mach. machine; machinery
mag. magazine; magnitude
maj. majority
Maj. Major
Maj. Gen. Major General
Man. Manhattan; Manitoba, Canada
man. manager; manual
mar. market; maritime; married
Mar. Marine; March
mat. maturity (bonds); matinee
math. mathematics, -cian, -cal
max. maximum
max. cap. maximum capacity
mb millibar
M b.m. thousand (feet) board measure
mc megacycle
m.c. marked capacity
M.C. Master of Ceremonies; Member of Congress; Military Cross
M/C marginal credit
Mcf million cubic feet (gas lines)
M c.f. thousand cubic feet
mch., mach. machine
m.c.p.s. megacycles per second; millicycles per second
m/d months after date
MD, Md. Maryland
M.D. Doctor of Medicine
M/D memorandum of deposit
mdse. merchandise

ME, Me.   Maine
M.E.   Mechanical Engineer; Military Engineer; Mining Engineer; Managing Editor
meas.   measure, -ment
mech.   mechanic, -s, -al
med.   medium; medicine; medical
memo   memorandum(s)
m.e.p., mep   mean effective pressure
meq   milliequivalent
mer.   mercantile; meridian
Messrs., MM.   Misters (Messieurs)
met.   metropolitan; meteorological; metal
metal., met.   metallurgy
Met.E.   Metallurgical Engineer
Mev.   million electron volts
Mex.   Mexican; Mexico
mf   millifarad (electricity)
mfd.   manufactured
mfg.   manufacturing
mfr.   manufacture, -r (pl. *mfrs.*)
mfst.   manifest
mg   milligram (metric)
m.g.d.   million gallons per day
mgr.   manager
Mgr., Monsig., Msgr.   Monseigneur; Monsignor
mh   millihenry
M.H.   Medal of Honor
mhcp   mean horizontal candlepower
mi.   mile(s), mill
MI, Mich.   Michigan
mid., mdnt.   midnight
Mid'n   Midshipman
mil.   military; mileage; million
min.   minute(s); minimum; minority; minister
min. B/L   minimum bill of lading
M.I.P.   marine insurance policy
misc.   miscellaneous
M.I.T.   Massachusetts Institute of Technology
mkt.   market
ml   milliliter (metric)
mL   millilambert
Mlle.   Mademoiselle (Miss)
mm   millimeter(s)
mm^2 square millimeter

mm³   cubic millimeter
Mme.   Madame (pl. *Mmes.*)
m.m.f.   magnetomotive force
mmfd   micromicrofarad
MN, Minn.   Minnesota
M.N.A.S.   Member of the National Academy of Sciences
mng.   managing
mo.   month(s) (pl. *mos.*)
MO, Mo.   Missouri
m.o.   money order; mail order
mod.   modified; moderate
mol. wt.   molecular weight
m.o.m.   middle of month
Mon.   Monday (M. in tabulations)
mot.   motor
MP   Military Police
M.P.   Member of Parliament (Britain); Mounted Police (Canada)
m.p.   melting point
M.P.C.   Member of Parliament, Canada
m.p.g., mpg   miles per gallon
m.p.h., mph   miles per hour
mr   milliroentgen
Mr.   Mister (pl. *Messrs.*)
Mrs.   Mistress or Madam (pl. *Mmes.*)
ms.,   megasecond, manuscript
MS., MSS.   manuscript; manuscripts
M/s, m/s   months after sight; meters per second
Ms.   Miss or Mrs.
MS, Miss.   Mississippi
M.S.   Master of Science
m.s.cp., mscp   mean spherical candlepower
msg.   message
Msgr., msgr.   Monsignor; messenger
M. Sgt., M/Sgt.   Master Sergeant
m.s.l.   mean sea level
MST, M.S.T.   Mountain Standard Time
Mt.   Mount; Mountain (pl. *Mts.*)
mt.   empty; megaton
MT, Mont.   Montana
MT, M.T.   mountain time
mt. ct. cp.   mortgage certificate coupon (securities)
mtg.   mortgage; meeting
mun.   municipal
mus.   museum; music; musical

m.v.   market value
MV   motor vessel

N

n.   net; news; normal; north; noon; note; noun; number
N.   north; Navy
na, NA   not available
N.A., n/a   no account (banking)
N.A., N.Am.   North America
N.A.M., NAM   National Association of Manufacturers
NANA   North American Newspaper Alliance, Inc.
NAS   National Academy of Sciences
nat., natl.   national
naut.   nautical
nav.   naval; navigation
n.b., N.B.   note well; take notice (L. *nota bene*)
NB, Neb.   Nebraska; northbound
NBC   National Broadcasting Company
NC, N.C.   North Carolina
n-c, NC   non callable (bonds)
N/C   new charter; new crop
NCO   noncommissioned officer
n.c.u.p.   no commission until paid
N.C.V.   no commercial value
n.d.   no date; next day's delivery
ND, N. Dak.   North Dakota
n.e.   not exceeding
NE   northeast
N.E., N. Eng.   New England
NEA   Newspapers Enterprise Association
NEA   National Education Association; National Editorial Association
n.e.c.   not elsewhere classified
NEC   National Electrical Code
NED   New English Dictionary (the Oxford English Dictionary)
neg.   negative, -ly
n.e.s.   not elsewhere specified
neut., n.   neuter
n/f   no funds (banking)
n.-f.e.   nitrogen-free extract
n.g.   no good
N.G., NG   National Guard
NH, N.H.   New Hampshire
n. hp., N. HP   nominal horsepower

NJ, N.J.   New Jersey
n.l.   natural log or logarithm; new line
NL   night letter (telegram)
N. Lat., n. lat.   north latitude
NLT   night letter cable
NM   night message
NM, N. Mex.   New Mexico
n/m   no mark
n. mi.   nautical mile(s)
NNE   north-northeast
NNW   north-northwest
No., no., Nos., nos.   number, numbers
No., N.   North; northern
n/o   in the name of (finance)
N/O   no orders (banking)
N.O.E.   not otherwise enumerated
N.O.H.P.   not otherwise herein provided
nom.   nominal; nominative
nom. std.   nominal standard
non pros.   he does not prosecute
non seq.   it does not follow (L. *non sequitur*)
n.o.p.   not otherwise provided for
n.o.s., N.O.S.   not otherwise specified
nos.   numbers
Nov.   November
np   nonparticipating (stocks)
n.p. or d.   no place or date
N.P.   Notary Public; no protest (banking)
n/p   net proceeds
N.P.L.   nonpersonal liability
n.p.t.   normal pressure and temperature
nr.   near
n.r.   no risk; net register
n.r.a.d.   no risk after discharge
n/s, n.s.   not specified; not sufficient; new series; new style
N.S.F.   not sufficient funds (banking)
n.t.   net ton; new terms (grain trade)
nth   indefinite (e.g., *nth degree*)
n.t.p.   no title page
nt. wt.   net weight
n.u.   name unknown
nv   nonvoting (stocks)
NV, Nev.   Nevada
NW   northwest

NY, N.Y. New York
NYC New York City

O

o. order; old
O pint, apothecaries'
oa., OA overall
o/a on account of
OASI old-age and survivors insurance
ob. died (L. *obiit*)
obit. obituary (pl. *obits.*)
O.B/L, ob/l order bill of lading
obs. obsolete; observatory
ob.s.p. died without issue (L. *obiit sine prole*)
oc. ocean; overcharge
o/c over-the-counter; overcharge
Oct. October
o/d on demand; overdraft
o.d. olive drab
o.e. omissions excepted
OE Old English
OED Oxford English Dictionary
off. office; officer
OH, O. Ohio
OK, Okla. Oklahoma
OK, OK'd, OK'ing, OK's correct
Ont. Ontario, Canada
O/o order of
op., opp. opinion; opposite
o.p. out of print
O.P., OP open, or floating, policy
op. cit. in the work cited (L. *opere citato*)
opd. opened (stocks)
opr. operate, -ing, -ion(s)
opt. optional; optician
OR, Ore., Oreg. Oregon
o.r. owner's risk (shipping)
o. & r. ocean and rail (transp.)
O.R.C., ORC Officers' Reserve Corps
ord. ordinance; order; ordinary
org. organization; organic
orig. original, -ly
o/s, OS out of stock

O/S   on sample; on sale or return
o.s. & d.   over, short, and damaged (transportation)
o.t.   overtime
o/t   old terms (grain trade); on truck
o.w., OW   one way (fare)
oz.   ounce(s)
oz. ap.   ounce, apothecaries'
oz. av.   ounce, avoirdupois
oz-ft.   ounce-foot
oz-in.   ounce-inch
oz. t.   ounce, troy

P

p.   page (pl. *pp.*); parallel; pence; per; pico (one trillionth); population;
   pressure
¶, ℙ   paragraph
PA,   Pennsylvania (also *Pa.*, *Penn.*, *Penna.*)
pa.   paper
p.a.   private account; particular average; by the year (L. *per annum*)
P.A.   purchasing agent; press agent; public-address system
P/A   power of attorney
P/Av.   particular average
Pac.   Pacific
P.a.C.   put and call (stock market)
p. ae.   equal parts (L. *partes aequales*)
pam.   pamphlet
paren.   parenthesis (pl. *parens.*)
part.   participating (securities); particular
pat.   patent, -ed
Pat. Off.   Patent Office
pat. pend.   patent pending
payt.   payment
PBX   telephone switchboard (private branch exchange)
pc.   piece (pl. *pcs.*)
P/C   price current; petty cash
p.c.   post card
pcl.   parcel
pct.   percent
pd.   paid; passed
per an., p.a.   by the year (L. *per annum*)
perp.   perpetual (bonds)
Per Pro., P.P.   on behalf of; by proxy (L. *per procurationem*)
pert.   pertaining

pet., petr.   petroleum
petn.   petition
pfd.   preferred (securities)
pF   picofarad (electricity)
Pfc.   private, first class
ph., PH   phase (1PH = single-phase)
Phar.D.   Doctor of Pharmacy
pharm.   pharmacist; pharmacy
Ph.B., B.Ph.   Bachelor of Philosophy
Ph.C.   Pharmaceutical Chemist
Ph.D.   Doctor of Philosophy
Ph.G.   Graduate in Pharmacy
P.I.   Philippine Islands
p. & i.   protection and indemnity
pk.   peck(s); pack, -ing; park (pl. *pks.*)
pkg.   package (pl. *pkgs.*)
Pkwy.   Parkway
p.l.   partial loss
pl.   place; plural; plate (pl. *pls.*)
P.L.   Public Law
P. & L., P/L   profit and loss
p.m.   afternoon
P.M.   Provost Marshal, afternoon
PM.   Postmaster
pm., prem.   premium
p.n., P/N   promissory note
P.O.   Post Office
PO   Petty Officer
P.O.D.   pay on delivery; payable on death
pol.   politics; political
p.o.o.   post office order
pop.   population
P.O.R., p.o.r.   pay on return
pos.   positive
pot.   potential
pow.   power
POW   prisoner of war
pp.   pages
p.p., P.P.   parcel post
ppd.   prepaid
PPI   plan position indicator
p.p.i.   parcel post insured; policy proof of interest
p.p.m.   parts per million
pr.   pair; price; printed

PR, P.R.   Puerto Rico; payroll
pref., pf.   preferred; preference; preface
prem.   premium
prep.   preposition; preparation
Pres.   President
prin.   principal
prob.   problem
prod.   product; produce, -d
Prof.   Professor (pl. *Profs.*)
pron.   pronunciation; pronounced; pronoun
prop.   property; proposition
Prot.   Protestant
pro tem.   temporarily
prov.   province; provision, -al
prox.   of the next month; proximo
pr. pf.   prior preferred (stocks)
prs.   pairs
P.S., P.P.S.   postscript; post-postscript
P/S   public sale
p.s.f., psf   pounds per square foot
psgr., pass.   passenger
p.s.i., psi   pounds per square inch
P.S.T., PST   Pacific Standard Time
pt.   part; pint; point; port (pl. *pts.*)
p.t.   private terms
P.T., PT   Pacific Time
P.T.A., PTA   Parent-Teacher Association (pl. *P.T.A.s, PTAs*)
ptg.   printing
p.t.o.   please turn over
pt. pf.   participating preferred (stocks)
pub.   public, -ation; published, -ing, -er
pur.   purchase, -r; purchasing
Pvt.   Private
p.w.   packed weight (transp.)
pwr., pow.   power
pwt.   pennyweight
P.X., p.x.   please exchange
PX   post exchange (pl. *PXs*)

Q

q   quintal (metric)
q., Q.   quart; query; question; quire

Q.E.D., q.e.d.   which was to be proved or demonstrated (L. *quod erat demon-*
   strandum)
Q.E.F., q.e.f.   which was to be done (L. *quod erat faciendum*)
Q.E.I., q.e.i.   which was to be ascertained (L. *quod erat inveniendum*)
qly.   quality
Q.M.   Quartermaster
qr.   quarter, -ly; quire
qt.   quart (pl. *qts.*)
qtr.   quarter, -ly
qty.   quantity
quad.   quadrant; quadrangle
ques.   question(s)
q.v.   which see (pl. *qq.v*) (L. *quod vide*)
qy.   query

R

r.   road; right
R.   Republic, -an; river; radius; Reaumur (thermometric scale)
®   Registered in U.S. Patent Office
R.A.   Rear Admiral; Royal Academy; regular army
R/A   refer to acceptor
racon   radar beacon
radar   radio detection and ranging
R. & D.   research and development
R.C.   Red Cross; Roman Catholic
R/C   reconsigned
rcd., recd.   received
rd.   road; rod; round
r.d.   running days
R.D.   rural delivery
rdp.   redemption
re   in regard to
R.E.   real estate
Rear Adm.   Rear Admiral
rec.   receipt; record; recipe
recd., rcd.   received
Rec. Sec.   Recording Secretary
ref.   reference; referred; referee; refunding
refr.   refrigerate, -ed, -ing, -or
reg.   regular; regulation; register, -ed
reg. sess.   regular session (of legislature)
R.E.O.   real estate owned (banking)
rep.   report; repeat; repair

Rep.   Republican; Republic; Representative (pl. *Reps.*)
req.   requisition; required
res.   reserve; residence; resort; resolution
ret.   retired; return
retd.   returned
rev.   review; revenue; revolution; revise, -ed, -ion
Rev.   Reverend (pl. *Revs.*)
rev. A/C   revenue account
revd., rev'd   reversed
revg., rev'g   reversing
rf., rfg.   refunding (bonds); refining (oil)
RF   radio frequency
R.F.D.   rural free delivery (see *R.D.*)
rg., reg.   registered
r.h.   right hand; relative humidity
rhp, RHP   rated horsepower
RI, R.I.   Rhode Island
R.I.   reinsurance
r. & l.   rail and lake (transportation)
r.l. & r.   rail, lake, and rail (transportation)
rm.   ream; room (pl. *rms.*)
r.m.s.   root mean square
R.N.   Registered Nurse
r. & o.   rail and ocean (transportation)
R.O.G.   receipt of goods
Rom., rom.   Roman; Romance; roman (type)
ROP   run of paper
ROTC   Reserve Officers' Training Corps
rotn. no.   rotation number
RP   reply paid (cables)
R.P.   return premium
R/p   return of post for orders
R.P.D.   Doctor of Political Science
r.p.m., rpm, r/m   revolutions per minute
R.P.O., RPO   Railway Post Office
r.p.s., rps, r/s   revolutions per second
RR   railroad (pl. *RRs*)
r.s.   right side
R.S.V.P.   please reply (F. *répondez s'il vous plait*)
rt.   right (pl. *rts.*); round trip
Rte., Rt.   Route
Rt. Rev.   Right Reverend
rva   reactive volt-ampere (see *var.*)
R/W   right of way

r. & w.   rail and water (transportation)

Ry.   railway (pl. *Rys.*)

S

s   stere (metric); seconds (e.g., *10″* or *10s*)

s.   silver; stock; shilling; son

S.   south; Senate bill (with number)

/S/   signed (before a typed signature)

s7d   seller 7 days to deliver (securities)

s/a   subject to approval; safe arrival

S.A.   South America; South Africa; Salvation Army; an incorporated company in France; a stock company in Spain.

SAE   Society of Automotive Engineers

SAGE   semiautomatic ground environment

S.A.I.   an incorporated company in Italy

S. Am.   South America, -n

s.a.n.r.   subject to approval, no risk (no risk until insurance is confirmed)

San.D.   Doctor of Sanitation

s. ap., sc., ℈   scruple, apothecaries'

s. and s.c.   sized and supercalendered

SAR   Sons of the American Revolution

Sat.   Saturday (Sa. in tabulations)

sav.   saving(s)

SB   southbound

s.b.   salesbook

S.B.   Senate Bill (State); short bill

S/B   statement of billing (transp.)

s.c.   small capital letters; same case (legal); sized and calendered; single circuit (electrical)

sc., sci.   science

sc., scil.   namely, to wit (see also *ss*)

SC, S.C.   South Carolina

S.C.   salvage charges

s. & c.   shipper and carrier

Sc.D.   Doctor of Science

sch.   schedule; school

S. Con. Res.   Senate concurrent resolution (with number)

s.cp., scp   spherical candlepower

s.d.   without date (L. *sine die*)

SD, S. Dak.   South Dakota

S. Doc.   Senate document (with number)

S.D.B.L.   sight draft, bill of lading attached

SE   southeast

sec   secant

sec., sect.   second; section (pl. *secs., sects.*)

sec., secy.   secretary

sec.-ft.   second-foot

sech   hyperbolic secant

sel.   selected, -tion

Sen.   Senate; Senator (pl. *Sens.*)

sep.   separate

Sept.   September (*Sep.* in tabulations)

seq.   the following; in sequence (pl. *seqq.*)

ser.   series; serial; service

serv.   service

sess.   session

S. & F.A.   shipping and forwarding

s.f.   sinking fund

Slc.   Seaman, first class

Sfc.   Sergeant, first class

sg., sig.   signature

S.G.   Surgeon General

sgd.   signed (see /*S*/)

Sgt.   Sergeant

sh.   share (pl. *shs.*)

SHF   superhigh frequency

shoran   short range (radio)

s. hp., shp   shaft horsepower

shpt.   shipment

shtg.   shortage

sh. tn.   short ton

sic   thus (Latin; no period)

sig.   signature

sin   sine (mathematics)

sing.   singular

sinh   hyperbolic sine

s.i.t.   stopping in transit (transportation)

S.J.D.   Doctor of Juridical Science (law) (see *J.S.D.*)

sk.   sack (pl. *sx*)

s.l.   salvage loss

S. Lat.   south latitude

sld.   sold; sealed; sailed

sltx, SLTX   sales tax

sm.   small

Sn., SN   Seaman

S/N   shipping note

s.o., S.O.   seller's option; shipping order; ship's option

So., S.   southern; south
soc.   society
sofar   sound fixing and ranging
sol.   solution; soluble; solicitor(s)
Sol. Op.   Solicitor's Opinion
S.O.L.   Shipowner's liability
sonar   sound, navigation and ranging
SOP   standard operating procedure
S O S   Help! (distress signal)
S.O.S.   Service of Supply (military)
sp.   species; special; spelling
s.p.   without issue (L. *sine prole;* law); single-phase
SP   shore patrol
S.P.   supra protest
SPAR   Coast Guard Women's Reserve
s.p.d.   steamer pays dues
spec.   specification(s); specimen(s)
spg.   spring (pl. *spgs.*)
sp. gr.   specific gravity
sp. ht.   specific heat
Sp. Op.   special opinion
s.p.s.   without surviving issue (L. *sine prole superstite;* law)
spt.   seaport
sp. term   special term (of court)
sq.   square (e.g., *sq. ft., sq. in.,* and so on)
sq.   the following (L. *sequens*) (pl. *sqq.*)
Sq.   Square (street)
Sr.   Senior; Señor; Sister
S. Rept.   Senate report (with number)
S. Res.   Senate resolution (with number)
SRO   standing room only
ss   namely (L. *scilicet;* law)
ss.   sections
SS.   steamship (pl. *SSs.*)
S. to S.   station to station
SSE   south-southeast
S.Sgt., S/Sgt.   Staff Sergeant
SSW   south-southwest
S.S.U.   standard Saybolt universal
St., Ste.,   Saint, Sainte (pl. SS.)
St.   Street; State; Store; Strait (pl. *Sts.*)
sta.   station; stamped (securities)
stat.   statistics; statutes
std.   standard

S.T.D.   Doctor of Sacred Theology
std. c.f.   standard cubic foot (feet)
stet   let it stand (L.)
stg.   storage; sterling
stk.   stock
Stk. Ex.   Stock Exchange
Stk. Mkt.   stock market
S.T.Lr.   Lector in Sacred Theology
st. mi.   statute mile(s)
stp.   stamped
S.T.P.   Professor of Sacred Theology
str.   steamer; store (pl. *strs.*)
S.U.   set up (freight)
sub.   substitute; suburb; subscriber, -ption
subj.   subject
subs.   subsidiary; subscription
Sun.   Sunday (*Su.* in tabulations)
sup.   superior; supply; above (L. *supra*)
supp.   supplement (pl. *supps.*)
supt.   superintendent
surg.   surgeon; surgery; surgical
s.v.   sailing vessel; under the word (L. *sub verbo*)
svc.   service
s.v.p.   if you please (F. *s'il vous plait*)
SW   southwest
S.W.   shipper's weights
S.W.G., SWG   standard wire gauge
sx   sacks
syl.   syllable(s)
syn.   synonymous
synd.   syndicate
sys., syst.   system

T

t   metric ton (*tn.* or *T.,* ordinary ton)
t.   temperature; town; troy; time
T., Tp.   township (pl. *Tps.*)
T.A.   Traffic Agent
tab.   table(s); tabulation(s)
T.A.G.   The Adjutant General
t.a.w.   twice a week (advertising)
t.b., T.B.   trial balance
TB   tuberculosis

tbsp., tbs., T.   tablespoon(s)
TC   Tax Court of the United States
T/C   until countermanded
T.D.   trust deed; Treasury Decisions
T/D   time deposit
TDN   total digestible nutrients
T.E.   Topographical Engineer; trade expenses
tech.   technical
tel.   telephone; telegraph; telegram
temp.   temperature; temporary
Ter.   Territory; territorial; terrace
tf., t.f.   till forbidden (advertising)
tg.   telegraph
tgm.   telegram
thou.   thousand
3-D   three-dimensional
Thurs., Thu.   Thursday (*Th.* in tabulations)
tkr.   tanker
T/L   time loan
t.l.o.   total loss only (marine insurance)
t.m.   true mean; trade-mark
tn., T.   ton (metric ton is *t*); town; train
TN, Tenn.   Tennessee
tn. mi.   ton mile (air freight)
T/O   transfer order
tonn.   tonnage
t.p.   title page
tr.   trust; trustee; transit; transfer; transpose
T.R.   tons registered (shipping)
trans.   translated, -tion, -tor
transp.   transportation
Treas., Tr.   Treasurer; Treasury
t.s., ts   tensile strength
T. Sgt., T/Sgt.   Technical Sergeant
tsp., t.   teaspoon(s)
TT   teletype, -writer
T.T.s.   telegraphic transfers (of money)
Tues., Tue.   Tuesday (*Tu.* in tabulations)
TV   television; terminal velocity
Twad.   Twaddell (hydrometer)
Twp.   township (see *T.*)
TWX   teletypewriter exchange
tx.   tax(es); text, -book
TX, Tex.   Texas

U

U., Univ.   University
U/A   underwriting account (marine insurance)
uc.; u.c.   uppercase
u.d., ut dict.   as directed (L. *ut dictum*)
UGT   urgent (cable)
UHF   ultra-high-frequency (television)
u.i.   as below (L. *ut infra*)
U.K.   United Kingdom
ult.   last month (L. *ultimo*); ultimate
un.   unifying; unified (bonds)
Un.   Union; United
UN, U.N.   United Nations
univ.   university; universal
unl.   unlimited; unlisted (securities)
up.   underproof (alcohols)
UP   United Press
u.s.   as above (L. *ut supra*)
U.S.   United States
U.S.A.   United States of America
USA   U.S. Army
USAF   U.S. Airforce
USAREUR   U.S. Army, Europe
U.S.C.   United States Code
USCG   U.S. Coast Guard
U.S.D.J.   United States District Judge
USMC   U.S. Marine Corps
USN   U.S. Navy
USNR   U.S. Naval Reserve
U.S.P.   United States Pharmacopeia
U.S.S.   United States Senate; U.S. ship
ut.   utilities
u.t., UT   universal time
UT, Ut.   Utah
U/w   underwriter

V

v.   volt; versus (also *vs.*); verb; volume
V.   valve; velocity
va, v-a   volt-ampere (electricity)
VA, Va.   Virginia
vac.   vacuum

val.   value; valuation
var   reactive volt-ampere
var.   variety; various; variant; variation
V.C.   valuation clause; Vice Consul
vel.   velocity
Ven.   Venerable
v.f., VF   video frequency (television)
VHF   very high frequency (television)
v.i.   see below (L. *vide infra*)
VI, V.I.   Virgin Islands
Vice Adm.   Vice Admiral
Vice Pres., V.P.   Vice President
vid.   see (L. *vide*)
VIP   very important person (pl. *VIPs*)
vis.   visibility (aviation)
viz.   namely (L. *videlicet*)
V.M.D.   Doctor of Veterinary Medicine
vol.   volume (pl. *vols.*)
v.o.p.   value as in original policy
vou.   voucher
voy.   voyage
v.p., vt. pl.   voting pool (stocks)
vs.   verse; versus
v.s.   see above (L. *vide supra*); volumetric solution
V.S.   Veterinary Surgeon
VT, Vt.   Vermont
vt.   voting (stock)
vv.   verses
v.v.   vice versa

W

w.   watt (electricity); week
W.   west
WA, Wash.   Washington (State) (Spell out Washington, D.C.)
w.a.   with average (insurance)
WAC   Women's Army Corps (pl. *WACs*)
w.a.e.   when actually employed
WAF   Women in the Air Force
war.   warrant (securities); warranted
WAVES   Women Accepted for Volunteer Emergency Service (Navy)
wb.   wheelbase
WB   waybill; westbound
w.d., wd   when distributed (securities)

w/d warranted
W.D. Western District
Wed. Wednesday (*W.* in tabulations)
wf wrong font (printing)
w.g. wire gauge; weight guaranteed
wh, w-hr., whr. watt-hour (electricity)
whf. wharf
whge. wharfage
whs. warehouse
whsle. wholesale
w.i. when issued (securities)
WI, Wis. Wisconsin
wk. week (pl. *wks.*); work
w.l. wave length (electricity)
W. Long. west longitude
W/M weight and/or measurement
WNW west-northwest
WO Warrant Officer
w.o.c. without compensation
w.p. without prejudice; weather permitting
wpc, w/c watts per candle
w.p.p. waterproof paper packing
w.r., wr with rights (securities)
w. & r. water and rail (transportation)
W.R., whr. rec. warehouse receipt
WSW west-southwest
wt. weight; warrant (pl. *wts.*)
WV, W. Va. West Virginia
w.w., ww with warrants (securities)
W/W warehouse warrant
WY, Wyo. Wyoming

X

x box(es); by (*4 × 6*); cross (*X-roads*); extra (*x-lge.*)
xc, xcp, x-c, x-cp ex or without coupon
Xch., X exchange
xd, xdiv., x-d, x-div. ex or without dividend
x in., x-i, x-in., x-int. ex or without interest
x pr., x-pr. ex or without privileges
xr, x rts., x-rts. ex or without rights
Xtal, xtl. crystal
xw ex or without warrants
XQ cross-question

Y

yb.   yearbook
yd.   yard (pl. *yds.*)
yd², sq. yd.   square yard(s)
yd³, cu. yd.   cubic yard(s)
YMCA   Young Men's Christian Association
yr., y.   year (pl. *yrs.*); your; younger
YWCA   Young Women's Christian Association

Z

z., Z.   zone; zero; zenith distance
zool   zoology, -ical

Frequently used government abbreviations follow.

ACDA	Arms Control and Disarmament
AID	Agency for International Development
ARS	Agricultural Research Service; Advanced Record System
BED	Bureau of Export Development
BIA	Bureau of Indian Affairs
BLS	Bureau of Labor Statistics
CAB	Civil Aeronautics Board
CAP	Civil Air Patrol
CCC	Commodity Credit Corporation
CEA	Council of Economic Advisers
CENTO	Central Treaty Organization
CEP	Concentrated Employment Programs
CETA	Comprehensive Employment and Training Act
CIA	Central Intelligence Agency
CIEP	Council on International Economic Policy
CONUS	Continental United States
CSC	Civil Service Commission
DARPA	Defense Advanced Research Projects
DCAA	Defense Contract Audit Agency
DOD	Department of Defense
DSA	Defense Supply Agency
EDA	Economic Development Agency
EEC	European Economic Community
EPA	Environmental Protection Agency
EXIMBANK	Export-Import Bank of the United States
FAA	Federal Aviation Agency
FAO	Food and Agriculture Organization (UN)

FAS	Foreign Agricultural Service
FBI	Federal Bureau of Investigation
FCA	Farm Credit Administration
FCC	Federal Communications Commission
FDA	Food and Drug Administration
FDIC	Federal Deposit Insurance Corporation
FHA	Federal Housing Administration
FHLBB	Federal Home Loan Bank Board
FIA	Federal Insurance Administration
FMC	Federal Maritime Commission
FMCS	Federal Mediation and Conciliation Service
FNMA	Federal National Mortgage Association
FPC	Federal Power Commission
FRS	Federal Reserve System
FTC	Federal Trade Commission
GAO	General Accounting Office
GATT	General Agreement on Tariffs and Trade
GPO	Government Printing Office
GSA	General Services Administration
GSP	Generalized System of Preferences
HEW	Department of Health, Education and Welfare
HUD	Department of Housing and Urban Development
IADB	Inter-American Defense Board
IAEA	International Atomic Energy Agency
ICC	Interstate Commerce Commission
	Indian Claims Commission
ICEM	Intergovernmental Committee for European Migration
IDA	International Development Association
IFC	International Finance Corporation
ILO	International Labor Organization
IMF	International Monetary Fund
IRS	Internal Revenue Service
ITA	Industry and Trade Administration
ITU	International Telecommunications Union
JEEP	Joint Export Establishment Promotions
JOBS	Job Opportunity in the Business Sector
MA	Maritime Administration
MAC	Military Airlift Command
NAB	National Alliance of Businessmen
NARS	National Archives and Records Service
NASA	National Aeronautics and Space Administration
NATO	North Atlantic Treaty Organization
NBS	National Bureau of Standards
NIH	National Institutes of Health

NLRB	National Labor Relations Board
NOAA	National Oceanic and Atmospheric Administration
NSA	National Security Administration
NSC	National Security Council
NSF	National Science Foundation
NTIS	National Technical Information Service
OAS	Organization of American States
OECD	Organization for Economic Cooperation and Development
OFCC	Office of Federal Contract Compliance
OIM	Office of International Marketing
OJT	On-the-Job Training
OMBE	Office of Minority Business Enterprise
ORD	Office of Rural Development
PHS	Public Health Service
PRC	Postal Rate Commission
PTO	Patent and Trademark Office
REA	Rural Electrification Administration
RRB	Railroad Retirement Board
SBA	Small Business Administration
SCS	Soil Conservation Service
SEATO	Southeast Asia Treaty Organization
SEC	Securities and Exchange Commission
SSA	Social Security Administration
SSS	Selective Service System
TOP	Trade Opportunities Program
TVA	Tennessee Valley Authority
UIS	Unemployment Insurance Service
UMTA	Urban Mass Transport Administration
UN	United Nations
UNESCO	United Nations Educational, Scientific, and Cultural Organization
UNICEF	United Nations International Children's Emergency Fund
USES	United States Employment Service
USIA	United States Information Agency
VA	Veterans Administration
VISTA	Volunteers in Service to America
WHO	World Health Organization
WIN	Work Incentive Program

18

Weights and Measures

Standard weights and measures are used in measuring lengths, quantities, and volumes and in determining avoirdupois, troy, and apothecary weights. The National Bureau of Standards is responsible for setting and encouraging acceptance of these standards in the United States. The weights and measures that follow correspond to those established by the Bureau.

CONTENTS

WEIGHTS
(The grain is the same in all systems.)

Avoirdupois Weight

27 11/32 grains = 1 dram (dr.)

16 drams = 437.5 grains = 1 ounce (oz.)

16 ounces = 7,000 grains = 1 pound (lb.)

25 pounds = 1 quarter

4 quarters or 100 pounds (U.S.) = 1 hundredweight (cwt.)

2,000 pounds = 1 short ton (T.)

2,240 pounds = 1 long ton

2,204.62 pounds = 1 metric ton

1 std. lime bbl., small = 180 lb. net

1 std. lime bbl., large = 280 lb. net

In Great Britain:

14 pounds = 1 stone

2 stone = 28 pounds = 1 quarter

4 quarters = 112 pounds = 1 hundredweight

2,240 pounds = 20 hundredweight = 1 long ton

Troy Weight

24 grains (gr.) = 1 pennyweight (pwt. or dwt.)

20 pennyweights = 480 grains = 1 ounce (oz.t.)

12 ounces = 5,760 grains = 1 pound troy (lb.t.)

1 assay ton = 29,167 milligrams, or as many milligrams as there are troy ounces in a ton of 2,000 lb. avoirdupois.

3,168 grains = 1 carat

(Pure gold is 24 carats fine.   Gold marked 14 carats is 14/24 pure gold by weight and 10/24 alloy by weight.)

Apothecaries' Weight

20 grains = 1 scruple (sc., ℈)

3 scruples = 60 grains = 1 dram (dr., ʒ)

8 drams = 1 ounce (oz., ℥)

12 ounces = 5,760 grains = 1 pound (lb.)

Weight for Precious Stones

1 carat = 200 milligrams

MEASURES

The Metric System. More than 90 percent of the world population lives in nations that are metric or are committed to the metric system. The United States adopted the metric system on December 23, 1975 by the passage of the Metric Conversion Act of 1975. The system is known as the SI system (for Systéme International d'Unités), and is simpler than any other scheme of measurement ever used. It is simple because each quantity, such as length (meter) or weight (gram), has its own unit of measurement and no unit is used to express more than one quantity. SI is based on the decimal system and follows a consistent name scheme for the base units for different types of measurement.

The unit of *length* is **meter** (m).
The unit of *weight* is **gram** (g).
The unit of *capacity* is **liter** (l).
The unit of *temperature* is **kelvin** (K).
The unit of *time* is **second** (").
The unit of *electric current* is **ampere.**
The unit of *light intensity* is **candela.**
The unit of *amount of substance* is **mole.**

Multiples and submultiples are always related to powers of 10 (Figure 18-1). **Deka** means ten times, **hecto** means a hundred, **kilo** means a thousand times, **mega** means a million times, and so on. **Deci** means a tenth of, **centi** means a hundredth of, **milli** means a thousandth of, **micro** means a millionth of, and so on. (Figure 18-2.) Metric abbreviations are the same for both singular and plural and are written in lowercase letters without periods, except for tera (T), giga (G), and mega (M). Square and cubic may be indicated by the exponents ^{2} and ^{3}.

Conversion from customary measurement to metric and vice versa may be made by using the figures in Figure 18-3 which permit a close approximation of the desired measure. In Figure 18-4, the metric unit is compared to the approximate size of an everyday unit of measurement.

THESE PREFIXES MAY BE APPLIED
TO ALL SI UNITS**

Multiples and submultiples	Prefixes	Symbols
1 000 000 000 000 = 10^{12}	tera	T
1 000 000 000 = 10^{9}	giga	G
*1 000 000 = 10^{6}	mega	M
*1000 = 10^{3}	kilo	k
100 = 10^{2}	hecto	h
10 = 10	deka	da
0.1 = 10^{-1}	deci	d
*0.01 = 10^{-2}	centi	c
*0.001 = 10^{-3}	milli	m
*0.000 001 = 10^{-3}	micro	μ
0.000 000 001 = 10^{-9}	nano	n
0.000 000 000 001 = 10^{-12}	pico	p
0.000 000 000 000 001 = 10^{-15}	femto	f
0.000 000 000 000 000 001 = 10^{-18}	atto	a

*Most commonly used

**Source: SBA Management Aids No. 214.

Figure 18-1   Metric multiples and submultiples used with metric base units of measurement.

Commonly-used Metric Prefixes and Their
Multiplication Factors

WEIGHT

1 kilogram = 1000 grams
1 hectogram = 100 grams
1 dekagram = 10 grams
1 gram = 1 gram
1 decigram = 0.1 gram
1 centigram = 0.01 gram
1 milligram = 0.001 gram

VOLUME

1 hectoliter = 100 liters
1 dekaliter = 10 liters
1 liter = 1 liter
1 deciliter = 0.1 liter
1 centiliter = 0.01 liter
1 milliliter = 0.001 liter

LENGTH

1 kilometer = 1000 meters
1 hectometer = 100 meters
1 dekameter = 10 meters
1 meter = 1 meter
1 decimeter = 0.1 meter
1 centimeter = 0.01 meter
1 millimeter = 0.001 meter

Figure 18-2   Metric prefixes used with weight, length and volume base units to show relationship by the factor 10.

Comparing the Commonest Measurement Units*

Approximate conversions from customary to metric and vice versa

	When you know:	You can find:	If you multiply by:
LENGTH	inches	millimeters	25
	feet	centimeters	30
	yards	meters	0.9
	miles	kilometers	1.6
	millimeters	inches	0.04
	centimeters	inches	0.4
	meters	yards	1.1
	kilometers	miles	0.6
AREA	square inches	square centimeters	6.5
	square feet	square meters	0.09
	square yards	square meters	0.8
	square miles	square kilometers	2.6
	acres	square hectometers (hectares)	0.4
	square centimeters	square inches	0.16
	square meters	square yards	1.2
	square kilometers	square miles	0.4
	square hectometers (hectares)	acres	2.5
MASS	ounces	grams	28
	pounds	kilograms	0.45
	short tons	megagrams (metric tons)	0.9
	grams	ounces	0.035
	kilograms	pounds	2.2
	megagrams (metric tons)	short tons	1.1
LIQUID VOLUME	ounces	milliliters	30
	pints	liters	0.47
	quarts	liters	0.95
	gallons	liters	3.8
	milliliters	ounces	0.034
	liters	pints	2.1
	liters	quarts	1.06
	liters	gallons	0.26
TEMPER-ATURE	degrees Fahrenheit	degrees Celsius	5/9 (after subtracting 32)
	degrees Celsius	degrees Fahrenheit	9/5 (then add 32)

*Source: SBA Management Aids No. 214.

Figure 18-3 Multiplication factors to use when making an approximate conversion from customary measure to metric equivalents and vice versa.

Measurement	Metric Unit	Approximate Size of Unit
Length	millimeter	diameter of a paper clip wire
	centimeter	a little more than the width of a paper clip (about 0.4 inch)
	meter	a little longer than a yard (about 1.1 yards)
	kilometer	somewhat further than ½ mile (about 0.6 mile)
Weight (mass)	gram	a little more than the weight of a paper clip
	kilogram	a little more than 2 pounds (about 2.2 pounds)
	metric ton	a little more than a short ton (about 2200 pounds)
Volume	milliliter	five of them make a teaspoon
	liter	a little larger than a quart (about 1.06 quarts)
Area	hectare	about 2.5 acres
Pressure	kilopascal	atmospheric pressure is about 100 kilopascals
Temperature	degree Celsius	see temperature scale below

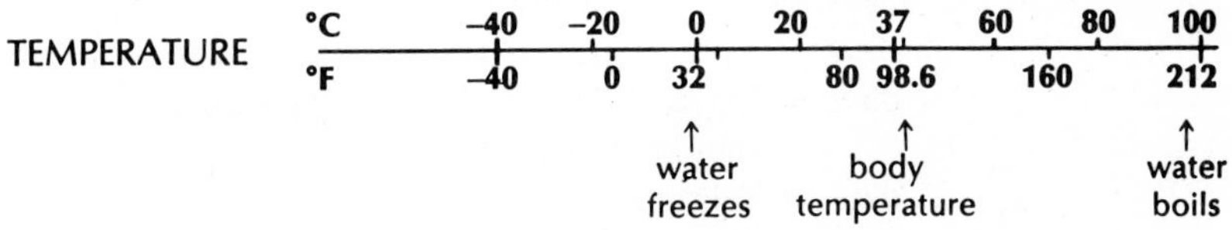

TEMPERATURE

°C	−40	−20	0	20	37	60	80	100
°F	−40	0	32		80	98.6	160	212

↑ water freezes   ↑ body temperature   ↑ water boils

Figure 18-4 Metric units of everyday measurements.

Circular or Angular Measure.

    60 seconds (") = 1 minute (')
    60 minutes   = 1 degree (°)
    30 degrees   = 1 sign (1/12 of a circle)
    60 degrees   = 1 sextant (1/6 of a circle)
    90 degrees   = 1 quadrant or right angle (1/4 of a circle)
   360 degrees   = 1 circle (cir.)

Common Units.

    12 units = 1 dozen (doz.)
    12 dozen = 1 gross (gr.)
   144 units = 1 gross
    12 gross = 1 great gross (great gr.)
    20 units = 1 score

Paper Measure.

    24 sheets = 1 quire (qr.)
    20 quires = 1 ream (480 sheets) (rm.)
   500 sheets = 1 commercial ream
     2 reams = 1 bundle (bdl.)
     5 bundles = 1 bale (bl.)

Time Measure.

    60 seconds (sec.) = 1 minute (min.)
    60 minutes = 1 hour (hr.)
    24 hours = 1 day (da.)
     7 days = 1 week (wk.)
    14 days = 1 fortnight
   4 1/3 weeks = an average month
    30 days = April, June, September, November
    31 days = January, March, May, July, August,
               October, December
    28 days = February (except for leap year
               every four years [1980], when it
               has 29 days)
   365 days = 1 common year (yr.)
    52 weeks = 1 year
    12 months = 1 year
   366 days = 1 leap year
    10 years = 1 decade
   100 years = 1 century
   1,000 years = 1 millennium

Temperature.

CELSIUS	FAHRENHEIT
0°	32° (Freezing point)
5°	41°
10°	50°
20°	68°
30°	86°
37°	98° (Normal body temperature)
40°	104°
50°	122°
60°	140°
70°	158°
80°	176°
90°	194°
100°	212° (Boiling point)

To compute Fahrenheit:

Multiply Celsius by 1.8 and add 32.

To compute Celsius:

Subtract 32 from Fahrenheit and divide by 1.8.

British Standard Measurement.

DISTANCE

1 kilometer = 0.621 mile	1 chain = 66 feet
1 furlong = 660 feet	1 hand = 4 inches
1 land League = 3 miles	1 mile = 1.609 kilometers

WEIGHT

1 stone = 14 lbs.
1 cwt. = 112 lbs.
1 kilogram = 2.2 lbs.

VOLUME

1 fluid ounce (Br.) = 0.961 fluid ounce (U.S.)
1 quart (Br.) = 1.201 liquid qts. (U.S.)
1 gallon (Br.) = 1.20094 gals. (U.S.)
1 bushel (Br.) = 1.032 bushels (U.S.)
1 quarter (Br.) = 8.256 bushels (U.S.)

Common Measures and Their Metric Equivalents

COMMON MEASURE	EQUIVALENT
inch	2.54 centimeters
foot	0.3048 meter
yard	0.9144 meter
rod	5.029 meters
mile	1.6093 kilometers
square inch	6.452 square centimeters
square foot	0.0929 square meter
square yard	0.836 square meter
square rod	25.29 square meters
acre	0.4047 hectare
square mile	259 hectare
cubic inch	16.39 cubic centimeters
cubic foot	0.0283 cubic meter
cubic yard	0.7646 cubic meter
cord	3.625 steres
liquid quart (U.S.)	0.9463 liter
dry quart (U.S.)	1.101 liters
quart, imperial	1.136 liters
gallon (U.S.)	3.785 liters
gallon, imperial	4.546 liters
peck (U.S.)	8.810 liters
peck, imperial	9.092 liters
bushel (U.S.)	35.24 liters
bushel, imperial	36.37 liters
ounce, avoirdupois	28.35 grams
pound, avoirdupois	0.4536 kilogram
ton, long	1.0160 metric tons
ton, short	0.9072 metric ton
grain	0.0648 gram
ounce, troy	31.103 grams
pound, troy	0.3732 kilogram

Miscellaneous Units of Measurement.

agate. A size of type between pearl and nonpareil, approximately 5 1/2 points.

Angstrom. One ten-billionth of a meter; used to calculate the length of light waves.

bale. A large compact bundle of goods; used as a unit of measure for certain commodities at fixed amounts, for example, a bale of cotton weighs 500 pounds.

Name	Abbreviation	Common Equivalent	Metric Equivalent
Linear Measure			
1 inch	in. or "	1,000 mils	2.54 centimeters
1 foot	ft. or '	12 inches	30.48 centimeters, 0.3048 meters
1 yard	yd.	3 feet (36 in.)	0.9144 meters
1 rod or 1 pole	rd., p.	5 1/2 yards (16 1/2 ft.)	5.0292 meters
1 furlong	fur.	40 rods or 1/8 mile (220 yds.)	201.168 meters
1 mile	mi.	8 furlongs or 320 rods (1760 yds., 5,280 ft.)	1609.3 meters 1.6093 kilometers
1 league		3 miles	4.828 kilometers
Square Measure			
1 square inch	sq. in.		6.4516 cm²
1 square foot	sq. ft.	144 sq. in.	929.034 cm² or 0.0929 m²
1 square yard	sq. yd.	9 sq. ft., 1,296 sq. in.	0.8361 m²
1 square rod	sq. rd.	30 1/4 sq. yd. 272 1/4 sq. ft.	25.2930 m²
1 acre	A.	160 sq. rd. 43,560 sq. ft.	40.4687 ares or 0.4047 hectares
1 square mile or 1 section	sq. mi. sec.	640 acres	258.9998 hectares or 2.5900 km²
1 township	T. or Tp.	36 sq. mi.	9324.0 hectares
Liquid Measure			
1 gill	gi.	32 fluid grams; 4 fluid ounces or 7.219 cu. ins.	0.1183 liter
1 pint	pt.	4 gills or 28.875 cu. ins.	0.4732 liter
1 quart	qt.	2 pints or 57.75 cu. ins.	0.9463 liter
1 gallon	gal.	4 quarts or 231 cu. ins.	3.7853 liters
1 barrel	bbl.	31 1/2 gals. (32 gals. in some states; 42 gals. for oil)	119.238 liters
1 hogshead	hhd.	2 barrels or 63 gals.	238.476 liters
Dry Measure			
1 pint	pt.	1/2 quart or 33.60 cu. ins.	0.5506 liter
1 quart	qt.	2 pints or 67.30 cu. ins.	1.1012 liters
1 peck	pk.	8 quarts or 537.605 cu. ins.	8.8096 liters
1 bushel	bu.	4 pecks or 2150.42 cu. ins.	35.2383 liters
1 barrel	bbl.	105 dry quarts or 7056 cu. ins.	115.6260 liters

Figure 18-5 Customary units of measurement common to the United States.

bushel. A unit of dry capacity used in the United States equal to 2,219.36 cubic inches.

board foot. A unit of quantity for lumber equal to the volume of a board 12″ × 12″ × 1″.

British Thermal Unit (BTU). A measure of heat equal to 252 calories or 0.00029 kilowatt-hours.

cable length. A maritime unit of length based on the length of a ship's cable and variously reckoned as equal to 100 fathoms, 1/10 of a nautical mile or 6,080 feet, or 120 fathoms.

calorie. A unit of heat equal to the quantity of heat required to raise one gram of water from 14.5°C to 15.5°C.

carat. An international unit of weight for precious stones equal to 200 milligrams; also used to indicate the purity of precious metals, such as 24 carats for pure gold.

chain. Often referred to as Gunter's Chain, it is a chain of 66 feet consisting of 100 links of 7.92 inches each; the unit of length used by surveyors.

decibel. A unit for measuring the loudness of sounds; it is equal to the smallest degree of sound detectable by the human ear. The human auditory range is about 130 decibels on a scale beginning at 1 for the faintest audible sound.

ell. A unit for measuring cloth, such as the English ell of 45 inches, the Dutch or Flemish of about 27 inches, or the Scottish unit of about 37 inches.

fathom. A unit of length equal to 6 feet based on the distance between the fingertips of a man's outstretched arms; used mainly for measuring the depth of water.

foot-pound. A unit of work equal to the raising of one pound of weight through a distance of one foot against the force of gravity.

freight ton. Cargo measuring less than 40 cubic feet per long ton or weighing less than 56 pounds per cubic foot.

great gross. A unit of quantity equal to 12 gross or 1,728.

gross. A unit of quantity equal to 12 dozen or 144.

hand. A unit of measure equal to 4 inches, used mainly for stating the height of horses.

hogshead. A large cask or barrel containing from 63 to 140 gallons.

horsepower. A unit of power equal in the United States to 746 watts and nearly equivalent to the English gravitational unit of the same name that equals 550 foot-pounds of work per second.

knot. One nautical mile per hour; used to express the speed of seagoing ships and of airplanes, to indicate the strength of water currents and the degree of intensity of air currents.

league. An English unit of about 3 miles.

link. One of the standardized links of a surveyor's chain, 7.92 inches long; serves as a measure of length.

magnum. A large wine bottle holding about 2/5 of a gallon.

micron. A unit of length equal to 1/1000 of a millimeter or about 0.000039 inch.

mil. A unit of length equal to 1/1000 inch or 0.0254 millimeter; used for measuring the diameter of wire.

nautical mile. Any of several units of distance used for sea and air navigation based on the length of a minute of arc of a great circle of the earth and differing because the earth is not a perfect sphere. The official international unit is 1,852 meters or 6,076.12 feet.

pica. A size of type equivalent to 12 points and a unit equal to 1/6 inch. Used in measuring composing materials, line and cut widths, and type-page dimensions.

point. A unit used to measure the size of type in printing that is equivalent to about 1/72 of an inch.

quintal. Any of various units of weight used primarily in Latin American and the Mediterranean countries; in the metric system a unit of measure equal to 220.46 pounds.

quire. A collection of 24 or 25 sheets of paper of the same size and quality, either not folded or having a single fold.

ream. Twenty quires or 480 sheets of paper, unless newsprint or book paper, which comprises 500 sheets.

span. The distance from the end of the thumb to the end of the little finger of the spread hand, or 9 inches.

stone. An official British unit equal to 14 pounds.

township. A piece of land that is bounded on the east and west by meridians 6 miles apart as its south border, has a north-south length of 6 miles, and forms one of the chief divisions of a U.S. public-land survey; 36 sections of 640 acres or 1 square mile each.

watt. A unit of electrical power equal to one volt multiplied by one ampere.

Metric Conversion Tables. The following five tables (Figures 18-6 to 18-10) provide for easy conversion from one unit of measure to another.

Conversion of Lengths

	Inches to milli- meters	Milli- meters to inches	Feet to meters	Meters to feet	Yards to meters	Meters to yards	Miles to kilo- meters	Kilo- meters to miles
1	25.4	0.03937	0.3048	3.281	0.9144	1.094	1.609	0.6214
2	50.8	0.07874	0.6096	6.562	1.829	2.187	3.219	1.243
3	76.2	0.1181	0.9144	9.842	2.743	3.281	4.828	1.864
4	101.6	0.1575	1.219	13.12	3.658	4.374	6.437	2.485
5	127.0	0.1968	1.524	16.40	4.572	5.468	8.047	3.107
6	152.4	0.2362	1.829	19.68	5.486	6.562	9.656	3.728
7	177.8	0.2756	2.134	22.97	6.401	7.655	11.27	4.350
8	203.2	0.3150	2.438	26.25	7.315	8.749	12.87	4.971
9	228.6	0.3543	2.743	29.53	8.230	9.842	14.48	5.592

Example: 1 in. = 25.4 mm

Figure 18-6   Conversion table of customary units of length to metric measurement and vice versa.

Conversion of Areas

	Sq. in. to sq. cm	Sq. cm to sq. in.	Sq. ft. to sq. m.	Sq. m. to sq. ft.	Sq. yd. to sq. m.	Sq. m. to sq. yd.	Acres to hec-tares	Hec-tares to acres	Sq. mi to sq. km	Sq. km to sq. mi.
1	6.452	0.155	0.0929	10.76	0.8361	1.196	0.4047	2.471	2.59	0.3861
2	12.90	0.310	0.1858	21.53	1.672	2.392	0.8094	4.942	5.18	0.7722
3	19.35	0.465	0.2787	32.29	2.508	3.588	1.214	7.413	7.77	1.158
4	25.81	0.620	0.3716	43.06	3.345	4.784	1.619	9.884	10.36	1.544
5	32.26	0.775	0.4645	53.82	4.181	5.980	2.023	12.355	12.95	1.931
6	38.71	0.930	0.5574	64.58	5.017	7.176	2.428	14.826	15.54	2.317
7	45.16	1.085	0.6503	75.35	5.853	8.372	2.833	17.297	18.13	2.703
8	51.61	1.240	0.7432	86.11	6.689	9.568	3.237	19.768	20.72	3.089
9	58.06	1.395	0.8361	96.87	7.525	10.764	3.642	22.239	23.31	3.475

Example: 1 sq. in = 6.452 sq. cm

Figure 18-7 Conversion of customary units of area to metric measurement and vice versa.

Conversion of Volumes or Capacities

	Fluid ounces to cu. cm.	Cu. cm. to fluid ounces	Liquid pints to liters	Liters to liquid pints	Liquid quarts to liters	Liters to liquid quarts	Gallons to liters	Liters to gallons	Bushels to hecto-liters	Hecto-liters to bushels
1	29.57	0.03381	0.4732	2.113	0.9463	1.057	3.785	0.2642	0.3524	2.838
2	59.15	0.06763	0.9463	4.227	1.893	2.113	7.571	0.5284	0.7048	5.676
3	88.72	0.1014	1.420	6.340	2.839	3.170	11.36	0.7925	1.057	8.513
4	118.3	0.1353	1.893	8.454	3.785	4.227	15.14	1.057	1.410	11.35
5	147.9	0.1691	2.366	10.57	4.732	5.284	18.93	1.321	1.762	14.19
6	177.4	0.2092	2.839	12.68	5.678	6.340	22.71	1.585	2.114	17.03
7	207.0	0.2367	3.312	14.79	6.624	7.397	26.50	1.849	2.467	19.86
8	236.6	0.2705	3.785	16.91	7.571	8.454	30.28	2.113	2.819	22.70
9	266.2	2.3043	4.259	19.02	8.517	9.510	34.07	2.378	3.171	25.54

Example: 1 fluid oz. = 29.57 cu. cm.

Figure 18-8   Conversion of customary units of volume or capacity to metric and vice versa.

Conversion of Volumes or Cubic Measure

	Cu. in. to cu. cm.	Cu. cm. to cu. in.	Cu. ft. to cu. m.	Cu. m. to cu. ft.	Cu. yd. to cu. m.	Cu. m. to cu. yd.	Gallons to cu. ft.	Cu. ft. to gallons
1	16.39	0.06102	0.02832	35.31	0.7646	1.308	0.1337	7.481
2	32.77	0.1220	0.05663	70.63	1.529	2.616	0.2674	14.96
3	49.16	0.1831	0.08495	105.9	2.294	3.924	0.4010	22.44
4	65.55	0.2441	0.1133	141.3	3.058	5.232	0.5347	29.92
5	81.94	0.3051	0.1416	176.6	3.823	6.540	0.6684	37.40
6	98.32	0.3661	0.1699	211.9	4.587	7.848	0.8021	44.88
7	114.7	0.4272	0.1982	247.2	5.352	9.156	0.9358	52.36
8	131.1	0.4882	0.2265	282.5	6.116	10.46	1.069	59.84
9	147.5	0.5492	0.2549	317.8	6.881	11.77	1.203	67.32

Example: 1 cu. in. = 16.39 cu. cm.

Figure 18-9 Conversion of customary units of cubic measure to metric and vice versa.

Conversion of Masses

	Grains to grams	Grams to grains	Ounces (avoir.) to grams	Grams to ounces (avoir.)	Pounds (avoir.) to kilo-grams	Kilo-grams to pounds (avoir.)	Short tons (2000 lb.) to metric tons	Metric tons (1000 kg) to short tons	Long tons (2240 lb.) to metric tons	Metric tons to long tons
1	0.0648	15.43	28.35	0.03527	0.4536	2.205	0.907	1.102	1.016	0.984
2	0.1296	30.86	56.70	0.07055	0.9072	4.409	1.814	2.205	2.032	1.968
3	0.1944	46.30	85.05	0.1058	1.361	6.614	2.722	3.307	3.048	2.953
4	0.2592	61.73	113.40	0.1411	1.814	8.818	3.629	4.409	4.064	3.937
5	0.3240	77.16	141.75	0.1764	2.268	11.02	4.536	5.512	5.080	4.921
6	0.3888	92.59	170.10	0.2116	2.722	13.23	5.443	6.614	6.096	5.905
7	0.4536	108.03	198.45	0.2469	3.175	15.43	6.350	7.716	7.112	6.889
8	0.5184	123.46	226.80	0.2822	3.629	17.64	7.257	8.818	8.128	7.874
9	0.5832	138.89	255.15	0.3175	4.082	19.84	8.165	9.921	9.144	8.858

Example: 1 grain = 0.0648 gr

Figure 18-10 Conversion of customary units of mass to metric and vice versa.

Signs and Symbols

+	plus		≐	approaches
−	minus		→	approaches limit of
±	plus or minus		∝	varies as
∓	minus or plus		‖	parallel
X	multiplied by; by (3″ X 4″)		⊥	perpendicular
·	multiplied by		∠	angle
÷	divided by		∟	right angle
=	equal to		△	triangle
≠	or ╪ ; not equal to		□	square
≈	or ≒ ; nearly equal to		▭	rectangle
≡	identical with		▱	parallelogram
≢	not identical with		O	circle; ⑤ circles
⇕	equivalent		⌒	arc of circle
~	difference		⟂	equilateral
≅	congruent to		≙	equiangular
>	greater than		√	radical; root; square root
≯	not greater than		∛	cube root
<	less than		∜	fourth root
≮	not less than		Σ	summation sign
≧	or ≥; greater than or equal to		!	or ∟; factorial product
≦	or ≤; less than or equal to		∞	infinity
‖	absolute value		∫	integral; ∫ extended integral
∪	logical sum or union		f	function
∩	logical product or intersection		∂	or δ; differential; variation
⊂	is contained in		π	pi
⊃	excluded from		∴	therefore
∈	is a member of; dielectric constant; mean error		∵	because
			‾	vinculum (above letter)
:	is to; ratio		( )	parentheses
∷	as; proportion		[ ]	brackets

{ }	braces	♄	Saturn
°	degree	♅	Uranus
′	minute; prime	♆	or ⯉ ; Neptune
″	second; double prime	♇	Pluto
‴	triple prime	♈	Aries
ℋℙ	horsepower	♉	Taurus
Δ	increment	♊	Gemini
ω	angular frequency, solid angle	♋	Cancer
Ω	ohm	♌	Leo
μ^{Ω}	microhm	♍	Virgo
M^{Ω}	megohm	♎	Libra
Φ	magnetic flux; farad	♏	Scorpio
Ψ	dielectric flux; electrostatic flux	♐	Sagittarius
ρ	resistivity	♑	Capricornus
γ	conductivity	♒	Aquarius
Λ	equivalent conductivity	♓	Pisces
ℛ	reluctance	☌	conjunction
⇆	electrical current	☍	opposition
⟨⁻⟩	benzene ring	△	trine
→	yields; direction of flow	□	quadrature
⇌	reversible reaction	∗	sextile
↓	precipitate	☊	dragon's head, ascending node
↑	gas	☋	dragon's tail, descending node
‰	salinity	①	Ceres
☉	or ☼ ; Sun	②	Pallas
●	or ⦻ ; New moon	③	Juno
☽	First quarter	④	Vesta
○	or ⦵ ; Full moon	⦿	rain
☾	Last quarter	∗	snow
☿	Mercury	⊠	snow on ground
♀	Venus	←	floating ice crystals
⊖	or ⊕ ; Earth	▲	hail
♂	Mars	△	sleet
♃	Jupiter	∨	frostwork

Symbol	Meaning	Symbol	Meaning
⌣	hoarfrost	®	registered in U.S. Patent Office
≡	fog	©	copyright
∞	haze; dust haze	c/o	care of
⊤	thunder	a/c	account of
⟨	sheet lightning	@	at
☉	solar corona	¢	cent
⊕	solar halo	*	asterisk
⍀	thunderstorm	†	dagger
⟍	direction	‡	double dagger
○	or ⊙ , or ⊙ ; annual	§	section
∞	or ② ; biennial	☞	index
♃	perennial	′	acute
♂	or ♂ male	`	grave
♀	female	~	tilde
□	male, in charts	^	circumflex
○	female, in charts	—	macron
℞	take (L. recipe); response (church)	˘	breve
$\overline{AA}$	or $\overline{A}$, or āā; of each	¨	dieresis
	(doctor's prescription)	⸜	cedilla
℔	pound	^	caret
℥	ounce	ˇ	caron
ℨ	dram	√	check
℈	scruple	√̌	double check
○	pint	□″	square inches;
ƒ℥	fluid ounce	□′	square feet
ƒℨ	fluid dram	#/□″	pounds per square inch
ℳ	minim	° ′ ″	degrees, minutes, seconds of an arc
&	or ⅋ ; and; ampersand	&c	and so forth; etc.
℔	per	¶	paragraph
#	number (before number);	₵	center line
	pounds (after number)	⬡	hexagon
/	virgule; solidus; separatrix; shilling; per	⟨⟩	an order set
%	percent	Π	product sign

Greek Alphabet

Name	Capital	Lower Case
Alpha	A	α
Beta	B	β
Gamma	Γ	γ
Delta	Δ	δ
Epsilon	E	ϵ
Zeta	Z	ζ
Eta	H	η
Theta	Θ	θ
Iota	I	ι
Kappa	K	κ
Lambda	Λ	λ
Mu	M	μ
Nu	N	ν
Xi	Ξ	ξ
Omicron	O	o
Pi	Π	π
Rho	P	ρ
Sigma	Σ	σ, ς
Tau	T	τ
Upsilon	Υ	υ
Phi	Φ	φ, ϕ
Chi	X	χ
Psi	Ψ	ψ
Omega	Ω	ω

Six-Year Holiday Timetable

(Includes provisions of the Uniform Holiday Bill, effective January 1, 1971 and 1978 legislation recognizing November 11 as Veterans Day.)

	1979	1980	1981	1982	1983	1984
New Year's Day	M Jan 1	T Jan 1	Th Jan 1	F Jan 1	S Jan 1	Su Jan 1
Lincoln's Birthday	M Feb 12	T Feb 12	Th Feb 12	F Feb 12	S Feb 12	Su Feb 12
Valentine's Day	W Feb 14	Th Feb 14	S Feb 14	Su Feb 14	M Feb 14	T Feb 14
Washington's Birthday	M Feb 19	F Feb 22	M Feb 23	M Feb 22	M Feb 21	M Feb 20
Ash Wednesday	W Feb 28	W Feb 20	W Mar 4	W Feb 24	W Feb 16	W Mar 7
Good Friday	F Apr 13	F Apr 4	F Apr 17	F Apr 9	F Apr 1	F Apr 20
Passover	Th Apr 12	T Apr 1	Su Apr 19	S Apr 8	T Mar 29	T Apr 17
Easter Sunday	Su Apr 15	Su Apr 6	Su Apr 19	Su Apr 11	Su Apr 3	Su Apr 22
Mother's Day	Su May 13	Su May 11	Su May 10	Su May 9	Su May 8	Su May 13
Memorial Day	M May 28	F May 30	S May 30	M May 31	M May 30	M May 28
Father's Day	Su June 17	Su June 15	Su June 21	Su June 20	Su June 19	Su June 17
Independence Day	W July 4	F July 4	S July 4	Su July 4	M July 4	W July 4

Labor Day	M Sept 3	M Sept 1	M Sept 7	M Sept 6	M Sept 5	M Sept 3
Rosh Hashana	S Sept 22	Th Sept 11	T Sept 29	S Sept 18	Th Sept 8	Th Sept 27
Yom Kippur	M Oct 1	S Sept 20	Th Oct 8	M Sept 27	S Sept 17	S Oct 6
Columbus Day	M Oct 8	M Oct 13	M Oct 12	M Oct 11	M Oct 9	M Oct 8
Veterans Day	Su Nov 11	T Nov 11	W Nov 11	Th Nov 11	F Nov 11	Su Nov 11
Election Day	T Nov 6	T Nov 4	T Nov 3	T Nov 2	T Nov 1	T Nov 6
Thanksgiving	Th Nov 22	Th Nov 27	Th Nov 26	Th Nov 25	Th Nov 24	Th Nov 22
Hanukah	S Dec 15	W Dec 3	M Dec 21	S Dec 11	Th Dec 1	W Dec 19
Christmas	T Dec 25	Th Dec 25	F Dec 25	S Dec 25	Su Dec 25	T Dec 25

Federal Holidays:

New Year's Day
Lincoln's Birthday
Washington's Birthday
Memorial Day
Independence Day
Labor Day
Columbus Day
Veterans Day
Thanksgiving
Christmas

Three-day Weekends:

Washington's Birthday
Memorial Day
Labor Day
Columbus Day
And any other legal holiday that falls on
    Friday, Saturday, Sunday, or Monday.

D

State Holidays

Note: When the holiday falls on Sunday, the Monday following is usually observed.

ALABAMA

Jan. 1, 19
Feb. 22
Mardi Gras*
April 13, 26
June 3
July 4
Labor Day
Oct. 12
Nov. 11
Thanksgiving
Dec. 25

ALASKA

Jan. 1
Feb. 12, 22
March 30
May 30
July 4
Labor Day
General election
Oct. 18
Nov. 11
Thanksgiving
Dec. 25

ARIZONA

Jan. 1
Feb. 12, 14, 22
May 30
July 4
Labor Day
Oct. 12
Election day
Nov. 11
Thanksgiving
Dec. 25

ARKANSAS

Jan. 1, 19
Feb. 22
May 30
July 4

Labor Day
Election days
Nov. 11
Thanksgiving
Dec. 25

CALIFORNIA

Jan. 1
Feb. 12, 22
Good Friday (noon to 3 p.m.)
May 30
July 4
Labor Day
Sept. 9
Oct. 12
General election
Nov. 11
Thanksgiving
Dec. 25

COLORADO

Jan. 1
Feb. 12, 22
May 30
July 4
Aug. 1
Labor Day
Oct. 12
General election
Nov. 11
Thanksgiving
Dec. 25

CONNECTICUT

Jan. 1
Feb. 12, 22
Good Friday
May 30
July 4
Labor Day
Oct. 12
Nov. 11

Thanksgiving
Dec. 25

DELAWARE

Jan. 1
Feb. 12, 22
Good Friday
May 30
July 4
Labor Day
Oct. 12
Election day
Nov. 11
Thanksgiving
Dec. 25

DISTRICT OF COLUMBIA

Jan. 1
Inauguration Day
Feb. 22
May 30
July 4
Labor Day
Nov. 11
Thanksgiving
Dec. 25

FLORIDA

Jan. 1, 19, Arbor Day
Feb. 22
April 26
Good Friday
May 30
June 3
July 4
Labor Day
Oct. 12
Nov. 11
General election
Thanksgiving
Dec. 25

*Held on Shrove Tuesday, the day before Ash Wednesday.

GEORGIA

Jan. 1, 19
Feb. 22
April 26
June 3
July 4
Labor Day
Oct. 12
Nov. 11
Thanksgiving
Dec. 25

HAWAII

Jan. 1, 30
Feb. 12, 22
Good Friday
May 30
June 11
July 4
Labor Day
Regatta Day
Primary and
  general elections
Nov. 11
Thanksgiving
Dec. 25

IDAHO

Jan. 1
May 30
July 4
Labor Day
Nov. 11
Thanksgiving
Dec. 25

ILLINOIS

Jan. 1
Feb. 12, 22
Good Friday
May 30
July 4
Labor Day

Oct. 12
Nov. 11
Thanksgiving
Dec. 25

INDIANA

Jan. 1
Feb. 12, 22
Good Friday
May 30
July 4
Labor Day
Oct. 12
Election day
Nov. 11
Thanksgiving
Dec. 25

IOWA

Jan. 1
Feb. 12, 22
May 30
July 4
Labor Day
Nov. 11
Thanksgiving
Dec. 25

KANSAS

Jan. 1
Feb. 12, 22
May 30
July 4
Labor Day
Oct. 12
Nov. 11
Thanksgiving
Dec. 25

KENTUCKY

Jan. 1, 19, 30
Feb. 12, 22
May 30

June 3
July 4
Labor Day
Oct. 12
Nov. 11
Thanksgiving
Dec. 25

LOUISIANA

Jan. 1, 8, 19
Feb. 22
Mardi Gras in
  New Orleans, etc.*
Good Friday
May 30
June 3
July 4
Aug. 30
Labor Day
Oct. 12
Nov. 1, 11
Thanksgiving
Dec. 25
Sat. P.M.

MAINE

Jan. 1
Feb. 22
April 19
May 30
July 4
Labor Day
Nov. 11
Thanksgiving
Dec. 25

MARYLAND

Jan. 1
Feb. 12, 22
Mar. 25
Good Friday
May 30
July 4
Labor Day
Sept. 12

*Held on Shrove Tuesday, the day before Ash Wednesday;

Oct. 12
Election day
Nov. 11
Thanksgiving
Dec. 25
Sat. P.M. (local)

MASSACHUSETTS

Jan. 1
Feb. 22
March 17 (local)
April 19
May 30
June 17 (local)
July 4
Labor Day
Oct. 12
Nov. 11
Thanksgiving
Dec. 25

MICHIGAN

Jan. 1
Feb. 12, 22
May 30
July 4
Labor Day
Oct. 12
Election days
Nov. 11
Thanksgiving
Dec. 25

MINNESOTA

Jan. 1
Feb. 12, 22
Good Friday
May 30
July 4
Labor Day
Oct. 12
Nov. 11
Thanksgiving
Dec. 25

MISSISSIPPI

Jan. 1, 19
Feb. 22
April 26
June 3
July 4
Labor Day
Nov. 11
Thanksgiving
Dec. 25

MISSOURI

Jan. 1
Feb. 12, 22
April 13
May 30
July 4
Labor Day
Oct. 12
Election days
Nov. 11
Thanksgiving
Dec. 25

MONTANA

Jan. 1
Feb. 12, 22
May 30
July 4
Labor Day
Oct. 12
General election
Nov. 11
Thanksgiving
Dec. 25

NEBRASKA

Jan. 1
Feb. 12, 22
April 22
May 30
July 4
Labor Day

Oct. 12
Nov. 11
Thanksgiving
Dec. 25

NEVADA

Jan. 1
Feb. 12, 22
May 30
July 4
Labor Day
Primary election
Oct. 12, 31
General election
Nov. 11
Thanksgiving
Dec. 25

NEW HAMPSHIRE

Jan. 1
Feb. 22
Fast Day
May 30
July 4
Labor Day
Oct. 12
General election
Nov. 11
Thanksgiving
Dec. 25

NEW JERSEY

Jan. 1
Feb. 12, 22
Good Friday
May 30
July 4
Labor Day
Oct. 12
General election
Nov. 11
Thanksgiving
Dec. 25
Sats.—Bank holidays

NEW MEXICO

Jan. 1
Feb. 22
May 30
July 4
Labor Day
Oct. 12
Nov. 11
Thanksgiving
Dec. 25

NEW YORK

Jan. 1
Feb. 12, 22
May 30
July 4
Labor Day
Oct. 12
General election
Nov. 11
Thanksgiving
Dec. 25

NORTH CAROLINA

Jan. 1, 19
Feb. 22
Easter Monday
April 12
May 10, 20, 30
July 4
Labor Day
Election day
Nov. 11
Thanksgiving
Dec. 25

NORTH DAKOTA

Jan. 1
Feb. 12, 22
Good Friday
May 30
July 4
Labor Day
Oct. 12
General election

Nov. 11
Thanksgiving
Dec. 25

OHIO

Jan. 1
Feb. 12, 22
May 30
July 4
Labor Day
Oct. 12
General election (P.M.)
Nov. 11
Thanksgiving
Dec. 25
Sat. P.M.

OKLAHOMA

Jan. 1
Feb. 22
April 13, 22
May 30
July 4
Labor Day
Oct. 12
Election day
Nov. 11
Thanksgiving
Dec. 25

OREGON

Jan. 1
Feb. 12, 22
Primary Day
May 30
July 4
Labor Day
Oct. 12
General election
Nov. 11
Thanksgiving
Dec. 25

PENNSYLVANIA

Jan. 1

Feb. 12, 22
Good Friday
May 30
June 14
July 4
Labor Day
Oct. 12
General election
Nov. 11
Thanksgiving
Dec. 25
Sat. P.M.

PUERTO RICO

Jan. 1, 6, 11
Feb. 22
Mar. 22
Good Friday
April 16
May 30
July 4, 17, 25, 27
Labor Day
Oct. 12
Election day
Nov. 11, 19
Thanksgiving
Dec. 25

RHODE ISLAND

Jan. 1
Feb. 22
May 4, 30
July 4
Labor Day
Oct. 12
General election
Nov. 11
Thanksgiving
Dec. 25

SOUTH CAROLINA

Jan. 1, 19
Feb. 22
June 3
July 4

Labor Day
General election
Nov. 11
Thanksgiving
Dec. 25

SOUTH DAKOTA

Jan. 1
Feb. 12, 22
May 30
July 4
Labor Day
General election
Nov. 11
Thanksgiving
Dec. 25

TENNESSEE

Jan. 1, 19
Feb. 12, 22
March 15
Good Friday
May 30
June 3
July 4, 13
Labor Day
Nov. 11
General election
Thanksgiving
Dec. 25

TEXAS

Jan. 1, 19
Feb. 12, 22
March 2
April 21
May 30
June 3
July 4
Labor Day
Oct. 12
Nov. 11
Thanksgiving
Dec. 25

UTAH

Jan. 1
Feb. 12, 22
Arbor Day
May 30
July 4, 24
Labor Day
Oct. 12
Nov. 11
Thanksgiving
Dec. 25

VERMONT

Jan. 1
Feb. 12, 22
May 30
July 4
August 16
Labor Day
Oct. 12
Nov. 11
Thanksgiving
Dec. 25

VIRGINIA

Jan. 1, 19
Feb. 22
April 13
May 30
June 3
July 4
Labor Day
Oct. 12
General election
Nov. 11
Thanksgiving
Dec. 25

WASHINGTON

Jan. 1
Feb. 12, 22
May 30
July 4
Labor Day

Oct. 12
General election
Nov. 11
Thanksgiving
Dec. 25

WEST VIRGINIA

Jan. 1
Feb. 12, 22
May 30
June 20
July 4
Labor Day
Oct. 12
General and
    special election
Nov. 11
Thanksgiving
Dec. 25
Sat. P.M.

WISCONSIN

Jan. 1
Feb. 12, 22
May 30
July 4
Labor Day
Oct. 12
Election days
Nov. 11
Thanksgiving
Dec. 25

WYOMING

Jan. 1
Feb. 12, 22
Arbor Day
May 30
July 4
Labor Day
General election
Nov. 11
Thanksgiving
Dec. 25

Twenty-four-Hour Military Time

The following chart compares the standard 12-hour time with the equivalent 24-hour military time. Only the first hour shown illustrates how the odd minutes of an hour compare. The same system applies to all hours.

12-hour Time	24-hour Time	12-hour Time	24-hour Time
1:00 a.m.	0100	11:00 a.m.	1100
1:07 a.m.	0107	12:00 noon	1200
1:15 a.m.	0115	1:00 p.m.	1300
1:30 a.m.	0130	2:00 p.m.	1400
1:52 a.m.	0152	3:00 p.m.	1500
2:00 a.m.	0200	4:00 p.m.	1600
3:00 a.m.	0300	5:00 p.m.	1700
4:00 a.m.	0400	6:00 p.m.	1800
5:00 a.m.	0500	7:00 p.m.	1900
6:00 a.m.	0600	8:00 p.m.	2000
7:00 a.m.	0700	9:00 p.m.	2100
8:00 a.m.	0800	10:00 p.m.	2200
9:00 a.m.	0900	11:00 p.m.	2300
10:00 a.m.	1000	12:00 midnight	2400

When speaking of military time, say:

0 one hundred, for 0100
0 one 0 seven, for 0107
0 one fifteen, for 0115
0 one thirty, for 0130
0 one fifty-two, for 0152
0 two hundred, for 0200
ten hundred, for 1000
ten 0 seven, for 1007
twenty-one fifteen, for 2115, etc.

Number of Days Between Dates

From Any Day of	To the Same Day of the Next											
	Jan.	Feb.	Mar.	Apr.	May	June	July	Aug.	Sept.	Oct.	Nov.	Dec.
January	365	31	59	90	120	151	181	212	243	273	304	334
February	334	365	28	59	89	120	150	181	212	242	273	303
March	306	337	365	31	61	92	122	153	184	214	245	275
April	275	306	334	365	30	61	91	122	153	183	214	244
May	245	276	304	335	365	31	61	92	123	153	184	214
June	214	245	273	304	334	365	30	61	92	122	153	183
July	184	215	243	274	304	335	365	31	62	92	123	153
August	153	184	212	243	273	304	334	365	31	61	92	122
September	122	153	181	212	242	273	303	334	365	30	61	91
October	92	123	151	182	212	243	273	304	335	365	31	61
November	61	92	120	151	181	212	242	273	304	334	365	30
December	31	62	90	121	151	182	212	243	274	304	335	365

When February has 29 days, add one day to the figure in the chart.

Simple Interest Tables *G*

($100 on a 360-Day Year Basis)

Time	1/4%	1/2%	3/4%	1%	4%	5%	6%	7%
1 Day	.0007	.0014	.0021	.0028	.0111	.0139	.0167	.0195
2	.0014	.0028	.0042	.0056	.0222	.0278	.0333	.0389
3	.0021	.0042	.0063	.0083	.0333	.0417	.0500	.0583
4	.0028	.0056	.0084	.0111	.0444	.0556	.0667	.0778
5	.0035	.0070	.0105	.0139	.0556	.0694	.0833	.0972
6	.0042	.0083	.0125	.0167	.0667	.0833	.1000	.1167
7	.0043	.0097	.0146	.0195	.0778	.0972	.1167	.1362
8	.0056	.0111	.0167	.0223	.0889	.1111	.1333	.1556
9	.0063	.0125	.0188	.0250	.1000	.1250	.1500	.1750
10	.0070	.0139	.0209	.0278	.1111	.1389	.1667	.1945
1 Month	.0208	.0417	.0625	.0833	.3333	.4167	.5000	.5833
2	.0417	.0833	.1250	.1667	.6667	.8333	1.0000	1.1667
3	.0625	.1250	.1875	.2500	1.0000	1.2500	1.5000	1.7500
4	.0833	.1667	.2500	.3333	1.3333	1.6667	2.0000	2.3333
5	.1042	.2083	.3125	.4167	1.6667	2.0833	2.5000	2.9167
6	.1250	.2500	.3750	.5000	2.0000	2.5000	3.0000	3.5000

Example: To find interest at 5 3/4% for 7 months and 20 days

	5%	3/4%
Add intererest for 6 months	2.5000	.3750
1 month	.4160	.0625
10 days	.1389	.0209
10 days	.1389	.0209
	3.1938	.4793
	.4793	
	3.6731	

Interest on $100 at 5 3/4% for 7 months and 20 days = $3.67

H

Decimal Equivalents of Fractions

	1	2	3	4	5	6	7	8	9	10	11	12	13	14	15	16
2nds	.5															
3rds	.3333	.6667														
4ths	.25	.5	.75													
5ths	.2	.4	.6	.8												
6ths	.1667	.3333	.5	.6667	.8333											
7ths	.1429	.2857	.4296	.5714	.7143	.8571										
8ths	.125	.25	.375	.5	.625	.75	.875									
9ths	.1111	.2222	.3333	.4444	.5556	.6667	.7778	.8889								
10ths	.1	.2	.3	.4	.5	.6	.7	.8	.9							
11ths	.0909	.1818	.2727	.3636	.4545	.5455	.6364	.7273	.8182	.9091						
12ths	.0833	.1667	.25	.3333	.4167	.5	.5833	.6667	.75	.8333	.9167					
13ths	.0769	.1538	.2308	.3977	.3846	.4615	.5385	.6154	.6923	.7692	.8462	.9231				
14ths	.0714	.1429	.2143	.2857	.3571	.4286	.5	.5714	.6429	.7143	.7857	.8571	.9286			
15ths	.0667	.1333	.2	.2667	.3333	.4	.4667	.5333	.6	.6667	.7333	.8	.8667	.9333		
16ths	.0625	.125	.1875	.25	.3125	.375	.4375	.5	.5626	.625	.6875	.75	.8125	.875	.9375	1.

Common Volume Formulas

/

Figure	Formula	Meaning of Letters
Rectangle	$A = ab$	a = base, b = height
Square	$A = a^2$	a = one side
Triangle	$A = \dfrac{ab}{2}$	a = base, b = height
Parallelogram	$A = ab$	a = base, b = height
Regular pentagon	$A = 1.720a^2$	a = one side
Regular hexagon	$A = 2.598a^2$	a = one side
Regular octagon	$A = 4.828a^2$	a = one side
Circle	$A = \pi r^2$	π = 3.1416, r = radius

J

Common Area Formulas

Figure	Formula	Meaning of Letters
Cube	$V = a^3$	a = one side
Pyramid	$V = \dfrac{ah}{3}$	a = area of base, h = height
Cylinder	$V = \pi r^2 h$	π = 3.1416, h = height, r = radius of the base
Cone	$V = \dfrac{\pi r^2 h}{3}$	π = 3.1416, r = radius of the base, h = height
Sphere	$V = \dfrac{4\pi r^3}{3}$	π = 3.1416, r = radius

Index

Quick Reference
to Frequently Consulted Subjects

(Contents on pages ix–xii—Full Index on page 747)